AF516397

India's Demography

India's Demography

Changing Demographic Scenario in India

P.K. Majumdar

RAWAT PUBLICATIONS
Jaipur | New Delhi | Bangalore | Hyderabad | Guwahati

ISBN 978-81-316-0569-1

Published by
Prem Rawat for **Rawat Publications**
Satyam Apts., Sector 3, Jawahar Nagar, Jaipur 302 004 (India)
Phone: 0141 265 1748 / 7006 Fax: 0141 265 1748
E-mail: info@rawatbooks.com
Website: www.rawatbooks.com

New Delhi Office
4858/24, Ansari Road, Daryaganj, New Delhi 110 002
Phone: 011 2326 3290

Also at *Bangalore, Hyderabad* and *Guwahati*

Typeset by *d'lines* DTP SERVICES, Jaipur
Printed at Nice Printing Press, New Delhi

Contents

List of Tables, Figures and Appendix

Tables

Figures

Appendix

India at a Glance

	India	South Asia	Low-Income Countries	
Population, midyear (millions) 2003–04	1064.4	1425	2310	
Provisional population total, 2011	1210.2			
Population density 2011	382/km^2			
Average Annual Growth, 1997–03				
Population (%)	1.6	1.8	1.9	
Labor force (%)	2.1	2.3	2.3	
Poverty (% of population below national poverty line)	19.3 (2007)			
Urban Population (% of total population)	28	28	30	
Life expectancy at birth (years)	63	63	58	
Infant mortality rate (per 1,000 births)	65	68	82	
Child malnutrition (% of children under 5)	47	48	44	
Access to improved water source (%)	84	84	75	
Illiteracy (%)	26 (2011)	41	39	
Gross primary enrollment (% of school age population)	99	95	92	
Male	107	103	99	
Female	90	88	85	
More Indicators on People				
Population Growth (%)	1.5 for the year 2003–04			
Fertility Rate (births per woman)	2.9 for the year (2002–03)			
Child immunization, measles (% of under 12 months)	67 for the year (2002–03)			
Technology and Infrastructure				
Fixed lines and mobile telephones (per 1,000 people)	51.9 (for the year 2002–03)			
Personal computers (per 1,000 people)	7.2 (for the year 2002–03)			
Internet users	16.6 million (for the year 2002–03)			
Key Economic Long Term Trends	***1983***	***1993***	***2002***	***2003***
GDP (US $ billions)	212.3	273.9	510.2	603.3

Cont'd…

...Cont'd

Average annual growth	*1983–93*	*1993–03*	*2002*	*2003*
GDP (%)	5.4	5.9	4.6	8.3
GDP per capita (%)	3.3	4.2	3	6.7
Exports of goods and services (%)	8	13.4	21.8	7
Structure of the Economy (% of GDP)	***1983***	***1993***	***2002***	***2003***
Agriculture	36.6	31	22.7	22.2
Industry	25.8	26.3	26.6	26.6
Manufacturing	16.3	16.1	15.6	15.8
Services	37.6	42.8	50.7	51.2
Private Consumption	71.8	67.4	65	64.9
General Government Consumption	10.6	11.4	12.5	12.8
Imports of Goods and Services	8.1	10	15.6	16
Average Annual Growth	***1983–93***	***1993–03***	***2002***	***2003***
Agriculture (%)	3.1	2.4	–5.2	9.1
Industry (%)	6.4	5.9	6.4	6.7
Services (%)	6.7	8.1	7.1	8.7
Private Consumption (%)	5.2	4.5	–0.8	7.6
General Government Consumption (%)	5.6	7.1	3.1	9.9
Gross domestic investment (%)	5.3	7.5	9.5	12
Imports of Goods and Services (%)	6.3	10.6	8.1	11.1
Prices and Government Finance	***1983***	***1993***	***2002***	***2003***
Consumer prices	14.4	5	4.1	3.7
Government Finance (% of GDP, includes current grants)	***1993***	***2002***	***2003***	
Overall surplus/deficit	–8.3	–10.2	–9.3	
Trade (US $ millions)	***1983***	***1993***	***2002***	***2003***
Total Exports	9861	22,683	52,512	62,952
Total imports	16,575	26,739	65,422	79,658
Balance of Payments (US $ millions)	***1983***	***1993***	***2002***	***2003***
Current Account Balance	–3595	–1526	3727	8160
Financing items (net)	2777	10160	13253	8820
Changes in Net Reserves	818	–8634	–16980	–16980

Preface

The fundamentals of demography have been discussed in some detail in *Fundamentals of Demography* written by the author. This volume is exclusively devoted to the history of population growth in India and how population-related events in India have been changing over the years, especially since independence. To draw attention of the readers to the qualitative and quantitative changes in various population indicators, a large number of statistical tables, charts and diagrams have been integrated. They have often been incorporated from the published data from Census, Sample Registration Records, National Sample Survey Reports, Family Planning Yearbook, National Family Health Survey reports, National Human Development Report, Report of National Applied Economic Research, Planning Commission statements put on the website and many other documents, downloaded from websites. Some of the tables are recast of the published documents, and the charts and figures either have been copied or drawn for the given data. Even some of the descriptions and interpretations covering some statistical tables have been borrowed from published documents.

Over 800 million people have been added between 1901 and 2001. But this addition has not been uniform throughout the length and breadth of the country. Whereas the Southern states grew faster till about 1960, the Central and Northern states picked up momentum since independence. Demographic parameters still are largely determined by four larger states – Bihar, Madhya Pradesh, Rajasthan and Uttar Pradesh (BIMARU states). Downward trend in population growth rate has remained steady since 1991. The intercensal data since 1991, more specifically after 2001, have given the assurance that the population and other projections are unlikely to be missed by a large margin this time.

A large space has been devoted to thrash out some of the major social and economic issues (Chapter 11) that confront India's developmental problems. While discussing Energy position in India, the most important input for industrial and social development, stress has been put on nuclear and other renewable sources of energy. A large space has also been devoted to one of the more vital affirmative steps taken to contain population growth, Family Planning (Chapter 13). Obviously, this is an issue that is exceedingly closely related to very many population-related matters – especially infant, child and maternal mortality, expectation of life, education and the economic strengths and weaknesses in different cross-sections of the Indian population. Performance of various states and population groups has been discussed. Growth and distribution of population by religion and cross-classification of these religious groups by sex, residence, education, birth and mortality rates, work participation rate, etc. have been dealt with in Chapter 4. The state of human development (HDI), poverty level (HPI), and gender discrimination (GEI) in various states have been discussed in Chapter 12. Chapter 14 gives a first hand idea about some important changes that have occurred between 2001 and 2011.

Some demographic parameters in India are changing very fast. A large part of our description and analysis of facts and figures often are based on data that are a little old, some are relatively current. Therefore, it may not be wise to relate events that refer to different time points especially since we did not try any time series, multivariate or other statistical analysis of data obtained from various sources. The reader therefore will need to try to visualize the broad trends that emerge from such assorted data and information. The sole intention of this book is to present a first hand picture of the visible socio-economic and demographic changes happening in India, especially since independence.

Kolkata **P.K. Majumdar**

1
Country Profile of India

Location and Boundaries

India is a multi-ethnic, multi-religious and multi-linguistic country having political boundaries with Pakistan in the West, Nepal, Bhutan, and China in the Northeast and Bangladesh and Myanmar in the East. Arabian Sea in the West, Indian Ocean in the South and Bay of Bengal in the East demarcate Indian peninsula. This subcontinent occupies much of Southeast Asia. The country's exact size is subject to debate because some borders are disputed. The Indian government lists the total area as 3,287,780 square kilometers, which includes the Pakistan occupied Kashmir (POK or Azad Kashmir, as it is called in Pakistan) and the total land area as 3,060,500 square kilometers. United Nations lists the total area as 3,287,263 square kilometers and total land area as 2,973,190 square kilometers. In either case, India is the seventh largest country in the world and about one-third the size of the United States. The great Himalayan range in the North and Northeast and the great water bodies on the other three sides have protected the Indian subcontinent against easy invasion in the past. Land boundaries total 15,200 kilometers. India shares common borders with Pakistan (3,325 kilometers; the Jammu and Kashmir border is 1,085 kilometers), China (line of actual control is 3,439 kilometers), Bhutan (605 kilometers), Nepal (1,690 kilometers), Burma (1,452 kilometers), and Bangladesh (4,339 km). Some regions remain the target of cross-border terrorism and some regions have so porous border with neighboring countries that illegal migration and trade vitiate India's social, political and cultural climate. Although India and Sri Lanka do not share a land boundary, the shortest distance between the two countries is only 64 kilometers across the Palk Strait. India's total coastline is 7,516 kilometers in length, which comprises 5,422 kilometers for the mainland, 132 kilometers for the Lakshadweep Islands and 1,962 kilometers for the Andaman and Nicobar Islands.

Climate

Six different climate regions can be seen in India. A vast majority of the population lives in *Humid Sub-tropical* (very warm summer) climate (Madhya Pradesh, Uttar Pradesh, Bihar, Jharkhand, most of the Northeastern states and part of West Bengal), followed by *Tropical Wet & Dry* (*Savannah*) (Maharashtra, a part of Madhya Pradesh, Chhattisgarh, Orissa, Andhra Pradesh and Tamil Nadu). Jammu & Kashmir, Himachal Pradesh, Uttaranchal, Sikkim and Arunachal Pradesh are in *Undifferentiated Highlands*; Punjab, Haryana, parts of Tamil Nadu, Karnataka, Maharashtra, Gujarat and Rajasthan are in *Semi-Arid region*; a part of Gujarat and most of Rajasthan are in *Desert or Arid region*; a part of the Southwestern India (Goa, part of Maharashtra and Karnataka) has *Tropical Wet climate*. People in this country lives in very different climatic conditions, from sub-zero temperature (Ladakh and many other places in Kashmir, Himachal Pradesh and Arunachal Pradesh) to temperatures as high as around 50°C (Jabbalpur, some parts of Orissa, Madhya Pradesh, Rajasthan and Gujarat). There are only a few inches of rainfall in Rajasthan as against Cherapunji in Meghalaya, which experiences the highest annual rainfall in the world. Average annual rainfall in the country as a whole is between 1,000 mm to 1,500 mm. Some parts of the Northwest receive a meager 150 to 300 millimeters of rain annually. Rain fall is very high in the Northeast and along the West coast (1,500 to 2,500 millimeters annually). Some regions are very rich in natural resources, some have very fertile lands, and some are more prone to natural calamities than most others.

Climate in India varies significantly from the permanently snow-capped Himalayas in the North to the tropics in the South. The country has four seasons. December to February is relatively dry and cool, March to May is dry but hot, from June to September predominating southwest maritime winds bring monsoon rains to most of the country, and in October and November there are retreating dry monsoons originating from the Northeast. Average temperatures range between 12.5°C to 30°C in the Northwest, 17.5°C to 30°C in the North and Northeast, and 22.5°C to 30°C in the South.

Land Use

In the year 2000, the total arable land and land under permanent crops put together was 1,697,000 square kilometers, and total irrigated land was 548,000 square kilometers (32.3% of total crop land). The total of non-arable land and land not under permanent crops was 1,276,190 square kilometers. An estimated 60 percent of cultivated land suffers from soil erosion, water-logging, and salinity.

Forest Area

Forest area covers 19.4 percent (some estimates put it at even less than 15%) of India's geographic area (63.7 million hectares). Nearly half of the country's forest cover is found in the state of Madhya Pradesh (20.7%) and the seven states (often called the Seven Sisters) of the Northeast (25.7%); the latter is however experiencing net forest loss. Forest cover in India has declined because of harvesting for fuel wood, mining, creating big dams and the expansion of agricultural land. However, of late the forest area has improved slightly.

Natural Resources

Commercially important natural resources include arable land, bauxite, chromites, coal (fourth-largest reserves in the world), diamonds, iron ore, limestone, manganese, mica, natural gas, petroleum, titanium ores and huge deposit of thorium (monazite), about one-third of the world reserve.

Economy

Agriculture still employs about 60 percent of the population, but accounts for only 20 percent of gross domestic product (GDP). From 1950 to 2000, share of industrial products increased from 15 to 27 percent of GDP. In the same period the Service Sector increased its share from 27 to 48 percent of GDP. Currently, service sector's share is close to 60 percent of GDP. In the 1980s and 1990s, private-sector initiatives increased noticeably, and information technology emerged as the most important addition to the modern hi tech organized labor. However, its growth, sky high at the moment, remains vulnerable to changes in foreign demand although the domestic market for information technology goods and services (computer and mobile telephones) is growing by leaps and bounds. Out-migration of workers in information technology is very high and the major destination states are Karnataka, Andhra Pradesh and Mumbai. A significant proportion of India's foreign exchange is earned through NRI remittance. India's foreign exchange reserve stood over $300 billion in June 2008.

Since 1980s, the liberalization measures—such as partial divestment of public sector industries and undertakings and reduced tariffs on imported capital goods—have been credited for 1990s annual economic growth rates of around 4 to 7 percent, nearly double the Hindu Growth Rate of 3–3.5 percent that characterized the previous 40 years. Since 2004, the economy is maintaining 8+ percent growth rates. Annual Foreign Direct Investment (FDI) has increased to around US$15 billion in mid 2007. India accounts for less than 1 percent of world trade in spite of having over 17 percent of the world's population. In 2002, the Gross Domestic Product (GDP) was US$496.8 billion (Rs 24.2 trillion). It has crossed US$1 trillion in mid 2007. In 2003, Purchasing Power Parity (PPP) per capita was US$2,880.

The States and the Union Territories

Prior to independence, there were hundreds of small and large princely states, which were accessed to Indian Republic after independence. Sikkim is India's last accession. Initially, there were fewer states many of which had large geographical area. State Reorganization Commission carved out many more states out of the existing ones to fulfill the aspirations of its peoples as also for administrative conveniences. The latest in the list are Uttaranchal (from Uttar Pradesh), Chhattisgarh (from Madhya Pradesh) and Jharkhand (from Bihar), all in 1990s. Originally, many of the Northeastern states were part of Assam. A further subdivision of some of the larger states cannot be ruled out.

Uttar Pradesh is by far the most populous state in the country with more than 166 million people (139 million after Uttaranchal was carved out; in 2011 it registered population strength of 200 million), which incidentally is more than the population of Pakistan, the seventh most populous country in the world. The population of undivided Uttar Pradesh (Uttaranchal included) is even greater than the population of Brazil, the fifth most populous country in the world and close to the population of Western Europe. Nineteen states now have populations over ten million, and 16 over 30 million. There are many states and UTs whose populations have not reached even the one million mark. Almost half of the country's population lives in five states, namely, Uttar Pradesh, Maharashtra, Bihar, West Bengal and Andhra Pradesh. While Uttar Pradesh and Maharashtra have held on the first two spots in terms of their ranking in 2011 as compared to that in 2001, Bihar has moved on to take the third position from its fifth position pushing West Bengal and Andhra Pradesh down to the fourth and fifth spots respectively.

As per 2001 Census report, there are 7 union territories and 28 others with full statehood. Of these 28 states, 16 are big ones; most of the smaller states are located in North and Northeast regions. These 16 states together covered over 930 millions (90.6% of India's 1027 millions population in 2001).

Population

Population of India has increased from 238 million to 1027 million in the 100 years, about 4.12 times the 1901 population size; the population density has increased from 73 in 1901 to 324 per square kilometer in 2001, nearly a 4.4 folds increase. Though the increase in population density has been fastest in Northern region (from 38 to 217 per km^2, a 5.71 folds increase), most of the states in this region, except Punjab and Haryana, have enough space for further growth of population. Population density is highest in the Eastern region where two most thickly populated states are located—West Bengal (904/km^2) and Bihar (880/km^2) as per 2001 census. Except Assam and Tripura, all the hilly states in the Northeastern region are still sparsely populated. Arunachal Pradesh is the least inhabited state (13/km^2) in the country. Most of the UTs, except Andaman & Nicober Islands (43/km^2), have very high population density. The estimated population of India in July 2005 is a little over 1080 million with annual growth rate of about 1.5 percent. Birth rate has fallen from 25.4 to 22.32 per 1,000 and IMR from 68 in 2001 to 56 per 1,000 in 2005. Life expectancy at birth in 2004 was estimated at 64 years, 63.3 years for males and 64.8 years for females.

Urban population (27.78% in 2001) in India has grown disproportionate to the degree of its industrialization and opening up of economy. There are as many as 393 cities (total number of urban agglomeration/towns is 4378) that have 100,000 or above population in India. There are 27 Municipal Corporations with more than 1 million populations (7 in Maharashtra and 5 in Uttar Pradesh). Western region, the smallest region with 16.04 percent of India's geographical area and only with two major states, Maharashtra and Gujarat, has as many as 8 Municipal Corporations each catering civic services to more than 1 million populations. Tamil Nadu (43.86%), Maharashtra (42.0%) and Gujarat (37.35%) are at the top and Himachal (9.79%), Bihar (10.47%) and Assam (12.72%) are at the bottom in the degree of urbanization in the state.

Languages Spoken

The major languages and the regional dialect in India are in excess of sixteen hundred. However, only 14 languages are granted scheduled status under the Constitution of India. Around 40 percent of Indians speak in Hindi or some dialect of it. Bengali, Telegu, and Marathi follow this in popularity. English still is the link-language and the most wanted language in India in higher studies, intra- and

Table 1.1

*Distribution of 10,000 persons by language, 1991**

Scheduled Languages	***Number of speakers (Per 10,000 persons)***	***Scheduled Languages***	***Number of speakers (Per 10,000 persons)***
Assamese	156	Oriya	335
Bengali	830	Punjabi	279
Gujarati	485	Sanskrit	1
Hindi	4,022	Sindhi	25
Kannada	390	Tamil	632
Kashmiri	1	Telugu	787
Konkani	21	Urdu	518
Malayalam	362	Scheduled Languages Total:	9,629
Manipuri	15	Non-Scheduled languages Total:	371
Marathi	745	TOTAL	10,000
Nepali	25		

*Excludes figures for Jammu & Kashmir where the 1991 census could not be conducted due to disturbed conditions.
Source: Registrar General of India, Census of India 1991 : Statement 3, Paper 1 of 1997-Language.

inter-state interactions, in judiciary and trade and commerce, especially since India became one of the most sought after destination for outsourcing because of brilliant skill of Indians in software technology as also for their fluency in English.

The Indian census lists 114 languages (22 of which are spoken by one million or more persons) that are further categorized into 216 dialects or mother tongues spoken by 10,000 or more persons. An estimated 850 languages are in daily use, and the Indian Government claims that there are more than 1,600 dialects.

Twenty-two languages are recognized by the Constitution for various political, educational, and other purposes: Assamese, Bengali, Bodo, Dogri, Gujarati, Hindi, Kannada, Kashmiri, Konkani, Maithili, Malayalam, Manipuri, Marathi, Nepali, Oriya, Punjabi, Sanskrit, Santhali, Sindhi, Tamil, Telugu, and Urdu. Numerous other languages are recognized by individual states but not officially recognized by the Central government. Linguistic issues related to education, employment, and politics are sometimes politically contentious. Indeed, some state borders are based on linguistic lines. The most commonly spoken languages are Hindi (40.2%), Bengali (8.3%), Telugu (7.9%), Marathi (7.5%), and Tamil (6.3%). The most commonly spoken languages in different states and UTs are presented in Appendix 1.1.

Religions

Although Hindus and Muslims together constitute about 94 percent of the India's population, the coexistence of four other major religious groups in the country namely, Christians, Sikhs, Buddhists and Jains is unique and enrich the 'unity in diversity' of this great nation. India has the grand distinction of being the land from where some of the important religions of the world—Hinduism, Buddhism, Sikhism and Jainism—originated. India is also the origin of some of the indigenous faiths/tribal religions that have survived even the onslaught of many major religions for centuries and are still holding their fort firmly.

The caste-class divide throughout the length and the breadth of the country adds an important social and political dimension to issues relating to the well-being of the population. Some states have remained out-migrating type for decades; some have become enriched through in-migration. The population characteristics of different states and regions are often so different that the aggregative picture of one-India often would suppress the fundamental differences that exist between different populations.

Hindus constitute 80.5 percent of India's population (lost 4.5% almost entirely to Muslims since 1951). They have overwhelming majority in most of the larger states; they are a minority in Punjab, Jammu & Kashmir and some other smaller states (most Northeastern states except Assam and Tripura) and union territory Lakshadweep.

Muslims (13.4% of total Indian population) are majority in Jammu & Kashmir. But they have a large share in the population in 9 other states (Assam, 31%, West Bengal, 25%, Kerala, 24.7%, Uttar Pradesh, 18.5%, Bihar, 16.5% and five other states Karnataka, Maharashtra, Jharkhand and Uttaranchal and Delhi have less than 15% but more than 10% Muslims in their total populations). In 1941, 23.8 percent persons in undivided India were Muslims. The proportion came down to 9.9 percent in 1951 census, the first Census after independence.

Christians' share to Indian population is around 2.34 percent (1.6% in 1941). They numerically dominate most of the Northeastern states (Nagaland, 90%, Mizoram, 87%, Meghalay, 70%,

Manipur, 34%). Some other states and UTs also have sizeable Christian population (Goa, 26%, Kerala, 19%, Arunachal Pradesh, 18.7%, and Andaman Islands, 22%).

The proportion of Sikhs in Indian population is only 1.9 percent (pre-partition proportion was 1.5%). Only in Punjab (60%) and UT Chandigarh (16%) they have significant share in the total population. Buddhists (only 0.8% of the total population) have significant presence in Sikkim (26%) and Arunachal Pradesh (13%). Jains (0.4% in the population) constitute between 1.1 and 1.3 percent in three states/UTs Rajasthan, Delhi and Maharashtra. Parshis, a very small community, are almost totally concentrated in Maharashtra. Population composition by religion for different states and UTs is presented in Appendix 1.2.

Caste-based enumeration of the population has not been carried out in India since 1931. In the last 75 years, some caste names have changed, quite a few new ones have emerged, several castes have merged with others or have moved up or down the social hierarchy, and many have become politically active. Caste being a sensitive issue, the proposition of caste-based census naturally provoked serious debate. The Home Ministry at the Center, which is in over-all charge of the Census enumeration, at some point of time was willing to include caste in the Census Schedule. Many political parties and the intelligentsia in general opined against a caste-based enumeration. They argued that enumeration of the population on the basis of caste is bound to be vitiated by vote-bank and reservation politics, leading to the inflation of population figures and the suppression or distortion of vital information on employment, education and economic status, among other things. The Anthropological Survey of India has identified 6,325 castes (7,500 if we include urban-rural differentiations). J.K. Bantia, the Census Commissioner 2001, defended the government's ultimate decision not to go for caste enumeration during the head-count planned for 2001, saying: "The Census as it is overloaded. Over five million tables are generated and analyzed even without caste enumeration." However, caste was included in 2011 census enumeration

Ethnic Groups

The exact number of ethnic groups depends on the source and method of counting. Scholars estimate that only the continent of Africa exceeds the linguistic, cultural, and genetic diversity of India. Seventy-two percent of the population is Indo-Aryan, 25 percent Dravidian, and 3 percent Mongoloid and others. Each of these groups can be further subdivided into various and changing combinations of language, religion, and, very often, caste. The Hindu caste system is technically illegal but widely practiced (generally more in rural areas) and comprises four major categories (*varnas*) that are found India-wide but are often subdivided into hundreds of sub-categories (*jatis*), many of which are often found only in specific areas. Similar hereditary and occupational social hierarchies exist within Sikh and Muslim communities but are generally far less pervasive and institutionalized. About 16 percent of the total population is "untouchable" (Scheduled Caste is the more formal, legal term; *Dalit* is the term preferred by "untouchables" and roughly translates to downtrodden); around 8 percent of the population belongs to one of 461 indigenous groups, called Scheduled Tribes for legal purposes, although the term *adivasi* is commonly used.

Early Empires

Whereas human settlement in India dates back to roughly 400,000 to 200,000 B.C., extensive urbanization and trade appear to have begun in the Indus River Valley around 3000 B.C. with the

Harappan civilization. From this period until the termination of British colonial rule in 1947, numerous empires ruled various parts of South Asia, often assimilating a rich collection of peoples and each adding its own contribution to an increasingly rich tapestry of cultures, ideas, and technologies. Indeed, many of India's current political, cultural, and economic traits have been influenced by historical events and trends, many of which pre-date European contact. Among the most influential early empires were the Aryans, who migrated from Persia to Northwestern India around 2000 B.C. and brought a new pantheon of anthropomorphic gods, an early form of Sanskrit language, a *tiered social system* essentially based on ethnicity and occupation, and religious texts that are an important part of living Hindu traditions. From 326 B.C. to around 200 B.C., the Mauryan Empire emerged as India's first regal power and ruled a large proportion of the then Indian territory with a highly centralized and hierarchical administration. For the next few hundred years, North and South India experienced a succession of ruling powers. From 320 A.D. to 550 A.D., most of North India was ruled by the Gupta Empire, which in contrast to the Mauryan Empire maintained a decentralized form of governance. As under the Aryans, Gupta authority was religiously legitimized, and it was in this period, called the Classical Age, that the multiple components of Hindu culture became crystallized into a more unified system of thought.

From the disintegration of the Gupta Empire to the mid-thirteenth century, various regional kingdoms emerged, and conflicts among them often led to their defeat but rarely to their total annihilation. In consequence, no highly centralized government emerged in South India, and South Indian villages enjoyed greater local autonomy than those in North India. During this period, South India engaged in flourishing trade with Arabs and Southeast Asia, which facilitated diffusion of Indian mathematical ideas to the Middle East and Indian art, literature, and social customs to Southeast Asia.

Islamic influence in South Asia emerged around 711AD as Arabs conquered part of Sindh (now in Pakistan), and by the tenth century the Punjab came under the control of Turk ruler Mahmud of Ghazni. By the thirteenth century, much of India had been periodically conquered, but rarely held for long, by a steady succession of Turk rulers, collectively referred to as the Delhi Sultanate or Mughal emperors. The most prominent Mughal ruler was Akbar, who ruled from 1556 to 1605. Akbar succeeded in political and geographic consolidation by using the powerful *zamindars* (landlords) to control local populations and collect revenues. But over time, the administrative capacities of later Mughal rulers suffered from overstuffed and excessively corrupt bureaucracies and huge, unwieldy armies.

2
Population Growth in India

2.1 Pre-Census Population in India

The world population stood at 1,600 millions at the beginning of the twentieth century. The same in India was around 240 millions, which was about 15 percent of the world total. At the end of the last century India's population stood at a little over 1,000 millions against the world total of 6,055 millions. That is, one in every six persons on this earth was an Indian disregarding those who had settled in other countries. India has only 2.4 percent of the world surface area and has to support over 16.7 percent of the World population today. By 2045, India is most likely to overtake China to become the most populous country on the earth with 17.2 percent world total. In the past 100 years, the average growth rate in India had consistently been higher, though by a small margin, than the average world population growth rate. UN estimate of average annual population growth rate of the world between 1990 and 2000 was 1.4 percent. The average growth rate in India in the same period was 1.93 percent. The large gap between the two averages is almost likely to be bridged by 2015 when the world average would come down to 1.1–1.2 percent and that of India would be 1.3 percent or even less. The populations of the ten most populous countries of the world are given in Table 2.1.

There was a time in the history of world population when 50 percent of the world population lived in this sub-continent. The demographers and population scientists have tried to estimate world population using variety of information for the period when regular censuses were not conducted (Table 2.2). The growth of world population in the last 12,000 years suggests that most regions were not as conducive as this sub-continent was to support human life system. Even in the remote past, it seems that the climate, natural vegetation and other natural resources were favorable to sustain human lives in this part of the world. To support the growing world population, the hitherto neglected regions had to be explored and make land habitable to create rooms for the enlarged numbers. That probably is the reason why India's share to world population had fallen as the world population grew. It came down to about 14 percent around the middle of the twentieth century. Since then, the trend has been reversed mainly due to the fact that the average growth rate in India has been in excess

Table 2.1
Population of 10 most populous countries

Country	*Reference date*	*Population (million)*
China	01.02.2000	1,277.6
India	01.03.2001	1,027.0
USA	April 2000	281.4
Indonesia	01.07.2000	212.1
Brazil	01.07.2000	170.1
Pakistan	01.07.2000	156.5
Russian Federation	01.07.2000	146.9
Bangladesh	01.07.2000	129.2
Japan	01.10.2000	126.9
Nigeria	01.02.2000	111.5

of the average world population growth rate. Table 2.2 shows how the world population has grown and how India's share has changed over time.

Learned guesses from various documents put the Indian population at around 100 million at the time of Ashoka, some 300 years before the birth of Christ, which was nearly half the world population at that time. From the scattered evidences available, scientists came to the conclusion that Indian population remained almost stationary between Ashoka's time and the beginning of the seventeenth century, i.e., for about 2000 years. The birth and death rates were almost the same – a shift of balance this or that way saw some small increase or decrease in the population. In times of peace and good harvest, the population growth gained some momentum. This favorable environment for growth lasted only for a short while. Within a few years draught, natural catastrophe, famine, epidemic and war created conditions non-conducive to sustained population growth. The growth curve

Table 2.2

Comparison of growth of population in India vis-à-vis world population

Year	*World population (million)*	*India's population (million)*	*Proportion of (3) and (2)*
1	*2*	*3*	*4*
0	200	100	50.0
1300 AD	400	50	12.5
1650	500	100	20.0
1750	700	190	27.1
1800	900	200	22.2
1820	1000	210	21.0
1850	1200	230	19.2
1900	1600	240	15.0
1930	2000	280	14.0
1950	2540	360	14.2
1960	3060	440	14.4
1970	3720	550	14.8
1980	4480	690	15.4
1990	5300	840	15.8
1999	5862	993	16.9

Source: UN 1949–50, 1959–62, Davis, 1953, US Bureau of Census, 1983, Census India, 1981, 1991, HDR 2001, UNDP.

Figure 2.1

Growth of world population vis-à-vis population of India, 1650–1999

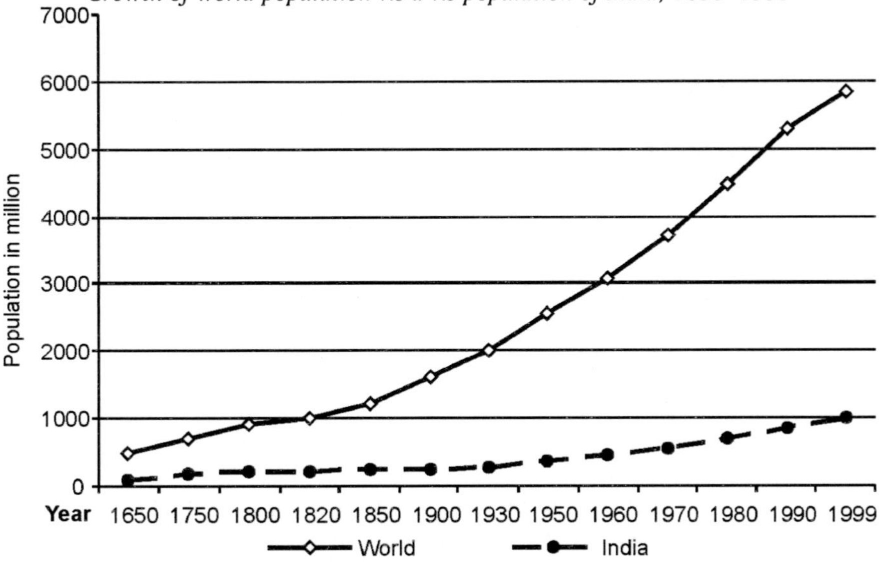

showed sudden drops. Instead of a smooth curve, it showed irregular fluctuations. Although a consistent upward trend is noticed since the beginning of the seventeenth century, the growth line became smooth only in early twentieth century.

The discovery of the Indus Valley Civilization (2500 BC – 1500 BC) through excavation by the Archaeological Survey of India, has thrown considerable light on the human habitations that grew up surrounding cities and towns in the West and Northwestern part of this sub-continent. The archaeological fingerprints of the civilization from the excavations have not been fully analyzed as yet. Once they are fully analyzed, it is hoped that they will throw significant light on the nature of human habitat that prevailed in that era. In the epics *Ramayana* and *Mahabharata,* we find mention of many kingdoms and the size of their populations. Already we have found archaeological evidences of some of these (Dwaraka, for example). We hope that a comprehensive picture about the social, economic and demographic characteristics existing in the distant past in this sub-continent would become available through archaeological surveys.

The Harappa and Mohan-jo-daro excavations reveal that India was in possession of a highly developed civilization with large and populous cities, well built houses, temples and public-buildings constructed by bricks and enjoyed many other amenities which the peoples of Mesopotamia and Egypt as far back as the 3rd or 4th millennium BC enjoyed. The Aryans came to India through the Northwest around 2000 BC. Mostly agricultural and pastoral, they used the animal-drawn plough and used irrigation and manures for cultivation. After arriving in India they made additional acquisitions, the most important of which was alphabetic writing borrowed from Semitic sources about 800 BC and the metal iron, acquired even earlier. So, in India some three to seven thousand years back there were peoples possessing a sufficient advanced knowledge and technology to support a dense population. Aryans found the soil and climate in India favorable for the application of their technology and many decided not to go back to the place of their origin.

We learn from the Rigveda, the earliest literature, that population was scanty and dispersed over wide areas in small villages. The Brahmanic literature (800–600 BC) around shows that some of the villages had grown into towns and capitals with an urban mode of life. The Buddhist literature also indicates that between the 7th and 4th century BC the economy of India was comparable to that of the later Middle Ages in Europe. Crafts and commerce were flourishing and were highly organized. In an ordinary town there used to live between 30 to 1,000 families and about 20 such cities existed in Northern India alone.

Arthashastra (The Principles of Governance, 325 BC), developed by Kautilya, one of the greatest genius in the history of political economy and administration, is the first historical treatise that presents evidences that population counts and registration of birth and death were indispensable part of administration at the time of the emperor Chandragupta. Kautilya firmly established population statistics as a measure of state policy for the purpose of taxation and induction of able-bodied persons to state army. *Arthashastra* contains a detailed description of methods of conducting population, economic and agricultural censuses. It also shows that classification of the population by caste and occupation was an important feature of these head-counts. However, the historians have not found any evidence of the same in most of the next 2000 years. The existence of dense population was confirmed by Alexander's army which invaded India in 327–326 BC. At that time even a small state had 37 towns each of which had populations over 5,000. The records of Chandragupta (321–297 BC) show that there was a standing army of 700,000 men, the maintenance of which must have required a substantial population. Under Ashoka (274–236 BC), the Indian civilization probably reached its summit due to efficient administration, the use of written commands, and abundant commerce.

During the Moghul period, extensive records were maintained on land, production, population, famines, etc. *Ain-e-Akbari* (administrative report) by Abul Fazal gives evidence of population count at the time of Moghul Emperor Akbar. The report also included comprehensive data pertaining to population, industry, wealth and many other characteristics of the state and its peoples. Prof. P.C. Mahalanobis has referred to these two treatises, *Arthashastra* and *Ain-e-Akabari*, as the first and second breakthrough in the Indian demographic statistics. Historians like W.H. Moreland, Romila Thapar, Shireen Moosvi, Irfan Habib, and others have examined intensely and carefully these two treatises and tried to throw light on the social, political and economic environment prevailing in those periods and also have made intelligent guesses of the population size, production process and distribution of the produces.

Very early in the British rule, the land surveyors discovered that population census was a general feature in the Moghul and the Maratha kingdoms. Dr Francis Buchanan has referred to a document, *Khana Shumari*, which mentioned the number of houses, households, businessmen, caste groups, agricultural implements, handlooms, and all that in a particular administrative jurisdiction. *Khana Shumari* is considered similar in many respects to the modern statistical tables. Kinsley Davis came to the conclusion after studying various archaeological documents, literatures and other historical documents that the population of India around 300 BC was between 100–140 millions.

The European merchants started to come to India in large numbers since the sixteenth century. For obvious reasons, such as defense, collection of revenues and taxes and employment of population in profitable trades and services, the East India Company was anxious to obtain reliable estimates of population in its Indian settlements. Moreland, the famous historian, estimated the total number of Indians in 1600 AD. For numerical basis of the estimation he concentrated, in the South, on the strength of the armed forces and in the North on the land under cultivation, on both of which subjects contemporary figures were available. Indirect estimates had been made, for example, of Fort St. George, Madras, for 1639 and 1648 by comparing revenues in 1639 and 1648, and for 1646 by adding reported famine deaths of 1647 to the estimate of 1648. A Census of some sort is mentioned having been taken in 1716 of Bombay, probably embracing only the Fort and a portion of the Island. The unsettled condition of the country, following the disintegration of the Moghul Empire, did not offer favorable conditions for systematic estimates of population. An estimate made of the company's possessions as late as the 1780's were discounted by H.T. Colebrooke.

The writings and dispatches by the merchants' document a very high population density in India in that period. They also reported that some of the cities had 200,000–500,000 populations. In 1793, Lord Cornwallis introduced *Permanent Settlement Act* for collection of land revenues. This administrative reform produced immediate results in two fronts – a better estimate of the amount of cultivable land and the agricultural produces thereof and a reliable estimate of the size of the population. Earlier in 1789, Cornwallis ordered for a district-wise account of population in the Bengal Presidency. Regretting that 'in India, no bills of mortality, nor registers of births, marriages and burials, afford data for calculation', Colebrooke built up an ingenious system of self-checking inferences based variously on area, density, sample counts, persons per household leases, ground rent, land under cultivation, area under each tillage, rent-rolls, and the yield and consumption of articles like cereals, pulses and salt. He presented a consolidated report (Remarks on the Husbandry and Internal Commerce of Bengal, 1794) on the size of population, size of the labor force and demand for consumer produces. Dr. Francis Buchanan and Walter Hamilton in 1808 conducted a mammoth survey on natural resources, social characteristics, population size, and distributions of the population by caste and occupation, etc. in the Bengal Presidency following the methods developed by Colebrooke. The microfilm of this 10,000 pages document has been preserved in the Indian Statistical Institute. In 1815, Walter Hamilton published the first Gazetteer. This gazetteer dealt with the population and related events prior to 1800. Some of the finest technical and methodological surveys conducted in this period are 'the censuses' carried out on the town of Allahabad (1824) and the city of Benaras (1827–28) by James Prinsep and of the city of Dacca (1830) by Henry Walters. Walter's census was perhaps the first complete census of an Indian city, which classified the population by sex and broad-age-groups, the houses and structures by building characteristics, storeys, other amenities, lodgers and inmates, and the population again by as many as 132 caste-occupations.

From the beginning of the nineteenth century, revenue and topographical surveys were conducted in various parts of the country. The surveys gave very important information on population size, natural resources, agricultural production, prices of consumer goods, labor wages, irrigation facilities, occupations, caste distribution, and others. Between 1836 and 1873 revenue survey was conducted in Bengal Presidency. The survey produced maps for each village and distribution of land and their uses in the villages. Statistical tables were also prepared for area of the village, population size, and agricultural and non-agricultural labors in the villages.

Table 2.3

Estimates of population of India, 300 BC to 1800 AD

Year	*Population (million)*	*Source*
320 BC	100	Romila Thapar
300 BC	100–140	Prananath, Kingsley Davis
	180	J.M. Datta
1100 AD	50	Desmond Annable
1200	51	
1300	50	
1400	46	
1500	54	
1600	100	W.H. Mooreland
	125	Kingsley Davis
	144	Shireen Moosvi
	150	Ifran Habib
1750	130	Chandrasekhar
	190	D. Bhattacharyya
1800	120	Win Playfair
	207	P.C. Mahalanobis & D. Bhattacharyya
	198	M.D. Morris
	200	Ifran Habib

Source: D. Bhattacharyya: Historical Demography in India, in, Symposium on Historical Demography, Indian Institute of Management, Bangalore, 1985.

Table 2.4

Estimates of the size of population in India between 1801 and 1871 (million)

Year	*Source*	
	Mahalanobis-Bhattacharyya	*M.D. Morris*
1801	207	196
1811	215	203
1821	205	211
1831	216	219
1841	212	228
1851	232	237
1861	244	246
1871	256	255

Prof. D. Bhattacharyya, after studying various documents and reports, has compiled a population table for India between 300 BC and 1800 AD.

There is considerable confusion and doubt about the size of population in India prior to 1800 AD because of lack of reliable supporting evidences. Since the beginning of the nineteenth century a large number of survey reports, region specific though, are available. Prof. Ashok Mitra in 1961 took a compilation project on the size of population in the pre-census days, 1801 and 1871. P.C. Mahalanobis and D. Bhattacharyya jointly and M.D. Morris produced estimates of population in different decades (Table 2.4).

2.2 Population Growth in Modern India

For the convenience of discussion, the history of population growth in modern India is divided into three periods – pre-1921, 1921–1951 and 1951 onwards.

2.2.1 Pre-1921 Period

Preparations for conducting complete census began in the middle of the nineteenth century. We can call 1850–70 as the preparatory phase in the history of periodic census in India. But for the Sepoy Mutiny in 1857 the periodic census could have been started earlier. The decade 1860–70 is worth remembering in the context of population count for various reasons. India was comparatively free from famines, epidemics and natural calamities which had remained integral parts of Indian life. The death rate dropped, growth rate improved. For this, a large proportion of the population in the 1870s was constituted of children aged 10 years or less. But nature took revenge in the very next decade. Famines and epidemics were widespread in various parts of the country. Madras Presidency was most affected. Death rates climbed, birth rates declined. A systematic and modern population census was conducted non-synchronously between 1865 and 1872 in different parts of the country. This effort culminating in 1872 has been popularly labeled as the *first population census* in India. The 1881 Census (first complete synchronous census) showed that although the population size compared to 1871–72 increased marginally, the proportion of infants and children dropped. It is to be remembered that a great change in birth or death rate in a decade continues to affect the population composition in the next four or more decades. The higher birth rates in the 1960s were felt in the 1980s. The increase in the proportion of girls in the child-bearing age resulted in the increase in birth rates. Between 1880 and 1920, death rates in the population fluctuated very frequently.

The great famine in 1896–97 took heavy tolls of life throughout the country. Immediately thereafter, plague took the form of epidemic, especially in Bombay Presidency. About 2 percent of the population died as a result of the famine and plague epidemic. The first decade of the twentieth century also saw famines and epidemics playing havoc in different parts of the country. Nearly the whole of Uttar Pradesh came under the siege of famine in 1907. Lives in Bengal and Bombay Presidency were badly affected by plague, and by malaria in Punjab and UP. However, these epidemics lasted only for a while. That is why the damage to the population in this decade was far less than that in the previous one.

The population growth rate recorded between 1881 and 1891 (1.5% per annum) was the highest growth rate ever registered till 1950. Between 1891 and 1901, the total population in India actually decreased. A slow increase in the population was registered in the next decade. The 1918–19 influenza epidemics took away lives of hundreds and thousands of people. Infants, young children and young pregnant women were the worst victims of this influenza epidemic. Just before this, cholera broke out in various parts of the country. In 73 districts, more than 30 in every 1,000 people died from these. In 42 other districts, the casualty was between 20 and 30 for every 1,000 people. Northern and Central India were the worst sufferers of this catastrophe. One million people died in 1896–97 from plague epidemic alone. Since then till 1918, about 0.5 million people died from plague every year. Between 1891 and 1921 the average death rate fluctuated between 45 and 50 per thousand – close to biological limit. The Southern part of India was relatively free from the effects of these killer diseases. The average death rate in this region was somewhere between 36 and 43.

During 1901–21, population in North India declined by 1.4 percent because of famines and epidemics. Population in the South increased fastest, by 11 percent. Population in Western region grew by about 9 percent. Population in Assam, Nagaland, Manipur, Sikkim and Tripura, grew fast in this period. The surge in population growth in Assam was due to its tea gardens receiving migrants from Bihar and elsewhere. Between 1911 and 1921, population of India actually declined by 0.8 million.

2.2.2 1921–1951

Prior to 1921 the population from time to time increased or decreased. Although the population has increased over the years, the growth has been exceedingly slow and uneven. Since 1921 the rise has been steady. For this reason the decade 1921–31 is very distinctive in the demographic history of India. Our problem so long had been how to prevent untimely deaths of millions of people in India. With 1921 a problem of different kind began to emerge – how to contain the population growth. Demographers and social scientists and even the political personalities apprehended this situation long back. Even if famine and epidemics were prevented, the steady rise in numbers would hasten increase in malnutrition and morbidity and act as impediment to development.

Gopalswamy, the Census Commissioner of India, 1951 rightly called the year 1921 as the **Great Demographic Divide** in the history of growth of population in India. The First World War created a condition for increase in agricultural and industrial production; employment situations also rocked high. India played a very important role in the two World Wars. India had to take the responsibility for supplying the basic necessities for the war. As a result, industries in India started to grow so also the trade and commerce. India's export trade increased by leaps and bounds. Food grains and other agricultural products increased simultaneously keeping the price under control. Purchasing power of the common man increased and since there was plenty of food available at reasonable prices, general health of the people improved, and resistance to common diseases also increased. The call for denunciation of foreign goods by M.K. Gandhi helped energize household and small-scale industries. The political environment prevailing lend a hand to organize the agricultural and industrial labor. The land reform movement gained some momentum. The British Raj had to concede some concession and autonomy to the provinces in the face of revolt against British rule fast spreading to every corner of the country. Gandhi's call for public health improvement and spread of education among the masses created a type of enthusiasm not seen before. This along with the improvement in communication and transportation network (for movement of military personnel, food and other commodities) facilitated to bring down general mortality level.

The end of the First World War was followed by a global economic depression. India was hard hit by this recession since the British Empire was much dependent on India for its economic strength. However, even this serious economic depression could not put a check on the population growth.

Gopalaswami has given some argument for this fast growth of population. For him, special programs undertaken for improvement of public health and enhancement of the health delivery system were the principal causes behind this high population growth. But there are differences of opinions among population experts. Modern demographers do not lay much credence on control of epidemics. They put stress on social and economic changes and on improvement in agricultural production, especially food grains.

The period 1920–40 may be regarded as the period of resurgence in India. A close coordination between social, political and economic activities was visible. The end of British Rule in India was only a matter of time. The signs of economic recovery were clearly visible. A good proportion of the agricultural labor slowly shifted towards non-agricultural enterprises. Size of the organized sector started to increase. Improvement in transport facilities, preservation of agricultural products and lending from cooperatives and other financial institutions on easy terms created an environment conducive to greater agricultural production.

Table 2.5
Population in India, 1901–2001

Year	*Persons (P)*	*Male (M)*	*Female (F)*	*F-M*	*Decadal growth rate*			*Crude death rate*		*Sex ratio*
					P	*M*	*F*	*M*	*F*	*(F/M)*
1901	238396327	120791301	117605026	–3186275				50.4	49.9	972
1911	252093390	128385368	123708022	–4677346	5.75	6.287	5.189	46.6	48.2	964
1921	251321213	128546225	122774988	–5771237	–0.31	0.125	–0.75	52.8	53.5	955
1931	278977238	142929689	136047549	–6882140	11.00	11.19	10.81	35.2	37.7	950
1941	318660580	163685302	154975278	–8710024	14.22	14.52	13.91	27.2	29.4	945
1951	361088090	185528462	175559628	–9968834	13.31	13.34	13.28	28.8	30.2	946
1961	439234771	226293201	212941570	–13351631	21.64	21.97	21.29	20.5	23.4	941
1971	548159652	284049276	264110376	–19938900	24.80	25.52	24.03	17.3	18.6	930
1981	685184692	354397884	330786808	–23611076	25.00	24.77	25.25	12.4	12.7	934
1991	843930861	437597929	406332932	–31264997	23.17	23.48	22.84	10.3		929
2001	1027015247	531277078	495738169	–35538909	21.69	21.41	22	8.9	8.1	933

Indian industries and trades with other countries grew fast because of the World War II. Many new industries were started. Employment situation in India was at its best in this period. New towns and cities came up. A sizeable proportion of the agricultural labor moved to industries. The rural-urban migration stream became strong. Infant and general mortality started to decline. Average expectation of life increased.

During 1921–51 the population growth in the Central region was somewhat low compared to that in India as a whole. High death rate and out-migration were the major factors behind this less than average growth in this region. The fast growth of industries in Western region, more specifically in Bombay and Baroda, attracted migrants from other regions. In-migration was an important cause behind the higher population growth in this region. Partition of India saw a redistribution of population between India and Pakistan. People coming from Pakistan far out-numbered those migrated to Pakistan. The share of Muslims in the total Indian population came down from 23.8 percent in 1941 to 9.9 percent in 1951.

Figure 2.2
Population in India, 1901–2001

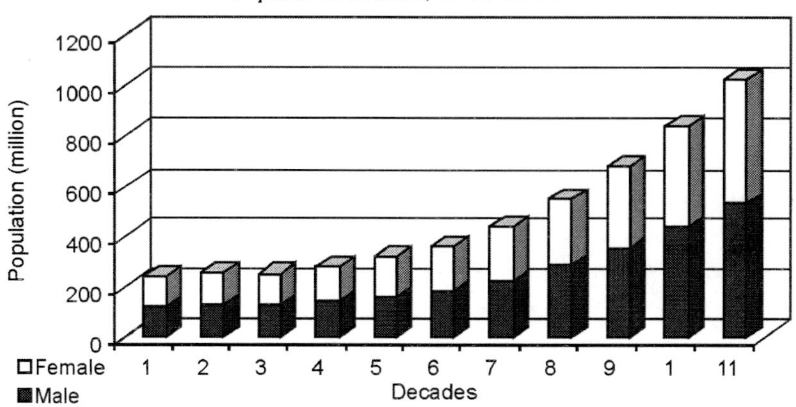

Figure 2.3
Decadal growth rates in India, 1901–2001

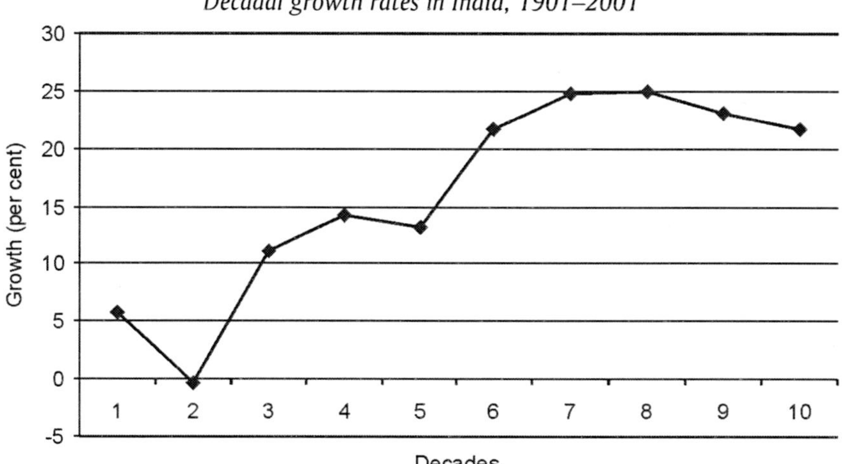

Table 2.6
Proportion of area and population of the states and UTs to the total area and total population of India, 1901–2001

*States/UTs**	*Area*	*Census Years*										
	1971	*1901*	*1911*	*1921*	*1931*	*1941*	*1951*	*1961*	*1971*	*1981*	*1991*	*2001*
1	*2*	*3*	*4*	*5*	*6*	*7*	*8*	*9*	*10*	*11*	*12*	*13*
Northern States	21.79	11.3	10.52	10.56	10.64	10.95	10.58	10.94	11.27	11.78	12.23	13.75
Haryana	1.35	1.94	1.66	1.69	1.63	1.65	1.57	1.73	1.83	1.88	1.93	2.05
Himachal Pradesh	1.69	0.81	0.75	0.77	0.73	0.71	0.66	0.64	0.63	0.62	0.61	0.59
Jammu & Kashmir	6.76	0.9	0.91	0.96	0.96	0.92	0.9	0.81	0.84	0.88	0.91	0.98
Punjab	1.53	3.15	2.67	2.85	2.87	3.01	2.54	2.54	2.47	2.44	2.39	2.37
Rajasthan	10.41	4.32	4.36	4.10	4.21	4.35	4.42	4.59	4.70	4.99	5.20	5.50

Cont'd...

Table 2.6 Cont'd...

1	*2*	*3*	*4*	*5*	*6*	*7*	*8*	*9*	*10*	*11*	*12*	*13*
Chandigarh*	—	0.01	0.01	0.01	0.01	0.01	0.01	0.02	0.05	0.06	0.08	0.09
Delhi*	0.05	0.17	0.16	0.19	0.23	0.29	0.48	0.61	0.74	0.91	1.11	1.34
Uttaranchal $												0.83
Eastern States	20.93	24.7	24.94	25.02	25.11	25.4	24.96	25.88	26.00	25.98	25.79	25.89
Assam	2.39	1.38	1.53	1.85	1.99	2.10	2.22	2.47	2.67	2.91	2.64	2.59
Bihar	5.29	11.5	11.23	11.19	11.24	11.04	10.74	10.57	10.28	10.21	10.2	8.07
Jharkhand $												2.62
Manipur	0.68	0.12	0.14	0.15	0.16	0.16	0.16	0.18	0.20	0.21	0.22	0.23
Meghalaya	0.68	0.14	0.16	0.17	0.17	0.17	0.17	0.18	0.18	0.20	0.21	0.22
Nagaland	0.5	0.04	0.06	0.06	0.06	0.06	0.06	0.08	0.09	0.11	0.14	0.19
Orissa	4.74	4.32	4.51	4.44	4.48	4.32	4.06	4.00	4.00	3.84	3.73	3.57
Sikkim	0.22	0.02	0.03	0.03	0.04	0.04	0.04	0.04	0.04	0.04	0.05	0.05
Tripura	0.32	0.07	0.09	0.13	0.14	0.16	0.17	0.26	0.29	0.3	0.33	0.31
W. Bengal	2.67	7.11	7.14	6.95	6.77	7.29	7.28	7.95	8.08	7.97	8.06	7.81
Andaman N. Is*	0.25	0.01	0.01	0.01	0.01	0.01	0.01	0.01	0.02	0.03	0.03	0.03
Arunachal Pradesh	2.54							0.08	0.09	0.09	0.10	0.11
Mizoram	0.04	0.03	0.04	0.04	0.04	0.05	0.05	0.06	0.06	0.07	0.08	0.09
Central States	22.42	27.5	26.81	26.2	25.5	25.27	24.73	24.16	23.71	23.83	24.24	24.07
Chattishgarh $												2.02
Madhya Pradesh	13.47	7.07	7.71	7.63	7.65	7.53	7.22	7.37	7.60	7.62	7.84	5.88
Uttar Pradesh	8.95	20.4	19.1	18.57	17.85	17.74	17.5	16.79	16.11	16.21	16.44	16.17
Western States	15.45	12.2	12.62	12.56	12.91	12.92	13.55	13.86	14.24	14.32	14.24	14.39
Gujarat	5.96	3.81	3.88	4.05	4.12	4.3	4.5	4.7	4.87	4.97	4.88	4.93
Maharashtra	9.35	8.13	8.52	8.3	8.59	8.42	8.87	9.01	9.2	9.17	9.33	9.42
Dadra & Nagar Haveli*	0.01	0.01	0.01	0.01	0.01	0.01	0.01	0.01	0.01	0.02	0.02	0.02
Daman & Diu (and Goa)*	0.12	0.21	0.21	0.2	0.19	0.18	0.16	0.14	0.16	0.16	0.01	0.02
Southern States	19.41	24.3	25.11	25.66	25.84	25.46	26.17	25.17	24.78	24.09	22.37	21.88
Andhra Pradesh	8.42	8.00	8.51	8.52	8.67	8.56	8.62	8.19	7.94	7.80	7.86	7.37
Goa											0.14	0.13
Karnataka	5.83	5.48	5.37	5.32	5.25	5.10	5.37	5.37	5.34	5.42	5.31	5.13
Kerala	1.18	2.68	2.84	3.10	3.41	3.46	3.75	3.85	3.88	3.71	2.37	3.10
Tamil Nadu	3.96	8.08	8.29	8.61	8.41	8.24	8.34	7.67	7.52	7.06	6.59	6.05
Lakshadweep*	—	0.01	0.01	0.01	0.01	0.01	0.01	0.01	0.01	0.01	0.01	0.01
Pondicherry*	0.01	0.1	0.1	0.1	0.09	0.09	0.08	0.08	0.09	0.09	0.09	0.09

$ Territories Uttaranchal, Jharkhand and Chhattisgarh have been carved out from Uttar Pradesh, Bihar and Madhya Pradesh, respectively.

Table 2.7

Changes in the proportion of the population of states, India 1901–2001

States/Union Territories*	1901–21	1921–51	1951–61	1961–71	1971–81	1981–91	1991–01	1951–81	1981–01	1901–01
1	14	15	16	17	18	19	20	21	22	23
Northern States	–1.44	43.9	25.7	28.56	30.34	27.6	36.74	110.6	74.46	492.6
Haryana	–7.94	33.30	33.79	32.23	28.04	27.41	28.06	126.50	63.15	455.2
Himachal Pradesh	0.41	23.70	17.87	23.04	22.46	20.79	17.53	77.62	41.96	313.8
Jammu & Kashmir	13.32	34.0	9.44	29.65	29.57	30.34	29.04	83.84	68.19	469.1
Punjab	–5.20	28.10	21.56	21.70	23.01	20.81	19.76	81.98	44.68	324.1
Rajasthan	–0.01	55.20	26.20	27.83	32.36	28.44	28.33	113.30	64.83	548.5
Chandigarh*	–17.40	33.80	394.10	114.6	74.95	42.16	40.33	1775.0	99.49	3877
Delhi*	20.36	257.0	52.44	52.93	52.41	51.45	46.31	255.30	121.60	3396
Eastern States	6.73	43.4	26.06	25.54	24.69	23.72	22.11	97.10	51.05	449.8
Assam	40.94	73.20	34.88	34.95	36.09	24.24	18.85	147.09	47.65	808.5
Bihar	2.90	37.90	19.76	21.33	23.90	23.38	28.43	80.04	18.54	303.4
Manipur	35.00	50.40	35.04	37.53	33.65	29.29	30.02	148.10	68.10	825.7
Meghalaya	24.05	43.40	27.03	31.5	31.25	32.86	29.94	119.10	72.63	677
Nagaland	56.38	34.10	14.07	39.88	49.73	56.08	64.41	262.90	156.60	2046
Orissa	8.31	31.30	19.82	25.05	19.72	20.06	15.94	79.38	39.20	356
Sikkim	38.48	68.50	17.76	29.38	50.44	28.47	32.98	129.00	70.83	1077
Tripura	75.65	110.0	78.71	36.28	32.37	34.30	15.74	222.40	55.43	1908
W. Bengal	3.15	50.50	32.80	26.87	22.96	24.73	17.84	107.20	46.98	473.2
Andaman N. Is.	9.89	14.30	105.2	81.17	63.51	48.7	26.94	506.5	88.76	1292
Arunachal Pradesh				38.91	34.34	36.83	26.21	—	72.69	
Mizoram	19.51	100.0	35.61	24.93	46.75	39.70	29.18	149	80.46	1292
Central States	0.54	35.6	18.86	22.49	25.38	24.40	22.80	82.54	52.76	361.8
Madhya Pradesh	13.71	36.00	24.17	28.67	25.15	27.24	24.34	99.95	15.73	358.3
Uttar Pradesh	–4.03	35.50	16.66	19.78	25.49	25.55	25.8	75.35	49.78	341.5
Western States	8.75	55.00	26.52	28.21	25.37	23.77	22.98	100.1	52.21	509.4
Gujarat	11.88	59.80	26.88	29.39	27.21	20.80	22.89	108.8	48.44	557.4
Maharashtra	7.52	53.50	23.00	27.45	24.35	25.73	22.57	95.91	54.10	499.2
Dadra & Nagar Haveli	27.87	33.80	39.56	27.96	39.78	33.57	59.20	153.70	112.60	861.6
Daman, Diu & Goa	–1.13	19.00	5.14	36.88	26.15	28.62	55.59	81.54	100.10	
Southern States	11.13	46.60	16.96	22.82	21.30	19.00	13.66	74.34	35.25	387.3
Andhra Pradesh	12.35	45.30	15.65	20.9	22.76	24.20	13.86	71.63	41.42	396.9
Goa									33.37	
Karnataka	12.09	45.00	21.57	24.22	26.43	21.12	17.25	87.49	42.00	403.3
Kerala	21.98	73.70	24.76	26.29	1 9.00	14.32	9.42	90.92	25.09	498.3

Cont'd...

Table 2.7 Cont'd...

1	*14*	*15*	*16*	*17*	*18*	*19*	*20*	*21*	*22*	*23*
Tamil Nadu	12.34	39.03	11.85	22.3	17.23	15.39	11.19	60.35	28.31	322.6
Lakshadweep*	–1.76	54.30	14.61	31.95	26.49	28.47	17.19	90.48	50.55	430.8
Pandicheri*	–0.89	29.90	16.34	27.81	28.07	33.64	20.56	90.54	61.10	387.7
INDIA										430.8

Table 2.8

Population growth rates in India, 1901–2001

Year	*Decadal Growth Rate*			*Growth rate relative to 1901 population*		
	Persons	*Male*	*Female*	*Persons*	*Male*	*Female*
1901	—	—	—	—	—	—
1911	5.746	6.287	5.189	5.746	6.287	5.189
1921	–0.306	0.125	–0.754	5.422	6.420	4.396
1931	11.004	11.189	10.810	17.023	18.328	15.682
1941	14.225	14.522	13.913	33.668	35.511	31.776
1951	13.314	13.345	13.282	51.466	53.594	49.279
1961	21.642	21.972	21.293	84.246	87.342	81.065
1971	24.799	25.523	24.030	129.936	135.157	124.574
1981	24.997	24.766	25.246	187.414	193.397	181.269
1991	23.168	23.477	22.838	254.003	262.276	245.506
2001	21.694	21.408	22.003	330.802	339.831	321.528

Table 2.9

Growth rate of population in India over the years

Year	*Arithmetic*	*Geometric*	*Exponential*
1901–11	0.58	0.56	0.56
1911–21	–0.03	–0.03	–0.03
1921–31	1.10	1.05	1.04
1931–41	1.42	1.34	1.33
1941–51	1.33	1.26	1.25
1951–61	2.15	1.98	1.96
1961–71[a]	2.48	2.24	2.22
1971–81[b]	2.47	2.23	2.20
1981–91[c]	2.39	2.20	2.14
1991–2001	2.14	2.00	1.93

Cont'd...

a. The reference date in 1971 census was 1st April 1971. In working out the decadal variations for 1961–71 and 1971–81, the change in reference date in 1971 census has been taken into account.
b. In 1981 Census, the reference date was 1st March 1981 in all states except Jammu & Kashmir where it was 6th May 1981. No census was conducted in Assam in 1981. However the interpolated population of Assam has been taken into account in calculating the growth rates.
c. The 1991 Census in Jammu & Kashmir could not be conducted. However, the projected population has been taken into account for the state in calculating the growth rate of All India.
Source: Office of the Registrar General, India.

Table 2.10
Average annual percentage growth rate of population by rural-urban origin

Year	*Rural*	*Urban*	*Total*
1901–11	0.64	0.04	0.58
1911–21	–0.13	0.83	–0.03
1921–31	1.00	1.91	1.10
1931–41	1.18	3.20	1.42
1941–51	0.88	4.14	1.33
1951–61	2.05	2.64	2.15
1961–71	2.19	3.82	2.48
1971–81[a]	1.93	4.61	2.47
1981–91[b]	2.00	3.65	2.39
1991–2001	1.79	3.12	2.13

a. The 1981 Census could not be held in Assam. The growth rates for 1971–81 and 1981–91 have been worked out on the interpolated population figures for Assam for 1981
b. The 1991 Census was not held in Jammu & Kashmir. Growth rate for 1981–91 is worked out with the projected population.
Source: Office of the Registrar General, India

2.2.3 1951—

The demographic change that took off in 1921–30 could not attain the needed momentum in the next two decades. However the social, political and economic changes, especially the arrival of antibiotics and insecticide sprays, accomplished concomitant to World War II created a very favorable stage for demographic transition that would auger population explosion in near future. Of course, the signal for such an exigency was noticeable around the later part of the nineteenth century. Eradication of diseases like plague and small pox, public health awareness, discovery of vaccines, penicillin and life saving drugs and enlargement of medical care and health services, more so after independence, brought down death rates very quickly. The improvement of rail and road connections, creation of a healthy buffer stock of food grains and making the public distribution system (PDS) more efficient helped to avert epidemics and famines in the country. The population of India grew by one and half times in the first half of the twentieth century. A phenomenal growth, nearly three-fold increase in population in the second half, amply suggests that India has been taking fewer years to pass through different stages of demographic transition. India's population growth during the twentieth century can be chartered and classified into four distinct phases:

- 1901–1921: Stagnant population
- 1921–1951: Steady growth
- 1951–1981: Rapid high growth
- 1981–2001: High growth with definite signs of slowing down

In absolute terms, the population of India has increased by a whopping 180.6 million during the decade 1991–2001. The absolute addition to the population during this decade is more than the estimated population of Brazil, the fifth most populous country in the world. Although, the net addition in population during each decade has increased consistently, the change in net addition has shown a steady declining trend over the decades starting from 1961. While 27.9 million more people were added in the decade 1981–1991 than between 1971–1981, this number declined to 17.6 million for the decades 1981–1991 and 1991–2001. This implies that as a result of the combination of population momentum and somewhat slowing down fertility, though India continues to grow in size its pace of net addition has been dropping.

Table 2.11
Population and its progressive growth rate, India 1901–2001

Census year	*Population*	*Decadal growth*		*Change in growth*		*Average annual exponential growth rate (%)*	*Progressive growth rate over 1901 (%)*
		Absolute	*Percent*	*Absolute*	*Percent*		
1	*2*	*3*	*4*	*5*	*6*	*7*	*8*
1901	238,396,327						
1911	252,093,390	13,697,063	5.76	—	—	0.56	5.75
1921	251,321,213	–772,177	–0.31	–14,469,240	–6.05	–0.03	5.42
1931	278,977,238	27,656,025	11.00	28,428,202	11.31	1.04	17.02
1941	318,660,580	39,683,342	14.22	12,027,317	3.22	1.33	33.67
1951[1]	361,088,090	42,427,510	13.31	2,744,168	–0.91	1.25	51.47
1961[1]	439,234,771	78,146,681	21.64	35,719,171	8.33	1.96	84.25
1971	548,159,652	108,924,881	24.80	30,778,200	3.16	2.20	129.94
1981[2]	683,329,097	135,169,445	24.66	26,244,564	–0.14	2.22	186.64
1991[3]	843,387,888	163,058,791	23.86	27,889,346	–0.80	2.14	255.03
2001	1,027,015,2477	180,627,359	21.34	17,568,568	–2.52	1.93	330.80

Notes:

1. In working out 'Decadal Growth' and 'Percentage Decadal Growth' for India 1941–51 and 1951–61, the population of Tuensang district for 1951 (7,025) and the population of Tuensang (83,501) and Mon (5,774) districts for 1961 Census of Nagaland state have not been taken into account as the areas were censused for the first time in 1951 and the same are not comparable.
2. The 1981 Census could not be held owing to disturbed conditions prevailing in Assam. Hence the population figures for 1981 of Assam have been worked out by 'interpolation'.
3. The 1991 Census could not be held owing to disturbed conditions prevailing in Jammu & Kashmir. Hence the population figures for 1991 of Jammu & Kashmir have been worked out by 'interpolation'.

Table 2.12 shows the relative share of population of the states and UTs to the total population of India as per 2001 census. It also provides the ranking of these states and UTs by population size in 1991 and 2001. It is seen that Uttar Pradesh is the most populous state in the country with more than 166 million people living in the state, which is more than the population of Pakistan, the sixth most populous country in the world. The combined population of Uttar Pradesh and Uttaranchal (until recently was a part of Uttar Pradesh) is greater than the population of Brazil. Nineteen states now have populations over ten million. Almost half of the country's population lives in five states, namely, Uttar Pradesh, Maharashtra, Bihar, West Bengal and Andhra Pradesh. While Uttar Pradesh and Maharashtra have held on to the first two positions in terms of their ranking in 2001 that in compared to 1991, Bihar has moved on to take the third spot from its fifth in 1991 pushing West Bengal and Andhra Pradesh to the fourth and fifth spots respectively.

Table 2.12

Ranking of states and union territories by population size, India 1991 and 2001

Rank in 2001	*States/UTs**	*Population 2001*	*Percent to total population of India*		*Rank in 1991*
			1991	*2001*	
1	*2*	*3*	*4*	*5*	*6*
1	Uttar Pradesh	166,052,859	16.17	15.60	1
2	Maharashtra	96,752,247	9.42	9.33	2
3	Bihar	82,878,796	8.07	7.62	5
4	West Bengal	80,221,171	7.81	8.04	3
5	Andhra Pradesh	75,727,541	7.37	7.86	4
6	Tamil Nadu	62,110,839	6.05	6.59	6
7	Madhya Pradesh	60,385,118	5.88	5.74	7
8	Rajasthan	56,473,122	5.50	5.20	9
9	Karnataka	52,733,958	5.14	5.31	8
10	Gujarat	50,596,992	4.93	4.88	10
11	Orissa	36,706,920	3.57	3.74	11
12	Kerala	31,838,619	3.10	3.44	12
13	Jharkhand	26,909,428	2.62	2.58	14
14	Assam	26,638,407	2.59	2.64	13
15	Punjab	24,289,296	2.37	2.40	15
16	Haryana	21,082,989	2.05	1.95	17
17	Chhattisgarh	20,795,956	2.03	2.08	16
18	Delhi*	13,782,976	1.34	1.11	18
19	Jammu & Kashmir	10,069,917	0.98	0.92	19
20	Uttaranchal	8,479,562	0.83	0.84	20

Cont'd...

Table 2.12 Cont'd...

1	*2*	*3*	*4*	*5*	*6*
21	Himachal Pradesh	6,077,248	0.59	0.61	21
22	Tripura	3,191,168	0.31	0.33	22
23	Manipur	2,388,634	0.23	0.22	23
24	Meghalaya	2,306,069	0.22	0.21	24
25	Nagaland	1,988,636	0.19	0.14	25
26	Goa	1,343,998	0.13	0.14	26
27	Arunachal Pradesh	1,091,117	0.11	0.10	27
28	Pondicherry*	973,829	0.09	0.10	28
29	Chandigarh*	900,914	0.09	0.08	30
30	Mizoram	891,058	0.09	0.08	29
31	Sikkim	540,493	0.05	0.05	31
32	Andaman & Nicobar Is.*	356,265	0.03	0.03	32
33	Dadra & Nagar Haveli*	220,451	0.02	0.02	33
34	Daman & Diu*	158,059	0.02	0.01	34
35	Lakshadweep*	60,595	0.01	0.01	35

The North Indian states have shown much faster rate of growth than the states in other regions, both between 1951–81 and 1981–2001 (Table 2.7). With the inclusion of Uttaranchal among the group of states in Northern region, this region now has the largest share of the landmass of India. The population density in this region is still low and therefore has the scope to increase its combined numbers. Southern states dominated the growth scenario in pre-independence days. However, after independence there was a total change in the demographic picture in India. The analysis of growth rates of the states starting from the decade 1951–1961 tells the real story of population growth in India. It took four decades even for Kerala to reach a decadal growth of less than ten percent from a high growth rate of 26.29 percent during 1961–71. Tamil Nadu also took forty years to reduce its growth from a high of 22.30 percent during 1961–1971 to 11.19 percent during 1991–2001. The growth rate in Bihar has shown an upward swing during 1991–2001 and the growth rates in Rajasthan, Uttar Pradesh, and Madhya Pradesh are now at a level where Kerala and Tamil Nadu were forty years back. Even if it takes four decades for these four states to reach the present levels achieved by Kerala and Tamil Nadu, it would be difficult for India to achieve a stable population by 2045. Therefore, it is imperative that some bold and path breaking initiatives are taken in reversing the trends of growth in these states, which at this stage do not show perceptible signs of abatement. Andhra Pradesh, however, has apparently shown an impressive fall in decadal growth rate by over ten percentage points and this success story does inspire confidence that it should be possible to cross all hurdles to achieve sharp declines in population growth. The percentage decadal growth of population in the inter-censal period 1991–2001 varied from a low of 9.42 in Kerala to a very high 64.41 in Nagaland. Delhi with 46.31 percent, Chandigarh with 40.33 and Sikkim with 32.98 registered very high growth rates; the small Union Territories of Dadra and Nagar Haveli and Daman and Diu also registered very high growth rates.

The growth rate in the Southern states fell behind the all-India average. Between 1951and 1981, they were 10 to 36 points behind others and 15 to 40 points behind in 1981–2001. Kerala experienced the highest growth rate among the Southern states both in 1951–61 and 1961–71. Since 1971, Kerala has curtailed its decadal growth rate drastically, from over 26 percent in 1971 to only about 9.42 percent in 1991–2001, a decadal growth often observed in the developed countries. From a 12.2 percent share of India's population, the Western region has 14.39 percent of India's total population in 2001. The primary reason for the higher growth rate in this region is in-migration from all other parts in India to the two most industrially advanced states, Maharashtra and Gujarat, especially after independence.

In the sixties and seventies of the last century, India experienced the highest decadal population growth, very close to 25 percent. States in the Northern region experienced the highest growth. Compared to fifties, the differences in growths between the regions and the states declined in sixties and seventies. Among the states Assam, Manipur, Meghalaya, Tripura, West Bengal (all in Eastern region), Haryana, Rajasthan and Madhya Pradesh grew fast. Both in Uttar Pradesh and Bihar out-migration kept the growth somewhat at a lower level. Tripura, Assam and West Bengal grew fast because of large-scale immigration from Bangladesh.

The Northern states continued to maintain their growth spree in the seventies as well. The Central region registered a high growth in the seventies and eighties because Uttar Pradesh, the largest state in India in terms of population, grew in excess of 5–6 percent both in seventies and eighties over its growth in sixties. Of the 35 states/UTs, population growth in eighties vis-à-vis 1961–71 declined in 19 states/UTs. Sikkim and Nagaland grew fastest; largest decline in growth was registered in Kerala, Orissa and Tamil Nadu.

Between 1901 and 1981, the populations of India grew by about 187 percent. The maximum growth has been in the Western India (237%), least in Central India (148%). One of the major reasons for smaller population growth in Central India is out-migration. Converse is the case with Western and Eastern states (growth 202%). Whereas the Eastern states received population from East Pakistan (Bangladesh since 1971), the Western states received population from all other states for reasons of industrial development in these states.

Figure 2.4

Contrasting growth rates in northern and southern states

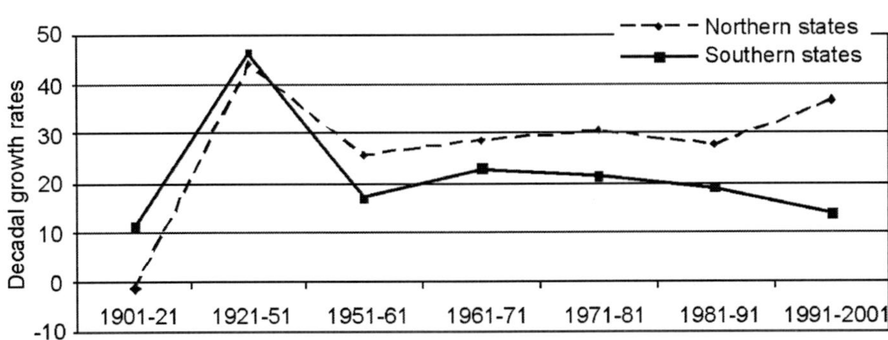

Since independence the population has grown fastest in North India, and slowest in the Southern states. India registered its highest decadal growth rate (25%) in 1981 census. In the last two decades the growth rate showed some decline. The 1991–2001 growth rate was 21.34 percent, which is a shade less than the growth rate registered in 1951–1961 (21.64%). However, a 21.64 percent increase in the fifties added only 78 million to the population of 1951; about the same proportional increase between 1991–2001added over 180 million to decadal base population just after 40 years. It took India hundreds of years to attain a population of 250 million in 1921, but it took only 80 years to add 750 million to the total of 1921.

Table 2.13

Population, percentage decadal growth and average annual exponential growth rates, India 1981–91 and 1991–2001

State/UTs*	Total population		Percentage decadal growth		Change in percentage decadal growth	Exponential growth	
	1991	2001	1981–1991	1991–2001		1981–1991	1991–2001
1	2	3	4	5	6	7	8
INDIA	846,387,888	1,027,015,247	23.86	21.69	–2.52	2.14	1.93
Jammu & Kashmir	7,803,900	10,069,917	30.34	29.04	–1.30	2.65	2.55
Himachal	5,170,877	6,077,248	20.79	17.53	–3.26	1.89	1.62
Punjab	20,281,969	24,289,296	20.81	19.76	–1.05	1.89	1.80
Chandigarh*	642,015	900,914	42.16	40.33	–1.84	3.52	3.39
Uttaranchal	7,113,483	8,479,562	24.23	19.20	–5.03	2.17	1.76
Haryana	16, 463,648	21,082,989	27.41	28.06	0.65	2.42	2.47
Delhi*	9,420,644	13,782,976	51.45	46.31	–5.14	4.15	3.81
Rajasthan	44,005,990	56,473,122	28.44	28.33	–0.11	2.50	2.49
Uttar Pradesh	131,998,804	166,052,859	25.55	25.80	0.25	2.28	2.30
Bihar	64,530,554	82,878,796	23.38	28.43	5.05	2.10	2.50
Sikkim	406,457	540,493	28.47	32.98	4.51	2.51	2.85
Arunachal	864,558	1,091,117	36.83	26.21	–10.63	3.14	2.33
Nagaland	1,209,546	1,988,636	56.08	64.41	8.33	4.45	4.97
Manipur	1,837,149	2,388,634	29.29	30.02	0.73	2.57	2.63
Mizoram	689,756	891,058	39.70	29.18	–10.51	3.34	2.56
Tripura	2,757,205	3,191,168	34.30	15.74	–18.56	2.95	1.46
Meghalaya	1,774,778	2,306,069	32.86	29.94	–2.93	2.84	2.62
Assam	22,414,322	26,638,407	24.24	18.85	–5.39	2.17	1.73
West Bengal	68,077,965	80,221,171	24.73	17.84	–6.89	2.21	1.64
Jharkhand	21,843,911	26,909,428	24.03	23.19	–0.84	2.15	2.09
Orissa	31,659,736	36,706,920	20.06	15.94	–4.12	1.83	1.48
Chhattisgarh	17,614,928	20,795,956	25.73	18.06	–7.67	2.29	1.66
Madhya Pradesh	48,566,242	60,385,118	27.24	24.34	–2.91	2.41	2.18
Gujarat	41,309,582	50,596,992	21.19	22.48	1.29	1.92	2.03

Cont'd...

Table 2.13 Cont'd...

1	*2*	*3*	*4*	*5*	*6*	*7*	*8*
Daman & Diu*	101,586	158,059	28.62	55.59	26.97	2.52	4.42
Dadra & Nagar Haveli*	138,477	220,451	33.57	59.20	25.63	2.89	4.65
Maharashtra	78,937,187	96,752,247	25.73	22.57	–3.16	2.29	2.04
Andhra Pradesh	66,508,008	75,727,541	24.20	13.86	–10.33	2.17	1.30
Karnataka	44,977,201	52,733,958	21.12	17.25	–3.87	1.92	1.59
Goa	1,169,793	1,343,998	16.08	14.89	–1.19	1.49	1.39
Lakshadweep*	51,707	60,595	28.47	17.19	–11.28	2.51	1.59
Kerala	29,098,518	31,838,619	14.32	9.42	–4.90	1.34	0.90
Tamil Nadu	55,858,946	62,110,839	15.39	11.19	–4.20	1.43	1.06
Pondicherry*	807,785	973,829	33.64	20.56	–13.08	2.90	1.87
Andaman & Nicobar Is.*	280,661	356,265	48.70	26.94	–21.76	3.97	2.39

Table 2.14

Distribution of states/union territories by range of percentage decadal growth, India 1981–1991 and 1991–2001

Percentage decadal growth	*Number of States/UTs 1981–91*	*Percentage of population to total population 1991*	*Number of States/UTs 2001*	*Percentage of population to total population 2001*
<18	3	10.17	10	34.08
18–21	3	6.75	5	7.91
21–24	3	17.81	3	16.97
24–27	8	48.97	4	2219
27–30	7	13.18	6	16.91
30 +	11	3.12	7	1.94

Table 2.15

Distribution of states/union territories by range of average annual exponential growth, India 1981–1991 and 1991–2001

Average annual exponential growth rate	*Number of States/UTs 1981–1991*	*Percentage of population to total population*	*Number of States/UTs 1991–2001*	*Percentage of population to total population*
1	2	3	4	5
< 1.0	0	0	1	3.1
1.0–1.4	3	10.17	5	17.43
1.5–1.9	5	16.94	9	21.46
2.0–2.4	11	64.28	8	46.71
2.5–2.9	10	7.07	6	9.64
3.0+	6	1.54	5	1.66

The growth of population in India, like that in all other developing countries, has been fast because of decline in mortality at all ages. The life expectancy at birth and fast decline in infant mortality rate are at the root of this fast population growth rate. Between 1901 and 1981, IMR declined from an estimated 232 to 125, a 47 percent reduction. In the 20 years since then, IMR has dropped by another 57 points, i.e., a 54 percent reduction. Life expectancy has increased from a meager 23.6 years in 1901 to 54 years in 1981 and then to over 63 years in 2001. Crude death rate has dropped from around 42 in 1901 to 8.5 in 2001. CBR in India declined from 49 per thousand populations in 1901 to about 36 in 1981. Between 1981 and 2001 CBR dropped by over 10 points. In the seventies when a massive sterilization program was forced on the people in the years of 'Emergency' and subsequent drop in sterilization rate as Janata government came into power, the demographers were pessimistic regarding substantial reduction in fertility. The fertility experiences in the last two decades clearly gave the indication that India definitely has entered into a faster take-off stage in fertility restriction. But for the indifferent performances in birth control in the four larger states Bihar, Madhya Pradesh, Rajasthan and Uttar Pradesh (nicknamed as BIMARU states, which together share 35.5% of India's population), the CBR in India would have been between 22 and 23 or even less. The growth rate in these four states in the last decade varied between 24.3 and 28.4 percent against the average growth rate of 21.34 in the total population. Except Assam and Tripura, all other Northeastern states registered alarming growth rate in the last decade. Population in the Northern states put together grew by 36.47 percent, whereas the Southern states together showed a growth of only 13.66 percent.

During 1991–2001, a decline of more than five percentage points in decadal growth rate from the previous census decade was observed in Andhra Pradesh, West Bengal, Arunachal Pradesh, Delhi, Mizoram, Tripura, Assam, Uttaranchal and Chhattisgarh, and also in the Union Territories of Lakshadweep, Pondicherry and Andaman and Nicobar Islands. These twelve states and Union Territories together account for only 22.61 percent of the country's population. In fact, among the major states, Andhra Pradesh has registered the sharpest drop (10.33) followed by Chhattisgarh (7.67) and West Bengal (6.89). Jammu & Kashmir, Himachal Pradesh, Punjab, Meghalaya, Orissa, Madhya Pradesh, Maharashtra, Karnataka, Goa, Kerala and Tamil Nadu and the Union Territory of Chandigarh have shown a decline of one to five percentage points in their growth rates during 1991–2001 as compared to that in 1981–1991. In Rajasthan and Jharkhand, the decline in percentage decadal growth is less than one percentage point. These two states account for 8.12 percent of India's population. Nearly two-thirds of the Indians live in states and UTs that registered a declining trend in growth rate.

Although, in the country as a whole, there has been an increase in net accretion in the population during 1991–2001 vis-à-vis 1981–1991; a few states and UTs have shown a reverse trend in this respect. The most significant drops in the net addition are seen in Andhra Pradesh, West Bengal, Kerala and Tamil Nadu. It is estimated that if these four states had added the same number of persons during 1991–2001 as they did in the previous decade, other things remaining the same, India would have added another 7.2 million more persons during this decade. This would have resulted in an increased decadal growth of India by almost one percentage point. Other things being equal, it appears that these four states together have been partly responsible for arresting the rate of growth of population of the country. On the other hand, Uttar Pradesh, Bihar and Rajasthan have together added about sixteen million more people during 1991–2001 than the number they added in the previous decade. These three states along with Madhya Pradesh account for about 42 percent of the growth of the country during 1991–2001, while during 1981–1991 their contribution in the growth was about 36 percent. At the other extreme are 16 states/UTs, which individually have not contributed even one percent to the growth of India's population during 1991–2001. As many as 14 states/UTs have registered a decline in growth in this decade as compared to that in the previous decade. These states/UTs together have 39.02 percent of India's population.

Of the 1027 million population in 2001, 48 percent were females and 52 percent males. A close look at the growth of rural and urban population in India over the years shows that urban population has been growing at a much faster rate vis-à-vis rural population, with average annual percentage growth rate for urban population being 3.65 percent during 1981–91 and slowing down to 3.12 percent during 1991–2001, whereas the same for rural population was 2 percent during 1981–91 and about 1.79 percent in the next decade. The growth rate of total population has been showing a declining trend in the last two decades. However, the percentage share of urban population has been growing continuously over the years with figures of 23.3 percent in 1981 to that of 25.7 percent in 1991 and 27.8 percent in 2001. It is estimated to reach around 36 percent by 2026. Obviously, net migration contributes very significantly in the urban population growth history.

An important feature of the decline in mortality rate in India is that it has been accomplished without a very great improvement in the economic front. The developed countries in the West took about 80 years to achieve a similar such decline in mortality which India could achieve only in 20 years. Decline in mortality has been more secular than decline in birth rate. Only 3 points differentiate between the CDRs for urban and rural population today. The minimum difference is in Kerala (0.3) and highest in Assam (4.0). But the same cannot be said about CBR. The difference is a loud high of 6.9 points, i.e., 33 percent higher in rural India. The difference is as low as 0.5 point in Kerala to a high of 9.9 points in Madhya Pradesh. The standard deviation for the Urban-Rural difference in CBR is 2.963 and that for CDRs in 16 larger states is only 1.053.

There have been considerable jurisdictional changes in the states/UTs after the 1991census on account of creation of three new states and a large number of new districts. The state-wise list of the total number of districts and the number of districts created after the 1991 census is given in Table 2.16.

Table 2.16

Statement showing the number of districts in the 1991 and 2001 census, number of new districts, affected districts and number of districts with no jurisdictional changes

*States/UTs**	*Number of districts*		*Number of new districts 2001*	*Number of districts affected due to*		*Number of districts without any geographical change*
	1991	*2001*		*Carving out of new districts*	*Geographical changes only*	
1	*2*	*3*	*4*	*5*	*6*	*7*
Jammu & Kashmir	14	14				14
Himachal Pradesh	12	12				12
Punjab	12	17	5	8	3	1
Chandigarh*	1	1				1

Cont'd...

Table 2.16 Cont'd...

1	*2*	*3*	*4*	*5*	*6*	*7*
Uttaranchal	9	13	4	6	1	2
Haryana	16	19	3	3	8	5
Delhi*	1	9	8	1		—
Rajasthan	27	32	5	5		22
Uttar Pradesh	54	70	16	19	8	27
Bihar	29	37	8	7		22
Sikkim	4	4				4
Arunachal Pradesh	11	13	2	2		9
Nagaland	7	8	1	1		6
Manipur	8	9	1	1		7
Mizoram	3	8	5	2		1
Tripura	3	4	1	2		1
Meghalaya	5	7	2	2		3
Assam	23	23			2	21
West Bengal	17	18	1	1		16
Jharkhand	13	18	5	5		8
Orissa	13	30	17	10		3
Chhattisgarh	7	16	9	6		1
Madhya Pradesh	38	45	7	7	2	29
Gujarat	19	25	6	8	2	9
Daman & Diu*	2	2				2
Dadra & Nagar Haveli*	1	1				1
Maharashtra	30	35	5	5		25
Andhra Pradesh	23	23			2	21
Karnataka	20	27	7	8		12
Goa	2	2				2
Lakshadweep*	1	1				1
Kerala	14	14			8	8
Tamil Nadu	21	30	9	6		15
Pondicherry*	4	4				4
Andaman & Nicober Is*	2	2				2
INDIA	**466**	**593**	**127**	**115**	**36**	**317**

A glance at the regional variation in population growth trend reveals that the extent of inter-state variation is still very high. Although most of the major states have registered a decline in growth rate in the last two decades, there are a few states including the populous states like Bihar,

Madhya Pradesh and Uttar Pradesh where the population growth rates still are at a higher level or where population is growing at a higher rate than the rates experienced in past decades. The growth rate in Bihar has shown an upward swing during 1991–2001 and the growth rates in Rajasthan, Uttar Pradesh, and Madhya Pradesh are now at a level where Kerala and Tamil Nadu were forty years back. Unless some drastic measures are taken it would be very difficult for India to achieve a stable population by 2045 or TFR 2.1 by 2010, as projected in the National Population Policy, 2000. All the BIMARU states are out-migrating type; yet their population pressure is increasing because of high birth rates. TFRs in these states are higher by 25 to 47 percent of the national average and they still have considerably smaller sex ratio in the population (F/M average around 912).

The story of population growth in India is fairly in tune with the classical theory of demographic transition. During most of the nineteenth century, India witnessed a fluctuating but ultimately more or less a stagnant population, which drifted into the twentieth century until 1921. Thereafter, the country as a unit passed successively through all the early phases of demographic transition and is now believed to have entered into the fourth stage (Blacker's Low Stationary Population), usually characterized by rapidly declining fertility and very low mortality. There are a few states where change in the absolute decadal growth shows a declining trend since 1981. The crucial question is: How long will this phase extend and when will India achieve a stable population? The National Population Policy (NPP), 2000, states that "the long-term objective is to achieve a stable population by 2045, at a level consistent with the requirements of sustainable economic growth, social development, and environment protection". It has been assumed in the policy document that the medium-term objective of bringing down the TFR to the replacement level by 2010 will be achieved. It is envisaged further that if the NPP is fully implemented, the population of India should be 1013 million by 2002 and 1107 million by 2010. However, in 2001 itself, India had already exceeded the estimated population for the year 2002 by about 14.5 millions. It will no doubt require a Herculean effort on the part of the government and the people to achieve the much-cherished goal of a stable population according the time-table.

The great diversity in population growths between regions and states call for an intensive examination of population policy in India. India urgently needs to address to these regional and sub-regional differences and relate the population situation in relation to social change and development. A decentralized population and development planning would be necessary to eliminate the disparity that still exists in demographic parameters between states and regions.

2.3 Future of Population in India

The national government, international agencies and demographers make different population projections at the country level from time to time. United Nations Population Division, the World Bank, the United Nations Population Fund etc. publish projections for the world population as well as for different countries.

The need for population projection in India, both at the Center and the states, was keenly felt in 1958 on the eve of the formulation of the Third Five-Year plan. Usually, the Office of the Registrar General and Census Commissioner, India undertakes the exercise of projection on behalf of the Planning Commission of India. The first Expert Committee on Population Projections was set up in 1958 under the chairmanship of the Registrar General, India to provide a set of population projections for India and the states. The projections up to 1971 were then made available to the Planning Commission. The projected populations proved to be far short of the actual population size as the

1961 Census results became available. The assumptions made in the projections about change in birth and death rate were far optimistic than what were happening in the real world. The Expert Committee was reactivated in 1963 for effecting a further revision of the projections and extending them up to 1981 taking into consideration the 1961 Census results as well as the Life Table for 1951–61. The Committee gave its report in 1964. Out of the three sets of projections namely high, medium and low, the second one was recommended for official use. This was again revised once 1971 Census data became available.

After the release of the five percent sample data of the 1981 Census, Expert Committee made another series of Population Projections in 1984. Population Projections for the period 1981–2001 were prepared under three assumptions on the basis of trends in fertility and mortality. The Sample Registration Data from 1964 onwards provided the trends in fertility and mortality in the country as a whole as well as for different states. Equipped with better relevant statistics, the Expert Committee published the projection report in 1988 and the medium projections were recommended for official use. In the light of the trends observed during 1980's in major demographic parameters, as revealed by the Sample Registration Scheme (SRS), the Planning Commission still had doubts if the future size of India's population would follow the levels projected by the Expert Committee. The Planning Commission set up a Standing Committee of Experts on Population Projections towards the end of October, 1988. This Committee reviewed the medium projections made by the Expert Committee in 1984, in the light of the further data available on fertility, mortality and contraceptive prevalence and submitted its report in 1989. The final population total in 1991 was fairly close to the projected population as estimated by the Standing Committee for that Census.

With the availability of age-sex distribution of population from the 1991 Census, the latest data relating to family planning performances and recent levels and trends in fertility and mortality as emerging from the SRS, the Planning Commission decided to go for a new set of population projections. The Technical Group on Population Projections constituted by the Planning Commission in 1996 under the chairmanship of the Registrar General, India worked with the following objectives [reproduced from Web Edition: of *Provisional Population Totals, Chapter 4* (*Population Projection*), Census of India 2001, Series 1, India, Paper 1 of 2001]:

- To review the methodology of Population Projections adopted in the past
- To prepare fresh projections of mortality status and parameters of fertility conditions based on changed pattern of contraceptive use and proportion of married females (1991 Census) and other characteristics
- To make population projections afresh up to 2016
- To prepare projections of the possible period when NRR = 1 will be achieved by the states/UTs and the country as a whole. The assumptions made to project the population of India up to 2016 are discussed below:
- The Technical Group considered the Total Fertility Rate (TFR) as the overall indicator of fertility. The earlier approach of taking NRR=1 as the replacement level of fertility was changed to TFR = 2.1. The TFR estimates based on the SRS data for India and major states were adopted. The lowest threshold of TFR was assumed to be 1.6. Two sets of TFR values from the SRS for India and major states for two time periods 1981–93 and 1985–93 were considered by the Group. On careful examination, the Group recommended the use of projected values of TFRs based on the period 1985–93 except for the states of Madhya Pradesh,

Punjab, Rajasthan and Uttar Pradesh. For these four states, the projected levels of TFR based on the period 1981–93 were adopted. The projected levels of TFRs assumed for India for the initial period 1996–2001 and terminal period 2011–2016 were 3.13 and 2.52 respectively.

- Although the SRS based sex ratio at birth of 110 for the period 1981–90, was found to be much higher than the internationally accepted sex ratio at birth of 105–106, yet the Technical Group recommended the use of sex ratio at birth as obtained from the SRS in view of the overall broad consistency and reliability of the SRS data.
- For projecting the mortality levels, initially the Group considered two sets of mortality projections. The first one was based on five-yearly abridged life tables constructed from SRS Age Specific Death Rates (ASDR) for the periods 1981–85 to 1989–93. The second set of mortality projections were considered by utilizing the projected survival ratios based on the observed ASDR value from the SRS. After examining the merits of the two sets of mortality projections, the later one, that is, the survivorship ratio method was recommended for undertaking the population projections. An upper limit of 70 years for the expectation of life for males and females was recommended for all India and major states except for Kerala and Tamil Nadu. The projected levels of expectation of life at birth for males were 62.30 years for the period 1996–2001 and 67.04 years for the duration 2011–2016. Similarly, for females, these figures were 65.27 years and 69.18 years respectively.
- In addition to considering the increase in the expectation of life at birth, the Group also considered the likely impact of AIDS on death rate. After considering the effect of likely deaths due to AIDS, it was found that future levels of the expectation of life at birth would have no significant impact from AIDS in the next 25 years.

Table 2.17

Projected values of expectation of life at birth, total fertility rate, and corresponding population projections for different periods

Indices	***Period***			
	1996–2001	***2001–2006***	***2006–2011***	***2011–2016***
	Projected expectation of life at birth			
Male	62.30	63.87	65.65	67.04
Female	65.27	66.91	67.67	69.18
TFR	3.13	2.88	2.68	2.52
Projected population	1012.4 (2001)	1094.1 (2006)	1178.9 (2011)	1263.6 (2016)

Note:
1. Population Projection for particular year is shown in millions
2. Figures in the parentheses indicate the end year for which the corresponding projections have been made

Source: Population Projections for India and States: 1996–2016. Registrar General, India

The population projections for each of the four Census years since 1971 by the various Expert Committees and the absolute and percentage variations from the final or provisional totals at the national level are presented below. The table shows some of the population projections for India made by different organizations and individuals in a period of 50 years after independence. These projections were made under different assumptions. By comparing these projections made over time and under different assumptions give us an opportunity to know the confidence with which we can use the projected population figures for various planning exercises. In 1971, the projected population was higher than the actual population totals while in 1981 it was just the reverse. The Standing Committee of Experts Projections in 1989 came closest to the actual population in 1991.

Table 2.18

Projected and actual/provisional population totals of India, 1971–2001 (in '000)

Year	*Projected population*	*Actual population*	*Difference*[6]	*Percent difference*[7]
1	*2*	*3*	*4*	*5*
1971	559,622[1]	548,160	–11,462	–2.05
1981	672,014[2]	683,329	11,315	1.68
1991	837,249[3]	846,388	9,139	1.09
1991	843,596[4]	846,388	2,792	0.33
2001	1,012,386[5]	1,027,015	14,629	1.45

Note:
1. Expert Committee on Population Projections, Registrar General, India, July 1968
2. Expert Committee on Population Projections, Registrar General, India, October, 1978
3. Expert Committee on Population Projections, Registrar General, India, January, 1988
4. Standing Committee of Experts Projections, Planning Commission, India, October, 1989
5. Population Projection for India and States, 1996–2016, Registrar General, India, New Delhi, 1996.
6. {Column (3)–Column (2)}
7. {Column (3)–Column (2)}*100/Column (2).

Table 2.19

Projected population of India in 2000/2001 by different individuals and organizations in the last fifty years

Sl.No.	*Year of projection/publication*	*Name of the individual/organization*	*Population projection for the year 2000/2001 (million)*
1	1950	K. Davis	790.0
2	1958	Coale-Hoover	1,146.0
3	1984	Office of the Registrar General, India	991.5
4	1985	Planning Commission/The Registrar General, India	986.1
5	1986	US Bureau of Census	1,023.7
6	1987	Department of International Economic & Social Affairs, UN	1,005.5
7	1989	Planning Commission	1,003.1
8	1996	Planning Commission/The Registrar General, India	1,012.4
9	1996	USAID	1,012.9
10	1998	Population Division, UN	1,007.0

Cont'd...

11	1999	Institute of Economic Growth, New Delhi	1,043.0
12	1999	Population Division, UN	1,013.7
13	2000	Population Foundation of India, New Delhi	1,011.8
14	2000	Dyson et al.	1,010.6

Assumptions:

Sl.No.1 No base year population. It was assumed that relatively high rate of natural increase observed between 1921 and 1941 would continue. Logistic method involving fitting a curve to the actual population growth was used. In this method, it is assumed that the social factors determining population growth in the area in question will remain constant in their effects.

(Source: The Population of India and Pakistan – By Kinsley Davis, Princeton University, USA, pp.88–90).

Sl.No.2 Base year population (1956): 384.0 millions. Fertility rates unchanged at estimated 1951 levels; Birth rate 43.2. Mortality risks unchanged at projected 1986 levels, M/F: 51.5/53.1

(Source: Population Growth and Economic Development in Low-Income Countries. By Ansley J. Coale and Edgar M Hoover, Princeton University, USA, pp.321–22).

Sl.No.3 Base year population (1981): 685.2 millions. The population in the age group 0–4 had been inflated to take into account the omission.

Mortality: Annual increase in expectation of life at birth(year/year):M/F–0.50/0.50. It will be 64.1 years for males and 64.7 years for females by 2001.

Fertility: Couple Protection Rate (CPR) may increase on an average at the rate of 1.3%. About 50 percent of the couples would be effectively protected by the year 2001.

Migration: Net migration negligible. Projection based on the above mentioned assumptions is termed as medium projection' as cited above. Projections based on lower couple protection rate (CPR) has been worked out and is termed as 'High projection' and was worked out as 1052.5 millions

Sl.No.4: Base year population (1981): 685.2 millions. In the age group 0–4, adjustments have been done for age distortion and omission based on Census Evaluation Study Projections based on lower CPR were worked out as 1021.9 millions.

Mortality: Annual increase of 0.50 and 0.55 years in expectation of life at birth for males and females respectively till it reached 60 years after which the respective improvements would be 0.45 years and 0.50 years. It will be 64.1 years for males and 65.6 years for females in 2001.

Fertility: CPR may increase on an average at the rate of 1.4 percent per annum. About 53 percent of the couples would be protected by the year 2001.

Migration: Net migration negligible.

Sl.No.5: Base year population (1981): 699.1 millions. Adjustment to the 1981 Census Total for 2.0 percent under enumeration was made The figure of High Projection is 1061.9 millions.

Mortality: Expectation of life at birth will be 60.7 years for males and 63.6 years for females in 2000.

Fertility: Total Fertility Rate will be 3.0 in 2000.

(Source: Demographic Estimates, Projections and selected Social Characteristics of the Population of India by Frank B. Hobbs, p.40)

Sl.No.6: No particular assumption for India has been mentioned.

(Source: Global Estimates and Projections of Population by Sex and Age – The 1984 Assessment, p. 269)

Sl.No.7: Base year population (1986): 762.9 millions.

Mortality: There is no mention about the adjustment of population. The expectation of life at birth for males will rise at the rate of 0.40 per annum till it reaches the age of 65. For females, the annual gain was assumed as 0.45 till the age of 65 years after which it is assumed to be 0.25 per annum. It will be 64.80 for males and 65.80 for females for the quinquennium 2001–2006.

Fertility: Estimated values of CPR during 2000 is 49.8 percent.

Migration: Net migration negligible.

Sl.No.8: Base year population (1996): 934.2 millions. In the age group 0–4, adjustments have been done for age distortion and omission based on Census Evaluation Study.

Mortality: Projected levels of expectation of life at birth was 62.30 years for males and 65.27 years for females during the period 1996–2001. Projected levels of Infant Mortality Rate was 60 during the same period.
Fertility: Projected levels of fertility was 3.13 for the period 1996–2001.
Migration: Net migration negligible.
Sl.No.9: No particular assumption for India has been mentioned.
Sl.No.10: No particular assumption for India has been mentioned.
(Source: World Population Projections to 2150, UN, p. 30)
Sl.No.11: Base year population (1991): 864 million as on March 1, 1991. This includes adjustment of 2.1 percent among males and 2.2 percent under count among females.
Mortality: Projected levels of expectation of life at birth was 63.68 years for males and 65.87 years for females in 2001.
Fertility: Projected Total Fertility Rate (TFR) in 2001 – 2.8
Mortality decline: Fast and medium fertility.
(Source: Population Growth in South Asia and its consequences, 1990–2051 – by Pravin Visaria and P.N. Mari Bhat, Institute of Economic Growth, New Delhi, Paper presented at the National Seminar on Economy, Society and Policy in South Asia: Retrospect and prospects at the dawn of the Next Millennium, Nov. 1999, Table 8)
Sl.No.12: No particular assumption for India has been mentioned.
(Source: World Population Prospects, The 1998 Revision, Vol. II, p. 453)
Sl.No.13: Base year population (1996): 934.2 millions.
Mortality: Projected levels of expectation of life at birth was 62.9 years for males and 64.9 years for females in 2001.
Fertility: Projected Total Fertility Rate (TFR) in 2001 – 3.1
(Source: Population Growth in 21st Century – India – by K.S. Natarajan and V. Jayachandran, Population Foundation of India, New Delhi, p. 19)
Sl.No.14: Base year population (1996): 934.2 millions.
Mortality: Crude Death Rate: 8.9 in 2001.
Fertility: Crude Birth Rate: 24.8 in 2001.
Average annual growth rate: 1.59 percent
(Source: India's Demographic and Food Prospects – State Level Analysis by Tim Dyson and Amresh Hanchate, Economic and Political Weekly, November 11, 2000, p. 4024)

The projection by US Bureau of Census, made in 1986, comes closest to the population total of India in 2001. The population projections for 2001 made by the planning commission in 1984 and 1985 had fallen short by 41 and 46 millions respectively. This is a clear indication that fertility did not decline as much as was anticipated. All the projections by individuals and organizations in late 1980s and in the 1990s fluctuate around 1013 million for 2001. Only the projection made as late as 1999 by the Institute of Economic Growth, New Delhi, who made adjustments to 1991 Census population totals, clearly overshoot the 2001 population total by about 26 millions.

For the Census 2001, however, the projected population by the Planning Commission in 1996 has fallen short by a little over 14.5 millions. The assumptions made about fertility in 1996 seem to suggest that the decline in growth of population may have fallen behind by about one year. This could also mean that either mortality had improved faster than was anticipated or fertility decline was a bit slower than assumed or a combination of both. Another possibility that exists is that the base year population itself needed a revision, taking cue from Post Enumeration Survey (PES). Most of the projections carried out on Indian population in the recent past have ignored migration since net migration for the country is very small compared to the population base.

The Technical Group on Population Projections constituted by the Planning Commission in 1996 also made population projections for different states and Union Territories (Table 2.20) and the country's population beyond 2001 (Table 2.22). Significant differences between the projected and the provisional population totals have been observed for the states of Rajasthan, Bihar and Jharkhand (combined), Gujarat and Maharashtra. For these four States taken together, the provisional figures exceed the projected figures by more than 16.2 millions.

Table 2.20

Projected and provisional population size of India, states and union territories as on March 1, 2001 (in '000)

*States/UTs**	*Projected population*	*Provisional population*	*Difference*	*Percent difference*
1	*2*	*3*	*4*	*5*
INDIA	1,012,386	1,027,0154	14,629	1.45
Jammu & Kashmir	10,071	10,070	–1	–0.01
Himachal Pradesh	6,805	6,0775	–728	–10.69
Punjab	23,794	24,289	495	2.08
Chandigarh*	907	901	–6	–0.67
Haryana	20,120	21,083	963	4.79
Delhi*	14,366	13,783	–583	–4.06
Rajasthan	54,509	56,473	1,964	3.60
Uttar Pradesh & Uttaranchal	174,290	174,532	242	0.14
Bihar & Jharkhand	101,819	109,788	7,969	7.83
Sikkim	570	540	–30	–5.18
Arunachal Pradesh	1,217	1,091	–126	–10.34
Nagaland	1,721	1,989	268	15.55
Manipur	2,569	2,389	–180	–7.02
Mizoram	972	891	–81	–8.33
Tripura	3,859	3,191	–668	–17.31
Meghalaya	2,484	2,306	–178	–7.16
Assam	26,492	26,638	146	0.55
West Bengal	79,992	80,221	229	0.29
Orissa	36,156	36,707	551	1.52
Madhya Pradesh & Chhattisgarh	81,189	81,181	–8	–0.01
Gujarat	48,971	50,5976	1,626	3.32
Daman & Diu*	142	158	16	11.31
Dadra & Nagar Haveli*	194	220	26	13.63
Maharashtra	92,057	96,752	4,695	5.10
Andhra Pradesh	76,392	75,728	–664	–0.87
Karnataka	52,719	52,734	15	0.03
Goa	1,627	1,344	–283	–17.39
Lakshadweep*	72	61	–11	–15.84
Kerala	32,530	31,839	–691	–2.13
Tamil Nadu	62,252	62,111	–141	–0.23
Pondicherry*	1,134	974	–160	–14.12
Andaman & Nicobar Islands*	394	356	–38	–9.58

Source: Population Projection for India and States, 1996–2016, Registrar General, India, New Delhi, 1996

Table 2.21
Distribution of states/UTs by the range of percent difference between projected and provisional population totals, 2001

Percent difference between projected and provisional population totals	*Number of states/UTs*	*Names of states/UTs**
–16 and higher	2	Tripura, Goa
–16 to –12	2	Lakshadweep*, Pondicheri*
–12 to –8	4	Himachal Pradesh, Arunachal Pradesh, Mizoram, Anadaman & Nicober Is.*
–8 to –4	4	Delhi*, Sikkim, Manipur, Meghalaya
–4 to 0	6	Jammu & Kashmir, Chandigarh*, Madhya Pradesh & Chhattisgarh, Andhra Pradesh, Kerala, Tamil Nadu
0 to 4	7	Punjab, Uttar Pradesh & Uttaranchal, Assam, West Bengal, Orissa, Gujarat, Karnataka
4 to 8	4	Haryana, Rajasthan, Bihar & Jharkhand, Maharashtra
8 to 12	1	Daman & Diu*
12 to 16	2	Nagaland, Dadra & Nagar Haveli*

Table 2.22
Projected population of India, 1996–2016

Year	*Projected population (in '000)*			*Percentage of Urban population*
	Persons	*Males*	*Females*	
1996	934,218	484,859	449,360	27.73
2001	1,012,386	523,780	488,606	28.77
2006	1,094,126	564,498	529,628	30.35
2011	1,178,889	606,744	572,145	31.99
2016	1,263,543	648,886	614,657	33.67

Source: Population Projection for India and States, 1996–2016, Registrar General, India, New Delhi, 1996

For most of the larger States the projected population totals underestimate the provisional totals (Census 2001). For most of them the Census figures exceed by more than 2 percent. The difference is negligible for the states Jammu & Kashmir, Uttar Pradesh and Uttaranchal (combined), Madhya Pradesh and Chhattisgarh (combined), Karnataka and Tamil Nadu. The projections have gone wrong mostly for the smaller states and Union Territories.

The National Population Policy 2000 has set up *immediate, medium* and *long-term goal* for stabilizing population of India, which is an essential requirement for promoting sustainable development with equitable distribution. The *immediate objective* is to address the unmet needs for contraception, health care infrastructure, and to provide integrated service delivery for basic reproductive and child health care. The *medium-term objective* is to bring the TFR to replacement level by

2010. The *long-term objective* is to achieve a stable population by 2045, at a level consistent with the requirements of sustainable economic growth, social development, and environmental protection. If the NPP 2000 is fully implemented, a population of 1107 million in 2010 is anticipated, instead of 1162 million projected by the Technical Group on Population Projections. NPP 2000 anticipates a growth described in the following table.

Table 2.23

Anticipated growth in population (in million)

Year	If current trends continue		If TFR 2.1 is achieved by 2010	
	Population	Annual increase in population	Population	Annual increase in population
1991	846.3	—	846.3	—
1996	934.2	17.6	934.2	17.6
1997	949.9	15.7	949.0	14.8
2000	996.9	15.7	991.0	14.0
2002	1027.6	15.4	1013.0	11.0
2010	1162.3	16.8	1107.0	11.75

Source: National Population Policy 2000 (Projection by Ministry of Health and Family Welfare)

To achieve the projection targets, NPP 2000 has urged that the following projections for CBR, IMR, and TFR must be met.

Table 2.24

Projections of CBR, IMR and TFR if the NPP 2000 is fully implemented

Year	CBR	IMR	TFR
1997	27.2	71	3.3
1998	26.4	72	3.3
2002	23.0	50	2.6
2010	21.0	30	2.1

Source: NPP 2000

There are only 9 states/UTs that have TFR ≤ 2.1. Only two bigger states, namely Kerala and Tamil Nadu, find place in this list. These states/UTs together share only 11.62 percent of India's population. There are 10 states/UTs (population share 46.52%) that have TFRs over 3.0. Among these are 4 BIMARU states that have TFR ranging from 4.0 to 4.7 (Madhya Pradesh 4.0, Rajasthan 4.1, Bihar 4.5 and Uttar Pradesh 4.7). Together their share to India's population is over 40 percent. All these states except Bihar have IMR over 79. It appears strange that Bihar with such high TFR has IMR below the national average of 68 (year 2000). These are backward states in most demographic, social and economic indicators. Other states/UTs in this high fertility category are Assam (3.1), Dada & Nagar Haveli (3.5), Tripura (3.9), and Meghalaya (4.8). The demographic performance of India in the coming years remains hostage to these few larger states. A massive uplift in socio-economic front in these states is what can save India from becoming the most populous country of the world even before the projected date.

3
Sources of Demographic Data in India

United Nations Convention on the Rights of the Child (CRC) (Article 7, 1989)

"The child shall be registered immediately after birth and shall have the right from birth to a name, the right to acquire a nationality and as far as possible, the right to know and be cared for by his or her parents."

What should be registered?

"Ensuring the right to a name and nationality and to know one's parents implies that registration should, as a minimum, include the child's name, sex, date and place of birth, and the name, address and nationality of both parents. While a person's name may be their most distinctive 'mark' of individuality – a right recognized in the CRC – additional data, such as family ties and nationality, promote the child's right to legal protection by parents and by the state."

Source: UNICEF 2002

3.1 Civil Registration System in India

Although registration of birth and death dates back to the time of Maurya Chadragupta, the first documentary evidence of registration was found in Goa. The Portuguese occupied and settled in Goa in 1510. It is in Goa where the oldest records of birth, death and marriage are found. In British occupied India, registration of marriage in 1604, birth in 1670 and death in 1720 were observed. But formal civil registration in India was introduced in the later part of the nineteenth century under British rule. Birth and death registration in India was started in 1860 primarily for evolving preventive measures against colossal loss of human lives due to frequent famines and epidemics throughout the length and breadth of the country. An Act in 1886 was passed for registration of birth, death and marriage all over the country. Registration however was not made mandatory. As such, the promulgation of the Act did not produce the desired result. The need for a more scientific documentation of vital events has from time to time been discussed and Commissions appointed (Health Survey and Development Committee, 1946, Vital Statistics Committee, 1949). Even as early as the publication of the third Census Report, the Registrar General and Census Commissioner G.F. Hardy wrote:

> It would appear hopeless for many years to come to expect anything like complete registration of births and deaths in India, and I would suggest that it would be well to concentrate efforts in this direction upon certain small but representative areas in various parts of India.

It took about 60 years to implementing Hardy's recommendations. Some serious talks began in the sixties of the last century when it was realized that the population projections in early fifties were miles behind the actual 1961 census figures. The assumptions made about parameters like birth and death rate, expectation of life etc. had little semblance with what was happening in the real world. The national planners realized that strict implementation of the Civil Registration Act throughout the country is a must but that would take quite sometime before the registration statistics could be trusted upon for analysis of demographic data and for population projection. National Sample Survey Organization (NSSO) under Planning Commission, set up in 1950, was entrusted with collection of various types of data through large-scale sample surveys. A new entity came into being in the form of Sample Registration Scheme (SRS) in 1964 under Registrar General of India for continuous registration of birth and death in selected sample blocks spread over the country throughout the year.

Since the promulgation of Registration of Birth and Death Act, 1969, registration of birth and death, especially in cities and urban areas has improved considerably. That a sizeable number of births now take place in hospitals, health centers and nursing homes, birth registration has improved noticeably both in rural and urban areas. The records of birth in these institutions are sent to the local registration authority routine. In urban areas, the cremation grounds and graveyards are under the direct control of the local municipality. Death certificates have been made obligatory for inheritance of property or putting up insurance claims and bank deposits. This aspect is yet neglected in villages where the local administration still is sloppy and less than efficient. Civil Registration centers under the control of the Office of the Registrar General of India are spread all over the country. The state health departments depute especially trained health workers to assist the municipalities in recording of the vital events. Copies of the forms used for birth and death registration is presented in Appendix 3.1.

Table 3.1

Percentage of births and deaths registration[2] (provisional) in different states

States	*Ref. year*	*Births*	*Deaths*	*States*	*Ref. year*	*Births*	*Deaths*
Andhra Pradesh	2001	55.8	58.5	Maharashtra	2000	91.1	71.5
Arunachal Pradesh	1999	81.7	28.4	Manipur	2001	45.9	25.3
Assam	2000	38.7	20.1	Meghalaya	2000	72.2	51.7
Bihar[1]	1995	18.7	25.6	Mizoram	2001	100	100
Chhattisgarh	2001	55.8	66.6	Nagaland	1994	94.6	52.1
Goa	2000	100	100	Orissa	2001	82.4	63.2
Gujarat	2000	88.8	60.4	Punjab	2000	92.2	82.5
Haryana	2001	75.5	70.6	Rajasthan	2001	39.6	55.8
Himachal Pradesh	2001	100	81.8	Sikkim	2000	80.0	41.4
Jammu & Kashmir	2000	68.1	49.5	Tamil Nadu	2000	93.5	73.0
Karnataka	2001	73.6	77.2	Tripura	2000	65.2	40.9
Kerala	2000	100	88.1	Uttar Pradesh[1]	1999	42.0	26.5
Madhya Pradesh	2001	38.2	48.3	West Bengal	1999	98.3	54.0

1. Bihar includes Jharkhand, Uttar Pradesh includes Uttaranchal
2. The level of birth/death registration is the percentage of registered birth/deaths estimated from births/deaths based on SRS rates.

Source: DRGSRS

Although about 40 years have gone by since the enactment of the Registration Act, the level of birth and death registration still remains poor. It is estimated that everyday some 70,000 babies are born and only 38,000 of these are registered. State disparities in birth registration coverage vary from 100 percent (Goa, Himachal Pradesh and Kerala) to as low as below 20 percent (Bihar). Registration of death in the states varies from 100 percent (Goa) to a low of 20 percent (Assam). The Working group on Birth and Death (2001) came out with the observation that at the national level 55 percent of births and 46 percent of deaths are being registered. Some of the states like Goa, Gujarat, Jammu & Kashmir, Karnataka, Kerala, Maharashtra, Mizoram, Punjab and Tamil Nadu and all the Union Territories except Dadra & Nagar Haveli have achieved above 90 percent registration of births. In some states as Andhra Pradesh, Assam, Bihar, Manipur, Meghalaya, Rajasthan and Uttar Pradesh the registration is below 50 percent.

It is interesting to note that for most states birth registration is better than registration of deaths. Birth registration certificate has been made mandatory for admission into schools. In a few states (Bihar, Chhattisgarh, Madhya Pradesh and Rajasthan) death registration appears much higher than birth registration.

Death registration is very important for the simple reason that a proper accounting of causes of death provides a direction to some of our health programs. The death trends from various causes of death can help the state decide on the preventable course to be adopted to check on the spread of certain diseases which in course of time may take virulent form. Section 10 of RBD Act 1969 makes the medical practitioners who attend the deceased during his/her last illness are legally bound to issue such certificate for cause of death as ascertained by him. Registrar after making necessary entries in the register is required to forward all birth and death certificates to the Chief Registrar within specified time limit. Unfortunately, birth and death registration, especially in rural India is still abysmally poor. Some of the reasons for the poor quality of registration are as under.

1. A very large proportion of Indian population, especially in rural area, is still illiterate.
2. More than 70 percent of Indians still live in villages where hospitals, doctors and trained midwives are not easily available; many births and deaths take place outside institutional care even today.
3. Although the government has taken steps to give proper training to the registrars of these local registration offices, they often are found to be lacking in motivation, seriousness and sincerity that are demanded of them for correct recording of all births and deaths in the prescribed forms.
4. Even when birth or death are registered, many of the columns relating to age at delivery (or at death), type of delivery, weight and height of the baby, any birth deformity, birth order, occupation and education of mother, religion and other information are left blank. Death certificates issued by doctors or hospitals often lack the clarity of the disease from which the patient succumbed.
5. The documents are poorly preserved.
6. There is no provision for recording marriages except when the marriage takes place in churches or when the individuals marry under Special Marriage Act or Hindu Marriage Act.

3.2 Census in India

3.2.1 Preparation for Modern Periodic Census

Counting of numbers is as old as the human civilization. Historians have shown that in the interest of running the administration and protect the territorial boundaries, the rulers of almost in all countries had to count their people who really were worth counting. The kings and emperors ruling a native state or the whole country, especially those who are remembered in the history for initiating better administration, had resorted to population counts from time to time. Most often these counts were directed for collection of taxes or for improving the military strength of the country or both.

(The reader is referred to Chapter 2 Population Growth in India, of this book, where history of Census in India has been discussed in some details.)

Gupta dynasty (300–600 AD) was the golden age in Indian history. Kautilya's *Arthashastra* is a shimmering example of how advanced and technically sound the population counts were in India some 2300 years back. The treatise depicts a very advanced level of analysis of the economic productive system and employment situations prevailing at the time of Maurya Chandra Gupta. Vincent in his book *Early History of India* wrote that population count at regular interval was a normal feature in Maurya Empire. The task of counting was reposed on to chosen civilians or the municipalities. In fact, there were full-fledged administrative units that collected throughout the year a variety of information on people and their livings to feed the general administration with the latest situation prevailing. There were also provisions for recording of births and deaths. There are ample documented evidences that show that counting of heads was in vogue during Maratha regime and Mughal rule, especially during Akbar's time.

Proofs are there that direct or indirect enumeration of population was a popular administrative feature in different parts of India even before the British took over the reins of administration from the Muslim emperors. In the early British period, the Madras Presidency was pioneer in many respects. Even before the attempt at a nation-wide population count in 1871–72, attempts were made to count people in various regions, provinces and even districts. The Registrar General of India published in 1972 the *Bibliography of Census Publications in India,* which documented a selected list of attempts made for population counts, most generally in some selected towns or districts since 1639. Because of disintegration of the vast Moghul Empire, the prevailing political and social environment was not conducive to population census in the entire country.

On the advice of the East India Company, an attempt was made in 1767 to ascertain the approximate population size in Madras Presidency. Similar attempts were made in other regions too. The scientific flavor of periodic census could not be expected in these coarse exercises. After the East India Company settled in India, the population censuses conducted between 1820 and 1830 were more scientific and better organized. Prof. Ashok Mitra in his book *India's Population Problems : Aspects of Quality and Quantity* praised highly the methodology followed in the censuses conducted in Allahabad (1824) and Benaras (1827–28) by James Prinsep.

The East India Company in 1849 planned to conduct census in the areas under their direct control. The then Government of India sent circulars to each of the regional administrative zones to conduct population census every five years with the help of the employees of the revenue section. After necessary preparations, the first census was conducted in 1851–52, the second in 1856–57, the third in 1861–62 and the last in 1866–67. This probably was the first serious well-planned attempt at complete enumeration in the history of modern India. From *Statistical Dispatch No.2*, July, 1856 it is gathered that the government of India had decided to conduct census enumeration simultaneously in all parts of the country. However, in 1859 the program to conduct such a complete census was dropped because of Sepoy Mutiny in 1857. Under the supervision of W.C. Plowdon a complete census was conducted in North Western Provinces on January 10, 1865. The team of enumerators visited every household in the province on the same day. Counting was done on religious affiliation, caste, sex, age, agricultural-non-agricultural labor, other occupations, etc. for the entire population. The census data were classified to yield the age distribution of the population.

3.2.2 Modern Periodic Census

Statistical organization moved fast at the close of this decade under the leadership of Lord Mayo, the Governor General. W.W. Hunter was appointed Director General of Statistical Survey in 1869. In 1865 the Government of India had agreed upon the principle that a general population census would be taken in 1871. W.C. Plowden had already worked out model census schedules and questionnaires in 1865. Under H. Beverley, the Registrar General, the years 1867–72 were spent in taking census by the actual counting of heads in as much of the country as was practicable. This series, commonly known as the Census of 1872, was not a synchronous project, nor did it cover all territories possessed or controlled by the British. Though based on uniform schedules it was not centrally supervised, moderated or compiled. It contained the rudiments of all basic demographic, social and economic tables. The undertaking stimulated the introduction into the Statute Book of the Bengal Births and Deaths Registration Act of 1873, to be followed later by the Births, Deaths and Marriages Registration Act of 1886 which would henceforth provide 'data for calculation', the lack of which H.T. Colebrooke had regretted in 1794.

The modern periodic census is largely a brainchild of Hunter, the father of modern periodic census in India. A program was chalked out to prepare statistics for various issues from data collected from the entire country. Although the 1872 population enumeration was carried out in most parts of India, 1872 census is not counted as the first of the *periodic synchronous census* in India for several reasons. The Census was incomplete since counting could not be done in quite a few regions. But more importantly, the counting was done on different dates even in the regions where counting could be done. Though imperfect on many counts, 1872 census is important even for today for various reasons. The 1872 census gave us a clear idea as to the administrative machinery needed for conducting such a mammoth exercise. It must be admitted that the administrative infrastructure that have gradually been evolved over the years, especially since independence, owes much to what were designed and followed by Hunter in 1872.

The first complete census of population was conducted in 1881, on a uniform basis throughout India providing the most complete and continuous demographic record for any comparable population. Since then the Census is being regularly held every ten years. These censuses have collected information on the distribution of population with respect to age and sex, its density, physical groups, urban and rural distribution, housing condition, migration, occupation, racial distribution, literacy, religion, physical deformities, civil condition and some others.

Population experts consider the type of census Hunter introduced in this country a "descriptive statistical system". Such statistical analysis provides demographic, social and economic characteristics of the population of the entire country and its constituent parts as well. Comparative study of two census data tells us the extent and the nature of changes that have taken place in these characteristics with time.

Till 1931 all the censuses generally followed the methods developed by Hunter. It was in 1941 census (seventh census) that Prof. P.C. Mahalanobis tried to introduce "analytical statistical system" in place of "descriptive statistical system" followed so long. Prof. Mahalanobis wanted that census data must be suitably used in economic analysis and in national planning purposes. To what extent the periodic census data have really been utilized or can be utilized in economic and other planning purposes remains a matter of intense debate. Those who oppose it do so on the ground that the census data lacks the kind of accuracy, precision, transparency and reliability needed for using them in planning exercises, least to speak of economic planning.

The Government of India emphasized the importance of population data and set up a Population Data Committee in 1944 to examine and advise on the available data relating to growth of population. This committee comprised of Mr W.M. Yeatts, the Census Commissioner of India in 1941 as Chairman and Sir Theodore Gregory, Professor P.C. Mahalnobis, Professor K.B. Madhava and Dr K.C.K.E. Raja as members. The Committee paid special emphasis to the statistical problems relating to the age tabulation of the 1941 census (which could not be completed because of financial stringency caused by the Second World War) and also made recommendations for the use of sampling methods for the estimation of vital statistics rates. In particular, they pointed out the use which could be made of the household lists prepared at the census as a sampling frame for obtaining demographic data and recommended their safe keeping.

The Bhore Committee (Health Survey and Development Committee, 1946), constituted for making plans for post-war developments in the health fields, made a comprehensive review of the field of population from the quantitative and qualitative aspects. It suggested the creation of a permanent office of the Registrar General of Vital and Population Statistics at the center and Provincial Superintendents in the Provinces with a view to improve the quality of population statistics. One of its chief recommendations was that "the population problem should be the subject of continuous study." Census Act was passed in 1948 and was placed on the Statute Book.

In 1949, the Government of India decided to initiate steps for improvement of Registration of Vital Statistics and further decided to establish a single organization at the Center in the Ministry of Home Affairs under the Registrar General and ex-officio Census Commissioner for India to deal with Vital Statistics and Census.

The administrative structure for census operation has not changed much since the days of Hunter. Definitely we are using more sophisticated tools for tabulation and analysis of enormous amount of data collected in every census. But the question that continues to foment is how far the use of improved analytical techniques could take care of the deficiencies in the census data. The inadequacy and lack of credibility of the census data appear obvious since the Government of India, who spends several hundred millions of tax payers' money on this gigantic periodic exercise, makes very little use of the census results in its planning exercises. The quality of census data is unlikely to improve much so long the government does not give due importance of this data in its planning exercises.

It was in 1881 the first complete census was carried out on the same day all over India. Ever since then complete census in India has been carried out every ten years. India like England followed *de facto* method till 1931. The census operation all over the country was completed in a single day by declaring the census day a holiday and the total transportation network throughout the country was deliberately put on hold so that people are forced to stay at the place where they were stationed on that day. *Post-enumeration check (PEC),* an integral part of modern census, to eliminate errors in enumeration, if any, was not a feature of the census operations till 1931. *De jure* technique was first employed in 1941 census. Counting on a single day was discarded. The census operation throughout the country was completed within two weeks although the counting continued to refer to a single day, that is, 31st March. Since 1951, persons continued to be enumerated at their usual place of residence if they had stayed there at any time within the specified period of 20 days; they were reckoned as 'visitors' wherever they were staying on the census night.

Till 1931 only a single schedule was canvassed for every household. From 1941 separate *individual slips* were employed for every member of the household. Earlier, all information about any individual in the household were transferred from the *household schedule* to another sheet. This transfer of information consumed considerable time and there was considerable chance of committing error in this process of transfer. Data are directly transferred to computers from the currently used schedules. A specific ID code used for the household and for each member of the household permits the data processor to locate the individual very easily.

The contents of the schedules used have changed over time. The 1872 census started with only 9 questions. The questions posed in census schedule are items that are commonly asked in enumerations in all other countries (sex, age, marital status, birth place, mother tongue, religion, education, occupation, etc.). Some of the questions were dropped in subsequent censuses; some of these reappeared at a later date. For example 'level of education' was dropped in 1891 census. It was reintroduced in 1941 census. "Nationality" was dropped in 1881, included again in 1951 (the first census after partition of India) and was dropped again in 1971 and subsequent censuses. Place of "last residence" was first introduced in 1971. "Caste" remained an important population classification criterion till 1941. Since 1951 census, the same was replaced by a question on "Scheduled caste/tribe" status of the respondents. In 1941, "Number of children born and age at first birth for every married woman" was canvassed and then dropped in subsequent censuses for the complexity of the question. Since 1971, age at marriage of every married woman and if any child was born in the past one year preceding the census date are being canvassed.

Not only the number of questions canvassed has changed, definition of some of the concepts has also undergone changes. It is for this reason some of the issues canvassed in different censuses are not comparable. "Occupation/work" has been canvassed in all the thirteen periodic censuses conducted till 2001. In the 1872 census no definition was offered for "Occupation". Even no attempt was made to enquire about the occupation of any woman. In 1881 census, whoever contributed (male/female/children) in some way or other to household income, were treated as having some occupation. "Occupation" was equated to "means of subsistence" in 1891 census. Since 1901, both "Primary" and "Secondary" occupations of individuals are recorded. In 1931, an altogether different question was canvassed – "Dependency status". The question has been dropped since 1961. In 1941, there were altogether 8 different questions covering occupation. Prior to 1961 census, the emphasis was on 'economic return'. Since 1961, 'nature of work' has been highlighted. The 'work status' of an individual at the time of census was decided on the basis of the 'nature of work' pursued and the 'number of days' one remained involved in it in a time frame defined prior to the date of census. Altogether 5 separate questions and 7 other related questions were canvassed to understand the nature of work and the work status. Workers were classified by several industrial categories. 'Secondary work' was omitted in 1961 census but reintroduced in the next census. Since 1971, a person is regarded as a 'worker' "... whose main activity is participation in any economically productive work by his/her physical or mental activity."

Table 3.2
Type of information collected through Census, 1872–1981

Information	*1872*	*81*	*91*	*1901*	*11*	*21*	*31*	*41*	*51*	*61*	*71*	*81*
Relation to Head of the household	—	—	—	—	—	—	—	—	×	×	×	×
Sex	×	×	×	×	×	×	×	×	×	×	×	×
Age	×	×	×	×	×	×	×	×	×	×	×	×
Marital status	—	×	×	×	×	×	×	×	×	×	×	×
Age at marriage of currently married women	—	—	—	—	—	—	—	—	—	—	×	—
Literacy	×	×	×	×	×	×	×	×	×	×	×	×
Level of education	×	×	—	—	—	—	—	×	×	×	×	×
Mother tongue	—	×	×	×	×	×	×	×	×	×	×	×
Any other languages known	—	—	—	—	—	—	×	×	×	×	×	×
Knowledge of English	—	—	—	×	×	×	×	×	×	—	—	—
Place of birth, district, rural/urban	—	×	×	×	×	×	×	×	×	×	×	×
Duration of residence in the place of enumeration	—	—	—	—	—	—	—	—	—	×	×	×
Nationality	×	—	—	—	—	—	—	—	×	×	—	—
Religion	×	×	×	×	×	×	×	×	×	×	×	×
Caste/Race/Tribes	×	×	×	×	×	×	×	×	—	—	—	—
Scheduled Castes/Tribes	—	—	—	—	—	—	—	—	×	×		
Displaced persons	—	—	—	—	—	—	—	×	—	—	—	—
Number of children born and age at first birth for ever married women	—	—	—	—	—	—	×	—	—	—	—	—
Current fertility	—	—	—	—	—	—	—	—	—	—	—	×
Infirmities	×	×	×	×	×	×	×	—	—	—	—	—
Main activity	—	—	—	—	—	—	—	—	—	—	×	×
Occupation/Means of subsistence or means of livelihood	×	×	×	×	×	×	×	×	×	×	×	×
Subsidiary occupation or means of livelihood	—	—	—	×	×	×	×	×	×	×	×	×
Dependency status	—	—	—	—	—	—	×	×	×	—	—	—
Employment status	—	—	—	—	—	—	—	—	×	×	×	×

Source: P.B. Desai: A Survey of Research in Demography, Popular Prakasan, Bombay, and Census of India, 1981.

Before 1951, population distribution was obtained for mother tongue, marital status, occupation and age by religion and caste. Such cross-tabulation of the population has been discarded since 1951. Instead, population has been cross-classified by occupation. Since 1951, statistical tables have been generated for various issues as education, occupation, migration, birth and death rate, etc. separately for urban and rural populations. The reports published by the Registrar General and the

Census Commissioner generally have four principal tables – General population Tables, Economic Tables, Social and Cultural Tables and Migration Tables.

The report of 1951 census was a complete departure from the pattern of previous census reports. This report attempted to interpret the past changes in the size and structure of India's population and to point out their implications for the level of living of the population. The report also made a plea for a reduction in the birth rate of the country. The 1951 census also attempted for the first time in the history of Indian census to make an assessment of the accuracy of the census count by a post enumeration check, PEC in the field.

The Census authority has been publishing since 1911 Primary Census Abstracts or Summary Tables soon after the completion of the enumeration. Besides these four tables, Special Tables are also been published since 1951. Six Special Table for Displaced Persons was published in 1951 to take a stock of the effects of partition of India in 1947. Such a table, however, has not been published in the subsequent censuses. In 1961, a special series of tables giving details of scientific and technical persons and house-related information were published. Fifteen special tables were published for scheduled castes and scheduled tribe's populations. Before 1961, statistics on migration were published under Social and Cultural Tables. Migration related statistics in India are published under a separate series since this census. In 1971, SC and ST related tables were not published. Instead nine special tables relating to fertility were published. Such tables were published in 1931 as well. But the data did not come from the census enumeration. A special survey provided the necessary information. Till 1951, classified series of population tables remained confined between 13 and 38. In 1961, it went up to 77. This number is increasing ever since.

1961 census under Prof. Ashok Mitra as Registrar General and Census Commissioner is really extraordinary in many respects. The population scientists are of the opinion that such well-organized and well-planned census on such a vast population is comparable only with the best of such exercises anywhere in the world. Prof. Mitra devoted considerable time in pre-census planning. He conducted workshops and seminars with population scientists, researchers and the potential consumers of census data. He discussed with them the details of the census, methodological and administrative issues. A careful analysis was done on the census schedules to be canvassed. Pre-testing was carried out with the draft schedules to test their relevance and efficacy. Detailed census maps for each census block, from state down to villages/smallest census units were prepared. The maps were so prepared that each enumerator could easily get a clear picture of the census block where he was to do the counting. Even the nature and number of tables to be prepared, the type of special tables needed for large cities were thought out in advance.

A novel feature of 1961 census was the undertaking of a large number of ancillary studies relating to rural craft, fairs and festivals and ethnographic surveys. The Census Organization, therefore, became the repository of a wealth of sociological information relating to the country. Special Socio-economic Surveys were undertaken in a large number of villages. For the first time in the history of Census of India, a Census Atlas was planned at the state level as well as at the national level. An attempt was also made for the mechanical tabulation of some of the data and consequently a moderate complement of mechanical data equipments like, Key punches, Verifiers, Sorters, Tabulators, Reproducers were obtained and household schedules of the 1961 census were tabulated on these mechanical equipments.

Private researchers did not have access to census data prior to 1961 census. Since 1961 the universities and the research institutions are allowed to use the census data for their research and for more intense analysis. Arrangements were made to help the researchers use the archives at the office of the Registrar General. Even some financial grants were made available for visiting and using vast census data, a large part of which even today remains unanalyzed.

The schedules of 1971 Census were further modified to suit the needs of the Government, Planning Commission, various demographic bodies and scholars. The new features of 1971 Census were : (i) attempt made to collect data on current fertility, (ii) migrational particulars with reference to place of last residence which yielded valuable and realistic data on internal migration, (iii) considerable departure in respect to economic questions. The main activity of a person was ascertained according as he spent his time basically as a worker producing goods and services or as a non-worker. A new concept of 'Standard Urban Area' was developed for the tabulation of certain urban data. Encouraged by the experience of 1961 Census, it was proposed to have a number of studies ancillaries to 1971 Census. It was planned to have a re-study of a number of villages and also to have intensive studies of about 200 towns and ethnographic studies of selected communities.

Since 1971 computers are being used for data compilation, storage and analysis. From this census a new question relating migration was canvassed – the last place of residence. With this information, proper identification of the migration streams by place of birth as well as by the last place of residence became possible. The place of work also gave an idea about the day-to-day movement of the population. Questions on age at marriage and if a child was born within a year prior to the date of census were introduced. SRS data on birth and death came to be used to supplement the census data.

In 1991 census, three different schedules were used – House list, Household schedule and Individual slip. In addition, a Post-Graduate Degree Holders and Technical Personnel Schedule (PGDHTP) were canvassed on behalf of the Council of Scientific and Industrial Research (CSIR). The House Listing was completed by September 1990. On the request of the Central Statistical Organization (CSO), an Enterprise List was also canvassed. The data collected on this list was handed over to CSO for analysis. The 1981 House List was revised in 1991 to include such items as: if the owner of the house stays in the said house, number of living rooms, materials used for the construction of the house, facilities for drinking water and electricity, toilet, etc. For the first time information on the type of fuel used for domestic purposes was collected in this census. This was done with a view to measuring the impact such fuel consumption could have on environment, forest resources and energy supply. The analysis would, it was hoped, suggest what alternative fuels could be recommended for use to prevent large-scale deforestation and environmental pollution. In the Individual Slip two questions were put for ex-military persons and the pensioners. In Causes of Migration, two more answers were included – on business ground and natural calamity like drought, flood, earthquake, etc. The 'individual slip' has been dropped in 2001 census. A full text of the census schedule, 2001 is appended (Appendix 3.2).

It is to be noted that many organizations and agencies took advantage of the periodic census to collect information, which they considered vital in the interest of national planning and/or getting a clearer picture about certain aspects of their interest. All these made the modern censuses very complex.

It was from 1991 census that the formula employed for calculation of literates changed. Earlier, 0–4 age group was considered illiterate. The proportion of literates in the population was calculated by the formula:

$$\text{Prop.of literates} = \frac{\text{No. of literates in the enire 5 + age group population}}{\text{No. of persons in the entire population}}$$

The revised formula is

$$\text{Prop. of literates} = \frac{\text{No. of literates in the entire 7 + age group}}{\text{No. of persons in the 7 + age group}}$$

This was done on the recommendation of the HRD ministry and the Planning Commission. The experts argued that the boys and girls in 0–6 age group, especially in rural India, should be regarded as illiterate even if they had some schooling. Their contention is that a boy or a girl could learn to read and write, only mechanically, even before they are 6. It is only when they are 7 years or more old, they learn with proper understanding. That is, a child of age < 6 would learn without retention, but a child in 7+ age would learn with retention. The denominator too has replaced "number of persons in the entire population" by "number of persons in 7+ age group in the population". The fall-out of this change of definition is that current literacy levels for various cross sections cannot directly be compared with those obtained in earlier censuses. They have to be adjusted according to this latest definition.

Organizing periodic census of population is a stupendous task for a vastly populated country like India. In the 2001 census over 2.3 million enumerators had to be employed. To conduct this gigantic exercise without compromising on quality, the Census Commissioner needs the support assistance of a vast army of specially trained and motivated enumerators and supervisors and huge amount of money.

Prior to independence there was not much scope to use the information realized through periodic census in economic and social planning of the country. That the census of population can have a significant role in development-oriented economic and social planning has never been questioned. Yet, the census output has not been utilized as an input in the developmental planning. The census data have customarily been used in a few political and administrative decisions: boundaries of the assembly segments, the dividing lines between rural and urban settlements, boundary lines while reorganizing states by languages spoken or some other characteristics, division between developed and underdeveloped regions, upgrading towns into cities, cities into mega cities, share of states to Center's revenue collections, etc. If we go through the Five Year Plans, it would be clearly visible that the Planning Commission has given far too little attention to census results than what it really deserves. Besides the periodical census, the Registrar General and other bodies conduct various types of sample surveys. Only a small fraction of this gold mine of information has been analyzed, what to speak of utilization.

The Census Commissioner repeatedly put advertisements in all the major dailies in the country drawing attention of the public to this vast exercise and its immense importance in the context of national planning exercises. The Census Commissioner asked for unstinted support and cooperation of the public in this exercise. Population experts and Planning Commission members have discussed threadbare the utility of census of population and these have been broadcast through TV networks and radio. The schedules to be used in the census have been published in newspapers so that head of every household can leave the information ready with someone in the house in case he happens to be away on the probable date of visit by the census enumerators. Even after this wide circulation of the message, common man often was not happy with what really had happened. There were protests through newspapers that the census enumerators did not take the matter with seriousness: there were reports that the enumerator did not visit their houses; house list number were seen on the wall although no one asked for the information mentioned in the house list schedule from any member of the house; many complained that their houses were not listed; many also complained that although the household schedule was filled up, the individual slip was not used (1991 census). The most common complaint was that the enumerators did not visit their houses for post-enumeration check. Many enumerators did not know if a university/college/school was a government organization or an autonomous body. In 1991 census, some of the potential users of the census data expressed their apprehension about the quality of the data. In the 1991 census, Indian Statistical Institute expressed its willingness to participate actively in some phase of the census operation. They asked the Census Commissioner to allow them to conduct enumeration with their trained staff in selected census blocks simultaneously with the enumerators appointed by the Census Commissioner. Alternatively, they suggested that they be given the responsibility for PEC to ascertain the trustworthiness of the census count. The Census Commissioner said "No" to this request.

Naturally, a serious question has been raised: Do we really need this mammoth exercise every ten years and drain the taxpayers' money? Even Prof. Mahalanobis thought that there was no need to conduct the census operations every ten years. The NSS and the SRS data are good enough to throw light on the population and its changing characteristics. The quality of the data collected through NSS and SRS are far superior to the population census data. Prof. Ashok Mitra also remarked

> … [T]he first question to ask is to what extent Population Census data are important in the planning exercise of the country, to what extent they have been utilized so far and to what extent they are likely to be used in the future.

It is high time that we look forward to some alternative to this periodic census of population covering over 1,100 million heads in 2011 census. Even the United States of America, which has less than one-third of the population of India, has been thinking for an alternative to house-to-house visit by enumerators. They tried mail questionnaire technique. Even in a cent percent literate country, the response to the mail questionnaire was disappointing.

3.2.3 Delays in Processing

Even though the first flash of results (provisional population totals) on population size by sex in the broad age categories 0 to 6 and 7+, density, and literacy among those aged 7+ are released soon after the completion of the fieldwork, undue delay in the release of all final tables undermines the immense utility of this gigantic exercise. Provisional population totals for 2001 Census were published within a month of the date of Census. To illustrate, the data on literacy for the age 15+ years, which is the internationally accepted minimum age for data on literacy, usually were available only after a gap of 4 to 5 years in the past. Although major population tables are available within 2 or 3 years of the census, the release-schedule needs to be advanced considerably. When the world's largest population count in China (last conducted in November 2000) could release final population totals within four months or when the US Population Census conducted in April 2000 could release data, which are all final, starting from December 2000, there can be no reason why India could not publish the final data on major issues within the same year of Census. The delay in release of final census data has been one of the most serious drawbacks in the past. Most of the information related to Census, current and recent previous, are now available on-line. They are now available in CD format as well.

Currently, census results for each state, district-wise, along with results for the entire country are published. Census publications since independence have increased enormously. The major reason for increase in the volumes of publication is the District Census Handbooks. These handbooks provide information about changes observed in the life style of people in the districts, the administrative changes and the social and economic developments in the past decade along with the usual information on current population distribution by various indicators. Simultaneously with the periodic census results, NSS and SRS results are published regularly. In recent years the Registrar General has undertaken various other studies based on samples. Causes of death, infant and child mortality, differential fertility, efficacy of the registration system, etc. are frequently covered in these sample studies. Between 1871 and 1970, that is in a span of 100 years the total number of census related publications was 2,653. Of these, 1,628 have come out between 1951 and 1970.

The results of the Population Census data are currently published in six broad categories indicating the nature of topics covered in each series. These are:

- A Series: General Population Tables
- B Series: General Economic Tables
- C Series: Social and Cultural Tables
- D Series: Migration Tables
- F Series: Fertility Tables
- H Series: Tables on Houses and Household Amenities

In addition, a number of Special Tables relating to SC and ST are published. On the request of the Planning Commission, HRD Ministry, Department of Science and Technology, Ministry of Defense (two questions were canvassed in 1991 Census on ex-servicemen), additional information are collected during Census and such information are passed on to the agency that requested for them.

Every population Census collects variety of information through household schedules during house listing operations. But some of the information, which could throw considerable light on socio-economic and cultural aspects, is not published for user consumption. They could be of much help in planning at the district or even lower level. After considerable debate and discussion, the Registrar General published some information relating to religion. There is a need to re-examine the issue of non-publication of information, such as cross-classification of data on religion, caste and language by literacy, work, migration, etc.

3.2.4 Population Census Stages

Present Census Operations in India are carried out in two phases – the House Numbering and the House-listing Operations followed by Head Count by personal visits. The objective of the House Numbering and the House-listing Operations is to systematically list out all the structures, houses and households throughout the country for preparation of a sound frame for conduct of the population enumeration. All the buildings and houses wherever necessary are numbered for easy identification at the time of actual enumeration. The House-listing for the 2001 Census was conducted in different states/UTs during April–September 2000.

The Population Enumeration 2001 was undertaken between 9th and 28th February, 2001 (both days inclusive) with a revisional round from 1st to 5th March, 2001. The census moment, the referral time at which the snapshot of the population is taken, was 00.00 hours of 1st March, 2001. Until the

1991 Census, the sunrise of 1st March was taken to be the census moment. The houseless population, as has been the usual practice, was enumerated on the night of 28th February 2001. In certain parts of the country, the population enumeration was carried out non-synchronously because of adverse climatic conditions or unforeseen contingencies arising at the last moment. Thus, in Jammu & Kashmir, and certain snow bound areas of Himachal Pradesh and Uttar Pradesh, the population enumeration was carried out during 11th to 30th September 2000 with a revisional round from 1st to 5th October 2000. The gigantic operation was carried out with over two million enumerators and supervisors engaged for enumerating over one billion people in about 220 million households living in 593 districts, 5564 Tahsils/talukas, 5161 towns and around six hundred forty thousand villages.

Several innovations have been introduced at almost all the stages of the 2001Census, right from the preparatory efforts to data processing and dissemination. We briefly mention the changes noticed in 2001 census.

3.2.4.1 Permanent Location Code Number PLCN

A system of Permanent Location Code Numbers has been adopted by assigning to each village within the state/UT a continuous series from 1 to N. Each village has been assigned an eight-digit code. The first six digits represent the code of the village as existing at the present census. The last two digits being '00' are kept for accommodating future changes in case of split of an existing village or creation of new villages etc. Since the PLCNs have been assigned to each village, tracing the precise location of village on account of future jurisdictional changes in the boundaries should not pose much of a problem.

3.2.4.2 Slum Enumeration Block

Slum Enumeration Blocks were identified for the first time in 2001census in each Municipal town having a population of 50,000 or more. Instructions were issued that these *Enumeration Blocks do not cut across ward boundaries or non-slum area*. It will thus be possible to compile and tabulate special tables for 'slums'.

3.2.4.3 Household, the Operational Unit of Enumeration

Census aims at enumerating every individual. But the operational unit in India is the physical entity of the household, which is generally understood as a group of persons commonly living together and sharing a common kitchen. A household may occupy an entire house, or more than one household may share a house. In organizing a census, one needs to locate every house and household. House numbering and house listing operation are taken up as preliminary to census enumeration a few months in advance. The staffs of the local authorities (school teachers, government and municipality employees, etc.) usually are employed for such operations. This house listing and numbering serves to identify every house and household, which the census enumerator is required to cover for census enumeration.

Special attention is given in the collection of *household information.* Income sources of the household, more specifically land and land ownership, are looked into. From 1961census, house listing, no matter if it was residential house or a house used for some other purposes has been made essential. This gives us reliable information about the number of houses in a block, a district and the whole country as also the purpose of construction and use of those houses. The house listing also informs us about the state of affairs about small-scale industries, household industries besides the total number of houses available on the census date. Industrial workers too are divided into two categories – those engaged in *household industries* and those in non-household manufacturing industries. Birthplace is classified as 'urban' and 'rural'. This makes evaluation of the strength of different migration streams possible. Region-specific demographic, social and economic distinctiveness are emphasized in the reports.

Keeping in view the requirements of data users and planners, the scope of House-listing was considerably expanded with the inclusion of new questions. The new features of the House-listing Schedule are listed below.

- The different uses of census houses have been standardized and grouped into ten main uses and assigned code numbers.
- Plastic has been added in the list of material of wall and roof of a census house, as it is often used for shelter in slums and shanties.
- In the previous census, the location of drinking water source was categorized into two locations viz. 'within premises' and 'outside premises'. In the 2001 Census, the source 'outside premises' was split further into two categories namely 'near the premises' and 'away from the premises'.
- The scope of question on availability of electricity was expanded to include six sources of lighting. Besides no lighting, this included sources like electricity, kerosene, solar, other oil and any other source.
- In 1991 Census, a question on availability of toilet facilities to the household was canvassed, while in 2001 Census, specific information on availability of latrine within the house by the type of latrine was sought.

The following new questions were added in the House-list Schedule for Normal Households.

- If the Census house was used for residential or partly residential purposes, the condition of the census house was to be categorized as good, livable or dilapidated based on the perception and response of the respondent.
- A question on number of married couple(s) living in the household was to be canvassed.
- Information was to be sought on the number of married couple(s) having independent room for sleeping.
- Information as to whether the waste-water outlet of the house is connected to 'closed drainage' or 'open drainage' or has no drainage to be connected.
- A question on availability of bathroom within the house was included.
- Information on availability of kitchen within the house was also to be sought.
- Availability of certain assets to the households namely radio/transistor, television, telephone, bicycle, scooter/motor cycle/moped, car/jeep/van were also to be recorded.
- It was to be enquired if any banking service was being availed by the household.

3.2.4.4 Houseless Population

Houseless population too is covered in Indian census. In some areas, particularly in some cities, there may be considerable number of pavement dwellers. Arrangements are made for covering them through a one-night enumeration by appointing special enumerators for the purpose. During the general enumeration, the enumerators try to locate the areas where there may be concentration of houseless population so that on the census night the charge officer can make arrangements for deputing adequate number of enumerators for single night enumeration.

3.2.4.5 Household Schedule

The Schedule has three parts. Part I contains the Location Particulars; Part II relates to Individual Particulars and Part III contains questions for Households engaged in Cultivation/Plantation. To facilitate quick tabulation for bringing out Provisional Population Totals, provisions of page totaling were made in the schedule itself for a few items namely population, males, females, population aged 0–6 years by sex, literates and workers and their categories by sex. Most of the questions canvassed during the 1991 Census, were retained for the 2001 Census, except the question on ex-serviceman, which was dropped in the 2001Census.

However, a number of new questions were added in the Household Schedule in view of the suggestions from policy makers, data users and researchers, while the scope of certain existing questions was enhanced. These modifications are:

1. Age at marriage was collected for males also, while it was collected for only ever-married females until the 1991 Census.
2. The type of educational institution attended was enlarged to include school, college, vocational institute, and other institute and literacy center.
3. The scope of the definition of 'work' was expanded to include production of milk for domestic consumption. In the 1991 Census, cultivation of certain crops even for self-consumption was treated as economic activity. The scope of the term 'Cultivation' was expanded in this Census to include certain other crops such as tobacco, fruits, all types of flowers, roots and tubers, potatoes, chilies and turmeric, pepper, cardamom, all types of vegetables and fodder crops etc. This meant that activities related to production of all the above mentioned crops for domestic consumption has been treated as work. Only five crops viz. tea, coffee, rubber, coconut and betel nuts have been classified under 'Plantation' in the 2001Census.
4. In 1991 Census, the question on seeking/available for work was canvassed for only non-workers. In 2001 census, this question was asked from the Marginal Workers as well. A question to elicit information on secondary work canvassed at the 1991 Census was dropped.
5. From among the categories of non-workers adopted at the 1991 Census, the category 'Inmates of institutions' has been dropped and 'Retired Persons and Rentiers' has been replaced by 'Pensioners'.
6. A new response category 'moved after birth' has been included in the question on 'reasons for migration' to bring out additional information on migration patterns. Natural calamities or distress migration as a reason for migration for last residence migrants included in the 1991 Census was to be covered under category 'Other'.
7. Number of children born alive to currently married women during last one year was to be collected for male and female children separately.

The following new questions were canvassed in the 2001 Census:

1. A question on total disability was canvassed in the 1981 Census which was dropped in 1991 census. In 2001 Census, a question to elicit information on total or partial disability was canvassed. The five types of disability on which information was to be collected are – in seeing, in hearing, in speech, in movement and mental.

2. A new question on 'Travel to place of work' was canvassed mainly for workers engaged in non-agricultural activities. Information on distance from the residence to place of work and mode of travel to place of work were to be collected under this section.
3. The Household Schedule has a new set of questions for Households engaged in cultivation/plantation – (i) Net area of land under cultivation/plantation, (ii) Net area of land irrigated and (iii) Tenure status. This question was not canvassed in the 1991 Census though canvassed in the 1981 Census in a slightly different form.
4. The signature or thumb impression of the respondent has been taken on the Household Schedule for the first time in the history of census.

The 2001 household schedule had 22 questions, many with number of break-ups.

3.2.4.6 Post-Enumeration Survey (PES)

Post Enumeration Survey (PES), which was earlier known as Post Enumeration Check (PEC), has become an integral part of the census operations in India since 1951. In earlier censuses, the Post Enumeration Survey used to be conducted only after the population enumeration. For the first time, a PES of the House-listing Operations was also conducted after the completion of the House-listing Operations in sixteen major states including Delhi in the 2001Census. The main objectives of the PES are (i) to get an estimate of under coverage of census houses, (ii) to get an estimate of under coverage of population and, (iii) to provide an estimate of the extent of the content error with respect to certain selected data items.

The sampling frame used for selection of samples for conducting the PES of the House-listing Operations were the sample units of the Sample Registration System (SRS) unlike the PES of the population enumeration, where the Enumeration Blocks (EB) are used as the sampling frame. In 1991 and earlier censuses, the PEC used to be conducted in certain selected states based on the criteria of the size of the population. However, in the last census, the PES was conducted in all the states and UTs of the country. In the 1991 Census, for measuring the content error, a ten percent sub-sample of households enumerated in census was selected from each EB and the usual residents in those households were listed along with certain particulars. But at the Census 2001, PES of all the households in the sampled EBs was proposed to be listed along with certain particulars. Since the PES estimation methodology is based on the assumption of independence between the PES and the census operations, wherever possible, the fieldwork in the states was to be carried out by the staff of the state governments, who would be specially trained for the purpose.

3.3 Census Legislation

For the success of an operation of such magnitude and importance as the Population Census, it is imperative that it should have the necessary backing of law. The Census Organization should be armed with necessary authority to have access to households and canvass the prescribed questionnaires and to expect the people to answer truthfully. The law should also protect the interests of the people by guaranteeing the secrecy of the information collected. Penalties for giving false answer or not giving answers at all to the census questionnaire are to be incorporated in the law. It should call upon the census officers to discharge their duties faithfully and should warn them against putting any question to a person that is not covered by the questionnaire. They would be required to record the answers as are given by the person enumerated. The census records shall not be open to inspection and also not admissible in evidence in a court of law. The answers ascertained at the census can be used only for statistical purposes.

The Census of India Act, 1948 empowers Central Government to notify the date for the census and to appoint a Census Commissioner and Superintendents of Census Operations in states. The Act enjoins upon every citizen to assist in conducting the census. The Act states that services of any citizen can be requisitioned for census work and makes it obligatory for every person occupying a house, enclosure, etc. to allow access to census officers and to allow them to affix to the place such letters, marks or numbers as may be necessary for census purposes.

3.4 Potential Areas where Census Results can be Used

The population census is the primary source of basic national population data required for administrative purposes and for many aspects of economic and social research and planning. The value of the census results is enlarged if they can be employed together with the results of other investigations, as in the use of the census data as a base of benchmark for current statistics. The usefulness of the census is also enhanced if it can furnish information needed for conducting other statistical inquiries.

1. *In Administration and Policy*

One of the most important administrative uses of census data is in the demarcation of constituencies and the allocation of representation on governing bodies. Detailed information on the geographic distribution of the population is indispensable for this purpose. The legal and administrative status of a territorial division often depends upon the size of its population. The social and cultural data provided by the census is employed to determine the total number of seats to be reserved for members of SCs and STs in the Parliament and the state assemblies in India. The district-level census data give information on the demographic and economic characteristics of the population at the district level. The study of the geographic distribution of the population, its size and other characteristics is essential for policy formulation for short and long-term economic and social objectives. Deliberations on employment and manpower planning, migration, housing, education, public health and welfare, social services, economic and social planning, and numerous other aspects of the life of the country, are facilitated if accurate information about the characteristics of the population is available for civil and other administrative divisions

2. *In Research*

The changing patterns of urban-rural concentration, the development of urbanized areas, the geographic distribution of population according to occupation and education, sex and age structure of population, social and economic characteristics of population are some of the issues of scientific interest, which are of importance both to research and practical problems of industrial and commercial growth and management.

3. *In Business and Industry*

The census data have many important uses for individuals and institutions in business and industry. It is very difficult to make a full assessment of the multiplicity of ways in which trade and business make use of the census data. A few uses of the census data can be mentioned. Life Insurance companies use age and sex-specific death rates in calculation of premiums to be paid by the policy-holder. Reliable estimates of consumer demand for variety of goods and services depend on accurate information on the size of the population and its distribution by age, sex, income and occupation since these characteristics heavily influence the demand for housing, furnishing, clothing, recreational facilities, medical supplies and so forth. Since the local availability of labor for production and distribution of commodities is important in determining the location and organization of enterprises, this calls for the need of the census data.

4. *In Sample Surveys*

Many issues on social and economic characteristics are not appropriate for collection in a full-scale census. They often are collected through sample surveys using census as the benchmark data. Inter-censal sample surveys are often used to collect current and detailed information on many topics, which are usually investigated at ten-year intervals in the population censuses.

The census often provides the frame for scientific sample design in connection with sample surveys; at the same time it provides benchmark data for evaluating the reasonableness of the over-all survey results as well as a base against which changes in the characteristics investigated in both inquiries can be measured. To permit comparison of census and survey results, the definitions and classifications employed should be as nearly alike as possible, consistent with the aims of each investigation. NSS in India frequently uses the list of census villages as frame for several social and economic surveys in rural India. SRS in India also utilizes the list of census villages and blocks as frame for the registration of births and deaths. Thus, the census provides the frame for subsequent sample enquiries during the inter-censal period.

5. *In Planning*

The census data is indispensable for social and economic planning of the country. The Planning Commission utilizes the census data on the distribution of population by age and sex classified by rural and urban regions, cities, town areas and social groups to analyze the growth of consumer demand and savings in the process of development. The census data also prove useful in national income estimates and estimates on differential personal incomes in rural and urban areas and the composition of rural and urban consumption groups of goods and services and income elasticity coefficients. An analysis of areas of different population size with different characteristics certainly serves as a basis for government plans and investigations in basic social capital. The data on economic activity and educational levels of the individual are important for manpower planning. The census data on population throw light on the housing needs. The census data can also prove their usefulness in the formulation of policies on education, health, agriculture, food, development of road, rail transport, and etc. The census data can be used for locating growth points.

6. *In Other Types of Censuses*

Certain information collected as part of a population census or incidental to it, can be most useful in housing, agricultural or establishment censuses taken at about the same time or near about as the population census.

7. In Civil Registration and Vital Statistics

Census data serve as denominators for the computation of vital rates, especially rates specific for characteristics normally investigated only at the time of the census. Conversely, census results, time-adjusted by vital and migration statistics, can provide estimates of the future size, distribution and other characteristics of the population of the whole country and sub-national levels. Further, census data on fertility can provide a benchmark check on the reliability of current birth statistics. It is consequently desirable that procedures for the collection of census data, vital and migration statistics be closely coordinated with regard to coverage, concepts, definitions, classifications and tabulations.

3.5 Provisional Population Totals

The Indian Census has a long tradition of releasing the population data on a tentative basis within days of the completion of the population enumeration. The population totals are built up by each enumerator right from the page totals of a few data items for each page of the Household Schedule, which are then consolidated at the EB level. The totals at various administrative levels are consolidated through a process of successive aggregation. The entire exercise is completed within a short span. The data items on which the provisional totals are compiled for each sex are Population, Child Population, Literate Population, Main Workers, Marginal Workers, Non-Workers and categories of Main and Marginal Workers, namely, Cultivators, Agricultural Laborers, Household Industry Workers and Other Workers. The actual processing and final tabulation of this huge volume of data takes time; therefore, provisional data relating to some key aspects of the population becomes very useful to the data users.

'The Provisional Population Totals', the first flash of census results, is rather raw and not subjected to the intensive checks and cross checks as are usual with census data. Therefore, the numbers given are somewhat tentative and the final figures are bound to be marginally different. The data user will have to keep this in mind. The data are best used to pick up some early demographic trends.

A complete census is a huge undertaking and requires many years to complete the whole tabulation program in India. By the time the data are published, its offer becomes outdated and cannot be used for many policy matters. In view of this, it becomes necessary to base the tabulation of census data on sample basis to provide quick estimates to the census data users. Both Provisional Population Total: India and Supplements: District Totals are available from the Office of the Registrar General and Census Commissioner, both in book form and in CD (in spreadsheet format – *xls*). Many tables with attended analysis are presented in Census website, mostly in PDF format.

3.6 Administrative Structure of the Census Organization

Before 1951 there was no permanent post for the Registrar General and therefore no permanent office as well. Just before the census date, someone from the Central government administration (a senior ICS or IAS officer) was temporarily appointed the Census Commissioner of India. A makeshift office was created with staff deputed from various secretariats. The Census Commissioner used to conduct the census operations with the help and assistance of other administrative units. Once the census was over, he went back to his secretariat and the temporary office dissolved.

Through Indian Census Act 1948, a permanent post of the Registrar General and Census Commissioner (RGCC) of India was created and he was given a permanent office as well. To assist the RGCC, post of Census Superintendent in each state were created. Initially, the posts of Census Superintendent were temporary; someone from the general administration was deputed to the post. Once the census was over, they would go back to their earlier office. At present there is a small but permanent office of the Registrar General in each state. Census programs are so devised that these offices can work in close cooperation with the state administration. The administrative machinery developed by Hunter is largely followed even today. This administrative set up has the advantage that it keeps down the expenditure on census operations. General administration closely cooperates with the Census Commissioner during the enumeration. Since personnel from state administration already have some link with the common man, many of the administrative problems likely to arise during the enumeration, could be tackled easily and effectively.

The administrative set up of the census organization has a pyramid structure. The Registrar General and Census Commissioner is at the apex of the pyramid. Census Superintendents from each state form the next line of hierarchy. The District Magistrates come next in the hierarchy followed by Sub-Divisional Officers and others. At the lowest rung are the enumerators.

- A **Census Block** has about 150 households. An **Enumerator** is given the charge of one such block (popularly called *beats*).
- A few blocks together constitute a **circle.** This is looked after by a **Circle Inspector**.
- Similarly, combining a few circles creates a **Charge** and the **Charge Superintendents** head these Charges.
- A few Charges constitute the **Sub-division** and an **SDO** remains in charge of this.
- The **District Magistrate** remains in charge of all the sub-divisions under him.
- The **Census Superintendent** remains responsible for the entire state.

The first Registrar General and Census Commissioner of India after independence was R.A. Gopalaswami.

Figure 3.1
Orgnizational structure of census operation

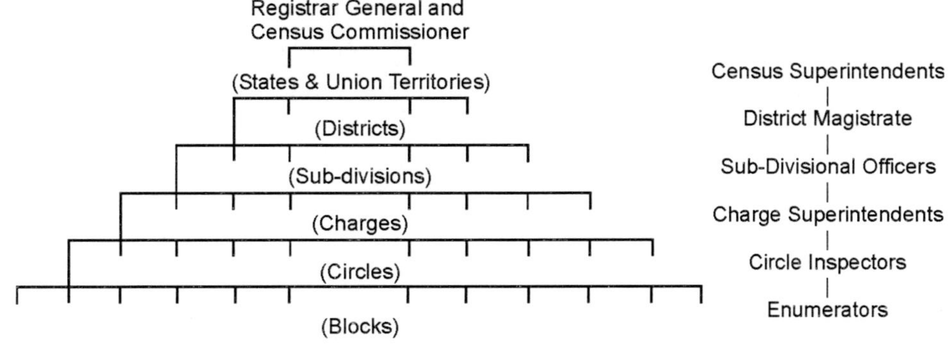

The following table presents the approximate number of field functionaries required for the conduct of the Census of India 2001.

Table 3.3
Census functionaries and their responsibilities

Name of Functionary	Responsibility	Approximate Number
Census Commissioner, India	In Charge of Census in India	1
Directors of Census Operations	In Charge of Census in states and Union Territories	30
Principal Census Officers	In Charge of Census in the District and supervising District Census Officers under him	710
District Census Officers	In Charge of Census in Districts	4.160
Charge Officer	In Charge of Census in a Charge below District	30,000
Supervisors	In Charge of six Enumerators	330,000
Enumerators	Undertakes enumeration of about 600 to 650 persons	2,000,000 (including Reserves)

3.7 National Sample Survey Organization (NSSO)

Periodic Census can cover only a few simple and readily documentable characteristics of a vast population. There are many complex social, economic, demographic, health, employment and landholding issues and their distribution and much other information, needed for national planning, could not be collected through census. NSSO in India, a permanent body under Planning Commission, was established in 1950 by Prof. P.C. Mahalanobis primarily to equip the planning commission and other planning bodies with such vital information. Initially, NSSO was attached to Indian Statistical Institute. National Sample Survey (NSS) is

> ... a continuing, multi-subject, integrated survey being conducted in the form of successive 'rounds', each round covering some topics of current interest in a specific survey period. The scope, period, sample design and program in each round are fixed by taking into account the requirements of its users and the resources available for the period.

NSSO also conducts some survey on ad hoc basis (Living Survey of the Middle Class and the Working Class, Post-census surveys of Population and Livestock, for example). NSSO also conducts pilot and exploratory surveys on various issues as also to develop survey schedules and sample designs to be used for some large-scale surveys. NSS often would collect concurrently data on past and the present on sample households. On the advice of the National Planning Commission, NSSO has been collecting information on birth, death and population in rural areas since 1958. Since 1973 (23rd round) urban areas have also been included in the project. Internal migration, fertility, causes of death, morbidity, infant mortality, housing, small scale industries, and caste-class factors in economic well-being, extent of poverty and many other issues are covered in various NSS rounds. National Human Development Report (Planning Commission) and India Human Development Report (National Council of Applied Economic Research, NCAER) have used extensively the NSSO data. NSSO and SRS data are used extensively in discourses related to Indian demography. NSSO data today remain the primary data for analysis and understanding of almost every issue relating to social and economic matters linking to population.

NSSO works in close collaboration with Indian Statistical Institute (Delhi and Calcutta). NSSO publishes the survey reports regularly. NSSO has collected data on innumerable topics in the last five decades. Only a fraction of this gold mine has been explored and analyzed. Couple Fertility (Dasgupta and others), Poverty in India (Dandekar and Rath) are some of the fine pieces of works on social demography.

3.8 Sample Registration Scheme (SRS)

The dismal failure to anticipate population growth rate in the 1950's forced the government of India to look for some alternative devices for obtaining an accurate picture of age-specific birth and death rates, area specific as well as for the entire country. Sample Registration System, directly under the control of the Registrar General, started functioning in 1964. Initially the sample registration scheme came into operation in selected rural areas of a chosen few states. Soon SRS was extended to both rural and urban areas of every state in India.

Villages and urban localities were selected based on 1961 Census data. In the selection of sample villages in rural India *one-stage stratified simple random* sampling was employed. For stratification, the natural divisions and size of the village population were used. A village or a part thereof formed the sampling unit for rural India. When a village had more than 2,000 persons, the village was so divided that the selected part had 1,500 persons or a figure close to that. In urban areas, *two-stage stratified random sampling* was employed, the first stage primary sampling unit (PSU) being the towns; the census-blocks constituted the second stage units. The towns/cities were grouped into five classes, viz. (a) towns with population below 20,000 (b) towns with population of 20,000 and more but less than 50,000 (c) towns with population of 50,000 and more but less than 100,000 (d) towns with population of 100,000 and more but less than 500,000, (e) cities with population of 500,000 and more but less than 1,000,000 and (f) each city with population 1,000,000 or more, treated as a separate stratum. The sampling unit in urban area is a *census enumeration block* with a population ranging from 750 to 1000.

A simple random sample of these enumeration blocks (EB) is selected without replacement from each of the size classes of towns/cities in each state/UT. Initially, 150 villages from every state came under SRS. It became fully operational during 1969–70 covering about 3,700 sample units. Continuing registration of birth and death were conducted in altogether 2,412 villages (or part thereof) and 1,268 census-blocks in urban areas. Thereafter the sample size has periodically been increased. At present SRS covers 6,671 sample units (4,436 rural and 2,235 urban) covering all states and Union Territories. These 6,671 sample units covered about 6.3 million population in 1999 for rural and urban areas combined in all the states and Union Territories where SRS was being implemented.

Of course this sample registration is in addition to the normal Vital Registration in the municipal offices. SRS covers about 0.7 percent of the total rural population. Number of sample units and population covered in India, states and UTs, 2000 is presented in Table 3.4.

The principal components of SRS are:

1. **Base-line survey** of the sample units to obtain usual resident population of the same sample areas. Prior to start of the continuous enumeration, a notional map of the survey area is prepared. Every house is given a number (house listing) and a household schedule is filled in to record the residential status and demographic particulars of every member residing in the household. Inmates of public institutions (hotels, hospitals) are excluded from the list. But households within the campus of the institution (doctor's quarter, manager's quarter) are

Table 3.4

Number of SRS sample units and population covered in India, states and union territories 2000

	Number of sample units			Population covered ('000)		
	Total	Rural	Urban	Total	Rural	Urban
1	2	3	4	5	6	7
INDIA	**6671**	**4436**	**2235**	**6284**	**4904**	**1380**
Bigger States						
1. Andhra Pradesh	310	210	100	306	240	66
2. Assam	275	200	75	244	200	44
3. Bihar	500	400	100	434	400	35
4. Gujarat	300	200	100	276	224	52
5. Haryana	180	110	70	212	161	52
6. Karnataka	375	260	115	359	285	74
7. Kerala	250	150	100	309	245	64
8. Madhya Pradesh	400	300	100	298	248	50
9. Maharashtra	375	200	175	343	237	106
10. Orissa	405	300	105	305	244	62
11. Punjab	200	120	80	177	128	49
12. Rajasthan	350	250	100	335	285	50
13. Tamil Nadu	375	200	175	355	237	119
14. Uttar Pradesh	650	450	200	644	541	103
15. West Bengal	475	300	175	471	362	109
Smaller States						
1. Arunachal Pradesh	56	50	6	46	39	6
2. Chhattisgarh	101	84	17	92	81	11
3. Goa	70	40	30	62	45	17
4. Jharkhand	139	92	47	120	95	25
5. Himachal Pradesh	190	140	50	101	73	28
6. Jammu & Kashmir	166	100	66	137	97	39
7. Manipur	150	100	50	134	98	36
8. Meghalaya	120	100	20	62	52	10
9. Mizoram	32	16	16	22	12	11
10. Nagaland	35	25	10	NA	NA	5
11. Sikkim	60	50	10	60	51	9
12. Tripura	75	60	15	30	24	6
13. Uttaranchal	35	22	13	30	24	6
Union Territories						
1. Anadaman & Nicober Is.	45	30	15	31	22	9
2. Chandigarh	30	5	25	25	6	19
3. Dadra & Nagar Haveli	25	20	5	25	22	3
4. Daman & Diu	17	15	2	19	18	1
5. Delhi	130	10	120	99	16	83
6. Lakshadweep	10	5	5	13	8	4
7. Pondicheri	40	20	20	36	23	13

covered. A list of pregnant women is also prepared during the base line survey. The events to 'visitors' occurring within the sample unit are recorded but not included in the list when calculating rates.

2. **Continuous (longitudinal) enumeration** of vital events pertaining to usual resident population in the sample units by the part-time enumerator. The enumerator maintains a Birth and Death record in prescribed form in respect to his area. He takes the help of the village priest, barber, village headman, midwife and such other functionaries and contacts these informants at frequent intervals and collects information about the occurrence of births and deaths. He is required to maintain a list of pregnant women, which helps him in netting of all the births. Despite all these efforts, the enumerator may fail to have information about some of the events. Therefore, he is required to visit all the households once in each quarter (in rural areas) and once a month (in urban areas) so as to ensure that all the events have been recorded
3. An independent **half-yearly survey** for recording births and deaths which occurred during the half-year under reference and up-dating the house-list and household schedule by a full-time Supervisor. He independently visits the households in the sample unit and records all particulars relating to births and deaths pertaining to usual residents and visitors, which have occurred within the last half-yearly period and records them in different forms. He also updates the 'house list', the 'household schedule' and the 'list of pregnant women'. This he does independent of the resident part-time enumerator. That is, he has no access to the records of birth, death and pregnancy prepared by the enumerator.
4. **Matching** of events recorded during continuous enumeration and those listed in course of half-yearly survey. On completion of the half-yearly surveys, two sets of data are matched case-by-case. This usually is done at the district or state headquarters. All the events are classified as matched, partially matched and unmatched.
5. **Field verification** of unmatched and partially matched events. Every partially matched or unmatched event is verified by a visit to the concerned households by a third person or jointly by the enumerator and his supervisor.

The main objective of SRS is to provide reliable annual estimates of birth and death rates at the state and national levels for rural and urban areas separately. It also provides various other measures of fertility and mortality. The advantage of the rigorous checking procedure in SRS, in addition to elimination of errors of duplication, is that it leads to a quantitative assessment of the sources of distortion in the two sets of records making it a self-evaluating technique.

SRS data have been proved trustworthy and reliable because of in-built checks in the system. SRS data slightly underestimate the vital events though rarely exceeding 5 percent mark. SRS data have become one of the most important data source for many demographic analysis, more specifically in projections and construction of Life Tables.

There has been a demand from some quarter that a few other demographic events as marriage, migration, family planning, cause of death, etc. are brought under the purview of SRS. Many population scientists have said against such a move and have argued that high quality of the current SRS data would have to be compromised if these other information were to be collected at the same go.

However to enhance the utility of SRS data, the following two initiatives have already been undertaken.

- Collection of additional data in SRS. Special schedules have been canvassed during July–December 2001 to collect additional data on 'Proof of age, registration of births and determining the residential status of the mother during pre- and post-natal period'. The report analyzing the additional data will be brought out separately.
- Integration of Survey of Causes of Deaths (Rural) in SRS. The Survey of Causes of Deaths (Rural) has been merged with Sample Registration System from 1st January, 1999 to give more impetus covering both rural and urban areas. The technique of causes of deaths reported will remain the same as "post death verbal autopsy".

Besides NSSO and SRS there are many other organizations and government agencies that collect and disseminate information on social, economic and demographic events. The Research Program Committee of the Planning Commission conducts surveys on many of these issues in large cities. The Family Welfare and the Health Department conducts surveys from time to time on such issues as birth and death rate, birth control, public health and sanitation, etc. The Directorate General of Employment and Training, Government of India regularly publishes employment related information. Central Statistical Organization (CSO), Council of Applied Economic Research (CAER), Indian Statistical Institute (ISI), Institute of Population Studies and many other public and autonomous bodies carry out large sample surveys on various issues. For comparative analysis these survey results often are used as base line data.

4
Composition of Population of India

4.1 Sex Composition

It is natural for a common man to believe that males and females in the population exactly balance each other. Little do they know how imbalanced the sexes are in different populations across the world. Sex ratio is an important social indicator to measure the extent of prevailing equity between males and females in a society at a given point of time. This has much to do with the interplay of sex differentials in mortality, sex selective migration, sex ratio at birth and at times the sex differential in abortion and in population enumeration. It has been estimated that at around 2000, the world had 986 females for every 1,000 males. The table below shows sex composition of 10 most populous countries in the world around 2000. Sex ratio in general is low in Asian continent and in other countries in the developing world. The sheer size of the Asian countries is responsible for bringing down the world average sex ratio to below 1,000 and preponderance of males in the global population. Pakistan, Bangladesh and China in recent years have shown signs of improvement in sex ratio.

The most important demographic features about India (in some other countries as well, China for example) that receive particular attention of the demographers is the increasing gender bias since the early days of census in the country – the small number of females compared to males. The number of females per 1,000 males is 933 in India in 2001 (a marginal improvement over 1991 Census estimate of 927) compared to a figure of 1,050 for Europe and North America and 1,022 for sub-Saharan Africa (Amartya Sen, 2001). Dreze and Sen (1996) have termed the low sex ratio in India as a "missing women" phenomenon: on the basis of sub-Saharan ratios, the number of "missing women" in India is estimated to be between 35–37 million.

Table 4.1
Sex ratio in population of selected countries

Countries	*Sex ratio (females per 1000 males)*
World	986
China	944*
India	933
USA	1,029
Indonesia	1,004
Brazil	1,025
Pakistan	938
Russian Federation	1,140
Bangladesh	953
Japan	1,041
Nigeria	1,016

* A recent report puts it at 117 males for every 100 females
Source: World Population Prospects (mid-year estimates), 1998 revision, Vol. 2, Sex and Age, United Nations.

In India, sex ratio in the total population has always remained unfavorable to women. What is more astonishing is that their proportion has consistently been declining throughout the last hundred years. The all-age sex ratio has declined from 972 females for every 1,000 males in 1901 to 927 in 1991. It has marginally increased to 933 in 2001. What is really appalling is the fact that the absolute differences between male and female populations have increased so much so that there were 35.5 million fewer females compared to males in 2001, i.e., male population was ahead of female totals by more than 6.6 percent. How badly the balance has gone against females is clearly visible in Figure 4.1. Surprisingly, the F–M gap has increased at a much faster rate after independence. There are already millions of surplus males whose destiny seems to resign them to permanent bachelorhood since their ghost brides never saw the light of the day. The single most worrisome feature is the decline in sex ratio in the 0–6 year age-group, from 945 in 1991 to 927 in 2001. Punjab (drop from 875 to 793) and Himachal Pradesh (drop from 951 to 897) are the major culprits in this regard although some decline is observed in most other states. The 7+ age group has registered a 12 point gain in sex ratio from 923 in the same period.

Figure 4.1

F-M in the total population, India 1880–2001

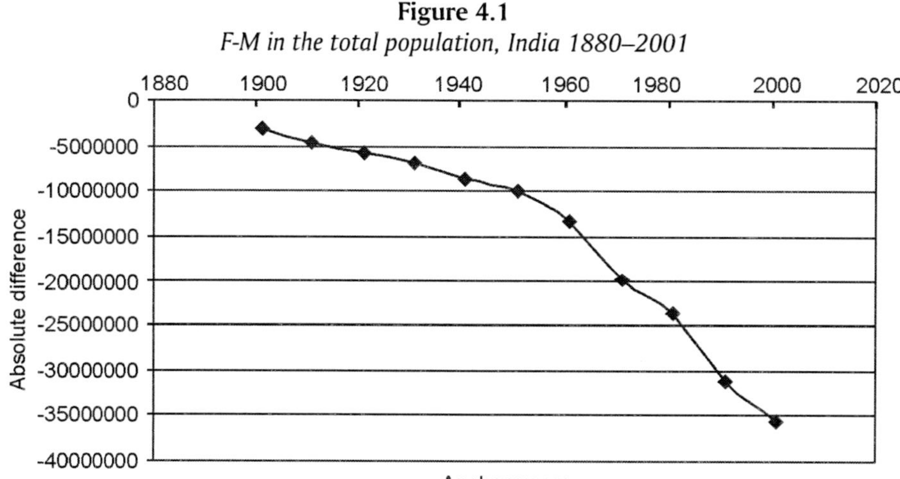

Table 4.2

Sex ratio in India, 1901–2001

Census year	*Sex ratio*
1901	972
1911	964
1921	955
1931	950
1941	945
1951	946
1961	941
1971	930
1981	934
1991	927
2001	933

Source: Census of India, 2001

Figure 4.2

Sex ratio in the total population in India, 1901–2001

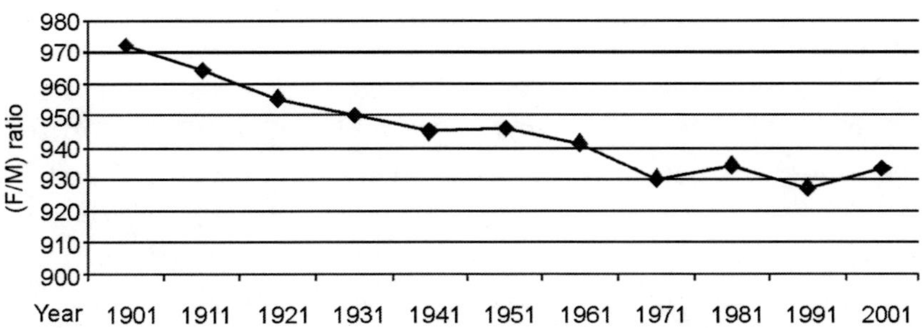

Table 4.3

Sex ratio (F/M) in total and child population in the states and union territories in India, 1991–2001

Code	States/UTs*	Total population		Child population(0–6)		Pop. aged 7 and above	
		1991	2001	1991	2001	1991	2001
1	2	3	4	5	6	7	8
	INDIA	**927**	**933 ↑**	**945**	**927 ↓**	**923**	**935 ↑**
1	Jammu & Kashmir	NA	900	NA	937	NA	894
2	Himachal Pradesh	976	970 ↓	951	897 ↓	980	981
3	Punjab	882	874 ↓	875	793 ↓	883	886
4	Chandigarh*	790	773 ↓	899	845 ↓	772	763 ↓
5	Uttaranchal	936	964	948	906 ↓	933	976
6	Haryana	865	861 ↓	879	820 ↓	862	869
7	Delhi*	827	821 ↓	915	865 ↓	810	813
8	Rajasthan	910	922	916	909 ↓	908	925
9	Uttar Pradesh	876	898	927	916 ↓	863	895
10	Bihar	907	921	953	938 ↓	895	916
11	Sikkim	878	875 ↓	965	986	860	858 ↓
12	Arunachal Pradesh	859	901	982	961 ↓	829	888
13	Nagaland	886	909	993	975 ↓	865	899
14	Manipur	958	978	974	961 ↓	955	981
15	Mizoram	921	938	969	971	911	932
16	Tripura	945	950	967	975	940	947
17	Meghalaya	955	975	986	975 ↓	947	974
18	Assam	923	932	975	964 ↓	910	926
19	West Bengal	917	934	967	963 ↓	907	929
20	Jharkhand	922	941	979	966 ↓	908	936
21	Orissa	971	972	967	950 ↓	972	976
22	Chhattisgarh	985	990	984	975 ↓	986	992

Cont'd...

Table 4.3 Cont'd...

1	*2*	*3*	*4*	*5*	*6*	*7*	*8*
23	Madhya Pradesh	912	920	941	929 ↓	905	918
24	Gujarat	934	921 ↓	928	878 ↓	936	927 ↓
25	Daman & Diu*	969	709 ↓	958	925 ↓	971	682 ↓
26	Dadra & Nagar Haveli*	952	811 ↓	1,013	973 ↓	937	779 ↓
27	Maharashtra	934	922 ↓	946	917 ↓	931	923 ↓
28	Andhra Pradesh	972	978	975	964 ↓	972	980
29	Karnataka	960	964	960	949 ↓	960	966
30	Goa	967	960 ↓	964	933 ↓	967	964 ↓
31	Lakshadweep*	943	947	941	974	943	943
32	Kerala	1,036	1,058	958	963	1049	1074
33	Tamil Nadu	974	986	948	939 ↓	978	992
34	Pondicherry*	979	1,001	963	958 ↓	982	1007
35	Andaman & Nicober Is*	818	846	973	965 ↓	790	830

Source: Census of India 2001, *Provisional Population Totals* (Web Edition)

Table 4.2 gives the trends in sex ratio in the population for the past hundred years. Table 4.3 presents the sex ratio in the total and child population (0–6 years) for 1991 and 2001 for the different states/UTs in India. The distribution of states and UTs by the different ranges of sex ratio in the child group and their share in the total population of the country in these ranges is shown in Table 4.4. The distributions of the number of states in 1991 and 2001 Census show some distinct variation – the equidispersed proportion of population in sex ratio categories is tilting towards higher categories.

Table 4.4

Distribution of states/union territories by range of sex ratio in India, 1991 and 2001

Sex ratio	*1991*	*Percentage of population to total population 1991*	*2001*	*Percentage of population to total population 2001*
880 & below	7	18.92	8	5.97
881–915	6	22.02	4	17.45
916–950	9	28.73	11	47.23
951–985	12	26.89	8	18.08
986 & above	1	3.44	4	11.27

In 1901, there were as many as 11 states and UTs that had sex ratio (F/M) in the population over 1,000. Except Kerala, all other states and UTs have shown a downward slide. Although the sex ratio in Punjab has consistently been low, it has shown a long-term upward trend. The sex ratio remained more or less stagnant in Haryana, Andhra Pradesh and Karnataka. West Bengal showed a decline till 1941 but made a gradual turnaround on an upward mode. It would be interesting to note that although the number of states/UTs with the sex ratio less than 916 remains almost the same, the percentage share of this population group has declined form about 41 in 1991 to about 23 in 2001. Similarly the number of states/UTs falling within the range of 916–950 marginally altered but the share of this population increased from around 29 percent to 47 percent. The push factor seems to have been effected through shifting a sizeable population from (951–985) category to 985+ group. The role played by these two groups of states/UTs appears to be the reason for the increase in overall sex ratio in the country.

Table 4.5

Distribution of states/union territories by below/above national level sex ratio in India 1991 and 2001

Sex ratio	*Number of states/UTs 1991*	*Percentage of population to total population 1991*	*Number of states/UTs 2001*	*Percentage of population to total population 2001*
Below national average	17	54.29	18	59.81
Above national average	18	45.71	17	40.19

Table 4.5 classifies the states and Union territories in two classes, namely below and above national average sex ratio. The number of states/UTs with sex ratio below national average has increased from 17 in 1991 to 18 in 2001. In fact, the proportion of population in the first category has increased from 54 percent to about 60 percent. In spite of the increase in the number and relative weight in the first category, the overall sex ratio of the country has improved. What could be the possible reason for this? It is observed that the highly populated states like Uttar Pradesh, Bihar, Rajasthan and Madhya Pradesh, which together constituted about 34 percent of India's population in 1991 and increased to 36 percent in 2001 lie in the category of below national average. Therefore, the increase in the overall sex ratio is possibly due to the relative larger increases in the sex ratio in these four populous states. The sex ratios in the total population have shown improvements in as many as 23 states/UTs. However, during the corresponding period the sex ratio in the child population 0–6 has increased in only four states and one UT. What really worries demographers and social planners is the fact that when the country is definitely showing signs of a brake on the growth of population and that there is a hint that the sex ratio in the population is improving, the sex ratio in 0–6 year age group has fallen sharply, by 35 points since 1981. The cascading effect of rapid decline in sex ratio in 0–6 age group is likely to haunt the composition of the population for a long time. All the Northern states and UTs – Punjab (875 to 793), Himachal Pradesh (951 to 897), Haryana (879 to 820), Uttaranchal (948 to 906), Chandigarh (869 to 845) and Delhi (915 to 865). Orissa (967 to 950), Maharashtra (946 to 917) and Gujarat (928 to 878) have also shown a huge decline in sex ratio in child population. Only 5 smaller states/UTs have improved this ratio between 1991 and 2001. It would not be surprising if the sex ratio in the population in a decade or two goes down again in view of the sharp drop in sex ratio in the 0–6 age group. The situation appears really gloomy if sex ratio for children below 5 years instead of below 7 years is taken up for projection. The sex ratio in 0–4 age group reached the lowest ever level, 901 in 2001 head count.

Consensus is developing among demographers, social planners, politicians and common man that the sharp decline in the child sex ratio may have substantial link with easy access to predetermination of sex and sex-selective abortions. Women's groups and health activists in Maharashtra successfully lobbied for a state level legislation against sex diagnosis in 1988. The government of India passed Pre-natal Diagnostic Techniques (Prohibition of sex determination) Act, better known as PNDT Act in 1994. This Act prohibits determination and disclosure of the sex of the fetus. License for installation of ultrasonography machines has been mandatory. In the last 12 years no one has been booked under the Act as yet. Throughout the country the sonologists have adopted several devices to communicate the sex of the fetus so that the law cannot book them.

In the mean time distress signal has already been sent to at least two of the Northern states, namely Haryana and Punjab for the shortage of marriageable girls in their local communities. This has resulted in a greater menace – girl-trafficking from other states taking the advantage of extreme poverty in their root families.

SRS has published sex ratio at birth for India and larger states for the period 1998–2000 (Table 4.6). At birth there were only 898 female babies for every 1,000 male babies born at the national level (M/F = 111). This is as low as 792 in Punjab and 797 in Haryana, a fact that probably gives credence to the assertion that sex selective abortion is rampant in many states in India. The highest sex ratio at birth is observed in Assam (984) followed by Andhra Pradesh (960) and West Bengal (952). Strangely, Kerala, often regarded as the demographic model to rest of the states, ranks only fifth in sex ratio at birth at 930 among the larger states. Its achievement in this regards goes further down to 8th spot in rural area though it occupies the first spot in urban area. There are as many as 6 bigger states (Bihar, Gujarat, Haryana, Punjab, Rajasthan and Uttar Pradesh) where the sex ratio at birth is below 900 point. The correlation between the sex ratio at birth with the same in the total population is a poor 0.666 and very poor with that in age 0–6, which is 0.579.

Table 4.6

Sex ratio by population groups and at birth by residence, 1998–2000

India and bigger states	*Sex ratio at birth*			*Sex ratio in*	
	Total	*Rural*	*Urban*	*Population*	*0–6 age group*
INDIA	**898**	**901**	**886**	**933**	**935**
Andhra Pradesh	960	956	972	978	980
Assam	984	986	962	932	926
Bihar	896	894	922	921	916
Gujarat	851	859	828	921	927
Haryana	797	807	755	861	869
Himachal Pradesh	902	907	823	970	981
Karnataka	942	952	917	964	966
Kerala	930	912	986	1,058	1074
Madhya Pradesh	907	908	903	920	918
Maharashtra	913	919	903	922	923
Orissa	928	932	885	972	976
Punjab	792	799	767	874	886
Rajasthan	877	885	830	922	925
Tamil Nadu	931	944	901	986	992
Uttar Pradesh	868	864	893	898	895
West Bengal	952	958	921	934	929

Source: Sample Registration System Statistical Report 2000

Let us take a closer look at the sex ratio in the population by states and the residential status of their peoples. There are as many as 27 states/UTs where sex ratios in the rural populations are better than that among their urban counterparts (Table 4.9). A better sex ratio in rural area is expected due to preponderance of male migration to urban areas. Only in four states (Haryana, Andhra Pradesh, Kerala and Tamil Nadu) and one UT, namely Lakshadweep, have rural sex ratio greater than that in urban area by a very small margin, 1.4 to 21.1 points. There are 14 states/UTs where the rural-urban difference is in the range 25 to 74 points. In 5 states/UTs, the differences in sex ratios are in excess of 100 points in favor of rural population. 4 smaller states in Northeastern region and 4 UTs (including Chandigarh and Delhi) have better to much better sex ratio in their urban populations vis-à-vis their rural populations (Table 4.7). When we compare the performances of the states against national average sex ratio in the population, there is hardly any significant change between 1991 and 2001; but more than 5 percent of the total population has gone below the national average in 2001 compared to that in 1991.

Table 4.7

Sex ratio in the population by states and residence[1], India 2001

*States/UTs**	*Sex ratio (females per thousand males)*			*Rural-Urban*
	Total	*Rural*	*Urban*	
1	*2*	*3*	*4*	*5*
INDIA	**932.9**	**945.8**	**900.2**	**46.6**
Jammu & Kashmir	899.8	926.9	822.4	104.5
Himachal Pradesh	970.4	991.2	797.2	194.0
Punjab	873.4	888.0	845.8	42.2
Chandigarh*	772.7	620.7	791.8	–171.1
Uttaranchal	963.3	1006	847.6	158.4
Haryana	861.2	867.0	847.2	19.8
Delhi*	821.0	809.5	821.9	–12.4
Rajasthan	922.1	932.1	889.9	42.2
Uttar Pradesh	897.8	903.6	876.3	27.3
Bihar	920.5	926.7	869.2	57.5
Sikkim	875.3	881.4	827.7	53.7
Arunachal Pradesh	893.6	905.5	848.5	57.0
Nagaland	909.1	932.1	809.0	123.1
Manipur	964.4	952.3	1003.7	–51.4
Mizoram	938.0	925.5	950.9	–25.4
Tripura	950.4	948.1	961.7	–13.6
Meghalaya	974.6	972.2	984.8	–12.6
Assam	932.0	940.1	878.2	61.9
West Bengal	933.6	950.1	892.5	57.6
Jharkhand	941.3	962.7	870.3	92.4
Orissa	972.2	986.4	895.0	91.4
Chhattisgarh	989.1	1005	930.3	71.7

Cont'd...

Table 4.7 Cont'd...

1	*2*	*3*	*4*	*5*
Madhya Pradesh	919.7	927.5	898.4	29.1
Gujarat	919.5	945.0	878.6	66.4
Daman & Diu*	709.2	584.6	983.2	–398.6
Dadra &Nagar Haveli*	811.0	850.0	690.7	159.3
Maharashtra	922.2	959.4	873.8	85.6
Andhra Pradesh	977.4	982.7	963.6	19.1
Karnataka	963.6	976.0	939.85	36.2
Goa	960.3	987.9	933.2	54.7
Lakshadweep*	947.3	956.7	935.6	21.1
Kerala	1058	1059.0	1057.6	1.4
Tamil Nadu	986.4	991.5	979.8	11.7
Pondicherry*	1001.0	990.4	1006.0	–15.6
Andaman & Nicober Islands*	846.1	861.7	814.7	47.0

1. Computed from Census data

Table 4.8

Range in sex ratio in the population by states and residence, India 2001

Range in sex ratio	*Number of states/UTs*	
	Rural	*Urban*
1000 and above	3	3
950–999	13	6
900–949	11	4
850–899	5	10
800–849	1	9
750–799	—	2
below 750	2	1

Table 4.9

Rural–urban difference in sex ratio in population

Range of difference	*Number of States/UTs*
125 and above	3
100 to 124	2
75 to 79	3
50 to 74	7
25 to 49	7
0 to 24	5
–24 to –1	4
–49 to –25	1
–74 to –50	1
–50 and larger	2

Against the poor performances in the general population and child population in particular, sex ratio in the population aged 7 years and more has shown a considerable rise since 1991 (Table 4.3). Even in states like Punjab, Uttaranchal, Himachal Pradesh and Haryana, where males far outnumber females, this proportion has gone up. Save for a few, most other states/UTs have either maintained their 1991 sex ratio level or have made some improvements in 2001 over 1991

Table 4.10

Sex ratio in total population and child population 1961–2001

Year	*Sex ratio in age group 0–6*	*Sex ratio in the population*
1961	976	941
1971	964	930
1981	962	934
1991	945	927
2001	927	933

level in 7+ age. This improvement in sex ratio, as the Census Commissioner has commented, may be related to increase in life expectancy of females at a much faster pace compared to that of males.

It is unfortunate that when as many as 23 states/UTs have improved their overall sex ratios in 2001, the sex ratio in child population has improved only in 4 states and 1 UT. The sex ratio in the child population has decreased faster than the sex ratio in the population since 1981. One thing is clear – the imbalance caused to early age-group is difficult to be rectified and would continue to distort the population for a long time to come. To say the least, demographically the sex ratio of 927 or 933 of the population in the age group 0–6 does not appear to augur well for the future of the country. Sex ratio of child population in the category 951 and above has sharply declined from 45 to 27 percent. The number of states/UTs with sex ratio in child population below 915 has increased from 4 in 1991 to 8 in 2001 and their share in the population in this category has also increased from about 4 to about 17 percent. Sharp declines in this regard have been noticed in Himachal Pradesh (951 to 897), Punjab (875 to 793), Chandigarh (869 to 845), Uttaranchal (948 to 906), Haryana (879 to 820), Gujarat (928 to 878) and Maharashtra (946 to 917). Most of the states where sex ratios in the child population have declined sharply are notoriously known for sex selective abortions.

The change in sex ratio in the population in some of the states is noticeably due to migration. Most dominant reason for out-migration is job. It is the movement of the semi-skilled labors that dominate out-migration. They generally migrate alone initially and bring their families only when they are reasonably protected in the job market. The skilled and professional persons generally migrate with their families. So, the receiving states tend to depress the sex ratio (F/M), the sending states tend to improve their sex ratio in the population. There are quite a few larger states like Bihar, Uttar Pradesh, Kerala, Tamil Nadu, and Rajasthan that traditionally send out people to other states and countries; the states like Maharashtra and Gujarat among others are currently the principal receiving states. Whereas sex ratio in the former states has improved in the last few decades, the latter mentioned states have consistently shown a depression in sex ratio. West Bengal had remained a steady destination from the neighboring and distant states and also from Bangladesh till 1971. The situation took a U-turn thereafter. The net migration (out – in-migration) has become negative since 1981 in the state. One of the major reasons definitely is labor unrest, flight of capital from the state and closure of many industries. In-migration is steadily on the rise in Maharashtra since independence.

The sex ratio in India has remained a mystery for demographers and social planners. When most of the developed countries have more or less a balanced sex composition, why did India have such an uneven sex structure? Some commonly cited reasons listed by the Census authority in India are:

- Neglect of the girl child resulting in higher mortality at younger ages
- High maternal mortality
- Sex selective female abortions
- Female infanticide
- Change in sex ratio at birth

The story of imbalance begins at the very beginning of life. It is now an established fact in nature that males exceed females at the time of birth. For every 1,000 male births there are about 950 female births. This deficiency of about 50 females per 1,000 males in every birth cohort is not easily compensated by higher death rates among males. Demographers, doctors and social activists have drawn our attention to some other factors that often are associated with poor health status of girls in our society:

- Child marriage
- Unscientific country method of delivery
- Women suffer from some diseases which are female-specific
- Indian women even today are reluctant and shy to consult doctors for their problems since most doctors are males
- Women in general are very casual in their habits of timely eating and rest
- They almost perform single handed all domestic activities putting immense pressure on their health
- The responsibility of nursing sick members besides other domestic work falls exclusively on women; they easily fall prey to diseases by contamination
- Their dish often is comprised of leftovers after all the members of the household have been served with better nourishing items in adequate quantity
- 'Son preference' and/or 'daughter aversion' among Hindus, the overwhelming majority religious community in the country.

There could be many other general and specific factors that have some effect on the sex ratio. Demographers have also referred to another important issue: Very young baby girls and very old ladies often are left out in head count.

We need to take a little closer look at the population data in the last century. Prior to 1921, death rates in India were almost at the biological limit. Various survey reports show that between 1891 and 1921 there were unprecedented deaths resulting from plague, cholera, small pox, and flue epidemic as also from some other diseases and famines or famine-like situations. It was the children, especially girls, women, particularly pregnant women who were the major victims in most of these catastrophes. The great famine in 1896–97 followed by plague epidemic, particularly in Bombay Presidency, took heavy toll on human lives. About 2 percent of the population died as a result. The beginning of the twentieth century saw a great many famines and epidemics. Nearly the whole of Uttar Pradesh came under the siege of famine in 1907. Bengal and Bombay Presidency were badly affected by plague, Punjab and UP by malaria. Women, girls and children remained easy victims from all such disasters. The influenza epidemic in 1918–19 took away lives of hundreds and thousands of people. Just before this, cholera became pandemic in various parts of the country. Between 1891 and 1921 the average death rate fluctuated between 45 and 50 per thousand, a near biological limit. The incidences of higher death rates in the child and young age population in one decade continue to influence the population, especially those in reproductive age group, for several decades. In a poor country like India where social customs often push girls and women to low priority, it is no wonder that such frequent epidemics and famines would greatly affect the sex and age composition for many years. Whenever a natural catastrophe or a famine-like situation happens, women and children have to bear the burden most.

Between 1901 and 1921 females lost by a huge 0.48 percent to males in addition to the lag already they had (0.67%) in the total population count in 1901 census. In the next 80 years they lost by another 0.58 percent in favor of the male population. In 1921, females were more than 2 percent point behind males in growth index with 1901 as base population (Table 4.11). In the next eight decades the growth index gap between males and females increased by another 16 points. The base period if shifted to 1921, the growth rates of males and females were almost the same in the next two decades. By the end of the century the gap increased to 9.5 points, base remaining unchanged at 1921. With the base changed to 1951, the growth index between the two narrowed down to 4 points in favor of males in a period of five decades.

Table 4.11

*Population growth index separately for males and females with different base periods**

Year	Base (1901) = 100			Base (1921) = 100			Prop. of Females to Total
	Persons	Male	Female	Persons	Male	Female	
1901							49.331
1911	105.746	106.287	105.189				49.072
1921	105.422	106.420	104.396				48.852
1931	117.022	118.328	115.682	111.004	111.189	110.810	48.767
1941	133.668	135.511	131.776	126.794	127.334	126.227	48.633
1951	151.465	153.594	149.279	143.676	144.328	142.993	48.620
1961	184.246	187.342	181.065	174.770	176.040	173.441	48.480
1971	229.936	235.157	224.574	218.111	220.971	215.117	48.181
1981	287.414	293.397	281.269	272.633	275.697	269.425	48.277
1991	354.003	362.276	345.506	335.798	340.421	330.957	48.148
2001	430.802	439.831	421.528	408.646	413.297	403.778	48.270

Table 2.6 Cont'd…

Year	Base (1951) = 100			Base (1981) = 100		
	Persons	Male	Female	Persons	Male	Female
1951						
1961	121.642	121.972	121.293			
1971	151.808	153.103	150.439			
1981	189.756	191.020	188.418			
1991	233.719	235.866	231.450	123.168	123.476	122.838
2001	284.422	286.359	282.376	149.889	149.910	149.866

* Computed from various Census Data

Between 1941 and 1951 the decadal growth rates for male and female populations were almost identical. Unfortunately, females lost 1.7 point in the very next decade. The same growth rate deficiency continued in the decade following. It was in 1981 census, for the first time we see that the decadal growth rate of females becomes comparable with that of males. But the momentum was lost in the very next decade only to be recovered in the final decade of the last millennium. Proportion of female population to the total population reached the lowest point in 1991. The growth index (base 1981) of males and females came to a level of parity in 2001. The 0.5 percent gain in female growth rate in the last decade saw the loss it incurred in 1981–91 decade nearly compensated. But the 3.5 points gap between males' and females' share in the population cannot be wiped out in the near future given the sex ratio among children (0–6 years) currently observed in the country.

Various survey reports since the sunup of Census in India unequivocally proclaimed that the young children and women were the principal victims of the recurrent epidemics and famine in late nineteenth and early twentieth century. But both young boys and girls (0–14 years) constituted around 39 percent of the total population even in the most difficult period (1891–1921) and their averages were somewhere between 39 and 38, and young girls' proportion in the population was only marginally short of boys'. There was huge gain in percentage point both by boys and girls in 1961 and 1971. But between 1971 and 2001, girls lost by a huge 8.4 percentage points, boys by 7.1 percentage points. This general fall in percentages for both probably was because of the aggressive campaign for birth control since the seventies.

But most remarkable thing has happened in the age group 0–4 years. Boys lost their initial advantage in numbers over girls at birth before they reached their fifth birthday. This was observed during the period when India was loosing her numbers to diseases and famines (Table 4.12, Figure 4.3). But boys started gaining their lost grounds after 1941 and the sex ratio (F/M) in 0–4 years dramatically dropped from 960 in 1991 to only 901 in 2001, a very extraordinary event by all counts! The 0–4 age group sex ratio had always remained above the "all-age sex ratio" except in the last decade. It had been declining steadily since 1941. Will this dip below a critical level have a significant role in population composition in the coming years? Can this loss be attributed to drastic improvement in natural sex ratio at birth due to increased use of sex determination prior to birth? The gains in sex ratio in 0–4 age group by girls in the years 1901–41 are lost in the very next age group; they lost by a low of about 58 points to as high as 93 points. The losses are of course low in the decades after 1941, between 30 and 38 points. The drop in sex ratio continued in the next age group as well.

Table 4.12

Sex ratio at different age groups, India 1901–2001

Census Year	*1901*	*1911*	*1921*	*1931*	*1941*	*1951*	*1961*	*1971*	*1981*	*1991*	*2001*
0–4	1029	1037	1044	1043	1012	989.3	992.2	975.6	978.9	960.2	901.7
5–9	959.4	956.4	961.6	951.8	953.5	968.8	960.3	942.3	940	934.2	915.8
10–14	829.1	822.4	825.2	848.7	851.3	908.4	876.1	879.4	897.8	888.3	902.3
15–19	917.7	918.2	898.3	940.8	923.1	946.3	929.5	877.6	886.2	892	880.3
20–24	1097	1080	1079	1068	1057	1016	1046	1003	977.8	969.6	953.6
25–29	984.7	974.3	977.3	984.3	991.9	946.3	975.4	1007	970.7	1006	944.8
30–34	985.1	975	978.1	951.8	959.2	959.2	927.7	972.7	963	955.1	983.5
35–39	909.8	856.5	865.6	880.8	888.5	887.1	878.3	899.3	949.5	900.1	977.5
40–44	988.4	963.6	970.3	903.5	914.7	898.2	888.7	877.2	880.5	870.7	916.7
45–49	896.8	864.7	835.7	865.3	862.6	843.4	853.5	845.3	891.9	884.2	892.5
50–54	1017	985	955.1	905.4	924.8	923.7	893.9	858.3	840	882.1	933.1
55–59	919.5	910	854.6	908.6	828.4	873.5	859.2	891.1	933.4	896.5	902
60+	1185	1144	1067	1049	1016	1018	992.3	945.6	947.7	923	1089
Sex ratio in population	**974**	**963**	**955**	**952**	**945**	**946**	**941**	**930**	**933**	**929**	**933**

Figure 4.3
Sex ratio (F/M) for 0–4 and all ages, India 1901–2001

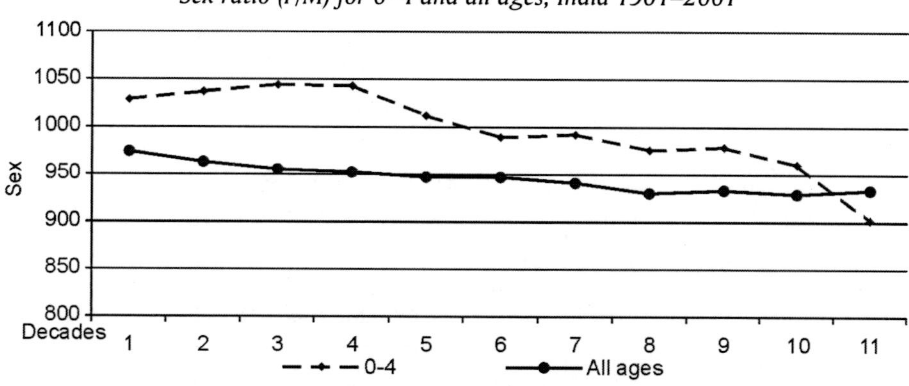

In demographic parlance it is said that the greatest risk of life of girls is in their reproductive age. The sex ratio in 15–19 years is almost reversed in the age group 20–24 in India. There were more females in this age group between 1901 and 1971, between 3 and 97 points over males. A near parity situation prevailed in the next age group (25–29), though females were consistently behind males in numbers. This observation is repeated till we reach age 60+. Females were comfortably ahead of males in the number count till 1951 and the ratio dropped to lowest ever to 923 in 1991, not known why, and a surprise 166-point gain in the very next decade. Whereas male population in 60+ age dropped from 6.7 percent in 1991 to 6.6 percent in 2001, the ratio for women in the same group shoot up from 6.7 to 7.7 percent in the same period.

The percentage composition of population for a census year often would hide many things than explain the nature of changes experienced by the population. We have tried to reconstruct the population composition by absolute numbers for the various age groups from the published age-sex group proportions (Tables 4.13A & 4.13B). The sums of these absolute numbers closely agree with the population totals reported for the census years. The surviving boys and girls in the age group (0–4 years) is most likely (save for reporting error) to be counted in 10–14 year age group in the next census. That is, the number recorded in 10–14 year age group, say in 1911 cannot exceed the number recorded in age group 0–4 years in 1901, except through massive immigration. But except between 1911 and 1921, the entries in 10–14 year age group (Male) are in much excess of the numbers recorded in 0–4 years in the previous count. Such anomalies are also observed with entries in (15–19), (20–24) and some other age groups when they are compared with appropriate age groups in the two successive censuses. With Females such anomalies are observed for 0–4 and some other age groups as well. The suspect figures appear under a shade. Immigration, if any, alone cannot explain such rise in numbers in various age-sex groups.

The demographers and the census authority need to find answers to the question to the anomalies observed in age composition in successive censuses and also why the sex ratio in 60 + age group declined from 1018 in 1951 to only 923 in 1991 and in the very next decade it gained by 166 points. That the expectation of life at birth for females has been increasing at a faster pace is also admitted by the Census Commissioner of India. If we go by the data published by the Census Commissioner, we observe that females are far behind in number count vis-à-vis males in all ages. This is contrary to what we should expect on the admission that life expectancy of females has been increasing at a faster pace than males.

Table 4.13A

Reconstructed population distribution by absolute numbers from table of proportions, Males

Age	1901	1911	1921	1931	1941	1951	1961	1971	1981	1991	2001
4	14736539	16818483	15168455	18009141	21442775	24489757	33265101	40334997	43590940	55137339	63221972
9	16548408	17332025	18767749	20010156	23243313	23376586	33038807	42323342	49615704	57762927	57377924
14	15461287	14892703	16068278	17151563	19478551	23191058	26250011	36642357	46426123	52511751	64284526
19	10508843	10912756	10797883	12291953	13094824	16883090	18556042	25280386	35085391	43322195	56315370
24	9542513	10655986	9898059	11720234	12603768	15027805	18329749	21587745	29769422	37633422	48346214
29	10629634	11554683	11054975	12577813	13749565	15398862	18556042	20451548	26579841	34132638	42502166
34	10267261	10784371	10669337	10862656	12440083	13543578	16066817	18463203	22327067	30631855	39314504
39	7368269	8088278	8226958.4	9576289	10639545	11873822	13577592	17327006	20555077	27131072	33470456
44	7972226	8345049	8098412.2	8432852	9657433	10946179	12219833	15054612	18783088	23192690	30282793
49	4590069	5007029	5141849	6288906	7365839	8534309	9730608	12498168	15947905	19254309	24438746
54	5435608	5777342	5784580	5860117	7038468	7792195	9051728	11077922	14175915	15753525	20188529
59	2174243	2310937	2442378	3144453	3928447	4823740	5204744	6817183	8859947	12690340	15938312
60+	5556400	6162498	6555858	7003555	9002692	9833009	12446126	16758907	23035862	29319061	35064287
Sum	**120791301**	**128642139**	**128674771**	**142929689**	**163685302**	**185713990**	**226293201**	**284617375**	**354752282**	**438473125**	**530745801**
%	100	99.8	99.9	100	100	99.9	100	99.8	99.9	99.8	100.1

Table 4.13B

Reconstructed population distribution by absolute numbers from Table of proportions, Females

Age	1901	1911	1921	1931	1941	1951	1961	1971	1981	1991	2001
4	15171048	17442831	15837973	18774562	21696539	24227229	33005943	39352446	42671498	52945181	57009889
9	15876679	16576875	18047923	19046657	22161465	22647192	31728294	39880667	46640940	53961013	52548246
14	12818948	12247094	13259699	14557088	16582355	21067155	22997690	32221466	41679138	46647021	58001366
19	9643612	10020350	9699224	11564042	12088072	15975926	17248267	22185272	31093960	38642262	49573817
24	10466847	11504846	10681424	12516375	13327874	15273688	19164741	21657051	29109239	36488697	46103650
29	10466847	11257430	10804199	12380327	13637824	14571449	18100033	20600609	25801371	34335133	40154792
34	10114032	10515182	10435874	10339614	11933096	12991412	14905910	17959506	21501143	29255971	38667577
39	6703487	6927649	7120949	8434948	9453492	10533578	11924728	15582512	19516422	24420609	32718719
44	7879537	8041021	7857599	7618663	8833591	9831339	10860020	13205519	16539340	20194747	27761337
49	4116176	4329781	4297125	5441902	6353986	7197945	8304721	10564415	14223833	17025350	21812479
54	5527436	5690569	5524875	5305854	6508962	7197945	8091800	9507974	11908325	13896586	18838050
59	1999285	2103036	2087175	2856999	3254480	4213431	4471773	6074539	8269670	11377322	14376407
60+	6585882	7051357	6998174	7346568	9143541.4	10006899	12350611	15846623	21831929	27061773	38171839
Sum	**117369816**	**123708022**	**122652213**	**136183597**	**154975278**	**175735188**	**213154512**	**264638597**	**330786808**	**406251665**	**495738169**
%	100.2	100	100.1	99.9	100	99.9	99.9	99.9	100	100.02	100

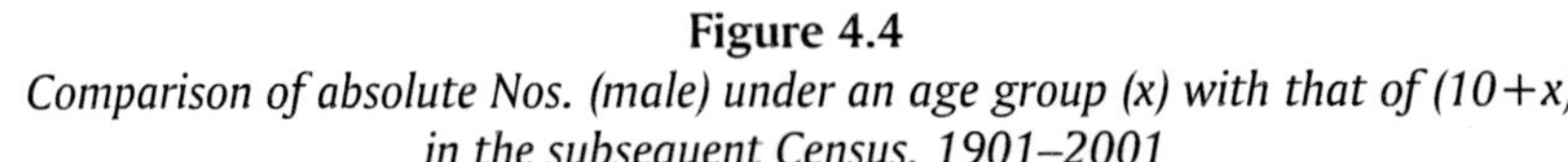

Figure 4.4

Comparison of absolute Nos. (male) under an age group (x) with that of (10+x) in the subsequent Census, 1901–2001

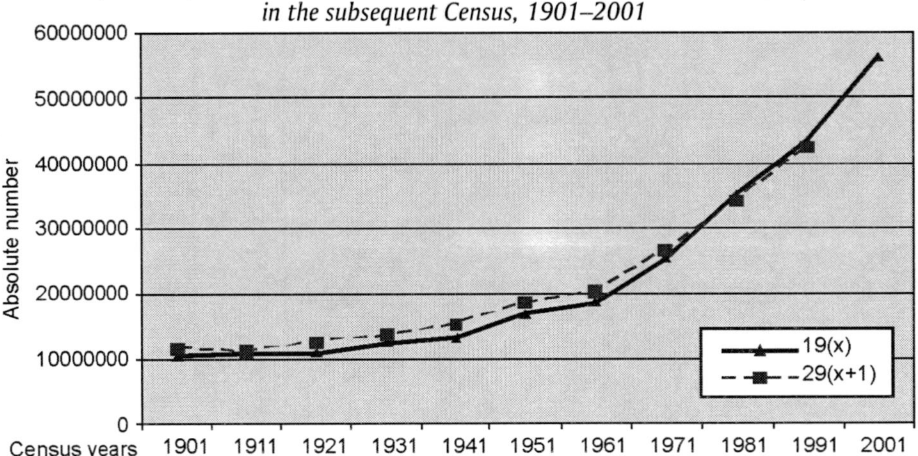

Figure 4.5

Decadal absolute growth by sex, 1901–2001

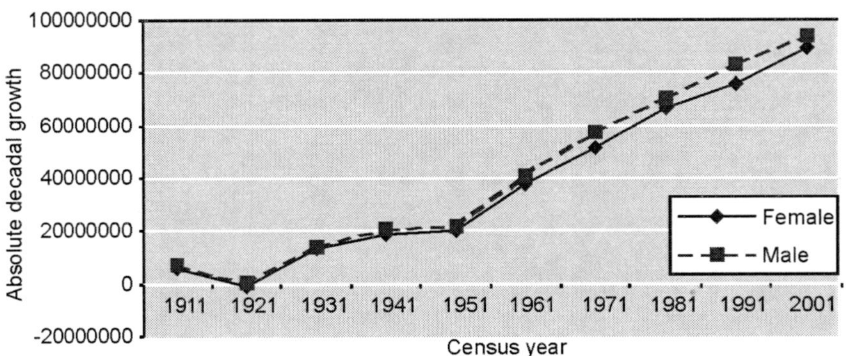

Although Females registered a higher annual growth rate (0.0199977) than Males (0.01958769) in the decade 1991–2001 and thereby improving the sex ratio a bit, the overtaking of males in annual population growth rate by females consistently in the coming years is unlikely to happen. The unusual loss in numbers in 2001 in 0–4 year age group will have a telling effect on the size of female population in higher ages quite for some time. With normal natural increase it is hardly possible for female population to catch up with the male population and therefore there is reason to worry about the fact that the sex ratio in the population is unlikely to improve much in the near future. There is already an ominous sign that the sex ratio in child population (0–6 years) showed a huge decline (18 points) between 1991 and 2001.

These and some other issues need to be discussed in greater detail to understand the apparent anomalies in the population data with its various breakups. Sex ratio at birth in general is in favor of males in all countries unless pregnancies are terminated on the basis of predetermination of sex. If abortions are based on sex of the fetus, the sex ratio is unlikely to improve.

Since independence health facilities and public health awareness have improved. Mortality from most of the killer diseases like TB, malaria, enteric diseases and others has largely been controlled. Mostly children and women frequent outdoor attendance in hospitals and health centers. Yet, it is the males who have benefited most by modern treatment of diseases and health management. The differences in improvement in health status between the two sexes as a result of expansion of public health program could have contributed to bridge the imbalance in the sex ratio. The age-specific female mortality in almost all ages between 0 and 35 years is still high.

4.2 Age Composition

The composition of Indian population by age and sex is presented in Table 4.14. Figure 4.6 shows the age distribution of Indian population, 2000 (SRS).

Table 4.14

Age distribution (in percent) of Indian male and female populations, 1881–2001

Popul. (mill)	*253.0*		*236.7*		*238.4*		*252.0*		*251.3*		*278.9*	
Age group	*1881*		*1891*		*1901*		*1911*		*1921*		*1931*	
	M	*F*	*M*	*F*	*M*	*F*	*M*	*F*	*M*	*F*	*M*	*F*
1	*2*	*3*	*4*	*5*	*6*	*7*	*8*	*9*	*10*	*11*	*12*	*13*
0–4	12.9	15.0	13.9	15.0	12.2	12.9	13.1	14.1	11.8	12.9	12.6	13.8
5–9	14.1	13.8	14.1	13.8	13.7	13.5	13.5	13.4	14.6	14.7	14.0	14.0
10–14	12.2	9.4	11.4	9.4	12.8	10.9	11.6	9.9	12.5	10.8	12.0	10.7
15–19	8.1	7.9	8.3	7.9	8.7	8.2	8.5	8.1	8.4	7.9	8.6	8.5
20–24	8.1	9.0	8.1	9.0	7.9	8.9	8.3	9.3	7.7	8.7	8.2	9.2
25–29	9.1	9.0	8.7	9.0	8.8	8.9	9.0	9.1	8.6	8.8	8.8	9.1
30–34	9.1	8.7	8.6	8.7	8.5	8.6	8.4	8.5	8.3	8.5	7.6	7.6
35–39	5.9	5.6	6.1	5.6	6.1	5.7	6.3	5.6	6.4	5.8	6.7	6.2
40–44	6.7	6.5	6.6	6.5	6.6	6.7	6.5	6.5	6.3	6.4	5.9	5.6
45–49	3.3	3.2	3.6	3.2	3.8	3.5	3.9	3.5	4.0	3.5	4.4	4.0
50–54	4.4	4.4	4.3	4.4	4.5	4.7	4.5	4.6	4.5	4.5	4.1	3.9
55–59	1.6	1.7	1.7	1.7	1.8	1.7	1.8	1.7	1.9	1.7	2.2	2.1
60 +	4.6	5.9	4.6	5.9	4.6	5.6	4.8	5.7	5.1	5.7	4.9	5.4
0–14	39.2	38.2	39.4	38.2	38.7	37.4	38.2	37.4	38.9	38.5	38.6	38.4
15–59	56.2	55.9	56.0	55.9	56.8	57.0	57.0	56.9	56.1	55.8	56.6	56.2
Median	20.0	20.0	20.9	20.9	21.1	21.1	21.5	21.5	21.3	21.3	21.2	21.2
15–49		50.3		49.9		50.6		50.6		49.6		48.8
Dep.ratio (Y)	69.8	66.4	70.4	68.3	68.1	65.6	67.0	65.7	69.3	69.0	68.2	68.3
Dep.ratio (O)	8.2	10.4	8.2	10.6	8.1	9.8	8.4	10.0	9.1	10.2	8.7	9.6
Dep ratio (T)	78.0	76.9	78.6	79.0	76.2	75.4	75.4	75.7	78.4	79.2	76.9	77.9

Cont'd...

Table 4.14 Cont'd...

Population (million)	***318.7***		***361.1***		***439.2***		***548.2***		***683.8***		***843.9***		***1027.0***	
Age group	***1941***		***1951***		***1961***		***1971***		***1981***		***1991***		***2000****	
	M	***F***	***M***	***F***	***M***	***F***	***M***	***F***	***M***	***F***	***M***	***F***	***M***	***F***
1	***14***	***15***	***16***	***17***	***18***	***19***	***20***	***21***	***22***	***23***	***24***	***25***	***26***	***27***
0–4	13.1	14.0	13.2	13.8	14.7	15.5	14.2	14.9	12.3	12.9	12.6	13.0	11.9	11.5
5–9	14.2	14.3	12.6	12.9	14.6	14.9	14.9	15.1	14.0	14.1	13.2	13.3	10.8	10.6
10–14	11.9	10.7	12.5	12.0	11.6	10.8	12.9	12.2	13.1	12.6	12.0	11.5	12.1	11.7
15–19	8.0	7.8	9.1	9.1	8.2	8.1	8.9	8.4	9.9	9.4	9.9	9.5	10.6	10.0
20–24	7.7	8.6	8.1	8.7	8.1	9.0	7.6	8.2	8.4	8.8	8.6	9.0	9.1	9.3
25–29	8.4	8.8	8.3	8.3	8.2	8.5	7.2	7.8	7.5	7.8	7.8	8.5	8.0	8.1
30–34	7.6	7.7	7.3	7.4	7.1	7.0	6.5	6.8	6.3	6.5	7.0	7.2	7.4	7.8
35–39	6.5	6.1	6.4	6.0	6.0	5.6	6.1	5.9	5.8	5.9	6.2	6.0	6.3	6.6
40–44	5.9	5.7	5.9	5.6	5.4	5.1	5.3	5.0	5.3	5.0	5.3	5.0	5.7	5.6
45–49	4.5	4.1	4.6	4.1	4.3	3.9	4.4	4.0	4.5	4.3	4.4	4.2	4.6	4.4
50–54	4.3	4.2	4.2	4.1	4.0	3.8	3.9	3.6	4.0	3.6	3.6	3.4	3.8	3.8
55–59	2.4	2.1	2.6	2.4	2.3	2.1	2.4	2.3	2.5	2.5	2.9	2.8	3.0	2.9
60 +	5.5	5.9	5.3	5.7	5.5	5.8	5.9	6.0	6.5	6.6	6.7	6.7	6.6	7.7
0–14	39.3	39.0	38.2	38.6	40.9	41.2	41.9	42.2	39.5	40.0	37.7	37.8	34.8	33.8
15–59	55.3	55.1	56.5	55.6	53.6	53.0	52.2	51.8	54.1	53.8	55.6	55.6	58.6	58.5
Median	21.3	21.3	21.1	20.8	20.0	19.9	19.6	19.6	20.4	20.6	20.9	21.0	22.0	22.8
15–49		48.8		49.2		47.1		46.0		47.7		49.3		51.8
Dep.ratio (Y)	71.1	70.8	67.6	69.4	76.3	77.7	80.3	81.5	73.0	74.3	67.9	68.0	59.4	57.8
Dep.ratio (O)	9.9	10.7	9.4	10.3	10.3	10.9	11.3	11.6	12.0	12.3	12.0	12.0	11.3	13.2
Dep.ratio (T)	81.0	81.5	77.0	79.7	86.6	88.7	91.6	93.1	85.0	86.6	79.9	80.0	70.7	71.0

*SRS Statistical Report 2000

Source: S.B. Mukherjee: *The Age Distribution of the Indian Population*, 1881–1961, East-West Pop. Institute. Others from Census of India, various issues

There is considerable variation in age-sex composition by rural-urban origin. The following Table 4.15 shows the current composition of India's population by broad age group, sex and residence. A very distinguishing feature of the trends is that if two trend lines were drawn for rural and urban population, separately for males and females, they would remain clearly separated, a fact that was noticed in earlier periods as well. That is, whether it is males or females alone, the age distributions for rural and urban populations still are largely different. Till 1941, females in 0–4 age group out-numbered males. But there was a rapid decline in the sex ratio (F/M) in 0–4 age thereafter and it reached an all-time low of 901 in 2001. This is going to influence the age-sex distribution and many other characteristics of the population for a considerable period. A sharp increase in the proportion of

Figure 4.6
Age composition by sex of Indian population, 2000

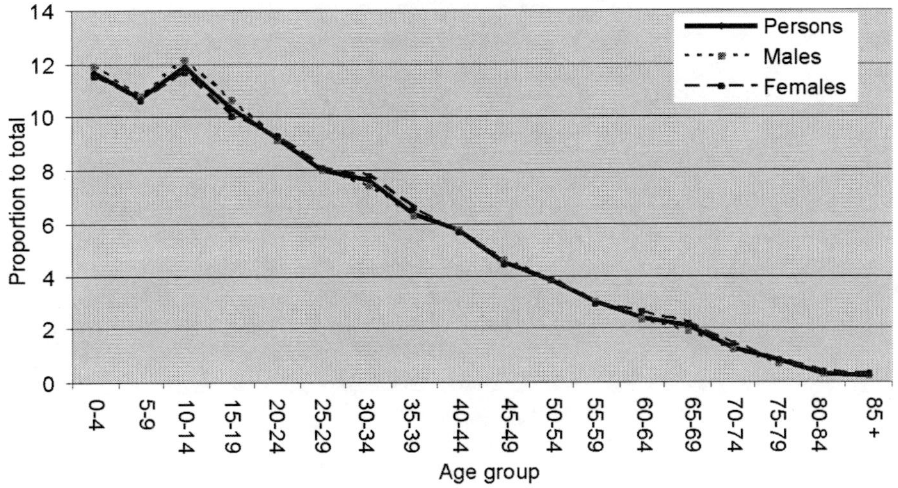

Source: SRS data, 2000

the active and old age group is noticed with the drop in the proportion in 0–14 year age group in the last decade. A similar drop was noticed with male children (but not so sharp) as a result of which median age for men also has increased in the population.

Table 4.15
Percentage of population by broad age groups, sex and residence, India 2000 (SRS data 2003)

		Broad age groups (yrs)						
Residence	***Sex***	***0–4***	***5–9***	***10–14***	***0–14***	***15–59***	***60+***	***65+***
Total	Persons	11.7	10.7	11.9	34.4	58.5	7.2	4.7
	Male	11.9	10.8	12.1	34.9	58.4	6.7	4.4
	Female	11.5	10.6	11.7	33.9	58.5	7.6	5.1
Rural	Persons	12.3	11.1	12.4	35.8	56.8	7.4	4.9
	Male	12.6	11.2	12.6	36.4	56.7	7.0	4.6
	Female	12.1	11.0	12.1	35.2	57.0	7.8	5.2
Urban	Persons	9.8	9.7	10.7	30.2	63.4	6.5	4.2
	Male	9.9	9.8	10.7	30.4	63.6	6.0	3.8
	Female	9.7	9.5	10.6	29.9	63.1	7.0	4.6

The population pyramids for the census data 1981, 1991 and 2001 are presented in Figures 4.7A–4.7C. Judging from the age-sex distribution for various census data, it appears that the population composition by age and sex in India is approaching the Type III pyramid.

Figure 4.7A

Population pyramid, India 1981

Figure 4.7B

Population pyramid, India 1991

Figure 4.7C

Population pyramid, India 2001

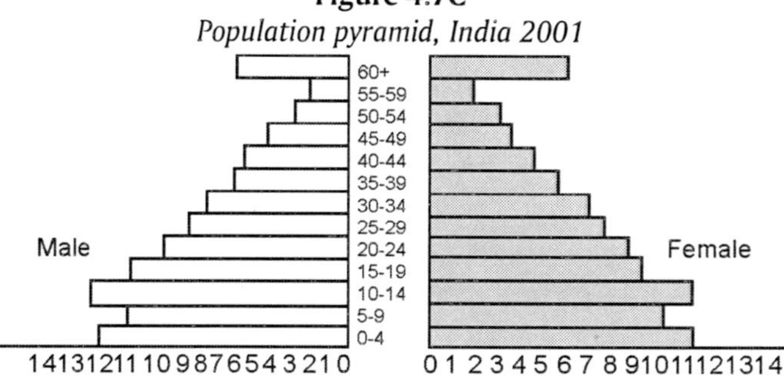

4.2.1 Median Age

The median age of the male population in India remained around 21 years till 1951 (Tables 4.14). It dropped appreciably in the next two decades and a turn around is seen from 1981. An almost similar trend has been observed in the movement for median age for females. The median age of the entire population has hovered around 20–22 years (even in the days of high mortality) in the last hundred and twenty years. India is 8 to 10 years behind the averages attained in the developed countries. With such a low median age, India's population should be considered "young".

A confusion arises between the median ages reported and the ones computed from the given age distribution of populations for various census years. Figure 4.9 and its accompanying data (computed median from age distribution) significantly differ from Figure 4.8. Whereas in Figure 4.8 both median age for male and female populations ran almost at the same dotted points till 1941, Figure 4.9 shows that the median age for the two groups were distinctly different almost through all the eleven time points – median age for females was behind males at only two census years, 1951 and 1961.

Figure 4.8

Reported median age of male and female populations, India 1901–2001

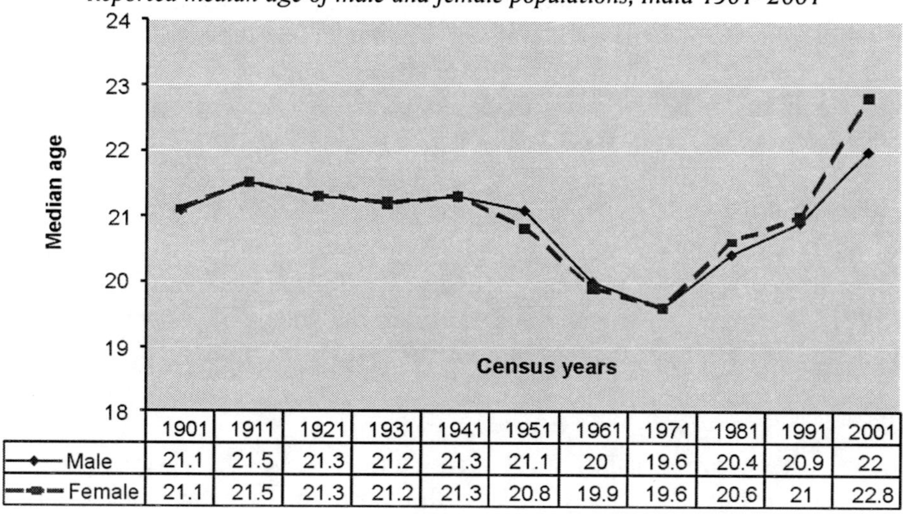

	1901	1911	1921	1931	1941	1951	1961	1971	1981	1991	2001
Male	21.1	21.5	21.3	21.2	21.3	21.1	20	19.6	20.4	20.9	22
Female	21.1	21.5	21.3	21.2	21.3	20.8	19.9	19.6	20.6	21	22.8

Figure 4.9

Computed median age for male and female populations, India 1901–2001

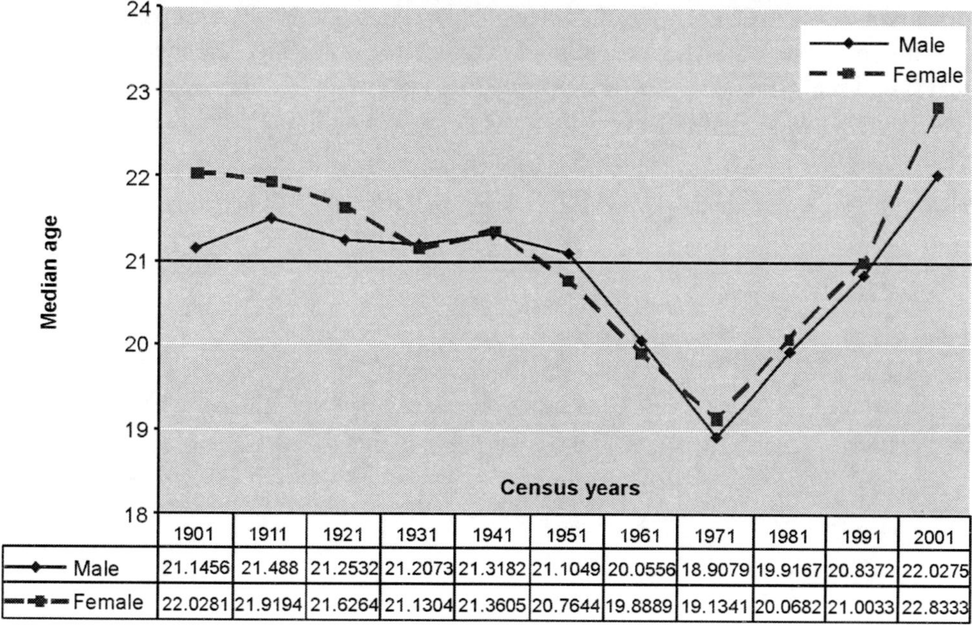

	1901	1911	1921	1931	1941	1951	1961	1971	1981	1991	2001
Male	21.1456	21.488	21.2532	21.2073	21.3182	21.1049	20.0556	18.9079	19.9167	20.8372	22.0275
Female	22.0281	21.9194	21.6264	21.1304	21.3605	20.7644	19.8889	19.1341	20.0682	21.0033	22.8333

The two graphs show three different trends – (1) 1901–41: the age points are more less at the same level, varying between 21 and 22 years; (2) 1941–1971: a rapid fall in the median age points from around 21 years to about 19; and (3) 1971–2001: a complete reversal of the previous segment's trend, median ages rising steadily, women consistently ahead of men. In a positive skew age distribution, the proportion of population in the young age group acts as the trendsetter. The near parallel line (Figure 4.8) between 1901 and 1941 is due to the fact that the proportion of the young age group in the population for males and females fluctuated around 38.5 percent and the proportion of population in the active age group remained almost at a stationary level. In the next segment we observe a steep rise in young age population, and a drop in the proportion in active age group (15–59 years), a fact that brought down the median age of the population (Table 4.14). This was the period when population in India was growing at a very rapid pace. Sometime since the middle of the 1970s, the young age group started to lose fast to other groups, the active age group quickly recovered its lost position and the old age group (60 + years) started to gain fast.

4.3 Dependency Ratio

Dependency ratios, separately for male and female populations for different census years are shown in the last three rows of Tables 4.14. Total dependency ratio rose to an all-time high of around 92 percent in 1971. Thereafter, there was a sharp drop in the young age population, which helped register an all-time low of 71 percent total dependency ratio in 2001 census.

4.4 Ageing

A silent revolution has occurred in the last 100 years – unseen, unheard, and yet so close. The biggest achievement of the century is longevity. All over the world, life expectancy has risen leading to a sharp rise in the number of older persons (Table 4.14 & 4.16). India was ranked fourth among the countries of the world in late 1980s and 1990s with a large elderly population; by the year 2001, it is likely to be second only to China in absolute size of elderly persons. While a drop in the proportion of population in the early ages is most certainly due to decline in fertility, the increase of the elderly population is definitely due to decline in mortality (the fast rise in life expectancy among females is at least partly due to decline in fertility with consequent decline in maternal mortality rate MMR).

Table 4.16

Crude birth rates (CBR), crude death rates (CDR), and expectation of life at age 60 (e_{60}^{0}) in Census years, 1961–2001

Census year	Decadal increase in		CBR	CDR	Proportion of population in				Growth of e_{60}^{0}	
	General population	Population in 60 +			Age 0–4		Age >60			
					Male	Female	Male	Female	Male	Female
1961	21.64	23.25	41.7	22.8	14.7	15.5	5.5	5.8	11.8	13.0
1971	24.80	32.39	41.2	19.0	14.2	14.9	5.9	6.0	13.6	13.8
1981	25.00	29.97	33.9	12.5	12.3	12.9	6.5	6.6	13.8	14.7
1991	22.19	28.94	29.7	10.7	12.6	13.0	6.7	6.7	14.5	15.5
2001*	17.77	38.46	23.7	8.4	11.9	11.5	6.6	7.7	15.2	16.4
1951–2001	170.29	273.89								

*Expert Committee projection

Between 1961 and 2001 population share of 0–4 age group dropped by 2.8 percentage points for males and 4 percentage points for females. In the same period the share of male population increased by 1.1 percent and female population by 1.9 percent in 60 + age group. The absolute number of 60 + persons increased from 24.7 million in 1961 to 75.9 million in 2001. The share of old age population in the total population has gone up by about 2 percentage points between 1901 and 2001 (Table 4.14). The growth was much higher in urban areas (from 3.7 to 21.1 million) than in rural areas (from 21.0 million to 54.9 million). The population of the elderly persons, both in percentage share and in absolute number is larger in rural area than in urban area. The old age dependency ratio has gone up by over 3 percentage points during 1901–2001.

Table 4.17
Population of 60 years and above, 1901–2025

Year	*Number of Older Persons*
1901	12 million
1951	19 million
2001	77 million
By 2025	a whopping 177 million!

Although the share of 60+ age group in the population has gone up by about 2 percentage point between 1901 and 2001, life expectancy in India has gone up from a meager 20 years in the beginning of the 20th century to over 63 years today. A sharp drop in death rate in all ages due to better nutrition, improved medical care and health facilities and declining fertility have made the miracle possible. In France, it took 120 years for the gray population to double from 7 to 14 percent. But in India, the gray population in absolute number has nearly trebled in just 40 years! By 2025 the number of old persons in the Indian population is likely to be around 177 million, about the size of the combined population of Japan and Republic of Korea.

With the disintegration of the traditional joint family, the natural support system for the senior citizens has literally crumbled. Only a very limited few senior citizens, mostly located in urban areas are fortunate to have retired from jobs in organized sector and have earned some retirement benefits. But a vast majority of 60+ years people are located in rural areas. Even when health does not permit, many of these senior citizens have to put in some kind of labor to earn a living. The fast-changing pace of life has added to the woes of the older persons. There will be more women than men in 70+ age if the current trends continue. Since most of them would be in rural areas without any income from savings, they will need support either from their children or the state. The state already has instituted old age and widow pension to economically weaker section. Here are a few stunning statistics relating to Indian senior citizens:

- 90 percent of older persons are from the unorganized sector, with no social security at the age 60.
- 47 percent elderly men and 9 percent elderly women (a total of 28% of total elderly persons) were expected to remain in the work force in 2001.
- 30 percent of older persons live below the poverty line and another 33 percent just marginally over it.
- 80 percent live in rural areas.
- 73 percent are illiterate, and can only be engaged in physical labor.
- 55 percent of women over 60 years are widows, many of them with no support whatsoever.
- There are nearly 200,000 centenarians in India.

4.5 Population Density

Pressure on the available civic amenities and natural resources in a region mounts as the population concentration in the region increases. One of the important indices of population concentration is the density of population. It is usually defined as the number of persons per square kilometer (or per square mile). The population density of India in 2001 was 324 persons per square kilometer, which means that 57 more people in 2001 live in the same space compared to the number that lived a decade back. The population living in per square kilometer in 2001 has gone up by 21.3 percent compared to that in 1991.

The 1971 base year population for various states is still taken as the criterion for plan allocation and sharing of revenues collected by the central government (initially this base line population was to be used till 2001; it has now been extended to 2025). The total number of seats in an Assembly as also a state's quota to send representatives to the Parliament and Assembly has been fixed on the basis of this base year population. For example, an Assembly segment in West Bengal roughly constituted of 150,000 eligible voters. The same assembly segment now has roughly twice as many people as there were in 1971. The abnormal rise in the size of population in some of the districts in West Bengal (mostly due to large scale infiltration from Bangladesh) has forced the election commission to redraw boundaries for Assembly segments. The districts of Burdwan, Hooghly and Calcutta (all in West Bengal) would lose their traditional quota for the Assembly in favor of these high-density border districts. Of the 126 assembly segments in Assam 42 old constituencies have been replaced by a similar number of new constituencies. A few districts have gained a few more seats and a few others have lost some as per the directives of delimitation commission. This has raised hue and cry among all political parties. Even the number of 'reserved constituencies' (for scheduled tribes) has been proposed to be increased because of large increases of ST population in many states in recent times. Of course this increase will be at the cost of unreserved constituencies.

The increase in population density saw establishment of many new municipalities, up-gradation of some municipalities into municipal corporations and creation of new districts and administrative blocks and police stations for the sake of administration, creation of new hospitals, schools, shopping complexes, expansion of transport network and a host of other things. Pressure on the land is mounting; ground water reserves are fast depleting because of lifting of hundreds and thousands of cubic feet of water to meet the requirements of farmers, industries and supply of drinking water to masses. The number of towns and cities in India has gone up from 1917 in 1901 to 4378 in 2001.

High increase in the density of population is a matter of great concern as it puts immense pressure on our natural resources putting severe constraints in our effort to improve the quality of life of the common man. Due to difference in climatic conditions, availability of resources, etc., density and distribution of population vary largely between states and UTs. Let us take a closer look at Indian states and UTs (Table 4.18 & 4.19) in matters of their population density and see how the same has changed over the years.

Table 4.18

Population by regions/states/UTs, India 1901–2001 (in million)

States/UTs	*1901*	*1911*	*1921*	*1931*	*1941*	*1951*	*1961*	*1971*	*1981*	*1991*	*2001*
1	*2*	*3*	*4*	*5*	*6*	*7*	*8*	*9*	*10*	*11*	*12*
INDIA	**238**	**252.1**	**251.3**	**279**	**318.7**	**361.1**	**439.2**	**548.2**	**685.2**	**843.9**	**1027.0**
Northern region	**26.9**	**26.52**	**26.54**	**29.7**	**34.89**	**38.2**	**48.05**	**61.78**	**80.71**	**103.2**	**132.69**
Haryana	4.62	4.185	4.247	4.55	5.258	5.669	7.599	10.03	12.88	16.29	21.11
Himachal Pradesh	1.93	1.891	1.935	2.04	2.262	2.383	2.811	3.453	4.248	5.148	6.08
Jammu & Kashmir	2.15	2.294	2.413	2.68	2.932	3.25	3.558	4.605	6.03	7.68	10.07

Cont'd...

Table 4.18 Cont'd

1	*2*	*3*	*4*	*5*	*6*	*7*	*8*	*9*	*10*	*11*	*12*
Punjab	7.51	6.731	7.163	8.01	9.592	9.172	11.16	13.54	16.72	20.17	24.34
Rajasthan	10.3	10.99	10.3	11.7	13.86	15.96	20.16	25.76	34.19	42.37	56.49
Chandigarh*	0.02	0.025	0.025	0.03	0.032	0.036	0.088	0.274	0.411	0.675	0.92
Delhi*	0.41	0.403	0.478	0.64	0.924	1.733	2.679	4.056	6.235	9.368	13.76
Uttaranchal											8.52
Eastern region	**58.9**	**62.87**	**62.88**	**70.1**	**80.94**	**90.13**	**113.7**	**142.5**	**178**	**217.6**	**264.97**
Assam	3.29	3.857	4.649	5.55	6.692	8.016	10.85	14.64	19.94	22.28	26.60
Bihar	27.3	28.31	28.12	31.4	35.18	38.78	46.43	56.35	69.96	86.08	82.88
Jharkhand											26.91
Manipur	0.29	0.353	0.377	0.45	0.51	0.578	0.791	1.096	1.439	1.857	2.36
Meghalaya	0.33	0.403	0.427	0.47	0.542	0.614	0.791	0.987	1.37	1.772	2.26
Nagaland	0.1	0.151	0.151	0.17	0.191	0.217	0.351	0.493	0.754	1.182	1.95
Orissa	10.3	11.37	11.16	12.5	13.77	14.66	17.57	21.93	26.31	31.48	36.66
Sikkim	0.05	0.076	0.075	0.11	0.127	0.144	0.176	0.219	0.274	0.422	0.51
Tripura	0.17	0.227	0.327	0.39	0.51	0.614	1.142	1.59	2.056	2.785	3.18
West Bengal	16.9	18	17.47	18.9	23.23	26.29	34.92	44.29	54.61	68.02	80.21
Andaman & Nicobar Is.*	0.02	0.025	0.025	0.03	0.032	0.036	0.044	0.11	0.206	0.253	0.301
Arunachal Pradesh							0.351	0.493	0.617	0.844	1.13
Mizoram	0.07	0.101	0.101	0.11	0.159	0.181	0.264	0.329	0.48	0.675	0.92
Central region	**65.5**	**67.59**	**65.85**	**71.1**	**80.53**	**89.3**	**106.1**	**130**	**163.3**	**204.6**	**236.93**
Chattishgarh											20.75
Madhya Pradesh	16.9	19.44	19.18	21.3	24	26.07	32.37	41.66	52.21	66.16	60.39
Uttar Pradesh	48.6	48.15	46.67	49.8	56.53	63.19	73.75	88.31	111.1	138.7	166.07
Western region	**29**	**31.81**	**31.57**	**36**	**41.17**	**48.93**	**60.88**	**78.06**	**98.12**	**120.2**	**147.79**
Gujarat	9.08	9.781	10.18	11.5	13.7	16.25	20.64	26.7	34.05	41.18	50.63
Maharashtra	19.4	21.48	20.86	24	26.83	32.03	39.58	50.43	62.83	78.74	96.74
Dadra & Nagar Haveli*	0.02	0.025	0.025	0.03	0.032	0.036	0.044	0.055	0.137	0.169	0.21
Daman & Diu (and Goa)*	0.5	0.529	0.503	0.53	0.574	0.578	0.615	0.877	1.096	0.084	0.21
Southern region	**58**	**63.3**	**64.49**	**72.1**	**81.13**	**94.5**	**110.6**	**135.8**	**165.1**	**188.8**	**224.71**
Andhra Pradesh	19.1	21.45	21.41	24.2	27.28	31.13	35.97	43.52	53.44	66.33	75.69
Goa										1.182	1.34
Karnataka	13.1	13.54	13.37	14.6	16.25	19.39	23.59	29.27	37.14	44.81	52.69
Kerala	6.39	7.159	7.791	9.51	11.03	13.54	16.91	21.27	25.42	20	31.84
Tamil Nadu	19.3	20.9	21.64	23.5	26.26	30.11	33.69	41.22	48.37	55.62	62.13
Lakshadweep*	0.02	0.025	0.025	0.03	0.032	0.036	0.044	0.055	0.069	0.084	0.10
Pandicherry*	0.24	0.252	0.251	0.25	0.287	0.289	0.351	0.493	0.617	0.76	0.92

Source: Various Census reports

Table 4.19
Area and population density of the states/regions, India 1901–2001

*Region/State/ UT**	*Area[2] in km²*	*Prop. to total*	*Population[1] Density*										
			1901	*1911*	*1921*	*1931*	*1941*	*1951*	*1961*	*1971*	*1981*	*1991*	*2001*
1	*2*	*3*	*4*	*5*	*6*	*7*	*8*	*9*	*10*	*11*	*12*	*13*	*14*
INDIA	**3169800.1**	**100**	**73**	**77**	**76**	**83**	**97**	**110**	**134**	**167**	**216**	**267**	**324**
Northern region	**649251.7**	**20.48**	**38**	**38**	**37**	**41**	**49**	**53**	**67**	**86**	**112**	**158**	**217**
Haryana	44199.1	1.39	105	94	96	103	119	128	172	227	292	369	477
Himachal[4]	55754.6	1.76	35	34	35	36	41	43	51	62	77	92	109
J & K[3]	101716.3	3.21	10	10	11	12	13	15	16	21	59	76	99
Punjab	50392.7	1.59	150	134	142	159	191	182	221	269	333	401	482
Rajasthan	342261.4	10.80	30	32	30	34	41	47	59	75	100	128	165
Chandigarh*	114.0	0.0036	193	162	159	174	198	213	1052	2257	3961	5620	7,902
Delhi*	1483.0	0.0468	273	279	329	429	618	1175	1790	2738	4194	6319	9,294
Uttaranchal	53330.6	1.68											159
Eastern Region	**688747.1**	**21.73**	**86**	**91**	**91**	**102**	**118**	**131**	**165**	**207**	**258**	**316**	**386**
A'chal Pradesh	83932.1	2.65							4	6	8	10	13
Assam	78348.3	2.47	42	49	59	71	85	102	138	186	230	284	340
Bihar	94180.5	2.97	157	163	162	180	202	223	267	324	402	497	880
Manipur	22323.7	0.704	13	16	17	20	23	26	35	48	64	82	107
Meghalaya	22389.0	0.706	15	18	19	21	25	27	34	45	60	78	103
Mizoram	21215.7	0.669	4	4	5	6	7	9	13	16	23	33	42
Nagaland	16572.0	0.523	6	9	10	11	12	13	22	31	47	73	120
Orissa	155537.8	4.91	66	73	72	80	88	94	113	141	169	202	236
Sikkim	7111.8	0.224	6	12	11	15	17	19	22	29	45	57	76
Tripura	10497.3	0.331	17	22	29	37	49	61	109	149	196	262	304
West Bengal	88740.2	2.80	193	205	199	215	204	299	397	504	615	766	904
Anadaman Is.*	8285.2	0.261	3	3	3	4	4	4	8	14	23	34	43
Jharkhand	79613.7	2.51											338
Central Region	**684131.6**	**21.58**	**89**	**92**	**89**	**97**	**109**	**121**	**144**	**176**	**221**	**278**	**361**
Madhya Pradesh	308087.3	9.72	38	44	43	48	54	59	73	94	118	149	196
Uttar Pradesh	241005.6	7.60	165	164	159	169	192	215	251	300	377	471	689
Chhattisgarh	135038.7	4.26											154

Cont'd...

Table 4.19 Cont'd...

1	*2*	*3*	*4*	*5*	*6*	*7*	*8*	*9*	*10*	*11*	*12*	*13*	*14*
Western Region	**508546.0**	**16.04**	**57**	**63**	**62**	**71**	**81**	**96**	**120**	**154**	**193**	**244**	**293**
Gujarat[5]	196112.4	6.19	46	50	52	59	70	83	105	136	174	210	258
Maharashtra	308128.2	9.72	63	70	68	78	87	104	129	164	204	256	314
Dadra-Nagar Haveli*	491.0	0.0155	50	59	63	78	82	85	118	151	211	282	449
Goa, Daman & Diu*	112.0	0.0035	133	136	131	142	151	156	164	225	705	906	1,411
Goa	3702.5	0.117									272	316	363
Southern Region	**636458.7**	**20.079**	**91**	**99**	**101**	**113**	**127**	**148**	**173**	**212**	**258**	**308**	**351**
Andhra Pradesh	275372.9	8.69	69	78	77	87	99	112	130	157	193	241	275
Karnataka	191759.9	6.05	68	71	70	76	85	101	123	153	194	234	275
Kerala	38875.0	1.24	165	184	201	245	284	349	435	549	655	747	819
Tamil Nadu	129939.0	4.10	148	161	166	181	202	232	259	317	372	428	478
Lakshadweep*	32.0	0.001	434	455	426	501	574	657	753	994	1258	1615	1,894
Pondicherry*	480.0	0.0151	513	536	509	539	594	661	769	982	1229	1605	2,029

Note:

1. The population of India includes the estimated population of entire Kach district, Marvin, Maliya-Miyana and Wankaner talukas of Rajkot district, Jodiya taluka of Jamnagar district of Gujarat state and entire Kinnaur district of Himachal Pradesh where population enumeration in 2001 could not be conducted due to natural calamity.

2. For working out the density of India and Jammu & Kashmir the entire area and population of those areas of Jammu & Kashmir, which are under illegal occupation of Pakistan and China have not been taken into account. Estimation of population density till 1971 was based on a total area of 3287780 sq. km (including Pakistan occupied portion of Jammu & Kashmir).

3. While working out the decadal growth of population of Jammu & Kashmir the population figures for 1991 have been worked out by interpolation as 1991 Census could not be held in this state owing to disturbed conditions.

4. Figures shown against Himachal Pradesh have been arrived at after including the estimated figures of entire Kinnaur district of Himachal Pradesh where the population enumeration in 2001 could not be conducted due to natural calamity.

5. Figures shown against Gujarat have been arrived at after including the estimated figures of entire Kach district, Morvi, Maliya-Miyana and Wankaner talukas of Rajkot district, Jodiya taluka of Jamnagar district of Gujarat state where the population enumeration 2001 could not be conducted due to natural calamity.

Population has grown faster in Northern region compared to most other regions. Yet population density has remained low in this area all the time. The death rates in this region were always on the higher side. Therefore, it is very likely that population densities in the states of this region will grow fast unless the common man embraces small family norm. Population density in the South had remained high since when population enumeration had begun. The population growth in this region has come down appreciably. The rate of increase in population density has slowed down of late. Around 1981, population density in the Eastern region had caught up with that in the Southern part of

India. Now this region has the highest population density (from 316 in 1991 to 386 in 2001), followed by Central region and Western region respectively, and the Northeastern region has the lowest density in the country (Table 4.19). West Bengal has the highest population density among the larger states at 904 per km^2, an increase of 137 persons per km^2 from the 1991 figure. The lowest population density is observed in Arunachal Pradesh (13 per km^2) and the highest in Delhi (9,294 per km^2). Bihar is now the second highest densely populated state pushing Kerala to the third spot in terms of ranking. Similarly, Punjab and Tamil Nadu have now interchanged their relative positions of tenth and eleventh spots respectively. Bihar would not have achieved this distinction had Jharkhand not being carved out of this state. The present Bihar is 1.77 times denser than what the undivided Bihar was in 1991.

4.6 Religious Divide of Population of India

Religion returns in Indian census provide a wonderful glimpse of the country's rich social composition and heritage, as many religions have originated and a few others of foreign origin have prospered in this soil. India's accommodative social and cultural systems have endeared some of the indigenous faiths/tribal religions to survive.

Prior to independence, religion data were cross-classified by many social and development parameters as education, age and marital status. However, only sex and residence have been used for cross-classification of Census data on religion since independence. There was a pressing demand from various quarters and political outfits and the National Minority Commission that religion data be published and cross-classified by socio-economic characteristics to assess the attainments and level of development of various religious communities, especially the minority communities. The National Statistical Commission 2001 also pressed for such cross-classifications.

The Working Group on Religion found out 1,700 names of religion that had appeared in the censuses of 1971, 1981 and 1991. The Social Studies Division of ORGI classified them into 7 main categories including 'others' plus those who did not return their religion.

Hindus and Muslims are the two major religious groups in India. Together they constitute about 94 percent of India's total population. In the last 40 years their combined share in the population has almost remained unchanged. Other religious groups have almost maintained their share at the same level. Whereas the Hindus lost about 2.9 percentage points between 1961 and 2001, the Muslims have gained by about 2.7 percentage points in the same period. Of the 1027 million population enumerated in 2001 Census, 828 million returned their religion as Hindus, 138 million as Muslims, 24 million as Christians, 19 million as Sikhs, 8 million as Buddhists, and 4.2 million as Jains. In addition, 6.6 million are included in "Other religions and Persuasions" including tribal religions that are not included into any of the six main religions. Population distribution by religion, sex, residence and child population is presented in Table 4.20.

The change of religious composition of India's population and the respective growth rates for the religious communities between 1961 and 2001, one based on data without any adjustments and the other by excluding the figures for Assam and Jammu & Kashmir where Census could not be conducted in 1981 and 1991 respectively is presented in Table 4.21.

Table 4.20

Population distribution by religion, sex, residence and child group, India 2001

Religion	*Residence*	*Total population*			*Population in 0–6 years*		
		Person	*Male*	*Female*	*Person*	*Male*	*Female*
1	*2*	*3*	*4*	*5*	*6*	*7*	*8*
All Religions	**Total**	**1,028,610,328**	**532,156,772**	**496,453,556**	**163,819,614**	**84,999,203**	**78,820,411**
	Rural	**742,490,639**	**381,602,674**	**360,887,965**	**126,470,497**	**65,407,648**	**61,062,849**
	Urban	**286,119,689**	**150,554,098**	**135,565,591**	**37,349,117**	**19,591,555**	**17,757,562**
Hindus	Total	827,578,868	428,678,554	398,900,314	129,326,464	67,199,939	62,126,525
	Rural	611,263,295	314,437,535	296,825,760	102,281,857	52,952,321	49,329,536
	Urban	216,315,573	114,241,019	102,074,554	27,044,607	14,247,618	12,796,989
Muslims	Total	138,188,240	71,374,134	66,814,106	25,893,059	13,279,540	12,613,519
	Rural	88,794,744	45,473,491	43,321,253	17,930,297	9,170,472	8,759,825
	Urban	49,393,496	25,900,643	23,492,853	7,962,762	4,109,068	3,853,694
Christians	Total	24,080,016	11,984,663	12,095,353	3,239,609	1,649,141	1,590,468
	Rural	15,893,958	7,943,541	7,950,417	2,320,828	1,181,359	1,139,469
	Urban	8,186,058	4,041,122	4,144,936	918,781	467,782	450,999
Sikhs	Total	19,215,730	10,152,298	9,063,432	2,459,486	1,377,375	1,082,111
	Rural	14,106,481	7,443,893	6,662,588	1,887,011	1,055,356	831,655
	Urban	5,109,249	2,708,405	2,400,844	572,475	322,019	250,456
Buddhists	Total	7,955,207	4,074,155	3,881,052	1,149,423	592,005	557,418
	Rural	4,893,610	2,499,409	2,394,201	745,792	383,450	362,342
	Urban	3,061,597	1,574,746	1,486,851	403,631	208,555	195,076
Jains	Total	4,225,053	2,177,398	2,047,655	448,663	239,980	208,683
	Rural	1,009,347	521,033	488,314	116,131	62,123	54,008
	Urban	3,215,706	1,656,365	1,559,341	332,532	177,857	154,675
Others	Total	6,639,626	3,332,551	3,307,075	1,193,273	603,979	589,294
	Rural	6,002,468	3,008,524	2,993,944	1,104,719	558,952	545,767
	Urban	637,158	324,027	313,131	88,554	45,027	43,527
Religion not stated	Total	727,588	383,019	344,569	109,637	57,244	52,393
	Rural	526,736	275,248	251,488	83,862	43,615	40,247
	Urban	200,852	107,771	93,081	25,775	13,629	12,146

Table 4.21
Proportion and growth rate of population by religious communities in India, 1961–2001

Religion	**A. Proportion**									
	Unadjusted					*Adjusted*				
	1961	*1971*	*1981*	*1991*	*2001*	*1961*	*1971*	*1981*	*1991*	*2001*
1	*2*	*3*	*4*	*5*	*6*	*7*	*8*	*9*	*10*	*11*
All religions	**100**	**100**	**100**	**100**	**100**	**100**	**100**	**100**	**100**	**100**
Hindus	83.4	82.7	82.6	82.0	80.5	84.4	83.5	83.1	82.4	81.4
Muslims	10.7	11.2	11.4	12.1	13.4	9.9	10.4	10.9	11.7	12.4
Christians	2.4	2.6	2.4	2.3	2.3	2.4	2.6	2.5	2.3	2.3
Sikhs	1.8	1.9	2.0	1.9	1.9	1.8	1.9	2.0	2.0	19
Buddhists	0.7	0.7	0.7	0.8	0.8	0.7	0.7	0.7	0.8	0.8
Jains	0.5	0.5	0.5	0.4	0.4	0.5	0.5	0.5	0.4	0.4
Others	0.3	0.4	0.4	0.4	0.6	0.3	0.4	0.4	0.4	0.7

	B. Growth Rate							
	Unadjusted				*Adjusted*			
	1961–1971	*1971–1981*	*1981–1991*	*1991–2001*	*1961–1971*	*1971–1981*	*1981–1991*	*1991–2001*
	12	*13*	*14*	*15*	*16*	*17*	*18*	*19*
All religions	**24.8**	**21.4**	**26.0**	**22.7**	**24.8**	**24.8**	**23.8**	**21.5**
Hindus	23.7	21.3	25.1	20.3	23.4	24.2	22.8	20.0
Muslims	30.8	22.9	34.5	36.0	31.2	30.8	32.9	29.3
Christians	32.6	13.7	21.5	22.6	36.0	19.2	17.0	22.1
Sikhs	32.3	26.0	24.3	18.2	32.0	26.2	25.5	16.9
Buddhists	17.1	23.8	35.3	24.5	17.0	25.4	36.0	23.2
Jains	28.5	23.1	4.6	26.0	28.5	23.7	4.0	26.0
Others	45.7	26.6	18.2	103.1	97.7	26.6	13.2	111.3

Table 4.22
Population composition by religion and residence, India 2001

Religious communities	*Urban*	*Rural*	*Total*
Not stated	200,852 (27.6)	526,736 (72.4)	727,588
Others	637,158 (49.6)	6,002,468 (50.4)	6,639,626
Jains	3,215,706 (76.1)	1,009,347 (23.9)	4,225,053
Buddhists	3,061,597 (38.5)	4,893,610 (61.5)	7,955,207
Sikhs	5,109,249 (26.6)	14,106,481 (73.4)	19,215,730
Christians	8186,058 (34.0)	15,893,958 (66.0)	24,080,016
Muslims	49,393,496 (35.7)	88,794,744 (64.3)	138,188,240
Hindus	216,315,573 (26.1)	611,263,295 (73.9)	827,578,866
All religions	**286,119,689 (27.8)**	**742,490,639 (72.2)**	**1,028,610,328**

Pakistan was carved out of undivided India in 1947 on the criterion of religion. Since then, religion has remained a touchy and volatile subject in Indian politics. The Indian government consciously tried not to highlight the progress and failures of various religious communities in diverse socio-economic parameters lest there were commotion and battle of words and wits between ethnic communities. Religious conversion, pampering of some religious groups, common civil law, abolition of special status to some state (Jammu & Kashmir) and many such issues often are behind many mass massacres, ethnic violence and political unrest in India. The 'minorities' have, in fact, become the 'vote bank' for many political outfits. 'Bhagalpur massacre' in Bihar, the 'Sikh massacre' in Delhi after the assassination of Indira Gandhi, the then Prime Minister of India, demolition of 'Babri Mashjid' in 1992 by Hindu fanatics, 'Godhra incident and its aftermath in Gujarat' in 2002 are some examples of communal violence. The target population in all these and most other violences had always been some minority community, most frequently the Muslims. The decision by the Census Commissioner to furnish in greater details the state of health of various religious communities on the basis of 2001 enumeration may have the backing and blessings of the Home Ministry of the NDA government. Rashtriya Swayang Sevaksangha, RSS, (Bharatiya Janata Party, BJP, is the political wing of RSS and was the dominant partner of National Democratic Alliance, NDA, which was in power at the Center at the time the Census held in 2001) saw in it a conspiracy to outbreed Hindus when the published erroneous report indicated that the Muslim population grew by 3 percent more over the growth rate registered in 1981–91 – a 16 percent growth advantage over Hindu's. The Census Commissioner had to withdraw the report on religious composition of Indian population on various demographic and social parameters for certain gross mistakes committed in the computation of growth rate for Muslims.

4.6.1 Growth Rate

The data on distribution and growth rate of population of religious communities since 1961 was published in October 2004. Unfortunately, the published data did not take into cognizance the fact that census could not be conducted in Assam and Jammu & Kashmir in 1981 and 1991 respectively. The unadjusted data suggested 36 percent growth rate for Muslims since 1991 census. The Hindu religious fanatics saw in it a conspiracy to outbreed Hindus.

The figures were subsequently modified. When analyzed on the basis of adjusted data (Table 4.20), it is observed that the Sikh population recorded the lowest decadal growth rate (16.9%) and also showed declining trend in growth since 1961–1971. The adjusted growth rate of Hindu population has come down from 22.8 percent in 1981–91 to 20.0 percent in 1991–2001. Similar trends are observed among Buddhists (growth rate of 36.0% in 1981–1991 to 23.2% during 1991–2001). The adjusted data showed that, Muslim growth rate declined from 32.9 percent during 1981–91 to 29.3 percent in 1991–2001. For Christians it increased from 17.0 percent in 1981–91 to 22.1 percent during 1991–2001. The Jain population also registered a growth rate of 26.0 percent against very low growth rate of only 4.6 percent during 1981–1991.

4.6.2 Rural-Urban Residence

Three-quarter of the total Jain population is concentrated in urban areas, mostly in Maharashtra, Rajasthan and Delhi. In fact, except Hindus (26.1%) and Sikhs (26.6%), all other religious communities have higher concentration in urban areas than the national average of 27.8 percent. 'Others'

(49.6%), Buddhists (38.5%), Muslims (35.7%) and Christians (34.0%) have higher concentration in urban area than both Hindus and Sikhs.

4.6.3 Sex Ratio

At the national level, Christians have the highest sex ratio, 1009, Sikhs the least, 893. Sex ratio among Muslim population at national level is 936 which is just above the national average of 933 for all religions while a shade lower is the Hindu population sex ratio of 931 (Table 4.23). Among the states, the highest sex ratio (1058) has been reported among the Hindu populations in Kerala followed by Chhattisgarh (990) and Pondicherry (987). There are as many as 4 states/UTs where sex ratio in the Muslim population is well above 1,000. Kerala is again at the top in the rank (1,082) followed by Pondicherry (1,097), Tamil Nadu (1,020) and Lakshadweep (1,002) for the Muslim population. Christians recorded a sex ratio of over 1,000 in as many as 13 states/UTs. The national average sex ratio of Christians is 1,009. Goa has returned the highest sex ratio of 1,107 among Christians followed by Pondicherry and Delhi. The Orthodox Church seems to have great command on Indian Christian community on matters related to birth. Sikhs have the poorest sex ratio (893) among all religious communities. The picture is horrendous in the 0–6 age group population (786). Delhi has returned the highest sex ratio among Sikh population (925) followed by Chandigarh (910). Both Sikhs and Hindus are behind the national average. Worst return for sex ratio in 0–6 age group is from Sikhs, followed by Jains (870) and Hindus (925). As many as 27 states/UTs have returned sex ratio in child population for Sikhs below 900. There are 9 states/UTs where child sex ratio for Sikhs is below 800. Christians returned the highest sex ratio in the child population, 964 (though 45 points below the same in the general population) followed by Muslims and Buddhists.

Table 4.23

Sex ratio in the general and child population by religion and residence, India 2001

Religion	*Total population*			*Population in 0–6 age*		
	Total	*Rural*	*Urban*	*Total*	*Rural*	*Urban*
All religions	**932.9**	**945.7**	**900.4**	**927.3**	**933.6**	**906.4**
Hindus	930.5	944.0	893.5	924.5	931.6	898.2
Muslims	936.1	952.7	907.0	949.8	955.2	937.9
Christians	1009.2	1000.9	1025.7	964.4	964.5	964.1
Sikhs	892.7	895.0	886.4	785.6	788.0	777.8
Buddhists	952.6	957.9	944.2	941.6	945.0	935.4
Jains	940.4	937.2	941.4	869.6	869.4	869.7
Others	992.4	995.2	966.4	975.7	976.4	966.7
Not stated	899.6	913.7	863.7	915.3	922.8	891.2

4.6.4 Child Population (0–6 Years)

A proxy estimate of the relative position of fertility among different religious communities can be had from the size of (0–6) year's population for the community. At the national level the proportion of child population stood at 15.9 percent in 2001 Census. Muslim population recorded the highest proportion of population in this age group at 18.7 percent followed by 18.0 percent in 'Others'. The lowest proportion of this age group was observed with Jains at 10.6 percent preceded by Sikhs at 12.8 percent. In fact, barring the Muslims and 'other religions', remaining religious communities had returned lower proportion in this age group compared to the national average. Generally it has been argued that in developing countries high female literacy rate usually has a positive dampening effect on fertility, other factors being constant. That is, there is a negative correlation between female literacy and fertility. This is observed with all religious groups, urban and rural, and in all states. This suggests that irrespective of religious affiliations, investment in female education would go a long way to bring down fertility faster.

Table 4.24

Percentage of 0–6 age group population by religion and residence, India 2001

Religious communities	*Urban*	*Rural*	*Total*
Others	13.9	18.4	18.0
Jains	10.3	11.5	10.6
Buddhists	13.2	15.2	14.4
Sikhs	11.2	13.4	12.8
Christian	11.2	14.6	13.5
Muslims	16.1	20.2	18.7
Hindus	12.5	16.7	15.6
All religions	**13.1**	**17.0**	**15.9**

Jain population has a very high female literacy. Their high concentration in urban areas and ascetic beliefs, and a high female literacy level presumably led to the lowest overall proportion of child population. In several districts this proportion was well below 10 percent. The Sikh population also showed a similar trend and their fertility level appears to be lower than that of other religious groups, except the Jains. Muslims, on the other hand, has higher proportion of children in age 0–6. This possibly has a correlate in their lower female literacy rate and their high concentration in rural areas. The past legacy of low female Muslim literacy, which is also true for the Scheduled Castes and the Scheduled Tribes, may have a decisive role in slowing down the pace of fertility decline.

At the state level, proportion of population in the age group 0–6 among Hindus is highest in Bihar and Rajasthan, both around 20 percent, and the lowest in Kerala at 10.8 percent.

Among the Muslims, Haryana has the highest proportion of population in the age group 0–6 (24.5%). Eight states, namely Uttaranchal, Haryana, Rajasthan, Uttar Pradesh, Bihar, Jharkhand, Assam and Meghalaya, have more than 20 percent child population among Muslims. Muslims in Tamil Nadu among the larger states have the lowest proportion of children (12.9%).

Among the major states Orissa has maximum child population (17.8%) while Maharashtra has the lowest (10.3%) among Christians.

21 states and Union Territories have child population proportion below 12 percent among Sikhs. Of these, nine states have returned less than 10 percent child population. Sikhs in Rajasthan recorded the highest proportion of child population (15.1%).

Jains have very low proportion of population in the age group 0–6. Among the major states, Jains have the highest proportion of children (12%) in Karnataka, and lowest in Gujarat, 9.2 percent.

Low fertility trend among the Jains is evident from the fact that except for two states, all others returned proportion of child populations below 14 percent.

Mizoram has returned the highest proportion of child population among Buddhists (20.5%) followed by Uttar Pradesh (19.9%). In Maharashtra the Buddhists have child population of 14.1 percent while that in Jammu & Kashmir is still low, 11.7 percent.

Among the major states, Tamil Nadu has a distinct and secular fertility pattern as none of the religious communities have more than 13 percent population in the age group 0–6 years and the range varies from a low of 10.4 percent among Sikhs to 12.9 percent among Muslims.

4.6.5 Literacy Rate

There are only a few states/UTs like Kerala, Pondicherry, Lakshadweep (all above 80%) and Andaman & Nicober Islands (above 70%) where literacy is generally high for all religious communities. Literacy rates in Bihar, Uttar Pradesh and Jharkhand for Hindus, Muslims and others are well below 60 percent. However, religion effects on literacy in most other states/UTs appear weak. Literacy seems to be functionally related to the general development level of the states/UTs rather than to the religious divide in the population.

Jains have the highest literacy rate (94.1%), followed by Christians (80.3%), Buddhists (72.7%) and Sikhs (69.4%). Hindus have a marginally higher literacy rate (65.1%) compared to the national average (64.8%). Muslims are way behind (59.1%) these four religious groups in literacy rates. Bihar has more Hindu illiterates than literates (47.9%).

Table 4.25

Literacy rates in the population by sex, residence and religion, India 2001

Residence	*Indians*			*Hindus*			*Muslims*			*Christians*		
	P	*M*	*F*	*P*	*M*	*F*	*P*	*M*	*F*	*P*	*M*	*F*
Total	64.8	75.3	53.7	65.1	76.2	53.2	59.1	67.6	50.1	80.2	84.4	76.2
Rural	58.7	70.7	46.1	59.1	71.7	45.7	52.7	62.3	42.7	74.6	79.5	69.7
Urban	79.9	86.3	72.9	81.3	87.9	73.9	70.1	76.3	63.2	90.9	93.6	88.3
	Sikhs			*Buddhists*			*Jains*			*Others*		
Total	69.4	75.2	63.1	72.7	83.1	61.7	94.1	97.4	90.6	47.0	60.8	33.2
Rural	64.2	70.6	57.2	66.9	78.8	54.6	87.5	94.2	80.3	43.9	58.2	29.5
Urban	83.6	87.5	79.2	81.6	89.8	72.9	96.1	98.4	93.8	75.3	83.8	66.5

Lakshadweep, where Hindus are a minority, has returned the highest literacy rate of 96.4 percent. Among the larger states, Kerala has the highest proportion of Hindu literates, over 90 percent. 7 states/UTs have returned over 80 percent literacy among Hindus. Among the major and more developed states, Karnataka and Gujarat have returned Hindu literacy rate only a little above the national average. 15 states/UTs have recorded 75 percent of Hindus as literates. 10 states/UTs have recorded Hindu literacy rate below the national average. Bihar has the lowest literacy rate among Hindus, 47.9 percent.

16 states/UTs have returned less literacy rates for Muslims than their national average (59.1%). Haryana has the lowest literacy rate among the Muslims (40%). Highest literacy rate among Muslims has been recorded in Andaman & Nicobar Islands (89.8%) closely followed by Kerala at 89.4 percent. There are 13 other states/UTs that have Muslim literacy rates over 70 percent. It is unfortunate that a predominantly Muslim state like Jammu & Kashmir has Muslim literacy rate below 50 percent.

Literacy rate among Christians is generally very good. 21 states/UTs have returned their literacy rates well above 75 percent; 19 of these have literacy rates higher than their national average (80.3%). Among the larger states Christians in Kerala and Maharashtra have literacy rates over 90 percent. Arunachal is the only state where Christian's literacy rate is below 50 percent.

32 states/UTs have recorded 70 percent or more literacy rates among the Sikhs. In as many as 13 of these states/UTs their literacy rate is as high as 90 percent or more. Surprisingly, Punjab, the home state of the Sikhs (over 70% of the population are Sikhs) has a poor record of literacy rate, 67.3 percent, even less than their national average of 69.4 percent.

The national literacy rate of Buddhists is 72.3 percent and as many as 16 states/UTs are above this mark. 5 states/UT's scoring above 90 percent level while another 5 are between 80 and 90 percent. Maharashtra has the highest Buddhist population in the country. Buddhists in the state have a literacy rate of 76.2 percent. The lowest Buddhist literacy rate was recorded at 44.9 percent in Arunachal Pradesh, the state with almost one-fourth of its population returning as Buddhist.

Jains have the highest literacy rate in the country (94.1%) also the highest male (97.4%) and female literacy (90.1%) rates. 29 states/UTs have literacy rates among Jains over 90 percent. It may be noted that the Jain population is urban-centric and most of them are engaged in business, industry and commerce. A very high proportion of them are professionals. Christians too have high literacy rates at the national level, 84.4 percent for males and 76.2 percent for females.

20 states/UTs recorded Hindu female literacy rates between 60 and 80 percent. The states like Bihar, Jharkhand, Uttar Pradesh, Rajasthan and Andhra Pradesh have Hindu female literacy rate below 50 percent.

Kerala has highest female literacy among Muslims at 89.5 percent. Haryana has returned the lowest Muslim female literacy rate at 21.5 percent preceded by Bihar (33%). In 15 states/UTs, Muslim female literacy rate is less than 50 percent; in 14 others it is above 60 percent.

The largest gap between male and female literacy at the national level is observed with Hindus (23 percentage points) followed by Buddhists (21.4) and Muslims (17.5). Gender gap is least among Jains, and that too at a very high level of literacy.

4.6.6 Work Participation Rate (WPR)

Work Participation Rate or percentage of workers to total population of India was recorded at 39.1 percent in the 2001 Census. The 'persons' column (P) in Table 4.26 refers to the proportion of persons for the religious group in the total work force, while entries under M (Male) and F (Female) refer to proportion in the work force to their *own population totals*. It is the 'Others' group that have recorded the highest WPR of 48.4 percent (although their share in the Indian work force is a meager 0.31%) followed by the Buddhist at 40.6, Hindus at 40.4 and Christians at 39.7 percent. Muslims have the lowest WPR, 31.3 percent at the national level preceded by Jains at 32.9 percent and Sikhs at 37.7 percent. Smaller presence of females in non-agricultural activity keeps the WPRs of women low in urban areas.

Table 4.26

WPR for different religious groups by sex and residence, India 2001

	Indians			*Hindus*			*Muslims*			*Christians*		
	P	*M*	*F*	*P*	*M*	*F*	*P*	*M*	*F*	*P*	*M*	*F*
Total	39.1	51.7	25.6	32.5	52.4	27.5	4.21	47.5	14.1	0.93	50.7	28.7
Rural	30.1	52.1	30.8	25.5	52.7	32.6	2.83	47.4	17.5	0.65	51.3	32.6
Urban	8.97	50.6	11.9	6.94	51.3	12.5	1.38	47.6	7.74	0.28	49.6	21.2
	Shikhs			*Buddhists*			*Jains*			*Others*		
Total	0.7	53.3	20.2	0.31	49.2	31.7	0.14	55.2	9.2	0.31	52.5	44.2
Rural	0.55	54.2	23.9	0.22	51.3	42.2	0.04	56.4	20.1	0.29	53.5	46.8
Urban	0.16	50.8	9.96	0.09	45.7	14.8	0.1	54.8	5.79	0.02	43.3	19.7

Among the Hindus, 15 states/UTs have WPR below 40 percent. The highest WPR for Hindus, over 60 percent, was from Mizoram and Lakshadweep. At the state level, 8 states/UTs have registered more than 50 percent WPR for Sikhs. Low WPR, less than 35 percent, was recorded in 23 states/UTs for Jains and 22 states/UTs returned low WPR for Muslims. In fact, WPR is less than 30 percent in 8 states/UTs, lowest around 23 percent for Lakshadweep and Kerala. In Sikkim and Mizoram, Muslim WPR is more than 50 percent. Interestingly, Lakshadweep has very high WPR, almost cent percent among Sikhs, Buddhist and more than 70 percent WPR among Hindus and Christians whereas the predominant religious group Muslims in the UT has the lowest WPR, only 23 percent. WPR among different states/UTs by different religious affiliations of persons especially in smaller states and UTs indicate that religious communities, which have higher WPR, are usually those that have smaller population share (but more male populations), indicating their migratory status.

The distinct feature of dominant male WPR among all religious communities is brought out sharply in these statements. Male WPR is highest among Jains, 55.2 percent, followed by Sikhs, 53.3 percent, and Hindus, 52.4 percent (Table 4.26). The lowest WPR for the male population is among the Muslims, which is also a healthy 47.5 percent. The female WPR on the other hand does not present a similar pattern across different religious communities. Female WPR was highest among 'Others', 44.2 percent, followed by Buddhists 31.7 percent and Christians 28.7 percent. The lowest female WPR was recorded among Jains, only 9.2 percent preceded by Muslims 14.1 percent. 27.5 percent of Hindu and 20.2 percent Sikh females had been reported as workers. In other words, whereas the gap between the male WPR at the national level was about 7 percentage points between the lowest and highest percent points among different religious groups, the same for the female WPR was as high as 35 percentage points (between 'Others' and Jains). Even among the major religions, the gap often was quite sharp.

The cross-tabs (see Appendix 7.1) present proportions of workers by four broad categories: cultivators, agricultural laborers, household industry workers and other workers by religious communities and by state/UTs. At the national level percentage of cultivators is highest at 49.9 percent among 'Others'. Of the six major religious groups, 33.1 percent of the Hindu workers are cultivators, followed by 32.4 percent of Sikhs and 29.2 percent of Christians. Only 20 percent of Muslims are engaged in cultivation. The same among the Jains is only 11.7 percent.

At the aggregate level, 26.5 percent of workers were Agricultural laborers (AL). Buddhists with 37.6 percent have most of their working population as AL followed by 'Others' with 32.6 percent and Hindus 27.6 percent. On the other hand 22.1 percent workers among Muslims, 16.8 percent among Sikhs, 15.8 percent among Christians, and only 3.3 percent among Jains are recorded in the category AL. All the last four proportions fell short of the national average. 82.5 percent workers among the 'Others' were engaged in agricultural activities either as cultivators or as agricultural laborers, followed by Hindus (60.7%) and Buddhists (58%).

8.1 percent of Muslim workers are in Household Industry (HHI), which is almost double the national average of 4.2 percent. 3.8 percent workers among Hindus, around 3 percent among Sikhs as well as Jains are in this category. Christian and Buddhist workers constituted 2.7 percent and 2.9 percent respectively as HHI in the 2001 Census return.

Earlier, workers were classified into 9 work categories. In 2001 Census, all those categories in the tertiary sector, namely Mining, Quarrying, Forestry, Plantation, etc., Manufacturing other than HHI, Construction, Trade and Commerce, Transport, Storage and Communication and other Services have been brought under one single category – Other Workers (OW). This really makes comparison between different census results difficult. There has been a shift in dominance from the traditional occupations to more hi tech occupations, especially in the manufacturing and service sectors. From around 68.4 percent of all workers engaged in the agriculture sector in 1981, the proportion has come down to 58.2 percent in 2001. In the same period, workers in the six categories clubbed into a single category OW have gone up from 33.6 percent to 37.6 percent.

For Jains, 81.7 percent workers are classified as OW, followed by 52.8 percent of Christians, 49.1 percent of Muslims. 35.5 percent of Hindu workers. Christians, Buddhists and Sikhs are behind Muslims but ahead of Hindus in the OW category of workers.

4.6.7 Fertility Differential

The differential growth rate among the religious communities, especially between Hindus and Muslims, has become a contentious issue among some political parties in India in recent times. Some political outfit even suggested that Hindus must adopt a 3-child norm instead of a 2-child norm currently advocated. Their fear that the Muslims in India have an agenda different from that in the mainstream population may not be totally unfounded.[1] The fertility rate of Muslim women is considerably higher than that of Hindu women. The National Family Health Survey (NFHS, 1998–99), shows that for India as a whole, TFR was 2.8 for Hindus and 3.6 for Muslims. The following tables are adapted from the NCAER Survey, 1994 conducted on a sample of 35,130 households spread over 1,765 villages and 195 districts in 16 States.

There is considerable difference between Hinduism and Islam in respect to the role of sons and daughters. The preference for sons compared to daughters in classical Hinduism is well documented in Hindu scriptures. The Hindu scriptures mainly see woman only in relation to the man, and give her an 'equal', 'exalted' position, as only a 'helpmate' within marriage and the family. The Mysore Population Study described one of the traditional Vedic blessings for married women popularly used in Karnataka 'May she bear ten sons, and make of her husband an eleventh!' which is also a good example of son-preference in Hindu society.

1. Average number of children per women in many Islamic countries (Iran, Algeria, Egypt, Indonesia, Bangladesh, etc.) has been brought down from 7–8 to around 3. The national government and many NGOs toiled hard to popularize birth planning in these countries. 'Islam is averse to birth control' is not really supported by Islamic literature. Only very recently a very influential and respected member of the Muslim Law Board (India) has advised the Muslims to take advantage of the scientific methods for birth control to ensure better care, health and education of their children.

Table 4.27

Fertility rates by population groups by religion in rural India

Social groups	CBR	TFR	Av. no. of children ever born to ever married women		
			Boys	Girls	Total
Religion					
Hindus	32	4.2	1.5	1.3	2.8
Muslims	39	5.8	1.8	1.5	3.4
Christians	20	2.1	1.2	1.1	2.4
Other minorities	28	3.9	1.6	1.4	3.0
Caste groups					
Scheduled Castes	35	4.7	1.6	1.4	2.9
Schedules Tribes	35	4.4	1.6	1.4	3.0

Source: NCAER Survey, India Human Development Report, 1999

Table 4.28

Contraception prevalence rate for ever married women (EMW) by population groups

Social groups	Termination method		Spacing method		% EMW using methods
	% EMW users	Vasectomy % to all	% EMW users	Loop/CopT % to all	
Religion					
Hindus	31.4	8.2	4.9	29.2	36.3
Muslims	16.5	7.4	8.2	18.7	24.7
Christians	35.1	11.1	13.0	33.3	48.1
Other minorities	32.7	12.6	13.7	38.9	46.5
Caste groups					
Scheduled Castes	29.5	13.5	4.4	36.5	33.9
Scheduled Tribes	26.7	9.6	4.7	19.1	31.4

Source: NCAER Survey, India Human Development Report, 1999.

Son-preference is also evident in Islamic society, which gives men a more prominent place than women within the family. Under Islamic law, sons are given twice as large an inheritance as daughters and a man's testimony in court is worth twice that of a woman. A feature of Muslim societies is that Muslim women gain respect and status when they marry and have children, thereby improving their bargaining position in the social structure (Youssef, 1978). Since women derive status from motherhood, even when divorced or rejected for a second wife, children represent a form of social insurance against the threat of divorce or polygamy.

The NCAER Survey fails to bring out any significant difference in 'son preference' between Hindus and Muslims, or for that matter any difference between the religious and caste groups though the survey clearly indicates that there is wide variation in TFR and average number of children born to women of various social groups. Muslim women are seen to reproduce more liberally than all other religious and caste groups. That they are more averse to birth control is also documented in the survey. The intensity of differences between Hindus and Muslims could be eased only a little in the national populations even though the proportion of Muslims living in urban areas (35.7% of the total Muslim population) are ahead of the Hindus living in urban areas (26.7% of all Hindus). There is not much difference in literacy rates of females between the two religious communities. Therefore, the difference in observed fertility rates of Hindus and Muslims may have something to do with the latter's aversion to embrace contraception to limit the family size.

5
Literacy in India

5.1 Introduction

Education is the central most acquired characteristic that helps bring personal endowments to an operative level and consolidate one's capabilities. The expansion of the knowledge-base through education provides one to look for logical alternatives in the face of constraints, widens choices and opportunities for leading a decent life. At the state or national level, it is a means to boost human capital and productivity and enthuse sentiment of 'oneness' among the masses so that a durable integration of people from all walks of life becomes possible. It is the single most important and critical investment, both for a family and for a nation is demonstrated by the fact that health and hygiene status of the population, especially children and mother, reproductive health care, infant and child mortality, empowerment of women, ease in adoption of new technologies and freedom from social and political dogma, improved productivity in agriculture and in all other sectors and many other aspects relating personal and national development have perceptible linkages with educational attainments.

UNDP studies show that productivity of a farmer, who has only four years of elementary education, is 8.5 percent higher than that of an average farmer with no education at all. Even in India "green revolution" started with educated farmers. In industry at enterprise level educated workers are more productive. Studies conducted on African countries have shown that the estimated rate of return on primary education (26%) is twice as high as the return from investment on higher education. Education also brings down inequality. Studies at international level have proved that one-fifth of income inequality can be explained by education alone. The studies also confirm that the poorer countries tend to gain higher rates of return than rich countries from investment in education. In India, the returns are somewhat different from those observed in African countries. Here the return increases as the level of education increases up to the secondary level. It is also observed that returns to women education far exceed that of men at middle and higher levels. Between 1983 and 1994, the return to women's education for primary and middle level declined; in the same period there was substantial return for secondary and college level education of girls.

5.2 Progress of Education in India

Under the British rule, progress of education in India was at a low key for various reasons. Formal education in India was initiated early in the nineteenth century. The British rulers wanted to make some Indians conversant with English to use them more effectively in administration. Formal education however remained confined to people living in big cities. They never thought of extending it to smaller towns and villages. Some educationists and social reformers (both Indian and English) decided to take education to masses even without any government support. However, both governmental and non-governmental programs could not get much headway due primarily to two reasons –

(1) very high child mortality and morbidity rates, and (2) masses' lack of conviction about utility of education in their everyday life.

If 1921 was to be regarded as the "Great Demographic Divide in India", then 1951 could be regarded as a "Divider" for progress in many areas including education. It was since 1951 that education in India gained some momentum, which it lacked under colonial rule. Directive Principles of the Constitution of India asks the state to provide free and compulsory education for all children until they complete fourteen years of age. To develop an educational policy, Commissions were appointed; opinions of public and educationists were solicited time and again. By amendment of the Constitution in 1976, education was brought in the Concurrent list (list of subjects for which the center and the states assume joint responsibility). This was an important step that called for a new sharing of responsibility between the union government and the states in this vital area. In 1985, the central government published a small book: *Challenge of Education: A policy Prescription*, and invited suggestions, comments and alternative proposals from educationists and social activists. The booklet tried to give a picture of the nature of growth in education in post-independence period. The National Policy on Education 1986 emphasized that the new thrust in elementary education will be on (i) universal access and enrolment, (ii) universal retention of children up to fourteen years of age, and (iii) a substantial improvement in the quality of education to enable all children to achieve essential levels of learning. The literacy rates obtained at the subsequent censuses and other parameters relating to spread of education give an account of the implementation part of government policies and programs. In the fast changing global market economy, no civil society can prosper without paying adequate emphasis on modernization of agricultural sector, adoption of capital-intensive industrialization, efficient communication and transport system, e-governance in administration, trade and commerce and urbanization. Education forms the most important input to one and all to appreciate the nature of changes occurring beyond the confines of one's immediate neighborhood and social milieu. The social, cultural and political environment of a nation undergoes certain irreversible changes. Only a knowledgeable person can take lessons from our previous mistakes and inefficiencies in some of the traditional systems and can develop a vision as to how to improve the quality of life by utilizing the scientific and technological innovations and discoveries. Education therefore is the most important investment in human capital.

The decades 1960 and 1970 were most ominous in India's socio-economic aspirations. Indian economy was severely damaged by three wars – with China in 1962, Pakistan in 1965 and its repeat in 1971 in the Bangladesh liberation war. India was facing a near famine situation in mid-sixties and had to import huge quantity of food grain from USA and other countries. After the death of Jawaharlal Nehru, the first Prime Minister of India, and the untimely death of Lal Bahadur Shastri who succeeded Nehru as Prime Minister, there was huge internal strife within the Congress party for the top executive position in the government. The economy as a whole, and social welfare schemes in particular, suffered.

Huge commitment for setting up heavy industries, the three wars, huge import bill for petroleum (and food grains at some points of time) and the political unrest slowed down some of our social and economic reforms programs. Added to this was the enormous growth of population in the fifties and sixties, which almost continued in the next decade in spite of draconian revision of the Constitution, curtailing the power of judiciary and taking administrative steps to force people to undergo sterilization during Internal Emergency declared by Mrs Indira Gandhi, the then Prime

Minister. Congress was thrown out in the next general election. Many reform activities (especially in family planning) became the casualty in the tussle for power between the key personalities within Janata Dal who came to power in 1977. Things started looking better since the eighties. After the assassination of Mrs Indira Gandhi, Rajiv Gandhi took over the legacy. It was during his premiership that the economic reform in the country was initiated, which found a desired shape at the hand of Dr Manmohan Singh, the Finance Minister in P.V.Narshima Rao's cabinet. The National Education Policy, 1986 sent a message about what India wants to do in expanding the population base of literate persons and improving the quality of education at all levels.

Information on education are gathered of every individual in all censuses. A person in the age group 7 years and above is treated as literate in census enumeration, if he/she can *both read and write* with understanding in any language. Prior to 1991 Census, children below five years of age were treated as illiterates. Several studies conducted by NCERT and other bodies have established that the ability to read and write with understanding is not ordinarily achieved until one had some schooling or at least some time to develop these skills. Literacy with retention, especially in rural areas, is likely to be achieved when the child is 7 years or more old. A child in an urban environment starts his formal and informal schooling much early. The environment provides the child with various inputs to become more knowledgeable than his counterparts in a village. She/he may become 'literate' even before attaining the age of literacy. However, keeping the larger canvas in mind, it was decided in the 1991 Census that all children in the age group 0–6, will be treated as illiterate by definition and the population aged seven years and above only is to be classified as literate and illiterate. The same criterion has been followed in the 2001 Census as well. It is not mandatory that to be treated as literate, a person should have received *any formal education or acquired any minimum educational standard.* A congenital blind person would be treated as literate if she/he can read and write in Braille.

5.2.1 Literacy Rate

Till 1981, literacy rate was calculated on the basis of proportion of literate persons aged 5 years and above to the total population of the country or state or some specific group. Since 1991 both numerator and denominator in the calculation of the proportion have been changed. The numerator now refers to 'literates in 7 years and above ages', while the denominator contains the 'entire population of 7 years and above'. To distinguish between the two indexes of literacy, the old literacy rate is referred to as "Crude Literacy Rate" and the one calculated since 1991 as "Literacy Rate".

$$\text{Crude Literacy Rate} = \frac{\text{Number of literate persons aged 5 years and above}}{\text{Total number of persons in the population}} \times 100$$

$$\text{Literacy Rate} = \frac{\text{Number of literate persons aged 7 years and above}}{\text{Total number of persons in 7 years and above in the population}} \times 100$$

The change in the literacy rates in India between 1901 and 2001 is presented in Table 5.1.

There was only a marginal increase in literacy between 1901 and 1931; an increase only by 4.15 percentage points in 30 years. The increase in literacy rate between 1941 and 1951 is barely perceptible. By the time India achieved independence, only 16.67 percent of the total population was literate, that is, an increase by only 7.17 percentage points in the two decades prior to independence.

Table 5.1
Literacy rate[1] in India by sex, 1901–2001

Year	Crude literacy rate[2]				Literacy rate[3]			
	Persons	*Males*	*Females*	*M–F*	*Persons*	*Males*	*Females*	*M–F*
1901	5.35	9.83	0.60	9.23				
1911	5.92	10.56	1.05	9.51				
1921	7.16	12.21	1.81	10.40				
1931	9.50	15.59	2.93	12.63				
1941	16.10	24.90	7.30	17.60				
1951[4]	16.67	24.95	7.93	17.02	18.33	27.16	8.86	18.30
1961[4]	24.02	34.44	12.95	21.49	28.30	40.40	15.35	25.05
1971[4]	29.45	39.45	18.69	20.76	34.45	45.96	21.97	23.98
1981[5]	36.23	46.89	24.82	22.07	43.57	56.38	29.76	26.62
1991[5]	42.84	52.74	32.17	20.57	52.21	64.13	39.29	24.84
2001[5]	55.30	64.13	45.84	18.29	65.38	75.85	54.16	21.70

Notes: 1. Data for 1901–31 is for undivided India.
2. The entire population is put in the denominator
3. The population in ages 7 and above is put in the denominator
4. Literacy rates for 1951, 1961 and 1971 are for persons aged 5 years and above
5. Literacy rates for 1981, 1991 and 2001 are for persons aged 7 years and above

Table 5.2
Revised estimates of literacy rates after modification of the definition of literacy rate, India 1951–2001(percentage)

Census year	Persons	Males	Females	Decadal growth		
				Persons	*Males*	*Females*
1951	18.33 (16.67)	27.16 (24.95)	8.86 (7.93)			
1961	28.31 (24.02)	40.40 (34.44)	15.24 (12.95)	9.98	13.24	6.38
1971	34.45 (29.45)	45.95 (39.45)	21.97 (18.69)	6.14	5.55	6.73
1981	43.56 (36.23)	56.37 (46.89)	29.75 (24.82)	9.11	10.42	7.78
Rural	36.01	49.59	21.70			
1991	52.11	63.86	39.42	8.55	7.49	9.67
Rural	44.69	57.87	30.62	8.68	8.28	8.92
2001	65.38	75.96	56.0	13.27	12.10	16.58
Rural	59.21	71.18	46.58	14.52	13.31	15.96
Urban	80.06	86.42	72.99			

Figures within parentheses indicate the rates were calculated on 5+ age group
Source: Census of India 1991 & 2001, National Human Development Report, 2002.

Figure 5.1
Growth of CLR in India by sex

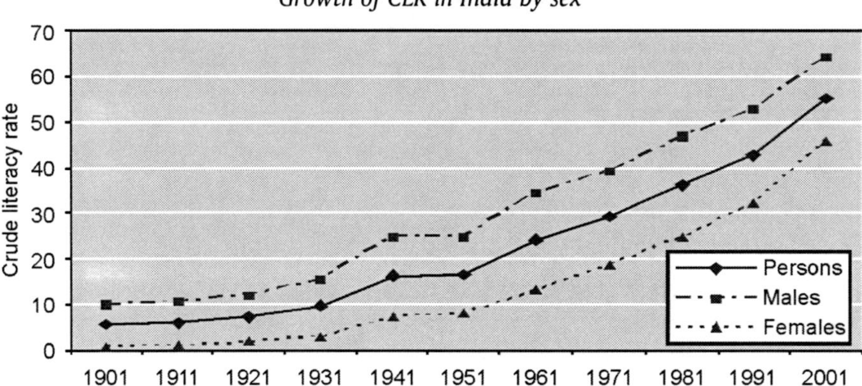

A rapid growth in CLR is observed in post-independence era. CLR crossed the 50 percent mark in 2001 Census. In the first 50 years of the last century the average annual growth of CLR was a meager 0.22 percent. In the 50 years thereafter the same grew by a healthy 0.77 percent per annum. There was an extraordinary jump between 1991 and 2001 – a decadal growth by 12.46 percentage points, the all-time high for any decade. Since the growth in terms of percentage points generally slows down as one approach the ceiling of 100 percent, the accelerated growth during 1991–2001 can be considered a great achievement. Another remarkable feature of the results on literacy in 2001 Census is that, for the first time, the absolute number of non-literates declined between 1991 and 2001. Between 1991 and 2001, while the number of literates increased by 203.6 million (that is, by 56.8%), the number of non-literates decreased by about 32 million (that is, by 9.7%). This many believe, is due to the policy initiative taken by the government of India in 1986. More significantly, this two-digit decadal growth has happened both with male and female populations.

UNESCO has remained actively associated with educational development and planning of 164 countries since 1990. They carry out regular survey with all these countries. UNESCO has set 2015 as the deadline for attaining 'education for all'. But their latest survey in 2007 clearly indicates that India, Pakistan and Bangladesh, which together have over 1,400 million populations today, could become the major road block for achieving the goal. Whereas India ranked 100 among these 164 countries in education front, the latest survey shows that it has dropped to 105th spot. It indicates clearly that whereas most other countries are gearing their machinery to achieve the 'millennium goal', India is failing in pursuing its goal. China, with current ranking at 62, is really miles ahead of India in literacy front. Even after India's Supreme Court judgment in 1992 declaring education as one of the fundamental rights, the executives have really done not much to honor this Apex Court verdict.

5.3 Differentials in Literacy Rates

It is a fact with every society that there is always a sectoral difference in adoption of an innovation. The more advanced sectors of the population are quick to adopt the innovation. Those sectors missing the bus may have to wait long enough to avail of the next opportunity. There would be a 'trickle down' effect to other sectors and this would gain in momentum when the government takes firm steps to spread the innovation to the masses. Since the early adopters would move fast to reach the summit, initial years or decades often would show the gap between the early adopters and late adopters widen. Once the late adopters gain in momentum, the gap would start to decline.

5.3.1 Change in Literacy Rate in India by State, Sex, Religion and Residence

Female literacy at the beginning of the last century (4th Census in India) was close to zero. In hundred years the female CLR is 46 percent (LR 54). The gap between male and female CLR increased to 22.07 percentage point (26.62 by revised definition) in 1981; a steady decline in the gap is noticed thereafter. The closing of the gap between male and female literacy rate is definitely due to the initiative taken by the governments and other agencies in creating more opportunities to attract girls into the formal schooling system as also due to the fact that male literacy in India has already reached a point any improvement from where is bound to be slow. It was only in the last two decades (1981–2001) that the growth rate of female CLR overtook the CLR of males. The male CLR moved upward by 17.24 percentage points as against female's 21.02 percentage points between 1981 and 2001. Since the national and state governments are working hard for empowerment of women in every walk of life, the gap between male and female CLRs is likely to drop faster in the coming decades. With 1951 as the base year, growth of CLR for women is an encouraging 478 percent; for males and for the total population respectively these are 157 and 232 percent. Another interesting observation from the Table 5.2 is that female CLR in 1951 was roughly 25 years behind the national average. In 2001, female CLR is well ahead of the national CLR recorded just 10 years back.

Table 5.3

Literacy rate by sex and residence in the mainstream population (7+ age) and in scheduled castes and scheduled tribes populations

	1981			*1991*			*2001*		
	M	*F*	*P*	*M*	*F*	*P*	*M*	*F*	*P*
Total	56.38	29.76	43.57	64.13	39.29	52.21	75.64	54.03	65.20
Rural	49.59	21.70	36.01	57.87	30.62	44.69	71.18	46.58	59.21
Urban			68			73	86.42	72.99	80.06
M-F gap	26.62			24.84			21.61		
R-U gap			32			28.3			20.9
SCs	31.12	10.93	21.38	49.91	23.76	37.41			
STs	24.52	8.04	16.35	40.65	18.10	29.60			

Figure 5.2

Literacy rates (7+ age) in India, 1981–2001

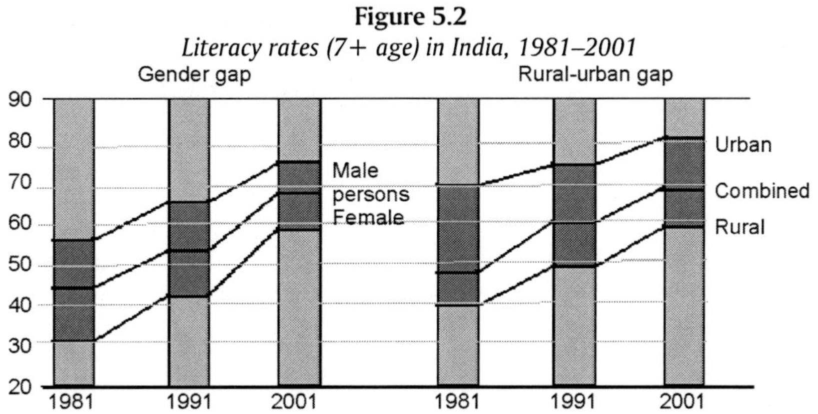

With the change in definition of literacy rate in 1991, the literacy rate in India looks a healthy 65.38 with males attaining the level of 75.85 and females, 54.16 in 2001. But this apparently fair achievement is overshadowed by the fact that the population of illiterates in 2001 was over 296 million, only about 50 million short of the total population of India in the 1951 census. That is, in the last 5 decades India still has almost the same number of illiterates as there were persons around 1947. In spite of the good performance in literacy in 1991–2001, the absolute number of illiterates could be brought down only by about 32 million from 328 million recorded in 1991 Census. The gender gap too has come down slightly compared to what it was in 1981 and 1991. The difference between the literacy rate of males and females of age 7+ was 26.62 in 1981; it dropped to 24.84 in 1991 and then to 21.70 in 2001.

There has been substantial improvement in literacy rate of females in the last two decades; it increased from 29.76 in 1981 to 54.16 in 2001, whereas the literacy rate of males increased from 56.38 in 1981 to 75.85 in 2001. However this good achievement is considerably spoiled by the fact that the number of illiterates in the population is still huge and the gender gap in literacy by absolute number is still increasing in spite of higher literacy growth rate of females (14.9% for females compared to 11.7% of males between 1991 and 2001).

Table 5.4

Absolute changes in literates and non-literates between 1991 and 2001

Literates/non-literates	*Persons*	*Males*	*Females*	*Gender gap M-F*
1	*2*	*3*	*4*	*5*
Literate				
1991	358,402,626	228,983,134	129,419,492	99563642
2001	562,010,743	336,969,695	225,041,048	111928647
Increase in 2001 over 1991	203,608,117	107,986,561	95,621,556	
Percent increase	56.8	47.2	73.9	
Non-literate				
1991	328,167,288	128,099,211	200,068,077	–71968866
2001	296,208,952	106,654,066	189,554,886	–82900820
Increase in 2001 over 1991	–31,958,336	–21,445,145	–10,513,191	
Percentage increase	–9.8	–16.8	–5.2	

Note:
1. To make the data comparable for the years 1991 and 2001, the figures for Jammu & Kashmir have not been included in both the years as no census in 1991 was conducted in the state due to disturbed conditions.
2. To make the data comparable the figures of literates and illiterates shown against 1991 and 2001 do not include the figures for entire district of Kachchh, Morvi, Maliya-Miyana and Wankaner talukas of Rajkot district, Jodiya taluka of Jamnagar district of Gujarat state and entire Kinnaur district of Himachal Pradesh where population enumeration in 2001 could not be conducted due to natural calamities

We need to take a closer look at the changes in absolute numbers to understand their likely impact on the future literacy trends in the country. Of the 836,650,839 persons recorded in the 1991 Census, as many as 686,569,914 persons (roughly the size of entire population of India in 1981) were aged seven years and above. Out of these, 358,402,626 were literate and 328,167,288 illiterates. The 2001 Census returned 858,219,695 (which is roughly of the same size of the entire population of India in 1991) persons as aged 7 years and above; 562,010,743 out of these are literates and 296,208,952 illiterates. There has been an increase of 171,649,781 persons in the age group 7 years and above during 1991–2001, while 203,608,117 additional persons have become literate during the decade. It means India has succeeded in clearing some of its backlogs in illiteracy in 1991–2001. The significant milestone reached in Census 2001 is that for the first time since independence, there is a decline in the absolute number of illiterates during a decade. This is a major shift in improvement rate in literacy status in India. The Census commissioner went on to hail this achievement and proposed to label 1991–2001 as the 'Literacy Decade'. He earnestly hoped that this trend could be made irreversible from now onwards. 53 percent of addition of the total number of literates in 1991–2001 came from males and the rest from females, a ratio closely similar to the ratio of male and female in the population.

It is a fact that the growth of literacy rate of females (14.9 points) was higher than that of males (11.7 points) between 1991 and 2001. But this aggregate statistic hides the fact that between 1991 and 2001, the increase in the absolute number of literate males far exceeded the increase in the number of literate females. While the number of literate males increased by 108.0 million in this decade, the corresponding increase in the number of literate females was by 95.6 million, which is 88.5 percent of the former. Since there were over 200 million illiterate females of age 7+ as against about 128 million illiterate males in 1991, the gap was too large to bridge. The 72 million gap has widened to 83 million by 2001. While the number of illiterate females decreased by 10.5 million, the number of male illiterates decreased by twice this number in the same period.

The reason for relatively slower rate of reduction of the number of illiterate females, partly at least, can be traced to the difference in enrolment ratios and dropout rates for boys and girls at the elementary school stage. According to the National Family Health Survey (NFHS 2), 85.2 percent boys and 78.3 percent girls in the age group 6–10 were attending schools in 1998–99. The same survey also found that while the median number of years of schooling was 5.5 for males in age 6 years and above, it was only 1.6 for females in the same age group. Ministry of HRD reported that among the total number of students enrolled in classes I–V in 1999–2000, only 43.6 percent were girls. Gross Enrolment Ratio was 104.1 for boys and 85.2 for girls. The drop out rate for girls also was a little higher, 42.3 percent against 38.7 percent of boys in classes between I and V.

That there has been an all round improvement in literacy, would be borne by the literacy rates attained by different age groups (Table 5.5) between 1961 and 1998–99. Literacy rate in all the age groups has almost doubled in the last 40 years. It has gained considerable momentum in the last two decades. The reason for higher decadal literacy growth rate in the younger age groups is obvious. It is the population in these age groups who benefited most from the initiative taken in the last two decades to fulfil the Constitutional pledge for free education for all below the age 15.

Table 5.6 gives population aged 7 and above and the absolute number of literates in 1991, and their absolute decadal and percentage difference between 1991 and 2001 for the states/UTs. The percentage decadal growth in population aged 7 years and above during 1991–2001 is 25.0 while the corresponding increase in the number of literates in this age group is 56.81 percent. Office of the Registrar General (1996) projected the population of those who attained age 7 years and above since 1991 Census at 239.81 million. The actual increase in number of literates between 1991 and 2001 (excluding Jammu & Kashmir) is 203.61 million, well short of the estimated figure. These figures suggest that a majority (about 85%) of children who attained age seven years and above after 1991 attended school at one point of time or other. This however can be confirmed only after age break-up of children attending schools becomes available.

Table 5.5
Literacy rates in different age groups, 1961–1998-99

Age group	*1961*	*1971*	*1981*	*1991*	*NFHS–2 1998–99*
10–14	42.3	49.6	56.3	68.5	81.8
15–19	38.4	51.3	55.5	65.7	76.9
20–24	33.6	44.7	52.0	57.9	67.0 a
25–34	28.5	34.8	45.0	50.9	56.9 b
35+	22.2	25.2	30.3	38.0	45.2 c
15+	27.8	34.1	40.9	48.2	58.6

(a) age group 20–29, (b) age group 30–39 and (c) age group 40 & above

Table 5.6
Decadal change in population aged 7 years and above and the number of literates, India 1991–2001

*State/Union Territories**	*Population aged 7 + in 1991*	*Decadal difference in population aged 7 + 1991–2001*	*% decadal difference in 7+ population 1991–2001*	*Number of literates 1991–2001*	*Decadal difference in number of literates 1991–2001*	*% decadal difference of literates 1991–2001*
1	*2*	*3*	*4*	*5*	*6*	*7*
INDIA[1,2]	**686,569,914**	**171,649,781**	**25.00**	**358,402,626**	**203,608,117**	**56.81**
Jammu & Kashmir	NA	NA	NA	NA	NA	NA
H'chal P'desh[3]	4,270,662	953,212	22.32	2,730,512	1,298,585	47.56
Punjab	16,975,724	4,258,080	25.08	9,932,116	4,921,694	49.55
Chandigarh*	546,245	245,376	44.92	425,060	222,148	52.26
Uttaranchal	1 5,809,288	1,350,881	23.25	3,354,695	1,820,481	54.27
Haryana	13,338,475	6 4,485,434	33.63	7,449,012	4,776,024	64.12
Delhi*	7,813,248	4,045,733	51.78	5,882,297	3,820,752	64.95
Rajasthan	35,146,498	10,875,521	30.94	13,549,088	14,537,013	107.29
Uttar Pradesh	105,103,376	30,477,441	29.00	42,789,501	34,980,774	81.75
Bihar	51,172,348	15,471,909	30.23	19,185,832	12,489,775	65.10
Sikkim	331,810	131,513	39.64	188,940	133,888	70.86
Ar'achal P'desh	681,933	209,129	30.67	283,610	204,186	72.00
Nagaland	,002,059	1706,405	70.50	617,736	528,787	85.60
Manipur	1,530,532	545,411	35.64	916,692	512,964	55.96
Mizoram	561,483	188,038	33.49	461,930	201,332	43.58
Tripura	2,260,083	504,073	22.30	1,365,980	670,179	49.06
Meghalaya	1,381,049	467,578	33.86	678,105	492,338	72.60

Cont'd...

Table 5.6 Cont'd...

1	*2*	*3*	*4*	*5*	*6*	*7*
Assam	17,992,811	4,295,348	23.87	9,516,393	4,811,147	50.56
West Bengal	56,515,668	12,572,679	22.25	32,609,397	15,212,360	46.65
Jharkhand	17,437,931	4,675,309	26.81	7,217,066	4,753,111	65.86
Orissa	26,312,235	5,214,134	19.82	12,915,917	7,137,868	55.26
Chhattisgarh	14,207,956	3,118,226	21.95	6,096,034	5,196,862	85.25
Madhya Pradesh	38,881,644	10,885,151	28.00	17,369,267	14,536,842	83.69
Gujarat[4]	32,946,120	8,573,192	26.02	20,284,486	8,765,533	43.21
Daman & Diu*	85,808	52,239	60.88	61,096	50,843	83.22
Dadra & N. Haveli*	110,140	71,138	64.59	44,834	63,996	142.74
Maharashtra	65,432,651	18,132,509	27.71	42,447,139	22,119,642	52.11
Andhra Pradesh	55,543,620	10,510,647	18.92	24,487,559	15,877,206	64.84
Karnataka	37,499,590	8,408,200	22.42	21,013,193	9,761,795	46.46
Goa	1,032,477	169,369	16.40	779,596	209,766	26.91
Lakshadweep*	42,243	9,492	22.47	34,548	10,733	31.07
Kerala	25,261,618	2,923,423	11.57	22,686,461	2,939,237	12.96
Tamil Nadu	48,410,887	6,882,283	14.22	30,336,235	10,288,163	33.91
Pondicherry*	697,390	163,429	23.43	521,213	180,234	34.58
A & N Islands*	234,312	77,279	32.98	171,086	81,859	47.85

Note:

1. For the sake of comparability the figures presented against India have been derived after excluding Jammu & Kashmir as the details for 1991 Census are not available since the Census of India 1991 could not be conducted in this state.
2. The figures shown against India exclude entire Kach district, Morvi, Maliya-Miyana and Wankaner talukas of Rajkot district, Jodiya taluka of Jamnagar district of Gujarat state and entire Kinnaur district of Himachal Pradesh where population enumeration in 2001, could not be conducted due to natural calamities.
3. For the sake of comparability the figures shown against Himachal Pradesh exclude figures of entire Kinnaur district where population enumeration in 2001, could not be conducted due to natural calamity.
4. For the sake of comparability the figures shown against Gujarat do not include entire Kach district, Morvi, Maliya-Miyana and Wankaner talukas of Rajkot district, Jodiya taluka of Jamnagar district of Gujarat where population enumeration in 2001, could not be conducted due to natural calamity.

N.A. stands for 'Not Available'.

There is a large variation among the states/UTs both in percentage decadal difference in 7 years and above population as well as in the percentage decadal difference in literacy between 1991 and 2001. Whereas the former varies from 11.57 percent (Kerala) to 70.50 percent (Nagaland), the latter shows very large variation among the states/UTs. Dadra and Nagar Haveli (142.74%) and Rajasthan (107.29%) have more than doubled their literacy in the decade under reference. A few other states that nearly doubled (80% or more) their literacy in the decade are Nagaland (85.60%), Chhattisgarh (85.25%), Madhya Pradesh (83.69%), Daman and Diu (83.22%) and Uttar Pradesh (81.75%). The states that were already advanced in literacy in 1991(Kerala, Lakshadweep, Mizoram, Goa for example), had very little to gain to improve upon their previous performances. Only 6 larger states contributed 76.91 percent toward the decrease in illiteracy between 1991 and 2001 (Andhra Pradesh

16.79%, Uttar Pradesh 14.09%, Maharashtra 12.48%, Rajasthan 11.46%, Madhya Pradesh 11.43% and Tamil Nadu 10.66%). These 6 states cover nearly half the population of India. Bihar on the other hand, is the only state among the larger ones where the number of illiterates increased from 31,986,516 in 1991 to 34,968,650 in 2001 (a difference of 2,982,134), negatively contributing by 9.33 percent to the kitty of literates. Unfortunately, in 7 states/UTs (Bihar, Delhi, Nagaland, Manipur, Chandigarh, Arunachal Pradesh and Dadra & Nagar Haveli) the absolute number of illiterates increased during the decade.

All the new states, Himachal Pradesh, Jharkhand and Chhattisgarh are ahead of the states from which they were carved out, in respect to both male and female literacy rates. Jharkhand and Chattishgarh, which are generally more backward, are the tribal parts of their mother states Bihar and Madhya Pradesh respectively; but it seems that in literacy they have benefited significantly from the educational programs of the missionaries as also by the initiatives taken by the respective state Departments of Tribal Welfare. Uttaranchal, comprised of hilly and tribal areas, though economically backward, is way ahead of Uttar Pradesh from which it was taken out, in the spread of education among its masses.

The literacy rate for different states/Union Territories and their respective ranks in 1991 and 2001 along with decadal growth is presented below.

Table 5.7

Sate literacy rates, 1991 and 2001

*State/UT**	*Literacy rate*		*Rank*		*Decadal difference in literacy rate*
	1991	*2001*	*1991*	*2001*	
1	*2*	*3*	*4*	*5*	*6*
INDIA	**52.21**	**65.38**			**13.17**
Jammu & Kashmir	N.A.	54.46	N.A.	33	—
Himachal Pradesh	63.94	77.13	11	11	13.19
Punjab	58.51	69.95	17	16	11.45
Chandigarh*	77.81	81.76	4	6	3.94
Uttaranchal	57.75	72.28	18	14	14.53
Haryana	55.85	68.59	22	20	12.74
Delhi*	75.29	81.82	6	5	6.53
Rajasthan	38.55	61.03	33	29	22.48
Uttar Pradesh	40.71	57.36	31	31	16.65
Bihar	37.49	47.53	34	35	10.04
Sikkim	56.94	69.68	20	17	12.73
Arunachal Pradesh	41.59	54.74	29	32	13.15
Nagaland	61.65	67.11	13	21	5.46
Manipur	59.89	68.87	16	19	8.97
Mizoram	82.27	88.49	2	2	6.22
Tripura	60.44	73.66	15	12	13.22
Meghalaya	49.10	63.31	24	27	14.21

Cont'd...

Table 5.7 Cont'd...

1	2	3	4	5	6
Assam	52.89	64.28	23	24	11.39
West Bengal	57.70	69.22	19	18	11.52
Jharkhand	41.39	54.13	30	34	12.74
Orissa	49.09	63.61	25	26	14.52
Chhattisgarh	42.91	65.18	28	23	22.27
Madhya Pradesh	44.67	64.11	26	25	19.44
Gujarat	61.57	69.97	14	15	8.40
Daman & Diu*	71.20	81.09	9	9	9.89
Dadra & Nagar Haveli*	40.71	60.03	32	30	19.33
Maharashtra	64.87	77.27	10	10	12.39
Andhra Pradesh	44.09	61.11	27	28	17.02
Karnataka	56.04	67.04	21	22	11.00
Goa	75.51	82.32	5	4	6.81
Lakshadweep*	81.78	87.52	3	3	5.74
Kerala	89.81	90.92	1	1	1.11
Tamil Nadu	62.66	73.47	12	13	10.81
Pondicherry*	74.74	81.49	7	7	6.75
A & N Islands*	73.02	81.18	8	8	8.16

Table 5.8

Ranking of states and UTs by literacy rate, sex-wise, 2001

Rank	Persons		Males		Females	
	States/UTs*	Literacy rate	States/UTs	Literacy rate	States/UTs	Literacy rate
1	2	3	4	5	6	7
1	Kerala	90.92	Kerala	94.20	Kerala	87.86
2	Mizoram	88.49	Lakshadweep*	93.15	Mizoram	86.13
3	Lakshadweep*	87.52	Mizoram	90.69	Lakshadweep*	81.56
4	Goa	82.32	Pondicherry*	88.89	Chandigarh*	76.65
5	Delhi*	81.82	Goa	88.88	Goa	75.51
6	Chandigarh*	81.76	Daman & Diu*	88.40	Andaman & Nicobar Is*	75.29
7	Pondicherry*	81.49	Delhi*	87.37	Delhi*	75.00
8	Andaman & Nicobar Is*	81.18	Maharashtra	86.27	Pondicherry*	74.13
9	Daman & Diu*	81.09	Andaman & Nicobar Is*	86.07	Daman & Diu*	70.37
10	Maharashtra	77.27	Himachal Pradesh	86.02	Himachal Pradesh	68.08
11	Himachal Pradesh	77.13	Chandigarh*	85.65	Maharashtra	67.51

Cont'd...

1	*2*	*3*	*4*	*5*	*6*	*7*
12	Tripura	73.66	Uttaranchal	84.01	Tripura	65.41
13	Tamil Nadu	73.47	Tamil Nadu	82.33	Tamil Nadu	64.55
14	Uttaranchal	72.28	Tripura	81.47	Punjab	63.55
15	Gujarat	69.97	Gujarat	80.50	Nagaland	61.92
16	Punjab	69.95	Haryana	79.25	Sikkim	61.46
17	Sikkim	69.68	Manipur	77.87	Meghalaya	60.41
18	West Bengal	69.22	Chhattisgarh	77.86	Uttaranchal	60.26
19	Manipur	68.87	West Bengal	77.58	West Bengal	60.22
20	Haryana	68.59	Madhya Pradesh	76.80	Manipur	59.70
21	Nagaland	67.11	Sikkim	76.73	Gujarat	58.60
22	Karnataka	67.04	Rajasthan	76.46	Karnataka	57.45
	INDIA	**65.38**	Karnataka	76.29	Haryana	56.31
23	Chhattisgarh	65.18	Orissa	75.95	Assam	56.03
24	Assam	64.28	**INDIA**	**75.85**	**INDIA**	**54.16**
25	Madhya Pradesh	64.11	Punjab	75.63	Chhattisgarh	52.40
26	Orissa	63.61	Dadra & Nagar Haveli*	73.32	Andhra Pradesh	51.17
27	Meghalaya	63.31	Assam	71.93	Orissa	50.97
28	Andhra Pradesh	61.11	Nagaland	71.77	Madhya Pradesh	50.28
29	Rajasthan	61.03	Andhra Pradesh	70. 85	Rajasthan	44.34
30	Dadra & N. Haveli*	60.03	Uttar Pradesh	70.23	Arunachal Pradesh	44.24
31	Uttar Pradesh	57.36	Jharkhand	67.94	Dadra & N. Haveli*	42.99
32	Arunachal Pradesh	54.74	Meghalaya	66.14	Uttar Pradesh	42.98
33	Jammu & Kashmir	54.46	Jammu & Kashmir	65.75	Jammu & Kashmir	41.82
34	Jharkhand	54.13	Arunachal Pradesh	64.07	Jharkhand	39.38
35	Bihar	47.53	Bihar	60.32	Bihar	33.57

States/UTs behind the national average are those in the shades

The highest and the lowest rank for all the three categories of literacy (namely, persons, male and female) are occupied by the same states, Kerala and Bihar respectively. The difference in percent attainment is from 90.92 to 47.53 for total population, 94.20 to 60.32 for males and 87.86 to 33.57 for females respectively. There are few other states that almost have similar rank in all the three categories indicating that the male-female gaps are either static or are declining. Mizoram and Lakshadweep sharing ranks between 2 and 3, Goa between 4 and 5, Jammu & Kashmir 33, Jharkhand between 31 and 34, Uttar Pradesh between 30 and 32, West Bengal between 18 and 19. Gujarat, an economically and industrially developed state has rank 15 both for 'person' and 'male' literacy, but its rank is a low 21 in female literacy. Among the major states, Maharashtra comes after Kerala with a literacy rate of 77.27 percent, followed by Tamil Nadu with 73.47 percent. There are 13 states/UTs where literacy rates are below the national average for 'persons'. 7 states/UTs are below the national average in all the three categories of literacy. Included in this list are some of the more populous states like Bihar, Jharkhand, Andhra Pradesh and Uttar Pradesh. Andhra Pradesh is the only state from the South, which is still doing badly in spite of some spectacular achievement in 1991–2001 in eradication of illiteracy from the state.

All the states and Union Territories without exception have shown increase in literacy rates during 1991–2001. 6 states/UTs have moved forward by more than fifteen percentage points during the decade. They are Rajasthan, Chhattisgarh, Madhya Pradesh, Dadra and Nagar Haveli, Andhra Pradesh and Uttar Pradesh (Table 5.6). Among the states/UTs, which had literacy rates of below fifty percent in 1991, Bihar is the only state in India in 2001 where literacy rate in the total population is still below 50 percent although literacy in the state in the decade has gone up by 10.04 percent. This is due to the very depressing female literacy rate (33.57%) in the state.

It is interesting to note that Kerala, Mizoram and Lakshadweep, which occupied the first three spots in literacy in 1991, retained their respective positions in the 2001 Census as well. The most significant improvement in ranking has been noticed for the states Chhattisgarh, Rajasthan and Uttaranchal. Chhattisgarh has surged forward from 28th rank in 1991 to 23rd spot in 2001, a jump in literacy rate from 42.91 in 1991 to 65.18 percent in 2001. Rajasthan moved ahead to take the 29th spot from the 33rd in 1991, improving its literacy tally from 38.55 in 1991 to 61.03 percent in 2001; Uttaranchal has moved from the 18th to the 14th rank, improving literacy from 57.75 in 1991 to 72.28 percent in 2001.

NSSO conducted a nation-wide survey (53rd round, January–December 1997). The following table provides a comparison between the Census 2001 and NSS 1997 estimates of literacy rates for different states by sex.

Table 5.9

Comparison of literacy rates from 2001 census with National Sample Survey (53rd round, January–December 1997) by sex

*States/ Union Territories**	*Literacy rate*						*Difference between Census and NSS*			*Rank of the entries in columns*					
	Census 2001			*NSS 1997*						*2*	*3*	*4*	*5*	*6*	*7*
1	*2*	*3*	*4*	*5*	*6*	*7*	*8*	*9*	*10*	*11*	*12*	*13*	*14*	*15*	*16*
	P	*M*	*F*	*P*	*M*	*F*	*P*	*M*	*F*						
INDIA	*65*	*76*	*54*	*62*	*73*	*50*	*3*	*3*	*4*						
Standard deviation	*10.6*	*8.58*	*13.5*	*14.67*	*11.4*	*18.6*									
Jammu & Kashmir	54	66	42	59	71	48	–5	–5	–6	31	29	31	24	24	24
Himachal Pradesh	77	86	68	77	87	70	0	–1	–2	10	8	10	12	11	13
Punjab	70	76	64	67	72	62	3	4	2	14	20	14	21	23	19
Chandigarh*	82	86	77	83	90	74	–1	–4	3	4	8	4	10	10	9
Haryana	69	79	56	65	76	52	4	3	4	17	15	22	22	21	22
Delhi*	82	87	75	85	91	76	–3	–4	–1	4	7	6	8	8	8
Rajasthan	61	76	44	55	73	35	6	3	9	26	20	27	28	22	30

Cont'd...

Table 5.9 Cont'd...

1	*2*	*3*	*4*	*5*	*6*	*7*	*8*	*9*	*10*	*11*	*12*	*13*	*14*	*15*	*16*
Uttar Pradesh & Uttaranchal	58	71	44	56	69	41	2	2	3	29	27	27	26	26	27
Bihar & Jharkhand	49	62	35	49	62	34	0	0	1	32	32	32	31	32	31
Sikkim	70	77	61	79	86	72	–9	–9	–11	14	18	16	11	12	12
Arunachal Pradesh	55	64	44	60	69	48	–5	–5	–4	30	31	27	23	26	24
Nagaland	67	72	62	84	91	77	–17	–19	–15	20	25	15	9	8	7
Manipur	69	78	60	76	86	66	–7	–8	–6	17	16	17	14	12	15
Mizoram	88	91	86	95	96	95	–7	–5	–9	2	3	2	3	3	1
Tripura	74	81	65	73	79	67	1	2	–2	12	13	12	17	19	14
Meghalaya	63	66	60	77	79	74	–14	–13	–14	25	29	17	12	19	9
Assam	64	72	56	75	82	66	–11	–10	–10	22	25	22	15	15	15
West Bengal	69	78	60	72	81	63	–3	–3	–3	17	16	17	18	16	17
Orissa	64	76	51	51	64	38	13	12	13	22	20	24	30	30	29
Madhya Pradesh & Chhattisgarh	64	77	51	56	70	41	8	7	10	22	18	24	26	25	27
Gujarat	70	80	59	68	80	57	2	0	2	14	14	20	20	17	21
Daman & Diu*	81	88	70	86	95	73	–5	–7	–3	7	6	9	6	5	11
Dadra & Nagar Haveli	60	73	43	49	66	30	11	7	13	28	24	30	31	28	32
Maharashtra	77	86	68	74	84	63	3	2	5	10	8	10	16	14	17
Andhra Pradesh	61	71	51	54	64	43	7	7	8	26	27	24	29	30	26
Karnataka	67	76	57	58	66	50	9	10	7	20	20	21	25	28	23
Goa	82	89	76	86	93	79	–4	–4	–3	4	4	5	6	7	6
Lakshadweep*	88	93	82	96	98	93	–8	–5	–11	2	2	3	2	2	3
Kerala	91	94	88	93	96	90	–2	–2	–2	1	1	1	4	3	4
Tamil Nadu	73	82	65	70	80	60	3	2	5	13	12	12	19	17	20
Pondicherry*	81	89	74	90	94	86	–9	–5	–12	7	4	8	5	6	5
A & N Islands*	81	86	75	97	100	94	–16	–14	–19	7	8	6	1	1	2

The literacy rates derived from the 2001Census compare well with those reported by the NSSO (1997) [Correlation between Census and NSS data: for Persons $r_{25} = 0.868$, for Males $r_{36} = 0.791$, and for Females $r_{47} = 0.916$]. If we go by the close agreement between the two sets of data, it would be reasonable to assume that the literacy rate at the national level which was around 62 percent in 1997 moved to 65 percent in 2001. With that assumption it follows then that the improvement during 1997 and 2001 for males and females respectively are 3 and 4 percentage points. That is, a close to 1 percentage point increases in literacy rate per annum in 1997–2001, irrespective of sexes. This is a little less than what one would expect had the average annual growth (about 1.3 percentage points) of literacy by census count roughly prevailed through the entire decade. In most of the smaller North-eastern states and the Union Territories, the NSS estimate probably contains more error than in the estimates in the larger states. That is, NSS observations give a fair estimate when the canvas is very large; it suffers from some limitations when using a smaller canvas for estimation. This would be evident from the fact that variability in literacy rates computed from NSS data is consistently larger than the corresponding values obtained from the census data. The correlation between Census ranks and NSS ranks for Persons, Males and Females respectively are 0.836, 0.803 and 0.901, which are closely similar to the correlations obtained from literacy scores.

A high positive correlation between these two sets of literacy data indicate that the ranks of the set of paired observations do not vary appreciably no matter if the paired observations were taken concurrently or at different points of time. Of the 32 states/UTs (since undivided states of Uttar Pradesh, Bihar and Madhya Pradesh only have been considered for this comparison), in 17 states/UTs the literacy estimates from NSS are in excess of the values that should have been obtained on the assumption of linear relationship between NSS and Census estimates.

In Northern India, the two reported rates perfectly agree for Himachal Pradesh, though the two estimates were taken at different time points. The Census literacy rates for Haryana and Punjab have shown an increase of 4 and 3 percentage points respectively, closely similar to that at the national level. Jammu & Kashmir, Delhi and Chandigarh have reported lower literacy rates at the Census by 5, 3 and 1 percentage points respectively, suggesting some over estimation by the NSS data. In the West, Rajasthan, Maharashtra and Gujarat have reported higher literacy rates by 6, 3 and 2 percentage points respectively at the Census of India, 2001 not quite different from what one would expect from the NSS result. Dadra and Nagar Haveli seem to have missed the mark by a large margin. Madhya Pradesh and Chhattisgarh and Uttar Pradesh and Uttaranchal taken together, have shown increase for the 2001Census by 8 and 2 percentage points respectively.

5 states/UTs viz., Kerala, Goa, Lakshadweep, Pondicherry and Andaman and Nicobar Islands have reported lower literacy rates at the Census of India, 2001, by 2, 4, 8, 9 and 16 percentage points respectively as per NSS data. The literacy rates pertaining to the states of Karnataka, Andhra Pradesh and Tamil Nadu have registered increase by 9, 7 and 3 percentage points respectively over the NSSO rates. In East, Orissa has recorded a maximum gain of 13 percentage points at the 2001 Census, while Sikkim and West Bengal have recorded lower literacy rates by 9 and 3 percentage points respectively. Bihar and Jharkhand taken together have reported the same literacy rates both in NSSO round and the Census 2001 indicating literacy rate remaining almost static in the period. In Northeast, six out of seven states viz., Nagaland, Meghalaya, Assam, Manipur, Mizoram and Arunachal Pradesh have recorded lower literacy rates in 2001 Census. The maximum difference between the Census and NSSO estimate is with Nagaland followed by Meghalaya and Assam where literacy rates are reported to have gone down by 17, 14 and 11 percentage points respectively. The variation in male and female literacy rates differs considerably from one state to another.

5.3.2 A Closer Look at Gender Disparity in Literacy and Variation between States and Districts

In the following table we examine the literate population by sex in India in 1991 and 2001 by the range of the levels of literacy attained by the states.

Table 5.10

Percent distribution of population and literates by literacy rates: 1991–2001

Range of literacy	No. of states/ UTs	Share of country's 1991 Population Absolute	%	Literates Absolute	%	No. of states/ UTs	2001 Population Absolute	%	Literates Absolute	%
					Persons					
Total	**34**	**836,650,839**	**100**	**358,402,626**	**100**	**34**	**1,014,651,658**	**100**	**562,010,743**	**100**
0–40	2	108,536,544	12.97	32,734,920	9.13		—	—	0	0
40–50	9	320,969,442	38.36	111,881,893	31.22	1	82,878,796	8.17	31,675,607	5.64
50–60	8	181,572,194	21.70	84,980,438	23.71	3	194,053,404	19.13	90,228,248	16.05
60–70	6	183,310,194	21.91	97,782,088	27.28	16	510,886,031	50.35	284,935,086	50.70
70–80	6	12,422,484	1.48	7,840,348	2.19	5	176,527,114	17.40	116,431,611	20.72
80+	3	29,839,981	3.57	23,182,939	6.47	9	50,306,313	4.96	38,740,191	6.89
					Males					
Total	**34**	**434,228,007**	**100**	**228,983,134**	**100**	**34**	**524,795,963**	**100**	**336,969,695**	**100**
0–40										
40–50										
50–60	10	208,042,806	47.91	92,254,860	40.29					
60–70	8	106,647,902	24.56	58,560,297	25.57	4	58,757,032	11.20	29,660,566	8.80
70–80	8	98,294,116	22.64	61,792,179	26.99	15	324,738,236	61.88	202,720,904	60.16
80+	8	21,243,183	4.89	16,375,798	7.15	15	141,300,695	26.92	104,588,225	31.04
					Females					
Total	**34**	**402,422,832**	**100**	**129,419,492**	**100**	**34**	**489,855,695**	**100**	**225,041,048**	**100**
0–40	10	204,531,943	50.83	43,641,327	33.72	2	52,772,983	10.77	14,906,863	6.62
40–50	10	98,761,703	24.54	37,070,972	28.64	4	106,293,909	21.70	37,540,310	16.68
50–60	6	78,314,264	19.46	34,188,190	26.42	9	167,650,340	34.22	77,102,225	34.26
60–70	4	5,366,131	1.33	2,977,855	2.30	10	138,328,614	28.24	77,188,227	34.30
70–80	3	639,268	0.16	397,535	0.31	6	7,979,142	1.63	5,163,802	2.30
80+	1	14,809,523	3.68	11,143,613	8.61	3	16,830,707	3.44	13,139,621	5.84

5.3.3 Between States Variation in Literacy and in Gender Gap

In 1991 Census, 11 states/UTs reported literacy rates 50 percent and below and had a share of 51 percent of the country's population. The number of states in this category has come down to only 1, Bihar, in 2001 Census, with a share of about 8 percent of India's population. The number of states/UTs having more than 80 percent literacy rate has increased to 9 in 2001 from 3 in 1991. There were 10 states/UTs recording male literacy rates in the range of 50–60 percent in 1991 census, accounting for 47.91 percent of the country's male population. This 'range category below 50' for level of literacy for males has disappeared altogether in 2001 since the minimum male literacy rate in the country (state taken as the unit) is over 60 percent now. The number of states/UTs having male literacy of 70 percent and above has gone up from 16 in 1991 to 30 in 2001. There were 20 states/UTs in the country where female literacy rate was 50 percent or less in 1991. These 20 states/UTs accounted for nearly three-fourth of the India's female population. In 2001, this is down to only 6 states with a share of about one-third of the country's female population. There were 8 states/UTs with more than 60 percent female literacy in 1991. 19 states/UTs are in this category in 2001 with a population share of 33 percent.

The decade 1991–2001 saw some significant reduction of gender gap in literacy rate (Table 5.7). State-level data indicate that in 1991, 5 states, namely Uttaranchal, Rajasthan, Uttar Pradesh, Chattishgarh and Jharkhand, which together had 27.36 percent of the 7 years and above age group population in India, had 30 percentage points or more gender gap in literacy rate in the population. In 2001, only Rajasthan, covering 5.36 percent of India's population in 7+ years, still has 30 percentage points gender gap in literacy. This is in spite the fact that literacy rates both for males and females in Rajasthan were higher than the male and female literacy rates in Bihar. On the other hand, 3 states Kerala, Meghalaya, Mizoram and UT Chandigarh had less than 10 percentage point gender gap in literacy in 1991. In 2001, one more state Nagaland has been added to this list. Except in Dadra and Nagar Haveli, the gender gaps in literacy rates in all other states/UTs have declined. In all the 34 states/UTs, female literacy rates have come up faster than male literacy rates; Dadra & Nagar Haveli is the only exception although both male and female literacy rates have increased there by large percentage points. Thus, the decade 1991–2001 registered a visible improvement in both male and female literacy rates with the latter having an edge over the former.

5.3.4 Between Districts Variation in Literacy Rate and Gender Disparity

The national level aggregative picture does not give any reasonably clear sign of change in literacy at the lower levels other than state. The variation in literacy rate and gender disparity at the national and state level often would gloss over the intrinsic variations that exists as we go down to smaller aggregative units. There shall be many villages in the country or some census blocks where 100 percent of the population are literate. Similarly, there would be some units, village or census blocks, where literacy rates are more than pathetic. In the following section we discuss literacy performances at district level.

Although the number of districts in 2001 census has increased to 593 from 466 in 1991, comparable literacy statistics for 577 districts for 1991 and 2001 are available.

Whereas the state-wise data gave the impression that by 2001 there was no state/UT where literacy rate in the population was still below 40 percent, the district level data indicate that there are a few pockets, 25 districts, where literacy rates in the population are still below 40 percent in 2001. The number of districts in 1991 where literacy rates were ≤ 40 percent was 145 (Table 5.11). These 145 districts, sharing about 26 percent of India's population, together contributed about 16 percent literates in the country. 360 districts in 1991 with 63 percent of national population, had literacy rates ranging from 40 to 70 percent and their share to literate population in the country was almost 60 percent. Only 25 districts (combined share was 5.40% of total population) in 1991 had literacy rates over 80 percent and they contributed 9.53 percent of literates in India. By 2001 there were as many as 443 districts (population share over 76%) in the range of literacy rate between 50 and 80 percent.

Table 5.11
Distribution of population of literates by range of literacy rate by districts of Indian states/union territories, 1991–2001

Literacy range	1991			2001		
	No. of districts	Population (%)	Literates (%)	No. of districts	Population (%)	Literates (%)
			Persons			
<10						
10–19.99	3	0.31	0.10			
20–29.99	42	6.37	3.20			
30–39.99	110	18.96	12.65	25	4.12	2.18
40–49.99	144	24.56	20.93	50	8.61	5.84
50–59.99	116	19.49	20.50	122	21.42	17.85
60–69.99	100	18.96	24.31	170	28.31	28.14
70–79.99	37	5.95	8.78	151	26.54	31.08
80–89.99	14	3.22	5.42	46	9.04	12.00
90+	11	2.18	4.11	13	1.95	2.93
Total	577	100%	100%	577	100%	100%
			Males			
<10						
10–19.99						
20–29.99	4	0.35	0.14			
30–39.99	27	4.10	2.29	1	0.07	0.03
40–49.99	77	12.98	9.08	19	2.73	1.60
50–59.99	134	21.76	18.49	41	6.58	4.67
60–69.99	150	26.58	26.62	105	17.83	15.17
70–79.99	114	21.45	25.58	187	33.24	32.81
80–89.99	55	9.89	13.35	194	34.74	39.57
90+	16	2.88	4.46	30	4.81	6.15
Total	577	100%	100%	577	100%	100%
			Females			
<10	3	0. 41	0.08			
10–19.99	100	15.03	5.89	2	0.24	0.08
20–29.99	125	23.56	14.52	40	6.19	2.75
30–39.99	122	18.64	16.61	76	13.20	8.29
40–49.99	84	15.05	17.43	124	22.36	18.19
50–59.99	73	15.16	21.72	136	22.03	22.45
60–69.99	37	5.79	9.74	117	20.25	24.78
70–79.99	17	3.15	6.34	59	11.43	16.24
80–89.99	11	2.54	5.96	16	3.38	5.57
90+	5	0.67	1.71	7	0.92	1.66
Total	**577**	**100%**	**100%**	**577**	**100%**	**100%**

Source: P.K. Bhargava (National Institute of Adult Education New Delhi): Changes in Gender Disparity in Literacy Rate during 1991–2001.

They together gave 77 percent of literate Indians. The number of districts having literacy rates over 80 percent increased from 25 in 1991 to 59 in 2001. These 59 districts (population share of 11%) together contributed 15 percent of literates to India. The top and bottom ten districts in level of literacy attained are presented below. Except one district from Pondicherry (Mahe), the other 9 districts in top tens are all from Kerala, the state recording the highest literacy rate in the country. Of the bottom ten districts, 9 are from BIMARU states (Bihar 1, Madhya Pradesh 2, Rajasthan 3, Uttar Pradesh 3) and 1 from Orissa.

Table 5.12

Top and bottom 10 districts in literacy rates, India 2001

Name of the district	*Top ten*	*Name of the district*	*Bottom ten*
Kottayam (Kerala)	95.72	Banswara (Rajasthan)	26.00
Pathanamthitta (Kerala)	94.88	Rampur (U.P.)	25.37
Mahe (Pondicherry)	94.10	Bastar (M.P.)	24.89
Alappuzha (Kerala)	93.87	Budaun (U.P.)	24.64
Ernakulam (Kerala)	92.35	Bahraich (U.P.)	24.39
Kannur (Kerala)	91.48	Jalor (Rajasthan)	23.76
Kozhikode (Kerala)	91.10	Barmer (Rajasthan)	22.98
Kollam (Kerala)	90.47	Korapur (Orissa)	22.66
Thrissur (Kerala)	90.18	Kishanganj (Bihar)	22.22
Thiruvanthapuram (Kerala)	89.22	Jhabua (M.P.)	19.01

For males, there were 61 districts, with 12.77 percent population share in the country, that had 80 percent and above literacy rates and they together contributed 17.81 percent of male literates in India in 1991. The respective figures in 2001 are 224, 39.55 and 45.72 percent. In fact, there are 381 districts with male literacy rates ranging from 70 to 90 percent sharing over 72 percent of Indian male literates.

Females have performed better than males in improving their literacy rate in the decade 1991–2001. There were as many as 103 districts in India where female literacy rates were below 20 percent (3 districts even had below 10% literacy) in 1991. In a span of 10 years, the number has come down to only 2. 377 districts (population share 64.64%) in 2001 have female literacy rates in the range of 40 to 70 percent and their combined share to total female literates in the country is impressive 65.42 percent. There are as many as 23 districts in 2001 compared to 16 in 1991 that showed female literacy rates above 80 percent.

5.3.5 Decadal Increase/decrease in Literacy Rate in the Districts

In 3 out of 577 districts a marginal decrease in literacy rate between 1991 and 2001 in the total population has been observed. The respective numbers for male and female populations are 7 and 2. This could have happened because more of the literate persons moved out to some other district. The largest number of districts registering a literacy growth rate in the range of 10 and 20 percentage points are Persons 367, Males 313 and Females 363. The decadal increase in Persons literacy rate over 20 but less than 30 percentage points is observed in 63 districts. For Males and Females, the numbers of such districts are 51 and 107 respectively. Females exhibiting over 30 percentage point's improvement have been recorded in 13 districts. Out of these 13 districts, 6 are located in Rajasthan alone, 3 each in Chhattisgarh and Madhya Pradesh and one in Uttar Pradesh.

Table 5.13

Decadal increase/decrease in literacy rates in 577 districts in India during 1991–2001

Ranges of decadal increase/decrease in Literacy Rate	*Number of districts*		
	Persons	*Males*	*Females*
Total	577	577	577
Negative growth	3	7	2
0.00–9.99	138	203	92
10.00–19.99	367	313	363
20.00–29.99	63	51	107
30.00 and above	6	3	13

Source: P.K. Bhargava: Changes in Gender Disparity in Literacy Rate during 1991–2001

5.3.6 Rural-Urban Gap and Gender Disparity

With improving literacy rates, regional inequality has declined. The decline is more noticeable since 1981. Whereas the literacy rate (Persons) in rural areas increased from 36 in 1981 to 59 percent in 2001, the same in urban areas increased from 67 to 80 percent in the same period. The rural-urban difference declined from 31 to 21 percentage points. In the same period, male literacy increased from 56 to 76 percentage points and female literacy from around 30 to 54 percent. The gender gap has declined from around 27 in 1991 to around 22 percentage points in 2001. The gender gap in rural areas is still very high, 24 compared to only 7 percentage points in urban areas. Inter-state inequalities in female literacy rate, though have been reduced, still remains high. In the high performing states/UTs like Kerala, Mizoram, Pondicheri, Lakshadweep and Goa, the gender gap is between 8–9 percentage points.

At the national level the gender gap is falling, but only very slowly. In 1961, the gender gap for persons aged 7 and above was 25 percentage points (28.3 percentage point in the adult group, 15+ years of age). There was 1 percentage point drop in the next decade but it stood at 26.6 percentage points in 1981 (29.1 in the adult population). There was a 5.1 points drop in gender gap between 1981 and 2001 (3.1 percentage points between 1991 and 2001) in 7+ year's age group (an almost identical drop in the adult group). The spurt of growth rate in literacy in the last two decades had a significant effect in reducing M-F gap in literacy.

Distribution of districts by range of male-females literacy gap is given in Table 5.11. It is observed from the data that 409 districts out of 577 (71%) had gender gap below 30 percentage points in 1991. The number has increased to 481 districts in 2001 (83% of the total number of districts). Less than 10 percentage point gap in male-female literacy rate has been observed in 45 districts in 2001 compared to 27 in 1991. The classified data also shows that in 1991, 26.4 percent of the total districts (152 districts) showed a gender gap in literacy rate less than 20 percentage points. The number of such district has increased to 219 (38% of the total districts) in 2001. This has happened since female literacy rate has risen faster during 1991–2001 and the gender gap in literacy rate has narrowed down in the advanced districts. Since male literacy rate has already reached a level from where further improvement would be slow, and since female literacy rate is still in the middle range, the gender gap can be wiped out faster in the coming years if steps were taken to improve the enrolment and retention ratio of girls in the school level. There are still a large number of districts (95, 16.4% of all districts) where gender-gap in literacy is over 30 percentage points.

Table 5.14

Distribution of districts by gaps in male-female literacy rate – India, 1991 and 2001

Ranges of male-female gap in literacy	*Number of districts 1991*	*Percentage to total number of districts in 1991*	*Number of districts 2001*	*Percentage to total number of districts in 2001*
Total	577	100.0	577	100.0
Less than 10.00	27	4.7	45	7.8
10.00–19.99	125	21.7	174	30.2
20.00–29.99	257	44.5	262	45.4
30.00–39.99	156	27.0	95	16.4
40.00 and above	12	2.0	1	0.2

The absolute difference between literacy rates of males and females can be used to compare performances of different states/districts in wiping out gender disparity when such comparisons are made for a fixed time point. When the overall literacy level is around 80 percent, a gender gap of 15 percentage points is not equivalent to a gender gap of the same magnitude when the overall literacy rate is 60 or so. Demographers are in the look out for an index that would help compare disparity between and within two time points. A very simple measure of Index of Gender Disparity, ID has been developed.

$$ID_i = ({}^{m}L_i - {}^{f}L_i) \times L_c/L_i$$

where ID_i = Index of gender disparity for the state i,

${}^{m}L_i$ = male literacy rate in the state i,

${}^{f}L_i$ = female literacy rate in the state i,

L_C = literacy rate in the country, and

L_i = literacy rate in the state i.

The multiplying factor L_c/L_i standardizes the gender gap. The same absolute gap but with L_i greater than, equal to or smaller than L_c, this formulation adjusts the value of the index. With L_i greater than L_c, the ID for the same absolute gender difference in literacy rate would be smaller than when L_c is greater than L_i. Some illustrations:

ID_{2001} for Kerala (base period 2001) = (94.2 – 87.86)× 65.38/90.92 = 4.56

ID_{2001} for Kerala (base period 1991) = (94.2 – 87.86) × 52.21/90.92 = 3.64

In the first computation L_c refers to literacy rate in the Indian population in 2001. When comparing intensity of gender disparity between two points, L_c in the computation may be taken as the literacy rate of the total population of the first time point. In the second computation this is what has been done, 65.38 in the first computation have been replaced by 52.21, the 1991 literacy rate in the entire population of India.

In the following table Index of Gender Disparity with different base years for the states and Union Territories is presented.

Table 5.15

Index of gender disparity for different states/union territories, 1991 and 2001

*States/ Union Territories**	*1991*			*Index of gender disparity*	*2001*			*Index of gender disparity base*	
	Total	*Males*	*Females*		*Total*	*Males*	*Females*	*2001*	*1991*
1	*2*	*3*	*4*	*5*	*6*	*7*	*8*	*9*	*10*
Jammu & Kashmir	N.A	N.A	N.A		54.46	65.75	41.82	28.73	22.94
Himachal Pradesh	63.94	75.41	52.26	18.9	77.13	86.02	68.08	15.21	12.14
Punjab	58.51	65.66	50.41	13.61	69.95	75.63	63.55	11.29	9.02
Chandigarh*	77.81	82.04	72.34	6.51	81.76	85.65	76.65	7.20	5.75
Uttaranchal	57.75	72.79	41.63	28.17	72.28	84.01	60.26	21.48	17.16
Haryana	55.85	69.1	40.47	26.76	68.59	79.25	56.31	21.87	17.46
Delhi*	75.29	82.01	66.99	10.42	81.82	87.37	75	9.88	7.89
Rajasthan	38.55	54.99	20.44	46.79	61.03	76.46	44.34	34.41	27.48
Uttar Pradesh	40.71	54.82	24.37	39.05	57.36	70.23	42.98	31.06	24.8
Bihar	37.49	51.37	21.99	40.92	47.53	60.32	33.57	36.80	29.38
Sikkim	56.94	65.7	46.76	17.37	69.68	76.73	61.46	14.33	11.44
Arunachal Pradesh	41.59	51.45	29.69	27.32	54.74	64.07	44.24	23.68	18.91
Nagaland	61.65	67.62	54.75	10.9	67.11	71.77	61.92	9.60	7.66
Manipur	59.89	71.63	47.6	20.95	68.87	77.87	59.7	17.25	13.77
Mizoram	82.27	85.61	78.6	4.45	88.49	90.69	86.13	3.37	2.69
Tripura	60.44	70.58	49.65	18.08	73.66	81.47	65.41	14.25	11.38
Meghalaya	49.1	53.12	44.85	8.79	63.31	66.14	60.41	5.92	4.73
Assam	52.89	61.87	43.03	18.6	64.28	71.93	56.03	16.17	12.91
West Bengal	57.7	67.81	46.56	19.23	69.22	77.58	60.22	16.40	13.09
Jharkhand	41.39	55.8	25.52	38.2	54.13	67.94	39.38	34.50	27.55
Orissa	49.09	63.09	34.68	30.22	63.61	75.95	50.97	25.68	20.5
Chhattisgarh	42.91	58.07	27.52	37.17	65.18	77.86	52.4	25.54	20.39
Madhya Pradesh	44.67	58.54	29.35	34.12	64.11	76.8	50.28	27.05	21.6
Gujarat	61.57	73.39	48.92	20.75	69.97	80.5	58.6	20.46	16.34

Cont'd…

Table 5.1 Cont'd...

1	*2*	*3*	*4*	*5*	*6*	*7*	*8*	*9*	*10*
Daman & Diu*	71.2	82.66	59.4	17.06	81.09	88.4	70.37	14.54	11.61
Dadra & Nagar Haveli*	40.71	53.56	26.98	34.09	60.03	73.32	42.99	33.03	26.38
Maharashtra	64.87	76.56	52.32	19.51	77.27	86.27	67.51	15.87	12.68
Andhra Pradesh	44.09	55.13	32.72	26.54	61.11	70.85	51.17	21.06	16.81
Karnataka	56.04	67.26	44.34	21.35	67.04	76.29	57.45	18.37	14.67
Goa	75.51	83.64	67.09	11.44	82.32	88.88	75.51	10.62	8.48
Lakshadweep	81.78	90.18	72.89	11.04	87.52	93.15	81.56	8.658	6.91
Kerala	89.81	93.62	86.17	4.33	90.92	94.2	87.86	4.56	3.64
Tamil Nadu	62.66	73.75	51.33	18.68	73.47	82.33	64.55	15.82	12.64
Pondicherry*	74.74	83.68	65.63	12.61	81.49	88.89	74.13	11.84	9.46
A & N Islands*	73.02	78.99	65.46	9.67	81.18	86.07	75.29	8.68	6.93
INDIA	**52.21**	**64.13**	**39.29**	**24.84**	**65.38**	**75.85**	**54.16**	**21.76**	**17.33**

When IDs are computed for years 1991 and 2001 on the basis of the respective year's population literacy rate, ID has marginally declined for all states and Union Territories except for Chandigarh. At the national level, gender disparity has declined by 3.08 percentage points. Least decline is observed for Delhi (from 10.42 to 9.88). Largest improvements are observed for Rajasthan (46.79 to 34.41) and Chhattisgarh (37.17 to 25.54). With 1991 as the base period, the decline in gender disparity is substantial. At the national level the decline in the index is 7.51 points. Index of disparity in 2001 (1991 base) is very small for the states Mizoram, Kerala and Meghalay; Rajasthan and Bihar, which displayed very high gender disparity in 1991 (above 40 percentage points), continue to be the toppers in gender discrimination in 2001 as well with mutual exchange of earlier rank position. The gender gap in literacy rate is relatively high in Rajasthan than in Bihar in 2001; yet the value of the index of gender disparity is higher (29.38) for Bihar than that in Rajasthan (27.48). A comparison of 1991 and 2001 data clearly indicates that gender disparity has been declining in all states. Such index of gender disparity can be studied at district or lower levels as well. L_c may refer to national total literacy rate or total literacy rate for the state. L_i of course would refer to total literacy rate for the district (or some other smaller unit).

We had to do a little bit of computation work for calculating the index of gender disparity. The index, which is a standardized measure of gender gap, does not throw much additional light on the performance of the states. The correlation between ID (1991) and Gender-Gap (1991) is 0.928 and that for the 2001 data is 0.961 (base year 2001) and 0.961 (base year 1991). The relative positions of the states remain identical whether we use 1991or 2001 total literacy rate in the country to obtain the value of the multiplying factor for computation of IDs for the states. The correlation study also confirms that the states that had higher index of gender disparity in 1991 continue to do so in 2001 as well. The correlation between the two sets of IDs is as high as 0.979. The gender disparity index is likely to be a more effective method of comparison between different districts or some other lower level aggregates.

5.3.7 Literacy among Scheduled Castes and Scheduled Tribes

Although the government consistently have followed a policy of positive discrimination for SCs and STs since independence, there is immense gap between policy prescription and its implementation at the ground level. In India, nearly one in every four persons is either a SC or ST. Policy of reservation in education and jobs has been extended to other backward castes (OBC) as well (22.5% for SC and STs + 27% for OBCs). In schools and colleges and in many government offices jobs reserved for these persons remain vacant year after year since there are only a few takers who conform to the very minimum educational criterion demanded from the job seekers. Indian Parliament is trying to bring legislation to force the private sector to accommodate these backward classes through some quota system. Reservation has become more of a political issue than a social one. The Ministry of Human Resources Development recent announcement that such reservations have to be strictly enforced in prime institutions like IITs, IIMs and in all medical colleges have created furor among the general category students all over India aspiring for admission to these prestigious institutions. In the face of strong opposition from the student community, the government has assured them that number of seats in the institutions would be suitably increased so that the absolute number of seats for the general category students is not brought down from the present level. Junior doctors and medical students resorted to mass agitation for days thus jeopardizing the health delivery system in most cities. The private players do not go by the caste or religious background of the job aspirants. They already have many workers who come from the so-called lower social background. They have a single agenda in today's extremely competitive market – 'improve the efficiency or perish'. The government at the center remains under pressure on the reservation issue from the partners in the government as also from the opposition bench.

Those who oppose reservation in the debate 'quota' versus 'merit' in higher level of education and highly professional jobs find ample support in the all-India sample survey conducted by NSSO in 1999–2000 on quality of education in the country. The survey showed that for every hundred SCs (rural urban combined) less than 4.5 passed the Higher Secondary examination. This percentage is about 5.5 for STs and a little above 6.5 among OBCs. The minimum level of education essential for any professional course (engineering, medical, management, and the like) is Higher Secondary. That is, 94–95 percent of SCs, STs and OBCs are ineligible even to seek admission in these courses. The picture is almost equally dismal for those who remain outside this 'reservation' system. Only about twelve and half out of every hundred in the unreserved category complete higher secondary education. Irrespective of caste/tribe/OBC status, only about 9.5 percent of boys and girls successfully cross the higher secondary level. Percentage of adults completing high school education in USA is 84 percent.

Even those among the SCs and STs who successfully pass HS examination discontinue further studies primarily due to economic reasons. As a result, a very large proportion of the 22.5 percent seats kept reserved for SCs and STs in most educational institutions remain vacant. Among IIT students only 7 percent are SCs and 3.5 percent STs, that is, more than half of the 22.5 percent seats reserved for SCs/STs remain vacant since there are not enough applicants who qualify (even after the cut-off point for them is brought down drastically) for admission into courses offered by IITs. Even if the current reservation of 22.5 percent is revised to 49.5 percent to include the backward communities including SCs and STs, the admission scenario is unlikely to change much. Unless more students from backward communities complete higher secondary education with reasonably good grade, there is little room for joy for the underprivileged and underachievers for 220 percent increase in seats under 'reserved' category.

The survey also points to the fact that only about a little over 5 percent of those who had per capita income less than Rs 350 per month in 1999–2000 could cross the barrier of HS examination. A good majority of this population were SCs, STs and OBCs. This tends to indicate that except those who really are brilliant and a few exceptional cases, very few from among the poor could take advantage of reservation in higher education. That is, income-educational attainment scenario prevailing in the country does not also support the much publicized demand that economic backwardness rather than caste/tribe status be taken as the criterion of reservation, if there should be any. It is the creamy layer in the backward communities that are taking advantage of reservation year after year. The Supreme Court also has asked to exclude this creamy layer from reservation category. Most political parties, however, are not agreeable to abide by these directives from the Apex Court.

Table 5.16

Literacy rates of SC/ST by sex and residence, All India

	Scheduled Castes			*Scheduled Tribes*		
	Total	***Rural***	***Urban***	***Total***	***Rural***	***Urban***
			Persons			
1961	10.87	8.89	21.81	8.53	8.16	22.41
1971	14.67	12.77	28.65	11.30	10.68	28.84
1981	21.38	18.48	36.60	16.35	14.97	37.93
1991	37.41	33.25	55.91	29.60	27.38	56.60
			Males			
1961	16.96	15.06	32.21	13.83	13.37	30.43
1971	22.36	20.04	38.93	17.63	16.92	37.09
1981	31.12	27.91	47.54	24.52	22.94	47.60
1991	49.91	45.95	55.60	40.65	38.45	66.56
			Females			
1961	3.29	2.52	10.04	3.2	2.90	13.45
1971	6.44	5.06	16.99	4.9	4.36	19.64
1981	10.93	8.45	24.34	8.0	6.81	27.32
1991	23.76	19.45	42.29	18.19	16.02	45.66

The government has passed a bill (National Rural Employment Guarantee Act, NREGA) in the Parliament to provide 100 days employment to one member from each rural family if she/he applies for a job and is willing to do any unskilled manual work. This step is likely to bring down the population below poverty line but is unlikely to create much asset out of this huge public spending. The government is in serious doubt if the scheme had a significant impact on rural poverty alleviation and also if any capital has been formed out of this huge spending of the tax payers' money. Even though some needy families are getting some money under this scheme, this huge spending is unlikely to make much impact on the education scenario in the country. The government needs to think about programs that would help enlarge educational facilities in schools at all stages without compromising on quality of education. Like the 'employment guarantee' scheme, the government can think of a scheme to fully finance education up to class 12 of at least one child from the economically weak and socially deprived families (including hostel charges wherever necessary) so that they get the necessary opportunity to acquire the essential skill and knowledge to compete for higher studies. That is, the 'intensity of formal education' must improve fast among all segments of the population. Once this is achieved, the need for reservation on the basis of caste or economic status would become irrelevant.

The literacy rates for Scheduled Castes and Scheduled Tribes are way behind the mainstream population with 37.4 and 29.6 percent respectively as per 1991 census. Less than one in every four SC women and less than one in every five ST women were literate in 1991. The position of SCs and STs in general and their women in particular is really pathetic in Bihar and Rajasthan respectively. Less than 10 percent of SC women in Bihar and less than 5 percent of ST women in Rajasthan were literate in 1991.

If the SC and ST populations are taken out of the population totals, the literacy rate for the rest would go up to 57.7 percent as against 52.11 percent for the total population in 1991. The situation was worse in 1981 when only 1 percent of ST females in Rajasthan were literate. At the other extreme is Kerala where nearly three-fourths of SC females were literate in 1991. The disparities between literacy rates both for males and females of SCs and STs were much higher than those in the rest of the population.

5.3.7.1 NCAER Survey

NCAER conducted a large sample survey in 1994 on households in 16 larger states in India. Such survey results generally should not be used for comparisons with results obtained from census counts, especially if the two reports refer to two different time points. Since such surveys make in-depth study in very many parameters of a population, they throw considerable light on the intricate relations that exist between the changing values of different parameters. The survey draws our attention to some basic questions regarding variability in attainment of literacy rate by different social and economic groups. Some observations from the survey are summarized below.

- Literacy rates increase and gender disparity decreases significantly as household income rises. The trend is particularly strong in poorer states.
- Age specific literacy rate is maximum (74%) in 10–14 year age group, followed by 70 percent in 15–19 age group. The literacy rate monotonically diminishes as we go up the age ladder. This is true for poverty line groups, landholding groups, occupational groups and social groups. With higher literacy rate the gender disparity also diminishes.
- The landless wage earners registered very low levels of literacy. There was not much difference in literacy rates between different land size groups.
- There is considerable variation between various social groups. SCs and STs have poor literacy rates, much behind the national average. Christians displayed highest literacy. Gender disparity in literacy rate is very wide among SCs and STs compared to that observed in other social groups. Literacy rates for SCs and STs are extremely low in Bihar, Rajasthan, Uttar Pradesh, Madhya Pradesh and Orissa. Gender disparity among Muslims is very wide in Uttar Pradesh.

- Village development has a strong link with levels of literacy attained. The least developed villages have lower level of literacy as well.

5.3.7.2 Adult Literacy

Current stock of human capital is better reflected in literacy and level of education of 15 years and older age segment of the population. Literacy in this segment of population is referred to as 'adult literacy'. It is one of the key indicators besides enrolment at various levels of schooling in computation of HDI by UNDP. As per NSSO 54th Round (January–June 1998) report, adult literacy rate in India was 57 percent, 50 percent in rural area and 78 percent in urban area. Urban male literacy rate was 86 percent, about 22 percent higher than that in rural area. 68 percent of urban adult females were literate, which was more than twice the ratio observed in rural area. There are quite a few larger states where female adult literacy in rural areas is still below 25 percent. Included in the list are the states like Bihar, Madhya Pradesh, Uttar Pradesh and Rajasthan – the BIMARU states. These states and Andhra Pradesh together had adult literacy (Persons) rate less than 50 percent. Like literacy rates in the general population, adult literacy rates for males, females and combined population between 1981 and 1995–96 have increased between 12 and 15 percentage points, females gaining the most. Almost similar observations are made for adult literacy rates in rural areas. The gap between male and female adult literacy is closing. But the same in rural areas remains nearly unchanged at around 30 percentage points. As a result, the male-female gap in adult literacy in the population is diminishing only very slowly. Both rural-urban and male-female gaps between 1981 and 1995–96 have declined by 1.7 to 2.6 percentage points, far less than the improvements noticed in the general population, especially in R-U gap.

Table 5. 17

Adult literacy (15 years and older) in India, 1981 to 1995–96

	1981			*1991*			*1995–96**		
	Male	*Female*	*Persons*	*Male*	*Female*	*Persons*	*Male*	*Female*	*Persons*
1	*2*	*3*	*4*	*5*	*6*	*7*	*8*	*9*	*10*
Rural	47.39	17.6	32.79	54.89	24.92	40.34	60.59	31.65	46.38
Urban	76.29	51.9	65.11	80.14	59.86	70.68	85.68	67.35	76.98
Combined	54.92	25.72	40.63	61.89	34.09	48.54	67.25	40.67	54.32
R-U gap	–28.9	–34.3	–32.32	–25.25	–34.94	–30.34	–25.09	–35.7	–30.6
Male-Female	29.2			27.8			26.58		

* NSSO 52nd Round, 1995–96

Source: National Human Development Report, India 2001

Literacy rate, especially adult literacy, gives an instant picture of the take-off status of a country or a state in its campaign for targeting a desired level of living for the common man. But the sustainability of the course of human development would depend upon the state of social infrastructure created in the country for this besides other resources as public health and hygiene, physical infrastructure, natural resources and the state-of-the-art technology available and resource allocation.

Figure 5.3
Adult (15+ age) literacy rate, India 1981–1995-96

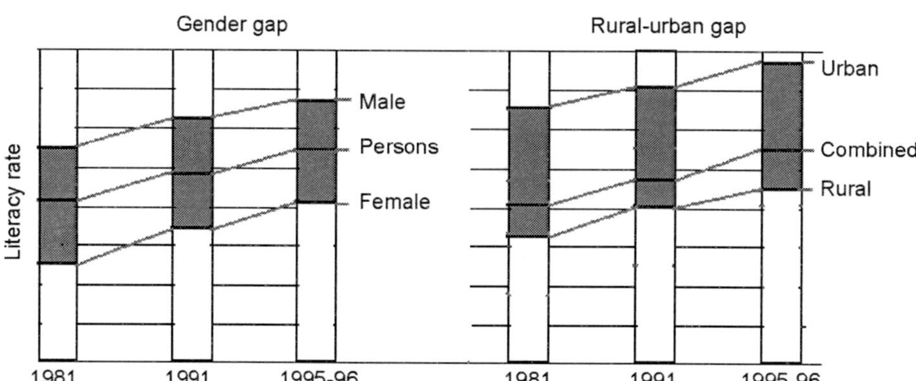

The industrially developed countries and the countries with high human development are seen to have achieved hundred or near hundred percent adult literacy. This they achieved through universalization of elementary education and creating the right type of infrastructure for achieving this goal. From time to time governments at the center and the states have talked about universalization of elementary education in India and assured government support for free education for children up to age 14 years. Policies have been framed to bring about substantial improvement in the quality of education imparted. These include improvement of school infrastructure, establishment of new schools in a manner that would prevent young children from walking distances more than one kilometer, provide midday meals at schools to attract more children to enroll in the school system, improve the teacher-pupil ratio, provide basic facilities in schools such as better school building with toilet and drinking water facilities and playground, provide adequate teaching aids, regular review of school curricula, regular training of teachers, periodic inspection, and many others to enable pupils to achieve desired levels and quality of schooling.

The 93rd Constitutional Amendment Bill, 2001 has reiterated fundamental right to free and compulsory education to children. Legislative measures have been taken for provisioning of public resources for improving accessibility of children to schools. Some states even have included in their education policy to supply free text books, schools bags, uniforms, especially to girls to encourage school enrolment and deter premature withdrawal of children from schools. By 2002, 14 states and 4 UTs have passed Acts making elementary education compulsory in the entire state or in some notified areas. Included in this list are the states Jammu & Kashmir, Haryana, Punjab, Rajasthan, Gujarat, Maharashtra, Uttar Pradesh, Bihar, Madhya Pradesh, West Bengal, Andhra Pradesh, Tamil Nadu, Karnataka and Kerala. The UTs Delhi, Chandigarh, Pondicheri and Andaman and Nicober Islands have also passed similar Acts. Even where such Act has been passed, it remains largely un-enforced because of tremendous pressure on the states' financial resources.

5.4 Logistic Support for Expansion of Education

Certain relevant statistics regarding post-independence spread of education in India is presented in Table 5.18.

Table 5.18

Growth of recognized educational institutions in India since 1951

Year	Primary	Upper primary	Sum 2 + 3	Index of growth
1	2	3	4	5
1950–51	209671	13596	223267	100.0
1956–56	278135	21730	299865	134.3
1960–61	330399	49663	380062	170.2
1965–66	391064	75798	466862	209.1
1970–71	408378	90621	498999	223.5
1975–76	454270	106571	560841	251.2
1980–81	494503	118555	613058	274.6
1985–86	528872	134846	663718	297.3
1990–91	560935	151456	712391	319.1
1991–92	566744	155926	722670	323.7
1992–93	572541	153921	726462	325.4
1993–94	572923	155707	728630	326.3
1994–95	581305	163605	744910	333.6
1995–96	590421	171216	761637	341.1
1996–97	598354	176722	775076	347.2
1997–98	610763	185506	796269	356.6

Table 5.18 Cont'd...

Year	High/Hr. Sec/Inter/ Pr.Jr. colleges*	Colleges for general education	Colleges for professional education	Sum 6 to 8	Index of growth	Universities#	Index of growth
1	6	7	8	9	10	11	12
1950–51	7416	370	208	7994	100.0	27	100.0
1956–56	10838	466	218	11522	144.1	31	114.8
1960–61	17329	967	852	19148	239.5	45	166.7
1965–66	27614	1536	770	29920	374.3	64	237.0
1970–71	37051	2285	992	40328	504.5	82	303.7
1975–76	43054	3667	*3276	49997	625.4	101	374.1
1980–81	51573	3421	*3542	58536	732.2	110	407.4
1985–86	65837	4067	*1533	71437	893.6	126	466.7
1990–91	79796	4862	886	85544	1070.1	184	681.5
1991–92	82576	5058	950	88584	1108.1	#196	725.9
1992–93	84076	5334	989	90399	1130.8	#207	766.7

Cont'd...

Table 5.18 Cont'd...

1	*6*	*7*	*8*	*9*	*10*	*11*	*12*
1993–94	88411	5639	1125	95175	1190.6	#213	788.9
1994–95	92252	6089	1230	99571	1245.6	#219	811.1
1995–96	98134	6569	1354	106057	1326.7	#226	837.0
1996–97	102183	6759	1770	110712	1384.9	#228	844.4
1997–98	107100	7199	2075	116374	1455.8	#229	848.1

*Includes institutions for Post-Matric courses
Includes Deemed Universities & Institutes of National Importance
Source: Annual Report 2000–2001: Ministry of Human Resources Development, Gvt. India.

In a little over 40 years after independence the number of educational institutions increased by over 300 percent. More than 70 percent of educational institutions were primary schools. The increase was fastest in the fifties and sixties, slowing down considerably since 1970. Since the announcement of the National Educational Policy 1986, founding of new schools, elementary and higher, gained considerable momentum. Between 1986 and 1998 over 132,000 new primary and upper primary schools came up; about 35,000 High/Higher Secondary schools and over 3,000 new colleges for general education were established in various parts of the country. Between 1950–51 and 1997–98, colleges for professional education increased from 208 to 2076, a ten-fold rise – about 1,100 such colleges came up in the five years between 1992–93 and 1997–98 alone. At the time of independence, India had only 27 Universities. By 1997–98, additional 202 Universities/Deemed Universities and Institutes of National Importance came up, 58 new Universities alone came up between 1985–86 and 1990–91.

In spite of the growth in number of primary schools, the number of schools per thousand populations has been declining.

Table 5.19
Number of schools per thousand populations

	Primary	*Upper primary*
1982–83	5.70	2.44
1992–93	5.75	2.69
1997–98	5.04	2.75

5.5 Enrolment in Schools

The central government, in partnership with the states and the local bodies, took up a program for universal education, in the name and style of *Sarva Shiksha Abhijan* (education for all). The major objectives are:

1. Five years of primary schooling for every child by 2007;
2. Eight years of schooling for all children by 2010;
3. Bridge the gender and social category gaps at primary stage by 2007 and at elementary education level by 2010; and
4. Universal retention by 2010.

To achieve these goals, Rs 6,000 million additional budgetary resources needed to be generated by the Central and state governments.

The flow or spread of education in a country is generally indicated by enrolment of children in schools. There are alternative measures, each capturing some aspect of the flow or spread of education.

Table 5.20
Sex-wise enrolment by stages since 1951 (in million)

Year	*Primary*			*Proportion of girls to boys*	*Index of growth of (4)*
	Boys	*Girls*	*Children*		
1	*2*	*3*	*4*	*5*	*6*
1950–51	13.8	5.4	19.2	39.1	100
1955–56	17.1	7.5	24.6	43.9	128.1
1960–61	23.6	11.4	35.0	48.3	182.3
1965–66	32.2	18.3	50.5	56.8	263.0
1970–71	35.7	21.3	57.0	59.7	296.9
1975–76	40.6	25.0	65.6	61.6	341.7
1980–81	45.3	28.5	73.8	62.9	384.4
1985–86	52.2	32.2	84.4	61.7	439.6
1990–91	57.0	40.4	97.4	70.9	507.3
1991–92	58.6	42.3	100.9	72.2	525.5
1992–93	57.9	41.7	99.6	72.0	518.8
1993–94	55.1	41.9	97.0	76.0	505.2
1994–95	62.3	46.8	109.1	75.1	568.2
1995–96	62.4	47.4	109.8	76.0	571.9
1996–97	62.5	47.9	110.4	76.6	575.0
1997–98	61.2	47.5	108.7	77.6	566.1

Table 5.20 Cont'd...

Year	*Middle/Upper Primary*			*Proportion of girls to boys*	*Index of Growth of (9)*
	Boys	*Girls*	*Children*		
1	*7*	*8*	*9*	*10*	*11*
1950–51	2.6	0.5	3.1	19.2	100
1955–56	3.8	1.0	4.8	26.3	154.8
1960–61	5.1	1.6	6.7	31.4	216.1
1965–66	7.7	2.8	10.5	36.4	338.7
1970–71	9.4	3.9	13.3	41.5	429.0

Cont'd...

Table 5.20 Cont'd...

1	*7*	*8*	*9*	*10*	*11*
1975–76	11.0	5.0	16.0	45.5	516.1
1980–81	13.9	6.8	20.7	48.9	667.7
1985–86	17.7	9.6	27.3	54.2	880.6
1990–91	21.5	12.5	34.0	58.1	1096.8
1991–92	22.0	13.6	35.6	61.8	1148.4
1992–93	21.2	12.9	34.1	60.8	1100.0
1993–94	20.6	13.5	34.1	65.5	1100.0
1994–95	24.5	15.8	40.3	64.5	1300.0
1995–96	25.0	16.0	41.0	64.0	1322.6
1996–97	24.7	16.3	41.0	66.0	1322.6
1997–98	23.7	15.8	39.5	66.7	1274.2

Table 5.20 Cont'd...

Year	***High/Higher Secondary***			***Proportion of girls to boys***	***Index of Growth of (14)***
	Boys	***Girls***	***Children***		
1	***12***	***13***	***14***	***15***	***16***
1950–51	1.3	0.2	1.5	15.4	100
1955–56	2.2	0.4	2.6	18.2	173.3
1960–61	2.7	0.7	3.4	25.9	226.7
1965–66	4.4	1.3	5.7	29.5	380.0
1970–71	5.7	1.9	7.6	33.3	506.7
1975–76	6.5	2.4	8.9	36.9	593.3
1980–81	7.6	3.4	11.0	44.7	733.3
1985–86	11.5	5.0	16.5	43.5	1100.0
1990–91	12.8	6.3	19.1	49.2	1273.3
1991–92	13.5	6.9	20.4	51.1	1360.0
1992–93	13.6	6.9	20.5	50.7	1366.7
1993–94	13.2	7.5	20.7	56.8	1380.0
1994–95	16.0	8.4	24.4	52.5	1626.7
1995–96	16.1	8.8	24.9	54.7	1660.0
1996–97	17.2	9.8	27.0	57.0	1800.0
1997–98	17.08	10.16	27.24	59.5	1816.0

5.5.1 *Gross Enrolment*

It refers to enrolment at a specified level of schooling, *irrespective of the age of the student enrolled*, to the population of children expected to be in the schools as per the prevalent norms. The national planners wanted at least one primary school in every village so that a child did not have to walk more than one kilometer to reach the school. But the promise is yet to be fulfilled. The government declared that all children below 14 years would be given education free of cost and that 100 percent of children in 6–14 years would be enrolled in schools. But the target has not been fulfilled till today. By 1984, 75 percent of children in age group 6–14 years were enrolled in the school system. The gross enrolment ratio in class I–V was 94.9 percent in 1999–2000. For some states this ratio exceeded 100 percent, more so in case of boys. But there was a huge drop in enrolment in VI–VIII; a meager 58.8 percent of those enrolled in I–V continued beyond this level.

From 19.2 million children enrolled in primary level in 1950–51, the number rose to about 109 million in 1997–98 (growth index 566%). The index of growth in upper primary classes is 1274 percent during the same period indicating that the drop out rates in I–V has fallen considerably. Even then 40 percent of those admitted in primary schools leave schools before completing the primary stage education. For every 100 boys admitted in primary schools there were only 39 girls in 1950–51. Towards the end of the last millennium the same rose to about 78. But the sex ratio in upper primary stage was still way behind that in the primary stage. Only about 8 of every 100 students admitted in primary schools reached secondary stage in 1950–51 (9.4% of boys and 3.7% of girls). The retention improved to 25 percent in 1997–98 (28% for boys and 21.5% for girls). The wastage when computed from upper primary stage has dropped from 52 percent in 1950–51 to 31 percent in 1997–98. Enrolment in secondary stage schools has risen by 18 fold between 1950–51 and 1997–98.

The statistics relating to rise in enrolment ratio published by different states are compiled at various levels. The sanction of additional posts of teachers, building additional classrooms, more teaching aids and equipments for the school, additional fund necessary to provide midday meals to increased number of children, etc. are all linked to the size of enrolment in a school. It is therefore no wonder that there often would remain a large gap between the number of children in the school registered and the actual number of students attending classes. Central and state government educational assistance under different schemes for districts or blocks or *panchayats* are also linked to the declared level of achievements recorded in enrollment of students. It is no wonder then that some inflation in enrolment is likely to happen at various stages of compilation. Even if it is assumed that the school registers really show the actual number of students admitted in various classes, there is no guarantee that all of them are attending their classes and the general attendance is satisfactory. It is a very common observation that the number of students swells in the school prior to serving the midday meal and thereafter the number drops drastically. A very large number of children, mostly from very poor socioeconomic background, leave the school after the midday meal is served.

NCAER in its 1994 survey found 71 percent enrolment rate for rural India as a whole with a gender disparity of 0.84 showing a deficit of 16 percent for girls. Enrolments are generally high in the Southern and Western states with low gender disparity. Though Bihar has the lowest level of enrolment (59%), Rajasthan has the highest gender disparity (46%) with an overall enrolment at 61 percent. Enrolment rate of children in schools was found lacking in families where there were no adult literate men or women. Enrolment ratio increased to 92 percent in households having both adult literate men and women. A very similar observation was made in a small survey conducted in 16 villages from four districts of West Bengal by the present author in as early as 1973–74. With only an educated female in the household, female enrolment was as high as 87 percent compared to 72 percent female enrolment in households where there were no literate women. In highly developed village groups the gender disparity was only about 7 percent.

The high literacy tradition in Kerala gives the state a distinctive status among all other states. It is the only state where the enrolment rate, even by gender and social groups, is unrelated to household income. In other states the variation is quite high with income groups. The question posed but not answered well is: Why enrolment ratio is poor among poorer households when primary and elementary schooling is provided free of cost and when such incentives as midday meal, free books and school bags and dresses in many states are provided to these children? Three possible reasons can be identified:

1. There is no demand for schooling. Some parents, who themselves are illiterate and poorly placed in society, do not realize the utility of education;
2. Inadequate schooling facilities and discriminatory treatment for children from low income and minority social groups; and
3. High direct and indirect costs of schooling.

5.5.2 Age-Specific Enrolment Ratio

It is defined as:

$$\frac{\text{Estimated enrolment in an age group}}{\text{Estimated child population in the age group}} \times 100$$

The ratio for the age group 6–14 years increased from 48.3 percent in 1981 to 55.3 percent in 1991. The Census data indicates that for rural areas the increase was from 42.2 percent to 49.9 percent and that for urban areas the same were 69.7 and 72 percent respectively. For boys, the increase was from 58 percent in 1981 to 62.1 percent in 1991; the same for the girls was from 37.8 and 47.9 percent. In Bihar, Rajasthan and Uttar Pradesh, the age-specific enrolment ratio was low, close to 40 percent. Kerala, Himachal Pradesh, Maharashtra and a few other smaller states and Union Territories registered over 70 percent enrolment in 6–14 year age group. There was considerable difference between male and female enrolment as also differences between the states.

A break-up for two age groups, 6 to below 11 years and 11 to 14 years is presented below. There is only a marginal improvement, only 4 percent in enrolment in 6 to less than 11 years age group. In urban area, the enrolment in the first group declined marginally between 1981 and 1991. Enrolment of urban boys has gone down by 2 percentage points. Enrolment of both rural and urban girls has improved by around 7 percentage points. The rural-urban gap in enrolment in 6–11 age group has declined by 5 to 7 percentage points (Table 5.23). The gap in the enrolment ratio between boys and girls also came down in this decade. Age specific enrolment ratio is much better in 11–14 years age group. There is 12 percentage points gain in enrolment ratio in this age group. The gain is maximum with girls in rural areas and a somewhat smaller gain is observed in urban areas. The gaps between rural and urban enrolment ratios both for boys and girls, though have declined by around 6 percentage points, still are very large.

Table 5.21

Age-specific enrolment ratios by sex and residence (percentage), 1981 & 1991

	Age group 6 to below 11 years						*Age group 11 to below 14 years*					
	1981			*1991*			*1981*			*1991*		
	B	*G*	*C*	*B*	*G*	*C*	*B*	*G*	*C*	*B*	*G*	*C*
1	*2*	*3*	*4*	*5*	*6*	*7*	*8*	*9*	*10*	*11*	*12*	*13*
Combined	55.3	38.5	47.2	56.6	45.4	51.2	62.0	36.7	50.0	71.1	52.2	62.1
Rural	50.6	31.4	41.3	52.3	39.3	46.0	57.6	28.1	43.7	67.6	44.4	56.7
Urban	72.8	64.9	69.0	70.7	65.8	68.3	76.6	64.5	70.8	81.0	73.6	77.5
Boys–Girls	16.8		11.2		25.3		18.9					
R–U gap	–22.2	–33.5	–27.7	–18.4	–26.5	–22.3	–19.0	–36.4	–27.1	–13.4	–29.2	–20.8

B – Boys, G – Girls, C – Children

Source: National Human Development Report, India 2001

Table 5.22

Age specific enrolment ratio for three most advanced and backward states/UTs by sex and residence, 1981–1991*

	Age group 6 to below 11 years						*Age group 11 to below 14 years*					
	1981			*1991*			*1981*			*1991*		
	C	*B-G*	*U-R*	*C*	*B-G*	*U-R*	*C*	*B-G*	*U-R*	*C*	*B-G*	*U-R*
1	*2*	*3*	*4*	*5*	*6*	*7*	*8*	*9*	*10*	*11*	*12*	*13*
Kerala	90	0.8	3.6	91	0.2	1.8	84	4.1	3.8	93	0.6	2.6
Lakshadweep*	82	5.6	–2.2	89	1.7	0.1	87	13.5	–1.3	88	5.7	–4.5
Pondicheri*	77	10.6	10.7	86	1.8	0.1	67	9.4	11.5	84	6.0	2.2
Rajasthan	34	18.5	20.2	39	14.0	18.2	40	31.0	30.8	52	41.2	26.7
Bihar	34	20.6	31.7	34	15.6	28.4	42	32.7	30.7	51	25.7	28.6
Arunachal	32	15.1	35.0	38	9.2	25.4	43	24.2	30.7	62	15.0	20.7

Source: National Human Development Report, India 2001.

Three top states/UTs in enrolment of children in 6 to below 11 years (1991) age group are Kerala (91.2%), Lakshadweep (89.2%) and Pondicheri (85.8%). They almost had the same ranks in 1981 as well. The difference in enrolment between boys and girls in these 3 states/UTs was virtually nil. Lakshadweep showed slightly better enrolment ratio both for 6–11 years and 11–14 years age group. The three backward states Rajasthan, Bihar and Arunachal Pradesh not only did poorly in school enrolment of children, there was huge gap between boys and girls and between rural and urban sectors in enrolment ratio for both the segments of children. The achievements of these 6 states/UTs in enrolment show almost a pattern similar to that observed in the ranking of the states/UTs in CLR in the general population. The other two BIMARU states, namely Madhya Pradesh and Uttar Pradesh have not performed any better than the two other constituents of BIMARU.

Net enrolment ratio overcomes the shortcomings of both gross and age-specific enrolment ratio. *Net enrolment ratio refers to the proportion of population of a particular age group enrolled at a specific level of schooling to the total population in that age group*. From the census data we cannot get this type of enrolment ratio. For this, we have to depend upon the Sixth All-India Educational Survey 1993 and the 52nd Round of NSSO (1995–96). As per the Educational Survey, 57.5 percent of children in age group 6–14 were enrolled in classes I–VIII. The ratio was 64 percent for age group 6 to less than 11 years and 44.8 percent for ages 11 to below 14 years. NSSO data for 1995–96 give a net enrolment ratio of 66 percent for classes I–V and 43 percent for classes VI–VIII. In rural areas this was 63 and 39 percent respectively. The corresponding ratios in urban areas were 78 and 58 percent.

Figure 5.4

Gender and rural-urban gap in age specific enrolment ratio

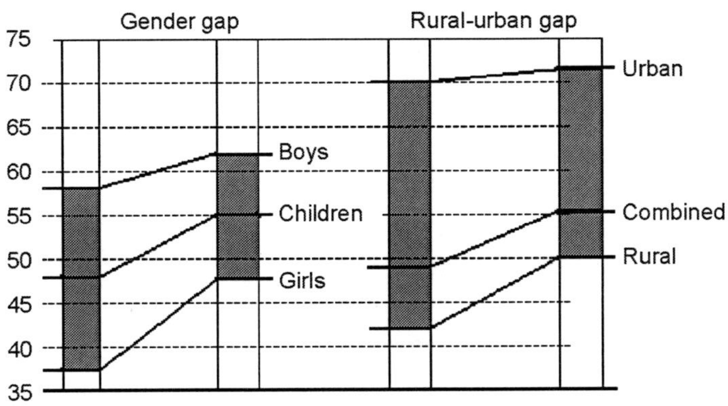

Table 5.23

Girls enrolled in various school stages, 1978 & 1993

Rural/ Urban	*I–V*			*VI–VIII*			*IX–X*			*XI–XII*		
	All	*SC*	*ST*	*All*	*SC*	*ST*	*All*	*SC*	*ST*	*All*	*SC*	*ST*
1	*2*	*3*	*4*	*5*	*6*	*7*	*8*	*9*	*10*	*11*	*12*	*13*
						1978						
Comb.	38.3	34.4	33.3	32.7	25.8	27.0	28.7	21.5	26.7			
Rural	36.2	32.7	32.8	27.8	22.0	25.1	21.9	17.1	24.1			
Urban	44.8	40.9	39.5	40.3	33.2	34.7	34.8	26.7	31.9			
						1993						
Comb.	43.2	41.7	41.5	39.6	36.3	35.8	36.5	32.3	32.1	35.9	30.3	27.6
Rural	42.0	40.5	41.0	36.4	33.0	34.0	32.2	28.9	29.9	29.8	25.5	26.3
Urban	46.7	46.0	45.5	45.1	42.7	42.7	41.7	37.4	38.2	39.7	34.0	29.6

SC – Scheduled Castes ST – Scheduled Tribes

Source: NCERT, 1999

NSSO data present higher enrolment ratio than the NCERT data. Girls (combined) enrolments in the three class categories have improved by 5 to 8 percentage points in 25 years. The increases in enrolments for girls in urban area are up 2 percentage points for I–V, 5.1 percentage points for VI–VIII and 6.9 percentage points for IX–X. An appreciable higher increase rates are observed in rural areas. The differences in enrolments observed between 'combined' and SC and ST girls declined noticeably in 1993 both in rural and urban areas. But this enrolment statistics of girls are not really reflected in the literacy rates attained by the respective population groups.

Drop out rate *is the percentage of students dropping out of classes in a given year.* Along with those not promoted to the next class, the drop out rate gives a picture of wastage in school education in spite of increases in the proportion of enrolment. It is to be admitted that drop out rate at national level has been declining. But there are considerable disparities between the states and regions in the drop out rates. The drop out rate is very high in Bihar, Jammu & Kashmir, Orissa, Rajasthan, Uttar Pradesh, West Bengal and most of the Northeastern states. The NSSO survey suggests that drop out rate increases cumulatively with level of education. It was estimated that 21 percent in the age group 5–14 years dropped out before completing primary level. Half the children dropped out attaining middle level (VI–VIII), over three-fourths before attaining secondary level and only 1 out of every 10 children enrolled could complete schooling. The drop out was least in families that were better off financially, and it was maximum in households coming from the lowest expenditure class. It has also been suggested that the students from poorer households drop out in the early stages in schooling. Students from better-off families drop out at later stages. Some surveys found that the drop out rate among the school-going children was maximum between the ages 12 and 15 years, presumably because they were asked to take up jobs to help the family.

Table 5.24

All-India drop-out rates at various school levels for different reference years

Class	*1981–82*			*1992–93*			*1998–99*		
	B	*G*	*C*	*B*	*G*	*C*	*B*	*G*	*C*
I–V	51.1	57.3	53.5	43.8	46.7	45.0	38.2	41.3	39.6
I–VIII	68.5	77.7	72.1	58.2	65.2	61.1	54.4	60.1	56.8
I–X	79.4	86.8	82.3	70.0	77.3	72.9	65.4	70.2	67.4

Figure 5.5

Drop-out rates (%) in various classes

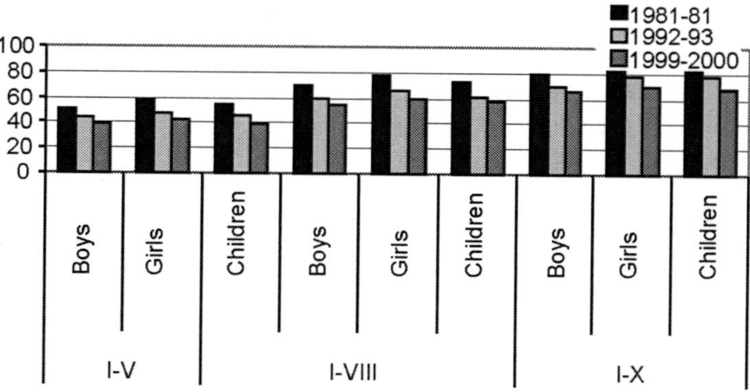

The states that have made rapid strides in raising literacy rates have done so by bringing down drop out rates apart from improvement in enrolment. Rajasthan, Madhya Pradesh, Haryana, Tamil Nadu, Maharashtra and Punjab have succeeded significantly in arresting drop outs. The drop out rates in bigger states like Bihar, West Bengal and Andhra Pradesh has remained stagnant and high.

5.5.3 Intensity of Formal Education

The enrolment rate does not really capture the flow or spread of education. Drop outs, students repeating the same class and poor and irregular attendance rates often nullify the claims of spread of education. The enrolment becomes meaningful only if the student is retained over successive classes. *Mean years of schooling* or *intensity of formal education* can give a better picture of the enrolment situation. In constructing this indicator, a weighted average of the share of class-wise enrolment in classes I–XII is taken, the weights increasing in successive classes from 1 to 12. This is then adjusted by the gross enrolment ratio for the population of children in age group 6–18 years. The more the higher enrolment ratio in higher classes, that is, the more the schools are able to retain children for a longer duration without drop out, and at the same time have a larger proportion of children of school-going age group, the better shall be the *Adjusted Intensity of Formal Education.*

At national level, the intensity of formal education was 4.03 years for students enrolled in 1978. It increased to 4.64 in 1993. For girls, it was lower for both the years – 3.76 and 4.46 years for years 1978 and 1993 respectively. For boys, the respective figures were 4.19 and 4.77. The gender gap decreased by 0.12 in 25 years. The intensity of formal education in rural areas in 1978 was about 73 percent of that in the urban areas. In 1993, it increased marginally to 77 percent. The adjusted intensity of formal education is estimated at 2.04 years in 1978 and 2.70 years in 1993. Between the two time points, the gender gap declined from 1.19 to 0.84 years (boys: 2.61 and 3.10 years). The R-U gap remained stationary at 1.6 years (urban: 3.20 and 3.81 years). Both unadjusted and adjusted intensity of formal education varied widely across states.

Table 5.25

Intensity of formal education by sex and residence, 1978 & 1993

	Rural			*Urban*			*Combined*		
	Boys	*Girls*	*Children*	*Boys*	*Girls*	*Children*	*Boys*	*Girls*	*Children*
	1	*2*	*3*	*4*	*5*	*6*	*7*	*8*	*9*
				1978					
Unadjusted	3.83	3.27	3.64	5.16	4.69	4.97	4.19	3.76	4.03
Adjusted	2.14	1.08	1.68	3.94	2.49	3.20	2.61	1.42	2.04
				1993					
Unadjusted	4.41	3.99	4.25	5.63	5.36	5.51	4.77	4.46	4.64
Adjusted	2.76	1.82	2.31	4.08	3.50	3.81	3.10	2.26	2.70

Source : National Human Development Report, India 2001

Among the major states, the unadjusted intensity of formal education in Bihar remained lowest both in 1978 and 1993 (3.28 and 3.97 years respectively). The adjusted values in Bihar for the respective years were 1.34 and 1.69 years respectively. Expectedly, Kerala was way ahead of other states both in unadjusted and adjusted mean years of schooling. The unadjusted mean years of schooling increased from 4.94 years in 1978 to 5.44 years 1993. The adjusted value went up from 3.79 to 3.94 years in the same period. Goa and two UTs Lakshadweep and Pondicheri had better averages in the respective years than the averages observed even in Kerala. The adjusted intensity of formal education in these three States/UTs respectively was 4.75, 4.81 and 4.84 in 1993.

The following table gives an indication as to how our achievements in the spread and intensity of education compare with world averages and selected few countries.

Table 5.26
Imbalance in the race for knowledge

Country/ development category	*Years of schooling*		*Enrolment ratio*				*Pub. edn exp as % of GNP (1993–96)*	*Scientists and engineers in R&D (per 100, 000 people)*
			Secondary		*Tertiary*			
	1980	*1990*	*1970*	*1997*	*1970*	*1995*		
1	*2*	*3*	*4*	*5*	*6*	*8*	*9*	*10*
High HDI	8.9	9.4	79	94	30	67	5.1	2827
Medium HDI	4.1	5.1	22	65	3	9	3.8	
Low HDI	1.8	2.8	8	28	1	2		
Republic of Korea	7.9	9.9		97	15 (1980)	68 (1997)	3.7	2193
Singapore	5.5	6.0		76	8 (1980)	43 (1997)	3.0	2318
USA	11.9	11.7		96	56 (1980)	81 (1997)	5.4	3676
INDIA	4.0	4.64		60			3.4	149
World	5.2	6.0	35	62	8	16	4.8	959

Source: Human Development Report, UNDP 2001.

NSSO and others have tried to ascertain the reasons for drop outs. Some of the reasons suggested are:

- Children/parents not interested to continue schooling
- Economic/family considerations – work for wages or looking after younger siblings
- Unfriendly/unattractive school atmosphere
- Doubt about the usefulness of schooling
- Inability to cope with studies
- Poor teaching standards
- Schooling becoming too expensive
- Physical punishment in schools, etc.

Pratichi Education Trust (founded by Prof. Amartya Sen) conducted a sample survey in 2001 in three districts of West Bengal covering 18 villages. The state has been under Left Front rule since 1977. Some of the disturbing observations in the survey are:

- A large majority of the parents are critical about the performance of the teachers. The dissatisfaction rate is three times more with primary school teachers (who are paid salary between Rs

5,000 – 10,000 per month + DA and other sops admissible) compared to teachers in Sishu Siksha Kendras (SSK) (consolidated pay of Rs 1,000 per month).

- On an average day only about half of the students attend the schools. The attendance of students in SSKs is much higher, around 65 percent.
- The absentee teachers' ratio (20%) is much higher in primary schools than in SSKs (14%). It is to be reminded in this context that most schools have only one or two teachers.
- Even when teachers come to schools, many of them would not take the allotted classes. (This scenario exists in secondary, higher secondary, college and university level education as well in West Bengal).
- The underperformance of primary schools is evident from the fact that a little less than half of the number of children interviewed took private tuitions. The rest who did not take private tuition did so for pecuniary reasons. (In secondary and higher education, private tuition has taken the form of epidemic and the government had to issue circulars to all types of schools asking the teachers to restrain from private tuitions. The circular was subsequently withdrawn under pressure from various quarters). 80 percent of students who could write their names were those who took private tuition. Appalling 7 percent students only could write their names who could not afford private tuition. In effect, even primary education has ceased to be free. The inequality between the rich and the poor starts operating at the very grass-root level of education.
- The primary school teachers often show less attention to those coming from poorer and socially backward families. The greater absenteeism of teachers or arbitrary reduction of school hour or declaring holidays are observed in schools that are numerically dominated by SC and ST students, especially when the teacher is from higher caste.
- Female teachers vis-à-vis male teachers, both in primary schools and SSKs are more caring and disciplined.
- Children of SC and ST communities often are made to sit separately in classes. This discrimination, even in a Left Front run state, is very disquieting. (There are newspaper reports that the upper caste students often boycott midday meals in some schools where lower caste persons cook the meal). Even though the midday meal scheme or free uniforms for girl students have not been extended to SSKs, the attendance of students in SSKs is generally better, more so for girls, presumably because the students in SSKs show greater degree of homogeneity than those attending primary schools.

Enrolment in higher education has increased fast. Number of persons seeking higher education has increased by an average of 10 percent per annum between 1950 and 1982. In the fifties and sixties the growth in enrolment was as high as 12.4 and 13.4 percent respectively. Since 1970, it has dropped sharply. Girls were far behind boys in the formal education system. Naturally, growth rate of enrolment of girls at all levels of education has been much higher than that of the boys. For example, there were only 16 girls for every 100 boys in the secondary stage in 1950. It went up to 42 in 1980 and over 75 in 1999.

In school and college level enrolment, Tamil Nadu was far ahead of others in 1960–61. Jammu & Kashmir, Madhya Pradesh and Bihar were far behind others. Since 1982–83, the picture has changed considerably. The enrolment ratio for boys, except for a few states, often is over 100 percent since many older boys are enrolled in lower classes. For girls, amazing improvement has been registered in Kerala, Himachal Pradesh, Punjab, Gujarat and Tamil Nadu.

5.5.4 *Accessibility to Schools*

Enrolment ratios and drop out rates have something to do with the distance a child has to walk to attend the nearest schools. The 1986 Education Commission assured that every village shall have a primary and upper primary school. Where this would not be possible, care would be taken to open new primary/upper primary schools at such locations so that no child would be required to walking more than 1 km distance. The All India Education Survey, NCERT, 1982 & 1999 gave the following information regarding accessibility to schools in rural areas.

Table 5.27

Accessibility to schools in rural areas, 1978 & 1993

	Population with primary schools			*Population with upper primary schools*		
	Within habitation	*Up to 0.5 km**	*Total up to 0.5 km*	*Within habitation*	*Up to 0.5 km**	*Total up to 0.5 km*
			All India 1978			
Number of states/UTs (%)	78.53	6.60	85.13	33.47	13.10	46.57
Above national level: Number	17	12	19	15	18	16
Below national level: Number	15	20	13	17	14	16
			All India 1993			
Number of states/UTs (%)	77.80	7.69	85.50	37.02	19.89	56.91
Above national level : Number	17	11	19	19	13	18
Below national level : Number	15	21	13	13	19	14

*But not within the habitation

Source: All India Education Survey, NCERT, 1982 & 1999

Increase of enrolment is partly related to the location of the school. When the school is located at a distance place, both children and parents show reluctance to enrolment. Pratichi Trust survey found a few villages that had no primary school within a radius of 2.5 km. The children had to walk to schools through the muddy ridges of paddy fields, cross highways or busy roads to reach the schools. In the monsoon months, they often are forced to stay at home.

In the 25 years between the two time points 1978 and 1993, no significant change has taken place as far as improvement of accessibility to schools in rural areas is concerned. About 22 percent of rural population still does not have a primary school within their habitation though 85 percent of the population does not have to walk more than 0.5 km to attend the nearest primary school. For the upper primary level, 43 percent of the children, still have to go beyond 1 km to attend the nearest upper primary school. Of the top 3 states/UTs in literacy rate, Kerala, Lakshadweep (it had 100% access to primary school within the habitat in 1978; since then it has come down to 86.32% in 1993) and Mizoram, only the last named state has made significant progress in easing accessibility to primary/upper primary schools. Punjab is the only state where 99 percent of the children do not have to walk more than 0.5 km to attend the nearest primary school.

Table 5.28

Availability of schooling facilities at primary stage in rural habitations, 1993 & 2002

State/UT*	Total number of habitations		Number of habitations having Primary Stage schooling facility				% increase in number of habitations having Pr. Stage Schooling facility over the 6th Survey (1993)	
			Within them		Up to 1 km*			
	1993	2002	1993	2002	1993	2002	Within them	Up to 1 km
2	3	4	5	6	7	8	9	10
Andhra Pradesh	62905	66528	43861	52218	55716	62475	19.05	12.13
Arunachal Pradesh	3834	4200	1436	1665	1804	2168	15.95	20.18
Assam	41179	67138	22448	29915	35300	56622	33.26	60.4
Bihar	64799	73030	37712	41418	59827	64935	9.83	8.54
Chhattisgarh	31098	37933	18287	23834	25862	34346	30.33	32.8
Goa	788	711	590	561	693	646	–4.92	–6.78
Gujarat	25749	33258	23285	25916	24656	31136	11.3	26.28
Haryana	7589	8839	6259	6916	7060	8123	10.5	15.06
Himachal Pradesh	35003	35844	7348	10329	20806	26877	40.57	29.18
Jammu & Kashmir	15176	20877	9072	10566	12214	16409	16.47	34.35
Jharkhand	45059	48465	17530	18648	36643	37399	6.38	2.06
Karnataka	48813	51853	29463	34971	40881	45845	18.69	12.14
Kerala	8745	6664	5390	4047	7191	5295	–24.92	–26.37
Madhya Pradesh	71178	85149	41531	58778	57750	75949	41.53	31.51
Maharashtra	72465	77800	46887	52626	61033	70929	12.24	16.21
Manipur	3369	3819	2489	2343	2959	3034	–5.87	2.53
Meghalaya	6576	7277	3677	5028	5003	6219	36.74	24.31
Mizoram	705	746	605	664	620	674	9.75	8.71
Nagaland	1277	1478	1035	1300	1117	1398	25.6	25.16
Orissa	73148	89682	35810	46220	60289	74370	29.07	23.36
Punjab	13345	14726	10785	11671	12774	13763	8.22	7.74
Rajasthan	63970	81014	32697	43271	47711	64678	32.34	35.56
Sikkim	1407	1390	709	735	1048	1083	3.67	3.34
Tamil Nadu	45139	53980	24132	29110	44516	47763	20.63	7.29
Tripura	6802	7556	2619	2835	5134	5732	8.25	11.65
Uttar Pradesh	191376	208932	56147	84749	153967	183772	50.94	19.36

Cont'd...

Table 5.23 Cont'd...

2	3	4	5	6	7	8	9	10
Uttaranchal	20749	25206	8387	11059	15454	21193	31.86	37.14
West Bengal	96511	115685	37009	40883	84636	106757	10.47	26.14
Andaman & N.Is.*	601	673	253	284	331	430	12.25	29.91
Chandigarh*	36	23	25	12	31	20	–52	–35.48
Dadra & Nagar Haveli*	489	460	157	195	401	394	24.2	–1.75
Daman & Diu*	67	82	31	33	64	71	6.45	10.94
Delhi*	271	179	177	107	234	179	–39.55	–23.5
Lakshadweep*	15	7	11	7	14	7	–36.36	–50
Pondicherry*	379	187	197	162	350	172	–17.77	–50.86
INDIA	**1060612**	**1231391**	**528051**	**653076**	**884089**	**1070863**	**23.68**	**21.13**

Source: National Human Development Report, India 2001

5.5.5 Types of Schools

Although providing mass education is a state responsibility, three types of elementary schools are available in all states, even in rural areas:

1. schools run and managed by state governments and local bodies,
2. schools run by private voluntary organizations/local associations/religious trusts that receive regular grants from the state (aided schools) and
3. private primary/nursery schools (often English medium) that do not receive any grant from the government.

Figure 5.6

Percentage of students in private schools

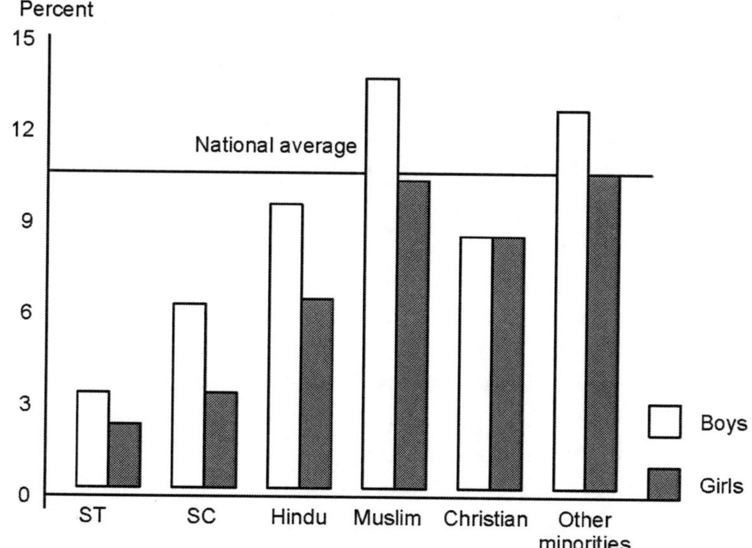

In rural India, NCAER survey estimated that about 68 percent of all school-going children attend government managed schools, another 22 percent government aided schools and only 10 percent going to private schools. There are inter-state variations in attendance of government and government aided schools. In many of the states a very high proportion of children in 6–14 years attend the government aided schools – Northeastern states (91%) and West Bengal (79%). Boys more often than girls attend private schools. Often private schools are a response to poor quality of education in public schools. The Fifth All India Education Survey by NCERT found only 2 percent of students at primary level attending private schools in 1986. National Council of Applied Economic Research in 1994 found this to have increased to about 10 percent. Uttar Pradesh (27%) and Punjab (20%) send a very high proportion of children to private schools. Private English medium schools in primary, secondary and higher secondary stages are increasingly attracting more students, especially in urban areas. These English medium schools are mushrooming in the cities and in other satellite towns in recent years especially after India proved her youth's talent in software technology and their expertise in written and spoken English to world community. Obviously, the high-income families are a very large majority among those who seek English medium education for their children. The Christian and the Muslim families send their children in large numbers to privately managed English medium schools or to schools run by their own fraternity both for medium of instruction and for the content (religious) of the school curricula. The share of government schools in all states is declining and the aided and private schools are going up as a result.

5.6 Public Spending on Education

5.6.1 Education Expenditure Ratio EER

Public expenditure for creation and maintenance of education infrastructure in the country has gone up considerably between 1980–81 and 1998–99. The education expenditure ratio, that is, percentage of public expenditure on education to the total public expenditure has increased consistently both at the central and the state level. For the former, the ratio has increased from 2.7 to 3.9 percent between 1980–81 and 1998–99; for the latter EER went up from 13.89 to 17.36 percent between 1980–81 and 1990–91 and only a very marginal increase between 1990–91 and 1998–99. In 1980–81 the states that spent most on education are Kerala (25.30%) followed by Punjab (16.99%) and West Bengal (15.92%). Lowest EER was recorded in Jammu & Kashmir (10.37%), Madhya Pradesh (10.82%) and Haryana (12.06%). In some of the Northeastern states EER was even below 10 percent. In 1990–91, Kerala (23.55%), West Bengal (22.95%) and Bihar (19.98%) had higher EER than all other states. Assam spent most (26.34%) followed by Bihar (21.16%), Tamil Nadu (19.76%) and Rajasthan (19.53%) on education in 1998–99.

Public spending on education has gradually increased from around 3.5 percent of GNP in 1985 to over 4.2 percent in 2000–2001 of which about 40 percent was spent on primary education and about 27 percent on secondary education. The share of higher education, especially in science and technology, has came down from 15.3 percent in 1985–86 to about 13.7 percent in 1995–97. It increased again to 15.4 percent in 2000–01. As percentage to total government expenditure it was about 11.6 percent. Various Education Commissions had recommended increase in public spending on education to 6 percent of GNP. In the developed countries public expenditure on education is often above 6 percent of GNP. However, in India, more than 75 percent of the allotted sum is spent on salary of teachers alone, and 10 percent on salary of non-teaching employees and other administrative heads. Although only around 28 percent of people live in towns and cities and they have better purchasing power than those living in villages, more than 55 percent of budgeted allocation on education is spent in urban areas.

Ratio of Expenditure on Education at state level to Gross State Domestic Product went up for all the states between 1980–81 and 1998–99 except in Kerala where it declined by a huge margin, –6.57 points. Even with this decline in EER, Kerala still holds rank 1 among the states/UTs with literacy rate over 90 percent. Assam increased its EER from 12.76 percent in 1980–81 to 26.34 percent in 1998–99. Even after allocating more funds for spread of education, the state's literacy ranking went down from 23 in 1991 to 24 in 2001. Rajasthan is the only BIMARU state, that improved its EER by a good 6.5 points between 1980–1981 and 1998–99 (from 13.07 to 19.53) and improved the state's literacy ranking by a big margin, from 33 in 1991 to 29 in 2001. Bihar, another BIMARU state increased EER by 8 points from 13.19 in 1980–81 to 21.16 in 1998–99, yet the state has the poorest literacy rate in the country, the only state having below 50 percent literacy in the population. Although West Bengal recorded a huge drop by 5.17 points in EER between 1990–91 and 1998–99 (from 22.95 to 17.78), the state improved the literacy ranking from 19 to 18. Even after increasing EER by 12.76 points, accessibility of primary schools within a distance of 0.5 km in Assam declined from 87.46 percent in 1978 to 80.20 in 1993. In West Bengal it dropped from 90.82 to 84.19, the drop in Bihar was by more than 10 percent. Teacher-pupil ratio in Bihar dropped from 1:41 in 1982–83 to 1:62 in 1997–98. Kerala cut down EER by 6.57 points but teacher-pupil ratio in primary schools improved from 1:33 in 1982–83 to 1:30 in 1997–98 and accessibility to primary schools remained almost the same.

As per the National Accounts Statistics (NAS), the share of private expenditure on educational services to the total private consumption expenditure increased from around 2.5 percent in the early eighties to around 3.5 percent in the late nineties. This rise could, at least partially, be due to the growing presence of private and missionary schools from kindergarten level to the vocational and professional colleges throughout the country.

State governments' average expenditure on Social Sector has gone up nearly by 4 percent between 1980–81 and 1998–99. An almost identical growth is observed in educational spending by states. Expenditure on health and other social services have come down to make room for increased 'amenities'. Of the 1.9 percent additional provision for 'Social Sector' by the central government in 1998–99 over 1980–81 allotment, 1.2 percent has gone to 'education' alone.

The nation-wide sample survey conducted by NCAER found that "free education" in rural India costs around Rs 378 per child per annum. A very large proportion of this expenditure is on books and stationery, school uniform, private coaching and fees. Expenditure for girls' education is less than that for boys'. Parents squeeze all their resources they have to send their sons to private schools to give them better education. NCAER observed that private elementary schooling was 230 percent more expensive than schooling in government and aided schools. Household expenditure on primary education increases as the household incomes rise. About 10 percent of the household expenditure goes on private tuitions and examination; 'other fees' share is about 19 percent; books, stationeries and uniform have the bulk share, about 67 percent. That is, an average rural household spends about Rs 40 on tuition per child and about Rs 270 on books etc. on the child per annum. West Bengal tops the list of states in spending sums on private coaching (36%) even for a child in elementary level of education. The same survey observed that 13–15 percent of expenditure on education per rural household is for fees in government and aided schools and 34 percent in private schools.

Table 5.29
Public spending on social sector – some critical ratios

State/Central Government	Social sector	Education	Health	Amenities	Other social services
		1980–81			
State Government	29.12	13.89	7.10	1.14	7.00
Central Government	6.30	2.70	1.40	0.40	0.80
		1990–91			
State Government	32.89	17.36	5.88	3.86	5.79
Central Government	6.40	3.50	1.50	0.40	1.00
		1998–99			
State Government	33.07	17.39	5.78	4.53	5.38
Central Government	8.20	3.90	1.80	1.00	1.40

Note:
1. The table entries are all public expenditure as proportion of Gross State Domestic Product.
2. Social sector expenditure includes all expenditure on education, health, amenities (water supply and sanitation, housing and urban development), other social services (including welfare of SC, ST & OBC; social security and welfare, etc.)

Source: National Human Development, India 2001

Table 5.30
Educational expenditure as percentage of GDP (at current prices) in India

Year	GDP at Factor cost (Rs crores)	Total educational expenditure (Rs crores)	Educational Expenditure as percentage of GDP
1	*2*	*3*	*4*
1950–51	9,547	114	1.19
1960–61	16,220	344	2.12
1970–71	42,222	1,118	2.65
1975–76	75,709	2,105	2.78
1980–81	130,176	3,859	2.96
1985–86	249,547	8,812	3.53
1986–87	278,258	9,807	3.52
1987–88	315,993	11,751	3.72
1988–89	378,491	13,871	3.66
1989–90	438,020	16,905	3.86
1990–91	510,954	19,791	3.87
1991–92	589,086	21,914	3.72
1992–93	673,221	24,722	3.67

Cont'd...

Table 5.30 Cont'd...

1	*2*	*3*	*4*
1993–94	781,345	27,530	3.52
1994–95	917,058	32,107	3.50
1995–96	1,073,271	37,097	3.46
1996–97	1,243,546	43,035	3.46
1997–98	1,390,148	49,032	3.53
1998–99	1,598,127	62,297	3.90
1999–00	1,761,932	70,197	3.98
2000–01	1,917,724	80,881	4.22

Source: Central Statistical Organization. Department of Education, Ministry of Human Resources & Development.

Table 5. 31

Percentage allocation of total (Center + State) budget for education by sub-sector of education (revenue accounts) for India

Year	*EE as % of GDP (at current prices)*	*Percentage of total budget allocation for*					
		Elementary education	*Secondary education*	*Adult education*	*University education*	*Technical education*	*Other educational programs*
1	*2*	*3*	*4*	*5*	*6*	*7*	*8*
1970–71a	2.65	15.4	29.1	2.2a	12.2	5.4 9	0.5
1975–76	2.78	46.2	31.3	0.8	13.4	4.4	3.9
1980–81	2.96	45.5	30.7	0.8	14.3	4.1	4.6
1985–86	3.53	46.2	30.8	1.2	14.0	4.6	3.2
1990–91	3.87	46.3	32.2	1.6	13.4	4.4	2.1
1995–96	3.46	48.3	32.8	0.8	12.3	4.1	1.7
1996–97	3.46	49.1	32.3	0.6	11.8	4.0	2.2
1997–98	3.53	49.6	32.3	0.5	11.8	4.0	1.8
1998–99	3.90	49.1	32.6	0.4	11.9	4.1	1.9
1999–00	3.98	45.6	34.0	0.3	13.5	4.0	2.6
2000–01b	4.22	47.2	30.5	0.4	15.4	4.1	2.4

a. Special education in 1970–71.
b. Revised estimates
Source: Department of Education, Ministry of Human Resources & Development.

The Pratichi Trust, besides covering 18 primary schools from three districts in West Bengal, conducted a survey on 196 households selected from all households from these villages. 89 of these households (45%) reported expenditure on private tuition. The cost of private tuition varied from Rs 20 to Rs 50 per month and the limits of months of private tuition varied from 6 to 12 months. The estimated minimum cost of private tuition per child in a year was Rs 120. Both NCAER and Pratichi Trust survey confirm that appointment of private tutors even at the primary level in rural areas is becoming the order of the day. Engaging private tutors for getting "free elementary education" must be a near universal phenomenon in cities and important urban centers. Many of the states excluded English at the primary level. But the rollback in some of the states in recent years would put more pressure on parents to appoint private tutors from the very beginning of a child's education career since most of the school teachers, especially in primary schools, are products of that era in some states when English in lower classes lost the favor of political patronage.

5.7 State of Health of Education in India

5.7.1 Infrastructure in Primary Schools

Most of the school buildings in remote areas are in a dilapidated condition. When a primary school needs at least 4/5 large rooms to accommodate students and teachers, many schools in rural areas have two or three rooms of which one room is used as the office-cum-teachers' room. Classes for new entrants often are held under the shade of a tree or in the open corridor of the school building. Classes are suspended whenever a storm or a threatening rain cloud appears. For years no maintenance work is done. It makes a mess whenever there is a heavy downpour. Often there are neither toilets nor drinking water facilities in the school premises. The physical atmosphere of the school is anything but attractive. The Pratichi Trust observed, "One of the schools we studied had no building at all, and eight of them had two classrooms to accommodate four classes, with an inescapable need for displacement." The survey also found that 18 schools surveyed (a total of 2,291 students enrolled) 4 of them had no doors and windows, 16 needed immediate repair, 16 had no toilet facilities, 6 were without any drinking water facilities and 4 schools had no blackboard.

Table 5.32

Infrastructure in primary schools

		Number of schools in 2002						*No. of Schools in 1993*	*Schools without building*	
		Pucca	*Partially pucca*	*Katcha*	*Tent*	*Open space*	*Total*		*1993*	*2002*
Primary	Rural	461941	70178	25888	857	14227	573091	507581	22365	15084
	Urban	65463	9124	2010	144	1549	78290	62874	1583	1693
	Total	527404	79302	27898	1001	15776	651381	570455	23948	16777
Upper Primary	Total	20175	32573	7215	171	3564	245274	162805	3121	3735
Secondary	Total	76529	10896	2903	106	327	90761	65564	333	433

Teacher-pupil ratio is an important factor in imparting quality education to students. Central government brings out selected educational statistics from time to time. Teacher-pupil ratio at various levels of schooling is brought out in Table 5.34. The formal statistics provided probably is calculated on the basis of sanctioned posts of teachers at different stages of schooling. It does not take into account the number of posts that remain vacant for years. The actual ratio should have been calculated on the number of serving teachers. Various Education Commissions at the state and central level have repeatedly drawn attention to this issue. Since the state governments have to pay salaries for teachers of government run as well as aided schools, most state governments go slow in filling up the vacant posts. There are numerous instances when a single teacher has to manage all the classes in the primary section. She/he has to manage teaching four classes simultaneously single handed besides performing the job of a clerk – keeping records and accounts, arrange midday meal, run to the office of the District Inspector of Schools or Panchyat office to coax them to release necessary funds, textbooks for children or the food grains for midday meals and etc. A teacher under such circumstance often has to spend all his/her time and energy on assignments not related to teaching. It is therefore no wonder that school attendance becomes thinner with time and drop out rate escalates. In secondary and higher education level, often schools and colleges are asked to perform with 50 percent or even less number of sanctioned posts of teachers. There are again other schools, few though, where there are 2 or more teachers in a primary school but not sufficient number of students.

It is a common complaint that there are fewer schools, especially in elementary level of education, than are needed to accommodate over hundred and ten million students in over six hundred thousand primary schools, that is, on an average 200 students per school (I–IV). That the growth of primary schools in relation to increase in the number of school goers has dropped sharply is evident from Table 5.19. The number of primary schools per thousand populations was 5.70 in 1982–83; the same has come down to 5.04 in 1997–98. By 2002, the total number of primary and upper primary schools rose to about 900,000 (about 20,000 without building) from around 730,000 in 1992–93. By 2005–06, another 250,000 new schools were added to the stock.

Table 5.33

Teachers in schools

Type of Schools	*Full time teachers*		*Para-teachers*		*Part-time teachers*		*% of female teachers**	*No. of full-time teachers (Sixth AIES)$*	*% increase from the 6th survey* (1993)*
	T	*F*	*T*	*F*	*T*	*F*			
1	*2*	*3*	*4*	*5*	*6*	*7*	*8*	*9*	*10*
Primary	1809661	699114	103270	47242	26715	13213	39.02	1623379	17.841
Secondary	958104	364386	37950	15765	19389	7724	38.17	829405	20.09

Note: * In Col. 8 and Col. 10 teachers include para-teachers but exclude part-time teachers.
$ There were no para-teachers.
T – total teachers, F – female teachers

Table 5.34

Teacher-pupil ratio at various stages of school education and number of schools per 1,000 population in India

1982–83			*1992–93*			*1997–98*		
Primary	*Upper primary*	*Secondary*	*Primary*	*Upper primary*	*Secondary*	*Primary*	*Upper primary*	*Secondary*
				Teacher-pupil ratio				
40	34	29	45	43	29	42	37	29
				Number of schools per 1,000 population				
5.70	2.44		5.75	2.69		5.04	2.75	

Source: National Human Development Report, India 2001

The National University of Educational Administration conducted a survey on 1,100,000 schools spread over all the 35 states and UTs. The State Report Card for 2005–06 brought out a few stunning revelations: 32,000 schools had no students (3% of all schools), 8,000 alone in Karnataka. 48 percent of these are primary schools located in rural area. 70,000 schools had less than 25 students (this includes schools in Kerala, which has over 90% literates in its population); the register of 1,70,000 showed enrolment of less than 50 students. More than 100,000 schools had only one teacher. In pursuance of universalization of education (*Sarva Shiksha Abhiyan*), many new school buildings have come up even in many remote villages since 2001. But the government forgot to appoint teachers to make many of these structures transformed into schools. UNICEF in 2002 reported a drop-out of 25 million children in the age group 6–13. This number has come down to around 12.5 million in 2005. There is a big doubt if the target of reaching universal education (primary level) for all can be reached by 2010. According to broad assessments made by the Department of Elementary Education and Literacy, Government of India, nearly Rs 600,000 million additional budgetary support will be required from the Central and the State Governments over next ten years for implementing this initiative.

Absenteeism among teachers is a very serious concern from the grass-root level to the top. Many primary and secondary teachers are also elected members of various local bodies. Many of them are important local leaders of different political parties. Their commitment often lies with their 'other democratic social responsibilities' and therefore they often would have to squeeze out time to come to the school and draw the salary. The teachers' unions often are successful in pressing for the rights of teachers to participate in different activities, hike in salaries and other facilities, transfer of teachers and the like but they rarely agitate for improvement of the infrastructure needed for imparting education to the young children or increase in the actual number of working days in schools or cut down absenteeism of teachers. With an average absenteeism over 30 percent, India is second only to Uganda among the countries of the world in teacher-absentee rate in educational institutions.

One of the major obstacles to making the primary school teachers dedicate their time in teaching alone is the 'other assignments' often imposed on them from time to time by various public agencies. We have already stated that many of the school teachers are active members in various *panchayat* bodies, cooperatives and other village groups besides being important members of local committees of different political parties. Both the central and state governments use the school teachers for preparation of voters' list, correction of such lists and in Census enumeration. They are extensively used for *panchayat*, assembly and parliamentary elections. Their long absence from schools for such reasons often affects the classroom teaching very badly.

5.7.2 New Schools

One very discouraging fact is that even though the state and the central governments are increasingly pumping more money on education and the governments, political leaders, educationists and social activists have time and again have pressed for a time frame for universalization of education, the primary education in the country still remains largely neglected. It is borne by the fact that not many new primary schools have come up between 1992–93 and 1997–98. The number of primary schools per 1,000 populations has gone down from 5.75 to 5.04. A part of the decline in number of primary schools of course is due to up-gradation of some primary schools to middle schools and middle schools to secondary schools. The decline is partially made up by increase in the availability of middle schools from 2.44 schools in 1982–83 to 2.75 schools per 1,000 children in 1997–98. Growth of various types of educational institutions has been presented in Table 5.18.

5.7.3 Quality of Education

Education has been regarded as the best social investment, given the synergies and the positive externalities that it generates for people in their well-being. Extent of literacy rate (especially in adult age group) attained is the usual indicator chosen for measuring development level attained by a country or a population group. But literacy is only a first step in learning and knowledge building. Primary education actually can lay a good foundation for the knowledge building function of education. The need for quality education becomes all the more important as more and more individuals become literate.

While informal education can take a specific few individuals to a great height, we need to address the issue from the masses' point of view who are imparted education formally through structured curriculum at schools. Worth of this formal education is captured in the quality of educational infrastructure (accessibility to schools, school ambience and building, games and recreational facilities, teaching instruments and course material, etc.). In addition, teacher-pupil ratio, training, motivation and competence of teachers, public spending on education, periodic inspection and appointment of a non-political specialists committee to advice on review of curricula and teaching practices are urgently needed. Simultaneously with attention paid to increased literacy rate, the effort should be on raising the level of educational attainment (intensity of education).

The most alarming aspect of primary education in India has been its awful poor quality. The most critical and sure proof of poor quality of education at primary and at almost all levels of education is the increasing dependence of students on their private tutors. To quote Professor Amartya Sen, "Private tuition has become a "regrettable necessity" even in elementary level of education". The joke : "I have as many private tutors as there are subjects plus one to look after my aggregate". It is a joke, but it really speaks about the health of education in many states in India. The Pratichi Trust survey found only 7 percent of students selected from classes III and IV who without the help of private tutors could write their names correctly. The success rate was 80 percent with those who were being tutored privately. It was a very disturbing observation from this very limited survey that if there was no assistance forthcoming from some member of the household and if the child comes from a very poor family, chances are very little that she/he would attain any level of education at all. Drop out rates will not improve unless the teachers are made accountable – they attend schools regularly and teach in the classes sincerely. The physical environment is to be made conducive to teaching; availability of teaching aids must be ensured; teachers must be given special training on how to deal with kids; female teachers be preferred in primary stage; stringent measure must be adopted against any social discrimination; performance of the teachers and the pupils be reviewed at regular interval.

Social discrimination is one of the major reasons why poorest of the poor and the SCs and STs have not enough literates in their communities. Even in a state run by the Marxists for over three decades at a stretch, who does not believe in any discrimination by religion or caste, such discrimination still persists at least in rural areas. Media reports show how caste Hindu students often boycott classes because they have to sit with lower caste students or students from very poor families. They would refuse to take midday meals that are cooked by lower caste people. Pratichi Trust survey report has been a rude shock to the Left Front Government in West Bengal. The report also highlighted how students from SC, ST and Muslim communities receive step-motherly treatment in classrooms. A common complaint received by the survey team is that "teachers only take care of the *babu* children". The SC, ST and Muslim students are made to sit separately in the class. Such discrimination makes them lose interest in education. This probably is a common scenario in many other states.

The survey also highlighted the fact that absenteeism of teachers is more in schools where SC and ST students numerically dominate and the teacher is from higher caste. Even some of the teachers did not hide their dislike for the presence of students from lower caste and very poor families in their classrooms. The situation could be more agonizing in some other states and regions where caste-class politics is openly practiced.

For improving the quality of college and university level education, the central and state governments have introduced a screening procedure (NET or SLET) to recruit good teachers in colleges and universities. The salary of the teachers and other facilities for personal accomplishment and up-gradation has been made more attractive. Some states even are conducting similar screening test for appointment of teachers in secondary and higher secondary schools. But no one seems to be really concerned about the quality of teaching at the grass-root level.

Although the literacy growth rates for most of the segments of the population have generally been satisfactory in the last two decades, an estimated 22 million illiterates (out of 160.6 million population addition in 1991) were added between 1981 and 1991 of which 16.31 million were females. At the end of 2001, India had 296,208,952 illiterate people in 7 years and above age group (a reduction by 31,958,336 over the number of illiterates in 1991), of which males' share was 106,654,066. A huge 189,554,886 females still remain illiterate (Table 5.3).

Today our illiterate population is 296.2 million, a little less than the population India had in 1951. This too has happened only because we have changed the definition of 'literacy rate' in 1991. Had we stuck to the earlier definition, the illiterate population could have exceeded the total population registered in 1961 census. This 296.2 million deficiency in literacy cannot be wiped out even in the next 30 or 40 years unless we make a concerted effort to bring every child in 6–11 year age group into formal education system, especially the girls. The central government needs to concentrate attention to some of the larger states – Bihar, Madhya Pradesh, Rajasthan, Uttar Pradesh and Andhra Pradesh. They together have a population over 441 millions. If to this the population of the breakaway regions are added (Jharkhand, Chhattisgarh and Uttaranchal), the total population would be close to 500 million. Except Uttaranchal (8.5 million), all these states have literacy rates well below the national average. World Bank was not wholly wrong when they predicted that the number of illiterates in India could reach 500 million by 2000 unless strict measures were taken to control the population growth rate and concentrate on school level education. The World Bank also predicted that 54 percent of the illiterates of the world in age group 15–19 would be Indians, that is, every second illiterate adult in the world would be an Indian. India even lags behind the average youth (15–24) literacy rate in the developing countries (71.8% against an average of 84.4% in the developing countries across the world), only a little above the percentage attained (65.2%) by the least developed countries in 1999. Though women education has received some attention in post-independence era, it is really difficult for the girls to catch up with boys since they started with a large handicap.

5.8 Higher Education

The present hi tech revolution owes fully to science and technology. Behind this enormous progress in science and technology lies man's creative brain and use of unlimited mental energy possessed by human beings. Education is the key for the fuller exposition of man's creative potential. Man uses the same for inventions, for discoveries. Education also empowers man with social obligation and responsibility, help develop his/her full potential and make him/her a mature personality. With education comes a higher need for achievement, puts the aspiration level high, offers him/her a wide range of choices, changes his/her tastes for goods and services and helps him/her assess the social environment, the traditional institutions like family, evaluate the traditional value system, and above all gives an insight to look into his limitations and potentials.

The great strides in technology have created an unlimited space to augur plans and programs for human development. Achieving this potential is dependent on the use of technology. The impact of modern technology has led to economic globalization, and economic globalization has enhanced technological innovations. Knowledge has always remained the king pin in our entire progressive endeavor. There is a global race for knowledge. Knowledge economy is at the forefront of global interaction. The fusion of computing and communication has broken the bounds of cost, time and distance. Genetic engineering (bio-technology) has opened a new vista for revolution in pharmaceutical and agricultural industries.

How equipped the developing countries are to participate in this global competitive environment? A partial answer to the question lies in the expansion of *tertiary education, especially in science* – education at the levels of university and higher levels of professional schools. How prepared are we to accept this challenge? A part answer to this can be had from our investment in technology creation. Table 5.35 shows the nature of imbalance that exists between developed and developing countries in the race for acquisition of knowledge and the relative position of India in the world perspective. Compared to the developed countries, enrolment in higher education both for boys and girls in developing countries is too small, especially the countries that have small size of population. India's large population base gives the country a very large number of persons who have the necessary knowledge and skill that can effectively contribute to attaining the country's developmental goal in spite the fact that only a small proportion of the country's youth completes the tertiary education. Although India spends around 4 percent of GDP on education (12.7% of government expenditure), it needs to provide more fund to improve the quality of education at all stages. The government spends about 40 percent of the total allocation on primary education and only 20 percent on tertiary education.

Quite a few of India's industrial giants are among the Fortune 500 industries in the world. A number of Indian multinational companies are expanding their organizational base beyond the domestic market. They are aggressively acquiring companies in foreign lands. India's exports have increased from 7 percent in 1990 to 14 percent of GDP in 2003; import in the same period has increased from 9 to 16 percent. Although the total debt service as percent of GDP has gone up from 2.6 to 3.4 percent between 1990 and 2003, primary exports as percentage of merchandise exports has declined from 28 to 22 percent in the same period. During 1990–2003, the manufactured exports have gone up from 71 to 77 percent of all merchandise exports and high-technology exports as percentage of manufactured exports have gone up from 2 to 5 percent. This is in spite the fact that FDI in India is only 0.7 percent of GDP compared to 3.8 percent in China. These speak quite a lot

Table 5.35

Relative strength of selected few countries in acquisition of knowledge and skill[1]

Country	Gross tertiary enrolment ratio		Professional courses enrolment as prop. of all tertiary enrolments[2]	Public spending on tertiary education as % of all levels	Education index	Researchers in R&D (per million)	Percentage of GDP spending on R&D
	Male	Female					
1	2	3	4	5	6	7	8
INDIA	5	8	20	20.3	0.61	120	0.8
Sri Lanka	4	6			0.83	197	
Pakistan					0.44	88	0,2
China	4	7			0.84	633	1.2
Brazil				21.6	0.89	324	1.0
Rep. of Korea	52	82	41	8.1	0.97	2979	2.5
USA	92	71		25.2	0.97	4526	2.7
Japan	36	44	20	14.9	0.94	5025	3.1
UK	56	49	21	20.6	0.99	2691	1.9
Singapore	31	37			0.91	4352	2.2

1 Data compiled from Human Development Report 2005

2 The courses referred to are those enrolled in natural sciences; engineering, mathematics and computer sciences; architecture and town planning; transport and communications, trade, craft and industrial programs; and agriculture, forestry and fisheries.

about the robustness of India's economy and its competitiveness in the manufacturing and service sectors. But unfortunately, Indian industries still are dependent on import of hi techs and sophisticated machines and tools. This is clearly observed from the fact that India spends only about 0.8 percent of GDP in R&D when the developed and high developing countries often spend over 2 percent of their GDP on the same. India has a meager 120 researchers in R&D per million; the advanced countries have several thousands researchers in R&D per million workers. China spends 1.2 percent of its GDP on R&D. But China outshines India in research; its output is 5 to 10 times India's in areas like material science, applied physics and computer simulation.

If we take look at the stock of scientific and technical personnel in India, we shall get an idea about the availability of technical manpower in the country. It has been increasing quite at a faster pace since economic reform started in 1991. The scientific and technical personnel were about 7.7 million in 2001 compared to 4.8 million in 1991. Category wise, "science graduates" account for the largest share of about 3.8 million (49.8%) followed by "engineering diploma holders" of about 1.4 million (18.9%) followed by 0.97 million (12.6%) "engineering degree holders". Total expenditure on R&D has been increasing over the years.

Table 5.36

Percentage distribution of literates by educational level and sex, 1991

	Total			*Rural*			*Urban*		
	Persons	*Males*	*Females*	*Persons*	*Males*	*Females*	*Persons*	*Males*	*Females*
	2	*3*	*4*	*5*	*6*	*7*	*8*	*9*	*10*
Total literates ('000s)	359,324	229,560	129,763	226,144	151,216	74,928	133,180	78,344	54,836
Below primary	25.2	23.8	27.8	29.2	27.2	33.2	18.4	17.1	20.4
Primary but below middle	28.7	27.3	31.4	31.6	30.1	34.8	23.9	21.9	26.7
Middle but below matric	20.9	21.2	20.4	21.0	21.6	19.7	20.8	20.5	21.3
Matric but below graduate	19.4	21.3	1.6	15.5	17.7	10.9	26.1	28.3	23.0
Graduate and above	5.7	6.4	4.5	2.7	3.4	1.4	10.8	12.3	8.7

Out of 359 million literates in 1991, about 20.5 million (5.7% of total literates) persons held graduation and higher degrees. UGC and NCAER accounts of enrolment of students in colleges and universities indicate that the total enrolments have jumped from 6.65 to 9.49 million between 1995–96 and 2003–04. The average growth rate of 4.5 percent between 1995 and 2000 has come down a little, to about 4.0 percent during 2000–03. The enrolment in medicine, engineering and natural science courses varied from 4.7 to 8.2 percent during 1995–2000. Although enrolment in science has increased from an average of 6.5 in 1995–2000 to 7.9 percent in 2000–03, enrolment in natural science courses dropped from 6.1 to 1.6 percent. Admission hike is observed for engineering (21.9%), medicine (10.1%) and agriculture (7.9%) in 2000–03. Even though the demand for courses in Arts increased from 4.0 to 6.2 percent, the admission in Commerce sharply declined from 6.0 (1995–96) to (–)7.5 percent in 2000–03.

Table 5.37

Gross enrolment in higher education (graduation and above)

Field of study	*Enrolment (in million)*			*Percentage distribution*			*Average growth rate (%)*	
	*UGC***	*UGC*	*NCAER**	*UGC*	*UGC*	*NCAER*		
	1995–96	*2000–01*	*2003–04*	*1995–96*	*2000–01*	*2003–04*	*1995–00*	*2000–03*
1	*2*	*3*	*4*	*5*	*6*	*7*	*8*	*9*
Science	1.91	2.62	3.29	28.8	31.1	34.6	6.5	7.9
Natural science	1.26	1.69	1.78	18.9	20.1	18.7	6.1	1.6
Engineering	0.40	0.59	1.07	6.0	7.0	7–11.2	8.2	21.9
Medicine	0.20	0.27	0.36	3.0	3.2	3.7	5.8	10.1
Agriculture	0.06	0.07	0.09	0.9	0.9	1.0	4.7	7.9
Arts	3.18	3.88	4.65	47.9	45.9	49.0	4.0	6.2
Commerce	1.13	1.51	1.20	16.9	18–7.8	12.6	6.0	–7.3
Others	0.43	0.44	0.36	6.4	5.2	3.8	0.5	–6.5
Total	6.65	8.44	9.49	100.00	100.00	100.00	4.9	4.0

Source: **UGC, "University development in India" basic facts & figures (1995–2000 to 2000–01)
*NCAER. National Sample Survey 2004.

It is, however, heartening to note that the gap in enrolment between males and females in higher education is fast thinning, especially in science and technology courses (Table 5.38). From a near zero girls enrolment in engineering education in 1950–51, there are now around 30 girls for every 100 boys admitted to engineering courses. Female participation in engineering courses has sharply increased keeping pace with economic reforms in India since 1991. This fast change is also noticed in medicine as well (from 41.6 in 1985–86 to 68.2 per 100 males in 2000–01). A very high percentage of girls in IT sector, especially in BPOs and Call Centers amply makes it clear that girls are in no way behind boys in science and technology education.

Table 5.38

Enrolment trend of females (per hundred males) in university education in major disciplines of education in India

Year	*Arts*	*Science*	*Commerce*	*Education*	*Engineering/ Technology*	*Medicine*[1]
1	*2*	*3*	*4*	*5*	*6*	*7*
1950–51	15.4		0.5	45.5	0.3	18.5
1960–61	22.3		2.8	48.1	0.4	25.6
1970–71	50.2	21.2	2.8	52.8	1.1	26.5
1980–81	59.7	38.9	18.5	98.8	4.6	29.9
1985–86	65.6	47.9	28.1	88.6a	8.1	41.6
1990–91P	65.5	58.3	31.6	79.2a	12.2a	52.1a
1995–96P	71.8	54.9	41.6	70.0	16.6	52.7
1996–97P	71.2	53.4	41.4	76.0	17.4	54.8
1997–98P	71.1	55.4	44.0	76.0	20.3	56.5
1998–99P	81.0	55.3	46.1	74.0	24.2	62.1
1999–2000P	81.3	60.0	50.7	74.2	28.3	61.0
2000–2001P	81.2	61.4	52.3	74.8	28.7	68.2

Note: Arts and science figures are combined for the years 1955–56, 1960–61 and 1965–66
1. Excludes dentistry, public health, nursing, midwifery & pharmacy
a. Only for degree level not post graduate
P: Provisional
Source: Department of Education, Ministry of Human Resources & Development.

The size of the scientific and technical personnel in India, which stood at 0.573 percent of the total population in 1991, has increased to 0.773 in 2000 (Table 5.39). Scientific man power has not kept pace with the growth of population and expansion of facilities for higher education. A section of the intelligentsia feels that entry into higher general education need be restricted and the resource thus saved spent on improving the quality of higher education.

Table 5.39

Stock of scientific and technical personnel in India ('000)

Category	Stock of scientific & technical personnel				
	1991	*1996*	*1998*	*1999a*	*2000a*
Engineering degree holders	546.7 (11.28)	704.5 (11.32)	798.4 (11.62)	845.6 (11.73)	969.5 (12.57)
Engineering diploma holders	873.9 (18.03)	1138.3 (18.29)	1255.5 (18.28)	1313.1 ((18.23)	1456.0 (18.88)
Medical graduates[1]	310.3 (6.40)	358.4 (5.75)	380.4 (5.53)	391.7 (5.44)	403.4 (5.23)
Agricultural graduates	168.4 (3.48)	202.3 (3.25)	216.5 (3.15)	223.8 (3.11)	231.2 (2.99)
Veterinary graduates	34.4 (0.71)	40.2 (0.64)	42.7 (0.62)	44.0 (0.61)	45.3 (0.59)
Science graduates	2430.3 (50.15)	3154.8 (50.68)	3479.3 (50.66)	3655.4 (50.74)	3837.7 (49.77)
Science post graduates	482.0 (9,94)	626.1 (10.05)	695.5 (10.13)	730.6 (10.14)	767.1 (9.95)
Total	4846.0 (100)	6224.6 (100)	6868.3 (100)	7204.2 (100)	7710.2 (100)
Total as % of total population	0.573	0.666	0.720	0.735	0.773

Note: Figures in parentheses refer to percentages
1. Included dental surgeons
a. Projected stock at the beginning of the year
Source: Institute of Applied Manpower Research, New Delhi.

Table 5.40

Scientific manpower in India

Year	Scientists, Engineers and technicians per thousand population	Scientists, engineers and technicians engaged in Research and Development, per thousand population	Scientists, engineers & technicians engaged in Research & Development as percentage of total no of scientists, engineers and technicians
1976	3.80	0.09	2.37
1978	2.97	0.10	3.37
1980	2.63	0.10	3.80
1985	3.43	0.20	5.83
1988	NA	0.22	NA
1990	3.76	0.27	7.18
1992	NA	0.22	NA
1994	NA	0.23	NA
1996	6.91	0.25	3.62
1998	NA	0.10	NA
1999	7.27	NA	NA

NA: Not available
Source: Research and Development Statistics, Department of Science & Technology.

Because of extreme financial constraints, even our prized institutions like IITs, IMAs, Medical Colleges, University Departments and institutions of excellence, exclusively or substantially financed by the government, have inadequate infrastructure, poor laboratories and workshops. They have not been upgraded since long. Hundreds and thousands of students sit for the tough screening tests. They spend in thousands for a period of two or more years, often neglecting the courses they were pursuing with a hope that they would be admitted for higher technical education in the subjects of their choice in these prime institutions. Considering the fast rising demand of scientific manpower in today's free economy and expanding global market and the fact that government has very little resources to create more such institutions to the level of rising aspirations of thousands of brilliant students, both central and state governments have allowed private fund managers to open engineering, medical and other colleges. Even some foreign universities have expressed their interest to have their campus in India. Every year more than 160,000 students go for higher studies in USA, UK, Canada, Australia and other countries which cost about US$4 billion from India's hard earned foreign exchange. Even though the Knowledge Commission has recommended campus facilities for foreign universities, the HRD ministry did not support the idea. Since there are fewer restrictions in admission to the privately established colleges, and since they are managed on a commercial perspective, the students have to spend even ten/twenty hundred thousands of money for admission in these privately run colleges. Many of them have no infrastructure, qualified faculties, laboratories, workshops and libraries. The government wanted to impose certain controls on the privately run colleges by way of a quota for the poorer students and re-determination of fee structure for various courses. The Supreme Court of India struck down the quota provisions on the ground that the government cannot impose or interfere in the admission policy of these colleges since they receive no financial aid from the government, provided these colleges follow a transparent admission policy.

Many of the universities and colleges, funded by the government have huge number of faculty positions lying vacant for years. Since these vacant posts are to be filled through Public Service Commission (for the colleges directly run by the government) or through College Service Commission (the aspirants are needed to qualify through NET or SLET to become eligible for appointment as college teachers), it takes hell of a long time to get these vacant posts filled up. Even instances are there that some departments did not have a single full-time teacher for years. These departments remained operational through part-time or guest lecturers. The faculties highly connected to IT and Computer technologies are the worst sufferers. The demand for IT and Computer technologists, especially software specialists, is increasing by leaps and bounds. The cream of the students is admitted in these courses. One of the principal reasons why there is always a dearth of qualified teachers in these departments is because the comparative advantage the IT and Computer specialists have in the corporate sector vis-à-vis in educational institutions. The entry-level salary for a college/university teacher is around Rs 35,000 per month, today which is by no means an inadequate pay packet in the context of general levels of living in the country. Since most of the graduates from these faculties are 'booked' through campus interview even before they have completed their courses with a fancy offer of fifty or sixty thousand or more buck a month (even the public sector undertakings PSUs are not behind the private corporate sector in this regard), it is no wonder that these departments fail to exert a pull on qualified persons to join the noble profession of teaching. Some of the multinationals would even offer them hundred thousand or more a month. Even a graduate software or IT engineer/diploma holder would have little difficulty of starting his/her career in a small business house at a monthly salary of Rs 20,000/25,000, a salary which was equivalent to salary of a senior Reader or a Professor of a University department a few years back. The government cannot hike the pay of the teachers in these high demand courses since the government cannot enforce one type of scale for these high demand courses and another for others. What is possible in a privately run institution is often not possible in state-run or aided institutions. Teaching in these specialized courses suffers as a result. Even the teacher-pupil ratio of 1:15, recommended by All India Council of Technical Education (AICTE), often cannot be maintained. The HRD ministry has asked the IITs, IIMs and other premiere institutions to increase admissions into the courses offered by them to accommodate 'quota' for OBC over and above the quota for SC and ST. But the ministry does not commit to proportional increase in the flow of fund necessary to hire additional teachers and other technical staff and for expanded infrastructural support.

The concept of "Virtual University", based on Web-based education using the Internet as a place for students, teachers, researchers and specialists engaged in many corporate houses to "meet", is looming large in the face of dearth of qualified teachers and necessary infrastructure (adequate number of quality education centers spread all over the country) in most of the developing countries. This really is a low cost distance education in technology courses that are evolving very fast, similar to one offered by Indira Gandhi National University (IGNU).

As of 2004, 27.5 percent of Indian population studied up to 10th class or above. The total number of graduates and higher professional degree and diploma holders in India is 48.7 million, or 4.5 percent of the total population. Out of 39.2 million graduates, 27.3 percent are from science faculties; out of 9.3 million postgraduates, 19.4 percent are from science. One-third of 300,000 Ph.D.s are from science and technology.

Human Development Report 2001 (UNDP) informs us that the advanced countries spend only 25 percent or even less of their budgetary allocation for education per capita on tertiary education in stark contrast to 66 percent of the same spent on tertiary education in developing countries. Public funding in India has been over 75 percent per capita in tertiary education. The skill shortage in the developed West is probably because of poorly subsidized highly expensive higher education in their country; their skill shortage in many sectors led to encouraging 'brain drain' from developing countries to man their universities, hospitals, IT and other hi tech industries and the R&D organizations.

On an average 100,000 professionals (from IITs, IIMs, premier medical colleges, universities and other institutions of excellence) from India move to USA, UK, Canada and many European countries every year lured by the fat salary and other perks and the excellent work environment offered. Operating costs plus the cost of replacement of physical and other facilities per student in these premiere institutions for a period of four years could be anywhere between US$15,000–20,000 bringing the revenue spending to US$2 billion every year. The government spends about US$3 billion (0.7–0.8% of GDP) on tertiary education from which about US$2 billion is lost due to 'brain drain'.

The government needs to spend more on elementary and secondary education – fulfill their commitment to have a primary school in every village, improved infrastructure and school environment and better teacher-pupil ratio – to improve the skill quality of students. Since public resources are limited, the government needs to develop some mechanism to recover the enormous sums spent on these "cream of the crop" that leave the country on the completion of their education and training in India's elite institutions.

The simplest way to recover this huge loss is to impose an exit tax to be paid by the employing firm while the visa is granted. This could be two months' salary, assuming an average annual salary of US$60,000 for these hired Indian professionals (actually such sums are often paid to placement agencies/head hunters). A few other alternatives can also be looked into.

- Every student admitted in high profile graduate and postgraduate courses are advanced education loan equivalent to the actual subsidy provided by the state. The student desirous of leaving the country would have to repay the loan amount in full.
- Some countries, US for example, tax individuals on the basis of their nationality, not their residence. India can negotiate bilateral tax treaties with 'brain drain' destination countries.
- The pharmaceutical companies and many other organizations are protected by Intellectual Property Right (patent right) in pricing their products for recovery of huge costs incurred in R&D for the product development. Government of India spends huge sums in developing their best talents. Therefore it has every right to ask for a compensation for these very high valued products under international agreements relating to Intellectual Property Right.

The success of Indian diaspora in Silicon Valley has already created a 'brand name' for Indian software programmers. 'Indian software specialists' send a signal for quality just as 'Made in Japan' labels signal quality in the manufacturing of electronic gadgets. The worldwide network of Indian professionals has already been investing in skill development at home. IT giants like Microsoft, IBM and others are opening up their India offices for smooth progress of their 'manufacturing facility'. Indian IT firms in US increasingly are showing interest in expanding information technology in India. Because of mass exodus of talents, India is likely to face huge shortage in qualified IT, management and other professionals which are in high demand in our domestic establishments. The government therefore is too eager to extend to these professional players necessary facilities to establish institutes of science and technology for skill development at home.

6
Urbanization in India

6.1 Introduction

The urban population of India was less than 11 percent of the total population in 1900, estimated at 250 million. The Indian urban population today is itself greater than this number. The world's urban population had increased to almost 2.9 billion in 100 years and constitutes about 46.5 percent of the world total. Thus the characteristics of life at the end of the twentieth century are qualitatively different from those at the beginning of it. The percentage of urban population in India (27.8) in 2001 was far behind the world average (46.5).

Table 6.1
Globalization – urbanization trend (percent)

Region	*Level of Urbanization*	
	1920	*2025*
World total	**19**	**61**
Less developed region	**10**	**57**
Africa	7	54
Asia	9	55
Latin America	22	85
More Developed Regions	**40**	**85**
Europe	46	83
North America	52	85
Oceania	47	75
INDIA	**11**	**38**

Source: UN, 2002

Till 1951 the definition of urban area was not very precise. 1951 Census defined an urban area as:

> [N]ormally an inhabited locality with a total population of not less than 5,000 persons. But places with somewhat larger population which do not possess definite urban character may not be treated as towns. At the same time, places with a smaller population with definite urban character (including generally all municipalities and cantonments and other places having a local administration of their own) may be treated as separate towns. The decision in the marginal cases rests with the State Governments in some states and Census Superintendents in others.

Presently, the criteria followed for classification of human settlements into rural and urban areas by the Indian Census authority can be summed up in the following lines:

> Places with a municipality, corporation, cantonment board or notified town area committee[1], also, all other places which satisfy the following criteria: a minimum population of 5,000; at least 75 percent of male working population engaged in non-agricultural pursuits; and density of population of at least 400 persons per square kilometer (1,000 persons per square mile), and a few urban characteristics.

In regards the male working population, only male main workers are considered. Workers engaged in agricultural activities: (i) Cultivation, (ii) Agricultural Labor, (iii) Livestock, Forestry, Fishing and Plantation, Orchards etc., are excluded for computing the percentage of workers engaged in non-agricultural occupation.

This definition of an urban area adopted in Indian Census is to an extent arbitrary and is not the same as used in other countries. There would be differences in the details, but they agree on certain fundamentals: the population density of the geographical or administrative area must be considerably high and that a majority of the population must be engaged in non-agricultural jobs.

There is some difference between the definitions adopted by the Census and that by the state administration. The state administration applies tax collection principle to the determination of rural settlements. The settlements left out thereafter are regarded as urban areas in the eyes of law and administration. A total reverse procedure is adopted in rural-urban demarcation in Census. In Census, urban areas are identified first; the rest of the human settlements are declared rural.

Many Indian demographers have expressed their discontent with the criteria followed in this classification and even have said that urban populations of different states are not strictly comparable since there was considerable differences between the states in the use of the criteria for classification of human settlements into rural and urban.

The urban criterion adopted in 1981 census differed slightly from that used in 1961 and 1971 censuses. In 1961 and 1971 censuses, the males working in activities such as fishing, logging etc. were treated as engaged in non-agricultural activities whereas in 1981 they were treated at par with cultivators and agricultural laborers. This definition has been followed in 1991 and 2001 census as well. Hence the rural-urban data in the last five censuses are just comparable. Earlier decades' data are not strictly comparable and this fact should be kept in mind while drawing inferences.

India's urbanization has increased at a much slower pace compared to many other countries in Asia. China and Indonesia, the other two larger developing Asian countries where the level of urbanization was even lower vis-à-vis India in 1951, have become more urbanized than India in 2001. One of the reasons for slow urbanization is that India applies more stringent criteria in classifying an area as urban compared to international standards. By international standards, the true level of urbanization in India may be somewhat higher than what the official figures indicate. For example, in 1991, there were 13,376 villages with population of 5,000 or more. Were these villages with 113 million people counted as urban, the level of India's urbanization in 1991 would have been 39.1 percent as against 25.7 percent accepted in 1991 Census.

Although migration, especially from rural areas remains an important component of urban growth, the natural increase of the urban population still remains the major factor contributing to India's urban growth. During 1991–2001, 55.8 percent of urban growth was due to natural increase. It is also a fact that due to steady decline in urban birth rate, its contribution to urban growth is on the

1. All places, which have been notified under law and have local bodies like municipal corporations, municipalities, municipal committees, municipal boards, municipal town committees, cantonment boards, notified areas, notified area committees, town committees, town areas, town boards, town municipalities, sanitary boards etc., irrespective of their demographic characteristics have been included in the category of towns.

decline. Last few head count results indicate that rural to urban migration has also slowed down and commuting to urban place of work from nearby rural areas is increasing both in response to relatively cheap transportation and higher housing and other costs involved in urban living.

Table 6.2

Estimates of relative share of natural increase, net migration and reclassification in the decadal urban growth, India 1961–1991

	1961–71	*1971–81*	*1981–91*
Urban Population Increase (million)	30.18	49.45	56.45
Estimated Share (million)			
Natural Increase	19.65	20.40	33.86
Net Migration	5.91	19.73	12.73
Reclassification	4.59	9.32	9.82
Percentage Share			
Natural Increase	65.21	41.75	59.98
Net Migration	19.58	39.40	22.62
Reclassification	15.21	18.85	17.40

Source: Census of India: Emerging Trends of Urbanization in India – An Analysis of 1991 Census Result, 1993.

6.2 Growth of Urban Centers and Urban Population

Three broad regimes of urbanization in India in the last hundred years can be deciphered: *period of low urbanization, period of medium urbanization and period of rapid urbanization.*

6.2.1 *Period of Low Urbanization (1901–31)*

In 1901, about 89 percent of India's population lived in villages. The urban population rose slowly from 10.8 percent in 1901 to around 12 percent in 1931. The little decline in urban population between 1911 and 1921 had something to do with plague epidemic – the towns and cities suffering the most. High urban deaths associated with evacuation from the affected cities and towns also had something to do with the fall in urban population in the said period. In fact, this was one of the major reasons why the urban population declined in some states. Bombay, Central India and Bengal were the worst sufferers. The other part of the explanation of this slow growth lies in very limited urban-based economic activities. The port-cities and a few mineral resource-based industrial towns attracted people for alternative jobs; the towns expanded as a result.

6.2.2 *Period of Medium Urbanization (1931–61)*

There was a considerable increase in urban population between 1931 and 1961, about 6 percentage point growth in 30 years. In the thirties, there was a fall in prices for agricultural commodities. At the same time India played a major role in providing necessary supplies for the World War II. The industrial and service sector grew significantly faster and attracted more people to join the new economic activities that were geared to production to meeting the needs of defense establishments. The metropolitan cities like Delhi, Kolkata and Mumby and those towns lying close to border areas grew really fast. By the middle of the 1940s it became quite clear that India was going to be divided on the facts of religion. People from East and West Pakistan started pouring into Indian cities and towns. India was more on the receiving end in this exchange of population. During 1951–61, the decadal growth rate sharply fell from 41.4 percent in 1941–51 to 26.4 percent even though the urban population in this decade grew by 17 million. If we look into the Table 6.4, it will be seen that there was an uninterrupted increase in towns and cities between 1901 and 1951. But there was a drastic drop in the count of towns in the next decade, from 3059 to 2699. This has resulted primarily due to adoption of a stricter norm for declaring an area as urban in 1961.

Often there is no one-to-one correspondence between growth of urban population and growth of urban centers. Prof. Ashish Bose has shown that 60 percent of the urban population in 1961 actually lived in settlements that had over 5,000 people, population density over 400/km^2 and 75 percent of the population were non-agricultural labors. The rest, 40 percent, lived in settlements that were *declared urban by administrative pronouncement*. Prof. Bose has also shown that the urban population growth during 1951–61 would have been 32.4 percent instead of 26.4 percent had the 1951 definition of 'urban' been followed in 1961 as well. Had 1961 definition been retrospectively applied to 1951 Census, the decadal urban growth rate would have been 30.7 percent instead of 41.4 percent. It is therefore not easy to relate the growth of urban population to the degree of urbanization. The growth of urban population since 1951, or more precisely after 1961, has largely been due to the launching of the First and Second Five Year plans which gave a big thrust to the growth of industrial and service sectors. Whereas migration was principally responsible for high urban and low rural population growth between 1941 and 1951, its impact on urban growth of population during 1951–61 was less pronounced. The scale of urban population growth had been slow in the first half of the last century. Most demographers and economists attribute this to slowness of economic development in India.

6.2.3 Period of Rapid Urbanization (1961–)

Urban population growth has been much faster since 1961. The average decadal urban growth rate in the last 40 years had been around 38 percent, reaching the peak growth in 1981 (46.4%) (Table 6.3). The decadal growth rate has been declining since. Most of the industrial, irrigation, power and other projects undertaken in the first two plans started to become operational since the middle of the sixties of the last century. That is, the programs of industrialization did have considerable impact in terms of population absorption in urban areas. The rural population in India grew at a very fast pace between 1951 and 1981 (an average annual increase over 2.2%). While the Sixth Plan projected the level of urban population to around 148 million, the actual level according to 1981 census was 156 million, that too excluding Assam and Jammu & Kashmir where census could not be conducted due to law and order and political reasons.

India's economic growth rate since 1970s has been led largely by the urban sector, especially the service sector since the 1990s. This would be evident from the comparisons of the contribution of agriculture, industry and service sector to GDP over the years (Figure 6.1). From about 32 percent in 1960s, service sector's contribution to GDP was almost 50 percent in 2000. Contribution of agriculture to GDP has been halved in the same period. Industry's share has improved only by about 8 percent.

Urban development has for obvious reason is getting more attention than rural development in the post-reform period. The physical and social infrastructure of the cities and adjoining areas need to be improved fast to attract private investors to establish new industrial units. The allocation of central plan funds clearly exhibits this.

Figure 6.1

Change in composition of India's GDP, 1960–2000

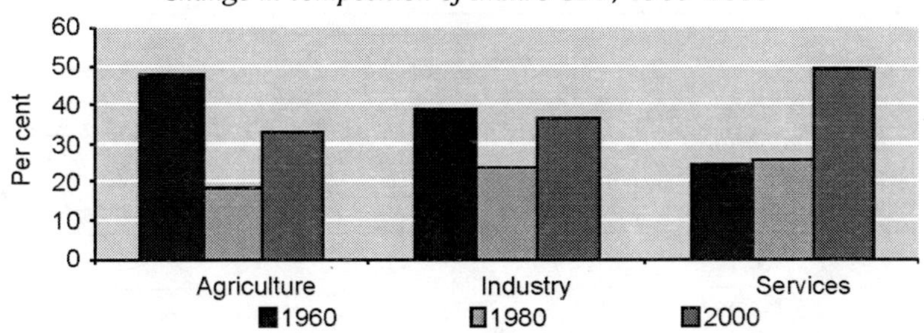

Figure 6.2

Central plan funds – Urban vis-à-vis rural (Rs million)

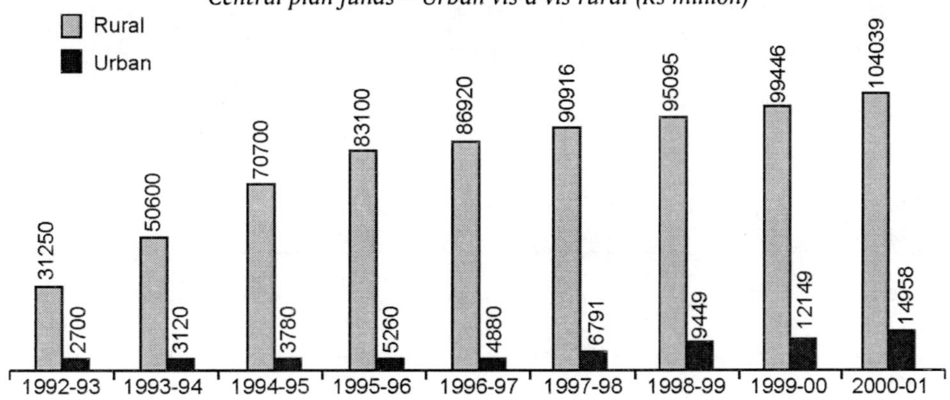

Table 6.3

Change of urban population in India, 1901–2001

Census year	***Population density (per km²) (R+U)***	***Percent of population***		***Decadal growth rate %***		***Exponential growth rate %***	
		Rural	***Urban***	***Rural***	***Urban***	***Rural***	***Urban***
1	*2*	*3*	*4*	*5*	*6*	*7*	*8*
1901	73	89.2	10.8				
1911	77	89.7	10.3	6.4	0.3		
1921	76	88.8	11.2	–1.3	8.3		
1931	85	88.0	12.0	9.9	19.1	2.29	2.95
1941	97	86.1	13.9	11.8	31.9	2.47	3.46
1951	110	82.7	17.3	8.8	41.4	2.17	3.72
1961	134	82.0	18.0	20.6	26.4	3.03	3.27
1971	167	80.1	19.9	21.8	38.3	3.08	3.64
1981+	216	76.7	23.3	19.7	46.4	2.98	3.84
1991*	274	74.3	25.7	19.6	36.2	2.98	3.59
2001	324	72.2	27.8	18.0	31.1	2.89	3.44

+ Includes Population (Projected) of Jammu & Kashmir.

* Includes Interpolated Population of Assam where census could not be held in 1981 due to disturbed conditions

Source: Census of India 1991, 2001

Table 6.4
Trends of urbanization, India 1901–2001

Census year	*Total population*	*Urban population*	*No. of towns/UAs*	*Percentage of Urban population to total population*	*Decadal Urban growth rate*	*Annual exponential growth rate*	*Annual gain in percentage of Urban population*	*Annual rate of gain in percentage of Urban population*
1	*2*	*3*	*4*	*5*	*6*	*7*	*8*	*9*
1901	238,396,327	25,854,967	1,827	10.85	NA	NA	NA	NA
1911	252,093,390	25,948,431	1,815	10.29	0.36	0.04	–0.06	–0.51
1921	251,321,213	28,091,299	1,949	11.18	8.26	0.8	0.09	0.86
1931	278,977,238	33,462,539	2,072	11.99	19.12	1.77	0.08	0.73
1941	318,660,580	44,162,191	2,250	13.86	31.98	2.81	0.19	1.55
1951	361,088,090	62,443,709	2,843	17.29	41.4	3.52	0.34	2.48
1961	439,234,771	78,936,603	2,365	17.97	26.41	2.37	0.07	0.39
1971	548,159,652	109,113,977	2,590	19.91	38.23	3.29	0.19	1.08
1981	683,329,097	159,462,547	3,301	23.34	46.14	3.87	0.34	1.72
1991	846,302,688	217,611,012	3,697	25.71	36.47	3.16	0.24	1.02
2001	1,028,610,328	286,119,689	4,378	27.80	31.45	2.73		

Note:
1. Includes the interpolated population of Assam for 1981; the total population is 18,041,248 and urban population is 1,782,376
2. Includes the projected population of Jammu & Kashmir for 1991; the total population is 7,718,700 and urban population 1,839,400
3.N.A; Not applicable
Source: Census of India, 1991, General Population Tables, Part II-A(i)

Figure 6.3
Urban decadal growth, India 1911–2001

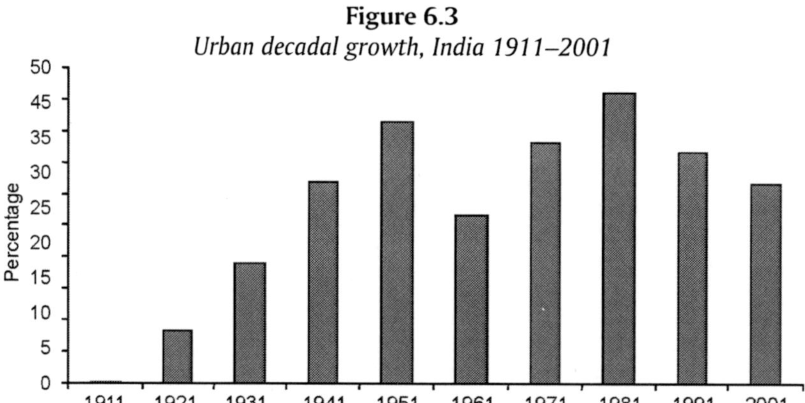

The degree or level of urbanization[2], defined as the proportion of people living in urban areas, witnessed a dramatic change in the decade of World War II, which also witnessed the partition of India and a massive transfer of population between Pakistan and India. In this transfer of population, India lost a large number of Muslims from its rural areas of the bordering states, as also from some

2. (U/P)*100 and urban-rural ratio (U/R)*100 are frequently used for measuring degree of urbanization. For every 100 ruralites there were 28 urbanites in India in 2001. This was only 11 in 1901.

other states having comparatively large Muslim populations. Cities and towns of bordering states in India had to bear the brunt of this population transfer most from the other side of the border. The sharp drop in urban growth rate during 1951–61 is largely due to declassification of a large number of towns in 1961. India saw a surge in urban population growth in the sixties and seventies mostly due to massive investment in the industrial sector. Since 1981 urban growth rate has decelerated considerably.

Table 6.5

India's population by sex and residence, 2001

	Population (absolute number)			*Population in proportions*		
	Persons	*Males*	*Females*	*Persons*	*Males*	*Females*
Total	1,028,610,328	532,156,772	496,453,556	100	51.7	48.3
Rural	742,490,639	381,602,674	360,887,965	72.2	71.7	72.7
Urban	286,119,689	150,554,098	135,565,591	27.8	28.3	27.3

Table 6.6

Districts, towns and villages in states/UTs, 2001

*State/UT**	*Districts*	*Towns*	*Villages including uninhabitated villages*	*Population as per Census 2001*		
				Male	*Female*	*Total*
1	*2*	*3*	*4*	*5*	*6*	*7*
Andhra Pradesh	23	210	28123	38527413	37682594	76210007
Arunachal Pradesh	13	17	4065	579941	518027	1097968
Assam	23	125	26312	13777037	12878491	26655528
Bihar	37	130	45098	43243795	39754714	82998509
Chhattisgarh	16	97	20308	10474218	10359585	20833803
Goa	2	44	359	687248	660420	1347668
Gujarat	25	242	18539	26385577	24285440	50671017
Haryana	19	106	6955	11363953	9780611	21144564
Himachal Pradesh	12	57	20118	3087940	2989960	6077900
Jammu & Kashmir	14	75	6652	5360926	4782774	10143700
Jharkhand	18	152	32615	13885037	13060792	26945829
Karnataka	27	270	29406	26898918	25951644	52850562
Kerala	14	159	1364	15468614	16372760	31841374
Madhya Pradesh	45	394	55393	31443652	28904371	60348023
Maharashtra	35	378	43711	50400596	46478031	96878627
Manipur	9	33	2391	1095634	1071154	2166788
Meghalaya	7	16	6026	1176087	1142735	2318822
Mizoram	8	22	817	459109	429464	888573

Cont'd...

Table 6.6 Cont'd...

1	*2*	*3*	*4*	*5*	*6*	*7*
Nagaland	8	9	1317	1047141	942895	1990036
Orissa	30	138	51349	18660570	18144090	36804660
Punjab	17	157	12673	12985045	11373954	24358999
Rajasthan	32	222	41353	29420011	27087177	56507188
Sikkim	4	9	452	288484	252367	540851
Tamil Nadu	30	832	16317	31400909	31004770	62405679
Tripura	4	23	870	1642225	1556978	3199203
Uttar Pradesh	70	704	107452	87565369	78632552	166197921
Uttaranchal	13	86	16826	4325924	4163425	8489349
West Bengal	18	375	40782	41465985	38710212	80176197
Andaman & Nicobar Islands*	2	3	547	192972	163180	356152
Chandigarh*	1	1	24	506938	393697	900635
Dadra & Nagar Haveli*	1	2	70	121666	98824	220490
Daman & Diu*	2	2	23	92512	65692	158204
Delhi*	9	62	165	7607234	6243273	13850507
Lakshadweep*	1	3	24	31131	29519	60650
Pondicherry*	4	6	92	486961	487384	974345

Many may view the deceleration in urban growth a welcome development. To many others it is a rather disturbing signal suggesting that slowing down the process of urbanization in India is a reflection of inadequacy in our economic policy. The economy seems to have generated too few jobs (*jobless growth*) to transfer people from rural to urban areas; inadequate urban infrastructure investment could also have worsened the situation. The lack of jobs compounded by a deteriorating quality of life may have discouraged the intending rural migrants searching for better livelihood in urban areas. The growth of industries and services has been in the broad range of 6 to 8 percent per annum in the 1980s and 1990s, while that of agriculture has been in the range of 2 to 3 percent in the same period. It may appear that the benefits of higher industrial and overall economic growth have not been as widespread as they should have been, and are not being shared with the intending urban immigrants. But it is a fact that, according to official estimates, the urban/rural per capita income ratio did not deteriorate in the 1980s and 1990s for which data are available. The reason behind slowing down of urbanization in India demands a careful study and analysis taking inputs from various economic and non-economic sources. Cost of living in an urban area, especially in bigger cities, is rising fast, especially in view of soaring land prices and shortage of accommodation for a fair level of living. With capital-intensive labor saving technology adopted by various establishments, demand for unskilled and semi-skilled labor fell drastically. If that is one of the reasons for slowing down migration of unskilled labor from rural areas, an equally important factor behind slowing down R-U migration is deceleration of agricultural productivity growth. Ironically, the slowing down of agricultural growth rate, save for a few regions, has prevented releasing agricultural labors in rural areas.

Table 6.7
Net domestic product (NDP) and population in rural and urban areas

	Net domestic Product (Rs billion)	*Population (million)*	*Per capita NDP (Rs)*
	1970–71		
Total	368	541	680
Rural	229	434	529
Urban	139	107	1294
Urban as a ratio of Rural	0.60	0.25	2.45
	1980–81		
Total	1103	679	1625
Rural	650	522	1245
Urban	453	157	2888
Urban as a ratio of Rural	0.70	0.30	2.32
	1993–94		
Total	7161	891	8037
Rural	3849	655	5876
Urban	3312	236	14035
Urban as a ratio of Rural	0.86	0.36	2.39

Note: NDP and per capita NDP are at current prices
Source: Central Statistical Organization

Table 6.8
Proportion of urban centers in the 16 larger states in India, 2001

	States	*Population (million)*	*Proportion to total population*	*Percentage of Urban population*	*Difference in urban growth rate between 1981–2001*
	INDIA	**1,027,015,247**	**100**	**27.78**	**4.46**
	1	*2*	*3*	*4*	*5*
1.	Kerala	31,838,619	3.10	25.97	7.19
2.	Tamil Nadu	62,110,839	6.06	43.86	10.88
3.	West Bengal	80,221,171	7.81	28.03	1.54
4.	Maharashtra	96,752,247	9.42	42.00	6.99
5.	Andhra Pradesh	75,727,541	7.37	27.08	3.83
6.	Punjab	24,289,296	2.37	33.95	6.23
7.	Karnataka	52,733,958	5.13	33.98	
8.	Himachal Pradesh	6,077,248	0.59	9.79	2.07
9.	Orissa	36,706,920	3.57	14.97	3.15
10.	Gujarat	50,596,992	4.93	37.35	5.27

Cont'd...

Table 6.8 Cont'd...

1	*2*	*3*	*4*	*5*
11. Assam	26,638,407	2.59	12.72	
12. Haryana	21,082,989	2.05	29.00	7.04
13. Rajasthan	56,473,122	5.50	23.38	2.45
14. Madhya Pradesh	60,385,118	5.88	26.67	6.36
15. Bihar	82,878,796	8.07	10.47	–1.99
16. Uttar Pradesh	166,052,859	16.17	20.78	2.77

Urban population started to grow since 1921. Usually, the scale of industrialization in a country determines the size of the urban population. But India, and most other developing countries, did not actually follow this principle of urban growth. Growth of urban population in India has considerably been due to migration of rural people in search of jobs. It is the rural *push factor* rather than the urban *pull factor* that is primarily responsible for growth of urban population. We may recollect at this point that employment market in India probably saw its best days during the period of World War II. Both industrial and agricultural sectors expanded rapidly because of war demands for variety of goods and services. But that momentum was lost at the end of the war although free India spent colossal amounts on heavy industries in the first two decades after independence.

Projected Urban Population. With the current definition of 'urban' remaining unchanged, the urban growth of population between 2000 and 2030 is likely to be as under.

Table 6.9

Projections of urbanization for the next 30 years

	2000	*2005*	*2010*	*2015*	*2020*	*2025*	*2030*
Total Population in millions	1017	1097	1174	1246	1312	1369	1417
Urban Population in million	281	315	355	402	456	517	586
Percent Urban	27.7	28.7	30.3	32.2	34.7	37.8	41.4

Source: World Urbanization Prospects: 2003 revision.

6.3 Classification of Urban Settlements

In Indian census, urban settlements have been classified into six categories on the basis of the size of urban population: Tables 6.10 and 6.11 show distribution of towns and cities by their size of populations.

Table 6.10

Classification of urban areas in India

Class of Urban area	*Population*
I	100,000 or more
II	50,000–99,999
III	20,000–49,999
IV	10,000–19,999
V	5,000–9,999
VI	5,000 or less

Table 6.11

Percentage distribution of urban population in India by size of town over the years

Category	*Population size*	*1951*	*1961*	*1971*	*1981*	*1991a*
Class I	100,000 & above	7.70	9.22	11.28	14.04	16.44
Class II	50,000–99,999	1.69	1.97	2.20	2.66	2.79
Class III	20,000–49,999	2.69	2.99	3.12	3.11	3.42
Class IV	10,000–19,999	2.33	2.26	2.10	2.13	2.02
Class V	5,000–9,999	2.25	1.20	0.88	0.79	0.67
Class VI	Less than 5000	0.53	0.14	0.09	0.11	0.07
Urban population as proportion to total population		17.32	17.98	19.92	23.39a	25.71b
Total population (million)		361.09	439.23	548.16	683.33a	846.30b

a. Includes the interpolated population of Assam in 1981.
b. Includes the projected population of Jammu & Kashmir in 1991
Source: Office of the Registrar General, India.

Table 6.12

Distribution of towns/UAs by their classificatory categories, India 1991 & 2001

Class	*Population size*	*1991*		*2001*	
		No. of UAs/Towns*	*%*	*No. of UAs/Towns*	*%*
Special Class	1,000,000 +	23	0.62	35	0.80
Class I	100,000 and above	277	7.49	258	5.89
Class II	50,000–99,999	345	9.33	401	9.16
Class III	20,000– 49,999	944	25.53	1,151	26.29
Class IV	10,000–19,999	1,170	33.65	1,344	30.70
Class V	5,000–9,999	740	20.01	888	20.28
Class VI	Less than 5,000	198	9.36	191	4.36
Unclassified			10*	0.23	
All classes (I to VI)	3697	100		4378	100
Urban population as percentage of total population			25.71		27.78

**UA : Urban agglomeration*
Source: Office of the Registrar General, India. (Population totals for India & States for the Census of India 2001).

Table 6.13
Percentage distribution of rural population by size of village over the years

Village size	*1961*	*1971*	*1981*	*1991**
Less than 200	3.83	2.68	1.78	1.69
200–499	12.55	9.91	7.49	7.78
500–999	18.33	16.45	14.21	16.76
1,000–1,999	19.80	19.90	19.25	25.74
2,000–4,999	17.22	18.68	20.09	29.80
5,000–9,999	5.05	5.94	6.90	11.21
10,000 & above	2.80	4.07	4.56	7.02
Rural population as percentage of total population	82.03	80.09	76.66	74.27
Total rural population (million)	360.30	439.05	523.87	628.69

*Jammu & Kashmir and Assam are excluded in the size-class distribution
Source: Office of the Registrar General, India.

Table 6.14
Growth of cities and urban population in India, 1961–2001

Year	*Size Class of Cities (Population in '000)*				
	All Urban areas	*Large (100+) Type I*	*Medium (20–99.9) Type II & III*	*Small (5–19.9) Type IV & V*	*Very small (<5) Type VI*
			Number of Towns		
1961	2700	107	657	1668	268
1991	3696	300	1292	1907	197
2001*	5161	423	1894	2617	227
			Urban Population (million)		
1961	78.9	35.1	25.3	17.6	0.9
1991	215.3	139.7	52.3	22.6	0.7
2001	285.4	172.0	81.9	30.1	0.8
			Urban Population (%)		
1961	100.0	44.5	32.1	22.3	1.1
1991	100.0	64.9	24.3	10.5	0.3
2001	100.0	60.3	28.7	10.5	0.3

*This number of towns and cities is much in excess of that reported by RGI, vide Table 6.11
Source: India Country Report : *Population and Development,* Department of Family Welfare, Government of India, 2004

Of the 393 cities with 100,000 or more population recorded in 2001 census, there are 35 cities (5 in 1951 and 23 in 1991) that have more than one million population and 3 cities, namely Mumbai, Delhi and Kolkata are given special status for each of them having more than 10 million populations.

Mumbai Municipal Corporation is the lone corporation, which alone caters services to as many as 11,914,398 people under its jurisdiction.

We have said earlier that census statistics for different periods often are not comparable primarily because definitions of terms and concepts often have changed. Two new concepts were introduced in 1961 and 1971 Censuses – *town group* in 1961 and *urban agglomeration* in 1971. In spite of these changes, certain prominent features in population redistribution are visible.

1. Number of class I cities have grown faster, even faster has been the growth of population in these cities; between 1961 and 2001, total number of urban localities in India has nearly been doubled, and the population multiplied by a factor of 3.62. Population has increased by 490 percent in class I cities, by 324 percent in class II & III towns, 172 percent in class IV & V towns, and population of class VI towns in 2001 is only 89 percent of the population they had in 1961.
2. Although the number of class II cities have increased considerably with time, the proportion of population in these cities have not increased by the same proportion;
3. The proportions of class III and IV urban centers have increased, but the shares of their populations to the total urban population have decreased;
4. The number of class V and VI towns has declined, especially after independence and so are their shares to total urban population.

The three major states that have very high urban population in the total population are Tamil Nadu (43.86%), Maharashtra (42.00%) and Gujarat (37.35%). In the other extremes are the states Himachal Pradesh (9.79%), Bihar (10.47%) and Assam (12.72%). West Bengal, the most populous state in the sense that it has the highest population density among the states, has slightly greater than the national average urban population. All the backward states have percentage of urban population below the national average (Table 6.8).

Table 6.15

Urban growth and share of natural increase in selected states in India

States	***Urban Growth (%)***			***Share of Natural Increase (%)***
	1961–1971	***1971–1981***	***1981–1991***	***1981–91***
	Relatively Rich States : Industrially advanced			
Maharashtra	40.8	40.0	38.7	57.0
Gujarat	41.0	41.4	33.6	69.9
	Agriculturally advanced			
Punjab	25.3	44.5	29.1	81.5
Haryana	35.6	59.5	43.1	62.1
	Relatively Poor States			
Bihar	43.9	54.8	30.4	85.5
Rajasthan	38.5	58.7	39.2	65.3
Orissa	66.3	68.5	36.1	60.7
Uttar Pradesh	30.1	60.6	38.9	62.8

Source: Census of India 1991

Though urban population growth has mostly been due to natural increase, internal migration and reclassification of towns too have important roles in urban growth of population, especially in the richer states. Industrially advanced states tend to receive more migrants in their cities and towns. Urban centers receive migrants searching for jobs. People also migrate from towns to cities often for certain facilities that are not available in district towns and other urban areas. Migrants tend to crowd the bigger cities and the metropolitans. But there are agriculturally advanced states like Haryana and Punjab which receive sizable migrant agricultural labors from neighboring states. Role of skilled migrants is quite important in urban population growth in poor states like Rajasthan, Orissa and Uttar Pradesh.

Of late, R-U stream of migration has weakened because of very high cost for accommodation and higher cost of living in cities. Improved road linkage and enlarged railway network have encouraged the growth of commuters to cities. In smaller towns, the growth of population is mostly due to natural increase. For this reason, their share to total urban population has been declining consistently. M.K. Premi studied urban population growth from 1971 census data. Premi observed that population actually decreased in 3.59 percent of towns and smaller urban areas; population increased only by around 15 percent in 10 percent of towns and other urban areas. Population growth in these urban centers was even smaller than the normal decadal natural increase. This suggests that about 15 percent of urban centers lost population due to out-migration. Premi called this type of suburban settlements as "out migrating towns". Even Kolkata, once a major destination for migrants, has been sending out people to other cities and metropolitans in large numbers in recent years.

Premi has worked out the nature of out-migration vis-à-vis in-migration in different classes of urban areas between 1961 and 1971. It is observed that the rate of out-migration is significantly high in smaller towns and cities than in the larger ones.

Table 6.16

Out-migrating towns by their sizes, India 1971

	Types of cities/towns						*All classes*
	I	*II*	*III*	*IV*	*V*	*VI*	
1	*2*	*3*	*4*	*5*	*6*	*7*	*8*
Number of towns	151	219	652	987	820	290	3119
Total population of towns (million)	53.38	14.7	19.95	13.96	6.20	0.90	10.91
Number of out-migrating towns	10	16	69	141	134	62	432
Population of out-migrating towns (million)	4.35	1.11	2.12	1.95	0.98	0.19	1.07
Percentage of out-migrating towns to total towns	6.6	7.3	10.6	14.3	16.3	21.4	13.9
Percentage of population of out-migrating towns to total urban population	8.1	7.5	10.6	14.0	15.8	20.9	9.8
Number of chronically out-migrating towns	1	6	17	74	56	8	162
Population of chronically out-migrating towns (million)	0.10	0.39	0.42	1.03	0.44	0.03	2.41
Percentage of chronically out-migrating towns to total towns	0.7	2.7	2.6	7.5	6.8	2.8	5.2
Percentage of population of chronically out-migrating towns to total urban population	0.2	2.7	2.1	7.3	7.2	2.8	2.2

Source: M.K. Premi: Urban Out-migration: A Study of its nature, Causes and Consequences. N.D.: Sterling Publication, 1980.

6.3.1 Regional and Inter-state Variation in Urbanization

Like most other demographic characteristics, urbanization and urban growth of population cannot be uniform in all parts of a country. But what is surprising is the magnitude of inter-state variation in urbanization, especially in the context of democratic indicators. The variation among the bigger states, as of 2001 data, is from a low of 9.79 percent in Himachal Pradesh to a high of 43.86 percent in Tamil Nadu (Table 6.8). Till 1981, Maharashtra was at the top in the proportion of urban population to the total population among the states. Tamil Nadu has taken up the top spot since. Percentage change in urban population between 1981 and 2001 ranges from (–)1.99 (Bihar) to 10.88 (Tamil Nadu). The drop in proportion of urban population in Bihar is mostly due to Jamshedpur, a 'million plus Steel City' going to Jharkhand after it was carved out of Bihar.

Table 6.17 below shows how the number of towns and cities in India has changed during 1901–2001. Between 1901 and 1951, the number of towns and cities has increased by about 60 percent. Recognition to 857 settlements recorded as 'urban' in the earlier censuses was withdrawn with the changed definition of 'urban area' adopted in 1961 census. However, in the same census 497 new settlements were accorded urban status. By 1981, urban settlements in India went up by 72 percent (base 1901). The number of urban settlements in all the regions except the Eastern region dropped substantially in 1961 Census. The change of the definition alone saw a near 60 percent increase in towns and cities between 1951 and 1961 in the Eastern region. Both in Central and Western regions urban status was withdrawn for 29 and 27 percent respectively of suburban areas. The Northern region has the least number of towns and cities, Southern the most. Tamil Nadu has the highest number of cities and towns, even much more than Uttar Pradesh, the largest state in terms of population. Actually Uttar Pradesh remains way behind in growth of urban population compared to most other states. Nearly 60 percent of India's urban population lives in 6 states – Uttar Pradesh, Maharashtra, Gujarat, West Bengal, Andhra Pradesh and Tamil Nadu. Highest urban population is observed in Mizoram and Chandigarh, the later a UT (Table 6.18).

Table 6.17

Number of towns in each class category, 1901 to 2001

Census Year	*Number of towns in each category in the last century*						
	Class I	*Class II*	*Class III*	*Class IV*	*Class V*	*Class VI*	*Total*
1	*2*	*3*	*4*	*5*	*6*	*7*	*8*
1901	24	43	130	391	744	479	1811
1911	23	40	135	364	707	485	1754
1921	29	45	145	370	734	571	1894
1931	35	56	183	434	800	509	2017
1941	49	74	242	498	920	407	2190
1951	76	91	327	608	1124	569	2795
1961	102	129	437	719	711	172	2270
1971	148	173	558	827	623	147	2476
1981	218	270	743	1059	758	253	3301
1991	300	345	947	1167	740	197	3696
2001	393	401	1151	1344	888	191	4368

Note. Class categories are as defined in Table 6.9.
Source: Census of India 2001.

Table 6.18

Distribution of cities and towns by their population size, 1991 & 2001

Population size	Number of cities and towns			
	1991	***%***	***2001***	***%***
One million and above	23	0.62	35	0.80
100,000 to one million	277	4.79	358	6.67
50,000 to 99,999	345	9.33	401	9.18
20,000 to 49,999	944	25.53	1,151	25.38
10,000 to 19,999	1,170	31.65	1,344	30.77
5,000 to 9,999	740	20.01	888	20.33
Below 5,000	198	5.36	191	4.37
All Classes	3697	100	4368	100

Table 6.19

Percentage of urban population over the years for states, union territories and India

State/UT*	***1971***	***1981***	***1991***	***2001***
1	*2*	*3*	*4*	*5*
Andhra Pradesh	19.31	23.32	26.89	27.08
Arunachal Pradesh	3.70	6.56	12.80	20.41
Assam	8.82	9.88b	11.10	12.72
Bihar	10.00	12.47	13.14	10.47
Chhattisgarh				20.08
Goa	25.56	32.03	41.01	49.77
Gujarat	28.08	31.10	34.49	37.35
Haryana	17.67	21.88	24.63	29.00
Himachal Pradesh	6.99	7.61	8.69	9.79
Jammu & Kashmir	18.59	21.05	23.83a	24.88
Jharkhand				22.25
Karnataka	24.31	28.89	30.92	33.98
Kerala	16.24	18.74	26.39	25.97
Madhya Pradesh	16.29	20.29	23.18	26.67
Maharashtra	31.17	35.03	38.69	42.40
Manipur	13.19	26.42	27.52	23.88
Meghalaya	14.55	18.07	18.60	19.63
Mizoram	11.36	24.67	46.10	49.50
Nagaland	9.95	15.52	17.21	17.74
Orissa	8.41	11.79	13.38	14.97

Cont'd...

Table 6.19 Cont'd...

1	*2*	*3*	*4*	*5*
Punjab	23.73	27.68	29.55	33.95
Rajasthan	17.63	21.05	22.88	23.38
Sikkim	9.37	16.15	9.10	11.10
Tamil Nadu	30.26	32.95	34.15	43.86
Tripura	10.43	10.99	15.30	17.02
Uttar Pradesh	14.02	17.95	19.84	20.78
Uttaranchal				25.59
West Bengal	24.75	26.47	27.48	28.03
Andaman & Nicobar Island*	22.77	26.30	26.71	32.67
Chandigarh*	90.55	93.63	89.69	89.78
Dadra & Nagar Haveli*		6.67	8.47	22.89
Daman & Diu*	37.56	36.75	46.80	36.26
Delhi*	89.70	92.73	89.93	93.01
Lakshadweep*		46.28	56.31	44.47
Pondicherry*	42.04	52.28	64.00	66.57
INDIA	19.91	23.34	25.71	27.78

a. Based on the projected population of Jammu & Kashmir by the Standing Committee of Experts on Population Projections. (October, 1989).
b. 1981 Census could not be held in Assam. Population figures for 1981 for Assam have been worked out by interpolation.
Source: Office of the Registrar General, India.

6.3.2 *Differences in Growth of Population by Type of Towns and Cities*

Populations in cities and mega-cities have grown much faster than the district level towns and the suburban areas. The larger agglomerations have grown much faster than the smaller ones. This is true both for urban and village level populations. Proportion of the population living in villages having less than 5,000 persons has been dipping consistently. Most of the larger units, both in rural and urban area, expanded their area and population at the cost of the smaller units.

To understand this vertical movement of population we need to study closely the *urban-urban migration stream.* Generally rural-urban stream receives most attention in studies on internal migration. We however need to take a longitudinal perspective rather than confining our attention to movements between the censuses alone.

Prof. Ashok Mitra, 1961 Census Commissioner, attempted a *functional classification* of the cities and towns in terms of types of goods and services they cater. He classified towns and cities into three groups:

1. Engaged primarily in manufacturing;
2. Engaged primarily in trade and transport; and
3. Engaged primarily in providing services.

He tried to estimate the number of people engaged in each of these three categories. He suggested that if the number of persons engaged in one of these categories is 20 percent more than those engaged in the other two categories put together, then the city/town was to be regarded as of that functional category. He made a finer division of the first category (manufacturing) of towns: (i) mining, plantation, (ii) artisans and (iii) manufacturing type. The second category of towns was further classified as (iv) trading and (v) transport town type. Such classification of towns is welcome although there is some reservation on the criteria he suggested for labeling a town by this or that category. K.B. Suri after analyzing the growth of towns during 1951–61 came to the conclusion that population in manufacturing type of towns grew fastest. Sherry, Dutt and Goel selected 2492 towns from the 1971 census, the towns that maintained their urban identity in 1961 Census as well. Keeping in mind the three categories of towns proposed by Prof. Mitra, they classified the towns by their predominant economic activities. Two independent ratings were carried out for all these towns for 1961 and 1971 with a view to compare if their economic ventures remained nearly the same in the two time points. To be exact, they wanted to see if the towns changed their modal industrial activity. They concluded that economic venture in 817 towns remained almost unaltered. But in others considerable changes were observed. The nature of change observed can be seen in the following summary table.

Table 6.20

Change in economic activities in Indian towns in the decade 1961–71

Industrial category	*The criteria for industrial categorization*	*No. of towns changed their category between 1961–71*
1	Very high emphasis on services, less emphasis on manufacturing, trade and commerce	96
2	Very high emphasis on services, moderate emphasis on manufacturing, trade and commerce	36
3	Optimum emphasis on services, moderate emphasis on manufacturing, trade and commerce	127
4	Very high emphasis on manufacturing, low priority on trade and commerce and services	62
5	Very high emphasis on manufacturing, moderate emphasis on trade and commerce and services	124
6	Optimum emphasis on manufacturing, moderate emphasis on trade and commerce and services	128
7	Very high emphasis on trade and commerce, low priority over manufacturing and services	153
8	Very high emphasis on trade and commerce, moderate emphasis on manufacturing and services	260
9	Optimum emphasis on trade and commerce, moderate emphasis on manufacturing and services	336
10	Optimum emphasis on all economic ventures	353

Source: Ashok Mitra: India's Population: Aspects of Quality and Control, N.D.: Abhinava Prakashan 1978.

Even though the government showed considerable interest for a faster take-off in manufacturing industries and for this the government spent billions for supply of basic materials (iron and steel, other metals and alloys) and made import of new technologies and machines easier, the industrialized towns seem to have gone in favor of trade and commerce and transport followed by a balanced development in all other industrial sectors. Service sector did not receive much attention till about 1980. Things started to change through computer and IT revolution in 1980s and 1990s. Bangalore became the Silicon Valley of India. India soon became one of the leading global players in software technology. India earns billions of dollars through out-sourcing today. Many giant global IT players are making India as their second home chiefly because of software skills of Indians as also because of comparatively soft payments they have to make for hiring software engineers and other technical persons.

The economic reforms initiated in India in 1991 slowly changed the scenario altogether. Even those political parties that fought tooth and nail against automation and computer use in designing, planning and data storage for fear of labor retrenchment and shrinkage in employment opportunities, realized their folly and are seen fighting for a space in IT and telecom sector (West Bengal, for example). IITs, IIMs, universities and private educational institutions expanded and upgraded their courses in computer science, information technology, bio-technology and management. The government allowed private players to play a major role in improving the tele-density in the country. Mobile phones in the country are increasing by leaps and bounds. Tariff, especially for ISD and STD calls, have drastically been slashed. DTP and PCO shops can be seen in every corner of a street in towns and cities. Already there are over 50 million telephone subscribers. Cellular telephones are making landline telephones largely redundant. The stiff competition among a large number of private players has brought down tariffs drastically. The government is determined to bring up the tele-density to around 30 percent by 2007. An estimated sum of $25 billion would be needed to achieve this goal. The government has decided to increase FDI in telecom sector from 49 percent to 74 percent to invite foreign capital in this capital-intensive program.

6.2.3 Slums

One of the major concerns for most developing countries has been unplanned growth of urban centers. The physical infrastructure (residential accommodation, parks and open space, roads, drinking water, drainage system, power supply, transportation network, etc.) in most cities and mega-cities is totally inadequate to support the fast rising urban population. Since most of the quality hospitals, educational institutions, entertainment houses and shopping malls besides hundreds of industrial and trading houses, government offices, retail chains and wholesale markets are located in big cities, they draw thousands of people on every working day from far and near making the city life really miserable.

The large-scale migration of unskilled, illiterate labor from rural areas and from other states in search of some kind of a living has been responsible for flourishing the slums. These migrants stay in "jhupris" violating all laws of the land, forcibly constructing some sort of a structure on public lands, on lands along the railway tracks or along the banks of the principal water channels carrying the city wastes. With time, these channels are encroached by the slum dwellers, solid garbage are thrown into these channels, waste plastic sheets and carry bags choke the drainage system, thus disrupting the carrying capacity of the drains and liquid waste carrying channels.

In the name of development, the fast growing real estate business is choking the cities with high-rise buildings violating all town planning norms. Cities get flooded and waterlogged even with moderate rains, disrupting transport and most other essential services. Take the instance of Mumbai and its adjoining areas on the 26th July, 2005. 94 cm rain in a single day brought the whole city and its suburbs under water. The low-lying areas went under 4–5 meters of water. Rail, road and air traffic came to a dead halt. There was no electricity in many areas, no drinking water and no supply of food. Thousands of people and domestic animals died, buildings collapsed and the situation became so alarming that even no organized rescue work could be carried out. Once the waters receded, epidemics followed. The medical teams, hospitals and nursing homes worked relentlessly but could not save lives of thousands.

Most often the slum dwellers have the blessings and active support of one political party or another. Within no time they get the ration card and the voter's ID card. They constitute the solid vote bank for some party. The party in power is unable to demolish these "jhupris" in spite of repeated orders from the High Court or the Supreme Court since many of these unauthorized settlements grew up at the behest of the ruling party. This generally is the picture in all big metropolitan cities like Mumbai, Kolkata, Delhi, Chennai and others. In these cities, the slum populations constitute about one-third of the total urban populations. These slum dwellers supply the necessary labor to the regular residents for their domestic services, and unskilled/semiskilled labor to innumerable small-scale industries and workshops. The major problem of the municipal or corporation authority in these mega-cities stems from the fact that the slum dwellers do not pay any municipal tax, yet the municipal corporations have to supply water free of cost, repair roads and attend to many other civic amenities catered to these slum dwellers.

There were 35 cities in India (2001) in million-plus population category. Of these the Census authority has published data relating to slums for the first 23 cities (ordered by population size, Table 6.23).

Table 6.21

Top 35 urban agglomerations/cities in India along with their populations, 2001

Rank	*Urban agglomeration/City*	*Population (million)*	*Rank*	*Urban agglomeration/City*	*Population (million)*
1	Greater Mumbai	16.37	19	Ludhiana	1.40
2	Kolkata	13.22	20	Kochi	1.35
3	Delhi	12.79	21	Vishakhapatnam	1.33
4	Chennai	6.42	22	Agra	1.32
5	Bangalore	5.69	23	Varanasi	1.21
6	Hyderabad	5.53	24	Madurai	1.19
7	Ahmedabad	4.52	25	Meerut	11.7
8	Pune	3.75	26	Nashik	1.15
9	Surat	2.81	27	Jabbalpur	1.12
10	Kanpur	2.69	28	Jamshedpur	1.10
11	Jaipur	2.32	29	Asansol	1.09
12	Lucknow	2.27	30	Dhanbad	1.06
13	Nagpur	21.2	31	Faridabad	1.05
14	Patna	1.71	32	Allahabad	1.05
15	Indore	1.64	33	Amritsar	1.01
16	Vadodara	1.49	34	Vijaywada	1.01
17	Bhopal	1.45	35	Rajkot	1.00
18	Coimbatore	1.45		TOTAL	107.88

Table 6.22

Cities (Municipal Corporations) with more than one million populations, 2001

	Name of City	State/Union Territory	Population			Sex ratio
			Persons	Males	Females	
	1	2	3	4	5	6
1.	Greater Mumbai	Maharashtra	11,914,398	6,577,902	5,336,496	811
2.	Delhi Municipal Corporation (Urban)	Delhi	9,817,439	5,378,658	4,438,781	825
3.	Kolkata	West Bengal	4,580,544	2,506,029	2,074,515	828
4.	Bangalore	Karnataka	4,292,223	2,240,956	2,051,267	915
5.	Chennai	Tamil Nadu	4,216,268	2,161,605	2,054,663	951
6.	Ahmedabad	Gujarat	3,515,361	1,863,886	1,651,475	886
7.	Hyderabad	Andhra Pradesh	3,449,878	1,773,899	1,675,979	945
8.	Pune	Maharashtra	2,540,069	1,325,694	1,214,375	916
9.	Kanpur	Uttar Pradesh	2,532,138	1,354,581	1,177,557	869
10.	Surat	Gujarat	2,433,787	1,372,307	1,061,480	774
11.	Jaipur	Rajasthan	2,324,319	1,239,711	1,084,608	875
12.	Lucknow	Uttar Pradesh	2,207,340	1,165,932	1,041,408	893
13.	Nagpur	Maharashtra	2,051,320	1,058,692	992,628	938
14.	Indore	Madhya Pradesh	1,597,441	839,843	757,598	902
15.	Bhopal	Madhya Pradesh	1,433,875	755,685	678,190	897
16.	Ludhiana	Punjab	1,395,053	789,868	605,185	766
17.	Patna	Bihar	1,376,950	749,868	627,082	836
18.	Vadodara	Gujarat	1,306,035	684,130	621,905	909
19.	Thane	Maharashtra	1,261,517	674,660	586,857	870
20.	Agra	Uttar Pradesh	1,259,979	674,902	585,077	867
21.	Kalyan-Dombivli	Maharashtra	1,193,266	633,395	559,871	884
22.	Varanasi	Uttar Pradesh	1,100,748	584,514	516,234	883
23.	Nashik	Maharashtra	1,076,967	579,638	497,329	858
24.	Meerut	Uttar Pradesh	1,074,229	571,074	503,155	881
25.	Faridabad	Haryana	1,054,981	580,548	474,433	817
26.	Howrah	West Bengal	1,008,704	547,969	460,735	841
27.	Pimprichinchwad	Maharashtra	1,006,417	543,436	462,981	852
	Total		73,021,246	39,229,382	33,791,864	861

Source: Census of India, 2001, Press Release on Rural – Urban distribution of population – India and states/union territories: 2001, 20 July 2001, New Delhi.

Table 6.23

Identified/estimated slum population of million-plus cities, 1991 & 2001 (in million)

City	1991				2001 #		
	Total Population	Slum Population		Percentage	Total Population	Slum Population	Percentage
1. Greater Bombay	12.60	4.32	*	34.30	17.07	5.86	34.30
2. Kolkata	11.02	3.63	*	32.93	13.11	4.31	32.90
3. Delhi	8.42	2.25		26.70	12.22	3.26	26.70
4. Chennai	5.42	1.53		28.13	6.98	1.96	28.10
5. Hyderabad	4.34	0.86		19.78	6.30	1.25	19.80
6. Bangalore	4.13	0.52		12.50	6.36	0.79	12.50
7. Ahmedabad	3.31	0.67	*	20.23	4.36	0.89	20.31
8. Pune	2.49	0.41	*	16.44	3.53	0.58	16.30
9. Kanpur	2.03	0.42		20.55	2.49	0.51	20.60
10. Lucknow	1.67	0.28		16.64	2.26	0.37	16.60
11. Nagpur	1.66	0.53	*	31.85	2.32	0.74	31.90
12. Surat	1.52	0.39	*	25.67	2.29	0.58	25.40
13. Jaipur	1.52	0.44	*	28.98	2.21	0.64	29.10
14. Kochi	1.14	0.28	*	24.55	1.54	0.38	24.80
15. Vadodara	1.13	0.21		18.31	1.71	0.31	18.30
16. Indore	1.11	0.17	*	15.33	1.54	0.23	15.20
17. Coimbatore	1.10	0.10		8.70	1.33	0.12	8.70
18. Patna	1.10	0.70	*	63.66	1.53	0.97	63.50
19. Madurai	1.09	0.20		17.99	1.31	0.24	18.00
20. Bhopal	1.06	0.15	*	14.11	1.53	0.21	13.99
21. Vishakhapatnam	1.06	0.27		25.20	1.67	0.42	25.20
22. Ludhiana	1.04	0.37		35.36	1.63	0.58	35.40
23. Varanasi	1.03	0.21		20.12	1.33	0.27	20.10
Total	71.00	18.87		26.57	96.63	25.48	26.37

Note
1. Classification of the size of cities is based on 1991 Census
2. Total is different because of rounding off the figures
3. *Based on the percentage identified slum population of 1981
4. # Estimated

Source: Central Statistical Organization, Compendium of Environment Statistics, 1997, M/o Planning & Program Implementation, GOI, New Delhi

Table 6.24

Identified/estimated slum population according to size-class category of units/towns in India during 1991

Size-class category of cities/towns	*No. of cities towns*	*Total population*	*Slum population*	*Slum population as percentage of total population*	*Percentage of total slum population*
>10 lakh population	23	709.97	188.66	26.60	41.30
5–10 lakh population	31	214.50	42.56	19.80	9.30
3–5 lakh population	39	151.24	28.60	18.90	6.30
1–3 lakh population	207	325.14	54.49	16.80	11.90
Total : class I	300	1400.84	314.30	22.40	68.80
50,000 to 99,999 population	345	236.29	47.15	20.00	10.30
<50,000 population	3052	520.58	95.23	18.30	20.90
Total	3997	2157.71	456.69	21.20	100.00

Source: A Compendium on Indian Slums,1996, Town and Country Planning Organization.

These 'million-plus' cities together had 71 million people in 1991. The estimated aggregate population in these cities in 2001 is 96.63 million, i.e., decadal growth rate is 36 percent. Both the slum and the non-slum urban populations have grown by almost the same percentage point – about 36 percent. More than 63 percent of the population in Patna (Bihar) lives in slums; less than 9 percent are slum dwellers in Coimbatore (Tamil Nadu) in the South. Bangalore (Karnataka), the heartland of IT industries in India, has about 12.5 percent slum dwellers.

Of the 23 'million-plus' cities 6 are located in two major Western states, Maharashtra and Gujarat. Maharashtra is the financial capital of the country. It has Head Quarters of most of the reputed industries and banks in India. Both Maharashtra and Gujarat are highly developed industrially and both attract people from every part of the country.

6.2.4 Economic Liberalization Impact

Once India accepted the policy of economic liberalization, the country needed huge domestic and FDI in manufacturing, petrochemical industries, mining, IT and telecommunication as also in education, health, construction of airports, roads and houses and in other service sectors. A good proportion of these infrastructure development programs are urban-centric. India has been spending billions on infrastructure development. Huge investments have already been made in the Golden Quadrilateral project connecting the four major cities – Delhi, Mumbai, Chennai and Kolkata. The National Highway Authority, which already has spent about Rs 300 billion in the last five years in road connectivity, would require Rs 1,700 billion in the next seven years to construct new roads, convert two-lanes into four-lanes, four-lanes into six-lanes. Most mega-cities are bustling with construction activities – fly-over, new connectors, housing complexes, special economic zones, etc. India has opened up its sky to private domestic and foreign players. To cope with the rising volume of air traffic new airports have to be built and the existing ones expanded and modernized. Private-public partnership (PPP) model in most of these modernizing processes has been accepted in principle to make India the destination for global players. Central and many state governments have entered into agreement with global giants for starting new industries and even in development of infrastructure on 'built, operate and transfer' (BOT) principle. Telecom is one sector in India, which is expanding very fast. Currently, there are more than 50 million telephone subscribers in the country; the major share of this number goes to mobile telephony. The government intends to increase the number of subscribers to 250 million by 2007 (which already have surpassed) for which a huge sum of $25 billion would be needed. The government is expecting that a substantial part of this sum would come from FDI. Global giants like ABN Amro are asking the Indian software giants to develop special software packages for their global banking business and operations. The whole of the Western world has targeted India for outsourcing. The Call Centers in India is growing fast. Except the manufacturing industries (steel, petrochemicals, etc.), power generation units and a few others, most hi tech industries (computer, telecom, hardware and software development, genetic engineering and bio-technology, and the like) require thousands of square meters of built-in space in urban areas, well connected by rail, road and air. India has no option but to concentrate immediate attention to growth and development of the major cities.

India's GDP has been growing at around 6–8 percent per annum since economic liberalization began in the country (over 8% since 2004). Since 1991, when the economic liberalization policy was adopted, India's foreign exchange reserve has gone up from near zero to over $300 billion in June 2008 (currently around US$1.5 billion is being added every week); the capital market has been attracting short and long term Foreign Institutional Investments (FII) and the exports are on the rise. Imports of goods and services have increased from 9 percent of GDP in 1990 to 16 percent in 2003; exports of goods and services in the same period have increased from 7 percent to 14 percent of GDP. Even when economy of some of the East Asian and Latin American countries crashed in the mid-nineties, Indian economy could withstand that global phenomenon. India already has started the second generation reform. Customs and excise duties have drastically been cut, tax reforms are in progress, bank interest rates have been brought down close to international level, 'one-window' principle has been adopted for clearing project proposals, tax holiday is being granted for projects undertaken in underdeveloped areas; the government is slowly but steadily withdrawing its direct involvement in trade, commerce and manufacturing except in some key areas; sick government industries are either being closed or sold at market prices. The government is destined to cut down the overhead cost by downsizing the government machinery. It is engaging reputed management consultants in some of its key sectors for their efficient running and the government is gradually withdrawing subsidy on petroleum products, food, fertilizers and power to farmers and domestic users. The National Intelligence Commission of USA has predicted (Mapping the Global Future) that China and India would largely control the world trade in this century.

The government of India believes that a GDP growth rate over 8 percent is absolutely necessary if India was to be reckoned as a global economic power. For this, huge FDIs are necessary besides domestic investments. Presently, China attracts over $40 billion a year in FDI against $5 billion in India (in 2006–07 it jumped to over US$15 billion). This has happened since China did the ground work by developing a very fine infrastructure – roads, highways, ports and harbors, airports, townships with modern amenities and abundance of power. India spends about 6 percent of GDP ($31 billion) on infrastructure. China spent about 20.6 percent of its GDP ($260 billion) in 2002 in infrastructure development according to estimates of Morgan-Stanley. In September 2004, Dr Manmohan Singh, India's Prime Minister, while addressing the New York Stock Exchange assembly said that India would need to spend around $150 billion in infrastructure development alone in the next 10 years and he admitted that without foreign assistance and their active participation such a gigantic development work could not be completed.

China did not hesitate to use a good part of the country's foreign exchange reserve in infrastructure development. Many economists in India, including Dr Montek Singh Aluwalliah, the Deputy Chairman of the Planning commission, have suggested that 10 to 15 percent of India's reasonably good foreign exchange reserve should be made available in infrastructure development. Hi tech capital-intensive industries will not generate as much job opportunities as industries did when they were labor-intensive. India will need to concentrate on rapid development of the existing urban centers with all modern facilities and also create new ones, and take every possible step to improve the skill quality of those who would man these hi tech projects. Without this the momentum of 8–10 percent GDP growth in the next 10 years would not be possible.

In housing and urban development alone India spends over 2.5 percent of GDP. The following table shows the plan outlay in housing and urban development. This is likely to go up further as India's economy gains the necessary thrust.

Table 6.25

Plan outlay in housing and urban development, India

Plan	*Total outlay*	*Housing and urban development*	*Percentage share in the total outlay*
		(Rs million)	
First Plan	20,688	488	2.1
Second Plan	48,000	1,200	2.5
Third Plan	85,765	1,276	1.5
Annual Plan (1966–69)	66,254	733	1.1
Fourth Plan	157,788	2,702	1.7
Fifth Plan	394,262	11,500	2.9
Annual Plan (1977–80)	121,765	3,688	3.0
Sixth Plan	975,000	24,884	2.6
Seventh Plan	1,800,000	42,295	2.3
Annual Plan (1990–92)	1,338,350	3,001	2.2
Eighth Plan	4,341,000	105,000	2.4

6.4 Rural-Urban Differentials

Even 60 years after independence, the rural-urban divide in most demographic characteristics still remains strong. Between the different urban centers (district towns, capital city, and metropolitan city) there is wide difference in economic, social and demographic characteristics. The manner in which the characteristics of a metropolitan city are changing, especially after the foreign capital started to flow, cannot be expected of a district town or suburban town.

Although the infrastructure in capital and metropolitan cities has changed greatly, certain basic demographic and social parameters of their populations have not shown substantial change. The population composition by religion, caste, language and even age has not changed much. However, considerable change is observed in sex ratio, family size, age at marriage, birth rate, literacy, income opportunities, etc. The areas where the differences between rural and urban areas still are large are:

1. Those in employment generally are a younger lot, between 15–45 years, in urban areas.
2. Women are fewer than males in urban areas (Table 4.9 & 4.22).
3. Death rates have declined greatly both in rural and urban India. Still there exists a clear 3 points difference in CDR between the two (Table 4.16).
4. Rural India is way behind urban India in all indicators of fertility; but the gaps are diminishing. The gap is only marginal in states that are really advanced in terms of Human Development Index, e.g., Kerala (Table 8.5 & 8.6).
5. People of religious faiths other than Hindus (and Muslims) appear to concentrate more in cities and larger towns (Table 4.21).
6. The average family size in larger cities is noticeably small compared to that in smaller towns and villages.
7. Literacy rates and levels of education are much higher in cities (Table 5.3). Persons with technical skill and training appears to concentrate in cities.
8. Persons in labor force in rural India are consistently 15 percentage points higher than that in urban India (Table 7.3). Proportion of urban male population in labor force is 6–7 percent lower vis-à-vis the rural male population (1983–2000). This surely is due to the fact that most urban youths join services only after completing certain level of education. That is, their entry age in remunerative jobs often is above 20 years. This generally is true in all countries, developed or developing. Whereas females in labor force in the rural population varied between 45.6 and 51 percent, urban females in labor force remained confined between 20.9 and 23.5 percent.
9. Service sector is very strong in cities and metropolitan areas.
10. A high vertical and horizontal occupational mobility is observed in urban areas.
11. Per capita income is noticeably high in urban areas.
12. The actual dependency ratio is much higher in cities and towns. However, there are more persons in 60 years and above age group in rural areas than in urban area. The difference is more than 1 percentage point in favor of rural senior citizens (Table 4.15).
13. Consumption expenditure pattern in families are quite different in rural and urban areas. The share of expenditure on food and related items still is as high as 60 percent of total expenditure in rural area. The shares of expenditure on food and non-food items for the urban people were evenly balanced till 1983. However, during 1983–2000 the expenditure share of non-food items has increased from 41 to 52 percent in urban areas.
14. Proportion of persons living below the poverty line in rural India has declined from 45.65 percent in 1963 to 27.09 percent in 1999–2000. The same in the urban population has dropped from 40.79 to 23. 62. The rural-urban combined proportion stood at 26.1 percent in 1999–2000 Persons below the poverty line in the country in 2006 is estimated at around 20 percent.
15. Urban people are more tolerant to other religious and caste groups. People from different communities work in the same factory or establishment, share the same neighborhood and even the same house for reasons of shortage of residential space and housing facilities.
16. Not only the populations in urban areas are growing faster, the urban areas too have expanded faster.

17. A large proportion of the urban populations are migrants. Their roots often are not deep-seated. They hesitate less to migrate to some other city or town where they have chance to earn better standard of living.

The following graphics show R-U differences in achievements in a few critical areas. The graphics indicate that though the rural-urban differences are declining in many areas, the differences still are very tall.

Figure 6.4
Rural-urban difference in some demographic indicators

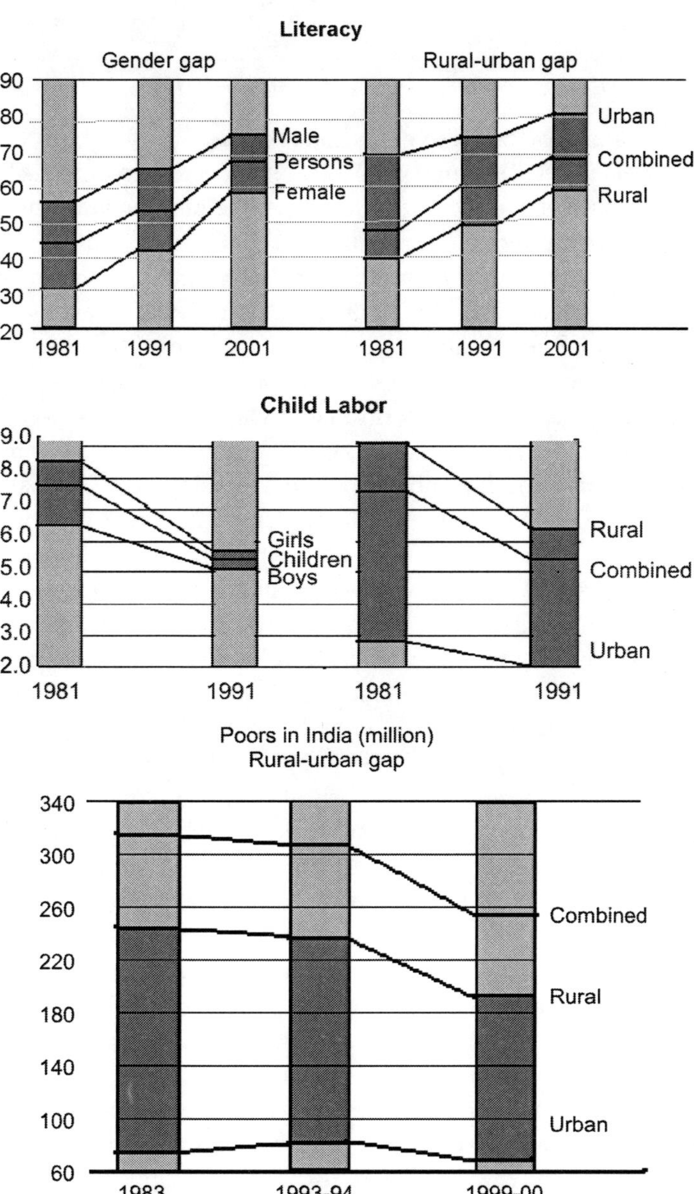

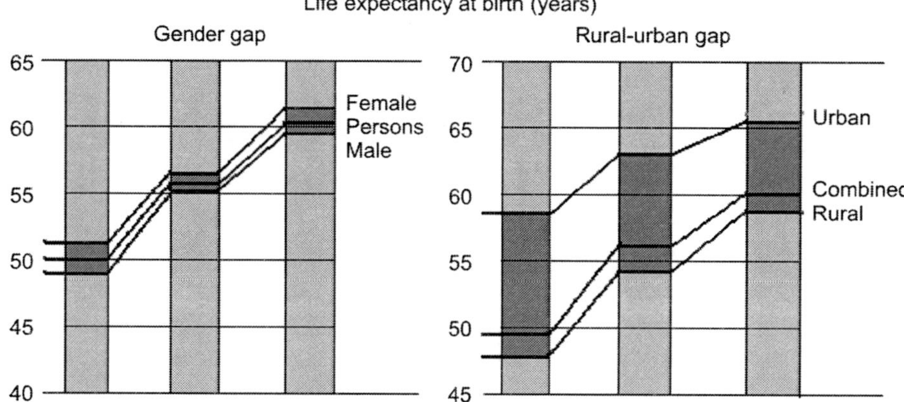

Not only the rural-urban gap between poors has declined over the years, the ratio of urban per capita Net Domestic Product (NDP) to rural per capita NDP decreased from 2.45 in 1970–71 to 2.32 in 1980–81 (Table 6.7). With economic reform in place, the ratio however has increased again to 2.39 in 1993–94 and possibly further higher in 2006.

The problem with most developing countries, including India, is that most of them are over urbanized in relation to the stage of their economic development and transition. Presently, about 28 percent of India's population lives in cities and towns. At this level of urbanization, the demographers feel that at least 50 percent of the total work force should have been in non-agricultural occupation. But about 60 percent of our workforce (73% in rural workforce) is still engaged in agriculture contributing only 20 percent to India's GDP. Urbanization in India has been much faster than it could accommodate those seeking non-agricultural employment. The pattern of urbanization followed in India has made concentration of population in larger and mega cities creating tremendous pressure on the civic amenities. The large presence of inefficient, poorly productive informal sector, rising slum dwellers and a very large floating population (commuters) are creating enormous pressure leading to virtual collapse of urban civic services. Poverty and display of wealth exists side by side. Growth of a very few selected urban centers is the result of demographic explosion rather than due to increasing economic base in these centers. Overcrowding in these big cities could have been avoided had other urban growth centers been nurtured. Funds made available for urban development are spent most on these big cities for better road and rail connectivity, erecting very many fly-overs to ease the movement of traffic, building many housing complexes, shopping malls, IT, education, entertainment and health parks. The government must realize that there is a limit to this type of urban development. Decentralized urban growth to redirect migration flows is urgently needed to save these mega cities from a virtual collapse.

The economic growth path India has opted would bring down the share of agriculture to GDP further. The labor force released from agriculture, lacking in education, training and skill, find their entry into the labor-saving employment market very difficult especially since unemployment even among the educated youth is mounting in urban areas. Increase in population in urban areas has forced the government to invest more and more on infrastructure development, especially in housing, roads, power generation and creating new townships with improved facilities to attract foreign and domestic investments. To develop new townships or economic zones and to improve connectivity between the growth centers and ports, the state governments have to acquire thousands of acres of land, which often would include some prime agricultural land. The displaced families are offered compensation for their land and the government would on occasions promise for alternative jobs and low cost housing facilities once the projects are through. Often governments violate the Land Ceiling Act in order to make thousands of acres of land available to the investors, especially foreign investors. Social tensions mount (Singur and Nandigram fiasco in West Bengal in 2006–08 are glaring examples) and the political parties cannot desist themselves from taking advantage of the dilemma in public mind generated by such decisions. The central government has been forced to start Rural Employment Guarantee Scheme to provide some relief to those who are displaced from their land either because of land acquisition for uses other than agriculture or for uneconomic fragmented land holding. As a result, most states have little resources left for developmental works in social sectors, especially in villages.

Some important features of urbanization in India can be traced:

- Growth in class I and special class cities indicates a lopsided urbanization.
- Urbanization remains largely a product of demographic explosion. The fast diminishing land-man ratio and uneconomic land holding have forced people, often without any education and skill, to look for an alternative livelihood in the urban areas.
- Even without strong industrialization and economic base, urbanization in India is taking place mostly due to rural *push* factor.
- Massive concentration of poorly educated people in cities has created huge growth of slums degrading the urban civic life. Due to lack of political will and appropriate relocation plans, these slums could not be demolished even wth Court intervention.
- Increased distress migration will only hasten urban decay.

6.5 The Future of Urban Population Growth

India's urban population is projected to rise from around 28 percent in 2001 to 38 percent by 2025 (Table 6.9), which means the total population living in urban areas could reach half a billion mark around that time. Maharashtra and Tamil Nadu, the more demographically and socio-economically advanced states, are likely to experience largest share of the population growth in urban areas; their rural areas vis-à-vis urban areas are likely to experience growth rates even more than the rate of natural increase due to return migration in the coming decades. By 2025 the number of the million plus club of urban agglomerations is likely to be around 70 from the present 35. Given the current pattern of distribution of urban population, these could hold about half of all the urban populations in India. How well the civic amenities can be provided to the rapidly growing populations in the old cities like Mumbai, Kolkata, Delhi or Chennai is anybody's guess, especially in view of the recent experiences when unprecedented rain played havoc in Mumbai and a few other cities in 2005. Real estate business and encroachment on canals carrying city wastes have become a very serious issue before the administration and town planners. Slum clearance would remain a serious challenge for the administration.

A centrally sponsored scheme of Integrated Development of Small and Medium Towns was initiated in 1979–80 to improve the physical infrastructure and also to provide essential facilities and services to slow-down the growth of large cities by developing new small and medium sized towns. This not only would ease the pressure cooker situation in the mega cities, it would strengthen the functional base of the urban economy in India. Keeping in mind the recommendations of National

Commission of Urbanization, a centrally sponsored scheme for infrastructure development of mega cities was initiated in 1993–94.

Migration and urbanization deserves greater attention in policy dialogues in achieving population and development goals in India. Access to services for urban poor and migrants needs to be addressed through focused interventions. It is encouraging to note that urban health is an emerging priority in the second phase of Reproductive Child Health (RCH) program. Both the government and the private sector need to organize institutional training programs to help the aspiring youth from rural and urban areas develop the skill necessary to find a place in the expanding industrial and service sectors.

7 Working Population in India

7.1 Introduction

The fruits of macroeconomic growth are distributed through employment generation and improvement in the quality of life of the commoners. The robustness of an economy is measured by its capability to generate additional employment as also its competence to sustain money wage returns on a long-term perspective. There is a paradigm shift in the type of employment generated as a country moves away from monopolistic tradition under a conservationist socialistic tradition to free-market economy relying heavily on e-governance and in the process the state's role increasingly becoming one of a facilitator than a participant in manufacturing, trade and commerce. The traditional sectors' contribution to country's GDP declines steadily and the empty space thus created is filled up by manufacturing and service sectors. An altogether new brand of employment is generated that emphasize on education and skill of the workers.

To transform from a predominantly agricultural economy, India embarked upon a public sector-dominated (basic and heavy industries besides public utilities as electricity generation, construction of dams for storage of water for power generation, irrigation, drinking water, etc.) industrialization strategy under the centralized investment planning in 1950–51. It was a period of restrictive external trade regime keeping an eye mostly on domestic consumption. Both external and internal competitions were not encouraged. Import of capital-intensive high cost technology restricted labor absorption in the industries which were built up. The outcome: Indian economy was trapped into a low "Hindu growth" syndrome of 3.5 percent real GDP growth over the thirty-year period 1950–51 to 1980–81 despite doubling the rates of gross domestic savings and investment. The decade of the 1980s, though considered as the beginning of economic liberalization and the emergence of the Indian economy out of the low growth equilibrium with real GDP, growth of employment in the organized sector showed considerable decline (Appendix 7.1). The private sector's contribution to generate employment was miniscule even in 1980s when public sector's contribution to employment generation even plummeted to 0.020 per annum (exponential) in the eighties compared to average 0.038 growth rate in the previous 20 years. Since 1991, while GDP growth rate has been commendable, the employment growth rate continued to decline even though the private sector appears to have grabbed the opportunity created by the 'new economic policy' to aggressively expand their industrial empire keeping eye both on the domestic and international market. Most impressive growth is observed, both in terms of money output and employment generation, in the service segment, especially in IT sector, which is totally dominated by private players.

The revolution in IT, communication and biotechnology (knowledge revolution) and also the role played by World Trade Organization (WTO) in changing the world trade practices have created a global employment market. The fast increase in knowledge-based industries and service sector all over the world requires that the young people spend more time in higher education and specialized training. This delays their entry into the employment market.

7.2 An Overview of the Employment Situation in India

The exact employment position in any country is a tricky question for several reasons. The determination of the size of the actual working force is not easy. It is comparatively easy to estimate the size of the population in the organized sector. In relation to the total workforce, employment in the organized sector in India reached a high of 7.93 percent in 1983 and since then it has declined to about 7 percent in 1999–2000 (Table 7.1). The 'organized labor force' not necessarily is totally non-agricultural or totally urban or urban non-agricultural. Whatever assumptions regarding composition of the 'organized labor force' are made, the rows 2 to 4 of Table 7.1 show that organized employment has declined over the years. Even if we take a look at the public sector workforce alone (rows 5 to 8), the same declining trend is observed. That is, public sector as employer has been steadily losing its share in generation of employment in the country in the last two decades after adopting economic liberalization policy in 1991.

Table 7. 1

Estimates of the relative magnitude of the reported organized workforce total (public plus private)

	1961	*1983*	*1993–94*	*1999–2000*
A. Total Organized WF as percentage of				
1. Total WF	6.41	7.93	7.32	6.98
2. Total Non-Agricultural WF	26.63	25.43	20.32	17.61
3. Total Urban WF	45.74	40.84	33.61	29.69
4. Total Non-Agricultural Urban WF	53.10	48.83	38.33	32.50
B. Public Sector WF as percentage of				
5. Total WF	3.74	5.44	5.20	4.80
6. Total Non-Agricultural WF	15.53	17.43	14.43	12.13
7. Total Urban WF	26.67	28.00	23.87	20.45
8. Total Non-Agricultural Urban WF	30.96	33.47	27.22	22.39

Adapted from S. Tendulkar: Organized Labor Market in India, Pre and Post-Reform (on line)

Reliability and trustworthiness of working population data in the unorganized sector, especially the agricultural labor, daily wage earner and the like, often remains suspect. Moreover, comparison of working population data for various periods of the same country or region or between different countries is not easy since the criteria for differentiating a 'worker' from a 'non-worker' had not been the same for different periods and for different countries. Between 1901 and 1931, persons whoever had 'a source of income' were included in the labor force in Indian Census. In 1981, a more pragmatic definition of worker was adopted. A person was to be considered a worker if he/she was found to be involved with any economic production system. His/her involvement in the economic activity can be physical or mental or both. Not only those who have direct involvement in the production system but also those others who are involved in the education and training of the work force or those who advise them on matters related to work or the managerial staffs that look after the affairs of the organization are also to be regarded as workers. The definition of 'worker' often has changed so much that inter-censal comparison poses a serious problem. For example, the definition of 'worker' in 1961 Census was so broad that students, even those engaged in household chores were regarded as 'workers'. The definition was changed in 1971 Census which resulted in deleting some 'activities' included in the list of occupations in 1961 Census from 'worker' categories. Consequently, there was a sharp drop in work participation rate, WPR, in 1971 (Table 7.2).

The computed WPR would differ depending on the entries both in numerator and denominator in the computation formula. One may put 'all workers' irrespective of their age in the numerator, or 'workers in the age group 15 years and above' or 'workers in age group 15–59 (or 15–65)' in the numerator. Similarly, the denominator may have 'total population' or 'population in the age group 15–59 (or 15–65)'. Obviously, the index WPR would differ depending upon what formulation one uses. Census reports are generally for 'all workers irrespective of age' in relation to the entire Census year population. A more pragmatic and comparable index (if we presume that all nations follow the guidelines of International Labor Organization, ILO, in respect to child-labor) would be WPR in relation to economically active population. NSSO uses the term Labor Force Participation Rate (LFPR), which is defined as "the proportion of persons in the age group 15 years and above who were either working (i.e., employed) on the usual principal and subsidiary status or seeking or available for work (i.e., presently unemployed)".

There are may different agencies who collect data on the work force and its composition in the country – the Registrar General, the Planning Commission, Director General of Employment and Training (DGET), Ministry of Labor, NSSO, Central Statistical Organization (CSO), Annual Survey of Industries (ASI), etc. There are always some differences in the estimates of work force in the country between the sources one use for obtaining the basic data. The most comprehensive industry-wise data for various states are published by ASI. Economists invariably use ASI data for time series analysis and complex model building. The estimated working population in 2001 by National Human Development Report 2001 (NHDR, 2001), under the aegis of Planning Commission is a little over 402 million. 55th round of National Sample Survey (large) puts it at 407 million in 1999–2000. Both ASI and DGET data are used to trace trends over time.

Table 7.2

Work participation rate by sex in the total population and in the economically active group, India 1901–81

	Sex	*1901*	*1911*	*1931*	*1941*	*1951*	*1961*	*1971*	*1981*
I. WPR in total population	Persons	46.61	48.07	46.92	43.7	39.1	42.98	32.93	33.45
	Males	61.11	61.9	60.52	58.27	54.1	57.12	52.51	51.62
	Females	31.7	33.73	32.67	27.63	23.3	27.96	11.97	13.99
II. Economically active population	Persons	59.03	60.33	59.64	60.19	57.1	54.41	51.99	53.93
	Males	58.93	60.35	59.84	60.59	57.6	54.77	52.18	54.06
	Females	59.14	60.11	59.44	59.77	56.6	54.03	51.8	53.78
III. WPR in relation to II.	Persons	78.95	79.81	78.65	71.95	68.5	78.99	63.32	60.22
	Males	103.7	102.6	101.1	96.17	93.9	104.3	100.6	92.67
	Females	53.6	56.13	54.96	46.23	41.2	51.74	22.91	25.28

Source: 1901–71 data are from Ashok Mitra: India's Populations: Aspects of Quality and Control, 1978; 1981 data refer to Main Workers only, Census 1981

Table 7. 3
Labor force participation rate LFPR, India 1983–2000 (percentage)

	1983			*1993–94*			*1999–2000*		
	Males	***Females***	***Persons***	***Males***	***Females***	***Persons***	***Males***	***Females***	***Persons***
Combined	87.1	44.4	66.5	85.4	42.6	64.5	83.5	38.5	61.8
Rural	88.7	51	70.3	87.6	48.8	68.8	85.4	45.6	66.2
Urban	82.5	23.5	55.4	79.9	23.4	53.3	78.6	20.9	51.1
Incidence of unemployment (as % of labor force)	2.3	1.3	2.0	2.1	1.7	2.0	2.5	1.8	2.3

Source: National Human Development Report 2001, Planning Commission, Government of India (data from 38th, 50th, and 55th round of NSSO survey on Employment and Unemployment Situation in India)

Figure 7.1
Persons in the labor force (percentage)

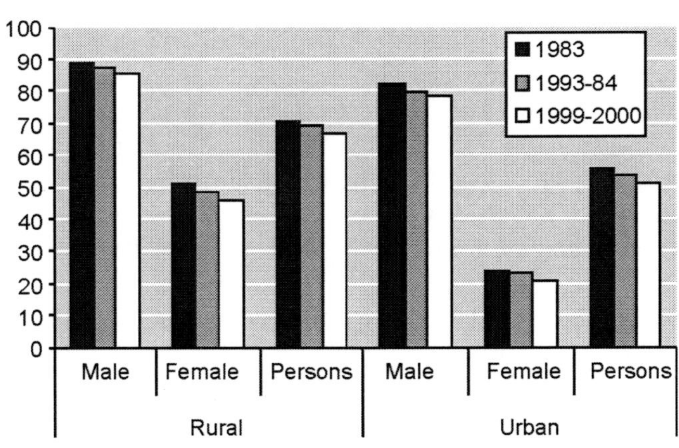

Table 7.4
Growth of employment between 1983 and 1999–2000

	1983 to 1993–94			*1993–94 to 1999–2000*		
	Males	***Females***	***Persons***	***Males***	***Females***	***Persons***
Combined	2.2	1.7	2.1	1.9	0.9	1.6
Rural	2.0	1.5	1.8	1.6	0.8	1.3
Urban	2.8	3.2	2.9	2.6	1.5	2.4

Source: Same as in Table 7.3

Till 1961, WPR for females was approximately half the WPR for males. Since 1971, there has been a sharp fall in female WPR. During the period 1983 to 1999–2000, LFPR for persons at the national level has declined from 66.5 percent to 61.8 percent; the decline has been more with females (from 44.4 percent to 38.5 percent) than with males (from 87.1 percent to 83.5 percent) (Table 7.3). The decline in LFPR growth rate has been very sharp in rural areas, especially since 1993–94 (Table 7.4). The covariance (CV) indicates (Table 7.5) that work participation of females varies widely among the states and UTs and an almost identical pattern is observed in this 17 years period as well. Low CV for males indicates that LFPR for males is almost similar in all the states and UTs.

Figure 7.2
Per capita adjusted income

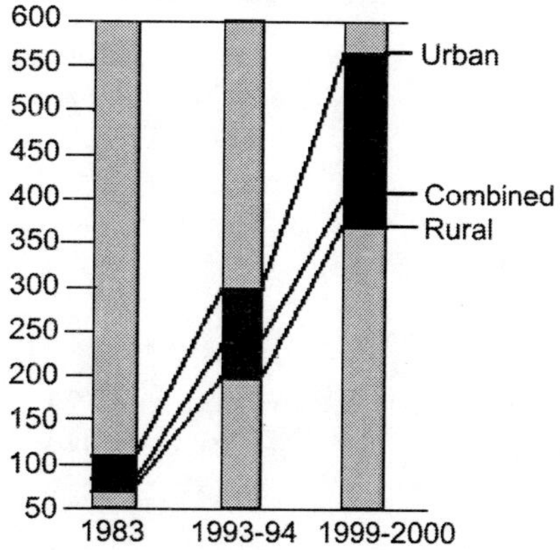

The decline in LFPR has been registered both in rural and urban areas (Tables 7.2 & 7.3). It may be mentioned here that the 17 years under scrutiny is the period of economic liberalization, which was started when late Rajiv Gandhi was India's Prime Minister. It took a firm shape in 1991 when Dr Monmohan Singh was India's Finance Minister. Labor force participation has significantly gone up in two Northeastern States, Mizoram and Nagaland (special economic packages from the Central government was granted for these two disturbed states) and in Lakshadweep, a union territory. Only a few states like Haryana, Andhra Pradesh, Himachal Pradesh, Rajasthan, Jammu & Kashmir and West Bengal besides a few smaller states in Northeastern region registered higher growth rates compared to the national average between 1983–1993 Table 7.5). Assam, Bihar and Punjab and a few smaller states and UTs, had growth rates better than the national average in the subsequent period. Most other states showed employment growth rate very close to the national average or behind it between 1993–94 and 1999–2000. Female employment growth in many states in this period was even negative (Haryana, Maharashtra, West Bengal, for example). Female LFPR in Mizoram has increased many folds between 1983 and 1993–94. Female labor participation in the state continued to increase in the succeeding period too. Tripura among the states and Delhi among the UTs have very few female labors in the working population. Himachal Pradesh, Meghalay and Nagalnd find LFPR of females above 60 percent. Between 1983 and 1993–94 female LFPR improved in 10 states/UTs. 8 states/UTs showed improved female LFPR in the period that followed. When compared with 1983 statistics, 1999–2000 data show an improvement in female LFPR only in 5 States/UTs (Assam, Orissa, Jammu & Kashmir, Maghalay and Mizoram). Female LFPR in urban area is far below (less than half) of female LFPR in rural area. Although labor participation rate in the 17-year period under examination has declined both for males and females, incidences of unemployment among males have marginally improved; for females the situation has worsened quite significantly.

Although the LPFR has declined over the years, more in urban areas, per capita adjusted income has increased substantially. In the process, income inequality between urban and rural population has increased manifold.

Table 7.5

Percentage distribution in labor force in India and states, 1983, 1993–94 and 1999–2000

*States/UTs**	*1983*			*1993–94*			*1999–2000*		
	M	*F*	*P*	*M*	*F*	*P*	*M*	*F*	*P*
1	*2*	*3*	*4*	*5*	*6*	*7*	*8*	*9*	*10*
Andhra Pradesh	89.7	58.1	74.1	87.8	60.3	74.2	85.1	54.2	69.9
Arunachal Pradesh				78.8	56.6	68.6	67.3	42.3	55.3
Assam	83.2	19.7	53.4	83.7	24.9	55.9	83.4	24.0	55.2
Bihar	87.6	36.0	62.5	84.8	25.1	56.3	85.2	26.3	57.3
Goa	82.1	57.1	69.8	77.7	35.2	56.8	77.4	24.6	51.0
Gujarat	86.0	48.5	67.7	86.1	45.3	66.3	84.9	44.6	65.4
Haryana	84.1	32.0	60.0	80.9	39.0	61.5	77.4	27.4	54.2
Himachal Pradesh	86.7	67.3	77.1	87.1	69.2	78.2	81.7	63.4	72.5
Jammu & Kashmir	88.0	36.1	64.1	83.7	49.4	67.5	81.2	38.5	60.7
Karnataka	87.3	49.8	69.1	86.5	49.8	68.6	85.0	45.4	65.6
Kerala	82.7	47.0	64.3	82.2	35.0	57.9	80.8	35.3	57.4
Madhya Pradesh	88.6	58.1	73.9	87.1	53.4	70.9	84.6	50.7	68.3
Maharashtra	86.4	54.2	70.9	83.0	53.0	68.5	82.1	46.3	64.8
Manipur	70.8	45.4	58.4	73.1	43.4	58.6	73.8	34.8	54.4
Meghalaya	89.4	61.5	76.0	89.0	65.2	77.4	85.0	62.1	73.6
Mizoram	82.4	9.5	48.4	78.8	43.6	61.9	78.5	48.7	63.8
Nagaland				68.0	31.4	50.8	74.1	60.6	67.6
Orissa	89.0	39.6	64.6	85.4	42.9	64.5	84.1	40.6	62.6
Punjab	87.2	39.8	65.1	84.3	27.4	57.6	82.2	33.9	59.4
Rajasthan	87.3	59.1	73.9	85.5	57.2	71.9	82.6	50.2	67.2
Sikkim	83.5	38.2	63.7	85.1	27.9	58.3	79.5	36.9	58.8
Tamil Nadu	88.6	53.3	71.1	85.6	54.1	70.0	83.6	47.6	65.7
Tripura	81.2	11.5	47.6	81.7	20.5	51.9	78.6	11.2	45.1
Uttar Pradesh	88.4	35.4	63.5	86.4	30.9	60.6	83.3	29.1	58.1
West Bengal	85.6	27.6	58.9	87.2	27.1	58.8	84.6	22.2	55.0
Andaman & Nicober Is.*	89.9	30.2	65.8	90.1	58.6	76.0	86.4	29.7	59.7
Chandigarh*	86.1	27.5	61.4	84.9	32.3	61.7	81.2	21.0	53.7
Dadra & Nagar Haveli*	84.2	77.3	80.8	90.7	76.5	83.8	92.7	53.2	73.0
Daman & Diu*	82.1	55.0	67.9	80.3	29.1	55.0	85.5	34.7	60.1
Delhi*	84.2	16.7	54.8	81.3	14.3	50.8	77.7	13.6	47.6
Lakshadweep*				82.2	25.5	54.7	81.9	33.1	57.8
Pondicherry*	84.0	39.0	61.6	79.9	30.8	55.5	79.8	29.2	54.3
INDIA	**87.1**	**44.4**	**66.5**	**85.4**	**42.0**	**64.5**	**83.5**	**38.5**	**61.8**
CV	4.38	37.6	12.2	5.54	37.0	13.5	5.51	35.3	11.6

Note:

1.Persons in the labor force or the labor force participation rate (LFPR) is the proportion of persons in the age group 15 years and above who were either working (i.e., employed) on the usual principal and subsidiary status or seeking or available for work (i.e., presently unemployed).

2. P for persons, M for males and F for females.

Source: NSSO 38th, 50th, and 55th Rounds on Employment and Unemployment Situation in India.

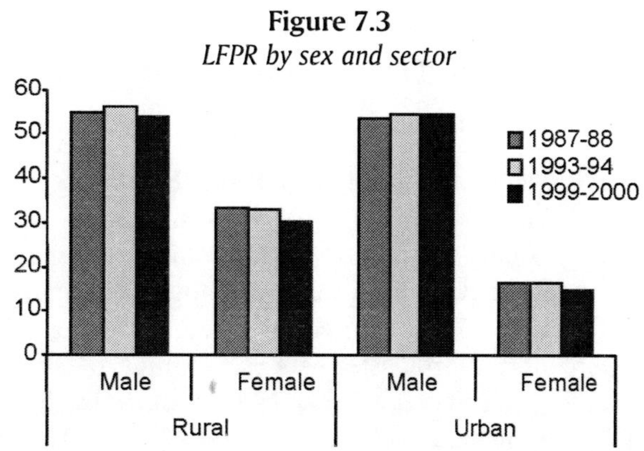

Figure 7.3
LFPR by sex and sector

These changes have to be seen in the context of demographic transition in each of these states as also the distribution of the population among various economic, religious and caste groups. Given the increase in the labor force in the nineties and decline of employment vis-à-vis in eighties, the intensity of unemployment increased both among males and females, especially in rural areas. LFPR is appreciably high among males, both in rural and urban areas, for the education groups 'below secondary level' and 'graduate and above' (Table 7.6). With some minor variation, the pattern has not changed much in the 17 years under review. For rural females a sudden increase in LFPR among educated girls below secondary level is observed in the same survey. Among urban females too a similar change is observed though LFPR for urban girls below secondary level was only about 50 percent of their counterparts in rural area. But unlike those in rural area, LFPR among graduate females in urban areas dropped significantly in 1999–2000. There is a wide gap in LFPR between males and females for all educational categories both in rural and urban areas.

Table 7.6
Labor force participation rates (LFPR) for educated persons by sex and residence in India

Year	*Education level*	*Rural*		*Urban*	
		Male	*Female*	*Male*	*Female*
1	*2*	*3*	*4*	*5*	*6*
1983	Literate below secondary	84.92	25.85	82.55	12.38
	Secondary & higher secondary	74.24	23.76	71.69	17.38
	Graduates & above	88.78	37.60	87.37	35.29
1987–88	Literate below secondary	83.80	26.35	81.25	12.78
	Secondary & higher secondary	74.20	26.30	70.70	16.20
	Graduates & above	91.10	39.90	86.40	37.70
1993–94	Literate below secondary	85.24	25.80	81.75	13.69
	Secondary & higher secondary	72.08	20.01	68.38	14.47
	Graduates & above	91.30	44.80	86.20	35.50
1999–2000	Literate below secondary	86.38	36.64	81.96	17.85
	Secondary & higher secondary	74.66	19.47	68.23	12.72
	Graduates & above	89.80	41.00	85.40	30.20

Note:
1. The LFPRs are for person of age 15 years and above.
2. The rates are according to the usual principal status.
3. The rates are based on the results relating to NSS 38th (1983), 43rd (1987–88), 50th (1993–94) and 55th (1999–2000) rounds respectively

Source: National Sample Survey Organization

7.2.1 NCAER Survey Findings

Some explanation of the gender disparity in employment, especially in rural India, can be found in the NCAER survey (1994). Although the estimates of work participation rate obtained from Census, NSSO and NCAER data are not comparable (as far as the magnitude of employment and unemployment rates are concerned), they closely agree with the patterns observed in the addressed populations.

NCAER computed two WPR estimates, one based on "usual status"[1] and the other "subsidiary status work participation". NCAER estimated 'usual status' male and female WPRs as 51.9 and 18.4 percent respectively for the entire country. The analysis of the survey data showed that CV for male WPR was only 6.8 compared to 56 percent for female WPR. The female WPR varied from a low of 4.6 percent in Northeastern states to a high of 38 percent in Himachal Pradesh. A few other low female WPR states are Bihar (9.1%) and Punjab (9.3%). Andhra Pradesh (37%) and Karnataka (31%) are the states where female WPRs are fairly high. Three low male WPR states are North-eastern states together (45.1%), Rajasthan (47.6%) and Bihar (48.4%); three high male WPR states are Andhra Pradesh (58.2%), Tamil Nadu (57.6%) and Gujarat (56.3%). The 'usual status' male WPR for the states closely matches the rates available from 1991 Census. But the 'usual status' female WPR is consistently lower compared with similarly defined rates from 1991 Census. When the 'usual and subsidiary status' are both used for estimating female WPR, the rate works out at 26 percent for the entire country, very close to 26.8 percent estimated from Census 1991. Major discrepancy between the two sets of estimates (Census and NCAER) is observed for the states West Bengal, Rajasthan, Uttar Pradesh, Punjab, Bihar and Orissa. NCAER attributed this discrepancy to cultural factors regulating female participation in productive work.

NCAER found that overall WPR is affected by the extent of participation of children in the labor force. WPR calculated on 15–59 age group presents a stable estimate. For this age group, 'usual status' WPR for males and females worked out as 82.7 and 29.5 percent respectively. With extended definition these changed to 83 and 41 percent respectively indicating that females more than males have larger 'subsidiary status'. Some important findings in the NCAER survey are

- Work participation rate decreases considerably as household income increases. While male WPR decreases from 85 to 79 percent, female WPR falls from a high of about 36 to 19 percent for the lowest (below Rs 20,000 per annum) and highest household income (Rs 86,000 and above per annum) categories respectively.
- A similar decline though not as steep was observed in the poverty group classification both among the 'usual' and 'subsidiary' status adult female WPRs suggesting that truly poor house-holds cannot afford to remain unemployed. The adult male WPRs were stable across poverty line group classifications.
- Male WPRs for large land holding families were smaller than that for landless wage earners. Female WPR was fairly high in landless families (52%) followed by marginal farmers (33%), small farmers (24%), medium farmers (22%) and large farmers (21%). Large land holding farmers employ hired hands frequently, requiring less assistance from female members and children of the household. Female and child labor participation rates are closely related to household income and ownership of assets like land.
- Female labor participation was high in smaller households (40%) than in larger households (21%). Household income effect produced larger CVs in larger households.

1. "Usual status WPR" is estimated from what persons usually do for a living for at least half the year. When persons report 'household duties' or 'student' or 'non-workers' as their main activity, a further probe often would reveal that they had undertaken some productive work though intermittently or only for a short while. Such an activity in NCAER survey was recorded as "subsidiary activity".

- Female labor participation is very high among STs (45%) and SCs (38%) compared to WPR of 30 percent in total rural female population.
- A large divide in female labor participation was observed among religious groups. Muslim women's participation was least, 16 percent, vis-à-vis 31 percent among Hindus and 37 percent among Christians.
- Non-worker–worker ratios were observed to be low in smaller households than in larger households.
- High income group (Rs 86,000 and above per annum) rural households were found to have larger household size (8.28) compared to 5.03 in the lowest income group (below Rs 20,000 per annum).
- When we look to the per capita income, the relation gets totally reversed. Household size was observed to be small in large per capita income households. Household size increased with per capita income dipping. Decline in household size attendant upon increase in per capita income saw a fewer female members in those households.
- The average size of a rural household is 5.7 (3 males and 2.7 females), and about 2.1 persons are engaged in productive activity (1.6 males and 0.5 females). That is, every earner has to support 0.7 male and 1.1 female non-earning members of the household. This dependency ratio is low among landless wage earners, SCs and STs, suggesting higher female and child labor participation among these population groups.

The growth rate of employment (Table 7.4) at the national level was 2.1 percent between 1983–1993–94 (1.8% in rural area and 2.9% in urban India). In the next six years, the national growth rate was a meager 1.6 percent (1.3% in rural area and 2.4% in urban area), which was even lower than the annual average population growth rate of 1.93 percent. The decline has been significantly high for females than for males. The growth rate of WPR has come down further since the last Census in 2001. The employment scenario obtained from 2001Census in the states and UTs is presented in Appendix 7.8.

7.3 Organized Workforce in India

It is sometimes more profitable to discuss labor from the view point of their activity status – wage and salary earners, self employed, casual and unemployed – rather than from occupational or industrial categories. Organized work force relates to those in 'wage and salary earners' who are engaged in production units registered under Factories Act, 1948.[2] They could be regular or hired contractual employees and their salaries often are in commensurate with their education and skill endowment. They in fact constitute a very privileged category of workers with several facilitating and mutually binding service conditions, giving them a high bargaining power. As per NSSO 1999–2000 survey, 'wage and salary earners' constituted only about 14 percent of the total work force in India (62% of them are in urban area), 'self employed' constituted 52 percent and 'casual labor' had a share of little less than one-third of the total work force. A little over 2 percent were 'unemployed'. Half of those earning wages and salaries were in the organized sector. Self-employment and casual labor statuses were more prevalent among rural than among urban labor force and among female than among male workers. The survey also showed higher unemployment rate in urban areas vis-à-vis rural areas.

The economy of a country must adapt to the fast changing global market in today's WTO regime and also to improve the life style of its masses. World GDP is dominated by the service and

2. The Factories Act applies to those units employing 10 or more workers and using power/20 or more workers not using power. Another Act – Employment (Compulsory Notification of Vacancies) Exchanges Act 1959 applies to all public sector establishments irrespective of their sizes and non-agricultural private sector establishments employing 25 or more workers.

manufacturing sectors, agriculture receding to the third spot. Though service sector has the largest share in national GDP, it thrives on the growth of the industrial sector (Table 7.8). The share of industrial workforce in India grew from 11.6 percent in 1961 to 17.3 percent in 1999–2000 of the total working population and its share to national GDP grew from 18.5 percent to 26.9 in 1993–94 prices. 1 percent growth in industrial workforce contributed to about 1.46 percent growth in GDP. But the most spectacular change has occurred in 'service sector'. From about 12.5 percent in 1961 its share jumped to 22.3 percent in 1999–2000 and in the process its share to GDP went up from 29.2 to 48 percent (Table 7.8) in the period (in 2006 the service sector's contribution is reported to be around 60%). That is, every 1 percent growth in service sector employment adds 1.92 percent to GDP. 1 percent of agricultural workforce contributed only 0.69 percent to GDP in 1961; it has come down to only 0.42 percent in 1999–2000. So the key to rapid growth of economy is largely dependent on expansion and modernization of industrial sector.

The technological uplift affects the urban work force more than the rural labor. To adapt new technology in the production system to remain competitive in domestic and international market, the establishments have to hire professionals and skilful persons, which are mostly available in urban areas, and have to pay hefty compensation to these hired hands for their professional eminence and skill. When technology is changing, enterprises have to invest in worker training to remain competitive. This can happen only when their workers are already better educated and have the basic skills, since that lowers the cost of acquiring new skills. So, it is no wonder that the demand of economic reform reaches the urban skilled workforce before it can percolate to other sectors.

Table 7.7

Classification of labor force according to usual principal plus subsidiary activity, 1999–2000

	Category of labor force	*Self employed worker*	*Wage and salary worker*	*Casual worker*	*Unemployed*	*Total*
	1	*2*	*3*	*4*	*5*	*6*
1.	Rural Males	53.96	8.70	35.63	1.71	100
2.	Rural Females	57.76	3.05	39.54	1.05	100
3.	Rural Persons	54.94	6.73	36.86	1.48	100
4.	Urban Males	39.59	39.81	16.09	4.51	100
5.	Urban Females	42.78	31.37	20.14	5.71	100
6.	Urban Persons	40.22	38.13	16.90	4.75	100
7.	Total (Rural + Urban) Males	50.23	16.77	30.56	2.44	100
8.	Total (Rural + Urban) Females	54.81	7.01	36.49	1.69	100
9.	Total (Rural + Urban) Persons	51.68	13.68	32.44	2.20	100
10.	Urban Share: Males	20.43	61.56	13.65	47.91	25.93
11.	Urban Share: Females	10.91	62.59	7.71	47.20	13.98
12.	Urban Share: Persons	17.24	61.73	11.54	47.74	22.15

Source: National Sample Survey Organization: "Employment and Unemployment Situation in India, 1999–2000", NSS 55th Round, Report No. 458

Table 7. 8

Percentage distribution of GDP at 1993–94 prices and total workforce in India by sectors: 1961, 1983, 1993–94 and 1999–2000

	Category of labor force	***Shares in Workforce (%)***				***Shares in GDP (%)***			
		1961	***1983***	***1993–94***	***1999–2000***	***1961***	***1983***	***1993–94***	***1999–2000***
	1	***2***	***3***	***4***	***5***	***6***	***7***	***8***	***9***
1.	Agriculture (A)	75.9	68	64	60.4	52.3	38.1	31.6	25.1
2.	Industry (I) (of which Manufacturing and Repair)	11.6 (9.5)	14.6 (11)	15.6 (11.5)	17.3 (12)	18.5 (10.9)	24.6 (15)	26.0 (15.9)	26.9 (17.1)
3.	Services (S)	12.5	17.4	20.4	22.3	29.2	37.3	42.4	48.0
4.	Total	100	100	100	100	100	100	100	100
5.	Share of Rural workforce in agriculture	86.1	81.5	78.4	76.3				
6.	Share of Female workforce in agriculture	85.7	81.1	77.5	75.4				
	Memo totals								
	(a) Workforce (million)	188.7	302.7	374.1	397.9				
	(b) GDP (Rs Crores)					204615	467331	788694	1150967

Notes:

1. GDP in agriculture and allied sectors(A) is a three year average centering on 1960–61(for 1961), 1983–84 (1983), 1993–94 and 1999–2000
2. Industry (I) includes mining and quarrying, manufacturing, construction and electricity, gas and water.
3. Services (S) include trade, hotels and restaurants, transport, storage and communication, finance, insurance, real estate, and business services and community, social and personal services.

Sources:

1. Census of India, 1961
2. National Sample Survey (Quinquennial) Rounds on Employment and Unemployment.
3. National Accounts Statistics, CSO

New technologies have created a large space for highly skilled and trained persons. Because of a very large population base, we still have plentiful of science graduates, engineers, doctors, IT and management specialists and bio-technologists. In fact, with knowledge explosion world over, this new generation of scientists and technologists truly have become members of a global village. However, it is sad to note that these exceptionally brilliant scientists and technologists (mostly products of IITs, IIMs and other reputed universities and institutes in India at a considerable cost) are lured to obtain jobs in USA, UK and other countries for higher pay packets and better work environment and also to prove their worth in the global market.

Five reputed institutes[3] recently conducted a survey on the effect of globalization in five countries, which included India as well. Their observation on Indian market is worth noting. There is a large market in India for technical and professional persons. But because of less than optimum infrastructure and unattractive pay, brain drain could not be checked. The intellectual assets of the country are lost in the process. The inadequacy of training programs for these technologists has also

3. Economic Policy Institute, Washington, Inter-trade Union Department of Statistics and Socio-economic Studies, Brazil, Institute of Applied Science, Norway, National Labor and Economic Development Institute, South Africa and Labor Studies Institute, South Korea

been brought under the scanner of the survey. The survey observed that the Indian institutes have failed to upgrade technologies and provide better facilities for training to these young professionals and entrepreneurs to keep pace with the fast changing world market scenario. This study also noticed that unemployment among the illiterates was far less than that among educated persons. Whereas only 0.2 percent of the illiterates were found fully unemployed, the same among the graduates were 8.8 percent and that for those completing the school education (HS) were 7.8 percent.

In the last 10 years or so PCOs, Xerox centers and DTPs have mushroomed even in the district towns and large villages. In West Bengal, for example, an estimated 130,000 PCOs are operating. With liberal bank financing, a significant number of skilled and semi-skilled youths have found some alternative occupations. Personal computers are fast becoming popular. The demand for computer mechanics (software and hardware) is growing fast. Some 10/12 years back there was hardly any dealer for computers even in district towns. The situation has changed in the last few years. One can easily find 6/7 such dealers within a radius of 2/3 km in important towns. Typewriting schools have been upgraded into computer training schools.

Between 1961 and 1981, the employment growth in the organized sector was around 3.2 percent per annum. About 60 percent of the labor force in the organized sector at this point of time was in government run organizations (mostly in administrative and other white collar jobs). A study in 1978 showed that about 15 million people were in the public sector, which constituted nearly 5.7 percent of the working population. Between 1951 and 1981 the annual average population growth rate was about 2.25 percent. But the job seekers in this period grew by around 3.0 percent per annum. That is, the country could not provide jobs to a sizeable number of aspirants. Only about 7 percent of the current Indian workforce is in the organized sector. Between 1961 and 1981, the exponential employment growth rate in the organized sector was 0.03 per annum, which dropped to 0.015 in the eighties and an all time low of just 0.005 in the first decade of economic liberalization (Appendix 7.1). Exponential growth rate in public sector dropped from 0.038 during 1961–81 to almost zero (0.001) in 1991–2001). Since 1991, there has been a decisive shift in the development strategy toward a closer integration with the world economy and greater reliance on private initiative and market-instruments. The private sector in India gained some momentum in the post-economic-reform period. They dominated employments in the manufacturing and service sector (Appendix 7.3). The process is still underway.

In 1991, 71.27 percent of the organized labor was in Public Sector – a little over 39 percent were State or Central government employees, the rest in quasi-government establishments like nationalized banks, educational and research institutes, public sector units, municipalities, corporations and other local bodies. Only about 29 percent of the organized labor force came from private sector. The share of the larger private sector establishments was 25.37 percent and the smaller ones contributed only 3.37 percent. By 2000, share of employment in public sector came down to 69 percent (Table 7.10). Dr Manmohan Singh in his new economic policy statement in 1991 made it clear that non-plan expenditure needed to be cut down to bring in fiscal discipline in the economy. Narsimha Rao government, of which Dr Manmohan Singh was the Finance Minister, and the subsequent governments at the Center took some steps to downsize Central government employees in a phased manner. 136,300 numbers of employments were curtailed in Central government establishments, that is, a 4 percent reduction between 1991 and 2000. Another 4.22 percent (151,000 in absolute numbers) employment was truncated in undertakings by the Central government. But increase in employment at the state level far exceeded this downsizing at the central level (4.87% increase in direct state government employment and 9.58% in organizations and institutions funded directly by state governments). In consequence, during 1991–2000 the percentage increase in public sector employment (Center plus states) was 1.35.

Table 7.9

Employment in the organized sector – All India 1961–2000 (million persons)

	1961	*1966*	*1971*	*1976*	*1981*	*1986*	*1991*	*1996*	*1998*	*2000*
Private	5.04	6.81	6.76	6.85	7.4	7.37	7.68	8.51	8.84	8.65
Public	7.05	9.38	10.73	13.32	15.48	17.68	19.06	19.43	19.54	19.31
Total	12.09	16.19	17.49	20.17	22.88	25.05	26.74	27.94	28.38	27.98
Proportion of males and females in the organized sector										
Male	89.1	88.7	89.0	88.2	87.8	87.0	85.9	84.2	83.0	82.4
Female	10.9	11.3	11.0	11.8	12.2	13.0	14.1	15.8	17.0	17.6

Source: Ministry of Labor, Director General of Employment & Training

Table 7.10

Employment in the organized sector, 1991 & 2000 ('000) A. Public sector

Year	***Government***		***Quasi-government***			***Total***
	Central	***State***	***Central***	***State***	***Local bodies***	
1	***2***	***3***	***4***	***5***	***6***	***7***
1991	3409.8	7112.9	3564	2658.3	2312.7	19057.7
%	(12.76)	(26.61)	(13.33)	(9.94)	(8.65)	(71.27)
2000	3273.5	7459.3	3413	2912.9	2255.1	19313.8
%	(11.71)	(26.68)	(12.21)	(10.42)	(8.07)	(69.08)
Employment growth	–136.3	346.4	–151.0	254.6	–57.6	256.1
% growth	–4.00	4.87	–4.22	9.58	–2.49	1.0134

B. Private Sector

Year	***Larger establishments***	***Smaller establishments.***	***Total***	***Grand Total (A+B)***
1	***8***	***9***	***10***	***11***
1991	6783.4	892.4	7675.8	26733
%	(25.37)	(3.34)	(28.71)	(100)
2000	7719.3	926.8	8646.1	27959.9
%	(27.61)	(3.31)	(30.9)	(100)
Employment growth	935.9	34.4	970.3	1226.9
% growth	13.80	3.85	12.64	4.59

Source: Employment Review, DGE&T, Ministry of Labour, Government of India.

The growth in private sector is good, especially in larger establishments. Some 935,900 additional employments were generated in larger establishments besides another 34,400 in the smaller companies during 1991–2000. The overall growth of employment in the private sector was 12.64 percent for the period 1991–2000. The average growth of employment in the organized sector (public and private) in this decade was 4.59 percent.

Table 7.11

Employment in the organized sector for 10 larger states, 1991 & 2000 ('000)

States	Central Govt.		Change % (3–2)	State Govt.		Change % (6–5)	Central+State		Change % (9–8)
	1991	2000		1991	2000		1991	2000	
1	2	3	4	5	6	7	8	9	10
INDIA	**6973.3**	**6686.5**	**–4.11**	**12083.9**	**12627.3**	**4.50**	**19057.2**	**19313.8**	**1.346**
Andhra Pradesh	458.1[6]	454.0[6]	–0.90[10]	930.0[4]	1049.4[4]	12.84[2]	1388.1[7]	1503.4[5]	8.31[2]
	(6.57)	(6.79)		(7.70)	(8.31)		(7.28)	(7.78)	
Bihar	735.0[3]	727.4[3]	–1.03[9]	725.6[6]	633.1[9]	–12.70[10]	1406.6[6]	1360.5[7]	–3.28[7]
	(10.54)	(10.87)		(6.00)	(5.01)		(7.38)	(7.04)	
Gujarat	278.6[9]	273.3[9]	–1.9[7]	681.9[8]	646.5[8]	–5.19[9]	960.5[9]	919.8[10]	–4.24[9]
	(3.40)	(4.09)		(5.64)	(5.12)		(5.04)	(4.76)	
Karnataka	338.6[8]	315.9[8]	–6.70[3]	678.8[9]	796.8[6]	17.38[1]	1017.4[8]	1112.7[8]	9.37[1]
	(4.86)	(4.72)		(5.61)	(6.31)		(5.33)	(5.76)	
Madhya Pradesh	540.0[5]	497.8[5]	–7.81[1]	883.9[5]	869.4[5]	–1.64[7]	1423.9[5]	1367.2[6]	–3.98[8]
	(7.74)	(7.44)		(7.31)	(6.89)		(7.47)	(7.08)	
Maharashtra	905.8[2]	835.9[2]	–7.72[2]	1375.8[2]	1454.0[1]	5.68[4]	2281.6[1]	2289.9[1]	0.364[5]
	(12.39)	(12.50)		(11.39)	(11.51)		(11.97)	(11.86)	
Rajasthan	254.2[10]	250.5[10]	–1.46[8]	698.6[7]	766.0[7]	9.65[3]	952.8[10]	1016.5[9]	6.69[3]
	(3.65)	(3.75)		(5.78)	(6.07)		(5.00)	(5.26)	
Tamil Nadu	430.2[7]	412.6[7]	–4.09[6]	1149.1[3]	1184.6[3]	3.09[5]	1579.3[3]	1597.2[3]	1.133[4]
	(6,17)	(6.17)		(9.50)	(9.38)		(8.29)	(8.27)	
Uttar Pradesh	719.6[4]	674.5[4]	–6.27[4]	1421.7[1]	1354.8[2]	–4.71[8]	2141.3[2]	2029.3[2]	–5.23[10]
	(10.32)	(10.09)		(11.76)	(10.73)		(11.23)	(10.59)	
West Bengal	961.3[1]	914.5[1]	–4.87[5]	613.7[10]	627.0[10]	2.17[6]	1575.0[4]	1541.5[4]	–2.13[6]
	(13.78)	(13.68)		(5.07)	(4.96)		(8.26)	(7.98)	
Total jobs	5621.4	5356.4		9105.1	9381.6		14726.5	14738.0	
% of total	80.61	80.11		75.35	74.30		77.28	76.31	

Table 7.11 Cont'd…

States/UTs	Private sector		Change (12–11)	Grand Total (Pvt + Pub)		Change (15–14)
	1991	2000		1991	2000	
1	11	12	13	14	15	16
INDIA	**7675.8**	**8646.1**	**12.64**	**26733**	**27959.9**	**4.589**
Andhra Pradesh	375.0[7]	568.4[6]	51.572	1763.1[5]	2071.8[5]	17.51[2]
	(4.89)	(6.57)		(6.60)	(7.41)	
Bihar	256.5[8]	253.3[9]	–1.257	1663.1[7]	1613.8[8]	–2.96[7]
	(3.34)	(2.93)		(6.21)	(5.77)	
Gujarat	700.0[4]	770.5[4]	10.075	1660.5[8]	1690.3[7]	1.80[6]
	(9.12)	(8.91)		(6.21)	(6.05)	

Cont'd…

Table 7.11 Cont'd...

1	*11*	*12*	*13*	*14*	*15*	*16*
Karnataka	430.0^{6}	750.7^{5}	74.581	1447.4^{9}	1863.4^{6}	28.74^{1}
	(5.60)	(8.6.8)		(5.41)	(6.66)	
Madhya Pradesh	245.2^{9}	226.5^{10}	–7.639	1669.1^{6}	1593.7^{9}	–4.52^{8}
	(3.19)	(2.62)		(6.24)	(5.70)	
Maharashtra	1365.9^{1}	1469.9^{1}	7.616	3647.5^{1}	3759.8^{1}	3.08^{5}
	(17.79)	(17.00)		(13.64)	(13.45)	
Rajasthan	231.1^{10}	259.1^{8}	12.124	1183.9^{10}	1275.6^{10}	7.75^{4}
	(3.01)	(3.00)		(4.42)	(4.56)	
Tamil Nadu	710.2^{3}	927.3^{2}	30.573	2289.5^{4}	2524.5^{3}	10.26^{3}
	(9.25)	(10.73)		(8.56)	(9.03)	
Uttar Pradesh	535.7^{5}	523.4^{7}	–2.308	2677.0^{2}	2552.7^{2}	–4.64^{10}
	(6.98)	(6.05)		(9.98)	(9.13)	
West Bengal	890.5^{2}	810.8^{3}	–8.9510	2465.5^{3}	2352.3^{4}	–4.59^{9}
	(11.62)	(9.38)		(9.22)	(8.41)	
Total jobs	5740.1	6559.9		20466.6	21279.9	
% of total	74.78	75.87		76.54	76.17	

Note. The superscript numbers indicate rank of states in respective classification categories.
Source: DGE&T, Ministry of Labor, Government of India, and National Human Development Report 2001

Table 7.12
Population of the 10 selected states, India 2001

States	***Population (million)***	***Percentage of total population***
INDIA	**1027**	**100**
Andhra Pradesh	75.69 (5)	7.37
Bihar	82.88 (3)	8.07
Gujarat	50.63 (10)	4.93
Karnataka	52.69 (9)	5.13
Madhya Pradesh	60.39 (7)	5.88
Maharashtra	96.74 (2)	9.42
Rajasthan	56.49 (8)	5.50
Tamil Nadu	62.13 (6)	6.05
Uttar Pradesh	166.07 (1)	16.17
West Bengal	80.21 (4)	7.81
Total	**783.92**	**76.33**

Note: Figures in parentheses indicate ranks.

We have in Appendix 7.3 the relevant data relating to working population by industrial categories in the organized sector, public and private. Over two time points 1991 and 2000 organized labor (public and private) for 10 larger states is presented in Table 7.11. These 10 larger states in India together shared over 76.33 percent of the total population of India in 2001 (Table 7.12). Their combined shares to the total workforce in 1991 and 2000 (cols 14 & 15 of Table 7.11) in the organized sector were just a little above 76 percent. There is, however, large variation among the states in the share of the workforce relative to their population size in both public and private sectors. In computing public sector employment, both direct and quasi government employments have been merged into one category, 'Central government employment'. Similarly, direct employments under state government, quasi government and local bodies have been put under 'State government employment'. Employments in larger and smaller establishments in private sector similarly have been put under 'Private sector employment'.

7.3.1 *Public Sector : Central Government*

In the last 50 years many of the central government offices had to be shifted either totally or partially from one state to another for administrative reasons or for distributive justice. So it is no wonder that such reorganization and relocation would have some effect on the state's share of workforce in central government concerns. The erstwhile NDA government at the center made a commitment for down-sizing various government departments in one of its budget sessions. A total of 10 percent posts, it said, would be allowed to lapse in a period of 5 years.

West Bengal, though has a population share of 7.81 percent (fourth in rank in population size), still has the distinction of the highest number of central government employees stationed in the state, much higher than its population share. This position has been maintained in both the years 1991 and 2000 even though the state lost about 46,800 employment opportunities in central government jobs during the period. Its share in the private sector dropped by over 2 percent (loss of around 80,000 jobs) in the same period (Table 7.11). Uttar Pradesh with highest population share (16.17%) in the country had only 10.38 percent of the central government employees working in the state. Between 1991 and 2000, it lost about 45,100 central government employees. Maharashtra, the financial capital of the country and head quarter of many leading industrial and trading houses, IT and other service providers, has a share of around 12.5 percent of central government employees, more than 3 percentage point relative to its population share (9.42%, rank 2). Madhya Pradesh, Bihar and Gujarat too had higher proportion of central government employees compared to their population share. As far as the relative spread of central government employees in these states is concerned, the pattern has not changed. The absolute size of central government has gone down in every state, the most in Madhya Pradesh (7.81%, 42,200 persons) followed by Maharashtra (7.72%, 69,900 persons) and Karnataka (6.7%). Andhra Pradesh lost only about 3,900 employees. At the national level, 4.11 percent (286,800 persons) decline has been observed in central government employment.

7.3.2 *Public Sector : State Government*

Whereas central government employment declined by close to three hundred thousands, state governments responsibility to pay salary and other benefits to its own employees, municipalities and corporations, schools and colleges, etc. increased by about 543,000 between 1991–2000. The net addition in employment in the Public Sector therefore was about 256,000. There was a very wide variation among the states – from a high negative growth of –12.7 percent in Bihar to a high positive growth of 17.38 percent in Karnataka. The growth rate was also positive in Andhra Pradesh (12.84%), Rajasthan (9.65%), Maharashtra (5.68%), Tamil Nadu (3.09%), and West Bengal (2.17%). The remaining states had negative employment growth rate in the public sector. Karnataka alone has created 118,000 employment opportunities between 1991 and 2000.

Annual exponential employment growth rate (Appendix 7.1) in public sector enterprises (Central plus State) was highest during 1961–81(0.038) and least during 1991–2001 (0.001). The largest drop was registered in 'finance, insurance and real estate' (from 0.119 to 0.006) followed by 'agriculture' (from 0.048 to –0.011) and 'electricity, gas and water supply' (0.052 to 005). Whereas public sector aggregate employment was most in Public Administration (community, social and personal services), the private sector employment was concentrated in the 'manufacturing sector' (Appendix 7.3).

7.3.3 Private Sector

Expectedly, the private players in the past have created most job opportunities in Maharashtra, West Bengal and Tamil Nadu following. When private sector employment (1991–2000) rose by such proportions as 74.58 in Karnataka, 50.57 in Andhra Pradesh and 30.57 in Tamil Nadu, all in the Southern part of the country, things did not go well with West Bengal where a heavy decline (–8.95%) in private sector employment was recorded. Flight of capital from West Bengal has been happening quite for sometime. Poor infrastructure, frequent strikes and 'bandhs' (often organized or supported by the ruling parties) and radical attitude of the labor unions against automation, computer and labor reform have contributed to the loss of confidence of private players. 'City of processions', a nickname for Kolkata, the capital city of West Bengal, clearly described the work culture and civic discipline in the state. Of late things have started to change a bit. The party in power for the last 34 years has of late realized that without fast industrial development and adoption of very latest technology, the state is doomed to go down in its economic health. The Chief Minister, Buddhadeb Bhattacharyya, reckoned as 'brand ambassador' for economic globalization even by the Center, rightly said, "Open up the economy or perish". To revitalize the state economy he said, "We need huge private investments, both domestic and FDI; we don't go by the color of the money".

Three other states that really did not do well in the private sector employment are Madhya Pradesh (–7.63%), Uttar Pradesh (–2.30%) and Bihar (–1.25%). The mammoth increase in private sector employment in Karnataka and Andhra Pradesh in the nineties definitely was due to the fact that these two states had already become IT hubs (Bangalore in Karnataka has been nicknamed as 'Silicon Valley' of India) and the IT sector in India is almost totally at the hands of private players. Only in recent years that Salt Lake City (Bidhannagar) in West Bengal is also becoming destination of many giant IT players. The private sector is to be credited with whatever growth of employment was observed in the organized sector in India during 1991–2000 (4.59%, Table 7.10).

The over-all losers in employment in the organized sector in the decade under review are Bihar, Madhya Pradesh, Uttar Pradesh and West Bengal. Maharashtra too has not done as well as one would have expected. This probably is due to the fact that the business houses in India are looking for alternative locations to widen their activity base. However, Maharashtra still remains the first choice for most of the private players. Maharashtra's share to total employment in the private sector is nearly double its percentage share in the total population. Chandra Babu Naidu, erstwhile Chief Minister of Andhra Pradesh had done everything to make the cities of the state as attractive as he could to create a center of attention for foreign and national IT giants. That left the rural Andhra largely neglected and Naidu had to pay a heavy price for that as his party lost badly in 2004 general election.

Women in general have poor representation in the organized sector (17.8%, Appendix 7.5). Bihar (6.8%), Uttar Pradesh (9.5%) and West Bengal (10.8%) have least female representatives in the organized sector; Kerala (39.5%), Assam (31.3%) and Karnataka (30.3%) find a large number of women workers in the organized sector.

7.4 Education and Skill among Workers

Of the 1367.2 million strong workforce in India, only 11 percent (40.2 million) can be categorized as human resource in science and technology (HRSTE) by educational qualification and a mere 7.3 percent – 26.8 million – by occupation (HRSTO). Only 3.9 percent of the workforce – 14.2 million – has a science/technology input in their education as well as the work they do. Only one-third of HRSTE are pursuing occupations related to their formal educational training. That is, two-thirds of this workforce is not truly gainfully employed – neither can the worker utilize his/her educational training nor can the management use his/her potential to the fullest extent. In 2004, only 35.2 percent of HRSTE held jobs requiring science and technology inputs, marginally more than 34.8 percent in 1991. Only 53 percent of those holding HRST jobs had the requisite educational qualification needed for their work. The share of postgraduates with science background among all unemployed postgraduates is about 63 percent. Among unemployed graduates, only 22.3 percent have studied science. The country is likely to face severe shortage in HRSTE workers since gross enrolment in natural sciences has shown a sharp decline from 6.1 percent in 1995–2000 to 1.6 percent in 2000–03 (vide Table 5.39).

7.5 Proportion of Workers in Different Work Categories

Table 7.13 presents the urban and rural break up of working population in India by their major work categories (2001). The first column refers to employment position in regards to the total population. 39.19 percent of the total population is actually in the workforce. Of this, 30.25 percent are from rural area (this would go up to 42 percent if the denominator of WPR consistd of rural population alone), and the rest (8.94%) from urban areas (the proportion would go up to 32% with WPR calculated on urban population). 51.85 percent of the total male population is in the workforce; these are again broken down into male rural (37.49%) and urban workers (14.35%). A similar break up of female workers in total female population is also presented. In the total working population (402,512,190 persons), 68.44 percent are male workers of which 77.2 percent are from rural areas and 22.8 percent from urban areas. The entries in the remaining four columns for each row are the break up of total workers represented by their respective col.3 entries as per the broad occupational categories.

Table 7.13

Total workers (main + marginal) and their categories, India 2001

Total : Rural/Urban	*Persons : Males Females*	*Total workers (Main + Marginal)*	*Cultivators*	*Agricultural laborers*	*Household Industry workers*	*Other workers*
1	*2*	*3*	*4*	*5*	*6*	*7*
Total	Persons	402,512,190 (39.19)	127,628,287 (31.71)	107,447,725 (26.69)	16,395,870 (4.07)	151,040,308 (37.52)
	Males	275,463,736 (51.85)	86,328,447 (31.34)	57,354,281 (20.82)	8,312,191 (3.02)	123,468,817 (44.82)
	Females	127,048,454 (25.63)	41,299,840 (32.51)	50,093,444 (39.43)	8,083,679 (6.36)	27,571,491 (21.70)
Rural	Persons	310,655,339 (30.25)	124,682,055 (40.14)	103,122,189 (33.20)	11,709,533 (3.77)	71,141,562 (22.90)
	Males	199,199,602 (37.49)	84,046,644 (42.19)	54,749,291 (27.48)	5,642,112 (2.83)	54,761,555 (27.49)
	Females	111,455,737 (22.48)	40,635,411 (36.46)	48,372,898 (43.40)	6,067,421 (5.44)	16,380,007 (14.70)
Urban	Persons	91,856,851 (8.94)	2,946,232 (3.21)	4,325,536 (4.71)	4,686,337 (5.10)	79,898,746 (86.98)
	Males	76,264,134 (14.35)	2,281,803 (2.99)	2,604,990 (3.42)	2,670,079 (3.50)	68,707,262 (90.12)
	Females	15,592,717 (3.15)	664,429 (4.26)	1,720,546 (11.03)	2,016,258 (12.93)	11,191,484 (71.77)

Figures in parentheses indicate percentages.
Source: National Human Development Report 2001, Planning Commission, Government of India

Earlier, workers were classified into 9 work categories clubbed into three sectors. The Primary Sector consisted of cultivator, agricultural labor, livestock, fisheries, forestry, etc. The Secondary Sector included mining and quarrying, manufacturing other than household industry and construction. Trade and commerce, transport, storage and communication and other services were included in Tertiary Sector. In 2001 Census, all those categories in the secondary sector, namely Mining, Quarrying, Forestry, Plantation, etc., manufacturing other than Household industries (HHI) and Construction, Trade and Commerce, Transport, Storage and Communication and other Services have been brought under one single category – Other Workers (OW). This really makes comparison between different Census results difficult unless further break-up of different categories becomes available. There has been a shift in dominance from the traditional occupations to more hi tech occupations, especially in the manufacturing and service sectors. From around 68.4 percent of all workers engaged in the agriculture sector (the primary sector) in 1981, the proportion has come down to 58.2 percent in 2001. In the same period, workers in the six categories clubbed into a single category OW have gone up from 33.6 percent to 37.6 percent. The non-worker to total worker population in India is 54.71 percent. Industry-wise break up for workers (not available for 2001 Census) at different time points gives a better picture how things are changing at the ground level. The service sector (Sl. No. 7 to 13, Table 7.14) has gained considerable momentum over the period and became the fastest growing sector since economic liberalization policy was adopted in 1991.

About 55 percent employments in urban areas are in the service sector followed by about 33 percent in manufacturing, construction and mining. Although 81.3 percent of female vis-à-vis 63.8 percent of male workers are still in agriculture and related activities, women are not far behind men in professional and technical positions as also in production related activities (Table 7.13).

Appendix 7.6 gives the percentage distribution of workforce by rural and urban origin and by industrial categories between 1972–73 and 1993–94 (NSS data). Appendix 7.7 shows the contribution of the service sub-sectors to national GDP for the years 1993–94 to 2001–02 (Economic Survey, 2002–03). The largest contribution to GDP comes from trade, restaurant and hotel industry. The progress of service sector growth has largely been in areas which themselves are dependent on the performance of others, especially the manufacturing sector. Whereas rural employment is still almost totally dependent on agriculture, the tertiary (service) and the secondary (industry) sectors provided over 80 percent employment in urban areas. Close to 60 percent of men in the urban workforce are in service sector. Women in urban area have traditionally been in the service sector. Women have consolidated their presence in the service sector further since adoption of the new economic policy. 36 percent of urban women workforce was in service sector in 1977–78; the proportion rose to over 46 percent by 1993–94.

The Task Force on Employment 2001 observed that of the 71 million employments generated between 1983 and 1993–94, half of then came from agriculture (net addition 36.17 million) and another 30 percent from the tertiary (service) sector. Between 1993–94 and 1999–2000, only 22.55 million new jobs were added: tertiary sector created 16.50 million and secondary sector 11.38 million jobs. However, some 5.33 million jobs were lost in the primary sector in the same period.

Labor absorption capacity of an economy is reflected by the degree of responsiveness of employment expansion to the state of economic growth in the country. This is generally expressed in terms of employment elasticity growth. Labor absorption capacity of a

Table 7.14

Percentage distribution of workers by industry

	Industry	*1961*	*1971*	*1981*	*1991 P*
1.	Agriculture	71.5a	71.6	66.5	66.5
2.	Forestry & logging	0.2a	0.1	0.2	0.2
3.	Fishing	0.3a	0.3	0.4	0.3
4.	Mining & quarrying	0.5a	0.5	0.6	0.6
5.	Manufacturing	9.5a	9.4	11.3b	10.0c
6.	Construction	1.5	1.4	1.6	2.0
7.	Electricity, gas & water supply	0.2	0.3	0.4	0.4
8.	Transport etc.	1.8	2.4	2.7	2.8
9.	Trade, hotels & restaurants	4.7	5.0	5.5	6.4
10.	Banking & insurance	0.2	0.3	0.5	0.6
11.	Real estate & business	0.1	0.2	0.2	0.4
12.	Public administration & Defense	2.0	2.8	2.7	3.1
13.	Other services	7.7	5.7	7.4	6.7

a. The estimates of the number of workers in 1961 for these industry groups relate to adjusted figures based on 1971 Census concepts
b. Includes community, social, personal services and activities not adequately defined
c. Including repair service
P: Provisional.

sector is closely related to the type of technology adopted. Both primary and secondary sectors show a large decline in their absorption capacity, the former declining from 0.99 in 1951–61 to 0.63 in 1981–91 and later declining from 0.68 to 0.26 in the same time period. The tertiary sector registered an increase from 0.46 to 0.66 in the same time frame. Although IT and telecommunication sectors are generating thousands of new jobs for the educated and skilled persons, the banking, insurance and some other service sectors may have to downsize their employee strength due to technology up-gradation to remain competitive in the market. The trend currently observed in the service sector growth could be maintained only if adequate demand impulses are generated in the other two sectors.

Table 7.15

Distribution of main workers by occupational classification, 1991

*INDIA***	*Percents Main Workers*		
	Persons	*Males*	*Females*
Professional, technical and related workers	3.6	3.4	3.9
Administrative, executive and managerial workers	1.0	1.3	0.2
Clerical and related workers	3.4	4.0	1.4
Sales workers	5.8	7.0	1.7
Farmers, fishermen, hunters, loggers and related workers*	67.7	63.8	81.3
Service workers	1.8	1.8	1.9
Production and related workers, transport equipment operators and laborers	15.5	17.4	9.0
Workers not classified by occupations	1.2	1.4	0.5

* Farmers include those classified as cultivators and agricultural laborers in census

** Excludes figures for Jammu & Kashmir where the 1991 census could not be held due to disturbed conditions

Source: Registrar General of India

7.6 Unemployment in India

Employment situation all over the world has been going through a bumpy period since the eighties. Given the increase in the labor force, a decline in growth of employment in the nineties vis-à-vis eighties has increased the incidence of unemployment. The index of unemployment, defined as *percentage of persons unemployed in the 15+ age group to the actual number of those in the workforce*, has increased at the national level, from 2 percent in 1983 to 2.3 percent in 1999–2000 (Tables 7.3 & 7.7). The incidence of unemployment is more in urban area (4.8% in 1999–2000) than in rural area (1.5% in 1999–2000). The NSS survey has brought out a stunning picture in the country. Unemployment has risen from around 26.5 million in 1999–2000 to 35.2 million in 2004–05. Among the major states, Kerala has the highest incidence of unemployment, nearly 8 percent throughout the period for which data are presented. This really is a contradiction since Kerala is a state where the social infrastructure is one of the finest in India and all demographic and social parameters indicate that the state already is in the final stage of demographic transition.

Table 7.16

Incidence of unemployment in selected few states and India, 1983 to 1999–2000

States	Residence	1983			1993–94			1999–2000		
		Male	Female	Person	Male	Female	Person	Male	Female	Person
Kerala	R	7.0	7.3	7.1	5.4	9.8	6.8	5.7	13.2	8.1
	U	9.4	15.1	11.2	6.6	18.5	10.2	5.5	19.9	10.0
	C	7.5	8.6	7.9	5.8	12.1	7.7	5.6	15.1	8.6
West Bengal	R	2.1	1.6	2.0	1.8	2.1	1.8	2.7	2.9	2.7
	U	8.1	12.8	8.8	6.3	15.1	7.9	7.2	9.7	7.6
	C	3.9	3.9	3.9	3.0	5.0	3.5	3.9	4.3	4.0
Tamil Nadu	R	2.3	1.1	1.8	1.8	0.6	1.3	2.7	1.0	2.0
	U	6.5	6.2	6.4	4.1	6.8	4.9	3.4	5.0	3.8
	C	3.7	2.1	3.1	2.6	2.0	2.4	2.9	1.9	2.6
Madhya Pradesh	R	0.3	0.1	0.2	0.7	0.2	0.5	0.7	0.2	0.5
	U	5.3	3.7	5.0	4.2	4.7	4.3	5.5	6.3	5.7
	C	0.9	0.1	0.6	1.7	0.5	1.3	1.5	0.3	1.1
Rajasthan	R	0.4	0.1	0.3	0.5	0.1	0.3	0.6	0.2	0.4
	U	3.7	0.9	3.0	1.8	0.4	1.5	2.6	1.9	2.5
	C	1.1	0.2	0.8	0.8	0.2	0.5	1.1	0.3	0.8
Uttar Pradesh	R	0.8	0.1	0.6	0.9	0.0	0.7	0.9	0.3	0.8
	U	3.9	2.7	3.7	3.3	0.6	2.9	4.3	3.3	4.1
	C	1.4	0.3	1.1	1.4	0.1	1.1	1.7	0.7	1.4
INDIA	R	1.4	0.7	1.1	1.5	0.8	1.2	1.7	1.1	1.5
	U	5.0	5.2	5.1	4.1	6.6	4.6	4.5	5.9	4.8
	C	2.3	1.3	2.0	2.1	1.7	2.0	2.5	1.8	2.3

Source: The 38th, 50th and 55th round of the NSSO on Employment and unemployment Situation in India.

The Director General of Employment and Training (DGET), Ministry of Labor maintains a live register of Employment Exchange in all the states. The Employment Exchange register was introduced to help the registered persons obtain at least a call letter from some establishments who are supposed to forward information on vacancies under Employment Exchanges (Compulsory Notification of Vacancies) Act 1959 to the appropriate authority. The names that are recorded in the register are mostly from urban areas with some level of educational attainment. Not all those who register with the Employment Exchange are unemployed; some register to obtain a better offer. Employment Exchange records therefore cannot by any stretch of imagination be thought of to reflect the unemployment situation prevailing in the country at a particular point of time.

Table 7. 17
Job-seekers registered with employment exchanges over the years in India

Year	*No. of jobseekers on live register (in million)*	*Percentage increase over previous year*	*Year*	*No. of jobseekers on live register (in million)*	*Percentage increase over previous year*
1961	1.833	14.1	1990	34.632	5.7
1966	2.622	NA	1991	36.300	4.8
1971	5.100	25.4	1992	36.758	1.3
1976	9.784	4.9	1993	36.275	1.3
1980	16.200	13.0	1994	36.691	1.1
1981	17.838	10.1	1995	36.742	0.1
1982	19.753	10.7	1996	37.430	1.9
1983	21.953	11.1	1997	39.140	4.6
1984	23.547	7.3	1998	40.090	2.4
1985	26.270	11.6	1999	40.371	0.7
1986	30.131	14.7	2000	41.344	2.4
1987	30.247	0.4	2001	41.996	1.6
1988	30.050	0.7	2002	41.177	–2.0
1989	32.776	9.1			

NA: Not available
Note: All the job seekers on the live register of employment exchanges are not necessarily unemployed
Source: Directorate General of Employment & Training, Ministry of Labor.

Rising unemployment is a common concern for all developing countries. The developed countries too have not been spared from this issue resulting from growth of high capital-intensive production system and service provisions. India after independence gave a lot of attention to development of heavy industries, power generation and expansion and modernization of railway network in the public sector for which the technical know-how and machinery were imported at huge costs. In capital-intensive growth path, generation of employment is limited. Heavy investment in industrial sector left the health of agriculture largely unattended. Attention to small irrigation, linking villages with market places and towns with all-seasons road for easy transportation of agricultural produces and expansion of small scale and household industries, which have the capacity to generate more employment, could not be given attention adequately. Bank interests and excise and other indirect taxes were so high that the farmers and the small entrepreneurs could not participate satisfactorily in this process of revitalization of Indian economy. Several hundred billions of rupees were invested in Public Sector Units (PSU). Poor policy implementation, bureaucratic delay and intervention and poor managerial skill made many of these PSUs sick. To infuse new blood to give a lease of life to these sick units, the government had to divert funds often at the cost of social infrastructure. The number of idle rural labors increased, rural-urban migration stream became uncharacteristically strong.

Prof. Mahalanobis, the chief architect of the first two Five Year Plans realized the limitations of employment generation by massive investment in heavy and big industries. He said,

In view of meagerness of capital resources there is no possibility in the short run, for creating much employment through the factory industries. Now consider the household or cottage industries. They require very little capital.

Through investment in small sectors and household industries, employment possibilities often would be more than ten times greater in comparison with the same investment in factory industries. The planners and politicians (their eyes were on their vote bank) were advocating expanding of labor-intensive methods to generate employment for the masses in the traditional sector.

Despite nationalization of leading banks in the country, the government had little option but to go in for large short and long-term loans from IMF, World Bank and other international fund managers. Government was the single largest borrower from our nationalized banks. India was in a debt trap since repayment of capital and interest to international agencies and national banks and high interest payment against small savings etc. cost India about 25 percent of her GDP. A time came in the late eighties when we had to send plane-loads of gold to London to get some foreign exchange for payment of annual interests to the foreign agencies. We (and many other developing countries) sometimes borrow from IMF or World Bank only to keep our commitments for repayment.

Our industries and factories needed technological up-gradation to improve productivity and to make our products competitive in the world market. To remain competitive, labor-intensive production process was to be replaced by capital-intensive highly automated systems. Large-scale use of computer and e-governance has changed the face of our industrial management within a very short span of time. Many factories that could not survive this competition were closed down making thousands jobless. Many new industries came up creating job opportunities but mostly for educated and skilled persons. Bank rates have drastically been cut to increase the availability of money in the market. Government was the principal beneficiary from this cut in bank rates. The large and small investors too benefited from this cut in interest rate as also from various other direct and indirect tax reforms. The common man, especially the elderly persons who had become dependent on interest income, suffered a lot.

In the last fifteen years, Indian economy has taken a new turn. The government has realized that it is not the job of the government to run industries, hotels and factories. The sick PSUs are being sold out or closed down. The government now has realized that the government's job is to provide the necessary physical and social infrastructure that would attract domestic and foreign investors to establish new factories so that very many newer products become available for domestic consumption and export. The government is trying hard to cut down its own avoidable expenses, concentrate more on infrastructure development and create an environment in which the market law would determine the growth of economy and employment. The experts believe that there would be a time gap before the fruits of economic liberalization reach the masses.

"Green Revolution" has given India food security but also has reduced employment in the agriculture sector. The more we use the new agricultural technology (tractor, thrasher and other implements along with chemical fertilizers, pesticides and improved seeds) and adopt better agricultural management, the less we depend upon animal energy and human labor. The greater use of modern agricultural technology is becoming imperative to push production at a higher level for food security since industrialization is reducing the gross land area for cultivation (2 to 4 million hectare acres of agricultural land was lost to industries and infrastructure development in the first decade of economic liberalization). There is no going back from modernizing our industry, trade and commerce as also agriculture. Before the full potential of the new economy is realized, India will have to pass through turbulent periods and the rate of creation of new jobs may not keep pace even with the declining rate of population growth.

NSSO survey in 1999–2000 estimated the number of earning members per 1,000 households (Table 7.18). Whereas only one male worker in the household was observed in 509 households for every 1,000 urban households surveyed, the same in rural areas was 277. But in rural areas the survey found 278 households having one male and one female worker for every 1,000 households, the same in urban areas was only 129.

Table 7.18

Per thousand distribution of households by number of usual status workers (ps+ss) of age 15 years and above in India during 1999–2000

Residence	*No. worker without any unemployed*	*No. worker with unemployed*	*Only one male worker*	*Only one female worker*	*Only one male & one female worker*	*Others*	*All*
Rural	44	2	277	49	278	351	1000
	(60328)	(2260)	(379431)	(66802)	(381323)	(480652)	(1370797)
Urban	69	7	509	36	129	250	1000
	(35193)	(3566)	(261476)	(18545)	(66089)	(128395)	(513264)

Source: National Sample Survey Organization, 1999–2000

Realizing the facts in the ground situation, especially in the rural area, the government has come out with legislation – National Rural Employment Guarantee Act (NREGA) – to provide at least 100 days employment for one adult member from a household at a wage rate agreed upon by the legislators and others. Already there are a few other schemes in operation in rural areas for poverty alleviation. All these would be brought under this new scheme. Implementation of the scheme is not going to be easy. The Central and the state governments will have to mobilize huge resources for implementation of this scheme. Many economists and social thinkers have expressed their doubts if such a huge investment would really create any permanent asset or if it would largely remain a kind of unemployment allowance.

Initially the employment guarantee scheme was started in 200 districts covering all the states. Since April 2007 another 130 districts have been added to the list. In the first year the central government provided 75 percent of the sum needed for operation of the scheme. In the second year the central government's share by the Act would come down to 50 percent. The implementation of the scheme is at the hand of the state governments. Those who register their names are to be given job cards after necessary verification. The state governments would remain bound to provide them 100 days work a year at an agreed minimum wage rate, failing which the state governments would remain honor bound to provide these eligible job-seekers unemployment allowance. It has been reported that almost all the state governments are far behind their targets and a large proportion of the funds released by the central government remain unutilized. The *panchayats* are the nodal agencies through which NREGA is implemented. They have failed to evolve sustainable development plans and projects that could be nurtured by the fund released under this scheme. Some of the major complaints regarding corruption and malpractices reported in media and surveys conducted by NGOs are as under:

1. A villager worked, say, for 4 days and was paid Rs 260, but the entry in the job card shows that he worked for 6 days and was paid Rs 390.
2. Job cards did not have photographs of the incumbent card holder pasted on them.
3. The secretary or the *sarpanch* collected the job cards from the villagers, made entries according to their sweet will, and returned the cards to the illiterate unsuspecting villagers.

The government knows well enough that this type of corruption may put a big question mark on the operational feasibility and on the intent of the Act. But the real obstacle for effective implementation of the NREGA is likely to come from the farmers, especially the small and marginal farmers. The profit from agriculture is already very low in a developing country like India, especially since restriction on import of agricultural products has been lifted, at least partially. Farming in India is still very labor-intensive and productivity of the land is very low by all standards. Since the margin of profit is very small, the small and marginal farmers would find it extremely difficult to raise the cost of hiring agricultural labor. NCAER survey has clearly shown how poorly the agricultural wage earners are paid across all regions. If the NREGA becomes fully operational, the wage workers would demand higher wages from their private employers since they already were receiving higher wages for the similar kind labor from the government. Those who can switch over to mechanized farming will do so to keep down their expenses and also increase productivity of their land to remain competitive in the market. The small farmers also would stop hiring labor as much as possible and try to put in their own labor to compensate the shortage of labor. A successful implementation of NREGA would ultimately raise the bargaining power of the wage labor; but that would add to the input cost of the farmer. The 'threat perception' of these farmers is real and that cannot be ignored by any economic and welfare logic.

It is also a fact that many of these small farmers (also big farmers) often are important functionaries of many *panchayats.* They probably would have their own agenda to see that such welfare schemes, detrimental to their personal interest, do not operate smoothly in their locality. They may even try to sabotage the employment program – corruption, pilferage, gross irregularities in book-keeping and other records and many others can be engineered to derail the project.

A nation-wide quick survey, however, convinced the government that the rural employment guarantee program has started providing dividend – it not only has generated employment opportunity among the rural poor creating a platform for reduction of poverty, it has created conditions for improvement of minimum wage rates, both in agricultural and non-agricultural jobs, in all the states. For example, the minimum wage rate in Uttar Pradesh has gone up from Rs 58 to Rs 100, in Nagaland from Rs 60 to Rs 100, in Jammu & Kashmir from Rs 45 to Rs 70, in Maharashtra from Rs 47 to Rs 72, in Madhya Pradesh from Rs 58 to Rs 72, etc. Inspired by this impressive performance, the government has decided to bring all the districts in the country under this program by 2007–08 fiscal. The survey also came out with the observation that the wage earners today are less burdened (about 30%) with the volume of work in comparison with the load of work they had to tolerate prior to this new program. The survey also confirmed that the profit margin for the farmers, who had to depend on hired labors, has come down in consequence to the rise in wage rate of agricultural labors.

It is the basic tenet of the economic theory that rules for raising the wage rate and enlarging the employment market cannot be imposed by law makers. The private sector would raise remuneration to get best out of the worker and at the same time the management would see that the same output (or more) is maintained even by curtailing labor. If the market does not provide the necessary support, the private investor may even refuse to increase the wage rates. The well-intended NREGA has created much confusion both among the beneficiaries from the Act and the already dwindling traditional labor market in the country. Raising the fund necessary to make the scheme operate is not going to be easy.

The Oil giants in the country are state owned. India has to import 70 percent of crude oil from the international market. The political parties, especially the Left, are against any price hike in petroleum products, electricity, and fertilizer or cut in employees' provident fund interest rate (EPF) or allow any part of PF to be invested in market share. Even after the price hike in petroleum and diesel by Rs 3 and Rs 2 respectively in August 2005 left the oil companies with an aggregate loss of Rs 30 billion a year. If petroleum prices are not allowed to rise in tune with cost of procuring it and if the state governments did not volunteer to cut the huge sales tax they levy on petroleum products, the profit making oil companies would become sick before long. Oil price in international market rose very fast (it reached $147 a barrel in July 2008). Presently, it has dropped to below $60 in the world market. Consumption of petroleum products is rising by a whooping 10 percent every year. The price of the crude will escalate again in near future. India's import bill on account of increase in oil prices are rising very fast. Because of administered prices, the distributors in the country incurred heavy losses even after the government reduced import taxes (some states reduced sales tax on petroleum products) on crude oil and issued oil bonds to the refineries and the major oil dealers. Even when the world price for crude comes down, the government takes time to cut down the retail prices to allow the oil companies to recover some of their losses.

With huge budgetary provisions for defense and debt payment, rising import bills on account of oil, commitment for huge investment in infrastructure development and progressive reform in direct and indirect taxes, the government will have to work hard and explore new areas for revenue generation (probably the service sector). This is not going to be easy in the era of coalition politics. The politics of compromise will delay economic and labor law reforms, which in turn could slow down the rate of GDP growth and allow the fiscal deficits to go beyond control. The global economic crisis in 2008 has hard hit the Indian economy. The GDP growth rate in 2008–09 came down to below 7 percent. There is no immediate relief to the unemployed youth, especially in urban areas.

7.7 Rural Employment

Participation in agriculture and traditional activities still remain the principal economic activity in rural India. A rural household has simultaneously several sources of income – own farm, artisan/industrial work, petty or organized business, salary and professional service, wage earning in agricultural and non-agricultural jobs, etc. A person may work on his own land and work in others' farm in his spare time, run a small grocery or tea stall or even may be serving as a school teacher. However, the largest share of household income, as the NCAER survey shows, comes from 'agriculture and allied activities' (55%, with CV 21) followed by 'salaries and professional services' (16.5%, CV 35.9) at the national level. Next in order are 'agricultural wage' (7.9%, CV 68.1) and 'non-agricultural wage' (6.3%, CV 49.9). These four economic activities put together account for more than 85 percent of income of an average rural household. Karnataka, Madhya Pradesh,

Maharashtra and Gujarat have relatively high levels of income from 'agriculture and allied activities' (ranging between 64.8 and 69.8%). 'Agriculture and allied activities' contribute the least to an average household's income basket in West Bengal (36.7%), Tamil Nadu (36.8%) and Northeastern states (37.7%). The percentage contribution of 'salaries and professional services' to household income is very high in Northeastern states (29.2%) and Himachal Pradesh (29%) and very low in Madhya Pradesh (8.7%), Karnataka (8.9%) and Andhra Pradesh (9.5%). Andhra Pradesh has the highest proportion of agricultural wage earners (19.7%) and least in Rajasthan (0.9%).

Figure 7.4
Share of rural household income

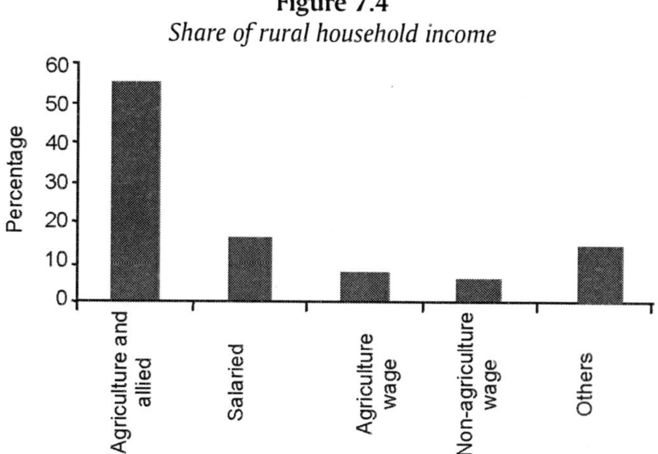

63 percent of rural households reported ownership of land. This proportion of reported ownership of land is as high as 91 percent in Himachal Pradesh, followed by Rajasthan (84%) and Kerala (79%) and as low as 34 percent in Tamil Nadu. Surprisingly, it was only 44 percent in Punjab, which is regarded as the 'granary' of India. In spite of all the good work done by West Bengal government in land reform and distribution of the vested and acquired land to landless poor, the reported ownership of land by households is only 53 percent. The average size of landholding for India as a whole works out at 4.5 acres per reporting household. The reported landholding size per household is quite high in Punjab (7.5 acres) and Rajasthan (7 acres). Although the reported household ownership of land in Kerala is 79 percent, the landholding size per household is a meager 0.9 acre. When the average landholding size is estimated for all rural households, the national average is only 2.8 acres. Rajasthan has the highest landholding per rural household (6 acres), followed by Madhya Pradesh (4.9 acres). Punjab's landholding estimate comes down to 3.3 acre per household. Lowest landholding per rural household was observed in Kerala (0.7 acre), Tamil Nadu (1.0 acre), West Bengal (1.5 acre) and Himachal Pradesh (1.5 acre).

NCAER's nation-wide survey in 1994 gives an absorbing account of the health of economy of rural India where 72 percent of the total population of India lives. The average size of rural household is estimated at 5.72 (from a low of 4.54 in Tamil Nadu to a high of 6.98 in Bihar), comprised of 3 male members and 2.72 female members (F/M = 0.906). On an average, there are 2.06 earning members (male 1.56 and female 0.50, F/M = 0.32) in an average family, which includes children, adult (15–59) and old age members. The least number of earning member per household is in the Northeastern states (1.52). West Bengal has the least number of earning members, 1.74 (average household size 5.74) per household among the bigger states and Himachal Pradesh the highest, 2.58 (average household size 5.75). CVs for these computed statistics are mostly below 10 percent. Adult (15–59) work participation rate in rural India is 83.1 percent for males and 40.7 percent for females. Percentage of adult male workers varies from 76.7 in Kerala to 86.8 in Madhya Pradesh (CV = 2.9). Proportion of female adult workers varies widely between the states and also between household income groups, social groups, occupational groups and literacy groups. Least

Figure 7.5

Adult work participation rate – rural India 1994

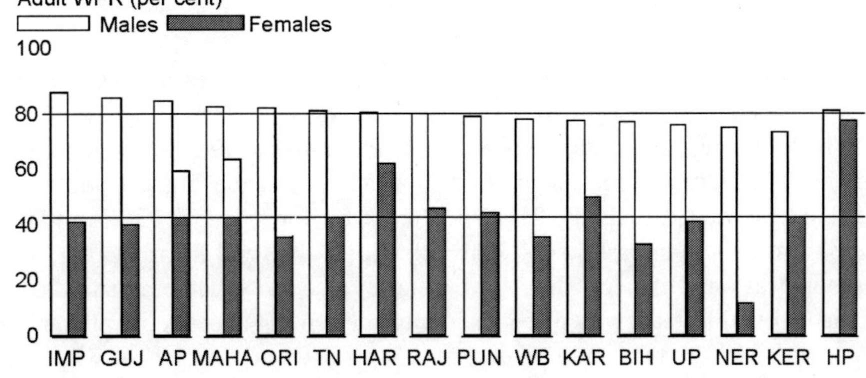

Figure 7.6

Income of rural households (Rs '000)

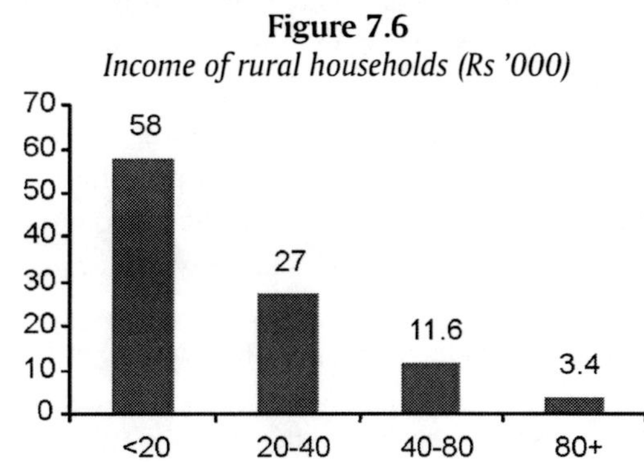

female adult workers are found in North-eastern states (11.5%) and highest in Himachal Pradesh (74.6%) with an average of 40.7 percent for all the states (CV = 33.7). Proportion of adult female workers is low both in the occupational groups 'cultivator' (15.6%) and 'salaried + professional + self-employed' group (10%). Women adult workers are found in large numbers among the landless wage earners (32.6%), in small household size groups (30.7% in households of size up to 4) and in low income households (21.7% in income group 'up to Rs 20,000 a year).

The NCAER survey also found that ownership of land is highest among Hindus (70%) followed by STs (69%) and least among SCs (47%). 57 percent of Muslim families owned land. Hindus have the largest landholding per household (5.1 acres), followed by Muslims (3.6 acres), SCs (2.8 acres) and Christians (2.0 acres).

The size of land holding in a household is strongly correlated with household income. The large landholding households have an average income about Rs 86,000 a year and 90 percent of it comes from 'agriculture and allied activities'. The marginal landholding households earn on an average Rs 19,586 per annum, 48 percent of which comes from 'agriculture and allied activities'. Those in the highest income category (Rs 86.000 and above a year), earns about Rs 148,000 a year and 81 percent of the income comes from 'agriculture and allied activities'. The households where annual income is less than Rs 20,000, about 67 percent of their income comes from 'agriculture and allied activities'.

The survey also observed that 58 percent of households in rural India had annual income less than Rs 20,000, the next higher category (Rs 20,001–40,000) covered 27 percent, and the highest category had only 3.4 percent of rural households. 70 percent of SCs and STs were in the lowest income category compared to 50 percent of all Hindu households. The national average of annual income per household from all sources is calculated at Rs 25,653. The high income states are Haryana (Rs 39,956) and Punjab (37,418). Orissa has the lowest per household income (Rs 17,208) followed by West Bengal (Rs 18,113) and Bihar (Rs 22,459). 90 percent of the landless wage earners and 65 percent of marginal land owners had less than Rs 20,000 household income per annum. 33 percent of the large landholding households had income over Rs 86,000 per annum.

Proportion of *adult wage earners* in the adult population gives an indication of employment stability. NCAER rural survey shows that 37.6 percent of all adult earners (CV 36.0) are wage earners. Adult wage earners among males and females are 35.3 (CV 25.6) and 42.8 (CV 59.9) percent respectively. Wage earning status for adults, both for males (19.5%) and females (12.5%), is comparatively low in Northeastern states. Andhra Pradesh has the highest adult wage earners (54.1%) as also female wage earners (68.2%), and Punjab the lowest (male 23.7% and female 12%). Madhya Pradesh (68.2%), Maharashtra (61.2%), Gujarat (59.7%) and Tamil Nadu (59.5%) employ adult females mostly as wage earners. The NCAER survey also show that feminization of wage labor is a fact in India across the states with a few exceptions. Even in the economically and industrially advanced states like Maharashtra and Gujarat, females mostly are in manual wage employment. Jawahar Rozgar Yojana and similar other programs, primarily targeted at SCs, STs and other vulnerable groups, probably has something to do with the high proportion of wage earners in the adult rural population.

The survey found that wage earning status of a person is closely related to household incomes. The proportion of wage earners dropped sharply as household incomes increased. It is the landless category with very poor financial background that provides the highest number of wage earning labors. Wage earning families are lowest among Muslims (31%) followed by Hindus (38%) and the Christians (43%).

The survey also estimated the average number of days of wage employment in agricultural and non-agricultural jobs in a year. On an average, wage employment in agricultural jobs is for 145 and 124 days respectively for males and females. In non-agricultural work the average person-days of employment are 157 for males and 133 for females. When the two types of works are combined, the person-days go up to 172 and 137 respectively for males and females. There is considerable inter-state variation in person-days employment among the wageworkers. For the STs and SCs access to wage employment is for 158 and 145 days respectively. Muslim wage earners work for highest number of days (187) in a year compared to Hindus 159 days and Christians 153 days. The study also observed that number of days of wage employment increases as the level of village development improves.

The key question is how much these wageworkers earn per day. There is large variation among the states as also in the nature of job on which the wage earners work. The agricultural wage work is least paying in Maharashtra (Rs 15.5) followed by Madhya Pradesh (Rs 16.6), Karnataka (Rs 17.3) and Orissa (and Rs 17.5). Highest payment for agricultural work is offered in Haryana (Rs 42) followed by Kerala (Rs 40.8) and Punjab (Rs 34.7). The all-India average for agricultural wage work is a meager Rs 20.9 per day, the price of 2 kg rice or wheat. Non-agricultural wage work is more paying in all states except in West Bengal and Kerala where non-agricultural wageworkers receive a little less than their counterparts in agriculture. There is considerable gender discrimination in wage rates both in agricultural and non-agricultural wage work and also between the states. At national level the male wageworkers in agriculture receive Rs 23.4 vis-à-vis female's Rs 16.4. Among the states, the minimum wage gap (Rs 1.3) between males and females is in West Bengal (males Rs 23 and females Rs 21.7). The gender gap in wage payment is very high (Rs 13) in Kerala (Rs 44.4 for males and Rs 31.4 for females). Both the states have Marxist Communists in government.

The non-agricultural wage rate is 36 percent more than that in agriculture. The all-India average for 'persons', males and females respectively are Rs 28.4, Rs 30.5 and Rs 18.7. Women are paid about 70 percent of what are paid to a male worker in agricultural work; they are paid about 61 percent of the paid amount to a male wage earner in non-agricultural works. Haryana pays the highest wage to a non-agricultural wageworker (Rs 46.0 for persons, Rs 46.4 for males and Rs 36.5 for females). Punjab comes next in order (Rs 40.7, 41.6 and 23.4 respectively for 'persons', males and females). In the other extreme are three closely comparable states – West Bengal, Orissa and Maharashtra. The wage rates for 'persons', males and females respectively in these states are (Rs 21.3, Rs 22.5, Rs 13.2), (Rs 21.4, Rs 22.5, Rs 14.5) and (Rs 21.5, Rs 24.3, Rs 13.9). Gender disparity is high in Northeastern states (males Rs 33.3, females Rs 16.1). In Maharashtra, females' wage share in non-agricultural work is only 57 percent of wage paid to males. Kerala pays highest daily wage of Rs 51.3 to male workers in non-agricultural work. Female workers receive Rs 27.6, which is only 54 percent of what a male worker normally receives.

These income and other statements are more than 14 years old (1994). Household income at current prices must have increased in these years, so also wage earnings from various sources, especially after the introduction of 100 days of wage work under NREGA.

Incidentally it may be mentioned that Communist parties are very strong both in the states West Bengal and Kerala (the Left Front was in power for the last 34 years uninterrupted in West Bengal and the CPI(M) led front comes back to power in Kerala almost every alternate assembly election). Kerala has consistently been advocating for better labor wages irrespective of the gender of the workers, no matter which party is in power. It has close to 100 percent literacy both among males and females and probably has the best possible social infrastructure in the country (demographic indicators confirm this). Left parties' pro-labor policy is at least partially implemented when the governments in Kerala are seen to secure a much higher wage rate for all types of wage workers. The Left parties are also very vocal against sex discrimination. West Bengal, on the other hand, has become a model for other states for its land reform achievements. Presently, economic reform has become the prime agenda with the government (the slogan 'reform or perish'). The government even has compromised its much lauded 'land reform and land distribution policy' ('industries cannot be built in air') to attract foreign and domestic investors to participate in the state's infrastructure development, petrochemical hub, manufacture of small cars and two-wheelers, health and knowledge park, new airport and sea port and a variety of other projects. The industry friendly attitude of the government has been highly appreciated by almost all federations of industries, commerce and trade. Earlier, the government had distributed agricultural land to thousands of landless labors; the sharecropper's right to till their land and obtain necessary bank loan for tilling their land have been guaranteed by legislation in the state. Yet, the anomalies in policy formulation and program implementation in these two states where the Communist parties have very broad mass base, really baffle us. The fact of the matter is that the gender disparity in wages is highest in one of their 'own' sates (Kerala). One of the very poor rates in the country for wage earners is in the state where they are in power for over 34 years and where the government's land reform policy has acclaimed praise even of the World Bank. The 'Singur episode' has put a serious question on the Left Front government's 'land acquisition' policy and has forced the government to develop a more democratic and transparent land acquisition policy (especially the fertile agricultural land) to support industrialization in the state.

7.8 Work Participation among Children

In 1995, a convention of the labor ministers from all developing countries was organized by ILO to chalk out an action plan to do away with child labor that still persists in almost all developing countries. In spite of the meet declarations, incidence of child labor could not be eliminated in most countries. ILO's estimate of child labor in the world is over 250 million; Asia alone contributes about 60 percent to total world child labor. As per the Indian Census reports, there were 10.75 million child workers in the age group 5–14 years in 1971, 13.64 million in 1981 and 11.28 million in 1991. Since the promulgation of The Child Labor Act in 1986, some decline in child workers has been observed. Our legislators have passed many Acts to eliminate child labor from various sectors; governments appointed many Commissions to suggest action plans to give back childhood to these unfortunate children. The reports have gathered dust; preventive Acts remain largely a show piece to exhibit to the world about our resolve to eliminate this cruel practice. When the question of implementation of the Acts arises, we find multiple of agencies through which the Acts are to be implemented. There is no coordination between these agencies and therefore the Acts remain largely a sacred document.

In spite of international regulations and commitment on restricting the use of child labor [The Child Labor (Prohibition and Regulation) Act, 1986, Factories Act, 1948, Plantation Labor Act, 1951, Mines Act, 1952 and many others], millions of children still are employed against a wage. Indian electronic media has brought out documentary evidences how these children have to work under extreme hardship and threatening hazardous conditions. NGOs and other social activists have rescued some of these poor children who had to work non-stop for 10–12 hours a day in a frightfully congested and inhospitable environment day after day. The government has asked to release all child labors from October 10, 2006.

Many developing countries have suffered in their trade with developed countries because of ILO's tag on child labor. Many countries in the West refused consignments from developing countries since child labor was employed in production of such export articles. Handmade textiles (silk clothes, the Kashmiri carpets, shawls and robes, etc.), crafts and many other novel indigenous products from India came under the scanner since many such industries use children at some stage in the production processes.

According to ILO, any person would be treated as economically active or gainfully employed if he/she would work on regular basis for which he/she would receive remuneration or of such labor resulted in output for the market. Census of India follows this definition to identifying child labor in India.

There is a lot of ambiguity in this definition. A child often is deprived to inculcate his/her capabilities and potentialities and use his/her childhood freedom to grow into a responsible individual. He/she would be asked to participate in many unpaid work – in household chores, looking after younger siblings and even in small family enterprises like small retail shops or seasonal agricultural work on the household farms. The ILO/Census definition cannot mark them as child labor. This problem of deploying child in domestic work or in household enterprises like agriculture, weaving, crafts, etc. is serious in the context that he/she is denied schooling because of the role he/she is asked to play to support the family. This is indeed a case of child labor but does not come under the purview of the Child Labor Act. There is another segment of the child population who are not enrolled in the school system and at the same time they are not counted as child labor although they generally have some work assignments, regular or occasional. This category of "no where children" is sizeable. Such pool of "no where children" becomes a ready source both in rural and urban areas, for employment in households or small-scale units like tea stalls, shops and restaurants and many other odd jobs at a fraction of market costs. This countless child labor remains uncounted because of our poor accounting system or because of sporadic nature of their association with the job market.

The official statistics show that the incidence of child labor has declined from 7.6 percent in 1981 to 5.4 percent in 1991. But the disguised child labor is many folds larger than what this accounting system admits. The 'no where children' group was as high as 52.9 percent in 1981; it dropped to 45.2 percent in 1991. That is, a total of 60.5 and 50.6 percent children in 5–14 years respectively were not attending schools in 1981 and 1991. The public policy and the action plan to combat the menace of exploitation of the child population must keep in mind that those who already are taken into account as child labor as also those who are not, remain a potential segment for exploitation. Child labor population by sex and residence for years 1981 and 1991 is presented below. Distribution of the working children (1991) by education and residence is presented in Table 7.20.

Table 7.19

Working children (%) in the age group 5–14, India 1981 & 1991

Residence	1981			1991		
	Boys	Girls	Children	Boys	Girls	Children
Rural	10.0	7.8	8.9	6.6	6.3	6.4
Urban	3.7	1.6	2.7	2.8	1.2	2.0
Combined	8.6	6.4	7.6	5.7	5.1	5.4

Source: National Human Development Report, 2001.

Table 7.20

Percentage distribution of working children by educational level for each sex and sector in India during 1991

Education level	Rural			Urban			Total		
	Male	Female	Person	Male	Female	Person	Male	Female	Person
1	2	3	4	5	6	7	8	9	10
Illiterate	72.38	82.63	76.38	56.10	68.38	59.34	70.37	81.59	74.59
Literate (without level)	11.39	7.90	10.03	15.21	13.26	14.69	11.86	8.30	10.52
Primary	12.60	7.74	10.70	20.68	13.94	18.90	13.61	8.19	11.57
Middle	3.32	1.63	2.66	7.14	4.01	6.32	3.79	1.80	3.04
Matriculation/Secondary	0.26	0.08	0.19	0.71	0.33	0.61	0.31	0.10	0.23
Higher Sec./Inter./Pre-University/Non-Technical/Technical cert./Diploma	0.05	0.02	0.04	0.16	0.08	0.14	0.06	0.02	0.05
Number (million)	4.96	3.17	8.13	0.70	0.25	0.95	5.66	3.42	9.08

Source: Office of Registrar General, India. Data relate to age group 5–14 years.

Highest percentage of working children (5–14 years) in 1981 was observed in Jammu & Kashmir (boys 15.3%, girls 15.5%) followed by Andhra Pradesh (boys, 14.8%, Girls 12.8%), Meghalaya (boys 13.5%, girls 10.7%), and Karnataka (boys 12.8%, girls 9.7%). Kerala (boys 1.5%, girls 1.5%) followed by Delhi (boys 2.8%, girls 0.6%) and Andaman & Nicober Islands (boys 3.9%, girls 1.5%) showed smaller percentage of working children in their populations. In 1991 (no census was held in Jammu & Kashmir), percentage of children of either sex in labor force came down in all states and UTs except in Mizoram, Dadra & Nagar Haveli and a few others. Dadra & Nagar Haveli was at the top (boys 10.5%, girls 16.1%) followed by Andhra Pradesh (boys 9.5%, girls 10.5%), and Mizoram (boys 9.0%, girls 9.8%) in proportion of working children in 1991.

Figure 7.7

Child labor (5–14 years) %

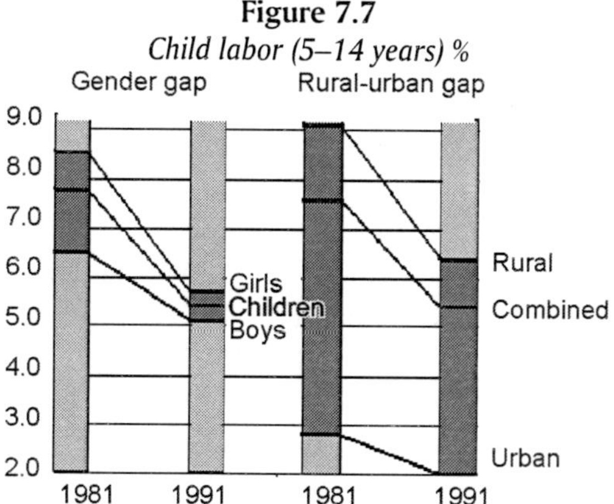

Figure 7.8

'No where children' (5–14 years) %

Of the 60.5 percent children who were either participating in labor market or those not enrolled/attending schools in 1981, 65.1 percent were from rural areas and 44 percent from urban areas. The proportion came down in 1991 to 50.6 (55.8% in rural and 34.3% in urban area). For girls, the proportion has declined from 67.2 percent to 57 percent. The proportion of working girls was smaller than that for boys, both in rural and urban areas (Table 7.20); but the proportion of 'no where girls' was much higher than the proportion of 'no where boys' at both the time points. This is so because it is the young girls who mostly get involved in household chores and looking after young siblings in addition to attending household farm activities. The gender gap has declined considerably between 1981 and 1991.

There is considerable variation in child labor among the states. The BIMARU states had more than two-thirds of the total number of children (75% for girls) in the combined category 'working children and no where children' in 1981. The proportion was much higher (at least by 5% for all children and 10% for girls) in rural areas in these states. Kerala had the least number of children in this combined category, 19.2 percent. Some other better-off states (ratio in the range 40–45%) were Gujarat, Maharashtra, Punjab and Tamil Nadu. The pace of improvement was rather slow in 1991 in most states. The 1991 census showed that 90 percent of the 'working children' were in rural areas. About 75 percent of them were illiterate (Table 7.20). Only a little over 3 percent had middle level or higher level education. Urban children had slightly better educational attainments.

Both boys and girls of the rural 'working children' were engaged in agricultural and allied activities, mostly in their household farms. Only 20 percent of urban boys and 30 percent of urban girls were engaged in farm sector. A larger proportion of girls than boys worked in household/domestic work; boys mostly worked in non-household industries, commerce, and trade and in urban areas. A smaller proportion of boys and girls also worked in service sector mostly as domestic helping hands.

NCAER study also throws light on child labor in rural India. The survey (1994) reported working status for 4.4 percent of boys and 3.5 percent of girls in age group 6–14 years. Most of these children were cash wage earners. The survey admits that child labor in reality was many times higher than what were admitted. The survey estimated that the child labors who earn either through wage or in some other forms in rural India alone could be over 10 million. This excludes all children that work as unpaid family workers. The incidence of child labor, the survey observed, was highest in rural Andhra Pradesh (boys 10.0%, girls 10.3%) followed by Karnataka (boys 7.7%, girls 7.8%), Maharashtra (boys 8.9%, girls 5.8%) and Tamil Nadu (boys 6.3%, girls 7.5%). The survey came to the conclusion that child labor was largely an outcome of extreme income poverty and lack of reasonable levels of adult earning. This is substantiated by the fact that with increases in household income child labor falls, especially female child labor. The largest number of child labor was found in landless wage earner category of households. Female child labor is lowest among large landowners, the salaried and the professionals. Child labor is found to be low in households having adults with better literacy levels. That is, when parents are literate and have some level of education; children are encouraged to go to schools. In a survey conducted in 1973–74 in 16 villages in 4 districts in West Bengal by the present author[4] observed that parents with some level of education do try to send their children to schools and generally do not make sex discrimination in this regard. The authors also noted that refusal to send children to schools or the cases of drop outs were very closely related to the very poor living conditions in these families.

Micro-level studies confirm that abject poverty both in rural and urban areas is the most important reason for children entering into labor market rather than going to schools. Initially, they are prompted by their parents to become wage earners to supplement the household income. Later, they find it difficult to leave work since his/her income becomes a regular part of family's budget as also the kind of independence the child develops because of realization of his/her earning potential. A female child, in school or out of it, shall have to extend her hand for household chores as also in the care of younger siblings. NSS studies confirm that incidence of female child labor is comparatively high in rural areas for most expenditure classes. An opposite picture is observed in urban areas. The safety and security of a girl independently walking around in the familiar environment of the village is better assured than when she has to go to places in an urban area.

Child labor is often related to non-accessibility of schools in the immediate neighborhood. Even when there is a school nearby, the environment of the school, quality of teaching, treatments meted out from teachers and other children (especially to those from lower social class and poor economic background), may dampen the child's interest in education.

Drop out, for whatever reason, enhances the probability of a child joining the labor market. The states where the drop-out rates at primary and middle levels are high, the incidence of child labor is also high. Bihar and Andhra Pradesh are examples where cumulative drop-out rates are exceptionally high as are the incidences of child labor. On the other extreme is Kerala where incidence of child labor and drop-out rates are least.

Child labor has a significant component in migration status of a family. Preponderance of child worker is found in families that have migrated to urban areas in search of a living. Given the unfamiliar environment and deprivation, children from these migrant families take up jobs in informal sector – in construction work, domestic help, rag picking, brick laying and other unskilled activities.

---

4. P K Majumdar and B Chaudhuri, *Faltering First Step*, Cosmo Pub., N Delhi, 1983.

The only remedial measure of this social nuisance is to create conditions that would force parents to send their children to schools and retain them in schools as long as possible. That is, every possible step must be taken (from improving the school environment to improved teacher-pupil ratio, quality of teaching and the school curricula) to improve the enrollment ratio at all levels of schooling and adopt measures to bring down drop-out rates, especially in lower and middle school levels. School timing may be adjusted to allow children to assist their household members in the peak agricultural season. Kerala presents a model for other states to emulate. Since the government has decided to abolish child labor totally and send the rescued children back to schools, the state has to think seriously about how to compensate these families who no longer would receive the kind of financial support from their children and yet they will have to spend a good amount for these children's daily requirements and for their schooling.

7.9 Work Participation among Elderly Persons

Sharp decline in mortality since 1950 and recent decline in fertility has contributed to the process of population ageing in India. Between 1961 and 2001 expectation of life at age 60 has increased by more than 3 years. The expectation of life at birth (e_0^0) is likely to go beyond 70 years by 2011 (Table 7.22). Between 1981 and 2001 the proportion of senior male citizens increased from 6.6 percent to only 6.7 percent, but the same for females increased from 6.6 to 7.7 percent. From 43 million of elderly person in 1981 to 57 million in 1991 and then to 74 million in 2001, the population of senior citizens may go beyond 113 million, accounting for nearly 9 percent of population in 2016. The proportion of elderly persons is much higher in rural areas (7.4%) than in urban areas (6.5%). Presently, females outnumber males in both areas, 7.8 percent against 7.0 percent in rural areas and 7.0 percent against 6.0 percent in urban areas.

High birth rates accompanied by high death rates even a few decades back kept the life expectancy of Indian men and women many years behind the present levels. All the Southern states have high proportion of 60+ age group persons in their populations. Kerala has about 9 percent of the total population in 60+ years age group. The observed ratio is generally low in Eastern and Northeastern states and high in the better-off states, viz. Punjab, Haryana and Himachal Pradesh. Surprisingly, the proportion of elderly in the total population is quite high, both for males and females, in Orissa, which is one of the poorest states in the country. Elderly persons have the least share in the total population in Assam (5.33%) among the bigger states; Arunachal Pradesh has the least share, 4.34 percent, among all states and UTs. As per 1991 data, in 15 states/UTs females had less than or equal to the expectation of life at birth of males in rural areas. In urban areas in 27 states/UTs, females have much higher expectation of life at birth than that of males.

Table 7.21

Expectation of life at age 60 (e_{60}^0) in the census years

	1961	*1871*	*1981*	*1991*	*2001*
Male	11.8	13.6	13.8	14.5	15.2
Female	13.0	13.8	14.7	15.5	16.4

Table 7.22

Expectation of life at birth (e_0^0), 1996–2011

Years	*1996–2001*	*2001–06*	*2006–11*
Male	61.5	63.1	71.0
Female	62.8	64.1	75.0

Figure 7.9

Gender and rural urban gap in elderly population

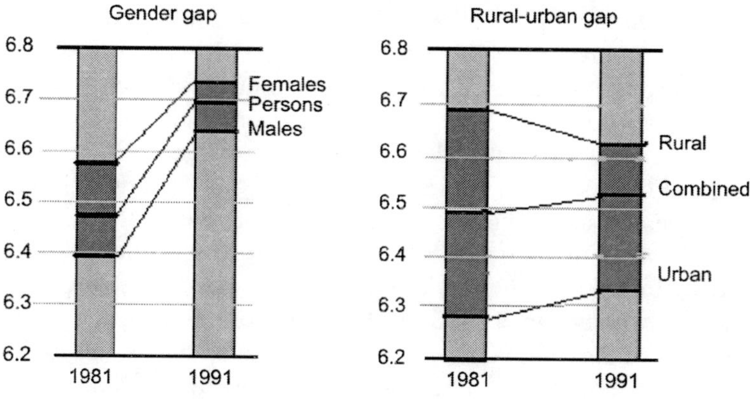

Table 7.23

Proportion of persons in 60+ and 65+ age group in the total population by sex and residence, 2001

		60+	*65+*
Combined	Persons	7.2	4.7
	Males	6.7	4.4
	Females	7.6	5.1
Rural	Persons	7.4	4.9
	Males	7.0	4.6
	Females	7.8	5.2
Urban	Persons	6.5	4.2
	Males	6.0	3.8
	Females	7.0	4.6

Table 7.24

Sex ratio in the elderly and general population by place of residence

Year	*Residence*	*60–64*	*65–69*	*70 +*	*60 +*	*All ages*
1961	Rural	975	971	1 062	1000	963
	Urban	939	916	1072	947	845
	Total	969	962	1 064	1000	941
1971	Rural	926	921	957	936	949
	Urban	908	895	978	928	858
	Total	923	916	961	937	930
1981	Rural	937	984	958	949	951
	Urban	933	994	1051	1000	878
	Total	936	986	976	950	935
1991	Rural	904	954	1025	958	958
	Urban	957	1009	1084	1016	897
	Total	916	966	1038	971	941
2001	Rural	956	952	1008	968	964
	Urban	1005	1 000	1060	1039	913
	Total	969	965	1022	987	947

Issues related to old age did not draw much attention of intelligentsia for the obvious reason that almost throughout the entire period of human life on earth elderly persons constituted only a very miniscule proportion in the total population in any country. Since early twentieth century, the proportion of aged in the population has increased due to rapid decline in mortality rates and consequent improvement in expectation of life. A fast decline in birth rates reinforced the ageing of the population in the developed countries. Prior to this, traditional social structure and prevalent joint family system in most societies could take adequate care of the elderly persons who took all possible care and used all their resources at their command to raise the family. It was the emotional bondage that gave the elderly people in the household an important role in the decision-making at the household level. But the modern industrial culture has forced young adults to leave their ancestral home and settle elsewhere and raise their independent families. Joint families broke; many nuclear families having the same roots came up. The elderly people became the marginalized 'Senior Citizens'. Social security of the senior citizens gradually became the responsibility of the state.

The size of the elderly population in India started to grow rapidly since the middle of the last century. Presently, it is growing twice as fast as the growth in the general population. This has happened because of increase in the expectation of life at all ages and declining young age population. Since 1961, the proportion of elderly persons in the population has gone up by over 1.5 percentage points. Traditional joint family system, which used to provide social security to the elderly and other dependents, has almost collapsed, especially in urban areas. In this changing scenario, how the care of the sick, the widow, the orphans and the elderly persons is to be ensured is becoming a headache for a welfare state. Despite the increased vulnerability of the aged, it is fortunate that this problem has not taken serious proportions in India as yet; nonetheless, it requires attention.

A large proportion of urbanites concentrate in organized sector. Therefore, they receive some compensation in the form of PF, Gratuity and Annuity/Pension in some cases. Some of them have alternative sources of one-time or regular monthly income (Life Insurance, Monthly Income Scheme in post offices, mutual fund investment, etc.). Still a large proportion of the elderly people in urban area do not have access to many of these retirement benefits or self-financing saving options. The situation is really grim in rural India. Even after attaining the age of retirement, they have to extend their working career no matter if they were fully physically fit or not.

Not many studies have been carried out on a larger canvas highlighting the problems of old persons in India. Some data are available relating to widows among the elderly females. While the percentage of widowers among the elderly males was about 15 percent, the percentage of widow population in 1991 Census was as high as 54 percent. A woman of age 60 years is expected to live 1.8 years longer than males. Given the usual age difference in marriage between the spouses, women surviving their spouses are likely to live as widows for about 6.5 years. That is, on an average a woman has to spend her life as widow for about one-tenth of her expected life span. Women in high life expectancy states are likely to spend more years as widow than in other states. The states where male-female age difference at marriage is large, there would be very many widows in the elderly female group. States like Karnataka, Kerala, Maharashtra and West Bengal will face serious problems in near future since these states will have to spend more on widows for a greater length of time since the differences in male-female marriage age in these and some other states are quite large.

NSSO survey conducted in 1995–96 draws the social planners' attention to many of the problems faced by the elderly persons, especially the rural elderly widows. The survey showed that 30 percent of males and 70 percent of females were economically fully dependent on others. High old age dependency, more specifically of females, was very high in West Bengal, Punjab. Assam, Haryana and Gujarat and marginally more for males in Karnataka, Punjab and Andhra Pradesh compared to the national average. The survey also showed that about 47 percent of the elderly persons in urban area and 63 percent of the same in rural area did not possess any financial assets to see them through the remaining years of their life. The gender disparity in possession of financial assets was 3.2:1 in rural area compared to 1.5:1 in urban area. The 1961 Census showed that WPR was 60 percent in the elderly males and 16 percent in elderly females. The rural-urban break up was 65 and 19 percent for males and females respectively in rural area and 43 and 6 percent respectively for males and females in urban area.

NCAER survey (1994) throws some light on the WPR of the elderly persons in rural area. The survey unfolds:

- The WPR is about 70 percent among males and 15 percent among females in 60 year and above age.
- Most males in all states continue with their occupational career even beyond 60 years of age. A small CV 9.3 indicates very little variation among the states in their WPR. Punjab and West Bengal have elderly male workers around 55 percent, lowest among the major states. The same in Madhya Pradesh and Himachal Pradesh are around 77 percent. West Bengal has the lowest elderly female WPR (3.2%).
- The variation is very large (CV 62) among the states in elderly females' WPR, which ranges from a low of 3.2 percent (West Bengal) to a high of 33.2 and 31.9 percent in Kerala and Himachal Pradesh respectively.
- Continuation of work participation is low in groups that have high household income or large landholdings. Among groups comprised of salaried and professional persons, elderly female WPR is low. This probably confirms that child and elderly women labor are responses to income poverty of households.

Studies have amply documented three major areas of social security for elderly persons – income security, health care and adequate shelter which need to be addressed by the state immediately. Studies also have shown that the fear of physical dependency (including being sick or disabled) rather than economic security remains the major cause of worry for the rural elderly. The survey also highlighted the inadequacy of the health care services of most states, especially for rural segments of elderly population. Kerala is an exemplary state which demonstrated that the civil society institutions (charitable trusts and community health care funds), the public health care system and private medical practitioners could collectively offer health care to senior citizens at affordable prices both in rural and urban area. Himachal Pradesh too has shown that public health care system can deliver basic health care and services even in rural area. Old age homes, a few though, at the initiative of the government and NGOs have come up in recent years. But there is a very wide gap in the demand and supply of such services. The prices for receiving such services often are beyond the reach of even the middle class families, what to speak of the rural poor. The government has to do a little bit of planning to improve the coverage and accessibility of the elderly persons to these services. Standardization of the services and a statutory check on quality of services rendered by these homes are needed.

Some preferences need to be given to the elderly persons in the public and private hospitals and some low cost workable medical insurance (subsidized for the very poor) plan for the elderly people need to be worked out (currently fresh health insurance cover is not offered beyond the age 60 years by insurance agencies). The whole medical fraternity needs to come forward and treat the senior citizens with a little bit compassion and understanding. Indian Railways are offering concession tickets for the senior citizens for undertaking long distance journeys for health care and other purposes. The same needs to be extended in air and long distance road travel. Tax concessions are also granted to the senior citizens who come under the direct tax net. Since medical bill is the single most expensive item for the senior citizens (who are not covered by medical insurance), the state may device mechanisms to give them some additional relief in their tax calculations.

India already has a good many laws that try to confer some compensation to the elderly people. However, very few are aware of them, especially the rural poor and the illiterates. Some such laws are The Hindu Succession Act, Hindu Adoption and Maintenance Act, The Employees' Provident Fund and Miscellaneous Provisions Act, The Payment of Gratuity and Pension Act, etc. The states also have passed legislations to protect the interest of the elderly people. For example, Himachal Pradesh Maintenance of Parents and Dependents Act, 1996 defines very specifically who the 'dependents' are (wife, parents and grand parents who are unable to maintain themselves). Tribunals in every district have been asked to determine the claims for maintenance within nine months from the date of filing the case. The Apex Court has also come out with the observation that the adult children in the family must look after their parents at their old age.

The government announced the National Policy for the Older Persons in 1999. The goal of this national policy is to strengthen the senior citizens' legitimate place in society and help them live their life with purpose, dignity, grace and peace. The policy prescriptions are:

- States to extend support for financial security, health care, shelter, welfare and other needs of elderly persons; provide protection against abuse and exploitation; make available opportunities for development of the potential of the older people; seek their participation and provide service to improve the quality of their life.
- Affirmative action in favor of elderly females to prevent their becoming victims of neglect and discrimination on account of gender, widowhood and age.
- Empowerment of older persons to enable better control over their lives and participation in decision-making.
- Increased budgetary support from the sate with equal attention to the rural and urban poor.

7.10 The Economic Growth Path India Is In

The world economic powers, especially the giant MNCs that virtually control world economy, are keenly looking at the economic growth and developmental activities of some of the developing countries to make some of them as their potential trading partners. USA produces enormous amount of food grains, much in excess of their own requirement, and exports the same to many countries at a much lower rate (50% or less of the cost price) to control the world food grains market. They still can increase food grains production but only at the cost of heavy revenue loss for the subsidy given to farmers. But the MNCs need to find new destinations to enlarge their business to keep their empire in one piece. Even a few decades back the MNCs were found to invest their capital mostly in the developed countries. Capitals flowed from USA to Japan, Japanese capital looked at the European and USA market and European capital flowed to USA. The capital flow from one developed country to another developed country was primarily for the reason that the risk factor involved in investment in a developed country was minimum. But because of stiff competition the profitability of investment in these countries (high wage rate and resource constraints increase the overhead cost bringing down the margin of profit) has come down drastically. Till recently, the industrial giants were at a great dilemma as to the profitability of taking their surplus capital to the developing countries, especially after what had happened to the economy in the East Asian countries like Korea, Indonesia, Malaysia and Thailand in the mid-nineties when the capital markets collapsed because of heavy withdrawals by FIIs. The shock wave after this economic disaster in the East Asian countries, also in Latin America, has made the multinationals cautious. They know that sooner or later they will have to come to the developing countries with their surplus capital for reasons of cheap labor, abundance of natural resources and less stringent environmental laws. They for the time are playing a wait and watch game and are studying the investment climate in these countries.

There is hardly any alternative than to go for large-scale industrialization for a faster economic growth of a nation. For rapid industrialization the country needs huge capital and high technology. Both the nature of technology and the capital necessary for investment in the industrial and service sectors remain the stumbling block for most developing countries like India. There is immense possibility for investment in these countries and they are earnestly negotiating with private industrial and business houses in the West to bring their capital and technology in their country for mutual benefits. Capital is trickling from the developed countries but the volume of FDI is still small to infuse fresh blood in their economy. The MNCs could have made huge profit from their investment in the developing countries; the developing countries too could have benefited from the new technology as also for creation of job opportunities for hundreds and thousands.

In view of the lukewarm attitude of the private investors from the developed countries, the developing countries are looking for capital from other developing countries. The United Progressive Alliance (UPA) government's 'look East' policy is an expression of National government's intent to expanding and improving bilateral trade relations as also to developing understanding between the neighboring countries so that each can invest in other countries for mutual benefits. Singapore, Indonesia, Korea, Malaysia, China and others are in our priority list. But such investments can only be in some limited areas, largely in infrastructure development, electronic goods, etc. Such cooperation between the developing countries is likely to reduce their dependence on Western world and Japan. This pattern of development was followed in the developed countries and it is highly probable that this pattern of mutual cooperation will succeed in the developing countries as well. Once such development model becomes a reality, the developed countries will have less reservation for investment in these countries because of improved infrastructure; they are likely to bring their latest technology along with capital. The Chief Minister of West Bengal has already given a push forward movement to Center's 'look east' policy when he signed MOU with the most influential business groups in Indonesia and Singapore. The groups assured to invest Rs 440 billion in a span of 15 years in West Bengal in various projects including manufacturing, logistic hub, Intelligence Park, hospital complex, shopping malls, hotels, trade center, construction of new roadways, etc. The logistic hub can be used as a 'dry port' both for internal and external trading. Once the Nathula Pass becomes fully operational, trading with China would improve fast. Kolkata has all the potential of becoming the 'nodal point' for trading with East Asian countries.

But investment in new townships, hospital complexes, hotels, shopping malls, etc. becomes meaningful in the context of industrial development. For creating large townships and logistic hubs, hundreds and thousands of acres of agricultural land have to be acquired. It is true that for setting up of industries, some agricultural land has to be sacrificed. But the more important question is: Would it be feasible for any government or the investor to pay them adequate compensation for their land

and property, relocate them to some other convenient place and provide them alternative livings on a long-term basis? Can the states and the country as a whole ensure food security even if a vast stretch of agricultural land is divested to various industries and for development of infrastructure?

Starting from UK and other Western countries in the past to the East Asian countries in the present have followed a developmental model in which at the first stage of transformation of a country's economy, the surplus labor in agriculture is absorbed in the industrial sector. Only after the industrial production has gained momentum, the improvement and expansion of the service sector comes up. The service sector's contribution to country's GDP often is regarded as an indicator of the stage of economic development the country is in. The major contribution to GDP of a developed economy comes from the service sector, followed by industrial sector and often less than 5 percent from agriculture. The following table shows the share of agriculture, industry and service sector to GDP along with a few other microeconomic indicators of a selected few countries for comparison. Although the statistics refer to years 1997 and 1999, they give a fair idea of how the growth of an economy is related to growth of these three principal sectors.

Table 7.25

Microeconomic indicators of selected few regions and countries

Country/ region	*% contribution to GDP*[1]			*Net FDI as % of GDP*[2]	*Goods and services as % of GDP*[2]		*Manu factured exports as % of merchan-dize exports*	*Debt ratio as % of GDP*[2]
	Agriculture	*Industry*	*Services*		*Imports*	*Exports*		
1	*2*	*3*	*4*	*5*	*6*	*7*	*8*	*9*
Least developed	33	25	42	3.0	28	18		2.8
East Asia	13	44	43	3.0	39	45	85	5.2
South Asia	25	29	46	–0.3	17	11		2.8
Industrialized countries	2	34	64				82	
Japan	2	38	60		9	10	94	
UK	2	31	67		27	26	83	
USA	2	27	71		13	11	83	
Indonesia	16	43	41	–1.9	27	35	54	12.5
Singapore		35	65	8.2			86	
China	19	49	32	1.0	19	22	88	2.1
Korea	6	43	51	2.3	35	42	91	10.6
Malaysia	12	47	41	2.0	97	122	80	5.9
Sri Lanka	22	26	52	1.1	43	35	75	3.3
INDIA	25	30	45	0.5	15	12	76	2.3
Pakistan	25	25	50	0.9	20	15	84	5.2
Bangladesh	24	27	49	0.4	19	13	91	1.7

1. 1997 data 2. 1999 data

Source: Human Development Report, UNDP, 1999 and 2001.

One thing from this find is clear – excessive dependence of GDP of a country on agriculture deters economic and social advancement. With rising population and increased demand for land for other uses as construction of roads and ports, new townships, IT parks, big track terminals and construction of dams, power plants and industries, there is hardly any alternative than to divert some agricultural land for use in non-agricultural purposes, especially when non-agricultural or poorly fertile lands still available can be used for expansion of certain types of industries only after a huge investment has been incurred on their connectivity (rail and road) with ports and important trading centers. Forest areas cannot be encroached upon any further for reasons of maintaining ecological balance. Land-man ratio is falling fast. The limited agricultural land available has to be used intensively and judiciously by applying modern agricultural implements and techniques to keep the productivity growing at a level that would at least wipe out the deficits likely to be incurred due to transfer of agricultural land for other important uses. Gradually, cultivation also would become capital-intensive creating a large proportion of agricultural labors surplus. We therefore need expansion of small scale relatively labor-intensive industries and select products keeping an eye on the domestic as well as the international market to absorb the surplus poorly educated and unskilled workforce from agriculture. The transition is not going to be easy. The conventional service sector (transportation and communication, container services, trade and commerce, etc.) will be called into play to support the growth of industrial production. Without an efficient supporting service sector, growth of industrial production cannot be sustained. Therefore, the service sector remains a major player in the transformation of a country's economy. The key role however is with the industrial sector. All industrially developed countries had at some point of time very high GDP earning from the manufacturing sector. However, in absolute terms, GDP growth from industries cannot go beyond a limit and that too if the service sector provides the necessary support. Therefore, the share of industries in a country's GDP either would remain stagnant or decline as industrialization gears up. The void created by agriculture's drop in GDP share has to be filled up mostly by the service sector. Some of the traditionally developed countries presently are emphasizing on export of technology and technical know-how since their giant industrialists find it convenient to establish fresh or relocate production units in the developing countries because of abundance of cheap labor and other resources as also because of soft environmental laws. The international markets often are seen to be flooded with consumer goods marked 'Made in China', Malaysia, etc. The countries like Japan, Korea and China have comparatively more export earnings from manufactured items than most other countries. China probably has the largest share of 'manufactured products' in the international market. Every third manufactured item one picks up in Wal-Mart or in any other shopping mall in Europe, USA or elsewhere, is marked 'Made in China'. Even the sophisticated electronic items developed in Japan and elsewhere are manufactured in China.

India has done remarkably well in the service sector than what the entries in Table 7.25 would suggest due to enormous kick-off in telecommunication, software development and business outsourcing in the past 10–12 years. That is, the service sector is growing much faster compared to the manufacturing industries. (Currently, service sector's share has gone up close to 60 percent of GDP in India, and the share of agriculture dropped to around 20%). China is far ahead of India both in domestic investment and FDI. Whereas domestic investment as percentage of GDP in India was only 24 in 1997, for China it was 38 percent. China had better domestic savings (43% of GDP) compared to India's 30 percent or a little more.

Both India and China made their development strides in the sixties of the century gone by. The two followed different political careers – China with communism and India with parliamentary democracy. There was considerable debate as to which of the two paths would yield quicker results. What China could achieve with their political set up could not be achieved in most democracies for intra- and inter-party dissentions, squabbles and contradictions. China has taken a big leap forward towards achieving its national goal at the shortest possible time and has already become a respectable player in international arena.

Though there has been good deal of doubt and controversy about their official statistics, there could be no doubt whatsoever that China at this point of time is miles ahead of India in most aspects that really matters to the economy of development. Their economy has been growing at 9–10 percent for the last few years (average of 8.2% compared to India's 3.2% between 1975 and 1999). One very good aspect of the robustness of Indian economy is that even when there was serious economic disarray (fall of capital market) all over the world in the mid-nineties and in 2008, India still could maintain an annual average economic growth rate of 6 percent in those difficult years. This achievement becomes laudable in the context of Kargil conflict with Pakistan and of imposition of sanctions by USA and other developed economies because of display of India's nuclear capabilities in the Pokhran 2 test in 1998. The average GDP growth rate in India since 2004 is a very healthy 8.5+ percent. The GDP growth rate during 2006–07 reached 9.2 percent – 2.3 percent in agriculture, 11.3 percent in industry and 11.2 percent in service sector. The national savings now stand at a healthy 32.4 percent and investment at 33.8 percent.

India has maintained a high economic growth rate in spite the fact that direct tax contributes only by 11.4 percent to national income (experts believe that this ratio should go close to 20%). In a country of over a billion people, only about 31.5 million people pay taxes (as recorded in 2006) although 54 million permanent account numbers (PAN – 10 digit alphanumeric number) were issued till July 2007. The higher number of PAN cards issued relative to number of actual tax payers is due to the fact that the government made it mandatory for everyone to quote the PAN number in any bank account, in purchase and sell of shares and securities, property transfer, passport and visa or bank loan. The number of tax payers in 2002 was 28.4 million.

China has made massive investments in infrastructure development, especially in roads, rail links and power generation. They work twice as fast as India does. In the beginning of the nineties, India was ahead of China in railway connectivity and carrying capacity of goods by train. But between 1991 and 2002, China expanded its railway network by 24 percent; Indian railways in the same period expanded only by about 1 percent. India no doubt has done magnificently well in road mileage; some 600,000 kilometers of road have been added in this ten-year period. While India was constructing national highways and roads to connect the towns and villages, China was busy in linking the important trade centers and ports with national highways. In 1976, per capita GDP in China was a meager US$101, far behind India at GDP per capita of US$250. In 1997, China went ahead of India with US$564 per capita against India's US$465. China was about US$100 behind India's per capita income even in 1990. But in the next 7 years, when India was still debating with her economic policy, China went ahead of India by US$100 dollars in per capita income. Between 1980 and 1999, China improved its HDI tally from 0.553 to 0.718; India improving its HDI from 0.433 to 0.571.

Private capital flows, particularly FDI, have helped some of the developing countries to grow and enhance their human development. Short-term speculative flow of domestic and foreign capital increases financial volatility and often has little long-term contribution to an economy. Attracting long-term capital inflows in the form of FDI is not easy. The country needs to reform its economic and labor policy, cut down the bureaucratic interferences, assure profit incentives and formulate an industrial policy that would encourage continuous technical up-gradation and least interference from the government and the labor unions. FDI flow in India in 1985, which was less than $1 billion, rose to $3.1 billion in 1997. At the beginning of this millennium it was hovering around US$5 billion. In 2006–07, it went up to over US$15 billion; exchange rate of rupee was very strong at around Rs 40 a US dollar (currently around Rs 45). In the early 1990s India removed restrictions on ownership, relaxing regulations on currency transactions, expedited approval of foreign investment proposals through "one-stop" coordination and persuaded the investors to import new technology. India developed a large number of export processing zones (EPZ), where the foreign and domestic investors were granted tax incentives and duty-free imports. Private-public partnership (including foreign companies) became a reality. Many special economic zones (SEZ) are coming up to boost industrial and urban development.

The path of economic reform initiated in 1991 has not been changed since though the succeeding governments changed hands quickly. Various coalitions of political parties came into power. But all of them respected the democratic traditions of the country. Even those who opposed vehemently against foreign investment in some critical sectors as information and telecommunication, insurance, banking and in modernization of airports had to soften their attitudes. The stability of the democratic set up in the country had never been questioned. Whatever the format of the government, maintaining political stability is most important in taking the economic reform to its ultimate goal. India has to go slow on 'labor reform' and cut in subsidy to petroleum products, electricity, fertilizers and irrigation because of strong opposition from most political parties and labor unions. This has prevented the government from spending more on the social sector – health and education.

China's leadership realized that their internal resources were too limited to make their economy grow at a rate that could help them throw a challenge before the world community for a respectable share in world's trade and commerce. Once they decided to invite foreign capitals, they were ready with all the necessary inputs to make China as the destination of the MNCs. Between 1990 and 1999, net FDI flows increased from 1.0 percent to 3.9 percent of China's GDP. In 1997 when FDI in India was only $3.1 billion, China with FDI $43.5 billion was well ahead of India and other developing countries. Currently, FDI in China is about 40 billion dollars per annum. FDI in India rose from 0.1 to 0.5 percent of GDP in the same period, and currently FDI flow is increasing fast. FDI presently accounts for 1 percent of GDP in India. The international and national fund managers have in recent years shown great respect for the resilience and sturdiness of Indian economy and the pace of economic liberalization at the hands of Monmohan Singh, Prime Minister of India and his Finance Minister P. Chidambaram and then Pranab Mukherjee. That India's capital market is growing fast is indicated by the fact that SENSEX in about 36 months has risen from around 5100 to 14,000. It took only 65 days to take SENSEX from 7,000 to 8,300 marks. By the end of October 2006, SENSEX crossed 13,000 and by July 2007 it crossed 15,000 marks. This certainly is an indicator of the type of confidence the domestic and foreign fund managers have in Indian economy.

Even though the governance of the country has changed hands quite frequently in the last 17 years, the successive governments have clearly gone ahead with India's economic liberalization agenda and have paved the way for increasing FDI's share in industry, telecom, insurance, and banking and in some others. The implementation of economic liberalization policy in India (foreign participation in insurance business, relaxing the upper limits of FDI in telecom and other sectors, partial disinvestments of profit-making PSUs and selling or closer of some loss-making units, power sector reform, gradual withdrawal of subsidies from fertilizer, food grains and from some other services, etc.) unlike that in China, often is beset with strong opposition from various political parties and labor unions. Some oppose it on grounds of national security (FDI in modernization of airport and telecom sector, for example), many others oppose it on the grounds that the MNCs will take over the Indian companies or the existing Indian companies will fail to survive in the competition against the hi tech industries established by MNCs and there would be severe retrenchment of labor if the government fully commits to a capital-intensive growth model. But India has already proved the resilience of its industrial giants when the Tatas, Birlas and many other companies including software companies took over many industrial giants in Europe and USA in recent years.

The success of capital-intensive growth depends on production efficiency. Neither our public sector nor our private sector manufacturing concerns can boast of in-house discipline and fine-tuned work-culture. The political and trade union leaders have opposed technology up-gradation on the fear that there would be labor retrenchment and that the government would sooner or later make

Table 7. 26

Man-days lost per thousand workers employed due to industrial disputes in manufacturing units in the public and private sector over the years in India

	Man-days lost per thousand workers employed				***Man-days lost per thousand workers employed***		
Year	***Public sector***	***Private sector***	***Total***	***Year***	***Public sector***	***Private sector***	***Total***
1961	115	1179	1022	1991	602	3275	2725
1966	548	2390	2041	1992	772	3877	3400
1971	309	2746	2301	1993	734	2363	2112
1976	404	2524	2102	1994	264	2436	2016
1980	938	3008	2534	1995	446	1488	1294
1981	4508	4490	4494	1996	514	2048	1782
1982	4219	11309	9547	1997	650	1964	1751
1983	1278	7142	5963	1998	419	1656	1464
1984	1538	7855	6595	1999P	210	2531	2170
1985	390	4155	3379	2000P	522	2248	1979
1986	1189	4828	4108	2001P	339	2658	2297
1987	2527	4807	4354	2002P	5	1786	1509
1988	2556	4109	3796				
1989	868	3903	3277				
1990	730	2643	2246				

P. Provisional

Source: Labor Bureau, Ministry of Labor.

sweeping changes in the existing labor laws to give company managements a free hand in hiring and firing workers. The trade union top leaders, most of who are political persons, often use the trade unions as instruments for bargaining political mileage rather than the true welfare of labors. Seldom do they use the democratic process in taking decisions about strikes and agitations. Even though they are vociferous for the democratic rights to stage protest against management, the same right is denied to workers for their choice between agitation and report to their duties as workers of the establishment. Such strikes often lead to lockouts or suspension of work. There are a few sates (West Bengal, for example) where the militant trade union activities had led to permanent closer of many industries and flight of capital to other states where trade union movements are not as militant as in some others (West Bengal lost about 127,000 jobs in the organized sector, 80,000 alone in private sector in the 1990s). With capital-intensive production units, such suspension of work would bring disaster to the production unit. The health of the highly costly equipments installed depends upon how efficiently the maintenance staff attends them. The 'call centers' and the organizations engaged in developing software on contractual agreement often have to be run 24 hours a day. A day's general strike may cost them millions of dollars. Frequent strikes and 'bandhs' and massive protests staged often against some political and economic decisions as also against some High Court or Supreme Court orders (against strikes and bandhs) totally jeopardize civic life and production. Table 7.26 shows how man-days are lost in the country on account of strikes, suspension of work or 'bandhs' frequently called by the trade unions and political parties.

In the eighties, man-days lost due to industrial disputes in the manufacturing units, both in public and private sector was enormous. It was a colossal loss to industrial productivity as well as the economy of the country. It is only in the post-reform period that things have started to improve both in public and private sector, more in the former.

In this era of coalition politics, no government can go ahead with their stated economic agenda if the coalition partners sing on a different tune. The political parties are keen to nurture their constituencies even if that meant down playing the national interest. The cost of crude oil in international market was US$10 per barrel in 1998. By 2002 it went up to US$30 a barrel. By June 2005 it was US$60 and by early 2006 it was $75 a barrel. It came down to around US$60 in December 2006, but climbed to $147 in July 2008. The Left parties would not allow the government to raise petrol, diesel, kerosene and LPG prices because that would hurt the common man. Even some coalition partners in the government were against any price hike since election in some of the key states was round the corner.

Morgan-Stanley has brought out a stunning find that the political and bureaucratic interference and unnecessary paper works in India escalates the cost in most developmental works by 50 to 100 percent point compared to that in China. The only service that is really cheap in India compared to that in China is telecommunication. The same report also states that China spends about 20.6 percent of the country's GDP on infrastructure alone (about $260 billion) compared to India's 6 percent of GDP.

The Indian government currently spends about US$31 billion in infrastructure development. It has been estimated that some US$150 billion would have to be invested in infrastructure alone in the next 10 years. India is about to launch a dedicated freight corridor between the four metropolises. Power sector in India has remained a disappointing performer. The 44 percent loss in transmission, distribution and theft is mind-boggling. The State Electricity Boards are making huge losses every year; yet they are neither allowed to retrench surplus labors nor raise the tariff. Electricity is supplied to farmers in most states at throw away prices or free of cost. Average return from agriculture is less than 50 paise per kWh.

We have over US$300 billion in foreign exchange reserve (June, 2008). This money is lying idle with RBI. A debate is mooting if a portion of this foreign exchange, say, $20 billion, should be used in infrastructure development. The Indian economy is robust enough to withstand the shock in the event the foreign investors (FIIs) decide to withdraw a large sum at quick notice (which is what had happened in East Asian and Latin American countries in mid-nineties and has happened in India in 2008 global economic crisis). China does not hesitate to use their foreign exchange reserve for infrastructure development projects.

In most of the developing countries, the proportion of agricultural workers in the total work force is fast declining. Even then roughly 70 percent of the people surviving on less than $1 a day live in rural area who depend wholly or partly on small-scale agriculture. A large proportion of GDP in these countries still come from agriculture (in India agriculture currently contributes about 20% to GDP). The decline in the proportion of agricultural labors in the total workforce and the decline in the importance of agricultural income in national economy run almost parallel. In the developed countries one percent rise in the agricultural population contributes one percent or more to national GDP. In the developing countries this is only 0.5 percent or a little more.

Food grain production in India since independence has increased by over four folds, but the economic health of agricultural labor has not changed much. Even though they are recorded as agricultural labors, a sizeable proportion of them do not find work round the year. In certain districts the absolute increase in the size of agricultural labor is really low. This has happened because of change in traditional cultivation practices. Paddy cultivation is most labor-intensive. In many areas the farmers have shifted from paddy to other cash crops. In some other districts, more land has been brought under paddy cultivation necessitating engagement of more labors.

There is often some disparity between the statistics supplied by different agencies. For example, UN Statistical Yearbook 1985 states that the proportion of agricultural labor to total work force in India in 1984 was 60 percent. But 1981 census report indicated the same as 68 percent. It really creates a doubt in mind if within four years such a drastic change in the proportion of agricultural population is possible. Census data of 1971 and 1981 indicate that the WPR for the respective years were 32.9 and 33.5 percent. But the UN Statistical Yearbook showed the 1980 and 1984 figures at 40 and 38 percent respectively although both the sources closely agreed with the 1970 figure. Demographic Yearbook 1956 reported that there were 10 and 6 percent workers respectively in industry and trade and commerce in India. However, in 1980 both the proportions appear to have increased by 8 percentage points.

The proportion of male agricultural population has been declining since 1981. The proportion has come down more significantly in some ages (15–29 years) many of them possibly migrated to urban areas in search of an alternative job. Since men are moving to off-farm employment at a faster rate, women make up an increasingly large proportion of the agricultural labor force in developing countries. Those below 15 years and those above 60 mostly are engaged in agriculture. This is true both for men and women labor. The literacy rate among the urban worker is quite high, more than 90 percent. Education often would delay the urban people to enter into the job market. Even those who have better education and training would have to wait for some more time for the right type of job thus delaying their entry into the labor market further. Competition level is very high in jobs that ask for education and special skill than are demanded by traditional occupations found in rural area.

The pressure on land is mounting fast due to growth of population as also due to diversion of agricultural land for other uses. This has resulted in transfer of more and more rural people, especially the younger educated males, to towns and cities in search of livelihood. This also has consequential effect in the fast increase of unorganized small-scale business and service sector (hawkers, unauthorized auto-rickshaw drivers, security and other service providers, especially in high-rise buildings and housing complexes, DTP centers and STD booths). Many of them have forcibly occupied (often with political patronage) government lands, and slums have come up fast in busy cities. In fact, in many important cities (Mumbai, for example), slum-dweller population often is around one-third of the total city population. The civic authority cannot deny them many of the basic civic amenities although the slum dwellers do not pay taxes for obtaining these services. They remain the vote-bank for one party or the other and therefore the government and the civic authorities remain reluctant to demolish these slums and unauthorized constructions in spite of the court order. A very recent example is the turmoil that was seen when the administration started sealing unauthorized shops and establishments in residential areas in Delhi by court order.

Economic globalization has put the developing countries like India in a great dilemma. These countries are becoming the obvious destinations of multinational giants for reasons of vast size of the potential consumers, cheap labor and excellent intellectual and natural resources. To take advantage of uninterrupted FDI flow, these countries need to develop the necessary infrastructure for expansion of trade and commerce and also concentrate on the social sector to provide skilled workers for the new class of jobs that are likely to come up. The cities and metropolis need to improve the within-and-between cities' road connectivity for faster movement of traffic and eliminate those human habitations, shops and unorganized, unauthorized markets that are clearly against the lifestyle commensurate with economic globalization.

UNDP Human Development Report lashed out at USA and the European Union for violating the WTO guidelines relating to agricultural subsidy in the developed countries. The report has highlighted how the developing countries have been pushed to the wall in this unequal competition in the international food grain market when agriculture in most developing countries still remains the principal component for their national income.

Agriculture was kept out of the ambit of open-door global economy quite for sometime. It was only in 1995 that agriculture was brought under the purview of WTO. Free trading of any commodity demands that the playing field is made transparent and competitive. That is, the cost of the product must not be kept low by dubious means. The cost input of a commodity varies from one country to another depending upon the technology they use and the cost of other inputs. Therefore, some countries would have some advantage over others because of their lower production cost.

However, the desirable competitiveness in the food grain market is easily destroyed when some countries violate the basic rules of international trading by providing huge subsidies to their producers and artificially keeps down the market price. The subsidy issue has been discussed in some detail in Chapter 13, *Fundamentals of Demography* by the present author.

Every one, from the treasury bench to those in the opposition, unequivocally acknowledges that for stability and faster growth of economy India needs huge capital. The government's own resources are fully exhausted especially after the Parliament passed the bill guaranteeing employment for the rural poor for at least 100 days a year. Subsequently the central government also asked the nationalized and private banks to write-off loans advanced to marginal farmers, which cost the exchequer over Rs 60,000,00 million. The national government in the past had declared amnesty to those who disclosed their undisclosed income. That did not work as well as the government had expected. The government levied cess of Rs 4 per liter on petroleum and diesel to create some sort of a fund for infrastructure development. The banks have been asked to reduce their non-performing assets (NPA) and take appropriate measures to get back the money they had advanced to individuals and industrial establishments. The results are not encouraging. The government promised to curtail some of its non-plan expenditure and bring in some discipline in spending. The government has succeeded in bringing down some of its internal debts as a result of reduced bank rates. The central government has been bringing down the number of government employees in a phased manner and already has reduced the number of central government employees by about 10 percent by 2003. However, instead of downsizing, almost all the states generated additional employments in public (4.87%) and quasi-public sector (9.58%) so that there was 1.0134 percent net increase in employment in the public sector between 1991 and 2000 (Table 7.10). The previous NDA government at the center took a bold step when it initiated the disinvestments policy of selected PSUs. But the UPA government decided to go slow on this because of intense opposition from the Left parties and also from some of its own constituent members since the coalition government was fully dependent upon support from the Left and other parties.

The government in principle has decided not to make investment directly on fresh industrial units. The government has seen that the revenue collected from the PSUs already disinvested is much more than the dividends received from these units before their sell out. Public-private joint venture is welcome, but the government wants to keep its share in such ventures to a minimum level so that the managerial skill of the corporate houses can be fully utilized. The government is organizing trade fairs in India and abroad and inviting business delegates from other countries and explaining to them what facilities and privileges can be extended to them if they would establish industries in this country and bring in the latest technology. Various Chambers of Commerce are also helping the government on this issue. The domestic players can play a significant role in the growth of industries, but it is felt that they would do better if they were tied with some foreign investors who could bring the latest technology and dollar.

Any investor, foreign or domestic, would like to invest in an area or in a state where there already exists good transportation facilities, ports close by and a developed market. That is, the existing infrastructure must be conducive to setting up of industries. There is a stiff competition among the states for attracting private investments. FDI is still not enough in India. Larger FDI is restricted to a few states, namely Maharashtra (about 16%), Gujarat (9%) and of late, Orissa (7%).

The major obstacle to large-scale industrialization in many states is the availability of land. Any big industry or a new township or hospital complex, or intelligence park would need thousands of acres of land at a stretch with necessary infrastructure support. We still have large area of arid land or land where agriculture is not profitable. We have thousands of factories that have been closed down long back. Since they are scattered all over an extended region, they can be acquired and given to smaller entrepreneurs, not to big investors. The only alternative is to acquire agricultural lands. Acquiring agricultural land for expansion of industries is posing problems in most states. The foremost issue in the dispute is adequate compensation for the acquired land and also how those who are evicted from their land (and also those who are attached to the land as agricultural wage workers) are going to be rehabilitated. Earlier, the government had acquired agricultural land for construction of roads and highways, power plants, hospital complexes, new townships and the like. In many cases the compensations given for the acquired land were far below the market price, even the evicted persons had to wait for years to get the compensation. The government promised rehabilitation of the evicted persons, a promise that had remained mostly unfulfilled. Another very important fact is that the political party in power often has a large mass base among the farmers. Displacement of farmers from their land would erode their support base from their constituency and the rival political parties would grab this opportunity to strengthen their base among these farmers (the case in example is acquisition of 1,000 acre of agricultural land for Tata motors in Singur in West Bengal). Once upon a time, the party currently in power in West Bengal fought tooth and nail when they were in opposition bench whenever the ruling party wanted to acquire agricultural land for industrial and other uses. The pro-farmer image of the party keeps a large section of the party members in dilemma if the party's current stand on industrial expansion at the expense of agriculture would not contradict its basic pro-poor ideology. The West Bengal government will need to acquire in the next two years about 100,000 acres of land (about 0.7% of total agricultural land in the state) for projects signed with domestic and foreign investors.

Such is the situation in West Bengal, one of the states run uninterrupted since 1977 by Left parties. A very heated discussion is going on if prime agricultural lands should be sacrificed to construct one of the largest logistic hubs in India. The Marxists will have to do a lot of explaining to its own party members, other parties in the Left Front and the farmers who are likely to be evicted from their land if such deals ultimately go through.

Most economists agree that the economics behind such acquisition of agricultural land be given primacy to sentiments. In all developed countries, industries have come up on agricultural lands and at places that are well connected with the ports, markets and other service providing centers. It may be argued that they could afford diversion of agricultural land to other uses since about 22 percent of the world population living in developed countries has a share of about 43 percent of the total arable and permanent cropland of the world (USA, Canada and Australia have abundance of farm land). In the world today, only about 11 percent of the total available land is arable and permanent cropland, the share of permanent cropland being a meager 0.75 percent. That is, agriculture remains confined to in less than 10 percent of the available cultivable land. The question is how much the nation as a whole is going to lose or gain from agricultural lands once they are converted into industrial hubs and consequent development of townships with all modern amenities. Urbanization and growth of industries go hand in hand. Both farmers and non-farmers benefit from such industrial-urban growth. According to an estimate by the Central Statistical Organization (CSO), India uses only 40 percent of the available land for cultivation. A modest estimate is that a farmer's net profit (taking into contemplation the cost of inputs – seeds, fertilizers, pesticides, irrigation and labor) from one acre of land with a single crop (paddy specifically) would be around Rs 2,000 per annum. With multiple crops and improved method of cultivation, the net profit from one acre of land could be anywhere between Rs 4,000 and Rs 6,000 per annum and that too with subsidized fertilizer and irrigation facilities. A modern industry on the same land can produce industrial goods worth several million rupees a year. The labor-days created by farming on one acre of land for single crop cultivation is about 100. With agricultural wage rate as low as Rs 60 per day, an agriculture wage earner can at best get about Rs 6,000 from it. For the rest of the days he would be forced to go for wage earning in non-agricultural sector. CSO report estimated that two or more crops are grown only in about 14 percent of agricultural land in India.

It is understood that the state government and the investors would jointly declare that those who are evicted from their land would be given employment in the industry at least for a few years besides paying adequate compensation for their land. As per the current market rate, the daily wage for a factory worker would be somewhere between Rs 100 and Rs 200 per day. If the private investors agree on this stipulated condition, the owners of the farm land will have little to worry about their living. Of course, a fear would always haunt those whose land was acquired that neither the investor nor the government would remain faithful to their commitment once the land deal was completed. This has been the common experience in similar land acquisitions earlier for purposes of road construction or for setting up of power plants, construction of dams or similar such public utilities.

The owner of the land may be given reasonable compensation (not at current market price, but at a likely rate for the adjoining lands once the industry becomes fully functional) and some of them could as well get wage jobs while the construction phase of the industry or the township continues. But one must not forget that there are other agricultural workers who are also intimately associated with the cultivation process. That is, the same farmland gave income security to a large number of people including the owner of the farm. Whereas the owner of the farm land would be doubly protected, at least for some time (one simple estimate shows that if the farmer is given a reasonably good price for the land acquired and if the farmer invests that money in monthly income scheme (MIS) in the post office, his interest income even in today's low interest regime would exceed the average annual income from the crop cultivated), the other agricultural wage workers (except share-croppers) would not come under the purview of this transaction. And it is very unlikely that these and other wage earners, mostly poorly literate and without any skill, would find entry into this fast track capital-intensive activities.

In international trading under the WTO regime, trade flows from one country to another of any merchandise including food grains would depend upon the comparative cost of production of the goods. Agricultural production in UK, for example, can feed its people only for three months. Even then UK does not try to increase food production for the simple reason that the country can import food grains and other agricultural products from Canada and Australia at a much cheaper price compared to the higher cost of production in UK. UK is very efficient in production of industrial goods and machinery and exports these products at prices much higher than their production costs, which gives them the leverage to import food grains. Singapore imports all its food requirements from other countries.

Agricultural productivity in India is still very low. Agricultural production here is largely dependent upon rain in the monsoon months. Agricultural production suffers in years that have less than average rainfall. Food grain production as a result of 'green revolution' was over 213 million metric tons in 2004. The short fall if any due to draught or flood can be taken care of by the buffer stock. But food production in 2005 dropped to 204 million metric tons as a result of change in the policy of cereal cultivation, and, in consequence, the buffer stock came down from 40 to 20 million metric tons. This has impacted many of India's welfare programs that are linked to food grain distribution from the central stock. There is enough land that can be brought under regular cultivation and generate employment. Even if agricultural land was not spared for construction of industries, such lands are to be made available for construction of houses, school buildings and health centers, roads, power houses, irrigation canals and others for mutual benefit of the villagers. In view of increased demand for industrial and other uses of agricultural land, many state governments have taken up plans to increase agricultural land by bringing more land under irrigation. The days are not far when capital-intensive cultivation would replace the labor-intensive agriculture in the country to improve the productivity per unit agricultural land. That will create a situation when there would be again a huge surplus of agricultural labor. Whereas the average annual industrial growth rate in India in the last decade was 8 percent or around, the average growth of agriculture was only about 2.3 percent. Since our agriculture is substantially dependent upon climatic conditions, agricultural production fluctuates a great deal. The fall in agricultural production is not so much related to how much of the agricultural land is given to industries or expansion of cities or in establishing new townships or industrial hubs. Increasing the productivity can compensate the loss if any of the farm land given to other uses. The per capita GDP can be improved only through rapid industrialization and diversification of industrial products. The additional employment can be generated only in the private sector and only through establishing many new industries. Though the small-scale industries (SSI) have more potential to generate employment, SSIs are struggling hard for their survival because of lack of necessary fund to modernize their units. This is in spite the fact that the government gives 12 percent subsidy, likely to be raised further, to the SSIs.

The foreign and domestic investors have reason to be worried about the work culture among our labors, especially in some states like West Bengal. The trade unions with the backing of political parties disrupt work every now and then. The highly capital-intensive plants cannot afford to lose working hours. The Indian economy is to be reformed fast; our mind sets have to be changed to take advantage of economic globalization. Since 1991, the successive governments have realized that large private investment, especially FDI flow, would remain a far cry if labor reforms were not carried out fast. But this is the most difficult hurdle that has to be cleared even by the strongest proponents of economic liberalization. The strongest opposition will come not from the other side of the treasury bench but from the 'comrades in arms'. Whatever labor laws we have today, and there are plenty of them, they are mostly directed to safeguarding the interest of 7 percent of the total workforce who are engaged in the organized sector, relatively very small number who have the greatest security in their job with various benefits accruing to them and to their families in comparison with those in the informal and unorganized sector. Dr Manmohan Singh has categorically admitted the stiffness of our labor laws in public. With a very 'limited mandate' and the realities of coalition politics, the top executives of the government have been forced to go slow on this vital issue. The government has set up a number of special economic zones where the usual labor laws largely remain inoperative. Earlier, those supporting the government from outside had opposed tooth and nail against foreign capital in banking sector and any bank reform that would put the nationalized banks into a stiff competition in the market. It is true that the nationalized banks vis-à-vis private banks played a very laudable role in India's development process although they have the largest non-performing assets (NPA). Entry of private players, especially the foreign players, in insurance business, was objected to presumably because that would end the monopoly of the Life Insurance Corporation of India in insurance business and the fear that the competition from the private players would force LIC to review its organizational structure and management policy. Retrenchment of surplus labor is on the card. The government's decision to invite FDI in telecom sector has also been resisted. They opposed downsizing of employment in public sector. But with time all these oppositions lost their vigor and the 'comrades in arms' grudgingly accepted the ground reality. Price hike of petrol and diesel in August 2005 was greeted in West Bengal by transport strike; normal life came to a halt for 48 hours. But the private transport operators in no other state showed a similar such agitation to express their unhappiness with the decision for the price hikes. The state government ultimately agreed on a price hike in road transports, but allowed the private transport operators an opportunity to impolitely show their might to jeopardize civic life in total disregard to the law of the land.

The Prime Minister in an interview to a foreign journal has spoken of the rigidity in our employment market. He, in the interview, spoke of softening the existing labor laws. The Prime Minister's Office (PMO) circulated a note in the recent past to different departments and states. Four major premises of the note are: a) the current labor laws be given a go bye in industrial establishments run by foreign investors, i.e., labor policy in these establishments be decided on the basis of dialogues between the employer and the employees; b) the state and the central government be given the power to absolve such establishments from giving any compensation in the event of retrenchment of labor; c) in 'public interest' the management shall have the freedom to appoint contract labors 'out sourcing', and d) the employer shall have the power to retrench employees in establishments that employ no more than 300 workers. The states like Maharashtra, Gujarat, Haryana, Punjab, Karnataka and a few others, where the presence of Left labor unions is nominal, have already shown their interest in these suggested changes. But it would not be easy to carry out these reforms in labor laws since some of the coalition partners' and the Left parties' fear that such labor reform will weaken the bargaining power of labor unions and ultimately affect their vote bank.

8

Trends and Differentials in Fertility in India

8.1 Introduction

India before independence was preoccupied with containing the high mortality and morbidity in the country. Till 1921, population in the subcontinent registered a chequered growth because of high death rates since plague, cholera, malaria and influenza epidemics were recurrent phenomena throughout the country. Although many social thinkers in India spoke forcefully about the consequences of high birth rate, no serious discussion on controlling birth rate followed since all attention got stuck in devising plans and strategies to control recurrent outbreak of killer diseases in various parts of the country. The study of human fertility largely remained a neglected field. It was in 1931 Census that a formal reference was first made about the possible consequences of 'devastating torrent of babies' and suggested that a long-term plan be adopted to stop the influx of babies. Family planning movement gained considerable momentum in the two decades following. Independent India took the issue in right earnest when family planning was included in the First Five Year Plan. It was realized that to control birth rate it was necessary to gather adequate knowledge about fertility behavior of the diverse cross section of people. In the two decades after independence, hundreds of fertility and KAP (knowledge, attitude and practice) studies were conducted. Unfortunately, the results of these studies have not been fully utilized in formulation of our population policies and programs.

Although the regular synchronous periodic Census is conducted since 1881, data relating to actual birth and death rate in the country remained very meager and unconvincing. Kinsley Davis has provided some estimate of birth rate in the subcontinent for the period 1881 to 1941. For the decades 1951–71, a number of demographers have come out with estimates of birth rate in the country. Since 1970, more reliable information on vital rates has become available through Sample Registration Scheme (SRS). Some idea about the birth rates prevailing at various time points between 1901 and 1981 can be had from Table 8.1.

Table 8.1

Estimates of birth rate in India, 1901–1981

Source	*Period*	*Birth rate*
Kinsley Davis	1901–11	49.2
	1911–21	48.1
	1921–31	46.4
	1931–41	45.2
Registrar General	1941–51	39.9
	1951–61	41.7
G.B. Saxena	1951–61	46.0
P.M. Visaria	1951–61	44.9
United Nations	1951–61	45.1
Registrar General	1961–71	41.1
Rele and Sinha	1961–71	41.0
Sample Registration Scheme	1970–72	37.2
	1975–77	34.2
	1980–82	33.8

The decline in fertility observed in these estimates is corroborated by sub-national studies. Mysore Population Studies, Standard Fertility Surveys sponsored by the Government of India, Calcutta Fertility Survey, etc. provided information on fertility behavior of various cross-sections of the studied populations.

We already have discussed earlier that registration of birth and death in India still lacks adequacy, coverage and depth for using them in statistical analysis. The Registrar General and Census Commissioner admitted that although the system of vital registration in India is more than 100 years old, registration of birth and death is still incomplete and faulty. As early as 1979, the Registrar General admitted that only 58 percent of births and 65 percent of deaths are formally registered. Birth and Death Registration Act, 1969 asks for compulsory registration of every incidence of birth and death in a family with the local registration office. The situation in municipal and city areas has improved considerably in recent years since a formal birth certificate from the registration authority needs to be submitted while seeking admission of children into schools (Chapter 3.1). In matters of property litigation, execution of a will or claiming PF and insurance benefits, etc. by the heirs of the deceased person have to be supported by death certificates from the registration authority. The situation has not improved much in rural areas since many of them are still unaware of the necessity for such registration as also due to the fact that they find no utility for such registration at the ground level. (The reasons behind incomplete and faulty registration have been discussed in Chapter 3 under Civil Registration.)

It is for this reason that birth and death related issues are not analyzed from the documents available from registration offices. Although the necessary infrastructure exists in most offices, the administration remains careless to take remedial measures to make the registrations really meaningful for all its uses. The Registrar General realized that it would take a stupendous effort to make the nation's on-going registration system respond to the need of the hour for a correct assessment of birth and death rates and their determinants and correlates, which are so vital in planning and projecting population changes. Under the direct control of the Registrar General, the Sample Registration Scheme (SRS) was initiated in 1964. Currently, this registration (over and above the continuing registration in the country) is carried out on 6,671 sample units, selected from all the big and small states and UTs, covering over 6.2 million people. (For a detailed discussion on SRS, the reader is referred to Chapter 3 of this volume.)

For estimation of birth and death rate in the total population as also in the states, the SRS data have been found quite dependable and satisfactory. For some issues related to birth, death, migration, employment, etc., NSSO and other sources of data are often utilized. For getting an idea about birth rates in the past, some especially devised methods (reverse survival or differencing method) are used on the age distribution of the population obtained from different census enumerations. Age distribution of the population showed irregular fluctuations till the middle of the last century. For getting a smoothed age distribution, the Indian Actuary followed the method of superimposition of the age distribution on the age distribution obtained in the next census. The crest and trough of one distribution were roughly in the opposite phases of the other distribution. The arithmetic average of the two distributions gave the smoothed age distribution of the year under scrutiny.

8.2 Crude Birth Rate

Till 1941 the crude birth rate (CBR) in undivided India was around its biological limit, fluctuating between 45 and 52. Objections were raised against comparability of these figures since the methods of estimation employed in various Censuses were not the same. S.B. Mukherjee employed Quasi Stable Population Model for estimation of birth, death and expectation of life for India as also for different states.

Table 8.2

Birth and death rates and average expectation of life, India 1901–61

Year	*1901*	*1911*	*1921*	*1931*	*1941*	*1951*	*1961*
CBR	47–49	48–50	48–50	46–48	44–46	42–44	43–45
CDR	47–49	42–44	48–50	36–38	32–34	30–32	25–27
Average life expectancy	21.48	23.65	21.07	28.61	32.94	34.61	38.28

Source: S.B. Mukherjee: The age distribution of Indian population: A reconstruction for the States and territories, 1976.

Table 8.3

Crude birth and death rates in India, 1901–2001

Year	*1901*	*1911*	*1921*	*1931*	*1941*	*1951*	*1961*	*1971*	*1981*	*1991*	*2001*
Birth rate	48.0	49.2	48.1	46.4	52.2	39.9	41.7	41.2	37.0	31.0	25.8
Death rate	48.0	42.6	47.0	36.3	31.2	27.4	22.8	16.1	12.7	10.0	8.5

Source: Various Census and SRS Data

With the Great Demographic Divide (1921) a new demographic regime took off in India. There was a major slash in death rate between 1921 and 1941 (around 16 points) and thereafter a steady decline in CDR. There is always a secular time lag before one observes the effect of change in death rate on birth rate. From nearly a stagnant population, India registered 1 percent average annual population growth rate for the first time since 1901 in 1941. The average expectation of life increased by about 12 years in the two decades (1921–41). But fertility declined only marginally. Fertility decline in India as also elsewhere remains a slow process unless the state adopts a fast track mechanism to bring down birth rate to a specified level within a target period (as has been done in China and Japan and even in India during the period of Emergency). Like death rate, decline of birth rate is also an irreversible process, except for some random fluctuations due to various unforeseen social and demographic factors and when a population reaches a threshold level (very low birth and death rate regime – incipient decline) after which depopulation may start if downward trend of birth rate continues.

Figure 8.1

Birth and death rates in India, 1901–2001

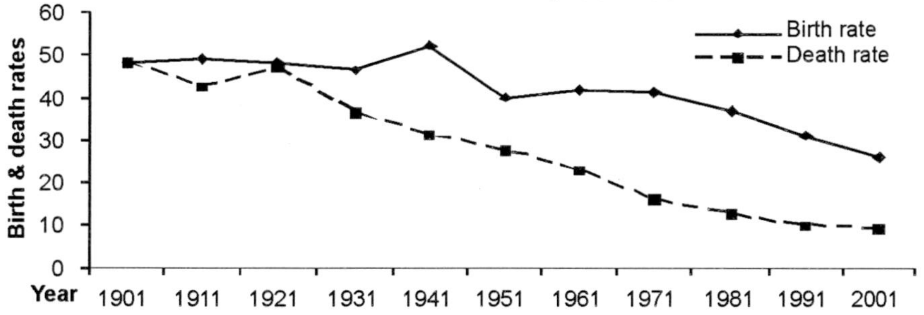

Prior to introduction of Sample Registration Scheme, there was no reliable mechanism to measure these demographic changes except at the time of Census. The sample surveys conducted by various agencies give us only an idea about some trend over a period, but such statistics cannot be used for reliable projections. NSSO data show that in the 1960s birth rate in urban area declined much faster vis-à-vis rural India. Though SRS took off in 1964, it took some time to develop and improve the recording mechanisms of births and deaths in the selected sample units. Since 1970 the quality of data on birth and death by SRS improved and the sample estimates became more and more reliable for population projections at the national level. At state or regional level, the sample estimates still are not consistently dependable.

The SRS report indicates that between 1988–1990 and 1998–2000 crude birth rates declined significantly, a 15 percent reduction at the national level – about 18 percent in urban area and 14.3 percent in rural India. The reduction was very low in the BIMARU states as also in Kerala, which already had the lowest birth rate among the larger states in India. Both West Bengal and Maharashtra showed about 25 percentage point decline in birth rate between these time points. Urban Punjab was well ahead of others in checking birth rate in this ten-year period.

Table 8.4

Percentage change in birth rate between 1988–90 and 1998–2000 by residence, India (SRS data, 2003)

Total			*Rural*			*Urban*		
1988–90	*1998–2000*	*% Change*	*1988–90*	*1998–2000*	*% Change*	*1988–90*	*1998–2000*	*% Change*
30.8	26.1	–15.1	32.3	27.7	–14.3	25.4	20.9	–17.9

The NCAER survey (1994) also observed significant variation in rural CBR among the states. The highest CBR 44 was observed in Rajasthan. High birth rates were also observed in Uttar Pradesh (38), Bihar (37), Northeastern states (34) and West Bengal (34). The Southern states had low CBRs ranging from 21 in Kerala to 28 in Tamil Nadu. CBR in these states could be, the survey suggested, due to higher age at marriage, higher levels of female literacy and wider use of contraception. Maharashtra (28), Himachal Pradesh (22) and Punjab (22) also showed lower fertility rates in their rural populations. The same survey also found high fertility rate among wage earners (35) and households with income below Rs 20,000 per annum (37). Not much variation in CBR (30–32) was observed among various size-class of landholding households. CBR was exceptionally high (45) among 'lower segment below poverty line group' and least (21) among 'upper segment above the poverty line' group. Muslims were found to have a very high (39) CBR compared to CBR 20 among Christians. SCs and STs both had CBR 35. Hindus reflected the national level average, CBR 32. Female literacy was also found to be closely related to their experienced birth rate. 'Non-literate households' gave the average CBR as 38 vis-à-vis 32 'both literate' households. A very unique observation was that when only the females in the households were literate, the CBR was lowest, 25. The NCAER survey also found an opposing trend in fertility with household income. Whereas CBR was observed to decrease with an increase in household income in many of the states, it *increased* with household income in Kerala and Gujarat. An indifferent behavior of CBR to change with household income was observed in most central Indian states.

Table 8.5

Percentage change in CBR between 1988–90 and 1998–2000 by residence and larger states, India (SRS data, 2003)

States	Total			Rural			Urban		
	1988–90	1998–2000	% change	1988–90	1998–2000	% change	1988–90	1998–2000	% change
1	2	3	4	5	6	7	8	9	10
1. Kerala	20.1	18.1	–10.0	19.9	18.1	–9.0	20.6	17.8	–13.4
2. Tamil Nadu	22.5	19.3	–14.2	22.9	19.8	–13.4	21.6	18.1	–16.3
3. West Bengal	27.9	20.9	–25.3	31.6	23.1	–26.9	18.7	14.5	–22.3
4. Maharashtra	28.5	21.5	–24.3	30.5	22.2	–27.3	24.7	20.5	–17.0
5. Andhra Pradesh	26.5	21.8	–17.9	26.8	22.2	–17.4	25.3	20.6	–18.4
6. Punjab	28.1	21.8	–22.4	28.7	22.9	–20.0	26.9	18.6	–30.9
7. Karnataka	28.2	22.1	–21.7	29.4	23.4	–20.5	25.0	19.2	–23.2
8. Himachal Pradesh	29.1	22.8	–21.6	29.7	23.3	–21.6	21.0	16.9	–19.6
9. Orissa	30.8	24.7	–19.8	31.4	25.3	–19.6	25.1	20.5	–18.4
10. Gujarat	29.3	25.4	–13.3	30.0	26.9	–10.2	27.7	22.0	–20.4
11. Assam	30.7	27.3	–11.0	31.3	28.2	–10.0	22.8	19.2	–15.6
12. Haryana	33.6	27.1	–19.4	34.9	28.1	–19.3	29.2	23.2	–20.3
13. Rajasthan	33.7	31.4	–6.9	34.8	32.8	–5.9	28.5	24.9	–12.7
14. Madhya Pradesh	36.5	31.1	–14.9	38.0	32.9	–13.5	30.3	23.4	–22.6
15. Bihar	34.8	31.5	–9.5	35.7	32.4	–9.1	27.5	24.6	–10.6
16. Uttar Pradesh	36.6	32.7	–10.7	38.0	33.8	–11.1	30.2	27.3	–9.7
INDIA	**30.8**	**26.1**	**–15.1**	**32.3**	**27.7**	**–14.3**	**25.4**	**20.9**	**–17.9**

Table 8.6

Crude birth rate by residence, India and larger states, 2000 (SRS data 2003)

State	Total	Rural	Urban	Rural-urban difference
1	2	3	4	5
1. Kerala	17.9	18.0	17.5	0.5
2. Tamil Nadu	19.3	20.0	18.1	1.9
3. West Bengal	20.7	23.0	14.1	8.9
4. Maharashtra	21.0	21.4	20.4	1.0
5. Andhra Pradesh	21.3	21.7	20.1	1.6
6. Punjab	21.6	22.7	18.6	4.1
7. Karnataka	22.0	23.3	19.1	4.2
8. Himachal Pradesh	22.1	22.5	16.9	5.6
9. Orissa	24.3	24.9	20.1	4.8

Cont'd…

Table 8.6 Cont'd...

1	*2*	*3*	*4*	*5*
10. Gujarat	25.2	26.8	21.9	4.9
11. Assam	26.9	27.9	18.6	9.3
12. Haryana	26.9	28.0	23.1	4.9
13. Rajasthan	31.4	32.8	25.1	7.7
14. Madhya Pradesh	31.4	33.4	23.5	9.9
15. Bihar	31.9	32.8	25.6	7.2
16. Uttar Pradesh	32.8	34.0	27.2	6.8
INDIA	**25.8**	**27.6**	**20.7**	**6.9**

Figure 8.2

Radar diagram of CBR of 16 larger states, India 2000

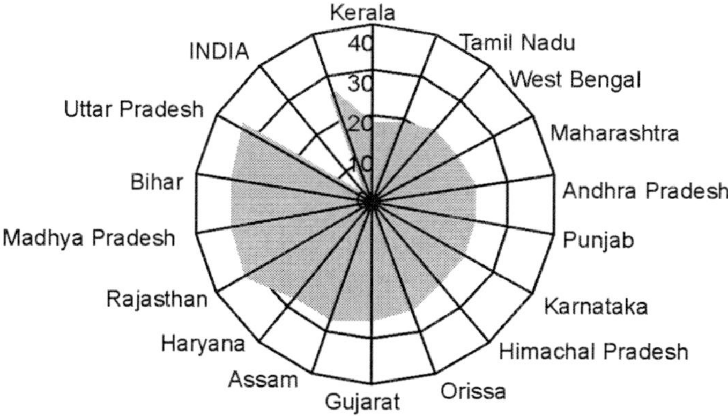

Vital rates based on Sample Registration Scheme by sectors for different states and UTs for 2001 have been presented in Appendix 8.1.

8.3 Age Specific Fertility Rates

CBR gives us only a first hand idea about the fertility situation prevailing in the entire population. The number in the numerator is the number of live births recorded in a given year; the denominator is the mid-year population size in the year – all ages and both sexes. In *age-specific fertility rate* ASFR, the entries in the numerator are the number of live births given by the mothers in a particular age group x and the denominator is the size of the mid-year female population of the same age group x, $i_x = 100B_x \, / \, ^f p_x$. ASFR is more meaningful for fertility analysis since the specific rates tell us which age group of females is showing changes in birth rates, which are relatively static. ASMFR is age-specific marital fertility rate, the denominator of which consists only the married women in the particular age group. From the age-specific birth rates (more specifically from ASMFRs), we can fairly accurately estimate the number of live births in the population – a vital component in population projection.

SRS data clearly indicate that birth rates slowly but steadily have been declining since the sixties (family planning movement got some momentum in this period). A comparison of 1978 data

Figure 8.3
CDRs of 16 larger states by residence, India 2000

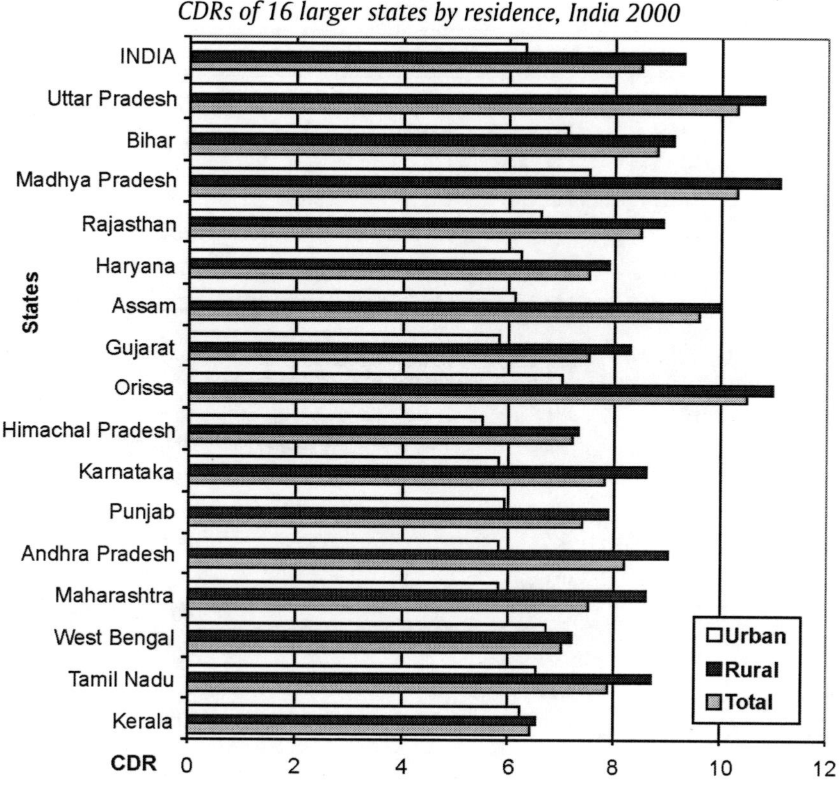

with that for 1972 (the time span includes the period of 'Emergency') clearly indicates that age specific fertility for all ages declined significantly, both in rural and urban areas. A part explanation for this decline is due to vigorous family planning campaign, leading almost to coercion, in 1970s prior to fall of the national government in 1977. Percentage of higher order birth rates also declined. When a comparison is made between 1978 data with that of 2000 (Table 8.8), it becomes evident that the pattern of age-specific fertility rates somewhat remained the same, but the intensity (the ordinate values) at different age groups changed. The changes are very large in 15–19 and beyond 30 year age groups both for rural and urban women.

The proportion of births among rural women in the age group 15–19 has been halved between 1978 and 2000; the same among urban women dropped to less than one-third (Table 8.9). This probably is due to larger increase in age at marriage in urban areas compared to that in rural areas. The first half of a girl's reproductive period (15–30 years) is still more important in terms of her contribution to population totals than the latter half, especially in tropical countries. 70–75 percent of all births are recorded in the age group 15–29 years. A large change has occurred among rural women in these 22 years – about 7 percent drop in fertility beyond the age 29 years. 20 to 29 years is the critical period in the life of an Indian woman when she remains most fertile. Women in this age group need to be targeted for birth planning. By the time a woman reaches 35, she almost has completed her fertility career. There is a steep rise in age specific birth rate between 15–24 and a sharp fall after 29. Table 8.10 shows ASFR by residence and educational level of women. The

Table 8.7
Age specific marital fertility rates, India and larger states, 2000 (SRS data)

States		*15–19*	*20–24*	*25–29*	*30–34*	*35–39*	*40–44*	*45–49*
1. Kerala		215.8	274.2	156.9	61.6	14.4	2.5	0.1
2. Tamil Nadu		291.4	288.9	153.5	55.6	16.7	2.4	0.3
3. West Bengal		276.8	257.5	146.1	69.1	27.3	13.3	6.0
4. Maharashtra		207.7	323.4	151.3	60.9	19.3	6.2	1.9
5. Andhra Pradesh		289.9	269.1	109.9	37.9	10.4	3.4	0.6
6. Punjab		259.9	377.1	205.2	64.5	21.0	3.5	1.4
7. Karnataka		290.4	313.2	165.3	60.2	22.5	8.1	2.1
8. Himachal Pradesh		314.5	338.5	185.6	44.9	18.2	5.5	0.0
9. Orissa		245.0	293.2	207.4	99.6	48.3	18.0	5.7
10. Gujarat		157.2	301.8	217.8	98.4	44.2	14.28	4.2
11. Assam		395.3	328.7	238.8	119.3	76.6	28.5	4.8
12. Haryana		242.9	355.7	192.3	81.3	30.2	17.1	4.7
13. Rajasthan		165.9	342.7	241.9	135.3	71.4	33.4	11.9
14. Madhya Pradesh		249.7	350.5	234.7	127.4	65.2	28.5	10.7
15. Bihar		210.2	303.4	269.0	164.1	111.4	53.2	20.2
16. Uttar Pradesh		203.1	358.9	273.7	193.3	130.3	57.8	23.1
INDIA	Total	232.4	315.7	205.0	107.2	57.0	24.0	9.0
	Rural	233.5	320.5	214.2	115.5	67.5	28.5	11.1
	Urban	225.5	299.2	179.7	82.7	30.1	11.6	3.6

Table 8.8
Age-specific fertility by residence, India 1978 & 2000

Age group	*15–19*	*20–24*	*25–29*	*30–34*	*35–39*	*40–44*	*45–49*
Rural (2000)	59.5	238.1	197.3	109.2	63.1	25.8	9.6
Rural (1978)	96.2	259.8	243.3	183.5	107.4	50.4	18.0
% change	–38.1	–8.4	–18.9	–40.5	–41.2	–48.8	–46.7
Urban (2000)	27.3	168.3	152.2	76.4	27.8	10.4	3.1
Urban (1978)	61.2	212.9	190.5	118.5	62.9	22.5	6.8
% change	–55.4	–20.9	–20.1	–35.5	–55.8	–53.8	–54.4

Source: Department of Family Welfare Yearbook, 1984–85; SRS Statistical report, 2003

Table 8.9
Cumulative proportions for the data in Table 8.8

Residence	*15–19*	*20–24*	*25–29*	*30–34*	*35–39*	*40–44*	*45–49*
Rural (1978)	16.2	41.2	63.7	80.5	91.8	97.6	100
Rural (2000)	8.5	42.4	70.4	86.0	95.0	98.6	100
Urban (1978)	21.5	51.9	74.2	87.7	95.8	98.9	100
Urban (2000)	5.9	42.0	74.7	91.1	97.1	99.3	100

cumulative data (Figure 8.5) indicate that rural population is about 20 years behind the urban population in fertility control. A true picture of real fertility performance is obtained from ASMFR.

Table 8.10

ASFR by level of education of women, India 2000 (SRS data)

Age-group	Education level of women								
	Illiterate	No formal education	Below primary	Primary	Middle	Class X	Class XII	Graduate and above	Total literates
1	2	3	4	5	6	7	8	9	10
					Total				
15–19	96.1	94.5	67.6	34.4	23.4	18.7	14.3	22.5	35.0
20–24	289.4	284.5	298.1	194.6	187.5	143.5	87.4	94.5	191.5
25–29	229.8	195.5	212.2	149.7	144.9	143.9	124.3	126.8	159.8
30–34	134.9	109.7	90.1	60.5	55.7	61.3	62.4	63.2	70.9
35–39	78.4	52.5	32.9	17.9	20.7	17.7	22.1	24.8	25.9
40–44	32.6	17.1	9.7	6.1	7.2	3.7	3.0	4.5	7.8
45–49	11.4	6.4	2.7	1.3	2.4	1.0	0.5	0.0	2.3
					Rural				
15–19	98.5	94.3	71.5	35.0	25.1	21.2	18.3	16.7	39.3
20–24	288.2	268.2	300.0	191.6	183.5	142.5	96.7	87.6	202.0
25–29	230.6	184.1	211.4	145.3	146.7	132.0	125.1	123.9	161.9
30–34	134.6	107.8	89.1	59.6	58.2	55.4	56.0	67.0	72.4
35–39	81.6	54.5	35.7	21.0	23.0	21.0	25.3	33.7	30.2
40–44	33.7	18.6	11.0	7.2	6.0	3.5	6.0	11.2	9.5
45–49	12.3	6.4	3.0	2.0	1.0	1.8	0.6	0.0	2.7
					Urban				
15–19	75.4	96.9	49.1	32.4	19.5	15.2	11.2	30.5	24.4
20–24	299.6	383.9	291.3	203.3	196.6	145.0	79.4	97.6	170.6
25–29	223.9	257.8	214.4	159.7	141.4	158.8	123.6	127.9	156.1
30–34	137.8	119.7	93.3	62.3	51.5	67.7	67.5	62.0	68.2
35–39	58.3	44.6	26.0	12.1	17.5	14.9	20.2	22.8	19.7
40–44	25.0	10.7	6.4	4.1	8.8	3.8	1.8	3.2	5.5
45–49	6.3	6.3	2.2	0.3	4.0	0.5	0.4	0.0	1.8

8.4 General Fertility Rate GFR

Besides CBR and ASFR, two other fertility indices are computed for a population or segments of it separately. Unlike in CBR in which the denominator consists of the entire mid-year population (M+F), General Fertility Rate GFR has mid-year female population in the age group (15–49) years

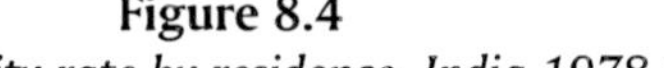

Figure 8.4

Age-specific fertility rate by residence, India 1978 & 2000

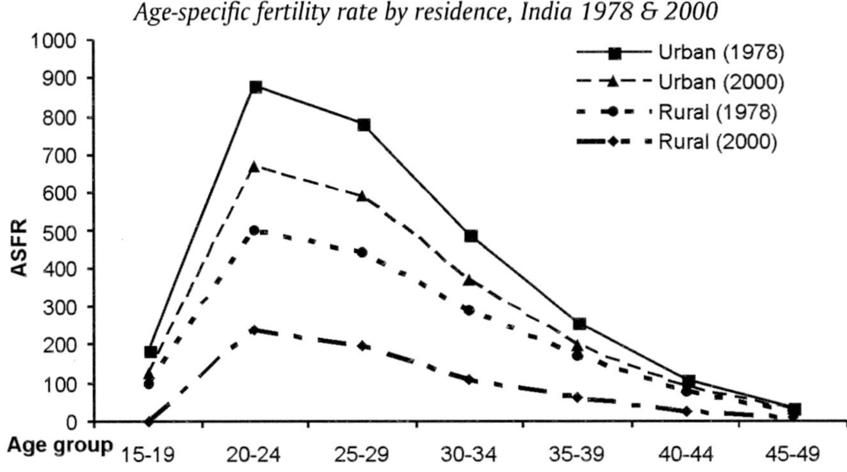

Figure 8.5

Cumulative ASFR for the data in Table 8.9

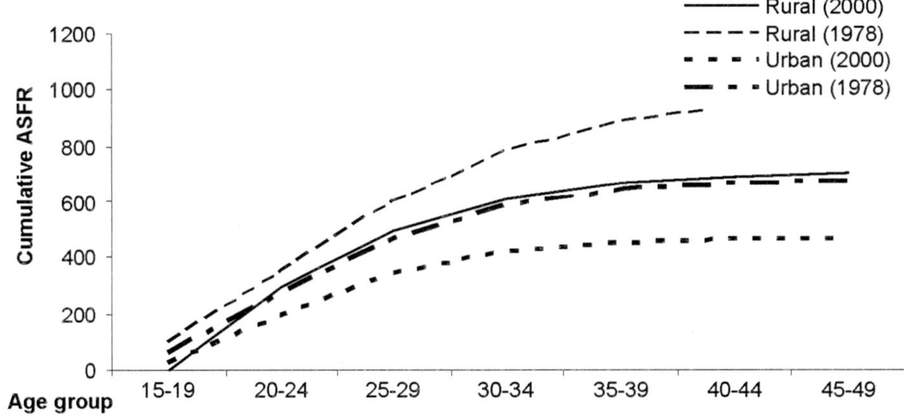

Figure 8.6

Age specific marital fertility, India 2000

Age group	15-19	20-24	25-29	30-34	35-39	40-44	45-49
Total	232.4	315.7	205	107.2	57	24	9
Rural	233.5	320.5	214.2	115.5	67.5	28.5	11.1
Urban	225.5	299.2	179.7	82.7	30.1	11.6	3.6

in the denominator. It is more refined than CBR and gives a better idea about the general fertility level in the population. GMFR has only the mid-year population of married girls (15–49) in the denominator. GFR and GMFR are presented in Table 8.13.

8.5 Total Fertility Rate TFR

ASFR, though the most important birth statistics for a population and for many demographic analyses, does not capture the general fertility situation prevailing in a population. Total Fertility Rate TFR has all the information contained in ASFR and at the same time it offers a general index of fertility (like CBR and GFR) for the entire childbearing women population. It is defined as the average number of babies born to a woman during her entire reproductive career (15–49 years), assuming that she would remain alive throughout her reproductive period and that she would produce babies at rates defined by ASFR exhibited in the population to which she belongs. It is defined as :

$$TFR = \sum_{15}^{49} ASFR, \text{ when single year age group is used, and}$$

$$TFR = 5 \times \sum_{15-19}^{44-49} ASFR, \text{ when a 5-year age interval is used.}$$

The multiplier 1,000 of ASFR is usually dropped while computing TFR. TFR and ASFR, as also Gross Reproduction Rate GRR are used extensively in population projections. TMFR gives TFR for the married women. TFR and TMFR for the Indian population, 2000 are given in the following table.

Table 8.11

Total Fertility Rate (TFR) by larger states and by residence, India 2000 (SRS data)

	States (1)		*Total (2)*	*Rural (3)*	*Urban (4)*	*Urban-Rural (5)*
1.	Kerala		1.9	1.9	1.8	–0.1
2.	Tamil Nadu		2.1	2.2	1.8	–0.4
3.	West Bengal		2.4	2.7	1.6	–1.1
4.	Maharashtra		2.5	2.6	2.2	–.0.4
5.	Andhra Pradesh		2.3	2.5	2.0	–0.5
6.	Punjab		2.4	2.6	2.1	–0.5
7.	Karnataka		2.4	2.6	2.0	–0.6
8.	Himachal Pradesh		2.3	2.3	1.8	–0.5
9.	Orissa		2.8	2.9	2.1	–0.8
10.	Gujarat		2.9	3.2	2.3	–0.7
11.	Assam		3.1	3.3	1.8	–1.5
12.	Haryana		3.2	3.4	2.6	–0.8
13.	Rajasthan		4.1	4.4	2.9	–1.5
14.	Madhya Pradesh		4.0	4.5	2.6	–1.9
15.	Bihar		4.5	4.7	3.4	–1.3
16.	Uttar Pradesh		4.7	5.0	3.5	–1.5
	INDIA	TFR	3.2	3.5	2.3	–1.2
		TMFR	4.8	5.0	4.2	–0.8

A change of almost similar nature and magnitude is observed both for GFR and TFR over the period for which the comparative statistics are obtained from SRS data. GFR, TFR and GRR (it is in a sense TFR for female births) by residence for India, 2000 is presented in Table 8.13.

Table 8.12

Percent change in GFR and TFR by residence between 1988–90 and 1998–2000

	Total			*Rural*			*Urban*		
	1988–90	*1998–00*	*% change*	*1988–90*	*1998–00*	*% change*	*1988–90*	*1998–00*	*% change*
GFR	127.1	104.2	–18.0	135.9	113.5	–16.7	99.2	77.7	–21.6
TFR	3.9	3.2	–18.2	4.2	3.5	–16.5	2.9	2.4	–18.7

Table 8.13

Some fertility indicators at a glance, India 2000

Indicators	*Total*	*Rural*	*Urban*
CBR	25.8	27.6	20.7
GFR	102.8	112.7	76.5
GMFR	139.2	148.8	111.1
TFR	3.2	3.5	2.3
TMFR	4.8	5.0	4.2
GRR	1.5	1.7	1.1

Source: SRS Statistical Report, 2003

Compared to the developed countries, the proportion of married women in the reproductive age group is much higher in the developing countries. About 10 percent of men and women in marriageable ages remain single for some reason or other. D. Ghosh in his book *Pressure of Population and Economic Efficiency in India* has shown that 80 percent of women in India in the age group 15–44 in 1931 were married. In the same time frame and in the same age group only about 50 percent of women were married in England and Welsh. 64 percent of all married women in India in 1931 were in the age group 15–30. The same in England and Welsh was only 33 percent. The demographers agree on the fact that the birth rate prevailing in a country depends largely upon what proportion of married women are there in the first half of the reproductive period.

With decline in mortality, the proportion of married women in the total women population increased fast between 1931 and 1961. In the decades thereafter, the proportion has come down considerably, especially in urban areas. The most significant reduction has occurred in ages between 10 and 24. That is, proportion of married women in the age group below 30 years has declined substantially and the proportion in 30 years and above age category has increased. Two reasons can be cited for this change: (1) there is a gradual upward revision in the age at marriage of girls, and (2) the average life expectancy of girls has increased considerably. In a survey conducted in 1978, it was observed that 43 and 44 percent of births in rural and urban India respectively came from those married women who were aged 25 years or less. Married women in the age category 30 years and more gave birth to only 33 percent of all babies born in rural area and 25 percent in urban area.

Table 8.14

Percentage distribution of females by age, marital status and residence, India (SRS data, 2003)

Never married			*Married*			*Widowed/Divorced/Separated*		
Total	***Rural***	***Urban***	***Total***	***Rural***	***Urban***	***Total***	***Rural***	***Urban***
				10+ age group				
30.0	29.1	32.5	59.7	60.5	57.4	10.3	10.4	10.1
				15+ age group				
17.6	15.9	22.3	70.3	71.8	66.1	12.1	12.3	11.6

TFR is the most preferred statistics in population projections all over the world. It captures all the information contained in ASFR of the population and also gives a close to real life picture of average number of children born to women who have just left the reproductive period. Replacement level of the population is achieved when the TFR in the population is 2.1. In India there are as many as 9 states and Union Territories that succeeded in bringing down TFR in their populations to 2.1 or below.

Table 8.15

Population profile of the states and union territories of India with TFR and some other statistics

State	*Population size (in million) as on 1 March 1999 $*	*Percent of total population*	*TFR 2000*	*IMR 2000*	*Contraceptive prevalence rate 1999*
1	*2*	*3*	*4*	*5*	*6*
INDIA	**981.3**		**3.2**	**68**	**44%**
A. TFR less than or equal to 2.1 (9 States/UTs, 11.4% of total population)					
Goa	1.5	0.2	1.0@	23**	27.1
Nagaland	1.6	0.2	1.5@	NA	7.8
Delhi*	13.4	1.4	1.6@	36**	28.8
Kerala	32.0	3.3	1.9	14	40.5
Pondicherry*	1.1	0.1	1.8@	21**	56.9
Andaman & Nicobar Islands*	0.4	0.04	1.9@	30**	39.9
Tamil Nadu	61.3	6.2	2.1	51	50.4
Chandigarh*	0.9	0.09	2.1@	32**	35.0
Mizoram	0.9	0.09	NA	23**	34.6
B. TFR > 2.1 but < 3 (13 States/UTs, 41.8% of total population)					
Manipur	2.21	0.2	2.4	25*	20.1
Daman & Diu*	0.1	0.01	2.5	51**	30.2
Andhra Pradesh	74.6	7.6	2.3	65	50.3
Himachal Pradesh	6.5	0.7	2.3	64	48.2

Cont'd...

Table 8.15 Cont'd...

1	*2*	*3*	*4*	*5*	*6*
Karnataka	51.4	5.2	2.4	57	55.4
West Bengal	78.0	7.9	2.4	51	32.9
Punjab	23.3	2.4	2.4	52	66.0
Sikkim	0.5	0.06	2.5	51**	21.9
Maharashtra	90.1	9.2	2.5	48	50.1
Arunachal Pradesh	1.2	0.1	2.8@	47**	14.0
Lakshadweep*	0.07	0.01	2.8@	37**	9.1
Orissa	35.5	3.6	2.8	95	39.0
Gujarat	47.6	4.8	2.9	62	54.5
C. TFR greater than or equal to 3 (10 States/UTs, 56.5% of total population)					
Assam	25.6	2.6	3.1	75	16.7
Haryana	19.5	2.0	3.2	69	49.7
Dadra & Nagar Haveli*	0.2	0.02	3.5@	61**	29.1
Tripura	3.6	0.3	3.9@	49**	25.2
Meghalaya	2.4	0.2	4.8@	52**	4.6
Madhya Pradesh	78.3	8.0	4.0	87	46.5
Rajasthan	52.6	5.4	4.1	79	36.4
Bihar	98.1	10.0	4.5	62	19.7
Uttar Pradesh	166.4	17.0	4.7	83	38.2
Jammu & Kashmir	9.7	1.0	NA	45*	15.0

@ Three year moving average TFR 1995–97
$ Population Projections by Technical Group on Population Projections, 1996
** Data refer to 1998
Source: Sample Registration System Statistical Report, 2003.

This profile really speaks how diverse the Indian population is in their birth control performances. Whereas some of the states/UTs have curtailed their birth rates so much so that their TFRs are well under the replacement level (Kerala, Tamil Nadu, Goa in the Southern region), there are several other states, mostly larger ones (BIMARU states alone account for about 40 percent of India's population), located in Northern and Central India, that are likely to take a few decades more even to bring down their TFR to the replacement level. High IMR and low contraceptive prevalence rate along with poor literacy rate among their people, more specifically among their female populations, seem to play a very important role in maintaining a higher level of TFR. The estimated urban TFR has been in replacement level in Kerala and Tamil Nadu (where the rural-urban differentials have virtually disappeared); the same in Andhra Pradesh, Karnataka, Maharashtra, Punjab, Orissa and West Bengal are very close to replacement level. In these states the rural TFR has also come down to around 3. NPP 2000 population projections are sure to miss the modest targets set for the country as a whole if the states/UTs mentioned in block C of Table 8.15 do not improve their track record in socio-economic indicators and mother and child health care fast. They will need much more investments not only in the provision of family planning services but in overall development and especially in the heath care for children and women in order to hasten the pace of fertility transition. Although the total fertility rate in India fell from 6.0 in the 1960s to 3.2 in 2000, it remains higher than that in most other Asian countries.

8.6 Nuptiality and Age at Marriage

There are ample evidences in epics and literature that in Vedic Age (2500 BC–1500 BC), the age at marriage of girls was substantially high, 16 years or more. They had enough freedom of movement, could educate them and actively take part in some occupation. They had the liberty to participate in all religious functions. From the Age of Brahmanas (1500 BC–500 BC), the social status of women started to fall. Though allowed education within the confines of parental house, their work participation was discouraged. Even with this change, their age at marriage did not change much. In the Age of Sutras and Epics (500 BC–500 AD) their status really declined. Marriage between Aryans and non-Aryans became inevitable. The non-Aryan girls without the knowledge of Sanskrit (the language of gods and goddesses), lost the opportunity of participating in religious activities and rites. They gradually came to be regarded as fit only for becoming mother and looking after the domestic affairs. They ultimately were denied any form of formal or informal education.

In Vedic Age and the Age of Brahmanas, sacred initiation (*upanayana*) at the age of 9 or 10, both for boys and girls in the higher section of society was a common practice. Girls, like boys, had to go through celibate life (*brahmacharya*) and through a regular course of education. Some even attained distinction in the realm of theology and philosophy and a significant number of women pursued teaching career. By and large, monogamy was the rule. Altekar in his book *Position of Women in Hindu Civilization* pointed out that since men were engrossed in the work of conquest and consolidation, women were allowed greater freedom in most walks of life and they enjoyed better social status. In the Age of Sutras and Epics, the age of sacred initiation came to be regarded as the right age for giving the girls in marriage. They lost all social freedom. No one thought it necessary that opinion of these illiterate and uneducated girls was necessary in the settlement of their marriages. Marriage now became irrevocable as far as wife was concerned even if her husband was insane or debauched. The child-marriage led to huge maternal mortality, especially when they were in their early adolescence. Around 500 AD widow remarriage took the form of a prohibition. Childless widow were forced to seek '*mukti*' (the divine salvation) by becoming *satee* (burning alive on the pyre of her late husband). By 700 AD, *Satee* became a part of rituals in Hindu society.

Even when Hindu society was undergoing through periods of turmoil and transition, Buddhism had kept up the tradition of giving a place of honor to women. Women were eligible for admission to the religious order – *Bhikshuni Sangha*. Many achieved distinction as teachers and scholars. They enjoyed prestige and respect in society. They even traveled abroad to preach Buddhism and were accepted as leaders of the order. The nunneries gave them the highest education and religious training.

At around 700 AD, foreign invasion, especially by Muslims, changed the then social scenario altogether. To save the Hindu girls from becoming easy pray to these invaders, the cultured Hindus imitated some of the customs and manners of the Muslims, and their girls were asked to follow 'purdah' system (custom of keeping the whole body including the face covered by a robe). Many cultured families were ruined by Turkish invaders and Muslim conquest. This dwindled down further the percentage of girls who could read and write. At the beginning of the British rule, female education had practically disappeared from the land of a great culture and Epic that gifted so many women luminaries to the mankind.

The British rulers enacted laws prohibiting killing of child (1802), abolishing *satee* (1829) and Hindu Marriage Act (1856) to restore some lost ground to women. But even after passing these laws, the position of Indian women did not show signs of much improvement. They still were thought as instruments for procreation. Hindus being the majority in the population, the other religious groups also succumbed more or less to the traditions of the mainstream Indians. Early marriage of girls, especially in villages and in backward communities, still continues. 13.8 percent of girls (16% in rural and 6.1% in urban area) still marry before the stipulated minimum age at marriage of 18 years.

Table 8.16

Percentage distribution of females by age at effective marriage and by residence, India (SRS data, 2003)

Total			*Rural*			*Urban*		
<18	*18–20*	*21+*	*<18*	*18–20*	*21+*	*<18*	*18–20*	*21+*
13.8	52.8	32.9	16.0	56.0	28.0	6.1	41.7	57.2

Unlike in Europe and other developed regions and countries, India could not develop a system of marriage registration even though successful implementation of the marriage laws of the land demands that every marriage is formally registered. Though the educated citizens generally have no objection to imposition of such a law, the political parties lack the will to do so for fear of loosing their vote banks in rural area and in the backward and minority communities. Most states as yet have not evolved fully functional administrative machinery (Goa is an exception) to ensure that no marriage goes unregistered. Registered marriages are still very few. The Apex Court in India has time and again asked all states to make marriage registration mandatory with proper legislation. The latest Supreme Court verdict on the issue came on 24 August, 2007. The legal fraternity believes that everything depends on how soon the Apex Court's ruling is implemented. Even many in the minority committee see the Apex Court's verdict as a step in right direction. They are fully aware that marriage under Islamic law is not valid for getting visa for a bride to go to any western country. The Muslim scholars did not hesitate to advocate all social marriages registered in this secular land of democracy. They even went on to say that there was no need to fear anything as the personal laws are not being interfered with. They have no doubt in their mind that such a legislation (and a commitment on the part of the government to implement the law) will help curb child marriages, help women who are deserted by their husbands, as well as in inheritance.

For obtaining an idea about changes in the age at marriage, we have to depend either on the Census data or data from sample surveys (NSSO or SRS) or on some indirect estimation. Prof. S.N. Agarwala calculated age at marriage of men and women as also their probability of remaining unmarried at various ages from the age distribution of the Census population and other related social characteristics. Table 8.17 is a partial reproduction of a) probability of remaining unmarried at selected age groups, and b) the average age at marriage of the synthetic cohort, for men and women.

Table 8.17

Probability of remaining unmarried at different ages and average age at marriage of males and females of a synthetic cohort

Age	*1901*	*1911*	*1921*	*1931*	*1941*	*1951*	*1961*
			Probability of women remaining unmarried				
5–9	0.889	0.890	0.907	0.858	0.919	0.946	0.947
10–14	0.543	0.555	0.603	0.487	0.763	0.827	.0804
15–19	0.158	0.163	0.192	0.157	0.270	0.289	.0290
20–24	0.046	0.045	0.056	0.034	0.063	0.071	.0057
25–29	0.030	0.023	0.029	0.015	0.023	0.048	.0018
30–34	0.028	0.018	0.024	0.008	0.014	0.031	.0009
35–39	0.028	0.013	0.020	0.007	0.012	0.031	.0003
Average age at marriage	12.77	13.07	13.53	12.52	14.94	15.38	15.43
			Probability of men remaining unmarried				
10–14	0.854	0.866	0.879	0.792	0.854	0.853	0.931
15–19	0.639	0.666	0.690	0.560	0.688	0.660	0.761
20–24	0.396	0.384	0.408	0.288	0.381	0.367	0.478
25–29	0.188	0.188	0.200	0.120	0.196	0.162	0.204
30–34	0.122	0.098	0.105	0.067	0.093	0.077	0.100
35–39	0.073	0.061	0.069	0.034	0.069	0.054	0.057
40–44	0.070	0.050	0.059	0.026	0.049	0.038	0.052
45–49	0.057	0.038	0.048	0.023	0.049	0.038	0.043
50–54	0.057	0.036	0.045	0.021	0.040	0:032	0.034
Average age at marriage	20.01	20.41	20/74	18.44	30.30	19.93	21.76

Source: S.N. Agarwala: *India's Population Problems*. ND, Tata McGraw Hill, 1972.

Although the age at marriage of girls gradually improved between 1901 and 1921, there was a surprise drop of the same between 1921 and 1931. One obvious reason was the 1917–18 influenza epidemics – the principal victims of which were children and pregnant women. There was a shortfall of eligible men and women for marriage in this decade. This shortfall was partially compensated by giving boys and girls to marriage early. But the more important reason according to Agarwala and many other demographers was the Child Marriage Restrain Act, 1929, popularly known as Sarda Act. Harbilas Sarda proposed this legislative step to restrain child marriage in India. Though the Act was passed in September 1929, it came into effect only from next April. The minimum age at marriage (MAM) of females was fixed at 14 years and that for males, 18 years. This six months gap between enactment and implementation of the Act prompted a spate of child marriage all over the country. The Sarda Act was reviewed in 1949 and MAM was raised to 15 and 21 years respectively for females and males. MAM for girls has again been revised to 18 years in 1976. There is a proposal that it be further advanced to 21 years for females and 25 years for males.

Table 8.18

Median and mean age at marriage of females, India 1901–2001

Census year	1901	1911	1921	1931	1941	1951	1961	1971	1981	1991	2001
Median age of females	21.53	21.42	21.13	20.63	20.86	20.26	19.39	18.63	19.57	20.50	21.54
Mean age at marriage	12.77	13.07	13.53	12.52	14.94	15.38	15.43	17.16	18.32	19.12	19.80

Table 8.19

Mean age at effective marriage of females by their residence, India, (SRS Data, 2003)

Total				***Rural***				***Urban***			
<18	***18–20***	***21+***	***All ages***	***<18***	***18–20***	***21+***	***All ages***	***<18***	***18–20***	***21+***	***All ages***
16.2	19.0	23.1	19.8	16.2	18.9	23.3	19.4	16.2	19.1	23.9	21.1

There has been a large drop in married females in the lower age groups, especially in 15–19 and 20–24 since 1961. At the younger age group of 15–19, fertility decline mainly reflects a rise in the age at marriage of girls, which increased from around 17 years in 1971 to around 20 years in 2001. Proportion of married girls in higher age groups, 30–49, has increased significantly. Marriage rate among the marriageable women too has dropped.

Figure 8.7

Median age of female population and their mean age at marriage, India 1901–2001

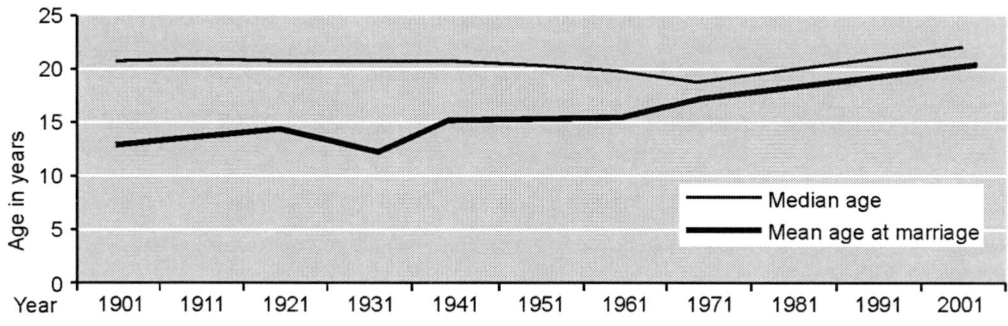

Figure 8.8

Median age for male and female population, India 1901–2001

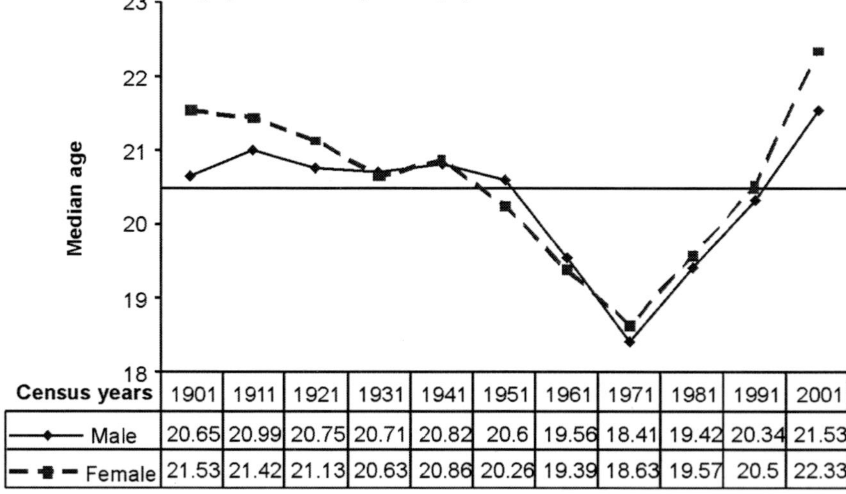

Table 8.20
Percentage of currently married females to all females for different age-groups over the years in India

Year	Age Group						
	15–19	20–24	25–29	30–34	35–44	45–49	15–49
1	2	3	4	5	6	7	8
1961	69.57	91.76	94.17	91.43	82.56	69.73	84.42
1971	55.41	88.83	94.95	94.00	88.07	78.03	83.40
1981a	43.44	84.46	94.35	94.86	90.76	83.15	80.74
1991b	35.28	81.81	93.97	95.14	92.75	87.56	80.18

a. Excludes Assam.
b. Excludes Jammu & Kashmir
Source: Office of the Registrar General, India.

Table 8.21
Mean age at fertility, India 1980 & 2000

	Total	Rural	Urban
1980	27.4	27.5	27
2000	28.2	28.3	27.8

Differences in the pattern of child bearing can also be measured in terms of the *mean age at fertility*. This is viewed as the age pattern a synthetic cohort of women follows assuming that they will go through similar fertility experiences through their reproductive period. Table 8.21 below shows the change of mean age at fertility between 1980 and 2000.

Table 8.22
Fertility rates by background characteristics

Background characteristics	Total Fertility Rate		Mean number of children ever born to ever married women aged 40–49 years	
	1992–93a	1998–99a	1992–93	1998–99
Residence				
Rural	3.67	3.07	5.13	4.73
Urban	2.70	2.27	4.16	3.78
Education				
Illiterate	4.03	3.47	5.26	4.98
Literate < middle school complete	3.01	2.64	4.50	4.06
Middle school complete	2.49	2.26	3.71	3.41
High School complete +	2.15	1.99	2.80	2.66
Caste/Tribe				
Scheduled Caste	3.92	3.15	5.40	4.85
Scheduled Tribe	3.55	3.06	4.81	4.74
Other Backward class		2.83		4.43
Other	3.30	2.66	4.76	4.20
Total	**3.39**	**2.85**	**4.84**	**4.45**

a. Rate for women aged 15–49 years.
Note: Total fertility rate for the three years preceding the Survey, and mean number of children by selected background characteristics
Source: National Family Health Survey; International Institute of Population Sciences.

The percentage of females who got effectively married before reaching 18 years of age is 13.8 at the national level and varies from a low of 1 percent (Himachal Pradesh and Punjab) to as high as 26.5 percent in Madhya Pradesh and 27.5 percent in Andhra Pradesh. The last two states have 30.8 and 31.6 percent rural women married before 18 years respectively. There are only three larger states viz. Andhra Pradesh, Bihar and Madhya Pradesh where MAM is still below 19 years. Kerala tops the states with 22.2 years as the mean age at marriage of women where 69.7 percent of women marry beyond 21 years. The average age of mothers giving birth to a baby in the year 1980 was 27.4 years (Table 8.21). It has increased to 28.2 years in 2000.

Rural-urban divide in fertility is still very strong. National Family Health Surveys (NFHS 1 & 2) clearly indicate that education of married women is key to their ultimate fertility behavior. Caste equation still plays a dominant role in fertility differentials.

8.7 Birth Order

SRS has been collecting information on order of birth and interval between current and previous live births since 1990. Not only is the number of children, spacing between successive children is important for health care both for the mother and the child.

The report of the Survey on Levels, Trends and Differentials in Fertility, conducted by RGI, 1979 showed that 5 or more live births constituted 33.24 percent of all births in 1972 in rural India, 29.54 percent in urban areas. The same came down to 25.05 and 20.82 respectively in rural and urban India in 1978. The first and second birth together accounted for 37.29 and 39.82 percent of rural and urban births respectively in 1972. The same went up to 39.82 and 49.08 percent respectively in 1978. The excesses during Emergency could have played some role in curtailing higher order births. The momentum gained in attaining small family norm still continues.

Table 8.23

Proportion of live births by birth order, India 1972, 1978 and 2000

Birth order	*Rural*		*Urban*		*Total (est)*		*Rural*	*Urban*	*Total*
	1972	*1978*	*1972*	*1978*	*1972*	*1978*	*2000*	*2000*	*2000*
1	19.85	23.48	21.60	25.75	20.26	24.01	32.1	38.4	33.4
2	17.44	20.63	18.22	23.33	17.62	21.26	26.3	29.6	27.0
3	15.70	17.49	16.19	17.88	15.81	17.58	17.9	15.9	17.5
4	13.77	13.38	14.45	12.22	13.93	13.11			
4 and above	**47.01**	**38.43**	**43.99**	**33.04**	**46.31**	**37.17**	**23.7**	**16.1**	**22.2**
5	11.24	9.69	9.52	7.93	10.84	9.28			
6 +	22.00	15.36	20.02	12.89	21.54	14.78			

Curbing of higher order births and consequent increase in the proportion of lower order births are important indicators for slowing down the population growth rate. The 2000 SRS data show that 4th and higher order births have come down by 52 percent in the last 28 years. There is about 13 percent increase in the proportion of 1st order birth since 1972. In 2000, 1st and 2nd order births together had a share of more than 60 percent of all births compared to a little over 37 percent in 1972. There is considerable variation in the first and second order births between the larger states. Uttar Pradesh had the lowest first order birth, 26.3 percent as against 47.8 percent in Kerala. Kerala had only 4.9 percent of 4th or higher order births, which in UP was still 33.9 percent. The first and the second order birth together shared 84.5 percent of all births in Kerala. The BIMARU states' share of first and second order birth varied from a low of 48 to a high of a little over 55 percent only.

Table 8.24

Percentage distribution of order of live births, India and larger states (SRS data 2000)

States	*Birth order*			
	First	*Second*	*Third*	*Fourth and above*
1	*2*	*3*	*4*	*5*
1. Kerala	47.8	36.7	10.6	4.9
2. Tamil Nadu	42.6	35.5	14.9	7.0
3. West Bengal	39.4	31.0	14.8	14.8
4. Maharashtra	36.6	30.8	18.0	14.6
5. Andhra Pradesh	47.6	34.4	12.9	5.2
6. Punjab	38.5	34.0	16.9	10.6
7. Karnataka	41.4	31.6	15.2	11.7
8. Himachal Pradesh	44.6	33.3	14.6	7.5
9. Orissa	33.4	27.6	19.4	19.6
10. Gujarat	37.0	29.2	18.1	15.8
11. Assam	35.1	26.0	15.2	23.7
12. Haryana	34.8	29.7	17.4	18.1
13. Rajasthan	30.7	25.5	19.0	24.9
14. Madhya Pradesh	29.8	25.8	20.1	24.3
15. Bihar	27.3	22.0	19.1	31.6
16. Uttar Pradesh	26.3	21.6	18.1	33.9
INDIA	**33.4**	**27.0**	**17.5**	**22.2**

It will not be out of context if we refer to a small study conducted by PG students of the Department of Sociology, Kalyani University, West Bengal on the birth statistics for the years between 1990 and 1997 obtained from Kalyani Municipal records. The study was based on the records for over 44,000 births registered with the Municipality in the years stated above with an average of over 7,300 birth records per annum. Though a small municipality, there are a few large hospitals within the municipal jurisdiction that caters health services to many adjoining villages and towns. The following Tables speak how some of the fertility indicators have changed even within a short span of 8 years.

Table 8.25
Age distribution of mothers, 1990–97 (municipal data)

			Kalyani Municipality			
Age	***1990***	***1991***	***1992***	***1995***	***1996***	***1997***
<18	10.64	10.07	10.20	8.77	9.04	9.34
22	40.39	39.21	39.09	40.85	40.66	41.36
26	30.67	31.1	28.96	30.47	30.55	29.35
30	13.65	14.01	14.95	14.55	14.25	14.54
<30	95.35	94.39	93.21	94.64	94.50	94.59
34	2.53	2.64	4.37	3.04	2.91	3.40
38	1.92	2.43	2.11	2.10	2.30	1.76
44	0.20	0.55	0.27	0.21	0.25	0.15
>44		0.08	0.04	0.01		0.02
N	7104	7607	7350	7189	7072	7840
$\overline{x}$	22.39	23.12	23.16	22.56	22.59	23.1
M/F among babies born to these mothers	107.8	108.0	110.7	104.6	108.4	107.3

Table 8.26
Proportion of live births by birth order, 1990–97 (municipal data)

Birth order			*Kalyani Municipality*			
	1990	***1991***	***1992***	***1995***	***1996***	***1997***
1st	57.56	53.27	57.87	61.44	54.63	63.25
2nd	26.28	33.94	27.88	27.40	34.14	27.64
1st +2nd	83.84	87.21	85.75	88.84	88.77	90.89
3rd	10.96	8.53	11.65	8.39	7.40	7.16
4th	3.51	2.49	2.92	2.16	2.38	1.34
<= 4th	98.31	98.23	99.72	99.39	99.10	99.39
5th	1.20	0.97	0.18	0.51	0.59	0.46
6th +	0.34	0.36	0.008	0.07	0.28	0.13

Although the municipal data are in no way comparable to the national level data, both national level data and the municipal data agree on some major points:

- There are both direct and indirect evidences that marriage of girls at an age less than 18 years have progressively been curtailed.
- Childbirth at both the ends of the reproductive period have been reduced, more so at the higher end.
- Completed fertility both at lower and upper end of the reproductive period is coming down.

- Age-specific fertility reaches its zenith somewhere between ages 20 and 24, both in rural and urban areas and continues at a high level till about 30 years. Thereafter the fertility falls sharply. A very nominal proportion of births remain after a woman attends 35 years.
- Higher order births have substantially been curtailed in the last two decades. The first two births account for over 60 percent of all births at the national level and more than 70 percent in urban areas. In the selected municipal area it is well over 90 percent.
- The mean age at effective marriage of females is on the rise. But beyond a point this may regress to a more satisfying level. Mean age fertility has marginally increased in the last 20 years.

8.7.1 Birth Spacing

From the viewpoint of health care of mother and her children, birth spacing is of vital importance. The distribution of second and higher order births by interval between the current and the previous live birth is shown in Table 8.27. At the national level, less than 1 percent of birth occurs within one year from the previous live birth. There is considerable variation between the states. Whereas 3.1 percent of birth occur within one year of the previous live birth in Himachal Pradesh, in Andhra Pradesh, Assam and Kerala this proportion is only 0.3. Kerala, West Bengal and Assam show 36 or more months gap between two successive live births on 53 or more percent occasions.

Table 8.27

Percentage distribution of interval between 2nd and higher births, India and larger states 2000 (SRS data)

	States	*Interval between current and previous birth (months)*			
		10–12	*12–24*	*24–36*	*36 +*
1.	Kerala	0.3	17.2	27.9	54.6
2.	Tamil Nadu	0.4	14.9	35.4	49.3
3.	West Bengal	0.5	13.0	33.5	53.1
4.	Maharashtra	0.8	26.6	37.4	35.2
5.	Andhra Pradesh	0.3	19.0	35.2	45.5
6.	Punjab	1.5	24.6	32.0	41.0
7.	Karnataka	1.0	35.2	34.0	29.8
8.	Himachal Pradesh	3.1	44.1	29.0	23.9
9.	Orissa	1.3	25.6	34.8	38.2
10.	Gujarat	1.1	34.7	29.2	34.9
11.	Assam	0.3	15.1	31.6	53.0
12.	Haryana	1.5	40.9	32.3	25.3
13.	Rajasthan	1.0	16.0	36.7	46.4
14.	Madhya Pradesh	0.9	21.5	37.4	40.3
15.	Bihar	0.7	26.1	31.6	41.7
16.	Uttar Pradesh	1.0	24.7	33.8	40.4
	INDIA	**0.8**	**23.1**	**34.1**	**42.1**

8.7.2 Medical Attention at Delivery

Health and education, more generally the social sector, have remained largely neglected in India. Political parties coming into power, either at the center or in states make huge commitment in their election manifesto and campaign that they would pay utmost attention to improving the social sector if they were put in to power. Whereas most of the developed countries spend over 5 percent of GDP as public expenditure on health and another 2 percent or so by private parties, public expenditure on health in India still remains below 1 percent of GDP. India has only about 50 doctors for every 100,000 people, which in the developed countries is well over 250; even the world average is around 125. It is therefore no wonder that a large majority of Indian mothers are denied institutional and specialist care for the birth of their babies. The rural–urban difference in institutional care is appalling. On the national level only about 25 percent of births happen under institutional care and another 29 percent under the care of doctors, nurses or trained midwives. Traditional birth attendants (*Dai*) still are responsible for around 46 percent of all births in the country. Only 17.5 percent of rural women receive institutional attention for their pregnancies; doctors, nurses and trained midwives attend another 28 percent. Even in urban areas more than 11 percent of all births take place under traditional attendants. The type of attention the Indian women receive in their pregnancy in the bigger states is shown below.

Table 8.28

Type of medical attention received (percentage) during child birth, India and larger states, 2000 (SRS data)

States	*Institutional*			*Doctor, nurse or trained midwife*			*Traditional birth attendants*			*Relatives or others*		
	T	*R*	*U*	*T*	*R*	*U*	*T*	*R*	*U*	*T*	*R*	*U*
Kerala	97.1	96.6	98.8	1.8	2.3	0.4	1.0	1.1	0.7	0.3	0.3	0.2
Tamil Nadu	64.8	52.5	92.7	21.7	28.2	7.0	7.8	11.0	0.6	6.1	8.7	0.2
West Bengal	35.8	27.2	76.1	14.2	12.9	20.0	50.0	60.0	3.3	0.7	0.7	1.0
Maharashtra	48.9	30.4	80.3	20.8	21.4	19.7	28.9	45.5	0.7	2.3	3.5	0.2
A. Pradesh	43.2	31.5	82.0	27.9	32.9	11.3	27.5	34.0	5.8	1.9	2.0	1.4
Punjab	13.1	13.0	13.5	86.2	86.1	86.5	1.2	1.3	0.6	2.0	2.4	0.2
Karnataka	49.2	38.2	80.5	27.0	31.0	15.9	13.6	17.2	3.2	11.4	15.1	0.7
H. Pradesh	24.5	22.5	57.0	26.8	25.9	41.9	47.9	50.8	0.9	1.1	1.1	0.7
Orissa	14.3	11.5	40.2	24.3	22.9	37.4	28.3	30.0	12.5	33.9	36.3	10.7
Gujarat	36.4	22.0	74.5	38.7	45.6	20.3	21.3	28.7	1.7	4.1	4.3	3.7
Assam	21.2	18.8	53.0	16.3	15.4	28.5	47.2	49.5	16.0	15.5	16.5	3.0
Haryana	25.1	20.5	45.3	68.1	71.1	54.5	6.7	8.0	0.7	0.6	0.6	0.4
Rajasthan	8.4	5.0	29.3	26.4	24.1	40.8	53.3	68.9	29.0	2.3	2.4	1.2
M. Pradesh	16.5	9.0	58.1	22.5	21.7	26.6	58.5	66.7	13.0	3.1	3.2	2.7
Bihar	15.9	14.2	31.8	19.8	17.5	42.0	62.6	66.6	24.4	1.9	1.9	2.1
U. Pradesh	8.4	6.3	20.4	42.4	38.4	66.2	49.8	55.9	13.8	0.3	0.2	0.4
INDIA	**25.2**	**17.5**	**55.3**	**29.0**	**27.7**	**34.1**	**42.6**	**50.9**	**10.0**	**3.9**	**4.5**	**1.1**

All the BIMARU states have poor track record of health care of pregnant women even in urban areas. Kerala has a near 100 percent of institutional care for pregnant women irrespective of their rural-urban origin.

8.8 Fertility Differentials

Marriage and age at marriage are two fundamental determinants that regulate birth rate, both at national and individual level in most orthodox societies since sex outside marriage is still a taboo in such societies. Their impacts are not so prominent in Western countries. Both marriage and age at marriage are organically related to many social, economic and cultural factors.

8.8.1 Urban-Rural Residence

For developing countries, *urban-rural fertility differential* still continues the major differential in the national and state scenario. In the more developed countries, urbanization has progressed fast making such a differential rather redundant. We have already seen how age at marriage, age specific fertility rate and other issues relating to birth are distinctly different for people living in rural and urban areas.

There are also considerable differences between larger cities and smaller towns in birth rates. The fast growth of population and increase in the density of population in metropolitan cities like Delhi, Bombay, and Kolkata are often more due to migration than due to natural increases. There is substantial difference between different regions as well. The Southern states are generally ahead in

Figure 8.9

Birth rates (CBR) for rural and urban areas for 16 larger states of India, 2000

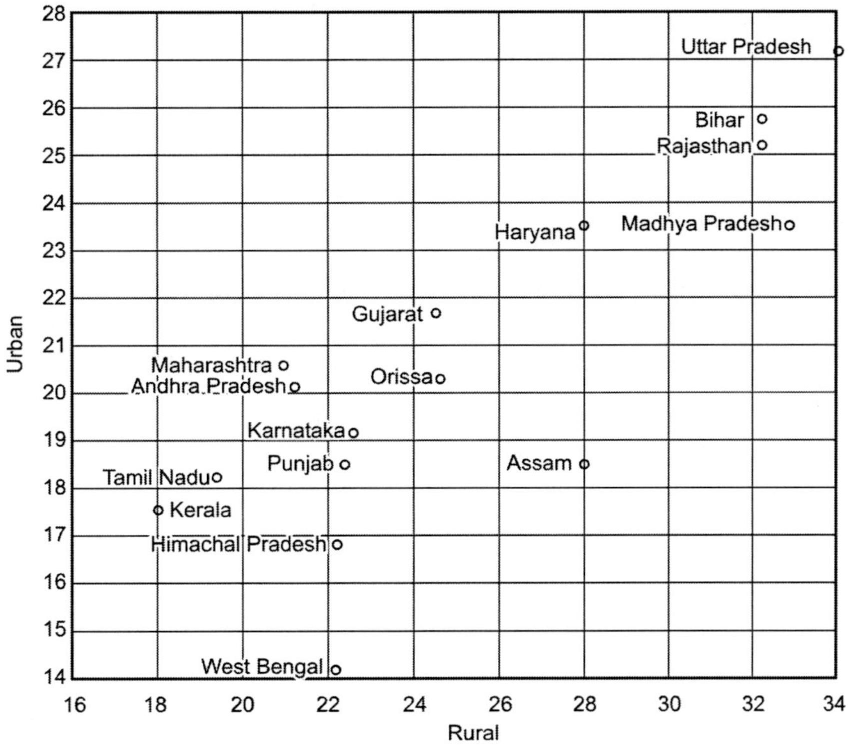

most birth indicators compared to other regions. Table 8.5 shows current attainments by different states in India in CBR as also the differences in CBR between urban and rural populations. The changes in CBR between 1988–90 and 1998–2000, presented in Table 8.4, also clearly indicate that a non-reversible trend of change in birth rate has already set in. It is likely to be strengthened further in the next few years. The rural women are behind urban women by 15–20 years in the attained fertility level of the latter.

There are some social and economic issues behind these rural-urban or regional differences. *Couple Fertility* (1955, NSS report No.7) study by Dasgupta et al. and the UN and Government of India sponsored *Mysore Population Study* (1961) in the fifties of the last century are considered hallmarks in the discourse of population analysis in India. These studies had set a few guidelines for our population planning exercises and in sample surveys conducted by NSSO and other official and non-governmental organizations for ascertaining the changing demographic profile from time to time. These studies highlighted the role religion, education, occupation, residence, age at marriage, etc. have on fertility pattern in Indian society. Traditional joint/extended family system has largely been disintegrated as India gradually moved away from agricultural to industrial economy as also for enforcement of Land Ceiling Act. The modern occupations demand better education and occupational training, option for jobs that push individuals away from one's familiar social milieu and remain prepared all the time to move to distance places at the shortest notice. A new family-culture is emerging that spun around the realization of the necessity for a small family. Childcare in a traditional joint family came under 'corporate' management. In the nuclear family this has totally been transferred to parents. Parents in a nuclear family often have no other option but to hire expertise from the market and pass some aspects of childcare to them. E.D. Driver and many others have shown that birth rate in a nuclear family is significantly smaller than that in a traditional joint family.

The impact of social and economic factors on birth is most often indirect. They have direct influence on marriage decisions and also the time for marriage. In societies that respect traditions and conventions, marriage and age at marriage play very important roles in birth regulations. S.N. Agarwala had shown that if the age at marriage of girls were increased by one year from the present minimum, that is, if married women did not give live birth before attaining age 20 years, 40 percent of births in the age group <25 years could be curtailed. C.R. Malakar, however, came to a different conclusion from his study. There could be only 11 percent reduction of birth if MAM for girls was revised to 19 years. Assuming that the age-specific fertility remained unchanged, the birth rate of women below 25 years could be reduced by 25 percent only by raising their marriage age to 21 years. Ashok Mitra also held the view that significant cut in birth could not be achieved by keeping the MAM of girls at 18 years. He recommended that in view of the health of the mother and the baby, MAM of girls needed to be raised to 22 years. By making 22 years the age at marriage, a woman is most likely to give birth to a baby when she is 24 or so. That would not only reduce the effective reproductive period, a significant proportion of the 'high fertility years' of Indian women (20–30 years) would be shortened. There are other demographers like Caseen who are not as optimistic as Agarwala, Malakar and Mitra were. By increasing the age specific fertility in the years remaining before attaining 30 years, the would-be mothers could make all calculations vulnerable. However, SRS and other survey data confirm that birth rate has fallen with the increase in the average age at marriage of girls. SRS since 1990 has been collecting information on the number of females who got effectively married during reference period of 'six months of each half-yearly survey'. Based on the information on females who got effectively married during the past one year, SRS is currently computing mean age at effective marriage for females.

Kinsley Davis has shown that before partition of India, there was hardly any difference between different religious communities in the average fertility level their women achieved. However, both Couple Fertility and Mysore Population Study gave evidence to the fact that religious faith of a person had something to do with her achieved fertility. In both the studies it was observed that the Muslims out-paced the Hindus and the Hindus out-spaced the Christians in this number game. Rele and Kanitkar however came to the conclusion from the analysis of data related to birth that if age at marriage and educational level attained by these married girls are kept at a controlled level (that is, if their effects are statistically eliminated) then the differences observed in average fertility of these various groups would disappear. That is, the ethnic groups that encourage education of girls also persuade people to give their daughters to marriage at a higher age

8.8.2 Education

Demographers unequivocally agree that education is the king pin for birth planning and control. A lot of survey has been carried out in the last 60 years, both in India and outside to understand the role education, especially women education, plays in controlling fertility. The Survey Reports on Levels, Trends and Differentials in Fertility (RGI, 1979) shows considerable differences in fertility by level of education of women.

Table 8.29

Social characteristics of female population and some fertility indicators, India 1978

	Residence	*GFR*	*GMFR*	*TFR*	*TMFR*	*GRR*
1	*2*	*3*	*4*	*5*	*6*	*7*
		Education level				
Illiterate	Rural	140.4	167.7	4.74	5.48	
	Urban	117.2	144.5	4.00	4.93	
Literate but below primary	Rural	122.3	175.9	3.85	4.98	
	Urban	106.7	139.1	3.27	4.96	
Primary and above but below matric	Rural	99.2	198.0	3.61	4.90	
	Urban	84.6	146.0	2.61	4.23	
Matric and above	Rural	81.3	186.4	2.48	4.67	
	Urban	75.4	144.1	1.88	4.01	
All literates	Rural	111.1	182.7	3.56	4.96	
	Urban	88.9	142.8	2.58	4.27	
		Occupational status				
All workers	Rural	112.6	148.5	3.85	4.91	
	Urban	62.8	103.7	2.25	4.11	
Non-workers	Rural	143.5	178.7	4.76	5.61	
	Urban	102.3	144.4	3.24	4.65	

Cont'd...

Table 8.29 Cont'd...

1	*2*	*3*	*4*	*5*	*6*	*7*
		Caste				
Scheduled caste	Rural	143.3	174.9	4.78	5.56	2.32
	Urban	122.2	163.1	3.88	5.03	1.86
Scheduled tribe	Rural	121.7	162.5	4.07	5.25	1.98
	Urban	111.3	154.9	3.62	4.97	1.73
Non-SC/ST	Rural	134.0	170.2	4.48	5.40	2.18
	Urban	97.5	141.3	3.04	4.53	1.46
		Religious groups				
Hindu	Rural	134.5	169.0	4.48	5.37	2.18
	Urban	104.1	137.0	2.97	4.37	1.44
Muslim	Rural	148.3	187.7	5.01	5.98	2.43
	Urban	122.9	176.6	3.98	5.53	1.93
Christians	Rural	99.0	153.5	3.34	5.07	1.62
	Urban	73.4	121.4	2.34	4.54	1.12
Sikhs	Rural	120.7	180.5	3.97	5.66	1.93
	Urban	98.9	150.5	3.03	5.07	1.47

Source: RGI: Survey Reports on Levels, Trends and Differentials in Fertility, 1979

There are considerable differences in various measures of fertility between literates and illiterates and between varying levels of literacy of women. A similar observation holds for rural and urban women holding education constant. SRS Statistical Report 2003 presents age and education level-wise fertility of Indian women for the year 2000 (Table 8.30). The literate-illiterate divide of female population does have some bearing on the fertility level attained. But the most intelligible difference in fertility behavior between an illiterate and literate woman is observed when the latter has a few years of schooling. Although the literate women definitely have lower ASFR, the graph below shows that level of fertility observed for a literate woman does not change much beyond primary level of schooling. The same trend is observed for rural as well as for urban females. Though the graph (Figure 8.10) has been drawn for a single age group (15–19), the pattern remains similar for other age groups as well. The most dominant factor across rural-urban divide is education.

Figure 8.10

ASFR (15–19) with level of education attained, India 2000

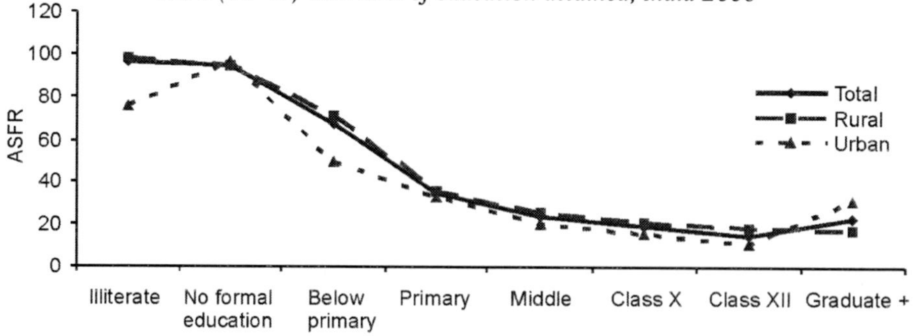

Table 8.30

Fertility indicators by level of education of women, India 2000 (SRS 2003)

Indicators	*Age group*	*Rural/ Urban*	*Illiterate*	*Literate*							
				Total literate	*Without formal education*	*Below primary*	*Primary*	*Middle*	*Class X*	*Class XII*	*Graduate and above*
1	*2*	*3*	*4*	*5*	*6*	*7*	*8*	*9*	*10*	*11*	*12*
% of women in the total population			44.9	55.1	3.5	11.7	11.2	14.1	8.0	3.6	3.0
Age Specific Fertility	15–19	Total	96.1	35.0	94.5	67.6	34.4	23.4	18.7	14.3	22.5
		Rural	98.5	39.3	94.3	71.5	35.0	25.1	21.2	18.3	16.7
		Urban	75.4	24.4	96.9	49.1	32.4	19.5	15.2	11.2	30.5
	20–24	Total	289.4	191.5	284.5	298.1	194.6	187.5	143.5	87.4	94.5
		Rural	288.2	202.0	268.2	300.0	191.6	183.5	142.5	96.7	87.6
		Urban	299.6	170.6	383.9	291.3	203.3	196.6	145.0	79.4	97.6
	25–29	Total	229.8	159.8	195.5	212.2	149.7	144.9	143.9	124.3	126.8
		Rural	230.6	161.9	184.1	211.4	145.3	146.7	132.0	125.1	123.9
		Urban	223.9	156.1	257.8	214.4	159.7	141.4	158.8	123.6	127.9
	30–34	Total	134.9	70.9	109.7	90.1	60.5	55.7	61.3	62.4	63.2
		Rural	134.6	72.4	107.8	89.1	59.6	58.2	55.4	56.0	67.0
		Urban	137.8	68.2	119.7	93.3	62.3	51.5	67.7	67.5	62.0
	35–39	Total	78.4	25.9	52.5	32.9	17.9	20.7	17.7	22.1	24.8
		Rural	81.6	30.2	54.5	35.7	21.0	23.0	21.0	25.3	33.7
		Urban	58.3	19.7	44.6	26.0	12.1	17.5	14.9	20.2	22.8
	40–44	Total	32.6	7.8	17.1	9.7	6.1	7.2	3.7	3.0	4.5
		Rural	33.7	9.5	18.6	11.0	7.2	6.0	3.5	6.0	11.2
		Urban	25.0	5.5	10.7	6.4	4.1	8.8	3.8	1.8	3.2
	45–49	Total	11.4	2.3	6.4	2.7	1.3	2.4	1.0	0.5	0
		Rural	12.3	2.7	6.4	3.0	2.0	1.0	1.8	0.6	0
		Urban	6.3	1.8	6.3	2.2	0.3	4.0	0.5	0.4	0
GFR		Total	128.1	87.9	117.1	124.3	80.4	74.8	72.3	63.9	71.4
		Rural	130.1	93.4	115.2	128.3	81.2	77.4	74.4	71.4	77.9
		Urban	113.8	77.6	126.3	111.7	78.2	69.8	69.8	58.3	69.3
TFR		Total	4.4	2.5	3.8	3.6	2.3	2.2	1.9	1.6	1.7
		Rural	4.4	2.6	3.7	3.6	2.3	2.2	1.9	1.6	1.7
		Urban	4.1	2.2	4.6	3.4	2.4	2.2	2.0	1.5	1.7

8.8.3 Occupation

In various Rounds, NSSO has collected data on employment and fertility. It has generally been observed that people engaged in traditional occupations have more children vis-à-vis in modern occupations, especially those that call for higher level of education and professional training. Employment of a person in a particular occupation or profession is closely related to his/her education and skill, rural-urban origin, income and expenditure habits, aspirations, etc. That is why it is very difficult to relate birth rate to a particular occupation or profession. However, women who are employed in gainful occupations, especially those in modern industrial sector, prefer to limit their family size. There is some evidence that occupation of women and the type of occupation of their husbands have some determining influences on birth rate. But the presence of such dominant factors as education and aspiration for better living often would obscure the importance of a particular occupation in determining the family size. Mysore Population Study, Couple Fertility Survey and the surveys conducted by NSSO all seem to agree on certain basic facts – a highly educated man usually has an educated wife; he marries late and the age gap between him and his wife is definitely not very large, often not exceeding 4/5 years. Such couples generally stay away from their ancestral houses and prefer a nuclear family than a traditional joint family. Not only the age at marriage of females in higher income group families in urban areas is high, the married couples produce fewer babies as well. The situation is somewhat different in a village setting. The average age at marriage of females in the poorest stratum is much higher than those in a well-to-do cultivator's family. Whereas the daily wage earners and the marginal farmers mostly live in nuclear family, a good many of the well-off cultivators still live in joint/extended families. High birth rate is still observed in well-off cultivator families.

8.8.4 Other Factors

There are other factors whose influences on fertility behavior have also been studied. Some political outfits in India have raised their voices against Muslims on the ground that their proportion in the national population is growing much faster than persons belonging to other religious faiths, more specifically the Hindus. It is a fact that since independence proportion of Hindus in the total population has declined from 85 to 80.5 percent; in the same period the Muslim population share in the national population has gone up from 9.9 to 13.4 percent. Muslims have the lowest literacy in the country. That probably explains why they still have a decadal growth over 29 percent when the Hindus have a decadal growth a little over 20 percent (1991–2001). They still have the highest fertility rates, much higher than the national averages (Tables 4.26 & 8.29). They have literacy rate 6-percentage point below the national average. Christians, the third largest religious group (2.34%) after Hindus and Muslims, are well ahead of all other major religious communities in all indicators of fertility. 80 percent of Christians are literate; even the Christian females have literacy rate above the literacy rate of males (all religions) at the national level. Both rural and urban women belonging to this community have commendable literacy rates. Jains, a very small community though (only 0.41%), has the highest level of literacy in the country (94.1%, even 80.3% rural women are literate). All these fertility differentials indicate that education probably is the single most important indicator of fertility.

Caste is an important issue in Indian politics. The Indian constitution has an important provision for positive discrimination in favor of Scheduled Castes and Scheduled Tribes. They together constitute a sizeable proportion of Indian population (about 25%, 16.48% and 8.08% respectively of the population in 1991 census). In spite of the privileges granted to them by India's Constitution, they still are far behind the mainstream population in most social and economic indicators. However they cannot be blamed much for taking a large share in the population growth of India. SCs are slightly behind non-SCs/STs in fertility reduction, but the tribal population of India is ahead of the mainstream population in all fertility indicators (Table 8.29). Most social and economic factors directly influence the age at which a girl is to be given to marriage. The key factor is the age at marriage.

9

Trends and Differentials in Mortality in India

9.1 Introduction

While rise in per capita income is an indicator of economic well-being of a country, health and education are probably equally if not more important indicators of a country's overall level of human development. Even though India's economy has been growing at a robust rate and mortality rates has declined at all ages and life expectancy increased to over 63 years, the health outcomes are anything but satisfactory. Premature death and widespread morbidity in the population, especially in the younger generation, among women and the older people have marred much of the advances India made in its economic and knowledge front. Infectious diseases, childhood illness and complications related to pregnancy and childbirth still galore in most parts of the country. There are serious discrimination against girls and women even in nutrition and health care.

India is in the phase of demographic transition where the population is still expanding but the growth rate has started declining because both fertility and mortality levels have been falling throughout the country for sometime and the mortality level already attained is such that further improvement in this depends largely upon how fast a reduction in IMR and child mortality are achieved. Kerala and Tamil Nadu are in late transition stage; Maharashtra, Karnataka, Punjab, West Bengal, Andhra Pradesh, Gujarat and Haryana are about to leave the mid-transition stage and the remaining other major states are between early and mid-transition stage. As is usual everywhere, fertility declines only after a persistent mortality decline over a considerable time. India's mortality level started declining since 1921 and the CDR fell from a high of 40–45 per 1,000 populations to around 32–33 at the time of India's Independence in 1947 and to 15 by 1971. The 2002 SRS estimate suggests that India's CDR has declined to 8.1. By 2007, it went down to 7.4 (rural 8.0 and urban 6.0). As it should be the case, reduction in the mortality level resulted in the rise in the rate of population growth, which reached almost 2 percent per annum during 1951–61. It remained fairly constant around 2.2 percent in the next three decades since decline in fertility was largely compensated by decline in mortality in most regions in India. In the decade 1991–2001, the birth rate fell faster (from 31.0 to 25.8) than the death rate (from 10.0 to 8.5) bringing about a decline in the rate of population growth to 1.93 percent per annum. According to the most recent estimate, the growth rate in 2006 should be around 1.5 percent per annum. The state of health prevailing in a country or in a population group is best indicated by (i) crude death rates, (ii) infant mortality rate, and (iii) life expectancy at birth.

Since independence, there has been considerable improvement in all the three indicators. Death rate has declined from 32–33 at the time of independence to less than 9 at the turn of the century, infant mortality declined from around 200 in 1940s to 63 in 2002 (55 in 2007), and expectation of life at birth doubled from 32 years to about 63/64 years in 55 years since Independence.

Three distinct phases of mortality history in India can be traced. Mortality was high and fluctuating till 1921 because of famines, epidemics and pestilences. It then declined slowly in the next 30 years. Preventive and curative technical know-how from the West, adoption of public health measures and control of communicable diseases and malaria eradication program, etc. were responsible for decline in death and morbidity rate in this period. There was only one notable famine since 1921 – the Bengal famine in 1943. Fatal diseases and epidemics were largely under control. Since 1951 mortality has declined fast. It fell considerably due to control of several major communicable diseases and the absence of major famines and epidemics and considerable improvement in the social and health infrastructure in almost every part of the country.

The governments at the center and the states are currently spending more on health care – number of hospitals in the country has increased four-fold between 1971 and 1998 and Primary Health Centers in rural areas increased by 453 percent (Table 9.2). One of the major determinants of the use of a health care facility, where it exists, is the distance one has to cover to reach the health center. This is especially relevant for women and children in rural areas. Overall, 47.4 percent villages had access to some health facility within the village and 38.9 percent villages had access to such facility within a radius of less than five kilometers. According to the Human Development Report (HDR), 1999, only 22 percent of villages had a sub-center within their village based on the population criteria. Coverage varied across Indian states. In Bihar, Orissa and Punjab, the proportion of villages with sub-centers was as low as 5–6 percent; less than 30 percent of villages had access to a PHC or hospital in Bihar, Gujarat and Madhya Pradesh. There was better coverage quantitatively in Tamil Nadu with 50 percent villages having health access, and the same in Maharashtra and Haryana, between 30–36 percent. Tamil Nadu, Kerala and Karnataka also had greater access to a hospital within five kilometers of the place of residence (HDR, 1999).

Table 9.1

Percent distribution of villages by distance from the nearest health center, India 1998–99

Distance	*PHC*	*Sub-Center*	*Hospital*	*Dispensary/Clinic*	*Any Health Facility*
Within Village	13.1	33.0	9.7	28.3	47.4
<5 km	28.4	39.7	25.0	32.4	38.9
5–9 km	29.2	16.3	25.1	17.4	9.7
10+ km	28.2	9.6	40.0	21.7	3.9
Median Distance (km)	4.9	1.3	6.7	2.4	

Source: National Family Health Survey II, 1998–99.

According to Central Bureau of Health Intelligence at the Ministry of Health and Family Welfare, the private sector accounted for about 57 percent of 11,174 hospitals in 1991. The same source reports that private sector share has gone up to 75 percent of a total of 18,218 hospitals in 2000. In 1998, a single hospital on average catered to the needs of a population in about 204 sq. km, which in 1971 was 810 sq. km. In reality, this increase in number of hospitals and other health services has not changed the scenario much at the ground level. In 1971, there were 64 beds in hospitals for every 100,000 persons. In 1998, the same has increased to 93 per 100,000 populations (it is around 350 in the developed countries). That is, from around one hospital bed for every 1562 persons in 1971, India now has one bed for every 1075 persons (Table 9.3). But most hospitals often do not have necessary infrastructure, equipment and medicines in their stores to cater to the needs of different categories of patients. The wards are over crowded. Consequently, infections easily spread from one patient to another. Most infectious disease (ID) hospitals in the country are "places of detention to persons dangerous to the community". There is a two-fold increase in registered doctors between 1971 and 1998 (from 27 to 54 per 100,000 populations) and a quantum jump on per capita expenditure on health from Rs 14 in 1971 to Rs 167 in 2000–2001 at current prices. Private health expenditure in India is about 4.2 percent of its GDP, which often in most of the developed countries is somewhere between 2 to 3 percent. All the modern health facilities in India are concentrated in bigger cities and metropolis. The well-known inequity in health sector is that rural areas with 72 percent of India's population account for only 25 percent of government health financing. Urban population thus receives more than five times of what the rural population receives in per capita terms. Consequently, the attainment of health indices has been very uneven across the rural-urban divide.

The PHC and their subsidiaries are often without doctors and other health attendants. Even the very commonly used medicines are not available in the PHCs. According to WHO, only about 35 percent of the population has access to essential drugs in India, which in the developed countries is 100 percent! Only 18 percent of all health expenditures are borne by the government, which makes India's health sector one of the most privatized in the world. While healthcare facilities have grown fast since 1990s, they are mostly in the private sector, often beyond the reach of the rural and urban poor. Hospitalization often imposes a cost burden of 60 percent of the annual income for an Indian on an average. The rich spends only a small fraction of their income on health, the poor has to bear a disproportionate burden for health services all over India. Evidence from NSS surveys show that the private sector accounts for most of the curative services. However, the poor still depends on the public sector for most health services, except out-patient care. 81 percent of out-patient care is provided by private hospitals. In the in-patient care too, the share of public sector has fallen from 60 percent in 1986–87 to around 45 percent in 1995–96. The World Health Organization standard for expenditure on public health is 5 percent of GDP. India's 0.9 percent expenditure of GDP on health is even less than the average for the poorer countries – 2.8 percent. The National Health Policy (NHP) 2002 set the goal of increasing public health expenditure from 0.9 percent to 2 percent of GDP by 2010. This calls for enhancement of states' health expenditure from 5.5 percent of total budget to 8 percent by 2010; and union expenditure from 1.3 percent of total budget to about 7 percent – almost six-fold increase. The National Common Minimum Programme 2004 (NCMP) of the UPA government at the Center set the target of increasing public spending on health care to 2–3 percent of GDP by 2009, with focus on primary health care. However, health is a state subject and therefore unless the state governments can raise enough resources for running the health show, which in most states are in shambles, there is little the Center can do to improve the health status of the common man. There is however a 'non-health' component – improvement in nutrition, sanitation, hygiene and housing – that could play a decisive role in improving the health status of the community.

Table 9.2

Number of hospitals, dispensaries and primary health centers in India

Year	Hospitals	Dispensaries	PHCS
1971	3862	9087	5112
1976	5025	12274	5328
1981	6804	16751	5740
1986	8067	25193	12934
1991	11174	27431	20450
1996	15170	25653	NA
1997	15188	25670	NA
1998	15501	22967	23179

Note: Information given in this table is as at the end of given calendar year.
PHC: Primary Health Centers.
NA : Not available
Source: Department of Health, Ministry of Health and Family Welfare.

Table 9.3

Availability of hospital beds and doctors and nursing personnel in India

Year	Number of beds per 100,000 population[1]	Number of personnel per 100,000 population			
		Doctors	Nurses	Auxiliary Nurse/mid-wives	Health visitors
1971	64.0	27	14	5	0.81
1976	78.9	31	18	8	1.11
1981	83.0	39	21	10	1.35
1986	91.0	41	27	14	1.71
1991	95.0	47	40	18	2.03
1996	91.0	51	61	30	2.84
1997	94.0	52	64	32	2.61
1998	93.0	53	70	35	3.34
1999	NA	54	NA	NA	NA

Note: 1. Information given in this table is as at the end of given calendar year.
NA: Not available.
Figures of doctors relate to allopathic doctors registered with the Medical Council of India. Similarly, figures of nurses relate to those who are registered with the Nursing Council of India.
Source : Department of Health, Ministry of Health and Family Welfare

Change in Crude Death Rate in the last hundred years has been described in Table 8.3. The picture of mortality situation in various states at the end of the last century is presented in the following table.

Table 9.4

CDRs by sex and residence of 16 larger states, India 2000 (SRS data, 2003)

State	Total	Rural	Urban	Urban-rural	Males	Females	Males-Females
1	2	3	4	5	6	7	8
1. Kerala	6.4	6.5	6.2	–0.3	7.4	5.5	1.9
2. Tamil Nadu	7.9	8.7	6.5	–2.2	8.6	7.2	1.4
3. West Bengal	7.0	7.2	6.7	–0.5	7.4	6.6	0.8
4. Maharashtra	7.5	8.6	5.8	–2.8	8.2	6.8	1.4
5. Andhra Pradesh	8.2	9.0	5.8	–3.2	8.9	7.5	1.4
6. Punjab	7.4	7.9	5.9	–2.0	7.7	7.0	0.7
7. Karnataka	7.8	8.6	5.8	–2.8	9.1	6.4	2.7
8. Himachal Pradesh	7.2	7.3	5.5	–1.8	8.2	6.2	2.0
9. Orissa	10.5	11.0	7.0	–4.0	10.8	10.3	0.5
10. Gujarat	7.5	8.3	5.8	–2.5	8.1	7.0	1.1
11. Assam	9.6	10.0	6.1	–3.9	9.9	9.2	0.7
12. Haryana	7.5	7.9	6.2	–1.7	7.9	7.1	0.8
13. Rajasthan	8.5	8.9	6.6	–2.3	8.4	8.6	–0.2
14. Madhya Pradesh	10.3	11.1	7.5	–3.6	10.3	10.3	0.0
15. Bihar	8.8	9.1	7.1	–2.0	8.6	9.0	–0.4
16. Uttar Pradesh	10.3	10.8	8.0	–2.8	10.1	10.4	–0.3
INDIA	**8.5**	**9.3**	**6.3**	**–3.0**	**8.9**	**8.1**	**0.8**

Figure 9.1

Radar plot of CDR of 16 larger states of India, 2000

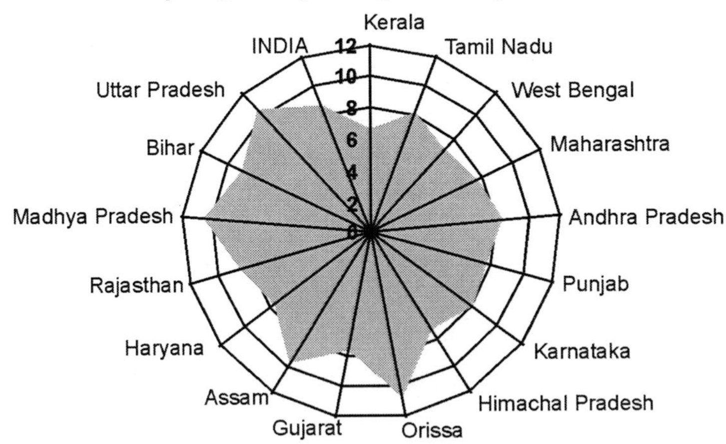

9.2 Mortality Differentials

9.2.1 Regional and Urban-Rural Differences

Progress and achievement in lowering mortality have been uneven in India as in other regions of the world. Mortality rates have been appreciably higher in rural areas vis-à-vis urban areas. Urban-rural mortality differences are so strong even today that the expectation of life of urban males and females in the late 1990s was almost 6 and 8 years respectively more than their rural counterparts. But more wide have been inter-state differences in mortality. In almost all demographic parameters the Southern states, especially Kerala and Tamil Nadu, are ahead of most other states. Both fertility and mortality levels are low in this region. Kerala in particular has done extremely well in almost wiping out the differences between rural and urban mortality (Table 9.4). West Bengal too has done well in bridging the gap between rural and urban mortality. But the success of Kerala in expanding health facilities to every corner of the state is proven by the fact that the state has brought down infant mortality rate to 13 per 1,000 live births (which could be an object of envy for many of the developed countries) and life expectation at birth above 70 years. Its general mortality rates are comparable to that of many of the first world countries. West Bengal, Himachal Pradesh and Punjab also have made significant progress in lowering mortality. At the other end of the spectrum are the states like Orissa, Madhya Pradesh and Uttar Pradesh with CDR still above 10 with large urban-rural differences. Although the Southern states have done really well in controlling mortality, it is strange that sex differences in mortality are among the highest in most of these states. Except Rajasthan and Bihar, the female mortality rate in all other states is smaller than that of male mortality rates. Although in the last 30 years all states have reported decline in mortality, the regional pattern of inter-state variations have persisted and call for region specific interventions.

Some of the major reasons for differences in mortality between rural and urban population are:

Figure 9.2

CDRs of 16 larger states by residence, India 2000

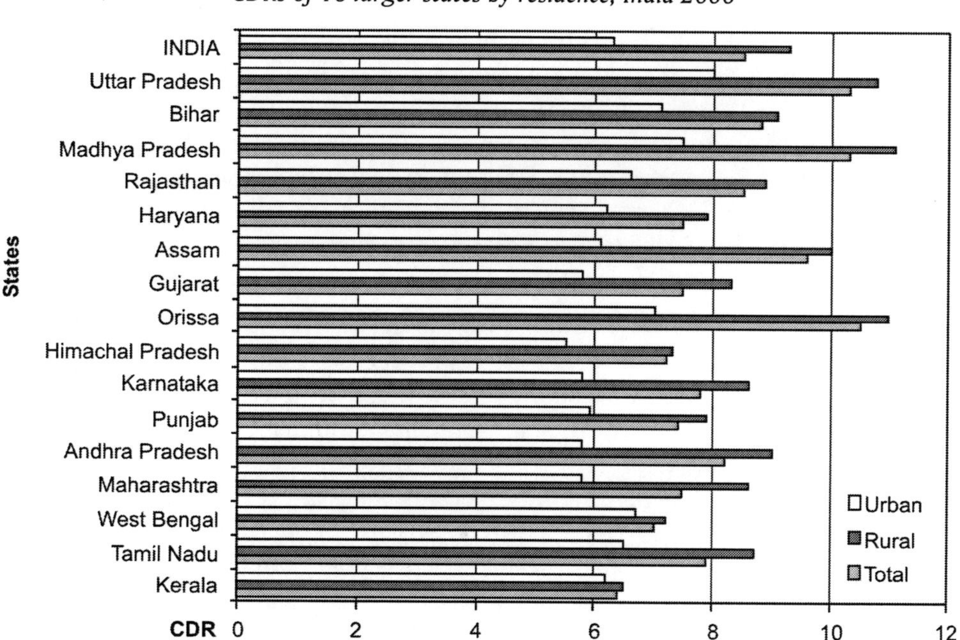

1. Unlike their rural counterpart, urban people are more health conscious, better educated and have better exposure to changes that are happening in medical science and technology.
2. A large proportion of the urban population is engaged in the organized sector. Many of them have insurance cover for health, receive health allowances from the employer or are entitled to receive reimbursement for certain kinds of health expenses.
3. The city-centric growth of various types of health institutions – private and public – also have helped the urban people to receive as much health support as are feasible through their family budget. In fact, about 75 percent of health budget of the government are spent in urban areas where only 28 percent of India's population live.
4. There is a statutory arrangement for supply of purified drinking water to all households in urban area. Even 60 years after independence many villages are without a tube-well.
5. There is some arrangement, often insufficient though, for collection of city wastes. There is some sort of drainage system for carrying liquid wastes and clearing the storm water during the monsoon days. These are almost totally absent in villages and smaller towns. Even after 60 years of independence only about 31 percent of India's population is supported by some sanitation facilities.

A comparison of death rates between 1988–1990 and 1998–2000 shows that of the 16 larger states 15 have reduced CDR. There is a marginal increase in CDR, both in rural and urban areas, in Kerala. In fact, Kerala has almost reached the biological limit and therefore such marginal increase in CDR is not unusual, especially since the proportion of deaths of senior citizens to total deaths in the state is very high (Table 9.8). This is also observed in those developed countries where CDR is as low as 5–6. All the BIMARU states have registered significant reduction in mortality in their populations. CDRs in urban area are down to below 8 per 1,000 populations in all the states.

T.N. Krishnan and P.G.K. Panikar have closely studied the demographic transition in Kerala. They have attributed the much lower death rates in the last few decades in Kerala compared to other states to the expanded health care facilities even to remote areas and people's eagerness to take advantage of the public health facilities. Prof. Ashok Mitra, Registrar General and Census Commissioner of 1961 Census, even after admitting that health care facilities have a significant role in controlling mortality in the population, was of the view that mortality primarily declines when every individual gets sufficient nutritious food and when adequate disease preventive measures are available to every segment of a population. To bring down death rates among infant and children, pregnant and young mothers, is to provide them nutritious food in adequate quantity and bring all of them under the care of preventive medicines. For the fast decline in mortality in Kerala, he found the following correlates that were not widely noticed in other parts of the country.

1. The erstwhile administrators of Travancor-Cochin, made it mandatory, even in the nineteenth century that everyone was to be vaccinated against certain diseases.
2. The administration was keen to keep the market place, temples and all crowded places (on festive occasions) clean and free from any garbage accumulating. This prevented spread of many communicable diseases.
3. Church and other welfare organizations, especially the 'Nair Society', kept watchful eye on prevention of tetanus among the newly born babies, particularly when the delivery took place at the hands of village midwives (*dai*). Kerala has the long tradition of low mortality among infants, children and maternal mortality.

4. Public health and hygiene in Kerala had been one of the best in the country. The civic society had always been active in keeping their residential locality clean. As a result, Kerala remained least prone to epidemics even when small pox, plague, cholera and malaria epidemics regularly broke out in other parts of the country.
5. The Rulers of the state made special drives to raise the level of health awareness among their subjects. People were made to learn that unsafe drinking water was the major source of many dreadful diseases. As a result, Keralites had remained comparatively free from gastro-intestinal diseases.
6. From the middle of the nineteenth century, the Rulers of the state made efforts to raise a big brigade of paramedical staff to keep watch over public health and hygiene. They were given intensive training in public health. These paramedical staff still remains envy of other states.
7. The Rulers of the state instituted intensive training in modern medicines to those doctors who sought license to practice medicine in the state.

Prof. Mitra was convinced that while other states were still busy in developing strategies to keep death rates under control, Kerala already had revolutionized its public health system, which brought down both mortality and fertility fast.

Table 9.5

Percentage change in CDR between 1988-1990 and 1998-2000 by residence and larger states, India (SRS data, 2003)

States	*Total*			*Rural*			*Urban*		
	1988–90	*1998–00*	*% change*	*1988–90*	*1998–00*	*% change*	*1988–90*	*1998–00*	*% change*
Kerala	6.2	6.4	3.8	6.1	6.5	4.9	6.3	6.2	–1.6
Tamil Nadu	8.8	8.1	–7.9	9.9	8.9	–14.4	6.9	6.6	–6.9
West Bengal	8.5	7.2	–15.6	9.3	7.4	–20.0	6.6	6.9	7.7
Maharashtra	8.1	7.6	–6.6	9.2	8.7	–8.4	6.1	5.7	–12.5
Andhra Pradesh	9.6	8.4	–12.5	10.3	9.2	–12.3	7.0	5.9	–16.9
Punjab	801	7.5	–7.8	8.7	8.0	–8.0	6.6	6.1	–11.4
Karnataka	8.6	7.8	–8.9	9.3	8.7	–9.4	6.5	5.6	–15.4
Himachal Pradesh	8.9	7.4	–17.2	9.1	7.6	–14.1	6.0	5.4	–10.0
Orissa	12.2	10.8	–12.0	12.7	11.2	–14.4	7.4	7.2	–3.9
Gujarat	9.9	7.8	–21.3	10.5	8.6	–21.1	8.4	6.0	–27.9
Assam	10.9	9.8	–10.4	11.2	10.2	–10.4	7.7	6.1	–24.1
Haryana	8.9	7.8	–12.4	9.4	8.2	–13.5	7.0	6.5	–4.3
Rajasthan	11.4	8.6	–25.1	12.2	9.0	–29.2	8.0	6.6	–16.0
Madhya Pradesh	13.3	10.9	–18.1	14.3	11.4	–20.5	8.7	7.6	–12.5
Bihar	11.8	9.0	–23.2	12.2	9.3	–24.6	7.4	6.9	–15.0
Uttar Pradesh	12.6	10.4	–17.2	13.5	10.9	–24.3	8.8	8.1	–12.0
INDIA	**10.3**	**8.7**	**–15.8**	**11.2**	**9.5**	**–17.9**	**7.2**	**6.4**	**–12.2**

9.2.2 Age-Sex Differentials

From demographic point of view the two most important specific death rates are age and sex specific mortality rates. A very disturbing feature in India's mortality situation has been the gender differentials – young girls experiencing higher mortality compared to young boys (Table 9.6). As per NFHS–2, female mortality rate below 5 years was slightly higher than male mortality rate (105 per 1,000 live births for females compared to 98 per 1,000 for male births). This pattern is found in rural areas and not in urban areas. When we compare the experiences of most countries of the world, the excess female mortality in India (and in some other countries in this sub-continent) is rather unusual. Many studies have shown that behavioral factors, including care-seeking practices operate against female children. Many micro level studies in India have shown that girls are less likely to receive medical attention compared to boys and when they at all receive care, it tends to be too late and inadequate. This is true as well for girls in 5–14 years age group both in rural and urban areas, more discrimination in the former. But there is a dramatic turnaround when children enter the active age group. Girls, while in their reproductive period, though they have an important additional risk factor – child bearing – have significant lower death rates than their male counterparts.

Table 9.6

Estimated death rates for some broad age groups by sex and residence, India 2000 (SRS data, 2003)

Age group	*Total*			*Rural*			*Urban*		
	P	*M*	*F*	*P*	*M*	*F*	*P*	*M*	*F*
1	*2*	*3*	*4*	*5*	*6*	*7*	*8*	*9*	*10*
Below 1	71.1	70.5	71.6	77.3	76.2	78.5	46.1	48.0	44.1
1–4	5.8	4.7	7.0	6.6	5.4	7.9	2.9	2.1.	3.7
0–4	19.5	18.6	20.6	21.7	20.6	23.0	11.5	11.3	11.7
5–9	1.7	1.5	2.0	2.0	1.8	2.2	0.9	0.7	1.2
10–14	1.3	1.2	1.3	1.4	1.4	1.4	0.7	0.6	0.8
15–59	4.3	4.9	3.8	4.6	5.1	4.1	3.5	4.2	2.8
60 +	47.3	52.6	42.3	48.3	54.1	42.9	43.6	47.5	39.9

Table 9.7

Age specific mortality rates over the years in India

Age group	*1971a*	*1976b*	*1981*	*1986*	*1991*	*1996*	*1997*	*1998*	*1999*	*2000*
1	*2*	*3*	*4*	*5*	*6*	*7*	*8*	*9*	*10*	*11*
0–4	51.9	51.0	41.2	36.6	26.5	23.9	23.1	22.4	20.4	19.5
5–9	4.7	4.8	4.0	3.3	2.7	2.3	2.1	2.1	1.8	1.7
10–14	2.0	2.4	1.7	1.6	1.5	1.3	1.2	1.1	1.2	1.3
15–19	2.4	2.7	2.4	2.3	2.1	1.6	1.7	1.8	1.9	1.9

Cont'd...

Table 9.7 Cont'd...

1	2	3	4	5	6	7	8	9	10	11
20–24	3.6	3.4	3.1	2.9	2.8	2.3	2.5	2.5	2.6	2.4
25–29	3.7	3.9	3.2	3.0	3.1	2.5	2.7	2.6	2.9	2.8
30–34	4.6	4.5	4.0	3.3	3.1	2.9	3.1	3.0	3.1	3.1
35–39	5.7	4.8	4.4	4.2	3.9	3.9	3.4	3.6	3.8	3.7
40–44	6.7	7.2	5.8	5.6	4.8	4.9	5.0	4.8	5.0	4.5
45–49	9.5	9.5	8.5	7.8	7.4	6.7	7.5	6.4	7.0	6.8
50–54	16.8	16.2	13.2	12.6	11.3	10.9	12.2	10.9	10.2	9.9
55–59	21.2	23.6	20.6	17.8	17.6	15.7	16.9	16.4	16.3	16.3
60–64	34.9	40.3	33.0	31.3	28.5	26.7	27.1	28.3	22.9	23.1
65–69	48.4	51.4	46.4	44.0	41.6	38.9	40.2	41.7	36.8	38.0
70–74	109.3	99.5	97.4	91.0	91.4	61.5	58.6	63.5	56.2	50.2
75–79						89.5	84.7	86.3	78.6	82.8
80–84						120.4	115.4	125.8	103.2	101.4
85+						182.2	190.1	206.0	165.8	164.7
All ages	14.9	15.0	12.5	11.1	9.8	9.0	8.9	9.0	8.6	8.5

a. Excludes Bihar and West Bengal. b. Excludes Jammu & Kashmir

Source: Sample Registration System; Office of the Registrar General, India.

Figure 9.3

Age specific death rate for the years 1971, 1986 and 2000

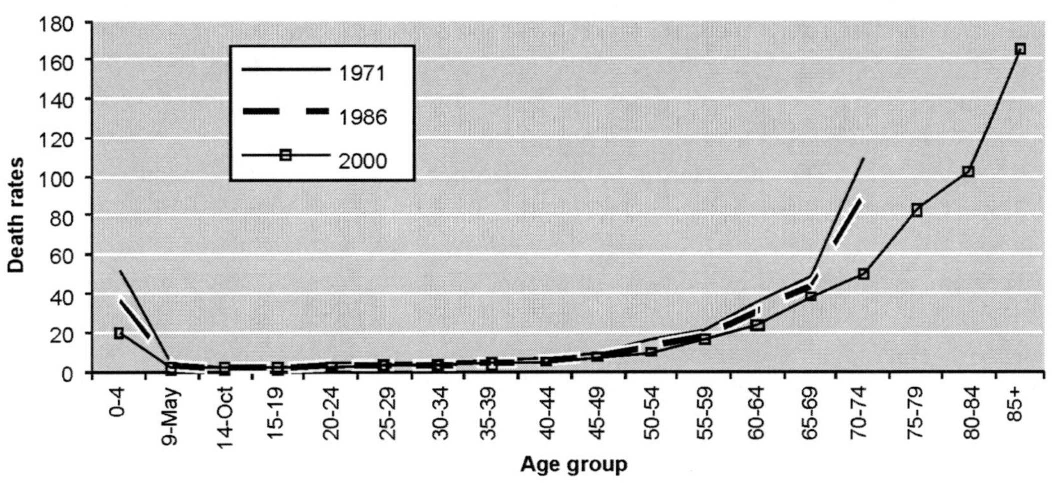

Table 9.8

Percent distribution of deaths by broad age groups, India and 16 larger states, 2000 (SRS data, 2003)

States	Broad age group					
	<1	*1–4*	*0–4*	*5–14*	*15–59*	*60 +*
Kerala	3.9	1.0	4.9	1.0	24.9	69.1
Tamil Nadu	12.4	1.5	14.0	1.8	36.8	47.5
West Bengal	14.9	4.0	18.9	3.2	31.0	46.9
Maharashtra	13.4	2.2	15.6	2.7	31.7	50.0
Andhra Pradesh	16.9	2.1	19.0	3.2	34.1	43.8
Punjab	15.3	3.1	18.4	2.0	30.8	48.7
Karnataka	16.0	3.5	19.5	2.3	37.4	40.8
Himachal Pradesh	15.7	3.1	18.8	1.3	25.6	54.4
Orissa	22.0	4.8	26.9	4.2	29.5	39.5
Gujarat	20.9	5.8	26.7	3.1	30.4	39.9
Assam	21.0	6.4	27.4	5.3	36.1	31.2
Haryana	23.8	5.5	29.4	3.1	29.3	38.2
Rajasthan	29.2	10.2	39.4	3.9	23.8	32.8
Madhya Pradesh	26.5	7.5	34.0	4.9	28.2	32.8
Bihar	22.3	9.2	31.5	5.4	26.1	36.9
Uttar Pradesh	26.6	10.1	36.7	4.4	25.2	33.7
INDIA	**20.5**	**6.3**	**26.8**	**3.9**	**29.6**	**39.6**

In all societies, mortality is highest among infants and a sharp decline is observed after the child crosses his/her first birthday. After the child attains the age 15 years, mortality gradually increases, very slowly though, till age 40 and thereafter the age specific death rate gets accelerated. By the age 70 years, the death rate is almost similar to that at age ‘0’. This is true both for males and females though there are minor differences in the dividing lines.

It is observed in all countries that at birth male babies slightly out-number female babies (105 male babies for every 100 female babies, though SRS in India reports 110 male babies for every 100 female babies). In most countries, the parity between male and female children is reached before they reach adolescent stage, i.e., mortality among male babies is considerably higher in the initial years. Since in most societies male members of a family are the principal earning members, they are exposed to external adversaries more often than the female members. It is quite natural therefore that the adult male members generally have greater risk of life than the females. In the developed countries, this invariably is true and for this reason sex ratio in their population is in favor of females.

That the sex ratio in population in India does not match the pattern observed elsewhere is matter of great concern. (This issue has been discussed in Chapter 4 in some greater detail)

As we take a close look at the graph (Figure 9.3) it becomes clear that between 1971 and 2000 there is a visible change at both the ends of the time scale. The plateau period (9 to 40 years), when death rates remained considerably low and there was only a smallish upward trend, seems to have been extended somewhat further in the 30 year period under consideration; it is around 55–60 years that a greater acceleration in death rate had taken place unlike around age 50 years observed in 1971. The pattern actually started to change in early eighties and it has become more pronounced at present. Till about 1980 females were behind males in life expectancy. Thereafter female life expectancy has increased much faster vis-à-vis male life expectancy. The sharp drop in death rate from around 52 to only 20 for the age group 0–4 years in just 30 years (IMR down by 50% in the said period) has taken away some of the sharpness in the drop in death rate at the initial years.

Although death rate in India has declined fast since independence, inter-state variations in death rates, more specifically death rates in the early years of life, is really stunning. The percentage share of death rate by deaths in 0–4 year age group is as high as 39.4 percent in Rajasthan compared to only 4.9 percent in Kerala (Table 9.8). All the BIMARU states' share of deaths in this age group to total deaths is well above 31 percent. Except in Kerala, death rate among very young children still is very high in all states. Kerala is way ahead of other states in checking mortality among children and infants. Though Tamil Nadu and West Bengal have done well in mortality reduction in the early years of life, they are behind Kerala by about 10 percentage points. Infant mortality in India still accounts for 20.5 percent of all deaths in the country and another 6.3 percent for deaths in 1–4 age group. Variation between the states in mortality is less pronounced in the age groups 5–14 and 15–59 years. Number of deaths in 5–59 years together accounts for only 33.5 percent of all deaths recorded. Proportion of old age deaths to all deaths is as high as 69 percent in Kerala to a low of 31 percent in Assam followed by Rajasthan (32.8%) and Uttar Pradesh (33.7%).

Earlier, a dying patient, more so in rural India, received very little attention from qualified medical professionals. Even in 1981, 39 percent of all deaths occurred where no professional doctor/hakim/vaidya attended the patient. Today 21 percent of all deaths occur either in hospitals or nursing homes or health centers and another 66 percent of deaths occur at home but attended by qualified practitioners. Obviously, patients dying without any medical attention are rare in urban areas. However, the same cannot be said about people dying in rural areas.

At the national level, institutional care before death was received by only 9.2 percent of all deaths in 1981. In 2000, it went up to 20.9 percent and it varied from 9.8 percent in Assam to 80.4 percent in Kerala among the bigger states. Another 65.9 percent at the national level received private medical attention at the time of death and 12.7 percent of all deaths did not receive any medical attention (4.7% in urban area). Orissa has the worst record where more than 44 percent people have to die without receiving medical attention whatsoever. But it is astonishing that the more advanced states like Tamil Nadu and Karnataka have as many as 36.1 and 31.2 percent respectively dying without receiving any medical attention. These three states are also at the top in the lists both for rural and urban deaths that succumb to their illness without receiving any medical aid. Maharashtra is the only state where nearly hundred percent of the dying urbanites receive at least some medical attention.

Table 9.9
Type of medical attention at death in India

Year	*Percentage distribution of deaths by type of medical attention received at the time of death*											
	Rural				*Urban*				*Total*			
	I	*T*	*U*	*O*	*I*	*T*	*U*	*O*	*I*	*T*	*U*	*O*
1	*2*	*3*	*4*	*5*	*6*	*7*	*8*	*9*	*10*	*11*	*12*	*13*
1981	6.5	25.6	25.1	42.8	20.4	44.2	11.4	24.0	9.2	29.2	22.4	39.2
1986	8.6	29.6	23.9	37.9	27.6	44.8	7.1	20.5	11.5	32.0	21.3	35.2
1991a	12.4	37.3	50.2	b	31.1	51.7	17.3	b	15.5	39.6	44.9	b
1996a	16.7	69.2	NA	14.1	35.7	59.5	NA	4.8	19.9	67.5	NA	12.5
1997a	16.8	69.3	NA	13.9	35.8	59.6	NA	4.6	20.0	67.6	NA	12.4
1998	16.9	69.1	NA	14.0	35.8	59.5	NA	4.7	20.1	67.5	NA	12.4
1999	17.2	69.1	NA	13.7	35.8	59.7	NA	4.4	20.7	67.3	NA	12.0
2000	17.4	67.5	14.6		35.9	58.9	4.6		20.9	65.9	12.7	

I: Death occurred in a hospital, dispensary, health center, other medical institution, etc.
T: Death occurred at home but was attended by a qualified practitioner.
U: Death occurred at home and was attended by an unqualified practitioner.
O: No professional doctor/hakim/vaidya attended (others).
a. Excludes Jammu & Kashmir.
b. Included in category U.
For 1996, 1997, 1998 & 1999 the following classification for type of medical attention is used.
I : Institution
T : Medical attention other than Institutes
O : No medical attention
NA : Not available
Source: Sample Registration System, Office of the Registrar General, India.

9.3 Infant Mortality and Life Expectancy

There was a time when consumption of sulfuric acid was regarded as the index of industrial development of a country. The arrival of computer and information technology has changed the computing index. Demographers too, even today, look at IMR of a country as an indicator of public health and hygiene as also the stage of socio-economic development a country is in. Utility of IMR as an index of level of prosperity is no longer tenable in the developed countries. With fast expansion of urban facilities, improved health infrastructure and expanding urban population base, IMR as an appropriate index of human development has lost ground. IMR in the high human development and high income countries has come down from around 22–25 to around 6–7 between 1970 and 1999. Top 30 high human development countries have IMRs ranging between 3 and 7 in 1999 as against 11–31 observed in 1970. Even the medium human development countries' IMR (India falls in this category) is sharply down from 142 in 1970 to 46 in 1999. China has brought down IMR from 85 to 33 in the said period. A small country like Sri Lanka had an IMR of only 17 in 1999. Even

Bangladesh is ahead of India in IMR reduction. Whereas IMR in India stood at 70 in 1999, IMR in Bangladesh was at 58 (HDR 2001).

Since 1921 general death rate in India has come down fast, especially after independence, primarily due to prevention of dreaded diseases like Tuberculosis, Plague, Malaria, Cholera and other water borne and communicable diseases. Added to this was a reasonable amount of food security to the teeming millions. But such measures alone were not quite effective in bringing down IMR fast. Birth weight of the babies born still remains a major concern for the social and health planners in India and in other developing countries. Though IMR has fallen for all states between 1961 and 2001, a faster decline has been observed between 1981 and 2001 compared to that in the previous 20 years. The decline of course is uneven across the states. What is disturbing is the fact that IMR in states like Tamil Nadu, Andhra Pradesh and Haryana have actually increased between 1981 and 2001. It is also disturbing that SCs and STs and other backward classes experienced much higher IMR vis-à-vis the upper castes/classes. The urban-rural and caste difference are also observed in child mortality. IMR over the years and by state and residence is presented in Tables 9.10 & 9.11.

Table 9.10

Infant mortality rate over the years by sector in India

Year	*Rural*	*Urban*	*Total*
1901–06c			215
1916–21c			219
1926–31c			178
1936–41c			161
1946–51c			134
1971	138	82	129
1976	139	80	129
1981	119	62	110
1986	105	62	96
1991a	87	53	80
1996	77	46	72
1997	77	45	71
1998	77	45	72
1999	75	44	70
2000	74	44	68
2001P	72	42	66

a. Excludes Jammu & Kashmir, and Mizoram.
c. S. Chandrasekhar: Infant Mortality in India 1901 to 1951
P. Provisional
Source : Sample Registration System; Office of the Registrar General, India

Table 9.11

Infant mortality rates (IMRs) by sex and residence for India and 16 larger states, 2000 (SRS data, 2003)

States	*Total*			*Rural*			*Urban*		
	P	*M*	*F*	*P*	*M*	*F*	*P*	*M*	*F*
1	*2*	*3*	*4*	*5*	*6*	*7*	*8*	*9*	*10*
Kerala	14	15	13	14	15	13	14	14	15
Tamil Nadu	51	49	54	56	53	61	38	40	37
West Bengal	51	54	47	54	56	51	37	45	28
Maharashtra	48	46	50	56	59	53	33	22	45
Andhra Pradesh	65	66	64	74	76	73	36	34	37
Punjab	52	45	61	56	47	68	38	39	36
Karnataka	57	65	47	68	77	59	24	32	16
Himachal Pradesh	51	57	44	52	58	45	35	34	38

Cont'd…

Table 9.11 Cont'd...

1	*2*	*3*	*4*	*5*	*6*	*7*	*8*	*9*	*10*
Orissa	95	98	92	99	101	96	66	74	56
Gujarat	62	59	67	69	66	73	45	41	50
Assam	75	66	83	78	69	86	35	29	41
Haryana	67	63	71	69	66	72	57	52	65
Rajasthan	79	76	81	82	81	83	58	48	68
Madhya Pradesh	87	81	93	93	85	102	54	64	43
Bihar	62	62	61	63	64	61	53	42	64
Uttar Pradesh	83	81	86	87	83	91	65	69	60
INDIA	**68**	**67**	**69**	**74**	**72**	**76**	**44**	**45**	**42**

P: Persons, M: Males and F: Females

About 50 percent reduction in IMR in India has become possible since 1971. This is true both for urban and rural populations. The rate of decline in infant mortality, considerably high in the 1970s and 1980s, slowed down in the 1990s. Trends in perinatal and infant mortality show a slow but steady decline, less for neonatal mortality (NMR) and almost no change in the rate of stillbirths. Each year 27 million infants are born in India. Around 10 percent of them do not survive to 5 years. In absolute terms, India contributes to 25 percent of the over 10 million under-five deaths worldwide every year. Nearly half of the under-five deaths occur in neonatal period.

Proportion of infant mortality to total deaths in a year still stands alarmingly high at 20.5 percent in India. Infant and child mortality claims 2.2 million lives every year. Rural IMR today is still around a level observed in urban area in the late 1970s. The following table shows how the different states succeeded in reducing IMR between 1988–90 and 1998–2000. Orissa, Assam and the BIMARU states still remain the poorer performers in reduction of IMR. Kerala is ahead of all other states (IMR 13 in 2007) and like in CDR it has almost succeeded in eliminating rural-urban differences in IMR by 2002. But in 2007 SRS recorded large rural-urban difference in IMR in Kerala. For every 100 male infant deaths there are 135 female infant deaths in Punjab, 125 in Assam, 114 in Madhya Pradesh and 114 in Gujarat to name a few states. In rural India the sex-ratio picture is: Punjab 145, Assam 125, Madhya Pradesh 120, Tamil Nadu 115, Gujarat 110 and Uttar Pradesh 110. But there are a few other states like West Bengal, Andhra Pradesh, Himachal Pradesh, Karnataka, and Orissa where female IMR is less than male IMR. Karnataka is the most distinguished state: there are only 72

Figure 9.4

Infant mortality rate in India

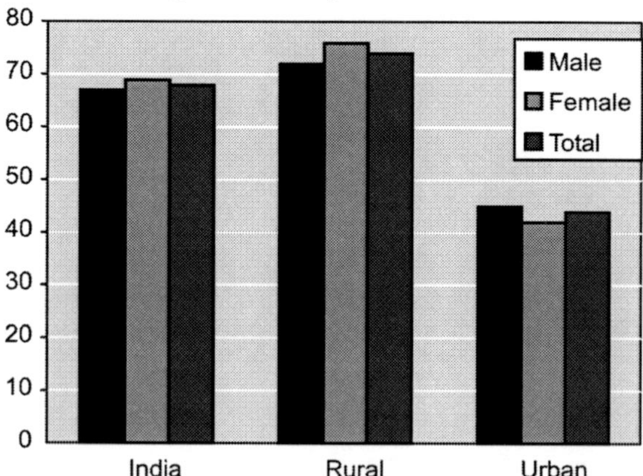

deaths to female babies for every 100 deaths to male babies before they celebrate their first birthday. This is true both for rural and urban areas.

Figure 9.5

Trends in infant and neo-natal mortality rates in India

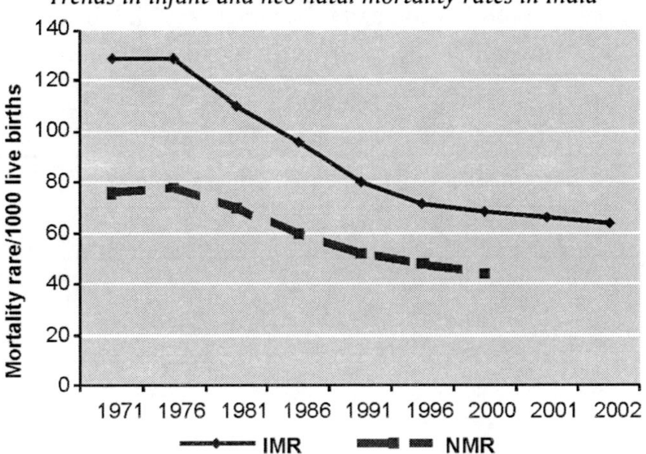

Table 9.12

Changes in IMR by residence for India and 16 larger states between 1988–90 and 1998–2000 (SRS data)

States	*Total*			*Rural*			*Urban*		
	1988–90	*1998–00*	*% change*	*1988–90*	*1998–00*	*% change*	*1988–90*	*1998–00*	*% change*
1	*2*	*3*	*4*	*5*	*6*	*7*	*8*	*9*	*10*
Kerala	22.0	14.7	–33.3	23.0	14.3	–37.7	17.3	15.7	-9.6
Tamil Nadu	67.0	52.0	–22.4	78.0	57.7	–26.1	43.7	39.0	–10.7
West Bengal	69.7	52.0	–25.4	75.7	55.0	–27.3	45.7	39.3	–13.9
Maharashtra	61.7	48.3	–21.6	68.7	57.3	–16.5	46.0	32.0	–30.4
Andhra Pradesh	78.0	65.7	–15.8	83.3	74.7	–10.4	57.3	37.0	–35.5
Punjab	62.3	53.0	–15.0	66.7	57.0	–14.5	49.3	39.0	–20.9
Karnataka	74.7	57.7	–22.8	84.0	69.0	–17.9	46.0	24.3	–47.1
Himachal Pradesh	74.3	62.0	–16.6	75.3	63.7	–15.5	38.0	37.7	–0.9
Orissa	121.7	96.7	–20.5	126.0	100.0	–20.6	71.7	65.7	–8.4
Gujarat	82.7	63.0	–23.8	90.7	70.0	–22.8	62.7	45.3	–27.7
Assam	88.7	75.7	–14.7	90.7	79.0	–12.9	56.0	35.7	–36.3
Haryana	80.3	68.3	–14.9	85.0	70.3	–17.3	61.0	58.0	–4.9
Rajasthan	94.3	81.0	–14.1	100.0	84.7	–15.3	61.0	59.0	–3.3
Madhya Pradesh	116.3	91.7	–21.2	124.3	97.7	–21.4	74.0	55.0	–25.7
Bihar	87.7	64.0	–27.0	89.7	65.0	–27.5	59.7	53.0	–11.2
Uttar Pradesh	113.7	84.0	–26.1	121.0	88.0	–27.3	74.3	65.3	–12.1
INDIA	**88.3**	**70.0**	**–20.8**	**95.3**	**75.3**	**–21.0**	**56.7**	**44.3**	**–21.8**

Table 9.12 shows that whereas 21 percent reduction in IMR has been possible in the ten year period at the national level, the states like Rajasthan, Haryana, Assam, Himachal Pradesh, Punjab and Andhra Pradesh remained under-performers. The high IMR states like Rajasthan, Haryana and Orissa did badly in bringing down IMR even in urban areas. NFHS II came out with the observation that infant and child mortality, both in rural and urban areas are high by a long way among SC, ST and other backward castes compared to the mainstream population.

Table 9.13
Infant and child mortality per 1,000 births, 1998–99

	Infant mortality	*Child mortality*	*Under five mortality*
	Urban		
Male	53.8	14.6	67.6
Female	44.3	19.7	63.1
Scheduled Castes	60.4	25.2	84.0
Scheduled Tribes	57.6	23.4	79.6
Other Backward Classes	51.2	16.3	66.6
Others	43.5	14.1	57.0
Low birth weight	66.6		
Very low birth weight	124		
	Rural		
Male	80.7	27.9	106.4
Female	78.6	41.7	117.0
Scheduled Castes	88.1	43.0	127.8
Scheduled Tribes	86.9	48.8	131.4
Other Backward Classes	82.2	32.7	112.2
Others	69.3	25.6	93.1
Low birth weight	78.2		
Very low birth weight	153.8		

National Family Health Survey II, 1998–99

Table 9.14
Birth weight and immunization statistics, All India

Birth Weight and height	*%*	*Year*
1	*2*	*3*
Prevalence of low birth rate (weight <2500 gm at birth)		
Total	23	1995–96
Urban	21	1995–96
Rural	24	1995–96

Cont'd...

Table 9.14 Cont'd...

1	*2*	*3*
Prevalence of under weight (weight for age) in < 3 years of age	47	1998–99
Prevalence of stunting (height for age) in < 3 years of age	45.45	1998–99
Prevalence of wasting (height for age) in < 3 years of age	15.5	1998–99
Immunization		
Eligible population (i.e., infants reaching their first birthday) that has been fully immunized according to national immunization policy	49.0	2001*
Infants reaching their first birthday who have been fully immunized against diphtheria, tetanus and whooping cough	52.1	1998–99
Infants reaching their first birthday who have been fully immunized against polymyelitis	41.7	1998–99
Infants reaching their first birthday who have been fully immunized against tuberculosis	69.1	1998–99
Women who have been immunized with tetanus toxoid during pregnancy	66.8	1995–96

* Press briefing by Minister of Health, 23 October 2001.
Source: NFHS II

9.3.1 Classification of Infant Mortality

Bourgeois-Pichat (1952) classified mortality into two causal categories – endogenous and exogenous infant mortality. The first category comprises "those cases in which the child bears within itself, from birth, the cause resulting in its death, whether that cause was inherited from its parents at its conception, or acquired from its mother during gestation or delivery". Exogenous infant mortality causes refer to "those cases in which the infant picks up the factors which causes its death in the environment in which it lives". McNamara (1982) described endogenous death as death that is caused by "factors such as the congenital malformations, the circumstances of prenatal life, and the birth process". Exogenous infant death is "caused by infection, parasitic and respiratory diseases, accidents and other environmental and external causes". Endogenous causes, which usually are the causes of neonatal death, may extend beyond the period of infancy to cause such degenerative diseases of later life as heart disease, cancer, diabetes and AIDS. It is the exogenous causes of death that is avertable through preventive medicines, education, medical knowledge and technology and better nutrition. Scientists are confident that deaths from intrinsic factors can also be controlled through gene therapy in the near future.

In the more developed countries *neonatal mortality* (death within the first 4 weeks) has the largest share in their IMRs. Causes of neo-natal mortality are primarily organic along with deficiency in nutrition during pregnancy or some injury at the time of birth. Exogenous factors are mainly responsible for *post-neonatal mortality* (age of one month to the first birthday). Nearly two-thirds of infant deaths in India happen within the first month of the child's birth. This ratio has almost remained at the same level as it was some 35 years back. Among the bigger states, Karnataka (71.0) registered the highest and Punjab (55.5) the lowest neo-natal death rates. Neo-natal mortality is more pronounced amongst male babies; mortality of male babies in post-neo-natal stage comes down considerably. On the other hand, female deaths are more common in the post-neo-natal stage (disaffection for female babies?).

Table 9.15
Child, infant, neo-natal, post-neo-natal and peri-natal deaths/still births per 1,000 births, India 2000 (SRS data, 2003)

	Mortality rates			*As percentage of infant deaths*		
	Total	***Rural***	***Urban***	***Total***	***Rural***	***Urban***
Child mortality rate (< 5 yrs)	20	22	12			
Infant mortality rate	68	74	44			
Neo-natal mortality rate	44	49	27	65.5	65.8	63.0
Early neo-natal mortality rate	32	35	19	47.4	47.8	44.7
Late neo-natal mortality rate	12	13	8	17.6	17.6	18.2
Post-neo-natal mortality rate	23	25	16	33.8	33.8	36.4
	Mortality rates			Still birth rate		
Peri-natal mortality rate	40	44	26	8	9	7

Early neo-natal mortality rate (within first 7 days of birth) forms a vital component and more specifically of the *neo-natal mortality rate.* Among the larger states Kerala (6) and Orissa (45) form the two extremes. In most states rural proportions of early neo-natal death is higher than that in urban areas.

Peri-natal mortality rate PMR (number of still births + early neo-natal deaths) at the national level is estimated to be 40, ranging from 26 in urban area to 44 in rural area. *Still birth rate* SBR is computed as the ratio of the number of still births to 1,000 live births. Punjab (22) has the highest proportion of still births and Bihar (3) the least. NSSO survey suggests a higher proportion of male peri-natal and stillbirths in India. This observation probably is true in all societies and in all populations.

The *post-neo-natal mortality* has fallen at a faster rate between 1970 and 2000, from 54 to 25 deaths per 1,000 births, i.e., by 54 percent. During the same period, the neo-natal mortality fell from 75 to 46, or by about 39 percent. This implies that the share of neo-natal mortality in infant mortality has increased over time. This is true the world over since neonatal mortality is inherently more difficult to control. Added to this is the fact that in large tracts of the country age at marriage and age at childbearing among women continues to be unacceptably low, increasing the risk of complications at the time of childbirth for both the newborn and the mother.

9.3.2 Causes of Infant Mortality

Even in 1981, about 64 percent of deliveries were conducted at home by untrained village *dai* or other untrained professional functionary or by relations and others excluding the above. The figure was staggering 73 percent in rural India and 34 percent in urban area. Even as late as 1999, 44 percent of deliveries (54% in rural area and 9% in urban area) happened at homes under no care of doctors or trained nurses or mid-wives. Only 26.6 percent of all births in 1999 took place under institutional care (only 18.2% in rural India). It is therefore no wonder that IMR and maternal mortality rate (MMR) in India are still so high in India. Injury at the time of birth and subsequent infection mostly are causes of neo-natal deaths. Peri-natal and neo-natal mortality rate cannot be improved without the deployment of a contingent force of paramedical staff in areas where institutional support system cannot be enabled.

Table 9.16
Type of medical attention at birth in India, 1981–1999

Year	Percentage distribution of births by type of medical attention at the time of birth											
	Rural				Urban				Total			
	I	T	U	O	I	T	U	O	I	T	U	O
1	2	3	4	5	6	7	8	9	10	11	12	13
1981	10.6	15.7	52.4	21.3	38.8	27.0	24.6	9.6	17.7	18.5	45.4	18.4
1986	14.3	17.7	48.3	19.7	47.8	25.0	18.6	8.6	20.7	19.1	42.6	17.6
1991	17.6	20.8	61.5	b	53.8	26.9	19.2	b	24.3	21.9	53.7	b
1996a	17.7	27.9	49.5	5.0	59.5	31.1	7.8	1.6	25.2	28.5	41.9	4.4
1997a	17.8	28.1	49.2	4.8	59.6	31.2	7.7	1.5	25.4	28.7	41.7	4.2
1998	18.0	28.2	49.2	4.6	59.6	31.4	7.6	1.4	25.4	28.8	41.8	4.1
1999	18.2	28.3	49.3	4.5	59.7	31.5	7.7	1.4	26.6	28.9	40.9	3.9

I: Institutions like hospitals, maternity/nursing homes, health centers, etc.
T: Delivery conducted in the home by doctor, trained dai, trained midwife, trained nurse, etc.
U: Delivery conducted in the home by untrained village dai or other untrained professional functionary.
O: Delivery conducted in the home by relations and others excluding the above.
a. Excludes Jammu & Kashmir.
b. Included in category U.
Source: Sample Registration System, Office of the Registrar General, India.

The Registrar General conducted the Infant and Child Mortality Survey in 1979. The survey exposed that only about 50 percent of children under age 5 in urban area received BCG vaccination (against TB) and 40 percent children were given Triple vaccine (diphtheria, tetanus toxoid and whooping cough). Only one in five received Polio vaccine. In village India the picture was dismal – 1 in every 4 children was given BCG, 1 in every 12 received Triple vaccine and only 1 in 40 were vaccinated against Polio. In the same survey a very strange observation was made – infant and child mortality was found to be quite high among mothers who were better educated (matriculation or more). The population scientists could not find any answer to this incomprehensible observation. The same survey also confirmed that infant and child mortality were closely related to family living standard.

It is to be noted that various public and private agencies collect the same type of data, in and around the same time span. Some differences are always observed between the reported statistics. The actual figures often would differ marginally, but the data patterns remain almost the same. In the following table we present IMR and Child mortality rate by background characteristics as compiled by the Central Statistical Organization (CSO) from National Family Health Survey II (1998–99). Girls are well ahead of their male counterparts in child mortality. This possibly confirms that they receive less attention and care even in their health matters from their parents compared to male children. Illiteracy and young age among mothers play a major role in infant and child mortality. IMR and Child mortality rates drop considerably with better education of mothers. Studies have clearly shown that even a few years of schooling for the mother can reduce as much as 40 percent of infant mortality. A woman with a high school education is more likely to have been cared for and nurtured in her own childhood and to have grown up with a sense of her own intrinsic value and identity. This definitely contradicts the observations made in 1979 survey conducted by the Registrar General that infant and child mortality were quite high among mothers who were better educated. The NFHS II data also suggest that IMR can be brought down fast if births took place under institutional care/supervision of doctors or trained paramedical staff. Some of the key findings of NFHS II are:

1. Malnutrition of women and children is a cause of concern. Child malnutrition ranges from 21 percent in Sikkim to as high as 65 percent in Madhya Pradesh. More than one-third women are undernourished. Obesity of women is fast becoming a serious issue, especially in cities.
2. About three-fourth of Indian children are anemic. Haryana (84%), Rajasthan (82%) and Bihar (81%) are at the top of the list. Half of Indian women are anemic.
3. Contraceptive use is lowest in Meghalaya (20%) followed by Bihar (25%) and Uttar Pradesh (28%). Himachal Pradesh, Punjab and West Bengal are at the top of the list with contraceptive use at 68, 67 and 67 percent respectively,
4. Not much improvement in antenatal check was observed between NFHS I and NFHS II. Two or more doses of BCG went up from 55 to 67 and iron and folic acid supplementation increased from 52 to 58 percent.
5. 42 percent of children aged 12–23 months received all the recommended childhood vaccines, up from 36 percent in NFHS I. 3 doses of polio vaccines were not received by 37 percent of young children
6. Discrimination in girls' health care still continues. Chances of dying of girls in 1–4 years are 50 percent more than that in boys.
7. Very low percentage of AIDS awareness was noticed in BIMARU states: Bihar (12%), Uttar Pradesh (20%), Rajasthan (21%) and Madhya Pradesh (24%). Awareness is as low as 40 percent nationwide.

Table 9.17

Infant mortality and child mortality rate by background characteristics, India 1998–99

Background characteristics	***IMR***	***Child mortality rate***
Sex of child		
Male	74.8	24.9
Female	71.1	36.7
Mother's education		
Illiterate	86.5	39.7
Literate < Middle complete	58.5	18.4
Middle school complete	48.1	10.5
High school complete and above	32.8	4.4
Medical care[1]		
No care	89.1	NA
One or two types of care	54.8	NA
All three types of care	34.8	NA

NA : Not available

1. Rates for the four-year period preceding the survey. Medical care is that given by a doctor, nurse, trained midwife, or other health professional in a hospital, clinic, or health center or care received at home from a health worker.

Source: National Family Health Survey, 1998–99; International Institute of Population Sciences

Figure 9.6
IMR and Child mortality by mother's education

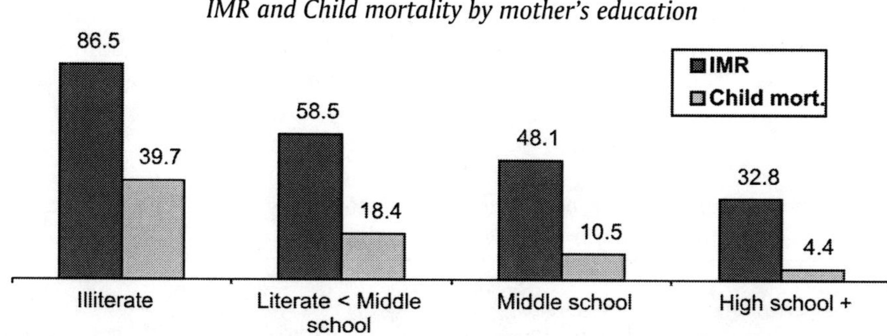

There is a strong belief, not without grounds though, that the chances of survival of a newly born baby are better in families with better life style. But the association between the two is not that obvious. For instance, newly born girls have better chances of survival in West Bengal than in Punjab, even though the average family income in Punjab is nearly twice as much as that in West Bengal. Similarly, Gujarat and Assam have very similar female IMRs in spite of wide differences in per capita incomes. It is not poverty alone that kills baby girls – the choices made consciously or involuntarily by her parents and family have a far greater role in their survival. Custom and tradition shape these choices. When resources are scarce, these can make all the differences between life and death. Significantly, micro-level studies have shown that baby girls are more likely to die in families where there is an older male sibling – strong circumstantial evidence of discriminatory care.

Pre-maturity, acute respiratory infections, diarrhea, anemia, neonatal tetanus and birth injuries account for approximately 70 percent of all infant deaths in India. The major causes of child mortality are acute respiratory infection (ARI), diarrhea, measles and malaria. Malnutrition is a major contributor to these deaths. Implementation of acute respiratory infections control program and essential newborn care have not received due attention from most states. In order to ensure that infant and child mortality is brought down rapidly, the state governments have been advised to focus on antenatal care and nutrition of pregnant mothers, essential newborn care to prevent the early neonatal deaths, control of deaths due to diarrhea and ARI and prophylaxis against Vitamin A and Iron deficiency anemia apart from immunization activities. Distribution of deaths due to specific causes of mortality peculiar to infancy is presented in Table 9.18 for India and a few selected states where IMRs are low and others where it is still very high.

The principal causes of infant death are pre-maturity and ARI including pneumonia (25% of all deaths). In the high IMR states it is higher by 5 to 10 percentage points. A slight excess of deaths due to cord infection (tetanus) is also observed in the latter group of states. There is a sudden surge of deaths due to congenital malformation in Kerala, the state where pre-natal and antenatal care is far superior to that in most other states.

One in every three of the world's malnourished children lives in India and about 50 percent of all child deaths in India are attributable to malnutrition (UNICEF). The proportion of low birth weight babies remains high at one third of all births (47% for babies < 3 years). Even after three-decade-old Integrated Child Development Scheme (ICDS), the percentage of underweight children (< 5 years) in India is at par with sub-Saharan Africa's. The promotion of early and exclusive breast-feeding is a well-recognized strategy for child survival. It is estimated that in India 28 percent of mothers initiate breast-feeding within one hour of delivery and only 39 percent practice exclusive breast-feeding till 6 months. While breast-feeding is still largely followed in rural India, especially among less educated women and having no independent occupation, with the more enlightened women in urban areas and among the educated class breast-feeding is not a standard practice. Enhancing early initiation of breastfeeding and intensifying nutrition is highlighted in Tenth plan.

Table 9.18

Percentage distribution of deaths due to specific causes under the major group "Causes Peculiar to Infancy" for selected states, 1996–98

States	*Year*	*Pre-maturity*	*Pneu-monia*	*Respira-tory infection of new born*	*Diarr-hea of new born*	*Cord infection (incl. tetanus)*	*Conge-nital malfor-mation*	*Birth injury*	*Others*
1	*2*	*3*	*4*	*5*	*6*	*7*	*8*	*9*	*10*
INDIA	1996	31.2	16.6	10.8	3.7	1.6	3.3	1.5	31.3
	1997	29.9	14.5	11.0	2.9	1.6	3.1	1.9	35.1
	1998	34.4	13.5	11.5	2.4	1.3	3.5	2.0	31.4
Kerala	1996	13.8	20.7	17.0	0	0	3.4	0	45.1
	1997	18.9	8.1	21.6	0	0	27.0	0	24.4
	1998	16.7	16.7	16.7	0	0	16.7	0	33.2
Maharashtra	1996	55.8	14.5	5.2	0.8	0	3.7	0.5	19.5
	1997	55.1	13.1	6.9	0.7	0.1	3.1	0.7	20.3
	1998	54.8	12.8	4.1	0.4	0	2.8	0.7	24.4
Orissa	1996	35.7	9.3	4.7	0	2.2	1.0	0	47.1
	1997	38.5	15.4	8.7	0.5	2.9	0	1.0	33.0
	1998	41.8	8.8	22.0	1.1	2.2	4.4	1.1	18.6
Madhya Pradesh	1996	35.6	22.2	12.0	3.3	1.9	3.0	0.4	21.6
	1997	27.6	21.7	7.1	2.1	0.8	2.4	1.6	36.7
	1998	37.7	20.5	14.8	2.5	2.0	3.4	2.8	16.3

Source: Registrar General, India

The Tenth Plan has set specific nutrition goals to be achieved by 2007. The major goals are:

1. Intensify nutrition and health education to improve infant and child feeding and caring practices so as to:
   (a) bring down the prevalence of under-weight children under three years from the current level of 47 percent to 40 percent;
   (b) reduce prevalence of severe under-nutrition in children in the 0–6 year age group by 50 percent;
2. Enhance Early Initiation of Breastfeeding (colostrums feeding) from the current level of 15.8 to 50 percent;

(a) Enhance the Exclusive Breast-feeding rate for the first six months from the current rate of 55.2 percent (for 0–3 months) to 80 percent; and

(b) Enhance the Complementary Feeding rate at six months from the current level of 33.5 to 75 percent.

9.3.3 Universal Immunization Program

Vaccination program is one of the key interventions for protecting children from life threatening conditions. Universal Immunization Program against six preventable diseases, namely, diphtheria, peritusis, childhood tuberculosis, polio-myelitis, measles and neonatal tetanus was introduced in the country in a phased manner in 1985, which covered the whole of India by 1990. Significant progress was made under the program in the initial period when more than 90 percent coverage for all the six antigens was achieved. However, relatively high drop out rates between the 1st and 3rd dose of Oral Polio Vaccine (OPV) has been observed in some states. In spite of massive drive for vaccination against the stated preventable diseases, only 42 percent of children received all the vaccines. The Ministry of Health and Family Welfare, has published immunization achievements in India since 1975–76. The same is reproduced in Table 9.19.

Table 9.19

Immunization of children against specified diseases in India, 1975–76 to 2000–2001

Year	Number of children immunized (million)			
	DPT	DT	Polio	BCG
1975–76	2.41	1.28	NA	NA
1980–81	7.15	10.23	1.61	NA
1985–86	15.18	12.53	13.19	6.62
1990–91	22.50	13.94	22.68	23.01
1995–96	22.56	10.49	22.78	24.13
1996–97	23.25	13.77	23.55	24.95
1997–98	23.74	10.05	23.98	25.42
1998–99	23.55	NA	23.93	24.54
1999–2000 P	23.56	NA	23.71	25.18
2000–2001 P	24.13	NA	23.61	24.70

DPT : Diphtheria, Peritussis (whooping cough) and Tetanus
DT: Diphtheria and Tetanus.
BCG: Bacillus Calemette Geurin.
P: Provisional.

Table 9. 20

Differentials in health status among states

Sector	Population BPL (%)	IMR/Per 1,000 live births (1999, SRS)	< 5 yr mortality per 1000 (NFHS II)	Weight for % of children under age 3 years < –2SD)	MMR per 100,000 (Annual Report 2000)	Leprosy cases per 10,000 population	Malaria +ve cases in year 2000 (in '000)
1	2	3	4	5	6	7	8
INDIA	**26.1**	**70**	**94.9**	**47**	**408**	**3.7**	**2200**
Rural	27.09	75	103.7	49.6			
Urban	23.62	44	63.1	38.4			
			Better Performing States				
Kerala	12.72	14	18.8	27	87	0.9	5.1
Maharashtra	25.02	48	58.1	50	135	3.1	138
Tamil Nadu	21.12	52	63.3	37	79	4.1	56

Cont'd...

Table 2.20 Cont'd...

1	*2*	*3*	*4*	*5*	*6*	*7*	*8*
			Low Performing States				
Orissa	47.15	97	104.4	54	498	7.05	483
Bihar	42.60	63	105.1	54	707	11.83	132
Rajasthan	15.28	81	114.9	51	607	0.8	53
Uttar Pradesh	31.15	84	122.5	52	707	4.3	99
Madhya Pradesh	37.43	90	137.6	55	498	3.83	528

Source: National Health Policy, 2002.

Table 9.21

Selected child health indicators, 1998–1999

Vaccination in children	***Percentage***
BCG	71.6
DPT (3 doses)	55.1
Polio (3 doses)	62.8
Measles	50.7
All vaccinations	42.0
None of these vaccines	14.0
Children chronically malnourished (stunted)	45.5
Children acutely malnourished (wasted)	15.5
Children underweight	47

Source: National Family Health Service II, 1998–99

Table 9.22

Percentages of children aged 12–23 months who had received specific vaccinations at any time before the interview, major states and All India, 1992–93 and 1998–99

	Type of Vaccination							
States	***BCG***		***DPT(3)***		***Polio (3)***		***Measles***	
	1992–03	***1998–99***	***1992–93***	***1998–99***	***1992–93***	***1998–99***	***1992–93***	***1998–99***
1	*2*	*3*	*4*	*5*	*6*	*7*	*8*	*9*
Andhra Pradesh	73.9	90.2	66.1	79.5	68.0	81.6	53.8	64.7
Assam	48.2	53.5	31.0	37.5	32.7	37.9	25.8	24.6
Bihar	33.9	37.7	29.1	24.2	31.6	41.0	14.6	16.6
Gujarat	77.1	84.7	63.8	64.1	62.9	68.6	55.9	63.6
Haryana	77.4	86.8	66.8	71.1	67.7	74.3	60.9	72.2

Cont'd...

Table 9.22 Cont'd...

1	*2*	*3*	*4*	*5*	*6*	*7*	*8*	*9*
Karnataka	81.7	84.8	70.7	75.2	71.4	78.3	54.9	67.3
Kerala	86.1	96.2	73.7	88.0	75.2	88.4	60.5	84.6
Madhya Pradesh	56.8	64.9	43.7	37.0	46.6	56.7	40.7	35.5
Maharashtra	86.9	93.7	83.1	89.4	81.6	90.8	70.2	84.3
Orissa	63.3	84.7	56.3	61.9	56.7	68.4	40.2	54.0
Punjab	77.4	88.7	73.6	82.0	73.4	83.6	64.8	76.5
Rajasthan	45.7	53.9	29.7	26.1	32.8	44.6	31.2	27.1
Tamil Nadu	91.7	98.6	86.5	96.7	85.3	98.0	71.6	90.2
Uttar Pradesh	48.9	57.5	34.1	33.9	37.1	42.3	26.3	34.6
West Bengal	63.1	76.5	51.9	58.3	56.0	61.7	42.5	52.4
ALL-INDIA	**62.2**	**71.6**	**51.7**	**55.1**	**53.4**	**62.8**	**42.2**	**50.7**

Note: The figures relate only to surviving children from among the two most recent births in the three years preceding the survey. The BCG vaccine provides immunization against tuberculosis; DPT provides immunization for diphtheria, pertussis (whooping cough), and tetanus. For DPT and polio the figures refer to those who had received a third vaccine dose.

Source: International Institute for Population Sciences (IIPS) and ORC Macro (1995, 2000).

Pulse Polio Immunization (PPI) was started 1995–96. This was the largest public health intervention program ever taken up, anywhere in the world. During 2000–01, 4 PPI rounds were conducted in Bihar, Delhi, Uttar Pradesh and West Bengal, 3 PPI rounds in 7 states of Assam, Gujarat, Haryana, Madhya Pradesh, Orissa, Punjab and Rajasthan and 2 PPI rounds in the rest of the 21 states. As a result of intensified rounds, polio cases have declined from 1,934 cases reported during 1998 to 265 cases in 2000. Polio eradication has become a distinct possibility in India, as number of new cases of Polio detected in July 2004 was only 34. Drop out rates for DPT and Polio vaccination continue to be a serious problem. NFHS II observed that 84 percent of children received first dose of Polio vaccination, but only 63 percent received all the three doses. First DPT was received by 71 percent; only 55 percent received all the three doses.

Polio vaccination still remains a very contentious issue among some segments of our population. Government of India has taken up a massive drive to eliminate polio from the Indian soil. Promotional programs have been arranged through electronic and print media. In some places house-to-house campaign is being carried out. Even some religious leaders have come out in open support of the polio vaccination program.

9.4 Expectation of Life at Birth

In most societies where men and women are treated equally and enjoy the same rights and freedom, women live longer than men do. Even though more boys are born than girls, there are more women than men in the adult and elderly populations. In the world scenario we see that on the average, women live five years longer than men. Even in sub-Saharan Africa, one of the poorest and most deprived regions in the world, women live 2.7 years longer than men do. Even for our next-door neighbors Sri Lanka and China (even though the recent reports suggest that sex ratio F/M is down to 100 females for every 125 males or even higher in some areas in China) the gap between female and male life expectancy is over 4 years in favor of females. In India, women currently outlive men by a little over one year and this turn around has happened only after 1980. Even a few decades back women in India did not seek timely advice from doctors for their health problems. Most of their illnesses remained unrecognized and therefore went unreported. The fact that the majority of doctors in rural areas are men is another deterrent. Women are reluctant to describe their problems to a male doctor, or allow themselves to be physically examined by men. Another important factor is that the health center may be at a considerable distance away making it difficult for a woman to reach it. The "social distance" between a woman and a health center, created by her caste and class status, is even a greater gulf than physical distance. Culturally too, women are conditioned from childhood to suffer in silence. Women think of going to a doctor or a health center only when they feel that they can no longer carry on.

There are hundred and one reasons why life expectancy among women was low or why it is not picking up as fast as it should in India. Their early marriage followed by repeated pregnancies (no respite to recover health) ruined their health. Surveys show that 50 percent of married women in India are anemic. Anemia is one of the few "female diseases" which can be a debilitating (sometimes deadly) disease, increasing women's vulnerability and limiting their capacities to function as full human beings; its symptoms – constant tiredness and lack of energy, loss of appetite and breathlessness – are often dismissed as "laziness" or "imagination" by others in the family.

Mother and Child Health care (MCH) has become an indispensable part of family planning movement in India since 1970s, which has done a lot good both to the health of the child and the mother. NFHS II found that 66.8 percent of women were immunized with tetanus toxoid during their pregnancy. Even with extended health support for the pregnant women, maternal mortality in India is many times more than what they are in the developed countries. According to SRS, there were 407

Figure 9.7
Prevalence of anemia among married women (%)

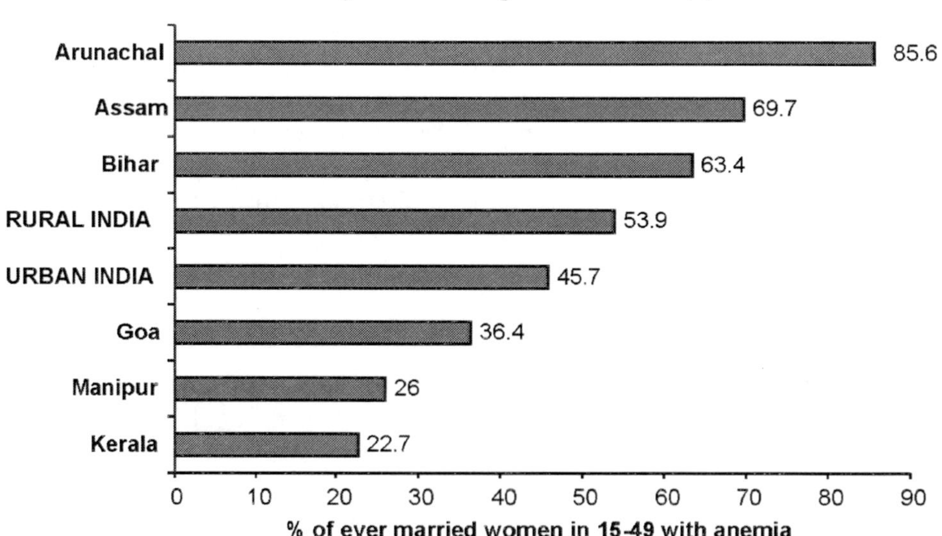

deaths to mothers either at the time of delivery or soon thereafter for every 100,000 live births in 2000. The same in 1991 was 437. NFHS II has obtained a much higher rate – 540 deaths per 100,000 live births (619 in rural area and 267 in urban area). Our neighbors China and Sri Lanka have MMR of 27 and 130 respectively. Maternal mortality statistics in India is terrifying – close to 300 mothers die everyday during childbirth or pregnancy-related causes. 40 percent of these deaths alone are in Uttar Pradesh. There is one maternal death every minute in Uttar Pradesh.

Table 9.23

Percentage of deaths by causes related to child birth & pregnancy, All India (rural)

Specific causes	***1985***	***1990***	***1995***	***1997***	***1998***
1	*2*	*3*	*4*	*5*	*6*
Abortion	11.5	11.8	17.6	7.3	8.9
Toxaemia	6.7	15.2	9.9	6.6	8.3
Anaemia	23.1	19.4	17.0	17.3	19.0
Bleeding of Pregnancy& Puerperium	15.9	23.7	28.9	27.6	29.6
Malposition of child leading to death of mother	7.7	7.1	4.0	10.7	9.5
Puerperal sepsis	13.9	8.1	8.5	13.0	16.1
Not classifiable	21.2	14.7	14.1	17.5	8.6

Source: Model Registration Scheme – Survey of Causes of Death (Rural) 1985, 1990, 1994, 1995 – A report. Causes of Maternal Deaths and their percent distribution to total maternal deaths by SRS 1997,1998 Registrar General, India.

Some states fare better than others. Haryana and Kerala lead with a life expectancy differential of 4.7 and 3.3 years respectively. Bihar, Orissa and Madhya Pradesh show a reverse pattern, with women having a lower life expectancy than men.

We have seen in the Life Table (*Fundamentals of Demography* by the present author) that there is a column marked e_x^0 telling us the probable number of years left on reaching age x. e_0^0 therefore refers to expectation of life at birth. Once the figures for 'Expectation of Life' become available, we can easily reconstruct the age and sex specific mortality in a population. Between 1921–31 and 1976–80 expectation of life for males was higher than that for females. This was in total contradiction to what one normally observes in most other parts of the world. High maternal mortality could have been the cause for this deviation. But there were and still are some behavioral factors, including care-seeking practices that operate against female children. This becomes quite evident if we compare the sex ratio for ages 0–14 years. Normally, the excess of male babies at birth is neutralized before reaching age 5 years. But even today there are fewer girls at every age between 0 and 14 years in India though there are variations between the states. This differential is more manifest in rural areas. Micro level studies in India have confirmed that girls are less likely to receive medical attention compared to boys and if they at all receive care, it tends to be too late and inadequate at times.

Table 9.24
Expectation of life at birth over the years, India

Year	Males	Females	Persons
1901–11	22.6	23.3	22.9
1911–21	19.4	20.9	20.1
1921–31	26.9	26.6	26.8
1931–41	32.1	31.4	31.8
1941–51	32.4	31.7	32.1
1951–61	41.9	40.6	41.3
1961–71	46.4	44.7	45.6
1971–75	50.5	49.0	49.7
1976–80	52.5	52.1	52.3
1981–85	55.4	55.7	55.4
1986–90	57.7	58.1	57.7
1987–91a	58.1	58.6	58.3
1988–92a	58.6	59.0	58.7
1989–93	59.0	59.7	59.4
1990–94	59.4	60.4	60.0
1991–95	59.7	60.9	60.3
1992–96	60.1	61.4	60.7
1993–97	60.4	61.8	61.1
1996–2000b	62.8	64.2	63.5
2000b	64.1	65.6	64.9

1. Census Actuarial Reports.
a. Excludes Jammu & Kashmir.
b. Ministry of Health and Family Welfare, Government of India
Note:
1. Figures for 1901–11 to 1961–71 are based on Census Actuarial Reports and for 1971–75 onwards on the basis of estimates from Sample Registration System.
2. Sample Registration System based abridged life tables 1986–90 (Occasional paper no. 1 of 1994)
Source: Office of the Registrar General, India.

Table 9.25
Life expectancy at birth by sex (2001–2006) for different larger states

	Life Expectancy at Birth (2001–2006)	
India/Major states	***Males***	***Females***
INDIA	***64.1***	***65.4***
1	***2***	***3***
Andhra Pradesh	62.8	65.0
Assam	59.0	60.9
Bihar	65.7	64.8
Gujarat	63.1	64.1

Cont'd...

Table 9.25 Cont'd...

1	*2*	*3*
Haryana	64.6	69.3
Karnataka	62.4	66.4
Kerala	71.7	75.0
Madhya Pradesh	59.2	58.0
Maharashtra	66.8	69.8
Orissa	60.1	59.7
Punjab	69.8	72.0
Rajasthan	62.2	62.8
Tamil Nadu	67.0	69.8
Uttar Pradesh	63.5	64.1
West Bengal	66.1	69.3

Source: Population Projection by Registrar General, India;(1996)

Figure 9.8
Life expectancy in India over the years

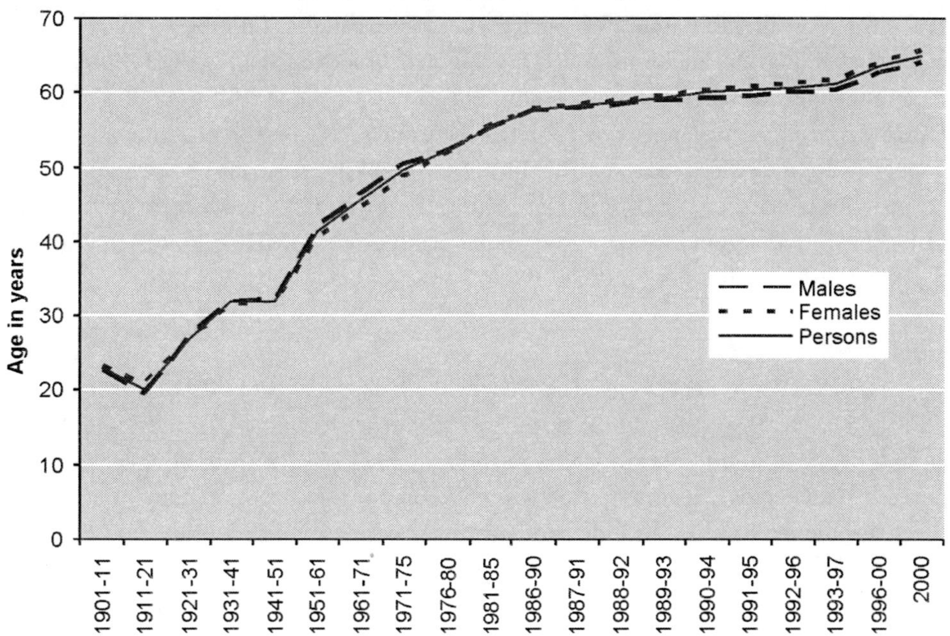

9.5 Causes of Mortality in the Population

In the quarter century after India's Independence, mortality fell considerably due to control of several major communicable diseases and the absence of major famines and epidemics. The decline in mortality continued in the last three decades of the 20th century and death rate fell to a little over 8 per 1,000 population at the turn of the century. This reduction in mortality, especially infant and child mortality, was evident in life expectancy at birth, which rose from around 50 years in around 1970 to around 64 years 30 years later (Table 9.24).

Generally speaking as mortality declines, there is a marked shift in the distribution of causes of death, from communicable diseases to those caused by non-communicable, degenerative ones (epidemiological transition). The available data on the causes of death in rural areas of the country show that India has succeeded in combating some of the communicable diseases very effectively, but some others continue to remain a major concern to the health system. The share of communicable diseases in rural India's cause of death profile fell from around 48 percent in 1969–71 to 22 percent by the mid-1990s. This decline has been due to prevention of deaths due to ailments such as gastro-enteritis, dysentery, tetanus and decline in diseases like leprosy. Intensive preventive and treatment measures to combat leprosy have resulted in a sharp decline in its prevalence rate and associated morbidity (3.7 per 10,000 in 2002) in states such as Tamil Nadu, Andhra Pradesh and Maharashtra. Due to re-emergence of malaria and persistence of tuberculosis, these two communicable diseases have remained potent causes of morbidity in spite of efforts to combat them through vertical disease control programs. The global warming has brought mosquito borne diseases in the developing countries where public sanitation continues to be abysmally poor. Dengue and Chickengunia almost took the form of epidemic in many states including the capital in India in 2006.

An important cause of death in the general population is related to maternal and peri-natal factors. Their combined share has remained around 14 percent of all deaths between 1969 and 1995. Although there is considerable doubt about the statistics available relating to maternal mortality, there could be no doubt that maternal mortality, for whatever reasons, is oddly high in India. No doubt the decline in fertility brought down maternal death to an extent. But something more has to be done to battle this needless wastage. The Reproductive and Child Health programs (RCH), initiated in 1997, specifically addresses maternal health by undertaking measures to promote institutional deliveries, providing emergency obstetric care and linking primary health care services to the first referral units. The government has set a few goals: bring down MMR from 407 in 2000 to 200 by 2007 and 100 by 2012; IMR from 70 in 2000 to 45 by 2007 and 28 by 2012.

9.5.1 Major Causes of Death

The trend of major "cause of death" based on Survey of Causes of Death (RGI 1964–94) is presented in Table 9.26 and Figure 9.9. The combined share of 'Fever', 'Digestive Disorder' and 'Coughs' was more than half of the total number of deaths in India in 1971. By 1991, their share dropped to just over 33 percent of all deaths. The major drop was registered for 'Fever' – 57 percent drop in 20 years. 'Coughs' remain the major killer in India; the drop was only a modest 17 percent between the two time points. Diseases under 'coughs' find an easy haunting ground in Uttar Pradesh and Rajasthan where almost without change over a time one-third of all deaths happen due to these diseases. Bronchitis and asthma maintained top rank over two decades accounting more than 8 percent of total rural deaths in India followed by TB of the lungs accounting 6.1 percent deaths. A much better achievement is noticed in containing deaths due to Digestive Disorder.

Violent death is rising at an alarming rate – from 3.9 percent in 1971 to 8.3 percent, a 213 percent rise in 20 years. It must have risen further in recent past due to increasing natural calamities (tsunami, earthquakes and super cyclones and heavy down pours in various parts of the country) and increases in rail and road accidents besides increase in the number of suicides and homicides and deaths from terrorist attacks in some areas (Jammu & Kashmir and Northeastern states in particular).

Table 9.26

Percentage distribution of 'causes of death' in rural India

Year	*A&I*	*Cbp*	*Fever*	*Dgd*	*Coughs*	*Dcns*	*Ocs*	*Cpi*	*Dcs*
1971	3.9	1.2	17.0	9.9	23.3	0.5	6.1	11.4	8.0
1976	4.6	1.1	11.6	9.7	20.7	3.4	7.8	12.7	7.9
1981	5.2	1.1	9.1	8.3	20.2	3.8	7.9	12.4	8.9
1986	6.5	1.0	9.5	7.3	20.2	4.0	8.7	10.4	9.6
1991	8.3	1.1	7.3	6.5	19.4	4.4	8.5	10.0	10.9

Abbreviations used: **A&I** – Accident & Injury (vehicular accident, drowning, suicide); **Cbp** – Childbirth & Pregnancy related (anemia, post-partum hemorrhage, abortion, toximia); **Coughs** (broncho-pneumonia, TB of respiratory system, pneumonia, asthma), **Dgd** – Digestive Disorder (gastro enteritis, cholera, dysentery, debility & malnutrition); **Dcns** – Diseases of Central Nervous System (meningitis, paralysis, convolutions) **Ocs** – Other Clear Symptoms (cancer, tetanus, jaundice, cerebral hemorrhage, urinary tract infection); **Cpi** – Causes peculiar to infancy; **Dcs** – Diseases of the Circulatory system; Fevers (typhoid, malaria, influenza, tuberculosis, septicemia, diphtheria).

Source: RGI, Survey of Causes of Death, Rural, 1964–94

Figure 9.9

Casuses of mortality, rural India

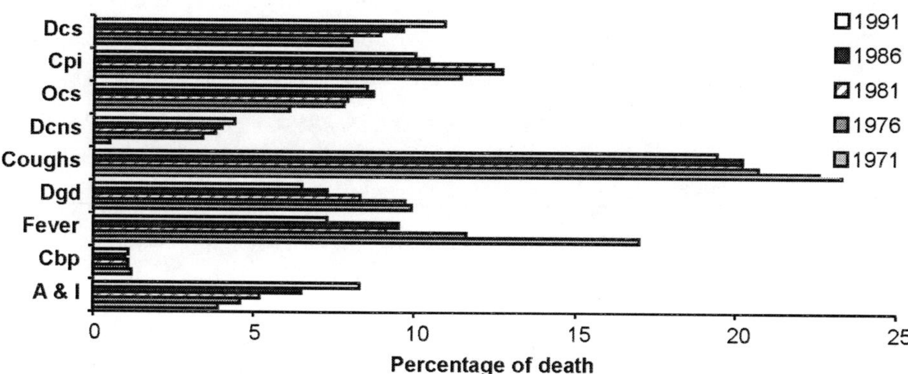

The following Table gives an idea about how the distribution of "Causes of Death", classified by International Classification of Diseases (ICD), has changed between 1992 and 1998.

Table 9.27

Percentage distribution of deaths in rural India by major causes of death over the years

S.No/ Code	*Major causes of death*	*1992*	*1993*	*1994*	*1995*	*1996*	*1997*	*1998*
1	*2*	*3*	*4*	*5*	*6*	*7*	*8*	*9*
1 R	Symptoms, Signs and Abnormal Clinical finding not elsewhere mentioned	26.4	26.2	24.3	18.6	20.6	19.0	18.4
2J	Diseases of the Respiratory System	14.4	14.4	15.1	16.6	17.8	16.4	17.2
3I	Diseases of the Circulatory System	7.9	7.6	8.2	9.5	10.9	12.1	12.5
4A	Infectious and Parasitic Diseases	12.7	12.5	12.0	11.9	10.2	10.0	9.6

Cont'd...

Table 9.27 Cont'd...

1	*2*	*3*	*4*	*5*	*6*	*7*	*8*	*9*
5P	Conditions Originating in the Peri-natal period	8.9	10.0	9.0	9.2	7.9	8.7	7.9
6G	Inflammatory Diseases of Central Nervous System	4.5	4.2	5.0	4.8	5.6	6.0	6.0
7X	With Venomous Animal Contact	5.0	4.7	5.0	6.0	5.5	5.9	6.7
8C	Neoplasm	3.2	3.1	3.9	4.2	3.9	4.3	4.3
9B	Viral infection	4.9	4.2	4.4	4.7	3.6	3.1	2.4
10D	Diseases of the Blood and Blood Forming Organs	2.9	3.1	3. 0	3.0	3.4	3.2	3.3
11V	External Causes of Mortality	2.1	2.1	2.2	2.4	2.1	2.3	2.2
12K	Diseases of the digestive System	1.4	1.4	1.6	1.6	2.0	2.1	2.1
13T	Injuries, Poisoning & Other Consequences of External Causes	1.2	1.3	1.3	1.4	1.1	1.4	1.3
14E	Metabolic Diseases	0.6	0.6	0.8	0.9	1.0	1.1	1.1
15N	Diseases of Genitourinary System	0.5	0.5	0.6	0.7	0.8	1.0	1.2
16O	Pregnancy, Childbirth and Puerperium injuries	0.9	1.1	0.9	0. 8	0.7	0.7	0.6
17W	Other External Causes of Accidental death	0.4	0.5	0.5	0.5	0.6	0.6	0.7
18F	Mental and Behavioral Disorders	0.3	0.6	0.4	0.5	0.5	0.5	0.6
19Q	Congenital Malformations, Deformations and Abnormalities	0.4	0.5	0.3	0.3	0.4	0.4	0.4
	Other Med. Certified Deaths	1.4	1.4	1.5	2.4	1.3	1.2	1.7

Source : Office of Registrar General, India : Survey of Causes of Death (rural) India (As per International Classification of Diseases –X revision).

Mortality from many of the communicable diseases has indeed declined but morbidity from some of them continues to remain high. Supply of potable drinking water and management of liquid and solid waste, still remain serious public health issue. Although mortality due to gastro-enteritis and dysentery has declined over time, diarrheal diseases continue to be an important cause of morbidity and mortality, especially among children. Oral rehydration therapy is becoming popular. The government has mobilized programs to reduce burden of morbidity and mortality attributable to vaccine preventable diseases. Poverty and malnutrition remain key health issues for the rural poor. Diseases related to environmental factors (e.g., respiratory diseases and cancer) are on the rise. Pollution from toxic industrial chemicals, from use of unprocessed fuels and emissions from vehicles all take their toll both in terms of increase in levels of morbidity and consequent mortality. India, China and many other developing countries have become dumping grounds for toxic materials and e-garbage from USA and other developed countries. The unscientific recycling of the scrapped computers and mobile phones releases carcinogens in the atmosphere. Changes in the life style as also the pressure of competition are reflected in the rise in deaths due to diseases related to circulation and nervous system.

On the basis of "Survey of Causes of Death, 1991" the states have been classified into three categories depending upon the disease-intensity of communicable diseases in the states.

Table 9.28
Communicable disease intensity zone (DIZ)

High disease intensity zone HDIZ	*Moderate disease intensity zone MDIZ*	*Low disease intensity zone LDIZ*
Assam, Madhya Pradesh, Uttar Pradesh	Bihar, Orissa, Rajasthan, Andhra Pradesh, Gujarat, Haryana, Punjab, Tamil Nadu	Kerala, Karnataka, Maharashtra

Source: RGI, Survey of Causes of Death, 1991.

The share of non-communicable diseases rose from 36 in 1969–71 to 55 percent in 1994–95. Bronchitis and asthma, cancers, heart attack, and paralysis are increasingly becoming important in the mortality profile. Though the figures pertain to rural areas, their share in the mortality profile of urban areas could be even greater, clearly reflecting the changing lifestyles. Tobacco use has become a major health risk. According to the NSS, 1998, nearly 45 percent of men and 7 percent of women aged 10 years and above were regular users of tobacco products. The use is greater among disadvantaged socio-economic groups and in rural areas. Another important cause of death relates to maternal and peri-natal factors. Their share to total deaths has not changed much during the period 1969–95. The RCH program initiated in 1997 specifically addresses maternal and child health.

Despite the welcome decline in mortality, there is still a huge scope for it to decline further in the decades ahead, especially in infant and child mortality. The low level of mortality achieved by Kerala clearly indicates that improvements elsewhere are possible. This would be true even if one makes allowance for the future impact of HIV/AIDS.

WHO publishes the burden of disease for different countries. Table 9.29 presents WHO estimates for 1998 for the burden of disease for India for selected diseases as also for the high as well

Table 9.29
Burden of diseases, WHO estimates 1998 (percent)

	India	*World*	*High income*	*Low income*
Communicable diseases, Maternal and Peri-natal conditions and Nutritional deficiencies	50.3	40.9	7.2	43.8
Infectious and Parasitic diseases	20.9	23.4	2.8	25.2
Tuberculosis	2.8	2.0	0.1	25.2
Sex Transmitted Diseases (STD)	1.8	1.2	0.4	1.3
HIV/AIDS	2.1	5.1	0.9	5.5
Diarrhaoel diseases	8.2	5.3	0.3	5.7
Childhood diseases	5.4	4.1	0.4	4.4
Malaria	0.2	2.8		3.1
Maternal conditions	2.9	2.3	0.5	2.5
Peri-natal conditions	8.7	5.8	1.9	6.2
Nutritional deficiencies	4.0	3.2	0.9	3.4
Non-communicable diseases	33.0	43.1	81.0	39.8
Injuries	16.7	16.0	11.8	16.4

Source: World Health Report, 2000.

as low/middle income countries by way of comparison. Half the burden of disease for India is accounted for by communicable diseases, maternal and peri-natal conditions and nutritional deficiencies. The share of communicable diseases alone is one fifth in the overall burden of disease. Moreover, the burden of disease in India for most traditional diseases is higher compared to both in high income and most other low/middle income countries. It is lower only for degenerative diseases, which forms a large part of the burden of disease in developed economies.

Over time with aging populations and decline in communicable diseases, the share of non-communicable diseases can only be expected to grow which will further strain the already constrained health system in India.

Infant mortality in India is still quite high and measures to significantly lower it are known, and tested. Combating childhood diseases such as respiratory tract infections and diarrhoeal diseases are well within reach requiring low technology and little investments. Universal immunization against vaccine preventable diseases such as tetanus, whooping cough and diphtheria as well as measles can save many lives. However health sector reforms that responding to issues of access, quality and ultimate satisfaction with service need to ensure that health for all does not remain a pipedream and goals articulated in the National Health Policy are achieved.

Three diseases need special mention in the changing pattern of causes of mortality – tuberculosis, malaria and HIV/AIDS.

9.6 Tuberculosis

Once a major killer disease, tuberculosis has been tamed by modern medicines. Every year on an average 2 million TB cases are reported in India, which is approximately one-fourth of all TB cases reported worldwide. TB still kills over 0.4 million Indians every year – a total that is greater than the combined death tolls from malaria, meningitis, hepatitis, nutritional deficiencies, leprosy, sexually transmitted diseases and tropical diseases, which cause about 258,000 deaths per annum in India (World Health Report 1999). National Tuberculosis Program (NTP) was initiated in India in 1962. It could not attain tangible achievement because of its over-reliance on X-rays for diagnosis, use of non-standard treatment regimens, low rates of treatment completion and lack of any systematic records of treatment outcomes. The Revised National Tuberculosis Control Program (RNTCP) was launched in 1993. The DOTS (Directly Observed Treatment, Short Course) strategy recommended by WHO was undertaken. The RNTCP is one of the largest public health programs anywhere in the world and has been a fairly successful one. The curative success rate with RNTCP is estimated at 89 percent in 2001. However, the emergence of HIV infection has complicated the TB scenario in India. People with HIV are more likely to actively develop TB and it is estimated that 7 percent of those infected with HIV also develop TB in India.

Asthma-bronchitis, TB of the lung and pneumonia are more prominent among the communicable diseases. Using wood as fuel for cooking coupled with poor ventilation and bad-housing conditions could be the cause for prevalence of asthma-bronchitis among rural women. TB prevalence is 131 per 100,000 in India while the world average is only 60. It still is one of the major killers in rural India. Lack of early detection, awareness, stigma about the disease to pursue treatment etc. is some of the reasons why TB prevalence rate could not be brought down fast. NFHS I (1992–93) reports that more than half of women aged 30 years and older suffer from risks of active tuberculosis.

9.7 Malaria

The resurgence of malaria, in spite of the vertical program since 1953 indicates that India needs to rethink about its strategies and develop close monitoring mechanism. As per National Malaria Eradication report, falciparum malaria has risen from 9.72 in 1972 to 35.5 percent in 1995, while the incidence of P. Vivax, the less virulent plasmodium, fell to 60–70 percent in the same period. There is evidence of increased resistance of falciparum parasite to chloroquine and other anti-malarial drugs. Although the number of deaths from malaria is not large, there is a concern over its morbidity effect which results in the loss of economic productivity.

Once a cause of frequent epidemics in rural areas, with greater urbanization, malaria has now stamped its presence in urban areas and other non-rural ecological environments. When National Malaria Control Program (NMCP) was started in 1953, 75 million malaria cases per year were reported of which 800,000 resulted in deaths. The NMCP was reshaped into National Malaria Eradication Program (NMEP) and by 1965 malaria was totally under control, thanks to DDT spray. 100,000 malaria cases were reported in the year with no report for death. From 1970 onwards, malaria has reemerged. The worst affected states in India as malaria reemerged in the 1970s were Bihar, Madhya Pradesh, Rajasthan, Uttar Pradesh, Orissa, Karnataka and Pondicherry. Now it almost arrives as an epidemic in nearly all the regions of India, more specifically in the poorer and more densely populated states like Uttar Pradesh, Bihar and West Bengal. In 2001, 2.01 million malaria cases were reported.

9.8 HIV/AIDS

In the last 30 years thirty new diseases have been discovered, HIV/AIDS is one of the deadliest. HIV (Human Immunodeficiency Virus) is lentrivirus. A man with HIV can live a long normal life before they develop full-blown AIDS (Acquired Immunodeficiency Syndrome) and during the gestation period they can cause rapid transmission of the disease through sexual relations. HIV is also a retrovirus, i.e., that it converts its genetic material from RNA to DNA when it inserts itself into a host's cell where it multiplies very rapidly. Adults between ages 25 and 40 are most vulnerable to HIV/AIDS. Human Development Report 1999 reported more than 33 million people living with HIV/AIDS in India at the end of 1998. In 2002, the number went up to 42 million. HIV infected population is more than 5.1 million in India in 2003. The prevalence rate among people in the age group 15–49 years is estimated at 0.8 percent (UNAID and NACO). Life expectancy in nine countries in Africa, where HIV prevalence rates were 10 percent or more (as high as 38.8% and 33.7% of population in ages 15–49 in Botswana

Table 9.30

Percentage of adults (aged 15–49) living with HIV/AIDS in selected countries by the end of 2001

Country	*Percentage of adults (aged 15–49) living with HIV/AIDS*
Botswana	38.8
Zimbabwe	33.7
South Africa	20.1
Kenya	15.0
Thailand	1.8
India	0.8
United States	0.6
United Kingdom	0.1
Pakistan	0.1

Source : UNAIDS and National AIDS Control Organization estimates.

and Zimbabwe respectively), has come down severely. AIDS is now a poor people's epidemic, with 95 percent of all HIV infected people are from the developing countries, especially the least developed sub-Saharan countries. In the high human development countries, the proportion was reported at 0.3 percent and the same in the least developed countries was as high as 4.3 percent. With no available cure in sight, HIV/AIDS has now become a major global phenomenon and has become a threat to India since the second highest number of HIV/AIDS infected people after South Africa are from India.

Figure 9.10
Reported AIDS cases, India 2003

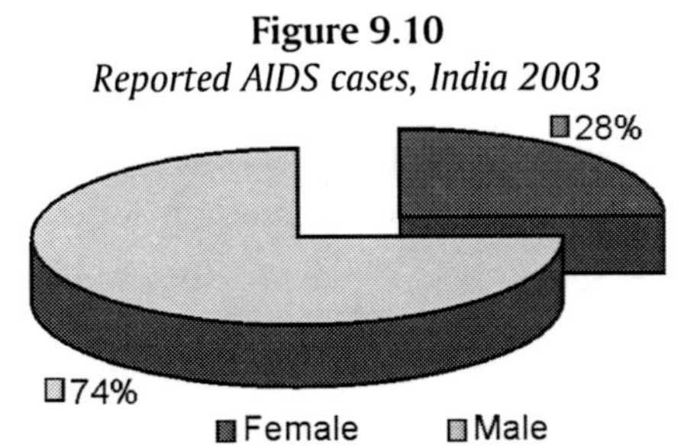

The first case of HIV in India was reported from Tamil Nadu as early as 1986. In the same year one more person infected with HIV was detected in Mumbai. It has rapidly spread since 1994. The number of people living with the disease has reached 5.1 million in 2003. (The estimated figures have been doubted by many. A recent survey suggests that HIV infected persons in India could be less than 2.5 million). Currently, every year about 0.6 million new cases of HIV infection in India are reported. Looking at the distribution of reported AIDS cases by sex in India, it is observed that in 2003, of the total reported AIDS cases, about 26 percent were females and 74 percent males. Nearly 60 percent of the reported cases were from rural areas.

The information collected on the transmission route from the AIDS cases reveal that in 86 percent cases the probable route of infection was through unprotected heterosexual sex, about 2.4 percent from infected blood or blood products, and about 2 percent of cases from sharing of needles/syringes associated with intravenous drug use. In about 3 percent of HIV cases, the transmission route was peri-natal or from mother-to-child. Among infants born to HIV-positive mothers, those who are breastfed for more than 15 months or who develop oral thrush (an oral and throat disease of infants) within six months after birth has an elevated risk of postnatal infection. Their risk is also increased if their mother has nipple or breast lesions during breastfeeding or if her immune system is compromised. Studies in Africa show that a large majority of childhood cases of HIV infection are acquired from the child's mother, whether before, during or after birth. Though measures such as antiretroviral medications and avoidance of breastfeeding reduce mother-to-child transmission, these interventions are often unavailable or impractical in the low-income families.

HIV has spread rapidly like fire among high-risk groups; levels of infection among commercial sex workers in Maharashtra reportedly increased form around 3 percent in 1987 to over 70 percent in 1997. Levels of HIV prevalence appear to be somewhat higher in the country's Southern states. But the single most severely affected location is the small Northeastern state, Manipur, bordering the so-called Golden Triangle region of South East Asia. HIV has spread in the state like fire by way of intravenous drug use, a practice not so widespread elsewhere in India.

Since AIDS is often associated in the minds of people with promiscuity and homosexual behavior, families and individuals conceal the illness for a long time for fear of discrimination and stigmatization that affect life in families, communities, workplaces, schools (infected children often are prevented from attending schools) and health care settings (even doctors and nurses refuse to attend HIV/AIDS patients). Tamil Nadu continues to account for the largest share of officially reported HIV/AIDS cases followed by Maharashtra, Andhra Pradesh, Gujarat and Karnataka. These five states account for about 80 percent of all reported HIV/AIDS cases in the country.

Figure 9.11
People living with HIV/AIDS in India

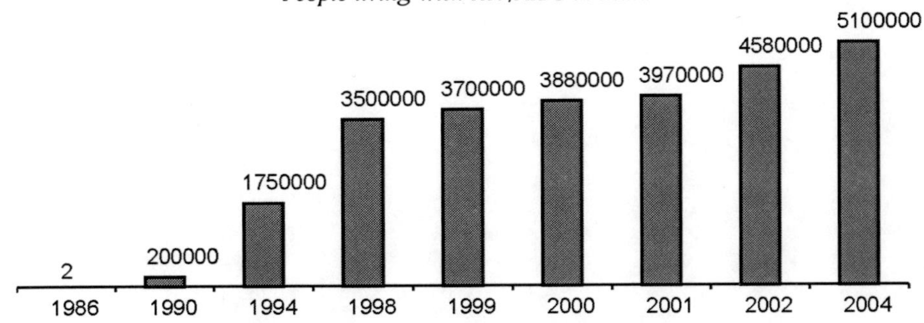

Figure 9.12
Percentage distribution of AIDS cases, India 2003

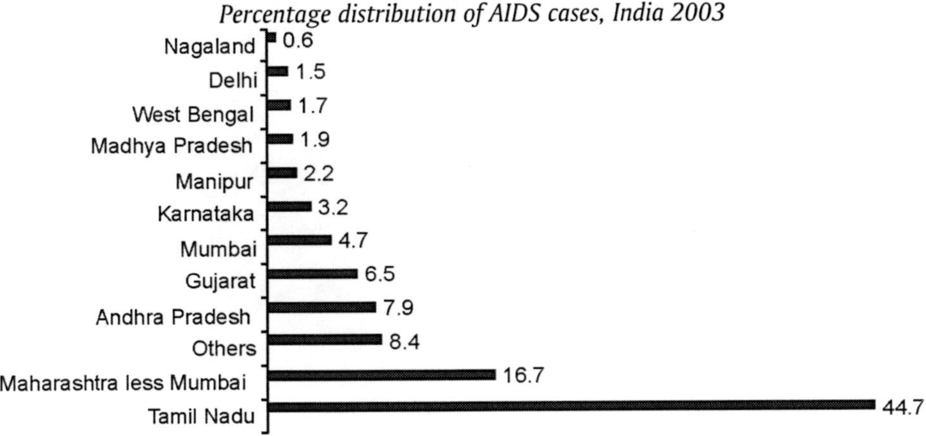

Table 9.31
HIV prevalence levels and officially reported AIDS cases

*State/UT**	*Percentage of patients testing positive for HIV at Sentinel sites 2002*			*Officially reported AIDS cases (as of 31st August 2003)#*
	Patients at sexually transmitted disease clinics	*Pregnant women at antenatal clinics*	*Patients at intravenous drug users clinics*	
1	*2*	*3*	*4*	*5*
Andhra Pradesh	30.4	1.3	NA	4339
Arunachal Pradesh	0.0	0.0	NA	0.0
Assam	0.8	0.0	NA	171
Bihar	1.6	0.3	NA	155
Chhattisgarh	0.8	0.3	NA	NA
Delhi*	3.2	0.3	7.2	821
Goa	11.3	1.4	NA	308

Cont'd...

Table 9.31 Cont'd...

1	*2*	*3*	*4*	*5*
Gujarat	6.2	0.4	NA	3562
Haryana	1.1	0.4	NA	313
Himachal Pradesh	0.4	0.0	NA	114
Jammu & Kashmir	1.0	0.1	NA	2
Jharkhand	0.1	0.0	NA	NA
Karnataka	13.6	1.8	2.3	1790
Kerala	2.5	0.4	NA	267
Madhya Pradesh	2.4	0.0	NA	1024
Maharashtra	7.8	1.3	39.4	11829
Manipur	9.6	1.1	39.1	1238
Meghalaya	0.9	0.0	0.0	8
Mizoram	2.6	1.5	1.6	51
Nagaland	2.4	1.3	10.3	343
Orissa	0.8	0.3	NA	128
Punjab	1.6	0.5	NA	248
Rajasthan	6.0	0.5	NA	826
Sikkim	0.0	0.1	NA	8
Tamil Nadu	14.7	0.9	33.8	24667
Tripura	1.4	0.0	NA	4
Uttar Pradesh	0.8	0.3	NA	1083
Uttaranchal	1 0.3	0.2	NA	NA
West Bengal	0.5	0.0	1.5	930
Andaman and Nicobar Islands*	2.6	0.0	NA	32
Chandigarh*	0.8	0.3	NA	750
Dadra and Nagar Haveli*	NA	1.0	NA	0
Daman and Diu*	NA	0.2	NA	1
Lakshadweep*	0.0	0.0	NA	0
Pondicherry*	2.0	0.3	NA	157
Total	**130**	**16**	**135**	**55169**

NA : Not available
#Experts believe these cases represent only a small portion of actual cases of AIDS in the country
Source : National AIDS Control Organization.

The national government has set up a separate body, National AIDS Control Organization (NACO), to combat this disease with the help of state health departments. Electronic and other media are extensively been activated to educate people about how they can prevent contracting HIV/AIDS. A debate even has now started if the government should come out with appropriate legislation asking people to get tested for HIV/AIDS before entering into matrimonial relations.

10
Migration in India

10.1 Introduction

The Indian census since 1961 has included questions on people's place of last residence and their duration of stay at the place of enumeration. Earlier, only birth place was recorded. Since inclusion of this question in the schedule, migrant is taken as, someone whose place of *previous residence* differs form the place where he/she was enumerated. Although the data miss out many movements, for example, within the same town (technically movement within the same town is not regarded as migration), they do capture the broad features of migration. Counting migration by birthplace does not capture fully the economic, social and political factors often closely associated with migration. Even today, most babies are born in maternal grandfathers' house, especially in rural middle class families in India. Geographical demarcation of many states and districts has changed over years. A large proportion of people in Punjab, West Bengal, Assam, Tripura and others were born in West Pakistan or East Pakistan (now Bangladesh). If place of birth is taken as the criterion, they are all immigrants. Carving out new states (Chhattisgarh, Jharkhand and Uttaranchal in the recent past) has changed the residence identity of many people.

The salient feature of the three censuses from 1961 to 1991 is that migration patterns have been changing only very slowly in India. Migrants accounted for about 27.5 percent of the total population in 1991, which in the years between 1961 and 1981 was around 30 percent. Women in India formed a great majority of internal migrants; 42 percent of the total female population had migrated from their previous place of residence to the place of enumeration. This proportion among males was only 14.7 percent. Women dominated the migration streams because of the practice of village exogamy prevailing in many parts of the country. At marriage women move to neighboring areas to live with their husbands' families. This explains why close to 60 percent of migration in India was reported to be intra-district indicating short distance moves. Another 25 percent of migration was inter-district but within the same state, which would also generally be short distance migration between adjacent districts. Only about 12 percent of migrants moved between the states.

At the initiative of the Planning Commission in India, many studies have been carried out on urbanization and migration. Agro-Economic Research Centers have conducted surveys on migration in many villages. NSSO keeps migration as a key topic in many of their survey rounds. Although most major analysis on migration is based on Census data, studies also are carried out on private or institutional initiative. For example, I.P. Desai conducted a survey in 1958 in Mahuva in Sourashtra and found that 56 percent of the habitants had settled there since 1900 or earlier, 15 percent came between 1901 and 1930 and 30 percent after 1931. Most people came from nearby villages, very few from distant places. The study also showed that 60 percent of the in-migrants had stayed in one another place, 24 percent in two other places and 16 percent in three or more places before finally settling in Mahuva. That is, the ultimate destination place was reached in stages. Most of these migrants decided to make Mahuva their home, 10 percent did not decide as yet and only 5 percent were seriously thinking of leaving the place. K. Patel found that two-thirds of laborers working in mills in Bombay had persons known to them intimately and were working in the same locality, 15 percent had close relations working in the place and another 17 percent had people from their villages staying in Mumbai. The study highlighted the importance of 'contact' in rural to urban migration. The study also showed that people both in the receiving and sending areas tried to take a compromised attitude towards the traditions of the sending and receiving areas. That is, there is some sort of cultural assimilation both for the in-migrants and the original inhabitants of the place. Studies on migration also revealed that there is always a dominant route for migration: the tea gardens in Assam received labor from Chotonagpur in Bihar, the coal mines in Chotonagpur received labor from Bihar and Uttar Pradesh, the brick fields in West Bengal have labors mostly from Bihar, etc.

K.C. Zacharia has made very valuable contribution on the nature of migration and its effect on the redistribution of the population, age and sex composition of the receiving and sending populations and some social and economic aspects of the migrated population. His study was based on the Census data from 1901 to 1931. He found that Bombay province received migrants from all over India. Out-migration far exceeded in-migration in the Southern states, that is, net migration in the Southern states was negative. Uttar Pradesh, Rajasthan and Punjab were out-migrating states. Though Punjab received agricultural labors from the nearby states, they themselves migrated in large number to distant places. Within the Southern states the dominating migration stream was Travancor-Cochin (Kerala) and Mysore (Karnataka) to Madras (Tamil Nadu). Bengal received people in large numbers from Orissa and Bihar, the latter two states basically being out-migrating type. In this period, Bengal sent its own educated men to different parts of the country. The migration streams identified by Zacharia for the period 1901–31 remain largely unchanged even today. Zacharia and Seetharam analyzed migration between 1951 and 1961 and came to the conclusion that two migration streams played major roles in population redistribution in India – one was from South to East and South-East and the other originating from North and moving towards North-West.

While studying rural-urban migration in Uttar Pradesh, T. Piplai and H. Majumdar came to the conclusion from their study of 1961 Census data on migration and some other migration studies that the magnitude of inter-state migration was far from very large when we take a look at the volume of internal migration observed in India. Most of the migrants concentrated in two of the then industrially developed states – Maharashtra and West Bengal. One-third of the out-migrants came from Uttar Pradesh and Bihar. In the first stage, the skilled persons and entrepreneurs migrated to the destination to take advantage of the opportunities that already exist or new ones created. Although the industry gets a boost through these migrants in their labor, the in-migrants soon enters into confrontation with the local people. This happens when the local people realize that they need to become interested in entering into similar such ventures or take advantage of the job opportunities created by the on-going and up-coming projects largely nurtured by those coming from some other states with a different linguistic origin. The demand for "Employment for the sons of the soil" arose because of conflict in interest between the local people and the settlers. Linguistic differences between the local community and the settlers often would lead to clashes and violence and different political outfits would try to take advantage of the situation. Even 60 years after independence the hard inequality in economic and social development remains among the states. In some instances even it might have intensified. The space between demand and creation of new jobs is widening everyday especially when employment opportunities in agriculture are progressively sinking. It is no wonder therefore that the local residents would demand all the jobs that are created in their state or in their locality for themselves.

Prof. Ashish Bose has analyzed migration related information collected in the 1961 Census with a view to relate these to prevailing social scenario all over the country. He tried to decipher the *modus operandi* of migration and bring out the original destinations of migration, measure the distance and volume of migration and the migration streams. We do not see much change in the characters of migration even when India was about to enter into a new phase of economic and social reconstruction. Neither the traditional streams of migration changed nor there was much change in respect to distance of migration. Bose drew our attention to an important feature of rural-urban (R-U) migration – the "return migration", that is, those who returned to their place of origin from the destination. He classified these migrants into three broad categories:

1. *The seasonal migrants:* Many people move to nearby towns and cities in search of some additional income or livelihood in the days when there is scarcity of job (lean season for agriculture) in villages. This cannot be called a distress movement.
2. *Target movers*: Some migrants move to towns and cities to earn certain amount of money within a specific time period. Once their goal is achieved, they return to their villages. Their stay in urban area may range from a few months to a few years depending upon how quickly their objectives are realized.
3. *The failures*: These migrants come to a city or a town with a well-defined objective. When they realize that their objectives could not be realized as easily as they had thought, they return to their villages disillusioned.

The first two categories deserve attention for economic analysis and social planning. These migrants retain their intimate contact with the villages where they hail from. They are unwilling to break their tie with their ancestral places in villages. If some alternative deal were made available in villages for the lean months, they probably would not have gone to towns to seek a livelihood. If rural development projects are properly implemented and small or medium-scale agro-industries are set up, the pressure of urban-ward migrations could be eased considerably.

Demographers seem to be divided in their explanations for different migration streams. Some stress on the *push factor* of the villages more than the *pull factor* of the destination responsible for out-migration. That is, the economically deprived section of the village people move to urban areas in search of a better and steady job prospect. Eames' observation of course was opposite of this. Edwin Eames observed that potential and pattern of migration are different for different caste communities. Potential for migration is more among the economically advanced higher caste groups. Victor D'Souza was of the view that different social groups try to asses with their own yard-stick, the availability of the specific nature of jobs and opportunity of earning before making any move. Because of linguistic, religious and caste barriers, the relatively economically disadvantaged people do not like to move to towns and cities alone; they migrate in groups. They try to stay together so that they can live among their own people and maintain a social climate closely similar to the one they had while they were in their villages. This migration in groups to the same destination is a common feature in Indian migration. In many cities and towns a bystander often would have a feeling that there are some pockets where the physical and social environment often would remind him of that of a village.

The Planning Commission initiated a survey on migration in the 1950s. The survey observed that the reasons behind and pattern of R-U migration was largely region specific. Although economic hardship was the most important reason behind such migration, some are attracted by the glamour of urban life style, for some it gives an opportunity to improve one's earnings, some move to towns and cities because it gives a better opportunity to pursue higher education and still for some others it is just because he was transferred to the place by his employer. 70 percent of in-migrants in Mumbai came in search of jobs from all parts of the country; 13.5 percent came for improving their earnings. The survey in Calcutta (now Kolkata) revealed that 50 percent of the migrants came to avail of the employment potential in the city as also because of abundance of facilities to improve one's life style; 43 percent migrated because of the 'push' factor operating in villages. A huge number of families came to West Bengal and Punjab from East and West Pakistan because of partition of India in 1947. N.V. Sovane reviewed closely the surveys conducted in some regions and came to the conclusion that income opportunity was the prime mover behind all migrations. Regarding occupation or profession of the migrants, his observation was that the intensity of migration was less among landless labor and more among those engaged in professions other than those tied to land. He also observed that proportion of unemployed among the migrants was fewer in large cities compared to that in smaller cities or towns. NSSO survey also confirmed this. One explanation for this phenomenon is that those who failed to secure jobs within a reasonable time, returned to their original/previous place of residence, which usually was their village (return migration). Prof. Ashis Bose after analyzing the NSSO data made the observation that for every 100 persons receiving a reasonable job in the city/town dragged 254 other persons to the city. To the observation that the proportion of unemployed among the migrants was small, he felt that this happened because "push" factor operated strongly both at the place of origin and destination. Commenting on the population distribution in Punjab, Gurudev Singh Goshal said that population density, per capita landholding and the inclination of the Punjabis in general to take risk at any point of time and for whatever other reasons propel them to migrate even to distant places. People from rural areas come to cities primarily in search of jobs, not for the glamour's of city life.

A study in 15 villages in Maharashtra by Demographic Training and Research Center found that marriage of girls contributed most both to in- and out-migration in villages. The young and educated persons dominated male migration. Villages tend to lose young and middle aged persons as a result of out-migration. More importantly, villages tend to lose talents. The problem of "brain drain" (recently, some are advocating the term "brain exchange") is not an issue only in international migration; it is equally ominous for those villages or states that send out talented youths and skilled hands in large numbers to cities or to different states. This has become a serious matter of discussion as Information Technology sector in some selected states expanded by leaps and bounds.

Research on migration has largely remained confined to R-U stream of migration. If 'migration for reasons of marriage' is discounted from the causes of migration, economics (search for job, better income, improvement in life style) remain the principal factor for male migration. Urban growth is to some extent related to level of industrialization, consequent upon a shift from agro-based economy to industrial economy. Therefore, study of migration has a strong component in the growth of economy and the distribution of the fruits of economic development among the masses. For this and many other reasons R-U stream has remained the focal point in most demographic, social and economic research.

An overwhelming majority of studies in migration have used aggregative data from the Census. The macro level studies give us trends in migration over a period of time, changes in the strengths of migration streams, inter-state variation in net, in- and out-migration, dominant reasons of migration as also the nature of region and state-specific population redistribution. Micro level studies are very few, often confined to very small pockets or some specific social groups. From the point of view of sociology and social demography, study of migration is to understand the changes in social environment and social organizations as also the activities in the political platform and how the disruptive forces operate in places where population density has changed and considerable alteration in the population composition has taken place due to migration. No credible report however has been published covering these social issues.

Most surveys in India have concentrated on inter-state migration, migration streams, volume of migration by distance and the effects urbanization and industrialization have on migration. India is a fast developing country with a very enviable cultural tradition. During the period of reconstruction after independence, it has taken variety of measures for a rapid growth in the economic and social sector. With rapid urbanization and industrialization and the multinationals' keen interest in the vast Indian market, the pace of life even for a common man has changed. In this fast changing scenario, many of India's traditional values have now become vulnerable; political and social instability galore; corruption at high places is at its peak; disruptive forces are becoming stronger everyday. How does migration fit into this fast changing state of affairs? It is time we take a comprehensive look at the prevailing situation and examine how migration fits into all these scheme of things.

10.2 International Migration

The 1981 Census informed us that about 8 million people, born in some other country, were living in India. A good proportion of these people were young or middle aged. Migration from Bangladesh still continues; both Hindus and Muslims are among these migrants. That illegal migration has become a serious issue is borne by the fact that decadal growth rates in some of the bordering districts of West Bengal and Northeastern states are much higher than the average population growth rates of these states. In 1981, number of such migrants in India was about 3.89 percent of all migrants, internal and international. In the total population their share was a little above 1 percent.

India has drawn people from all over the world even in the distant past because of its abundant resources. Indians too had established trade relations with many countries and many Indians in course of time had settled there. Between the first and the ninth Census (1951), net international migration, in-migration (immigration) of foreign nationals and out-migration (emigration) of Indians, was insignificant. Even the population exchanges between Pakistan and India during partition in 1947 was evenly balanced. Nearly 7 million people were involved from either side in this population exchange. Although Nepal, Bhutan and Sri Lanka are our next door neighbors, size of immigration from these countries or emigration to these countries are nominal. The 1971 Census recorded about 9.4 million people in India who were born in other countries. After Bangladesh Liberation War in 1971 the absolute number of immigrants had dropped. In 1971, these immigrants constituted 5.64 percent of all migrants and their share in the total population was 1.7 percent. The high percentage of immigrants was mostly due to 1965 war with Pakistan. In fact, trans-boundary movement from East Pakistan, now Bangladesh, has never stopped because of political unrest in that country as also because of the discriminatory stand on Hindus taken by the administration from time to time. Between 1961 and 1971, nearly 1.8 million people migrated to India from East and West

Pakistan. Among the immigrants only 0.07 million were from Nepal, Malaysia, Sri Lanka and Myanmar.

The Northeast has over 500 ethnic groups owing to frequent migrations and invasions. Migration of population creating demographic changes is an issue of concern. In the 20th century under British rule, immigration and in-migration, particularly into Assam, North Bengal and Tripura, was probably to the extent of 30 percent of the population, of which about two-thirds were from East Bengal. This trend continued even after independence. In 1971, again there was a major exodus from East Pakistan to Northeast and West Bengal, the majority of whom never returned owing to the situation which led to the Indo-Pak war. Thereafter, major agitation in Assam led to slowing down of immigration but did not totally stop it, most probably due to vote-bank politics.

The effects of immigration are that Tripura, which had a tribal majority in the early 20th century, is now a tribal minority state with consequent long drawn insurgent movement. Sikkim now has a Nepalese majority; Assam has about 40 percent immigrant population, about 30 percent from Bangladesh and the rest from West Bengal, Bihar, UP and Rajasthan. The communal disharmony is largely to blame for Ulfa, Bodo, Karbi and Dimasa insurgencies

If migration is counted 'by place of last residence', the proportion of migrants from outside India to total migrants was 4.48 percent in 1971. In 1981, this dropped to 2.97 percent. The 1991 Census data shows 2.5 percent of total migrants had their last residence in some other country (mostly Pakistan and Bangladesh).

There is no reliable data on the volume of emigrants from India. As early as the beginning of the nineteenth century, Indians started going over to many places on contractual assignment. A sizeable proportion of them had made these countries their homes. They are living there for many generations. But their exact number is never known. Many Indians have been going to USA, Canada, UK and some other countries in the West to pursue higher education. Many of them ultimately settled there and obtained citizenship of the country. The Missionaries are sending many destitute and orphans to Europe and other countries to their adopted parents. The immigration laws in most of these countries had been tightened to curb illegal immigration. But with globalization of economy, the developed countries have relaxed visa for certain categories of persons, mostly the highly educated and technical persons. These countries have become the destination of skilled, scientific and technical persons from the developing countries, especially from India and China. Persons with highly specialized education and training are increasingly becoming the citizen of the global village.

There are hardly any university or research institution in USA and UK, which are not manned significantly either by the Indians or by the Chinese. In UK, there are probably more Indian doctors than the British doctors. Many aeronautic engineers and computer specialists from India are in many important positions in NASA. Indian scientists and engineers, especially in the IT sector, are in high demand from all over the world.

There was a time, not very long ago though, the best of the Indian students invariably would do their graduation in science and pursue higher education most possibly in Physics or Chemistry or Mathematics. But today the cream of these best prefers IIT or IIM, which are among the best professional institutions in the world. The government has done everything possible to provide the IITs and IIMs the best infrastructure and the best teaching and training facilities to attract the talented youths to join these institutions. Banks are more than eager to provide hefty educational loans to those enrolled in these premier institutions. The big industries and corporate bodies offer them lucrative jobs even before they have completed their courses. But it is sad to note that many of these IIT and

IIM trained engineers and management specialists do not hesitate to allow USA or UK or some such countries to buy them at hefty prices for their specialized skills. It is true that these Indian scientists, technologists and management specialists are among the best paid persons in USA, UK, Canada or Australia. This 'brain drain' (or 'brain exchange') has escalated more after Indian talents proved that they are one of the best in software technology. The Indian government has been trying hard to prevent the colossal loss of brainpower. Corporate giants in India are trying hard to hold them back in India, but they too cannot pay them the salary and other parks that the multinationals offer them without any hesitation. It would be simplistic to say that the Indian talents are lured by the robust compensation the multinationals offer for hiring their skill. Money offered is important, but no less important is the freedom to work and the excellent working environment that are offered in USA or UK or Canada or Europe. Even our corporate giants cannot insure the latter two because of the general work culture in the country and frequent interferences from powerful trade unions under the banner of this or that political party. When our Public Sector engages these scientists, technologists and other super-specialists, they soon become mere administrators. The organization seldom uses their scientific skills true to their potential. Many scientists came back from abroad to serve the cause of the nation. But the work environment in which they were asked to work soon disillusioned them. Disheartened as they were, they had to go back to the country from where they returned.

The structural adjustments in the last twenty years or so that are going on in the developing economies has created a regime that is looking for more openness and greater trade relations with the rest of the world. The desire to become an important participant in global economy, India has opened the floodgate for internal and international migration both for skilled and semi-skilled labor. Though the exact number of Indian emigrants to various countries in any specific year is not exactly known, Ministry of Labor, Government of India and International Labor Organization provide some data of emigrants from India to a few selected countries. An estimates of the total number of emigrants from India is presented below.

Table 10.1

Total emigration from India, pre- and post-reform

Year	*Emigration*	*Year*	*Emigration*	*Year*	*Emigration*
1986	114,000	1992	417,000	1998	355,000
1987	125,000	1993	438,000	1999	199,000
1988	170,000	1994	425,000	2000	243,000
1989	126,000	1995	415,000	2001	279,000
1990	144,000	1996	414,000	2002	368,000
1991	202,000	1997	416,000	2003	466,000

Source: Annual Report 2003–04, Ministry of Labour, Government of India.

North America and the Middle East draw a very large number of migrants from India. Each country has stringent Immigration Laws. Even then illegal immigration remains a serious problem for most of these countries, especially the developed ones. The following two tables show the skill composition of Indian Immigrants to North America and the Gulf countries.

Figure 10.1

Total emigrantion from India, 1986–2003

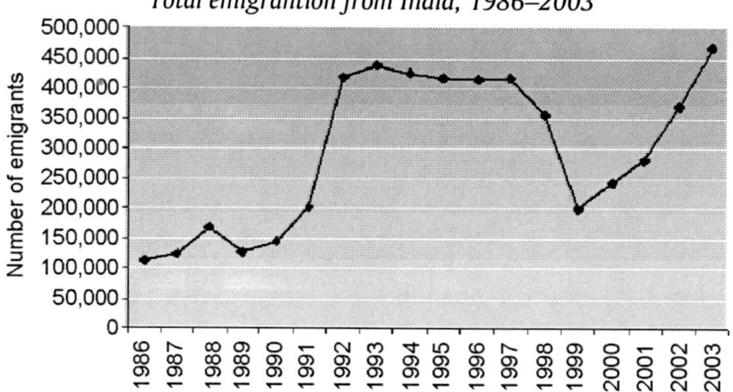

Table 10.2

Skill composition (percentage) of Indian immigrants to USA and Canada

Occupation	*1971–75*		*1976–79*		*1980–85*		*1986–90*	
	US	*Canada*	*US*	*Canada*	*US*	*Canada*	*US*	*Canada*
Professional & Technical	43.4	11.1	26.9	3.5	15.7	2.8	13.5	2.1
Administrative & Managerial	2.1	1.3	4.7	0.7	5.2	0.7	5.8	1.5
Clerical and Sales	2.7	5.5	4.2	2.6	3.7	1.5	4.2	1.7
Service	1.1	1.3	1.0	0.6	2.2	0.7	4.5	0.9
Farming and allied	0.3	4.9	1.7	1.3	2.7	3.7	3.3	4.7
Skilled Workers	2.2	14.0	3.3	3.2	2.9	2.4	2.5	4.1
Dependents/Unclassified	48.2	57.8	58.2	75.7	67.6	69.4	66.2	64.8
Total Number	72,912	42,632	76,561	30,271	98,179	32,657	142,140	46,647

Source: Annual Report, Ministry of Labour, Government of India: various issues.

Table 10.3

Skill composition (percentage) of Indian immigrants to the middle-east

Occupation	*Percent of total*	
	1984	*1986*
Unskilled Workers	43	40.1
Construction	41.7	34.6
Farms and Household	1.3	5.5
Skilled Workers	41.8	47
Construction	22.3	21.5
Others	19.5	25.5
White Collar Workers	3.6	6.5
High-skilled Workers	3.2	5.2
Medical	1.3	1
Technical and Supervisory	1.9	4.2
Other	8.4	1.2
Total number	205922	113649

Source: Annual Report, Ministry of Labour, Government of India.

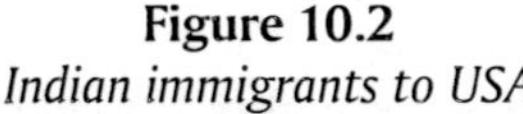

Figure 10.2
Indian immigrants to USA

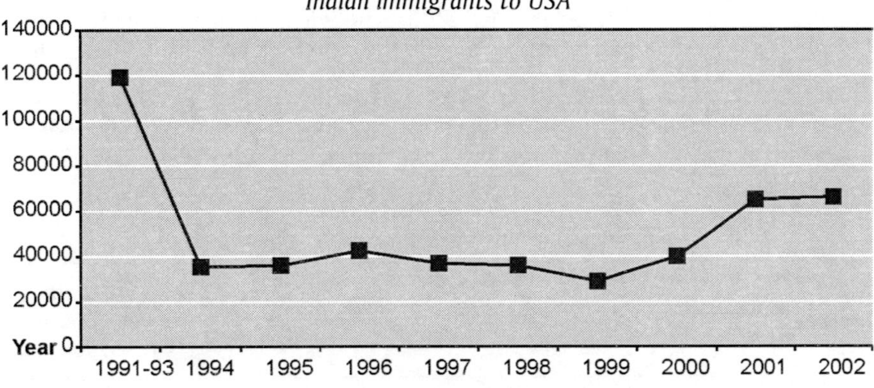

Figure 10.3
Indian immigrants to Soudi Arabia and UAE

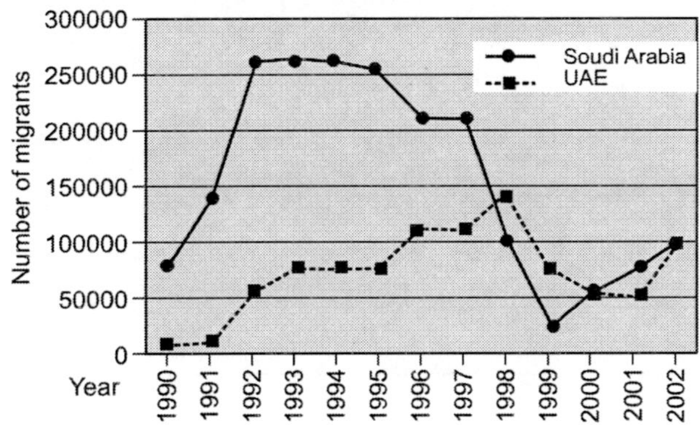

The decision for international migration depends on a number of factors: foreign returns vis-à-vis domestic returns to work-effort, the wages offered by the destination country discounted by the differences in cost of living in the sending and destination countries, domestic and foreign market conditions, the production technology demanding skill and professionalism in the native country vis-à-vis destination countries and a host of personal and social factors. There is no uncertainty that skill-premium across the globe, especially with globalization and trade liberalization, has increased considerably. Although a large outflow of skill from the developing countries is causing some concern in the skill basket of the sending country, it has a plus point as well – inflow of remittances adds substantially to the foreign exchange reserve of the country.

For India, the migration in the post-reform period has been substantial, especially to USA (Figure 10.2). The other most important destination for Indian migrants is the Gulf countries. In the years immediately after reform was started, the Indian immigrants to Gulf countries increased although the trends tapered towards the end of the decade. The drop in the number of Indian immigrants in some of the Gulf countries was partly due to extradition of illegal immigrants as also due to job-cuts in the Gulf-states. The Gulf countries still remain the major destination for emigrants from India for various kinds of skilled, semi-skilled and unskilled jobs. The drop in the number of emigrants from India in late nineties was largely due to drop in Indian immigrants to Gulf countries in those years. Emigration has picked up again (Figure 10.1). A large contingent of immigrants in Gulf countries are from Kerala. Whereas the highly skilled and professionals persons chose USA, Canada and Europe as their destination, it was mostly the unskilled and skilled labors that went to the Gulf countries. If economics of poverty played a dominant role in emigration to the Gulf countries, it was probably better pay along with the desire to improve one's skill quality and obtain better recognition in the world community that inspired Indian talents to move to USA, UK, Canada, etc.

Table 10.4
Indian immigrants' remittances over the years

Type of remittances	*Remittances (US$ million)*			
	1990–91	*1992–93*	*1996–97*	*2001–02*
1. Workers' Remittances (a to f)	1655	3410	11626	11533
(a) Family Maintenance	626	730	2518	
(b) Repatriation of savings	1027	1604	1935	
(c) Migrants transfer	2	0	11	
(d) Gold and silver	0	1076	2718	13
(e) Foreign currency bonds transferred to residents	0	0	1017	0
(f) Local withdrawals/redemptions of NRI deposits	NA	NA	3427	3444
2. Gifts and donations, etc.	429	454	809	659
Total (1 and 2)	2083	3864	12435	12192

N.A. Not Available
Source: Reserve Bank of India Bulletin, various issues
(Adapted from Rajat Acharyya and Saibal Kar: Trade Liberalization, Migration and Poverty (on line)

10.3 Migration Streams in Internal Migration

The salient feature of the three censuses from 1971 to 1991 is that migration patterns have been changing very slowly in India. Migrants accounted for 27.5 percent of the total population in 1991, more than 2.5 percentage points drop from the proportions in previous two Censuses. The R-U migration stream in India remains almost as strong as in any other country. It is a naked truth today that agriculture alone cannot sustain the growing size of job-seekers in almost all countries. Per capita land available for cultivation is getting smaller everyday. The huge number of households holding less than 2 acres of agricultural land speaks why India's job potential in agriculture is simply bleak. That is, agriculture cannot provide jobs to the rising numbers in rural areas. Industrialization has given a new hope for our teeming millions. Urban-ward movement is getting stronger everyday in all countries since industrialization has created varieties of job opportunities. All the desired facilities – health, education, entertainment, trade and commerce, etc. are concentrated in urban areas. In most developing countries a large share of their GDP is spent in developing and expanding urban areas. For better communication facilities, the address of most of the industrial establishments and business houses is one of these urban centers.

Table 10.5

Percentage distribution of migrants in different migration streams for each sex over the years, India

Sex	*Year*	*Rural to Rural*	*Rural to Urban*	*Urban to Urban*	*Urban to Rural*
Male	1961	56.7	25.7	13.0	4.6
	1971	53.5	26.0	14.0	6.5
	1981	45.6	30.0	17.4	7.0
	1991	43.4	31.6	17.8	7.2
Female	1961	81.3	9.7	5.8	3.2
	1971	77.7	10.5	6.7	5.1
	1981	73.3	12.5	8.7	5.5
	1991	72.2	13.5	8.8	5.5
Person	1961	73.7	14.6	8.1	3.6
	1971	70.3	15.3	8.9	5.5
	1981	65.2	17.6	11.2	6.0
	1991	64.5	18.4	11.2	5.9

Note:
1. Table excludes persons who were born outside India.
2. 1981 figures exclude Assam State where 1981 Census could not be conducted due to disturbed conditions prevailing at that time.
3. 1961,1971,1981 and 1991 figures are based on place of birth and excludes the unclassifiable figures.
4. 1991 figures excludes Jammu & Kashmir as no census could be held there.

Source: Office of the Registrar General, India

'Rural to Rural' migration stream has steadily declined from around 74 percent in 1961 to 64.5 percent in 1991. This is true both for male and female rural populations. That the R-R migration has remained most dominant among women clearly indicates that a very high proportion of these movements must have been due to marriage considerations. Even today 60 percent of migration among women takes place within the same district. Decline in the R-R migration ratio for females probably has something to do with family decisions as also to the migration decisions of the principal earning members, most generally by their husbands. Marriage as a reason for R-R migration of females has increased by about 4 percent between 1981 and 1991 and share of 'family movement' as a cause for migration declined by about the same percentage point. Expectantly, R-U migration has increased over the years, so has U-U migration. The latter type of migration mostly relates to skilled population. Proportion of women involved in these two streams of migration too has increased but their proportion remains less than half of that of males involved in these migrations. Over the years, 'Urban to Rural' stream of migration (share of return migrants must be very high in this stream) has declined fast between 1961 and 1981 and thereafter it has remained almost steady at around 6 percent. Migration streams in Table 10.5 are based on 'place of birth' whereas that of Table 10.6 are based on last residence.

The greater the level of industrialization the stronger becomes the R-U stream. The stronger the R-U stream, faster becomes the growth rate in urban areas with consequent increase in population density in cities and towns. Whereas growth of population in villages is entirely dependent on natural increase (minus out and return migrations), growth of urban population is significantly dependent upon the volume of net migration. Since urban-ward movement is primarily for seeking jobs and for trade and commerce, male population dominates in urban areas, resulting in weak F/M ratio in the urban population. The age distribution of the urban population is also different from that in rural area. Even the newly emerging urban areas have a different age-sex population composition compared to that in the older cities and towns. Population in urban areas, especially the emerging ones, is "young" compared to those in older cities and in rural areas.

The following table gives a comparative picture of internal migration by place of last residence in India between 1971 and 1991.

Table 10.6

Percentage distribution of migrants by place of last residence for each sex over the years

Place of last residence	*1971*			*1981*			*1991*		
	M	*F*	*P*	*M*	*F*	*P*	*M*	*F*	*P*
1	*2*	*3*	*4*	*5*	*6*	*7*	*8*	*9*	*10*
A. Migrants within the state of enumeration to total migrants	74.0	88.6	83.9	76.8	89.5	85.7	76.6	89.4	85.8
(i) Migrants who have resided elsewhere in the district of enumeration to total migrants (short distance)	49.0	69.0	62.6	48.5	66.7	61.3	47.9	60.3	60.5
(ii) Migrants who have resided in other districts of the state to total migrants (medium distance)	25.0	19.6	21.3	28.3	22.8	24.5	28.7	24.1	25.3
B. Migrants who have resided in other states of India to total migrants (long distance)	18.0	8.0	11.2	18.0	8.5	11.3	18.5	8.8	11.5
C. Migrants who have resided in other countries to total migrants (international)	8.0	3.4	4.9	5.2	2.0	2.9	4.9	1.8	2.7
Total Population (million)	284	264	548	354	331	685	438	406	844
Migrant Population (million)	53.9	113.9	167.8	62.5	145.2	207.7	64.3	167.8	232.1
Migrant Population as % of Total Population	19.0	43.1	30.6	17.7	44.2	30.3	14.7	41.3	27.5

Source: Office of the Registrar General, India.

Migration in India mostly remains confined to within the state – from 83.9 percent in 1971 it has gone up to 85.8 percent in 1991. Of this proportion, the short distant migrants' share (movement within the same district of enumeration) is 60.5, the remaining 25.3 percent are for medium distance (between two districts of the same state) migration. A good majority of women (60.3%) are short distance migrants. 89.4 percent of the migrant women move within the same district compared to 76.6 percent of men. Inter-state migration has remained around the same level (11.2 – 11.5%) during 1971–91. International migration (previous residence was some other country) has declined by 45 percent during this period.

There are three components of urban growth viz., the natural increase, net migration and the area classification, i.e., addition of new towns minus declassification of existing towns. The extension of boundaries of towns tends to influence the urban growth. The natural increase reflects the role of *demographic momentum*; migration is sensitive to economic growth. Table 10.7 shows the natural growth rate between 1971 and 1999 separately for rural and urban areas. Though there was huge difference in birth rates between rural and urban India in the 1970s, this has narrowed down since. Along with lower birth rate, death rate in urban areas has also been low. The death rate too in rural areas was quite high compared to that in urban areas. This indicates that there was not much of a difference in the decadal natural growth rate (1970s and 1980s) in rural and urban India. The natural increase in rural area has increased during 1981–90, but it remained almost at the same level as in 1971–80 in urban area. This is a clear indication that slowing down of urbanization in India cannot be accounted for by natural increase alone. The share of natural increase to urban population in the 1980s has increased and the share of migration declined. The natural increase further dipping (15.75) in the urban areas during 1991–2000, net decadal migration remaining almost at the same level, slowed down the urbanization process in the 1990s.

Table 10.7

Trend in natural Increase and decadal growth in rural and urban areas, India 1971–1999

Year	*Decadal growth rate*		*Natural increase*	
	Rural	*Urban*	*Rural*	*Urban*
1971–80	19.7	46.4	19.99	19.27
1981–90	19.6	36.2	21.64	19.49
1991–99	18.0	31.1	19.57	15.75

Source: RGI: Sample Registration Bulletins.

Whereas decadal growth rates in rural areas had been close to the natural increase, natural increase account for about 50 percent or even less of the decadal growth rate in urban areas. The difference between the two growth rates in favor of urban area must be due to migration from rural areas as also to an extent by extension of boundaries of urban areas or by reclassification of some rural pockets as urban as and when they met the criteria accepted for declaring a habitat urban. The growth rates in rural areas have consistently remained behind the growth rate expected from the natural increase alone. The net migration (out-migration – R-U migration including the return migration) in rural areas is essentially negative; in addition there is a constant revision and declassification of towns as also villages.

Urban growth and the share of natural increase in selected states of India are presented in Table 10.8. The urban growth at all-India level has declined during 1981–1991 decade (Table 10.7). This trend is largely visible for most of the states of India for the period 1981–1991, irrespective of the stages of development they were in. The poorer states like Bihar, Orissa, Uttar Pradesh and Rajasthan that registered very high urban growth rate during 1971–81 (55 percent and above) compared to that in 1961–71 (marginally in Orissa as well), registered declined growth rate, to below 40 percent levels. The states like Maharasthra and Gujarat, which are industrially advanced states, and the agriculturally developed states like Punjab and Haryana also registered decline in urban growth during 1981–91, a sharper decline in the latter two agricultural states, probably due to greater mechanization in agriculture. The share of natural increase is very high in urban growth both in relatively poor and rich states in India. This clearly shows that the urbanization in India in recent times is predominantly led by demographic momentum. The impact of economic momentum in terms of pull factors is mostly confined to big cities. Even in these large cities the space is getting limited to new entrants due to ever increasing size of the informal sector and growing nativism. The increasing nativity has been pronounced in Maharashtra, Orissa, Tamil Nadu, Uttar Pradesh and West Bengal.

Table 10.8
Urban growth and share of natural increase in selected states of India

States	Urban Growth (%)			Share of Natural Increase
	1961–1971	1971–1981	1981–1991	1981–91
		Relatively Rich States		
Industrially advanced				
Maharashtra	40.8	40.0	38.7	57.0
Gujarat	41.0	41.4	33.6	69.9
Agriculturally advanced				
Punjab	25.3	44.5	29.1	81.5
Haryana	35.6	59.5	43.1	62.1
		Relatively Poor States		
Bihar	43.9	54.8	30.4	85.5
Rajasthan	38.5	58.7	39.2	65.3
Orissa	66.3	68.5	36.1	60.7
Uttar Pradesh	30.1	60.6	38.9	62.8

Source: Census of India 1991

The estimated share of natural increase, migration and reclassification of the towns for the Census years 1971 to 1991 is presented in the following table.

Table 10.9
Components of urban growth, India 1971–1991

Percent share	1971–81	1981–91
Natural Increase	41.7	59.9
Net Migration + Changes in Municipal Boundaries	39.4	22.6
Reclassification	18.8	17.4

Source: Census of India 1991.

Migration and changes in municipal boundaries had a share of about 40 percent in urban growth during 1971–81, about the same level as the natural increase. Their share comes down to less than 23 percent in the decade 1981–91 and the share of natural increase has risen by about 50 percent compared to what it was in 1971–81. The share of new towns adjusted for reclassified towns has almost remained unchanged in these two decades. The truth is that urbanization has lost momentum since 1981 and the major reason is that the size of new rural-urban migrants in 1980s has declined significantly. The share of migrant population to total urban population, which was highest in Maharasthra in 1981 (48%) dropped to only 34 percent in 1991. Sharp drops (close to 11%) are also observed in West Bengal and Orissa. Kerala, the most demographically developed state and Uttar Pradesh where demographic parameters of development is one of the worst, displayed very low ratio of migrant population to total urban population both in 1981 and 1991. It must not be lost sight of that proportion of migrants in the total population in 1991 dropped by around 2.5 percent compared to the proportions registered in 1981. This is reflected in the share of migrants in the total urban population as well as in the share of decadal migrants (inter-censal) to total migrants in India and in the larger states. At the national level inter-censal urban migrants has declined by over 5 percent. Except Gujarat where inter-censal urban migrants in 1991 increased marginally among male migrants, all other states experienced decline in male urban migrants. The lowest inter-censal urban migrants for males and females in 1991 were in West Bengal, most possibly due to closure of thousands of industries and flight of capital to other states where the labor problems were less. The picture remained almost unchanged in West Bengal in 1981 as well. In 1981, the share of inter-censal female migrants to total urban migrants exceeded that of males in three states, viz. Gujarat, Punjab and West Bengal.

Table 10.10

Trend in migration into the urban areas, 1981–1991

States	*Percentage of migrants to total population**		*Percentage of inter-censal urban migrants to total urban migrants*					
			1981			*1991*		
	1981	*1991*	*Male*	*Female*	*Total*	*Male*	*Female*	*Total*
1	*2*	*3*	*4*	*5*	*6*	*7*	*8*	*9*
INDIA	**38.8**	**32.2**	**48.7**	**45.2**	**46.9**	**43.1**	**40.2**	**41.6**
Andhra Pradesh	38.6	34.5	57.3	54.1	54.9	49.3	46.0	47.5
Assam		38.6				44.1	42.2	43.2
Bihar	38.5	31.8	53.1	42.3	53.1	42.3	32.3	35.9
Gujarat	39.6	38.1	42.1	44.7	43.5	42.6	41.8	42.2
Haryana	46.8	43.6	51.5	46.7	48.9	46.3	42.0	43.9
Himachal Pradesh	58.8	58.9	63.6	57.4	60.8	58.1	50.9	54.6
Karnataka	37.9	32.8	52.6	47.1	49.7	48.6	44.7	46.6
Kerala	25.0	25.5	53.9	48.0	50.4	48.3	43.7	45.5
Madhya Pradesh	41.8	39.1	53.6	46.8	49.9	45.5	41.5	43.2
Maharashtra	48.3	33.8	44.3	44.4	44.3	40.3	41.0	40.7
Orissa	47.7	37.0	59.9	52.6	56.4	49.4	43.4	46.3
Punjab	42.6	40.1	42.4	53.3	41.7	41.0	38.9	39.8
Rajasthan	32.9	30.0	55.9	43.2	48.5	49.3	39.0	43.1
Tamil Nadu	35.8	28.2	51.9	49.9	50.8	40.9	40.8	40.8
Uttar Pradesh	28.8	22.3	49.9	36.4	41.6	44.1	35.5	38.6
West Bengal	39.4	28.5	31.3	33.4	32.3	28.3	32.1	30.3

*It includes international migration also.

Source: Census of India 1991.

A major reason for drop in R-U migration is increasing unemployment rate in urban areas. This is likely to increase further as industrialization in India is rapidly taking the capital-intensive path contrasted to the labor-intensive growth path of earlier days. The unemployment data available from National Sample Survey show that unemployment in urban areas vis-à-vis rural areas increased during 1983–1987. Unemployment rate was more in the metros, more so for females. In fact, unemployment among them had increased faster vis-à-vis males in urban areas. This is an important factor dampening the rate of rural to urban migration in the country during 1980s. The more recent data on the growth of employment in organized sector shows that the average growth in employment was only 0.87 percent per annum during 1991–1999 in spite of impressive growth of GDP during the said period (over 6 percent per annum). With IT sector emerging as the major service provider in the metros, the natives of the metros have opportunities to prepare themselves with the required skills for the type of jobs that are created. The migrants from rural areas faced an upheaval task to compete with the natives of the metros or bigger cities. Rate of employment generated in hi tech industries is inadequate even to accommodate the labor force due to natural increase in the cities and metros. The situation looks very ominous for prospective migrants. In view of this changing scenario in the employment sector, it is no wonder that strong sentiments are becoming progressively visible against migration from villages or from other states. A demand is brewing up especially in the developed states for reservation of jobs for the native applicants. The arrival of more FDI would bring with it more advanced technology and less dependence on human labor. The local entrepreneurs would need to improve their skill quality to remain competitive in the market. This is the immediate fall out of globalization of economy. It is only a matter of time that the government revises its labor policy giving more freedom to the big players to manage their labor force (hire and fire). A number of export processing zones (EPZ) have already come up where the existing labor laws have little or no relevance. The 'trade union specialists' have realized that their hay days are over. Production cannot be destabilized through 'work to rule', 'pen down' or frequent strikes. The urban population growth rate is destined to slow down further in the coming years. Even some states like West Bengal, which had been run by a combine of Left parties since 1977, has been in the process of inter- and intra-party dialogue if the IT sector in Salt Lake city, which has many international and national IT giants and many BPO and Call Centers that run 24 × 7, can be treated as 'essential service sector' to protect them from the purview of aggressive trade union activities. Even CITU (Center for Indian Trade Union), affiliated to CPI (M), has agreed that they will open their wing in this IT hub, but would not indulge in coercive tactics to disrupt the functioning of IT and BPO companies.

10.4 Reasons of Migration

Women in India formed the overwhelming majority (72%) of those recorded as migrants in 1991 Census. 41.8 percent of the total female population had migrated from their previous *place of residence* to the *place of enumeration*. This proportion among males was only 14.7 percent. Women dominated the short distance migration stream because of the practice of village exogamy prevailing in many parts of the country. At marriage, women move to neighboring areas to live with their husbands' families. This explains why more than 60 percent of migration in India was reported to be intra-district indicating short distance moves. Only about 12 percent of migrants moved between states.

Table 10.11
Percentage distribution of migrants in India by reasons for each sex

Reasons for migration	*1981a*		*1991b*	
	Male	*Female*	*Male*	*Female*
Employment	31.0	1.9	27.0	1.8
Education	5.3	0.9	4.8	0.8
Family Moved	30.2	14.5	26.6	11.0
Marriage	3.1	72.4	4.0	76.1
Others	30.4	10.3	37.6	10.3
Total number of migrants (million)	62.5	145.2	64.3	167.8

1. For 1991 include business, natural calamities like drought, floods, etc.
a. Excludes Assam.
b. Excludes Jammu & Kashmir.
Source: Office of Registrar General, India.

Reasons for migration and distances and streams of migration are closely interlinked. Urban-ward movement is primarily for seeking employment or for taking a chance to improve upon one's skills and for better living. Most of the urban-ward movements in search of employment do not involve the entire family. Only when the earning member is reasonably settled in the new location, the other members of the family may join him. That is why the proportion of women in R-U migration is small and that is also the reason why the sex ratio in urban population is male biased. In U-U movement, especially when the migrant is skilled or professionally qualified, usually the other members of the family also move simultaneously or shortly after the principal member has settled reasonably and acquired a reasonable accommodation for the entire family. That is why 'family moved' remains a significant reason behind all types of migration, more so for U-U migration. All dependent members therefore come under this category of movers. Percentage distribution of migrants by reasons of migration is presented in Table 10.11. The 1991 data clearly indicate that urban areas have lost some of its charm as job provider to surplus labor from villages.

11
Economic Well-being
Some Acute Problems in India

11.1 Introduction

Economic health of a nation and the well-being of its citizens have conventionally been tried to be understood through indicators like its GDP growth or percapita GDP growth. Employment data for any population are suspect for various reasons. More suspects are the data on income (or expenditure) of a person. One can fairly accurately obtain information on income for persons in the organized sector, especially the income of tax-paying segment of the workforce. But for those in the unorganized sector or in self-employment category (doctors, engineers, lawyers and other professional persons, business men and others), there is always a chance that the income returns are far from what they are in reality. GDP growth or per capita GDP growth can be regarded as a good index of economic well-being when the distribution of income in the population is not very skewed. In most countries, even the developed ones, the income distributions are often extremely skewed. Questions regarding the aptness of using the aggregate data (mean or median) for all the segments of the population are quite legitimate. Income distribution in India is highly skewed. Even though India has a huge number of multi-millionaires (quite a few of them even figure in Fortune 500, 36 persons have wealth exceeding 1,000 million dollars), the official statistics inform us that about 20 percent of Indians still live below the poverty line (over 300 million when the poverty line is less than $1 a day), millions have no stable shelter to live under, thousands of villagers have to walk miles to fetch drinking water; a whooping majority of the villagers have no toilets in their houses; many families call the day as the sun sets in since they neither have electricity in their houses nor have the money to buy kerosene to burn the lamps.

We have seen earlier that there has been a gradual decline in the labor force participation rates, both in urban and rural areas, over the years, especially since 1980. The decline is likely to continue, or even may increase as economic liberalization gains further momentum and labor laws are modified to promote faster growth of the capital-intensive sectors, especially in areas where export promotion is encouraged. The agriculture sector too has to be revamped to improve the productivity level so that food grains production from 213 million tons of the present to close to 260 million tons in the next five years can be achieved. Not very much can we do to increase agricultural production by bringing more land under cultivation. In reality, huge amount of agricultural land has to be transferred for non-agricultural uses (industries, roads, airports, special economic zones, and etc.) as industrialization gains momentum. Per unit agricultural production in India is one of the lowest in the world. More fallow lands have to be brought under cultivation to make up the growing losses for land transfer for other uses. The fragmented lands have to be brought under a common larger holding with the intention that by using tractors and other mechanical devices production per unit land can be increased. More land has to be brought under irrigation so that instead of one crop, two or more crops can be had through crop rotation. That is, instead of animal energy and human labor, we increasingly have to rely on technology and improved management to increase agricultural production. More people are likely to be displaced from agriculture for allocating land for industries, construction of new roads and highways, and to develop industrial hubs and new towns. We discuss briefly some of the major problems originating from or leading to the poor health of our economy.

11.2 Per Capita Consumption Expenditure

Per capita income works well for evaluation of the well-being of populations with a regular income either from service or from self-employment. A large segment of rural people are wage earners or casual labors. A very large proportion of these people belong to the BPL category. In the recent past, attempts have been made for state and district level estimates of per capita income (in State Human Development of Madhya Pradesh, Karnataka and some other states, for example). The methodological approach followed in these estimations remains debatable. The direct incomes normally are under reported, more so when individuals have more than one source of income or if they have no fixed source of income at all. The rich would play down income to avoid paying taxes. Perks and other benefits (travel allowance, medical allowance, house rent paid by the employer or free accommodation, and subsidized ration, etc.) and returns from investment in banks and securities are less likely to be reported in household income surveys. The poor, on the other hand, would also understate income with the hope that their households would become eligible for various kinds of subsidies, direct or indirect, announced by the government under poverty alleviation and other welfare schemes. Household income survey in all likelihood would give per capita income considerably smaller than the actual. Net State Domestic Product (NSDP) normally would contain many types of income that do not accrue at the household level. Profits from public and private sector undertakings, for instance, would not get distributed to households. Value added by many other sources (mining, forest products, and other natural resources) enter into National Accounting. Only a very nominal proportion of this may get transferred to households through wage payments for their involvement in some of these operations.

It is on these counts, many economists believe that 'consumption expenditure' is a better option to understand the income status of households for consumption is believed to be influenced by past savings as well as prospects of future income. Consumption data often would include at least a part of the public expenditure on services as health, education and nutrition, which generally find no mention in income data. NSSO collects consumption data in various Rounds. National Council of Applied Economic Research (NCAER) conducted a sample survey on 33,000 rural households in 1994 (which included consumption-expenditure survey) and the report of the survey was published as *India Human Development Report,* 1999.

In the following table is presented per capita NSDP (yearly average) data at constant prices (1980–81) as also the NSSO data (monthly averages) on per capita consumption expenditure. Data are adapted from National Human Development Report 2001.

Full data for all states and UTs show no uniform pattern over the period at sate level. The range of variation was as large as 69 percent of monthly consumption expenditure (at current prices) at the national level in 1983 (70 and 67% respectively in rural and urban areas). The same in 1999–2000 at the national and urban level dropped to 64 and 43 percent although it increased by about 6 percentage

Table 11.1
Per capita NSDP and per capita consumption expenditure (Rs)

	1983			*1993–94*			*1999–2000*		
	Rural	***Urban***	***Total***	***Rural***	***Urban***	***Total***	***Rural***	***Urban***	***Total***
NSDP (India)			1790			2337			2480
Advanced States									
Punjab			2884			4019			4389
Maharashtra			2558			4189			5032
Backward States									
Bihar			999			1038			1126
Orissa			1399			1549			1666
Range of variation among the major States									
INDIA			1665			2981			3263
NSSO (India)	112.31	165.80	125.13	281.40	458.00	328.18	486.08	854.95	590.98
Advanced States									
Punjab	170.30	184.38	174.26	433.00	510.70	456.59	742.43	898.82	792.07
Haryana	149.14	183.97	157.03	385.0	473.90	407.67	714.37	912.07	767.89
Backward States									
Bihar	93.76	139.50	99.53	218.30	353.00	236.78	384.72	601.89	417.18
Orissa	97.48	151.35	104.06	219.80	402.50	245.94	373.17	618.48	413.71
Range of variation among the major States									
INDIA	76.54	44.82	74.73	214.70	176.8	219.81	369.26	371.44	378.36
Inflation and inequality adjusted per capita consumption expenditure									
INDIA	78.90	111.01	86.59	87.90	124.27	97.53	98.49	143.49	111.28

Sources: Central Statistical Organization for NSDP. NSS 38th, 50th and 55th Rounds on Household Consumer Expenditure.

points in rural areas; that is, variation in average per capita consumption expenditure in rural areas among the states has increased. Inequality and inflation adjusted per capita consumption expenditure shows a 25 percent increase (from Rs 78.90 to Rs 98.49) in rural areas and 29 percent in urban areas (Rs 111.01 to Rs 143.49) between 1983 and 1999–2000. Among the major sates Bihar, Madhya Pradesh, Orissa and Uttar Pradesh consistently remain below the national average in per capita consumption expenditure at all the time points; similarly, Punjab, Haryana, Kerala and even Rajasthan have consistently remained at higher than the national average. Such clear trends could not be observed for the other larger sates. In per capita monthly expenditure, the Christians are well ahead of other religious groups.

Figure 11.1
Inequality unadjusted for per capita expenditure (Rs)

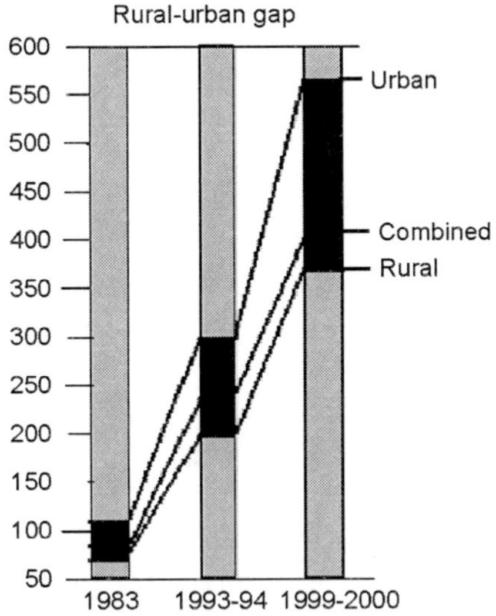

Rural-urban gap

600
550
500
450
400
350
300
250
200
150
100
50

Urban
Combined
Rural

1983 1993-94 1999-2000

The story told in the Table 11.3 is that the marginalized majority of the Indian population has little choice of their own as to where to use the money they earn. Poor people all over the world are forced to spend a very large share of whatever they earn on food-related items alone. A decline in proportion of expenditure on

Table 11.2

Per capita monthly expenditure in Rs (NSSO data)

	Hindu	*Muslim*	*Christian*	*Buddhist*	*National*
1993–94	676	620	838	583	682
2004–05	1,586	1,459	2,263	1,512	1,605

Table 11.3

Food and non-food items in per capita consumption expenditure (percentage)

INDIA	*1983*		*1993–94*		*1999–2000*	
	Food	*Non-food*	*Food*	*Non-food*	*Food*	*Non-food*
Rural	**65.56**	**34.44**	**63.18**	**36.82**	**59.41**	**40.59**
More on food compared to national average						
West Bengal	73.94	26.06	66.82	33.18	65.90	34.10
Orissa	73.72	26.28	68.06	31.94	64.11	35.89
Bihar	73.63	26.37	71.00	29.00	66.54	33.46
Assam	73.37	26.63	72.26	27.74	67.63	32.37
Less on food compared to national average						
Punjab	58.67	41.33	57.92	42.08	52.29	47.71
Andhra Pradesh	60.24	39.76	59.58	40.42	60.50	39.50
Rajasthan	60.52	39.48	62.78	37.72	59.50	40.50
Kerala	61.64	38.36	60.45	39.55	53.70	46.30
Urban	**58.69**	**41.31**	**54.65**	**45.35**	**48.06**	**51.94**
More on food compared to national average						
Bihar	66.14	33.86	62.92	37.08	57.24	42.76
Orissa	65.13	34.87	57.79	42.21	56.95	43.05
Assam	63.77	36.23	59.68	40.32	55.38	44.62
West Bengal	60.90	39.10	55.93	44.07	52.28	47.72
Less on food compared to national average						
Andhra Pradesh	54.57	45.43	53.84	46.16	47.44	52.56
Rajasthan	57.58	42.42	56.65	43.35	50.85	49.15
Punjab	55.92	44.08	53.03	46.97	47.12	52.88
Maharashtra	57.53	42.47	53.02	46.98	45.31	54.69
Scheduled Castes						
Rural	67.08	32.92				
Urban	62.05	37.95				
Scheduled Tribes						
Rural	70.12	29.88				
Urban	62.95	37.05				

Source: NSS 38th, 50th and 55th Rounds on Household Consumer Expenditure.

food items to total expenditure is taken as an indicator of development and economic prosperity. In 17 years between 1983 and 2000, spending on *non-food* items has increased by about 6 percentage points in rural area and by about 7.5 percentage points in urban area and urban spending on non-food items has marginally overtaken spending on food items.

This small change in spending behavior has a lot to do with the declining proportion of people living below the poverty line (BPL) as also because of government's increased spending on social sector.

The NSS survey shows that rankings of the sates on average consumption expenditure for procuring food almost have remained unchanged, especially those in the two ends. The poorer sates like Orissa, Bihar, Assam, Madhya Pradesh and Uttar Pradesh still are behind national per capita consumption expenditure. It is no wonder that their names feature among the sates where people spend most on food. But it is surprising that the people in West Bengal, which has per capita consumption expenditure nearly at par with national level, should be spending such a big share of their earned income on food. It is also surprising that Rajasthan and Andhra Pradesh, which have per capita consumption expenditure lower than that of the national average, should find their names along with the sates like Punjab, Kerala and Karnataka where people spend less on food vis-à-vis non-food items. The share of expenditure on food among the Scheduled Castes and Scheduled Tribes was consistently higher both in rural and urban areas in 1983 for which data are available,

The per capita household consumption expenditure has been increasing over the years with the figures for 1999–2000 for rural and urban areas being Rs 494.9 and Rs 914.6 respectively. Consumption on food alone was Rs 278.6 in rural area and Rs 400.6 in urban area. In 1999–2000, about 59.4 percent of the total consumption was on food related items in rural area; in urban area, it was somewhat smaller at 48.1 percent. The share of food in total consumption has been decreasing down the years both in rural and urban area. In rural area, the consumption figure for food items was 72.9 percent in 1972–73 compared to 59.4 percent in 1999–2000. Similarly, for urban area, it was 64.5 percent in 1972–73 and 48.1 percent in 1999–2000.

11.3 Income distribution and the Consumer Market

NCAER has been conducting Market Information Survey of Households (MISH) since 1985. *India Market Demographics Report 2002* observes definite structural changes in income distribution – high income class is expanding fast, middle income classes, especially in rural areas, are also growing, and there is a fast decline in the low income class. During the post-reform period, the rate of growth of the upper-income class was much higher vis-à-vis decline in the size of the low-income class. The growth of the top-most income class after 1995–96 has been of the order of about 19 percent. The size of the low-income households in urban area has dropped in the post-reform period. A 15 percent decline in the share of low-income households was observed in Karnataka, Punjab, Haryana, Kerala and Tamil Nadu.

The income distribution of households by occupation of the head of the households from the MISH data shows that a very large majority of the households under the stewardship of wage earners or cultivators or housewives or artisans or petty shopkeepers are in the low and lower-middle income classes; the households under the care of salaried persons are almost equally divided between (Low + Lower Middle) and (Middle + Upper Middle + High). It is only the households headed by professionals and businessmen that are on the higher side of the scale divisions of income class.

Table 11.4
Income distribution (in percent) of households by head's occupation, 1999–2000 (All India)

Head's Occupation	***Income class***					
	L	***LM***	***M***	***UM***	***H***	***All***
Housewife	29.99	35.88	19.62	9.08	5.42	100.0
Cultivator	38.31	36.48	13.32	6.19	5.69	100.0
Wage earner	56.25	33.81	8.41	1.08	0.46	100.0
Salary earner	14.91	33.29	24.12	13.22	14.47	100.0
Professional	6.23	16.72	23.62	25.32	28.11	100.0
Artisan	32.51	39.56	20.87	4.63	2.43	100.0
Petty shopkeeper	23.50	36.00	20.74	10.11	9.64	100.0
Businessman	0.42	4.48	23.35	33.07	38.68	100.0
Others	26.41	30.59	21.39	11.99	9.63	100.0
Total	36.37	34.20	15.44	7.10	6.89	100.0

L, Low, LM, Lower middle, M, Middle, UM, Upper middle, H, High income class.
Source: NCAER: India Market Demographics Report 2002.

MISH also found that the salaried class households took a major share in the revival of consumer markets in 1999–2000 after a drop in 1997-98 – 1998-99 presumably due to the sanction imposed on India by USA and other countries after the Pokhran nuclear test as also because of markets becoming volatile due to crash of economy in some of the East-Asian and Latin American countries for a massive withdrawal of FIIs from their capital markets during the middle of the nineties.

Even without any perceptible income rise, the salaried class households, because of their high level of awareness and proclivity to consume, took gleefully the economic space created by Consumer Finance by banks and other financial institutions, especially since bank rates have been cut quite significantly. Consumer finance has remained key to the growth of market economy in all developed countries and Indian market responded very positively since the market realized that income boom alone is not sufficient to lure consumers to try various non-traditional consumer products. The industries and the service sectors through its salaried class, numbering over 35 millions, assured by their fixed and regular income (a leverage that they have in their household budgets) would remain the main force that would provide the needed momentum for the market growth. Both ownership and purchase data on consumer durables indicate that the product composition is getting transformed and households, both in rural and urban areas, prefer high priced products to medium-priced durables. The rural markets are also growing fast. But their performances would be largely dependent upon infrastructural development (more specifically to penetration and uninterrupted power supply in villages and road connectivity) and performance of agriculture.

11.4 Unemployment and Poverty

The growth of employment (Table 11.5) for persons in 15 years and older, both in rural and urban areas has declined in the nineties compared to that in eighties. The extent of decline in growth for persons has been similar in rural and urban areas. The drop in employment has been more for females, more in urban areas. At the state level employment growth rates have been noticed to be higher than that at the national level in Himachal Pradesh, Jammu & Kashmir, Rajasthan, West Bengal and Andhra Pradesh during 1983 to 1993–94. In the subsequent period only Punjab, Bihar and Assam did not only improve their performances over the previous period, employment growth rates in these states were higher than that at the national level.

Table 11.5

A. Growth of employment, 1983 to 1999–2000 (percent)

	1983 to 1993–94			*1993–94 to 1999–2000*		
	Male	***Female***	***Person***	***Male***	***Female***	***Person***
Rural	2.0	1.5	1.8	1.6	0.8	1.3
Urban	2.8	3.2	2.9	2.6	1.5	2.4
Comb.	2.2	1.7	2.1	1.9	0.9	1.6

B. Incidence of Unemployment, 1983 to 1999–2000 (percent)

	1983			*1993–94*			*1999–2000*		
	Male	***Female***	***Person***	***Male***	***Female***	***Person***	***Male***	***Female***	***Person***
Rural	1.4	0.7	1.1	1.5	0.8	1.2	1.7	1.1	1.5
Urban	5.0	5.2	5.1	4.1	6.6	4.6	4.5	5.9	4.8
Comb.	2.3	1.3	2.0	2.1	1.7	2.0	2.5	1.8	2.3

1. The incidence of unemployment is defined as the percentage of persons unemployed in the age group 15+ years on the usual principal and subsidiary status to the total number of persons in the labor force.

Source: NSSO on Employment and Unemployment Situation in India, 38th, 50th and 55th Rounds.

With increase in the population size, the size of the labor force also increased. A decline in growth of employment during nineties vis-à-vis eighties, incidence of unemployment in the later part of nineties increased. Incidence of unemployment was more acute in urban areas, especially among females compared to that in rural areas. Analysis of results of NSS 55th Round shows employment growth rate declining from 2.1 percent during 1983–94 to 1.6 percent per annum during 1994–2000. The decline in employment growth rate observed even when GDP growth rate remained high, indicates a decline in labor intensity in production. The growth rate became negative since 1999–2000 (jobless growth).

Among the major states, Kerala, which incidentally has the highest Human Development Index (HDI) in India, has the highest incidence of unemployment, nearly at 8 percent for all the time points for which the aggregate data are presented. Only in two states Haryana and Karnataka there was a secular decline in incidence of unemployment. For other states no such clear trend is visible. In most states (except Punjab and Tamil Nadu) the incidence of unemployment is higher in 1999–2000 than what it was in 1983.

Persons below the poverty line dropped from 54.88 percent in 1973–74 to 44.48 percent (rural – 45.65%, urban – 40.79%) in 1983 (Table 11.5). In 1999–2000, about 27.1 percent of populations in rural area and about 23.6 percent of urban populations were still living below the poverty line. The state-wise figures indicate that during 1999–2000, Orissa had 47.1 percent of the population below the poverty line followed by Bihar at 42.6 percent. The percentage of BPL population was lowest in Jammu & Kashmir in 1999–2000, about 3.48 percent, followed by Goa at 4.40 percent. The NSS (55th round) suggests that unemployment has soared to 35.2 million in 2004–05 from around 26.5

million in 1999–2000. Though unemployment level has increased fast, poverty level has come down to around 21 percent. The earlier surveys conducted by NSSO seem to suggest that the level of poverty in India has been halved between 1977–78 and 1999–2000. As per the 57th NSS Round, chronically hungry households in rural India were 0.5 percent; it was 0.1 percent in urban area. Seasonal hunger (getting enough food only in some months) in rural area was 16 per thousand households and 3 per thousand in urban households. The Tenth Plan documents also suggest that poverty ratio in India is likely to come down to 19.3 percent in 2007 (21.1% in rural and 15.1% in urban area). By 2012, this is likely to drop further to 15 percentage points.

Figure 11.2
Number of poors (millions), rural-urban gap

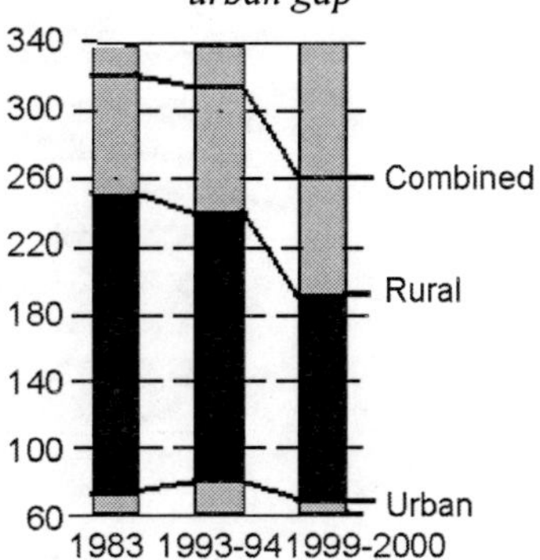

Table 11.6
Number and percentage of population below poverty line, India 1973–2000

	Rural			Urban			Combined	
	No. of persons (million)	*% of persons*	*Poverty line (Rs)*	*No. of persons (million)*	*% of persons*	*Poverty line (Rs)*	*No. of persons (million)*	*% of persons*
1	*2*	*3*	*4*	*5*	*6*	*7*	*8*	*9*
1973–74	2,61.290	56.44		60.05	49.01		321.3	54.88
1977–78	2,64.247	53.07		64.65	45.24		328.9	51.32
1983	251.957	45.65	89.5	70.94	40.79	115.65	322.9	44.48
1993–94	244.031	32.27	205.84	76.34	32.36	281.35	320.4	35.97
1999–2000	193.243	27.09	327.56	67.01	23.62	454.11	260.3	26.10
2007[1]	170.50	21.10		49.60	15.10		220.1	19.30

1. Tenth Plan Projections
Source: National Human Development Report 2001, Planning Commission, Government of India.

Figure 11.3
Estimate of incidences of poverty in India

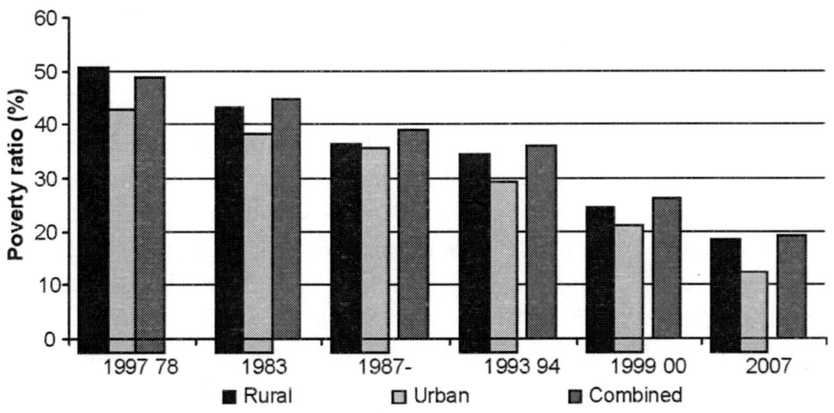

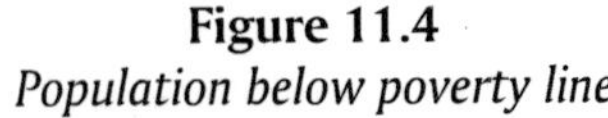

Figure 11.4
Population below poverty line

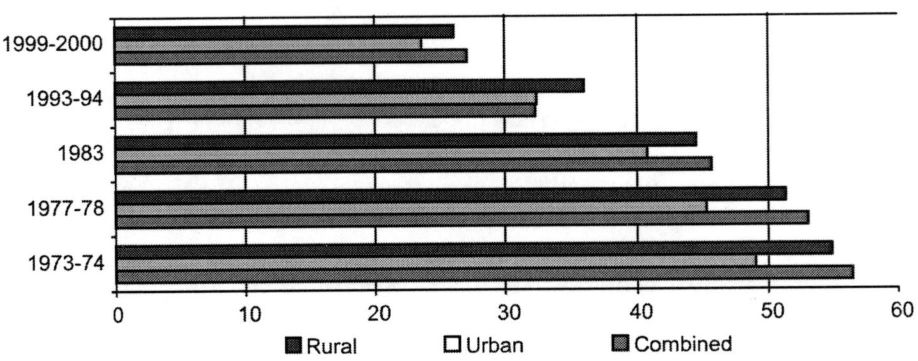

Table 11.7
Percentage of population below poverty line in four selected states

	Orissa			*Bihar*			*Punjab*			*Himachal Pradesh*		
	1983	***1993–94***	***1999–00***	***1983***	***1993–94***	***1999–00***	***1983***	***1993–94***	***1999–00***	***1983***	***1993–94***	***1999–00***
						Rural						
% of persons	67.53	49.72	48.01	64.37	58.21	44.30	13.20	11.95	6.35	17.0	30.34	7.94
Poverty line (Rs)	106.3	194.0	323.9	97.5	212.2	333.1	88.6	233.8	362.7	88.5	233.8	367.4
						Urban						
% of persons	49.15	41.64	42.83	47.33	34.50	32.91	23.79	11.35	5.75	9.43	9.18	4.63
Poverty line (Rs)	124.8	298.2	473.1	111.8	238.5	379.8	101.0	253.6	388.2	102.3	253.6	420.2
						Combined						
% of persons	65.29	48.56	47.15	62.22	54.96	42.6	15.18	11.77	6.16	16.4	28.44	7.63

Source: Planning Commission, India.

National Human Development Report treats Human Poverty Index (HPI) as a measure of intensity of deprivation. Like Human Development Index (HDI), HPI is also a composite index involving three factors, viz. health, educational and economic. This has been captured through the proportion of population not expected to survive beyond age 40 (Health), proportion of illiterate population and children not enrolled in schools (Educational), and proportion of population below the poverty line, proportion of the population without access to safe drinking water, sanitation and electricity, proportion of population deprived of medical attention at birth and full vaccination for children in age group 12–23 months and proportion of population living in *kutcha* houses (Economic). There are many publicly provided goods and services or benefits for which consumption share for a person cannot be measured even approximately. The proportion of population not able to attain a specified level of expenditure on all counts is identified as poor. The minimum consumption expenditure necessary for attaining an average energy (food related, items) norm of 2,400 and 2,100 kilo calories (kcal) per head per day in rural and urban areas respectively, defines State Specific Poverty Line. HPI estimates reflect the deprivational perspective on development. HPI takes values from 0 to 100. It means the higher the value of HPI (closer to 100), the greater the deprivation. For computation of HPI and other indices, please refer to Chapter 12 of this volume.

At the national level, the incidence of poverty on Head Count (HC) Ratio declined from 44.48 in 1983 to 26.10 in 1999–2000 and then to 10.3 in 2007 (Table 11.8). Of this over 18 points decline, nearly 10 points have come in six years after 1993–94, i.e., in the period when economic reforms in India started to take a definite shape. In absolute terms, India had fewer poor (260 million) in 1999–2000 than six years back (320 million). Almost similar percentage point decline of poor was observed in rural and urban areas between 1983 and 1999–2000. The decline was faster (8.7%) in urban area between 1993–94 and 1999–2000 compared to 5.2 percent in rural area in the same period.

Table 11.8

Trend of decline in rural and urban poverty in India

	Percent of the population			*Absolute numbers (in million)*		
	Rural	***Urban***	***Combined***	***Rural***	***Urban***	***Combined***
1977–78	53.1	45.2	51.3	264.3	84.6	328.9
1983	45.7	40.8	44.5	252.0	70.9	322.9
1987–88	39.1	38.2	38.9	231.9	75.2	307.1
1993–94	37.3	32.4	36.0	244.0	76.3	320.3
1999–00	27.1	23.6	26.1	193.2	67.1	260.3
2007*	21.1	15.1	19.3	170.5	49.6	220.1

*Projected
Source: 10th Five Year Plan.

In 1983, Orissa, Bihar, West Bengal and Tamil Nadu among the major states had more than 50 percent of their populations living below the poverty line. The latter two states reduced their poor by 50 percent by 1999–2000. None of the states and UTs currently has more than 50 percent of their populations below their respective poverty lines. Orissa and Bihar still continue to be the major states that have more than 40 percent BPL population. Only two smaller states, Jammu & Kashmir (3.48%) and Goa (4.40%), and one UT Daman & Diu (4.44%) have almost succeeded in eliminating the poor from their populations by 1999–2000. Haryana (8.74%), Himachal Pradesh (7.63%), Punjab (6.16%), Chandigarh (5.75%) and Delhi (8.23%) must have by now been successful in eliminating households below the poverty line. Of the 35 states/UTs, percentages of populations below the poverty line in urban area were found to be less than 10 percent in 15 states/UTs in 1999–2000. Only one state Himachal Pradesh had rural poverty level below 10 percent. There were as many as 10 states (no UTs) where percentage of population below poverty line in rural areas was above 40 percent. Among the BIMARU states, Rajasthan has done really well to reduce the population of poor by more than 50 percent, from 34.46 in 1983 to 15.28 in 1999–2000. The state has performed even better in reducing poverty in the rural population (from 33.50 in 1983 to 13.74% in 1999–2000). Rural Orissa and rural Bihar continue to be the poorest among rural areas. Orissa, Madhya Pradesh and Bihar have the largest number of poor in urban areas.

World Bank in 2006 has given head count ratio (HC) for different countries and different regions within the same country. This report puts poverty in Orissa and Bihar at 40 and 41 percent respectively, which are similar to that in Malawi and Ghana in Africa. Proportion of poor is only 5 percent in Haryana and 2.4 percent in Punjab far less than that in Columbia and Brazil which are considered high medium developed countries. It is really strange that there is so much difference in incidences of poverty between states of the same country as are observed between Punjab or Haryana and Orissa or Bihar. The World Bank also observed that 78 percent families in India still take advantage of public distribution system (PDS), but only 1 out of every 10 people said that they were satisfied with the quality of commodities supplied through PDS. The World Bank also came out with the observation that only 16 percent of the 78 percent families who send their children to government aided schools expressed their satisfaction with teaching in these schools.

Even with a GDP growth rate in excess of 6 percent (the growth rate in the years 2004–2006 was over 8 percent and around 9 percent thereafter) employment growth rate has fallen; it even became negative in the final years of the last millennium. This is not quite unexpected in the era of economic globalization since to remain internationally competitive, the industrial, service, transport and communication and even the agricultural sector have to be transformed from labor-intensive to capital-intensive production system. In its eagerness to attract massive private investment, domestic and foreign, the state has to make very big stride in infrastructure development. A developing economy under the press of reform is always short of funds for investment in the social and agriculture sector. The benefits of higher GDP growth do not easily percolate to the rural poor. In a democratic set up, globalization does not really help the political party in power to receive electoral support. In India, hundreds and thousands of acres of agriculture land, even the prime lands, had to be acquired to develop special economic zones (SEZ), industrial hubs, IT, health and education parks, and for construction of roads, bridges, ports, houses, etc. Such lands can be acquired often at the cost of loosing electoral support from those who had been displaced from their only asset, the land. Even the political parties in opposition make this their campaign issue during electoral battle. Since industrialization and economic globalization is an irreversible process, whichever party comes into power through negative campaign against the erstwhile party in power, soon will have to go ahead with more drastic measures to achieve the objectives of economic reform. Given the time to settle, the new industrial masters would have to participate even in the social sector development in their own interest – to expand the domestic market for their produces.

India's economic reform was started in the 1970s when the major capital markets were deregulated. The private and corporate investors, the Foreign Institutional Investments (FII) and Foreign Direct Investment (FDI) since 1991 has given India a very healthy looking foreign exchange reserve (over $300 billion in June 2008). FDI inflow in India has seen a dramatic rise in recent years – from 4 billion dollars in 2000–01 to 32.43 billion dollars in 2007–08. Despite the fact that India needs huge investment, private and foreign, in the infrastructure, the national leaders are hesitant to use any part of this foreign exchange reserve for this or other purposes for the fear that the private players, especially FIIs, can wipe out this reserve in a matter of days. In fact, all the Central Banks across the world face the same problem. The experiences of East Asian and Latin American countries in mid-1990s and the meltdown of USA and European markets in 2008 have made India and others cautious since a crash in the capital market due to capital flight triggered by a few important investors may put the country under a serious debt trap, especially if a sizeable proportion of the foreign exchange reserve was invested for infrastructure development.

11.5 Transition from Agriculture to Industrial Economy

Transition from a predominantly agricultural to industrial economy is never easy. A reasonably good health of industries depends on a number of complex factors – punctuality in attendance and discipline in certain personal and collective habits, a set of secular values, sanctity of contracts, continuous enrichment of skills, and uninterrupted supply of inputs, both human and material. It is a historical truth that industrialization tends to weaken certain social bonds found in a traditional society which creates an atmosphere of psychological stress and insecurity.

Industrial advancement depends in large measure upon the accumulation of capital. In early phase of industrialization, transfer of surplus labor in huge numbers from traditional agricultural sector provided the necessary support system for this accumulation of capital. In holding the society together the role of the state became very important in this protracted period of transition – from agriculture to industry.

It is a fact that industrial revolution did not take place over all parts of the world at the same time. The countries all over the world are at different stages of industrial transition as they are with the stages of demographic transition. There are many countries where it is yet to come. The circumstances that helped or withheld this transition have indeed been dissimilar. Many of the countries which are considered industrial giants today had carried out this transition through harsh authoritarian measures. It is a fact that in larger countries (on number count), the early phase of industrialization unfolded not under a truly democratic set up (in Europe or elsewhere). Even Stalin's Russia and China's single party dictatorship were ruthless in acquiring farm land for infrastructural development for rapid growth of industries. This is not to admit that some kind of authoritarianism is necessary to create an environment so that the transition can take place relatively smoothly.

The rural economy prior to rise in free private enterprises or capitalism was generally poor but it was rather free from mass unemployment. Mass unemployment was unknown in the Middle Ages except when there was war, natural catastrophe and visitation of famine and epidemics. It is a historical truth that industrialization at its initial stage did not portray a rosy picture for the common man, especially the rural poor. In this regard no one would dispute with the observations made by Bertrand Russell when he wrote, "… I do not think any student of economic history can doubt that average of happiness in England in the 19th century was lower than it had been a hundred years earlier". The experience in the process of transition, as Keynes remarked, is a movement from a low-level equilibrium position to an expectedly higher-level equilibrium, a parallel observed in demographic transition. That is to say, reaching a stable equilibrium is almost unreachable. Labor surplus and intensity of unemployment therefore has to be seen relative to the technology we are employing and the nature of commodities that are brought to the market for the consumption of the common man. Therefore it is no wonder that the specter of involuntary unemployment continue as long as the transition continues. The economists however believe that even the rising capital-intensive labor-saving growth of industry would in the long run absorb the surplus labor since the industries and the state would have to undertake programs to enhance the skill quality of the common people to see that there is no shortage of skilled labor in industries and the industries would be too willing to invest their capital for expansion of existing facilities and/or put in their surplus for diversification of their manufactured products.

The misery that visited the common man in England and other countries in Europe and elsewhere in the early phases of transition had happened in spite the fact that they could send their surplus labor for exploitation abroad (to USA, Australia and many other countries in South America and Africa). When the disruptive potential of industrialization was at its worst, the West still could dump the 'troublemakers' in their established colonies. The West did inflict a great amount of misery on itself and its colonies to climb to the height it has currently achieved. The technological developments and fierce global competition have forced the common man to acquire the needed skills lest they miss the bus. The smaller population base and slow growth rate came handy to tide over the threat of surplus labor and unemployment and maintain a reasonably stable social order in Western countries.

Most of the developing countries have realized that they too have no option but to embrace capital-intensive industrialization if the support system for their citizens were to be consolidated and life style of the common man improved. They cannot afford to embrace the labor-intensive technology in this age of global competition and economic liberalization. Since technologies for up-gradation of their industries and diversification of products are now readily available from the developed countries, of course at a high premium, the transition from traditional agriculture to industrialization in these countries is to be achieved as smoothly and quickly as possible. The infrastructure development to support industrialization is not going to be easy for them. If huge capital investment is the single most important impediment to augur this infrastructure development program, the other formidable obstacle comes from farmers whose agricultural land, often their only asset for survival, has to be acquired by the state pushing more people jobless in countries where unemployment rate and social unrest are fast mounting because of fast declining land-man ratio. Land acquisition for construction of roads, ports, industrial hubs, housing complexes, special economic zones (SEZ), etc. will have considerable impact on the availability of land for cultivation. Food security for many countries would be at stake unless massive investments are made on irrigation, crop rotations are introduced to prevent loss of fertility of the soil and soil erosion and better scientific method of cultivation and agricultural management are adopted. These countries are dependent on international funding agencies like World Bank, IMF etc. for most of their developmental activities. Funds by these institutions are released often on the condition of protection of the existing forest land at all costs and that protection of environment must be assured.

The harsh methods adopted by the Western countries and more recently by China, for protecting social solidarity and promoting industrialization are incompatible with democratic norms. The social fabric of India with its great traditions and incomparable cultural diversity probably could not have been held together by any system other than the political framework of a democratic constitution. Pre-independent India was divided into innumerable native states having their own independent administrative machinery. India has been ruled in the last 2500 years by various kingdoms including the British Rulers. But none of these kingdoms could bring all these native states under the rule of a common administration. It is through the democratic constitution framed by the Constitutional Assembly of independent India that all these diverse entities were brought under a single umbrella – the Republic of India. There is no other way of holding this country and its vast masses together. We have made very many changes in our Constitution without deviating from the basic tenets and fundamental rights which constitute the fundamentals of our Constitution. There was no other way of holding this country and its peoples together and thwart civil war and further fragmentation of this land. India has witnessed rise of many political parties and their combines coming into power at the center as well as in the states, which include the communist parties who had strong reservation in parliamentary democracy. Every political party, however, paid due respect to the democratic set up envisaged in our Constitution.

It is a historic exception when India attempted industrialization under a democratic political set up after independence. No country of India's size and cultural diversity ever attempted industrialization through democratically elected governments. The pattern of growth and the path of industrialization followed in India is distinctly different from the model followed in the West. The first phase of industrialization (first three Five Year Plans) was relatively smooth since construction of heavy industries, thermal and hydro power plants, construction of dams etc. was under public sector. There were plenty of fallow lands, fewer cultivable lands had irrigation facilities for which the farmers had to depend mostly on monsoon rains for cultivation. At that stage, land-man ratio was better enabling employment opportunities for the rural poor. The momentum gained in the first phase of industrialization could not be maintained because of political turmoil that was widespread over a decade. The regional parties increasingly became strong in various parts of the country. Green Revolution in India raised the food grain production from 72 million metric ton (MMT) in 1965–66 to 213 MMT in 2004–05, more than three-fold rise in less than 40 years although area under cultivation increased by no more than 7–8 percent. However, the area brought under irrigation increased from around 20 percent to over 40 percent. Food grain production increased from 630 kg/hectare to over 1,600 kg/hectare. Modern farm practices (HYV seeds, chemical fertilizers, increased mechanization in agriculture) were key to this whooping rise in food grain production.

Even though the total farm land area dropped by 2 to 4 million hectares since the beginning of economic liberalization in 1990–91 for diversion of agricultural land to infrastructure and industrial development, it did not affect the total agricultural output of the country. But this has resulted in sizeable decline in average operational holding and increase in the proportion of small and marginal farmers. The proportion of cultivators and agricultural workers to the total workforce in the country has come down from 67 percent in 1991 to 58 percent in 2001. But what is disparaging is the fact that unemployment at the national level is rising alarmingly. The latest NSS report shows that national level of unemployment was 35.2 million in 2004–05 compared to 26.5 million in 1999–2000. West Bengal, the Leftist ruled state for the last 34 years, made in recent years a serious attempt to acquire agricultural land for construction of highways, ports, chemical hubs, IT park, new townships, manufacturing industries (land acquisition for Tata's small car project at Singur, Hooghly district, shifted since to Gujarat due to mass agitation against forced land acquisition from unwilling farmers), new large and small steel plants. The acquisition of agricultural land, especially the high fertile lands, has met with strong opposition from political parties of all shades and colors, the intelligentsia and the farmers. This only shows how difficult it would be for the state to pursue a smooth transition from agriculture to rapid industrialization. The slogan "agriculture is our base, industry our future" could not convince the farming community irrespective of their political divide. Even a much exalted financial compensation package could not pacify the mood of those losing their only asset in this take over. Neither the investor nor the state can assure an alternative job for those who lose their land. Education and skill requirement of the proposed hi tech industries are serious obstacles for most of the displaced labor to finding an entry opportunity in these establishments.

It has given a sigh of relief to the state administration to learn that the total number of unemployed persons in West Bengal has declined to 3.34 millions in 2004–05 from 4.0 millions in 1999–2000, a creditable achievement considering the quantum jump of unemployment at the national level in the same period. However, West Bengal still accounts for about 10 percent of all unemployed in the country. This unemployment reduction does not mask the pitiable state of unemployment situation in the state, which is reflected in a news item that 253 candidates with honors or postgraduate degrees applied for a contract job (Rs 2,600 + allowance) that requires only a class VIII pass certificate. Job responsibilities listed are washing and cleaning glass apparatus and cleaning of rooms/tables in a microbiology unit of a Public Health laboratory. Taking cue from the example of the resistance offered at Singur and Nandigram (where the chemical hub was proposed to be created), the political parties are planning to thwart any agricultural land acquisition at any part of the state for setting up industrial hubs, townships, power plants, etc. This is primarily because the government did not put up their 'industrial policy' for close scrutiny by the opposition parties and for public debate – even those in the treasury bench, the intelligentsia and the common man.

The extensive all-India media coverage of the Singur and Nandigram episode, especially in the electronic media, has encouraged political and social activists in other states to intensify the 'save farm land' campaign. It is highly likely that many other states (Orissa is already experiencing the heat over the Posco deal), which have very little surplus land, would also witness similar such agitations where the governments are planning to make some change in the land-use pattern followed so long. The central and state governments need to review the compensation package for any land take-over. West Bengal government presently ascertains the current market value of the acquired land and adds 10–20 percent or even more over and above this as the compensation package. The price of the agricultural land where Tata's small car project was coming up had sharply gone up in the last few years because of better road connectivity and other facilities. Had the proposed factory become operational, many other smaller companies and realtors would have liked to set up their units or housing complexes adjacent to the factory. The price of land in and around Singur would have gone up by many times. Prof. Amartya Sen felt that governments need to work out a compensation package for any acquired land not on the basis of current market value but on the basis of its future price, say, 5 years from the date production starts, and also what alternate employment opportunities can be offered to the families losing their land. The fall-out of Singur episode is already visible. The land owners are demanding higher prices for their land, which were acquired even 18 years back (but not fully compensated) for expansion of Indian Iron and Steel Company (IISCO) at Burnpur, else they want their land back.

The economic liberalization started in 1991 has encouraged private investors, domestic and overseas, to invest huge capitals in certain infrastructure and various types of industries and service sector. Foreign exchange reserve of India rose from near zero in 1991 to over US$300 billion by June 2008 and the Indian currency was going very strong at around Rs 40 a US$1 from more than Rs 45 even a few years back. Indian currency has risen by more than 12 percent against the dollar in 2007 alone. India, in fact, was hit by a double barrel of rupee appreciation and continuous dollar (US) inflows. It became a problem not only for exports but also for the entire industry. China and India continue to rank first and second spot in FDI. Investment from developed and developing countries continues to name China and India as their most preferred destination for investments. India will continue to attract investors in the value added services and information technology.

A stiff competition is going on among the states to attract these investors to put their money in their state, offering various types of incentives – land of their choice, tax holidays, adequate supply of power and water at subsidized rates, and etc. For this and other reasons, the government needs to prepare an inventory of lands and land map, the type of industries suitable in different regions, chalk-out a detailed industrial development plan and submit it to debate and discussion, and do the ground work to make people realize that agriculture alone cannot solve the problem of mounting unemployment or ensure a better standard of living of the people. Unless a more congenial environment is created, even the investors who signed MoU with the state governments may try to relocate their proposed industry or other plans to some other states which are offering better terms and conditions.

The central government, though advocates 'economic reform with a human face', cannot afford to going slow on its economic agenda. The existing labor laws often are inadequate to push forward the productivity of the capital-intensive industries. The government could not go ahead with 'labor reforms' because of strong opposition from different political parties, labor unions and even from its own treasury bench members. To achieve a sustainable double digit GDP growth, 'labor reform', withdrawal/reduction of subsidies (in power, irrigation and fertilizer in agriculture) and provisioning of huge fund for social infrastructure (health, education and population control) are urgently needed. The government needs to review the Land Reform Act of 1894 in order to make land acquisition and its transfer more transparent. Opinions abound that the investors must be asked to directly negotiate with the land owners and the government's role would be to ensure that the land owners are paid adequate compensation.

The population pressure on land in India is incomparably more adverse than what it was in most developed and developing countries. India has no substantial outlets for its surplus population. The globalization has only created routes for 'brain drain'. Its impact is likely to be felt in hi tech industries, IT and biotechnology sector, and even in universities, research institutions and higher levels of civil services. It is true that the service sector is currently absorbing a large number of educated and skilled workers and it has the potential to absorb many more at an accelerated rate. But the supply side is unlikely to meet all their demands since there is shortage of educational and training institutes to equip the educated youths with the necessary skill. Many such institutes at the initiative of private enterprises have come up, but the quality of teaching and training imparted in these institutes at a very high cost often is miserable. In view of rupee getting stronger in relation to dollar, there is some decline in India's export earning. To maintain the growth momentum in industrial production, expansion of the domestic market obtains vital importance.

Most of the newly established industries make use of labor saving technology. Unless very many such industries come up quickly in all regions, it is unlikely that these industries can help in a big way in reduction of unemployment. The pressure of unemployment may lead to acute social problems, even civic strife. The declaration by some regional political parties – "We shall ruthlessly oppose establishment of industries on agricultural land" – does not portray a rosy picture for the smooth transition; both rightist and leftist extremist forces are appearing as destabilizing factor. A democratically elected government cannot remain ambivalent to rising unemployment in the country and the social tension mounting in consequence. The disruptive forces will take advantage of the brewing discontent among the masses. India cannot solve the unemployment problem overnight through lop-sided capital-intensive industrial-urban development. Along with urban-centric industrial development, India needs to pursue village level small scale industries and dispersed growth centers to offer employment to educated rural youth. Billions of tax payers' money is spent on the development of cities neglecting the countryside. We often use our natural resources for manufacturing of products which are meant only for the consumption of our rich people or for export. Unless employment-poverty is addressed sincerely, serious attention is given to improvement of the social sector, the domestic consumer base for various products and utilities will not expand in spite of high GDP growth.

11.6 Food and Nutrition

One of the major and persistent problems in most developing countries is food security and distribution of the available food grains. At the time of independence, only 42.8 million metric tons of food grains were produced in India for the consumption of 350 million people. Availability of per capita food grains (rice, wheat, other coarse grains and pulses together) at that point of time was only 394 grams per day. 60 years down the line the situation has improved to some extent. Food grain production has increased by about 5 times and population by 3 times. Even today the availability of food

Table 11. 9

Per capita availability of food grains and other selected commodities in India

Year	*Net availability of food grains per day (figures in grams)*[1]			*Per capita availability of*		
	Cereals	*Pulses*	*Total*	*Edible oil (in kg)*	*Sugar (in kg)*[2, 3]	*Cotton Cloth (in.sq. meter)*
1	*2*	*3*	*4*	*5*	*6*	*7*
1980–81	417.3	37.5	454.8	5.3	7.3	11.0
1989–90	431.5	41.1	472.6	6.5	12.3	14.6
1990–91	468.5	41.6	510.1	6.6	12.7	15.1
1991–92	434.5	34.3	468.8	6.4	13.0	13.7
1992–93	427.9	36.2	464.1	6.8	13.7	15.6
1993–94	434.0	37.2	471.2	7.1	12.5	15.9
1994–95	457.6	37.8	495.4	7.8	13.2	15.2
1995–96	443.4	32.8	476.2	8.0	14.1	16.3
1996–97	466.0	37.1	503.1	9.0	14.6	16.2
1997–98	414.2	32.8	447.0	7.6	14.5	15.9
1998–99	429.2	36.5	465.7	9.8	14.9	13.1
1999–00	422.7	31.8	454.4	10.3	15.6	14.2
2000–01	392.5	30.0	422.5	9.6	15.8p	14.2
2001–02	463.7P	33.4P	497.2P	10.1	16.53P	14.8

Notes:

1. Production figures relate to agriculture year, which is July–June.
2. Relates to actual release for domestic consumption
3. Up to 1965–66 the sugar season was November–October. It has changed since to October–September.

P: Provisional.

Source: Directorate of Statistics and Economics, Report of Agricultural Cooperation, Ministry of Agriculture – Compendium of Textiles Statistics, Ministry of Textiles.

grains per capita per day is below 500 grams (Table 11.9). Between 1980–81 and 1998–99 food grain production has gone up from 129.59 MMT to 203.4 MMT, but the advantage of 73 MMT of additional production between the two time points could increase the availability of food grains per day per capita by a meager 11 grams. Since agriculture even today is largely dependent on monsoon rains, food grain production displays large variations, year on year. Per capita availability of food grain was highest in 1990–91 (510 gm) and the least in 2000–01(422gm). That is, growth rate of food grain production on the average just could match the population growth rate in the country. Availability of edible oil and sugar has doubled during this period. Availability of cotton cloth has increased by about 14 percent.

11.6.1 Land Use

Land use in the country since independence has undergone a sweeping change. Land under agriculture has almost doubled, forest cover has dwindled to less than half, and large tracts of fertile agriculture and forest land have been diverted to build roads, create dams, cities and other settlements. To understand the food situation in the country and nutrition status of a common man prevailing in the post-independence period, we need to take a look at how much the increase in food grain production is related to increase in the total cropped area, area under cultivation (million hectares, mha) of different crops, net area under irrigation, production (million tons) and yield

Table 11.10

Area, production and yield of food grains – All India

Year	*Area (million hectares)*	*Production (million tons)*	*Yield (kg/hectare)*	*% coverage under irrigation*
1950–51	97.32	50.82	522	18.10
1955–56	110.56	66.85	605	18.50
1960–61	115.58	82.02	710	19.10
1965–66	115.10	72.35	629	20.90
1970–71	124.32	108.42	872	24.10
1975–76	128.18	121.03	944	26.50
1980–81	126.67	129.59	1,023	29.70
1985–86	128.02	150.44	1,175	31.40
1990–91	127.84	176.39	1,380	35.10
1991–92	121.87	168.38	1,382	37.40
1992–93	123.15	179.48	1,457	37.40
1993–94	122.75	184.26	1,501	38.70
1994–95	123.86	191.50	1,546	39.60
1995–96	121.01	180.42	1,491	40.50
1996–97	123.58	199.44	1,614	
1997–98	123.85	192.26	1,552	
1998–99	125.36	203.04	1,620	

Source: Planning Commission, Government of India: Indian Planning Experience – A Statistical Profile, 2001.

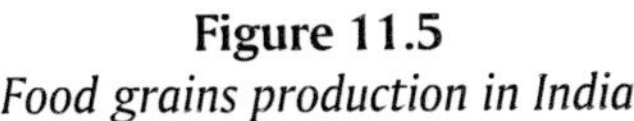

Figure 11.5
Food grains production in India

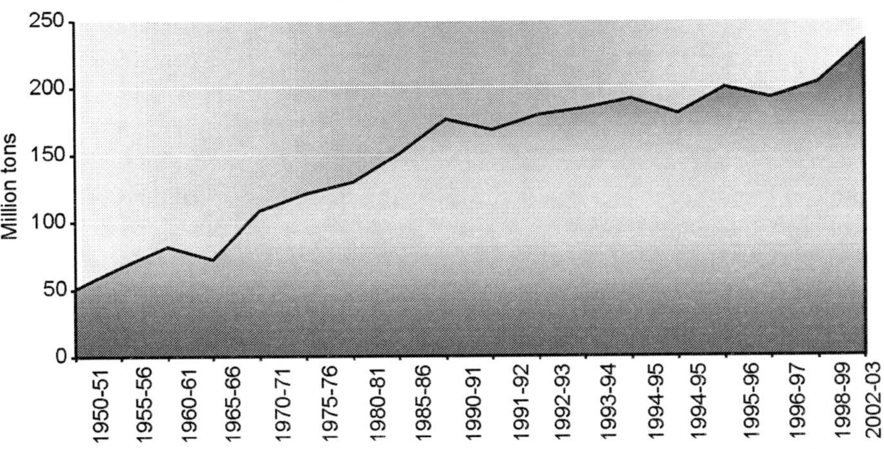

(kg/hectare) as also the consumption expenditure of different classes of households. In 2000, the total arable land and land under permanent crops combined was 1,697,000 square kilometers, and total irrigated land was 548,000 square kilometers (32.3%). The total of non-arable land and land not under permanent crops was 1,276,190 square kilometers.

Although the yield per hectare land has increased three-fold between 1950–51 and 1998–99, a lot increase in food production during the period has been done through bringing more land under cultivation (30% increase in land area for cultivation). The average yield has increased because more than 40 percent of the crop land today has irrigation facilities compared to only 18 percent in 1950–51. We are behind the average world yield level for almost in all crops and even behind China in yields in all crops except in potato. The following table definitely is an indication that India has the potential to increase its total food production by bringing more land under irrigation and by improving the yield per unit area of cultivation through better agricultural management.

Table 11.11
Yield of selected crops – An international comparison (yield in kg per hectare)

Crop	*World*		*India*		*Mexico*		*USA*		*China*	
	1979–81	*1990*	*1979–81*	*1990*	*1979–81*	*1990*	*1979–81*	*1990*	*1979–81*	*1990*
1	*2*	*3*	*4*	*5*	*6*	*7*	*8*	*9*	*10*	*11*
Wheat	1,886	2,570	1,545	2,117	3,822	4,179	2,291	2,656	2,047	3,179
Paddy	2,757	3,557	1,858	2,691	3,447	3,780	5,167	6,173	4,244	5,728
Pulses	674	863	461	553	719	661	1,633	1,693	1,223	1,475
Sugarcane	56,566	61,329	52,105	64,140	66,016	99,695	81,668	76,800	54,170	59,897
Course grains	2,207	2,548	694	892	1,990	2,240	5,377	6,308	2,604	3,538
Potato	14,167	15,098	12,639	15,873	12,677	12,587	30,387	32,484	10,888	11,588

Source: FAO Production Yearbook, 1990.

Figure 11.6

Cross tab of area and production over time (1951–1999)

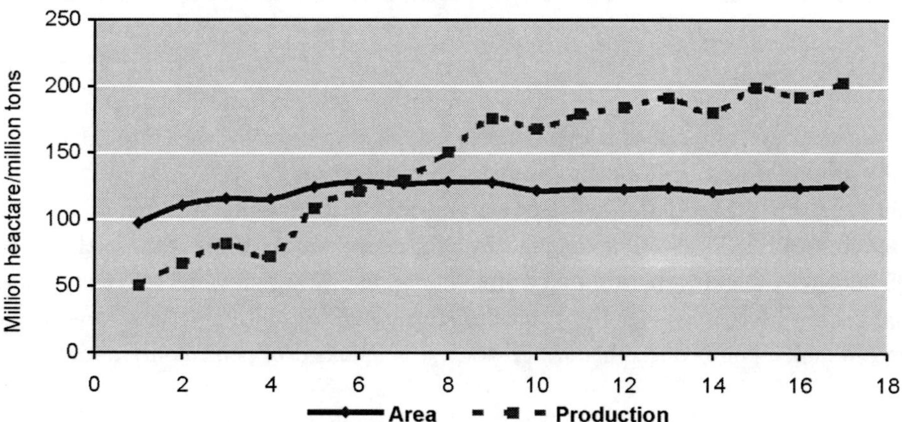

Table 11.12

Key statistics on area and production of agricultural products

	India	*India's rank in world production*	*India's share in world production*	*India's share in exports*	*USA*	*China*	*Brazil*
1	*2*	*3*	*4*	*5*	*6*	*7*	*8*
Arable land (mill. ha)	161	2			175	124	54
Irrigated land (mill. ha)	55	1			27	54	2.92
Production (in million tons)							
Wheat	65	2	12	0.02	56	86	6
Rice and paddy	124	2	22	1.8	10	186	13
Coarse grains	29	3	4	Negligible	318	144	45
Milk	91	1	16	Negligible	77	23	23
Fruits	47	2	10	Negligible	29	78	36
Vegetables	82	2	10	Negligible	38	423	8
Edible oilseeds	25	3	7	Net importer	95	49	49
Pulses	15	1	21	Net importer	1	5	3
Sugarcanes	245	2	21		27	93	411
Tea	0.85	1	28	12		0.8	0.08
Cattle (million)	186	2	16		95	106	192

Source: FAO 2004 and Radobank Analysis.

Table 11.15 shows how food production has increased through two major crop seasons – *Kharif* and *Rabi*. Extensive cultivation of major crops is carried out during the monsoon months (*Kharif*) in all parts of the world taking the advantage of abundant rain water. Even if additional water is needed, it can be had from rivers, canals, ponds and other reservoirs that store rain water. There is practically no need for lifting ground water for irrigation in monsoon season in most regions. On the contrary, *Rabi* crops require huge amount of water, a major part of which is provided through canals from the dams and the ground water. In 1950–51, net irrigated area was only 20,853,000 hectares in India; by 1995–96 this went up to 53,510,000 hectares – about one-third of which was irrigated through canals under state control, 17,937,000 hectares through deep and shallow tube-wells (33.5%) and 11,860,000 hectares of land were irrigated from other wells (22%), the latter two use ground water as their source (Table 11.16). Till 1960–61, around 18 percent of cultivable land was irrigated using water stored in tanks, ponds and other water-bodies. This has dropped to only about 5.8 percent in 1995–96.

The benefits of the expansion of irrigation facilities, especially through lifting of ground water, have not reached the poor small and marginal farmers. Their small land holding does not permit them to take advantage of irrigation during non-monsoon months to increase production from unit land. Over 78 percent of farming households in 1991 had less than 2 hectares of operational holding (59% had less than 1 hectare). They together operated around 33 percent of the land under cultivation.

Table 11.13

Distribution of landholding – All India

Category of holdings	*No. of operational holdings ('000)*		*Area operated ('000 hectares)*		*Average size of operational holdings*	
	1985–86	*1990–91*	*1985–86*	*1990–91*	*1985–86*	*1990–91*
1	*2*	*3*	*4*	*5*	*6*	*7*
Marginal (Less than 1 ha)	56,147 (57.8)	63,389 (59.4)	22,042 (13.4)	24,894 (15.1)	0.39	0.39
Small (1.0 to 2.0 ha)	17,922 (18.4)	20,092 (18.8)	25,708 (15.6)	28,827 (17.4)	1.43	1.43
Semi medium (2.0 to 4.0 ha)	13,252 (13.6)	13,923 (13.1)	36,666 (22.3)	38,375 (23.2)	2.77	2.76
Medium (4.0 to 10.0 ha)	7,916 (8.2)	7,580 (7.1)	47,144 (28.6)	44,752 (27.0)	5.96	5.90
Large (10.0 ha and above)	1,918 (2.0)	1,654 (1.6)	33,002 (20.1)	28,659 (17.3)	17.21	17.33
All holdings	97,155 (100.0)	106,637 (100.0)	164,562 (100.0)	165,507 (100.0)	1.69	1.55

Note : Figures in brackets indicate the percentage of respective column to totals (percentages on the basis of absolute values).

Source : Agricultural Census 1990–91.

Table 11.14

Per thousand distribution of rural households by size class of land cultivated in the years 1986–87, 1992–93 & 1998–99

Size class of land cultivated (figures in ha)	Households			Population		
	1986–87	1992–93	1998–99	1986–87	1992–93	1998–99
1	2	3	4	5	6	7
Up to 0.40	544	575	632	472	509	573
0.41–1.00	173	171	168	179	179	182
1.01–2.00	139	135	112	158	155	128
2.01–4.00	86	76	59	108	95	74
4.01 & above	58	43	30	82	61	43
Total	1000	1000	1000	1000	1000	1000

Source: Employment and Unemployment Situation in India, NSS 55th round (July 1999 – June 2000) NSS Report No. 458–I.

Table 11.15

Kharif and rabi crop production over the years – All India

Year	Kharif			Rabi		
	Area[1]	Production[2]	Yield[3]	Area	Production	Yield
1	2	3	4	5	6	7
1966–67	78.21	48.89	625	37.09	25.34	683
1970–71	82.36	68.92	837	41.96	39.5	942
1975–76	83.15	73.89	889	45.03	47.14	1047
1980–81	83.21	77.65	933	43.46	51.94	1195
1985–86	81.80	85.25	1042	46.22	65.19	1410
1990–91	80.78	99.44	1231	47.06	76.95	1635
1991–92	78.02	91.59	1174	43.85	76.79	1751
1992–93	77.92	101.47	1302	45.23	78.01	1725
1993–94	75.81	100.4	1324	46.94	83.86	1787
1994–95	75.19	101.09	1344	48.67	90.41	1857
1995–96	73.60	95.12	1292	47.42	85.3	1799
1996–97	74.34	103.92	1379	48.24	95.52	1980
1997–98	74.15	101.58	1370	49.7	90.68	1825
1998–99	74.07	103.35	1395	51.29	99.69	1944

1. Area in million hectares 2. Production in million tons 3. Yield in kg/hectare.

Source: Ministry of Agriculture, Government of India

Figure 11.7

Area under kharif and rabi crop

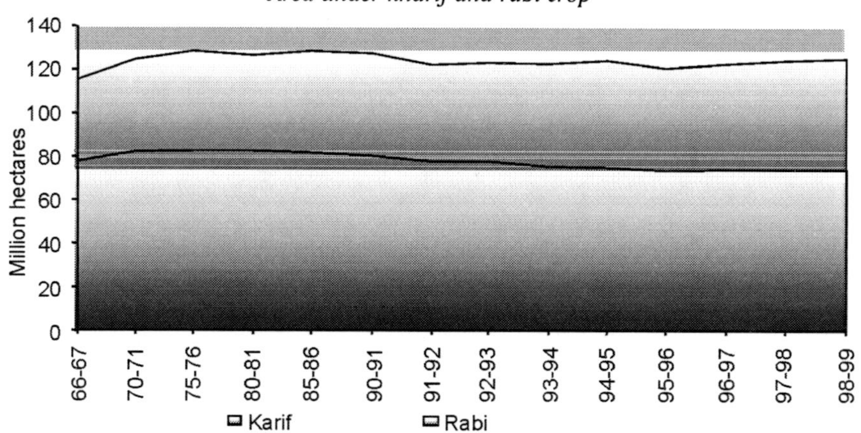

Figure 11.8

Kharif and rabi food grains production

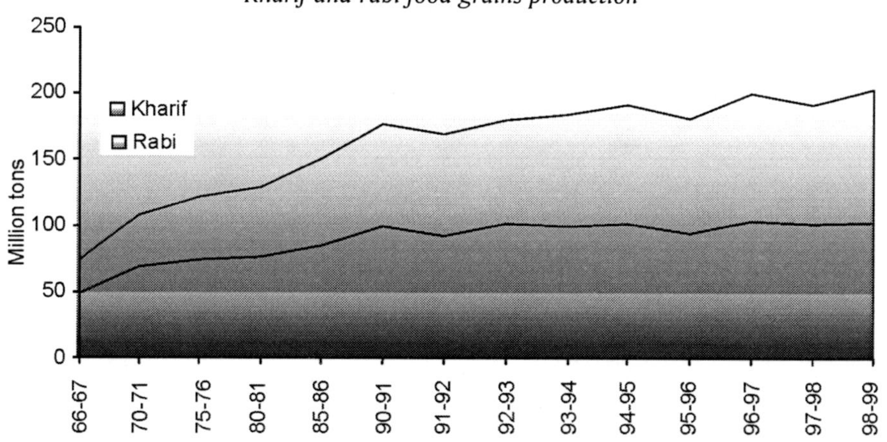

Table 11.16

Area irrigated by source – All India (area '000 hectares)

Source	*50–51*	*60–61*	*70–71*	*80–81*	*90–91*	*91–92**	*92–93**	*93–94**	*94–95**	*95–96*
1	*2*	*3*	*4*	*5*	*6*	*7*	*8*	*9*	*10*	*11*
Government Canals	7,158	9,170	11,972	14,450	16,973	17,327	17,001	16,653	16,799	16,882
	(34.3)	(37.2)	(38.5)	(37.3)	(35.3)	(34.7)	(33.8)	(32.4)	(31.7)	(31.0)
Private Canals	1,137	1,200	866	842	480	464	456	485	481	560
	(5.5)	(4.9)	(2.8)	(2.2)	(1.0)	(0.9)	(0.9)	(0.9)	(0.9)	(1.0)
Tanks	3,613	4,561	4,112	3,182	2,944	2,991	2,854	3,170	3,276	3,111
	(17.3)	(18.5)	(13.2)	(8.2)	(6.1)	(6.0)	(5.7)	(6.2)	(6.2)	(5.8)
Tube wells		135	4,461	9,531	14,57	15,118	15,814	16,376	17,190	17,937
	(0.6)	(14.3)	(24.6)	(29.7)	(30.4)	(31.4)	(31.9)	(32.4)	(33.5)	(33.5)

Cont'd...

Table 11.16 Cont'd...

1	*2*	*3*	*4*	*5*	*6*	*7*	*8*	*9*	*10*	*11*
Other Wells	5,978	7,155	7,426	8, 164	10,437	10,869	11,105	11,220	11,722	11,860
	(28.7)	(29.0)	(23.9)	(21.1)	(21.7)	(21.8)	(22.1)	(21.9)	(22.1)	(22.2)
Other Sources	2,967	2,440	2,266	2,551	2,932	3,048	3,065	3,435	3,533	3,460
	(14.2)	(9.8)	(7.3)	(6.6)	(6.1)	(6.2)	(6.1)	(6.7)	(6.7)	(6.5)
Total (Net irrigated area)	20,853	24,661	31,103	38,720	48,023	49,867	50,295	51,339	53,001	53,510
	(100)	(100)	(100)	(100)	(100)	(100)	(100)	(100)	(100)	(100)

Note:
(i) Figures in brackets are percentages to total net irrigated area.
(ii) Included under Other Wells as separate figures were not collected during this year.
(iii) *Provisional.

Over exploitation of ground water for irrigation, industrial use and for supply of drinking water in areas where surface water is not available in required quantity, is resulting in falling ground water table in many countries. Environmentalists, agricultural scientists and hydrologists are stressing on Integrated Water Management (IWM) for water conservation and the quantity of water that we draw for various uses. They are asking us to shift our attention from productivity of land to increasing productivity of water use. For each drop of water, we should aim at increasing the value added and welfare derived from its use. In agriculture, this means promoting practices that achieve more output per unit of water consumed. With more crops from each drop, there is a need for use of fewer drops. There is considerable scope to increase the productivity of water in agriculture. Productivity gains can be achieved from improved agricultural practices and improved water delivery services and switch over to such crop that requires relatively small water in the areas where water resources is scarce. Increasing agricultural productivity of water will free up more water for nature; it will reduce scarcity giving more opportunities to poor, and with a poverty focus, can improve their incomes and livelihoods.

A popular recommendation is to concentrate food production in rain fed rather than in irrigated areas. The total cultivated area of the world is about one billion hectares, of which only about one-third is irrigated. A 10 percent increase in the productivity of rain fed agriculture can have twice the impact as the same increase in irrigated area. Since the beneficiaries would be largely the poor farmers in marginal areas, this is an enormously attractive idea.

India therefore needs to concentrate its agricultural activities when water for irrigation is not a problem. But unfortunately, area under *Kharif* crop has shrunk from over 78 million hectares (mha) in 1966–67 to 74 mha in 1998–99 (a large part of this one-crop land has been diverted to other uses). During the same period, area under *Rabi* crop has gone up from 37 million hectares (mha) to over 51 mha, a 38 percent increase over 1966–67 level. Yield for *Kaharif* crop has more than doubled during the period and the *Rabi* crop yield has gone up by nearly three times. One needs to look for new varieties that can provide greater yields for each unit of water consumed and other inputs. Waste water from industries, after elimination of toxic substances and salinity, can be used for irrigation in nearby agricultural fields.

Figure 11.9

Kharif and rabi crop yield

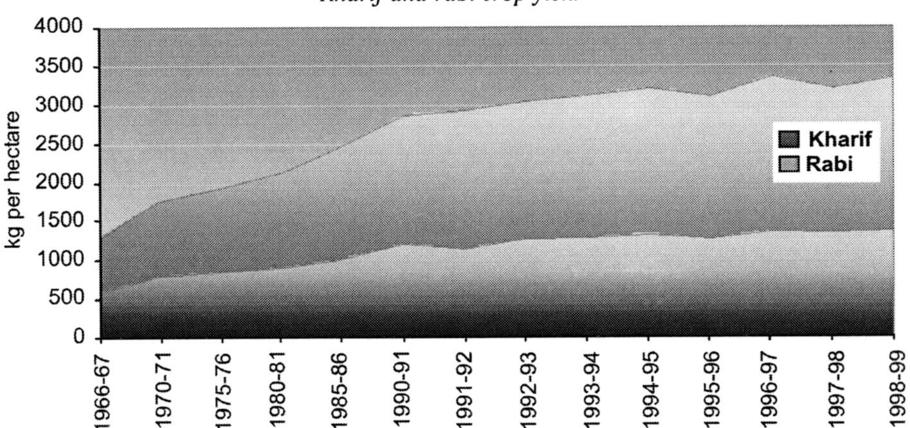

We take a look at how production and yield of major crops improved since independence.

Table 11.17

Break-up of per capita net availability of food grains in India (in kg)

Year	*Rice*	*Wheat*	*Other Cereals*	*Cereals (2 to 4)*	*Gram*	*Pulses*	*Food grains (5 + 7)*
1	*2*	*3*	*4*	*5*	*6*	*7*	*8*
1951	58.0	24.0	40.0	122.0	8.2	22.1	144.1
1956	68.7	22.5	40.7	131.9	10.6	25.7	157.6
1961	73.4	145.9			11.0	25.2	171.1
1966	59.1	34.8	37.5	131.4	6.7	17.6	149.0
1971	70.3	37.8	44.3	152.4	7.3	18.7	171.1
1976	68.5	29.1	39.2	136.8	7.4	18.5	155.3
1981	72.2	47.3	32.8	152.3	4.9	13.7	166.0
1986	77.4	55.1	25.8	158.3	5.9	16.0	174.3
1991	80.9	60.0	29.2	171.0	4.9	15.2	186.2
1992	79.2	57.9	21.5	158.6	3.7	12.5	171.1
1993	73.4	51.2	31.6	156.2	3.9	13.2	169.4
1994	75.7	58.2	24.5	158.4	4.3	13.6	172.0
1995	84.7	62.8	23.9	171.4	5.5	13.9	185.3
1996	77.4	65.0	22.9	165.3	4.2	12.0	177.3
1997^P	80.7	65.0	27.2	172.9	4.7	14.0	186.9
1998^P	79.6	61.4	24.2	164.6	5.0	12.1	176.7

Notes: Figures in respect of per capita availability given above are not strictly representative of the actual level of consumption in the country.

Source: Planning Commission, Government of India, Indian Planning Experience – A Statistical Profile, 2001.

Figure 11.10

Per capita availability of food grains (in kg)

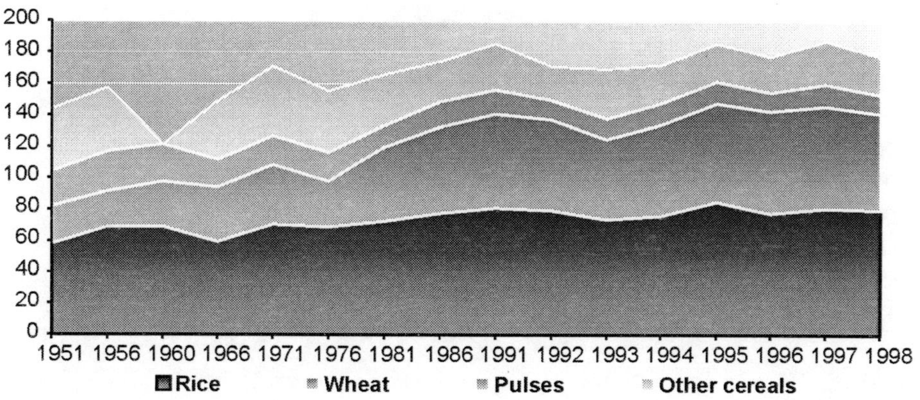

Table 11.18

Per capita availability of food grains and other selected commodities in India

	Net availability of food grains per day (Figures in grams)[1]			Per capita availability of other commodities		
Year	*Cereals*	*Pulses*	*Total*	*Edible oil (in kg)*	*Sugar (in kg)*[2, 3]	*Cotton cloth (sq. meter)*
1	2	3	4	5	6	7
1980–81	417.3	37.5	454.8	5.3	7.3	11.0
1989–90	431.5	41.1	472.6	6.5	12.3	14.6
1990–91	468.5	41.6	510.1	6.6	12.7	15.1
1991–92	434.5	34.3	468.8	6.4	13.0	13.7
1992–93	427.9	36.2	464.1	6.8	13.7	15.6
1993–94	434.0	37.2	471.2	7.1	12.5	15.9
1994–95	457.6	37.8	495.4	7.8	13.2	15.2
1995–96	443.4	32.8	476.2	8.0	14.1	16.3
1996–97	466.0	37.1	503.1	9.0	14.6	16.2
1997–98	414.2	32.8	447.0	7.6	14.5	15.9
1998–99	429.2	36.5	465.7	9.8	14.9	13.1
1999–00	422.7	31.8	454.4	10.3	15.6	14.2
2000–01	392.5	30.0	422.5	9.6	15.8p	14.2
2001–02	463.7p	33.4p	497.2p	10.1	16.53p	14.8

Notes :

1. Production figures relate to agriculture year which is July–June.
2. Relates to actual release for domestic consumption
3. Up to 1965–66 the sugar season was November–October and after that it has changed to October–September.

Source: Directorate of Statistics and Economics, Report of Agricultural Cooperation, Ministry of Agriculture Compendium of Textiles Statistics, Ministry of Textiles.

Figure 11.11
Availability of per capita food grains (in gms)

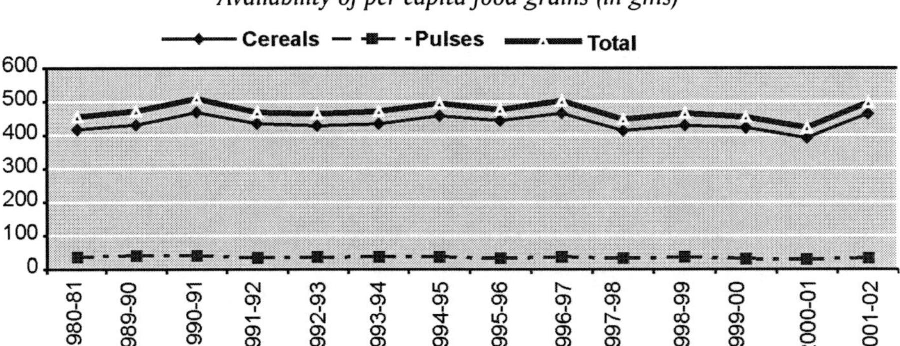

Though crop production is a little higher in *Kharif* than in *Rabi* season (Table 11.15), yield per hectare is 38 percent more in the latter. In the 1960s, *Rabi* crop was grown in less than 50 percent of the cultivable land because of very restricted irrigation facilities. Net irrigated area has increased from 20,853,000 hectares in 1950–51 to 53,510,000 hectares in 1995–96. Irrigation through shallow pumps and deep tube-wells came in a big way since early seventies and presently more than one-third of the cultivated lands come under this type of irrigation. Ground water reserve is declining fast as a result. A better access to electricity, often practically free of cost in certain states, has also led to enormous loss of ground water.

11.6.2 Cereal Consumption

It is generally accepted that dietary patterns have changed in India over the last thirty years. Consumption of coarse cereals has declined in favor of rice and wheat. Also, cereals as a whole now account for a smaller share of total food consumption. However, the NSS, which is the main source of data for demand analysis, differs considerably from the estimates of food availability by other sources. As against the usual assessment that cereals production and availability has increased significantly over the last thirty years, the NSS shows massive decline in availability of cereals for consumption – from 175 kilograms per capita per annum (kpca) in 1972–73 to only 147 kpca in 1999–2000. Both NSS and the Planning Commission admitted that cereal production flattened out in the nineties and then dipped sharply. The official availblity of food grains for per capita consumption, after making necessary provisions for seed, animal feed, waste, industrial use, etc., almost remained at the level of 155 kpca between 1987–88 and 1995–97 and then dropping sharply to 142 kpca in 2001.

There is no doubt that per capita consumption of cereals is much less than what it was a decade or two ago. Production of coarse cereals has dropped since 1971–72 and has remained almost stagnated after 1981. NSS data indicate that consumption of *coarse cereals* has declined from 50 kpca in 1971–72 to around 14 kpca in 2000.

Unlike coarse cereals, there is a sustained growth of rice and wheat production. Growth of rice production has decelerated to just about the population growth rate after the 1980s. Over time, rice and wheat consumption has almost become equal across all income classes. The NSS data show that consumption of rice/wheat among the 20 percent poorest population in rural India was only 76 kpca

Figure 11.12

Share of food items in the consumption basket

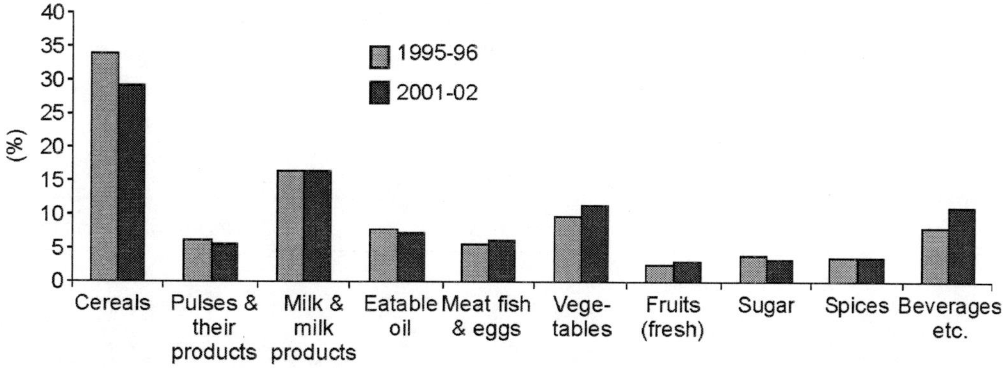

Source: NSSO data and Radobank analysis

in 1972–73, less than half of the 180 kpca consumed by the richest 20 percent of the rural population. The consumption of the poorest lot increased by 40 percent in 1987–88 (107 kpca), while consumption of the richest segment remained at the same level as of 1972–73. In urban area, consumption of the poorest quintile increased by 20 percent, from 90 kpca in 1972–73 to 108 kpca in 1987–88. Consumption of the uppermost urban quintile increased from 132 kpca to 135 kpca during the same period. Consumption of rice/wheat by the poorest 20 percent of rural population increased from around 107 to 116 kpca between 1987 and 1999–2000; the same in the urban area increased from 108 to 116 kpca. Steady decline in rice/wheat consumption by the richest segment in rural (from 180 to 156 kpca) and urban population (135 to 120 kpca) has been reported by NSS.

The decline in cereals consumption does not mean that there was a total decline in food consumption. National Accounts Statistics (NAS) confirms a 6 percent reduction in per capita real price expenditure (1993–94 prices) on cereals between triennia ending (TE – consecutive three years) 1987–88 and TE 2000–2001, but per capita real price expenditure on all food items taken together increased by 16 percent. NAS reported increase in expenditure on non-cereal food items except pulses (edible oil, sugar, vegetables and a large increase, about 45 percent on animal products – milk and milk products, egg, meat, fish, etc. and other 'food items' as spices, tea, and outside eating). NSS generally agrees with NAS observation on expenditure on non-cereal food. Average calories intake estimated by NAS rose from below 2,000 kcal in the seventies to over 2,400 kcal (1995–97) and then declined to 2,200 kcal in 2001. NSS data show the peak in calorie intake in 1988–89 and a slow decline thereafter till 1998 and then rising sharply to a little below 2,200 kcal in 2000. Although a common man's dish today contains more varied items than it had in the 1970s, cereals still today provide about 60 percent of the calories (1,250 kcal/day) from our foods and beverages, 58 percent of total proteins and about 13 percent of total fats (having come down from 66, 65 and 20 percent respectively in 1981). Cereals account for only a small share (about one-third) of total food expenditure but contribute very significantly to nutrition than many other expensive items in our food basket. The poorer people (the bottom 40% in rural population) amass 75 percent of calories from cereals. That is, as we move away from cereals, we have to spend more for every unit of nutrient so that increase in calories and the protein ingestion from these varied items is less than the increase in food expenditure.

We present below the report on protein and calories intake by National Nutrition Monitoring Bureau (NNMB). The data furnished do not really agree either with NAS or NSS data for the estimated calories for different time points though it generally agrees with the pattern of change suggested by NAS and NSS data. The Bureau data indicate that protein in a common man's dish has steadily declined between 1975 and 2001.

Table 11.19
Average daily intake of proteins and calories in India

Year	*Proteins (in grams)*	*Calories (in kilo calories)*
1975	63.6	2,296
1980	62.8	2,404
1988–90 b	61.8	2,283
1991–92 c	54.1	2,139
1993–94 d	55.8	2,187
1994–95	55.8	2,172
1996–97 e	54.0	2,114
2001 f	50.7	1,955

a. During 1983 the surveys were conducted on a sub-sample of NSSO 'Central' sample in only four states viz. Andhra Pardesh, Gujarat, Orissa and Tamil Nadu.
b. Results are based on Repeat Surveys conducted earlier during 1975–79 to study changes in consumption and nutritional situation.
c. Report of NNMB (1993). During the years 1991 & 1992, surveys were conducted on a sub-sample of NSSO 'Central' sample in the states of Kerala,Tamil Nadu, Karnataka, Andhra Pradesh, Maharashtra, Gujarat, Orissa and West Bengal.
d. Report of NNMB (1996) represents the simple average at state level estimates of consumption for the state of Kerala,Tamil Nadu, Karnataka, Andhra Pradesh, Maharashtra, Gujarat, Madhya Pradesh, Orissa.
e. During 1996–97 Second Repeat Surveys were conducted in the State of Kerala, Tamil Nadu, Karnataka, Andhra Pradesh, Maharastra, Gujarat and Orissa (NNMB II Repeat Survey).
f. Figures are based on NNMB survey on "Diet and Nutritional Status of Rural Population" carried out in the year 2000–2001.
Source: Annual Reports of National Nutrition Monitoring Bureau.

A close approximation to nutritional status of the population can be had from people's consumption expenditure. During 1999–2000, about 64.4 percent of households in rural areas were in the Monthly Per Capita Expenditure (MPCE) class of less than Rs 525, the same for urban areas was at 61 percent. The urban people have some edge over their rural counterparts in MPCE class distribution in their populations.

Figure 11.13
Average daily calories intake

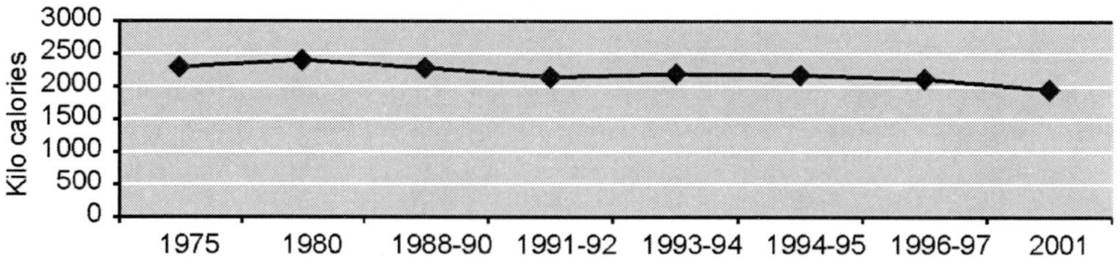

Kilo calories
3000
2500
2000
1500
1000
500
0
1975 1980 1988-90 1991-92 1993-94 1994-95 1996-97 2001

Table 11.20
Per thousand distribution of households and population by MPCE class in India during 1999–2000

Rural			*Urban*		
MPCE class (Rs)	***Households***	***Population***	***MPCE class (Rs)***	***Households***	***Population***
000–225	44	52	000–300	38	52
225–255	42	50	300–350	37	50
255–300	87	100	350–425	75	96
300–340	90	100	425–500	86	101
340–380	93	103	500–575	86	99
380–420	92	97	575–665	91	100
420–470	100	102	665–775	96	101
470–525	96	93	775–915	103	100
525–615	111	103	915–1120	113	100
615–775	113	99	1120–1500	130	101
775–950	61	50	1500–1925	67	50
>950	71	50	>1925	77	50
All classes	1000	1000		1000	1000

MPCE: Monthly Per Capita Expenditure.
Source: Employment and Unemployment in India, 1999–2000, NSS 55th Round.

11.6.3 Household Size and MPCE Class

The NSSO survey (59th Round) shows that household size was largest for the lowest MPCE bracket. The largest households, 6.9 members, had an MPCE less than or equal to Rs 225 and the smallest households, 4.1 members, had an MPCE over Rs 950. The average household size declined steadily with the rise in MPCE. The survey also indicates that farmers' incomes have failed to keep pace with increase in expenditure-income for all rural households, which also include non-agricultural activities. In 2003, the MPCE for farmer households at national level was Rs 502.83 as against Rs 554.15

Figure 11.14
Households in different MPCE classes

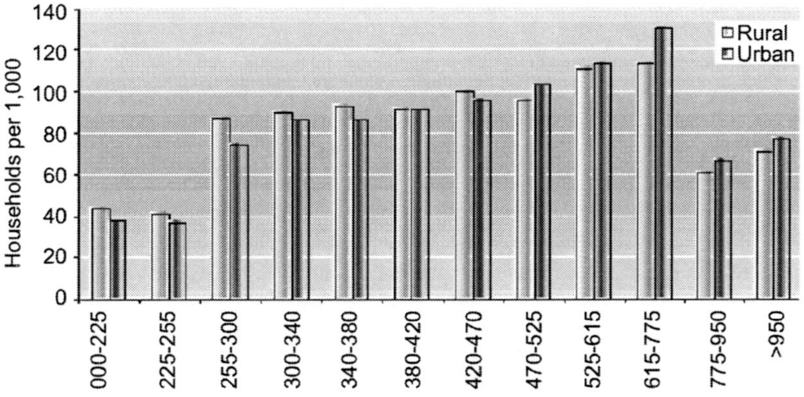

Households per 1,000
140
120
100
80
60
40
20
0
Rural
Urban
000-225
225-255
255-300
300-340
340-380
380-420
420-470
470-525
525-615
615-775
775-950
>950

for all rural households. In absolute terms, the farmers spent less on food items per month (Rs 278.74) compared to Rs 298.57 by all rural households. Assam farmers spend most on food (65% of their MPCE), followed by Jharkhand (64%), Bihar (62%) and West Bengal (61%).

Table 11.21

Per capita household consumption expenditure (Rs) over the years in India

Year	Rural		Urban	
	Food	Total	Food	Total
1954–55	9.9	15.0	13.7	24.7
1959–60	14.1	20.0	16.9	27.5
1964–65	19.3	26.4	22.7	36.0
1969–70	25.6	34.7	33.1	50.4
1973–74	39.7	53.0	47.9	70.8
1977–78	44.3	68.9	57.7	96.2
1983	73.7	112.5	97.0	164.0
1986–87	92.6	140.9	129.0	222.0
1990–91	133.3	202.1	185.8	326.8
1994–95	188.9	309.4	271.5	508.1
January – December 97[a]	231.9	395.0	320.2	645.4
January – June 98[a]	232.4	382.1	339.7	684.3
July 99 – June 2000	288.8	486.1	443.2	971.6
July 2000 – June 2001[a]	278.6	494.9	400.6	914.6

a. The results are based on thin samples.
Source: National Sample Survey Organization (NSSO).

Nagaland has the highest percentage of farmers in the high MPCE bracket (36 percent, MPCE > Rs 950) and also the highest per capita expenditure on education (Rs 77.21). Surprisingly, Kerala, where over 90 percent rural people are literate, farmers are the lowest spenders on education (Rs 42.36) though they have the highest MPCE (Rs 900.59). They, however, spend highest in medical bill (Rs 97.98). The survey also noted that 22 percent of farmers in Orissa, 11 percent in Jharkhand, 8 percent in Madhya Pradesh and Chhattisgarh and 6 percent in Bihar have MPCE less than or equal to Rs 225.

11.6.4 Public Distribution System (PDS)

Although crop production in India is closely related to rains in the monsoon months, per capita availability of food grains have remained close to 500 grams quite for some time. Had the food grain been equitably distributed and those in BPL category had the purchasing power to buy from the open market wheat, rice, sugar and kerosene, which are sold to them through the ration shops at a very subsidized price, there should have been no incidence of death from starvation. The starvation problem is not so much in urban area as in rural area since most urbanites on average have better purchasing power and can procure their requirements from the open market. The rural poor are totally dependent on the supplies through the fair-price shops under public distribution system (PDS).

The real magnitude of starvation in a country is difficult to estimate. A close approximation to the magnitude of starvation and hunger probably can be had from the study of depth of perception of deprivation and injustice. National Sample Survey has come out with a report (February 2007) of perceived inadequacy of food consumption in rural households. On the basis of answers received, the survey households were included in one of the three categories: a) households having adequate food throughout the year; b) households having inadequate food during some months of the year; and c) households having inadequate food throughout the year. The NSS findings are summarized in Table 11.22 for the major States in India.

Table 11.22

Number of households (per 1,000) with inadequate food in rural India

States	Inadequate food during some months of the year	Inadequate food throughout the year	Food grain production per capita (tons/year)*
Andhra Pradesh	6	0	0.18
Assam	17	36	0.15
Bihar	20	8	0.03
Chhattisgarh	26	0	0.29
Gujarat	3	0	0.12
Haryana	0	0	0.62
Jharkhand	6	1	0.10
Karnataka	3	0	0.12
Kerala	22	3	0.01
Madhya Pradesh	15	5	0.26
Maharashtra	10	0	0.11
Orissa	48	13	0.19
Punjab	8	1	1.00
Rajasthan	0	0	0.31
Tamil Nadu	1	1	0.07
Uttar Pradesh	14	3	0.26
West Bengal	106	13	0.20

* Computed by Abhirup Sarkar: *Grain of truth*, The Telegraph, 28 October 2007.

There are only six states that have moderate to large surplus of food grains produced. The deficit states are dependent on import of food grains from other states or from the central food stock. The central government also allocates food grains to different states for running various welfare programs for the rural and urban poor. Most seasonal starvations are reported from West Bengal (10.6%), Orissa (4.8%) and Chhattisgarh (2.6%). Bihar, where estimated per capita food grain production is as low as 30 kg/year, has reported only 2 percent seasonal starvation and 0.8 percent starvation round the year. In spite of moderately good food grain production in West Bengal and Orissa, about 1.3 percent of rural people reported starvation throughout the year in these states. Most starvation cases have however been reported from Assam (3.6%). In this connection it is worth noting that the NSS survey also found that whereas 16 states drew 90–100 percent of their allotted quota for BPL from the central food stock for disbursement through the PDS in 2006–07, West Bengal could draw only 68 percent of their allotment. Maharashtra, Karanataka and Kerala, where per capita food grain production though quite low, could provide 19.8, 18.2 and 15.6 kilograms of rice respectively per month to every BPL household in their states. The same in West Bengal was only 3.4 kilograms on average. While a very large proportion (between 35 and 79) of the rural households (BPL+APL) in most rice-eating states like Tamil Nadu, Andhra Pradesh, Karnataka and Kerala received rice from fair-price shops, only 13 percent of the same received rice from the ration shops in West Bengal, a traditionally rice-eating state. Even the people of Gujarat and Maharashtra, which are not really rice-eating states, are better treated by their respective governments in the supply of rice through their public distribution chains. That is, PDS in most other states are far more efficient compared to that in West Bengal.

The PDS has remained operational throughout the country for about 50 years. Presently, the ration shops mostly deliver wheat, rice, sugar and kerosene to BPL families. Even the highly subsidized rations and various other poverty eradication programs currently under operation have failed to arrest starvation. The public impression is that the state machinery is hand in glove with the unscrupulous traders, local politicians and their collaborators. People have reason to believe that the ration shop owners often sell a large proportion of the subsidized food grains and kerosene allotted for the poor in the open market. Even truckloads of food grains from FCI godowns move out for unknown destination. The poor have to purchase the same items from the open market at a very high price. This is one of the major reasons why the market price is going up even though the inflation is reasonably under control and the GDP growth rate is really high in the country.

There are signs that the public distribution system is on the verge of collapse in many parts of the country not because there is shortage of food grains in the country but because of indifference or lack of vigil on the part of the local administration. The first sign of *food riot* appeared in a state where power for governance has remained vested for long 34 years on a political combine that claim to have their support base among the downtrodden – the rural and the urban poor. The incidences in Singur and Nandigram in West Bengal over land acquisition issue had already sent a distress signal to the farmers all over the state. Opposition political outfits took advantage of this rising public anger. Closely following these came the mysterious death of Rizwanur Rahman and a very partisan handling by the top police officials of the marriage under Special Marriage Act between Rizwanur, a Muslim boy, and Priyanka Todi, the daughter of a wealthy Hindu businessman. The Calcutta High Court asked the government to handover the case to CBI for an impartial investigation. The unprecedented spontaneous public anger over this unfortunate death of Rizwanur has put the government in the doc. While the Left parties were organizing for a mass movement against the government at the center for the price hike of essential commodities, a visible anger was fuming in their own backyard for the collapse of the PDS in the state for the rampant corruption in the distribution channels. Ration shops were burning, commodities looted and the ration dealers forced to sign agreement that they would pay appropriate compensation to all the ration card holders under their jurisdiction. Few lives have been lost, some from police firing. This spontaneous revolt, akin to a 'food riot', has not been witnessed anywhere in the country. The unfolding saga of ration riots in this state reminds many of the Bengal famine (man-made scarcity). Whereas the victims remain the same – the poverty stricken people – the color of the perpetrators have changed over the years. Food sector is not the only public department infested with corrupt practices. It is quite likely that such spontaneous mass movements against land acquisition for private industrial houses and lack of vigil over the public distribution system soon may spread to some other states.

The reader can easily observe from the data given above that there is not much correlation between starvation and per capita food production in the states. The low food grain producing states like Karnataka and Gujarat have very low level of starvation; relatively high food grain producing states like Madhya Pradesh, Uttar Pradesh and Chhattisgarh reportedly have large number of instances of starvation.

The problem, it appears, is not with production but with distribution along with lack of purchasing power of the rural and urban poor. Some are of the opinion that the system is useful in situations of scarcity of food grains. They say that PDS has outlived its utility as there is no real threat for food shortage in the country. It would be better if the government winds up the PDS and pays a cash equivalent to the amount of subsidies in food and fuel prices offered to those living below the line of poverty.

11.6.5 Household Expenditure Pattern

NSS collects data on total consumption per capita for a period of 30 days covering broad consumption categories as food, clothing, fuel and lighting, etc. Pattern of expenditure for rural and urban populations appear significantly different. Share of expenditure on food to total monthly expenditure is significantly small in urban areas. Urban people have to pay more on miscellaneous goods and services, especially in rents and taxes than their rural counterpart. An average person from rural area spends only 57 percent of what an average urban person spends in 30 days.

Table 11.23

Percentage distribution of total consumption per capita (at current prices) for a period of 30 days according to broad group of items of consumption by sector for India

Item	*1972–73*	*1977–78*	*1983*	*1987–88*	*1993–94*	*1999–2000*
			Rural			
Food total	72.9	64.3	65.6	64.0	63.2	59.4
Fuel and light	5.6	6.0	7.0	7.5	7.4	7.5
Clothing	7.0	8.7	8.6	6.7	5.4	6.8
Misc. goods & services[1]	8.7	10.3	12.5	14.5	17.3	19.6
Non-food total	27.1	35.7	34.4	36.0	36.8	40.6
Total	100	100	100	100	100	100
Total consumption (Rs)	44.2	68.9	112.5	158.1	281.4	486.1
			Urban			
Food total	64.5	60.0	59.1	56.4	54.7	48.1
Fuel and light	5.6	6.4	6.9	6.8	6.6	7.8
Clothing	5.3	7.1	7.6	5.9	4.7	6.1
Misc. goods & services[1]	19.2	14.6	20.5	23.2	27.5	31.5
Non-food total	35.5	40.0	40.9	43.6	45.3	51.9
Total	100	100	100	100	100	100
Total consumption (Rs)	63.3	96.2	164.0	249.9	458.0	855.0

1. Includes rents and taxes

Source: National Sample Survey Organization

11.7 Housing Problems

11.7.1 Housing Stock

Housing ranks next only to food and clothing in importance in developing countries like India. That we could not provide sufficient employment opportunities to our rural and urban poor to create a situation that would enable them to buy reasonable amount of food and other basic necessities to improve their quality of life is borne by numerous facts – about 20 percent of the population still lie below the poverty line, about 50 percent of children below age 5 suffer from malnutrition, about one-third of babies born are under weight and about 15 percent of the population even today are not expected to survive beyond age 40 years though the expectation of life at birth at national level has risen to around 64 years. Prevalence of certain diseases (communicable and parasitic) among the rural and urban poor is definitely related to the poor state of their shelter, congested living conditions and other housing amenities that are far below the minimum standard accepted nationally and internationally.

The households and housing stock between 1951 and 2001 is presented in the following table. The number of houseless households has dropped considerably between 1981 and 1991.

Table 11.24

Households and housing stock in India (million)

Year	*Number of households*	*Number of occupied residential houses*	*Deficit in houses*
		Rural	
1951	53.6	54.1	–0.5
1961	68.9	65.1	3.8
1971	79.6	72.7	6.9
1981	90.9	86.1a	4.8
1991b	111.6	107.9	3.7
2001	138		
		Urban	
1951	12.3	10.3	2.0
1961	15.6	13.8	1.8
1971	20.9	18.0	2.8
1981	28.9	27.6a	1.3
1991b	40.4	39.1	1.3
2001	53		
		Total	
1951	65.9	64.4	1.5
1961	84.5	78.9	5.6
1971	100.4	90.8	9.7
1981	119.8	113.7a	6.1
1991b	152.0	147.0	5.0
2001	191		

a. Excludes Assam

b. Excludes Jammu & Kashmir.

Source: Population Census, Office of the Registrar General, India.

Table 11.25
Number of homeless households and population by sex and residence in India

	Number of homeless households	Homeless population		
		Male	Female	Person
1981[a]				
Rural	420,409	970,358	753,753	172,4111
Urban	209,520	406,154	212,689	618,843
Total	629,929 (0.526)[c]	1,376,512	966,442	2,342,954
1991[b]				
Rural	305528	709,291	572,606	1,281,897
Urban	216917	471,077	254,515	725,592
Total	522445 (0.344)[c]	1,180,368	827,121	2,007,489

a. Excluding Assam.
b. Excludes Jammu & Kashmir
c. Proportion to households living under regular shelters.
Source: Office of the Registrar General, India.

Deficit in houses rose steadily between 1951 (1.5 million) and 1971 (9.7 million). Thereafter, thanks to the economic space created by consumer finance by banks and other financial institutions as also the proactive government policies for rural housing as a part of the rural development program, the deficit has progressively come down. Construction of multistoried buildings and innumerable new townships, IT, health and knowledge cities have given a boost to the construction sector. Among the states, Maharashtra has the highest number of households (about 19 million) followed by Andhra Pradesh (about 16 million) and West Bengal (about 15 million).

11.7.2 Housing Structure

Since 1961 Census, issues relating to housing have gained considerable momentum. The available data permits analysis of three aspects of quality of housing and shelters, namely living space, quality of construction and the essential civic amenities available to these houses. Although proportion of households living in one room has declined much between 1981 and 1991, majority of the Indians, both in rural and urban areas, still live in one-room accommodations. The pattern of housing units by number of rooms is no different in urban areas from that in rural areas. Over 71 percent of households still live in houses with two or less rooms. Average number of households residing per living quarter is usually 1. But the 1991 urban data show that in some instances more than one households were found to share the same living quarter. Average size of households has remained unchanged at around 5.5.

Table 11.26
Distribution of households (%) according to the number of rooms occupied

No. of rooms	Rural		Urban		All areas	
	1981	1991	1981	1991	1981	1991
1 room	44.28	40.82	45.80	39.55	44.72	40.49
2 rooms	28.87	30.65	27.84	30.37	28.62	30.58
3 rooms	12.23	13.50	12.21	14.82	12.22	13.85
4 rooms	6.30	6.92	6.33	7.77	6.31	7.14
5 + rooms	5.80	7.05	5.70	6.97	5.78	7.02
No exclusive room & unspecified	2.42	1.06	2.12	0.52	2.35	0.92

Source: Office of the Registrar General.

The Census data classify houses by materials used for construction of walls and roof separately. A house will be treated *pucca* when burnt brick, GI or other metal sheets, stone or cement concrete are used for the roof and the walls. A wall is considered *kutcha* if the material used includes grass, leaves, bamboos, un-burnt brick or mud. A roof would be considered *kutcha* when the material used is grass, leaves, reeds, bamboo, thatch, mud, un-burnt brick or wood. When the wall is *kutcha* but the roof is *pucca* or the roof is *kutcha* but the walls are *pucca*, the house is classified as *semi-pucca*.

Table 11.27
Households by type of housing structure

	1981			1991		
	Rural	Urban	Combined	Rural	Urban	Combined
Kutcha	40.55	13.50	34.04	33.76	9.56	27.44
Semipucca	36.93	21.80	33.29	35.65	17.69	30.95
Pucca	22.53	64.70	32.67	30.59	72.75	41.51

Source: Census of India 1991.

Figure 11.15
Household by housing structures

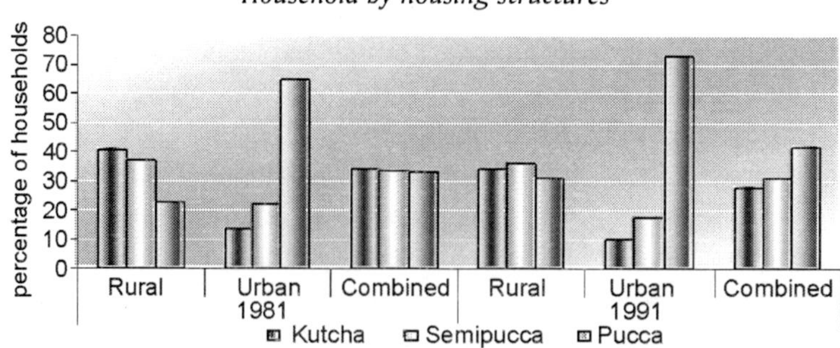

At the national level the share of households living in *pucca* houses has gone up by 8 percent both in rural and urban areas. The share of households living in *semi-pucca* houses has declined only moderately. Punjab among the major states has the largest number of *pucca* houses, both in urban and rural areas (88 and 72% respectively in 1991). Orissa stands at the other extreme where only about 19 percent of urban and 13 percent of rural households are accommodated in *pucca* houses. There are very many states where a large proportion of people live in *semi-pucca* houses (Madhya Pradesh 65%, Karnataka 41%, Maharashtra 36%). Materials used for construction of a house have great deal to do with the local topographical and climatic conditions. Mud plasters and un-burnt brick is used in high altitude places to insulate from very cold winter. In the Northeastern region bamboo/wood is available in plenty and therefore very many houses are constructed using bamboo/wood as the stock material. Wooden structure is preferred in earthquake prone areas.

NSS data are available for the years 1986–87 to 2000–01 on the distribution of households by the type of housing structure. Although the two sets of data (Census and NSS) do not fully agree on the actual intensity of the characteristics for different time points, both indicate that *pucca* houses both in rural and urban areas are gaining popularity. According to NSS data, percentage share of *kutcha* houses has declined from about 50 percent in 1986–87 to 30 percent in 2000–01 in rural area and the share of *pucca* houses has jumped from 17 to over 38 percent in the same period. An 18 percent gain in the share of pucca houses is noticed in urban area and the share of kutcha houses has dropped from 17 to a little over 7 percent in the same period. NFHS II also collected data on quality of houses. This survey found nearly 32 percent of the households lived in *pucca* houses at the national level (25% in rural area and about 66% in urban area) in 1998–99. The national level estimates from NFHS II are considerably lower than are reported either in Census 1991 or in NSS estimates. Whereas the Census 1991 put 56 percent of households in Kerala living in *pucca* houses, NFHS II puts the same at 80 percent. NFHS II also recorded only 53 percent of households in Punjab living in *pucca* houses contrasted to 77 percent reported in 1991Census.

Table 11.28

Percentage distribution of households by type of housing structure

Characteristics	*Percentage of households*								
	1986–87	*1987–88*	*1988–89*	*1991*	*1992*	*1993*	*1993–94*	*1994–95*	*2000–01*
				Rural					
I Type of structure									
Pucca	17.2	19.5	27.1	26.5	26.7	32.3	29.2	29.6	38.4
Semi pucca	33.1	31.9	33.5	34.6	35.3	36.0	38.1	37.9	31.6
Kutcha	49.6	48.6	59.3	38.9	37.8	31.7	32.7	32.4	30.0
II Living in rented dwellings	NA	2.9	3.3	3.8	3.9	NA	3.9	3.6	4.3
				Urban					
I Type of structure									
Pucca	57.2	57.9	71.1	66.8	67.3	73.8	70.7	70.4	75.2
Semipucca	25.7	24.3	18.0	22.8	22.5	17.9	19.5	20.0	17.4
Kutcha	17.0	17.8	10.9	10.2	10.2	8.3	9.9	9.5	7.4
II Living in rented dwellings	NA	36.1	37.0	36.6	35.1	NA	35.6	35.9	33.7

Source: NSS reports.

11.7.3 Housing Amenities

11.7.3.1 Toilets

Even more than 60 years after independence when Indian economy seems to be on a track of high growth path, the dark patches in our civic life galore everywhere. As of 1998, 83 percent of rural households and over 25 percent of urban households still had no toilet facilities. Majority of the dwelling units, save in the mega cities and larger towns, sanitation facilities for disposal of wastewater and solid wastes are wanting. The general poor health condition and higher morbidity levels in the country have to a considerable extent roots in the lack of sanitation, particularly sewage and disposal of solid wastes including 'night soils'. NFHS II also provides data on access to toilet facilities. This survey found 64 percent of households in the country were without any toilet facility in the premises in 1998–99, which is a fair improvement over Census 1991 figure of 76 percent, of course if the two data are roughly comparable. At the state level, Andhra Pradesh, Bihar, Madhya Pradesh, Orissa, Rajasthan, Tamil Nadu and Uttar Pradesh were below the national average on this count. 85 percent of households in Kerala had access to within household toilet facilities, much above the national average of 36 percent found in NFHS II.

Table 11.29

Availability of electricity, drinking water and toilet facilities to households, India 1991

	Number of households		
	Total	***Rural***	***Urban***
1	*2*	*3*	*4*
Total No. of Households (in'000)	151,003	111,539	39,493
Households having the following facilities (%)			
(a) Electricity	42.4	30.5	75.8
(b) Safe Drinking Water	62.3	55.5	81.4
(c) Toilet	23.7	9.5	63.9
(d) Electricity and Safe Drinking Water	30.4	18.7	63.6
(e) Safe Drinking Water and Toilet	18.2	5.6	53.9
(f) Electricity and Toilet	20.4	6.5	59.4
(g) All the three facilities	16.1	3.9	50.5
(h) None of the three facilities	24.5	31.3	5.4

Source: Census India 1991

11.7.3.2 Safe Drinking Water

Census of India treats a household as having access to safe drinking water if the household receives drinking water through tap or a hand pump/tube-well situated within or just outside the premise. Millions of Indians suffer from water-borne diseases because of lack of access to safe dinking water. Government has promised to evolve mechanisms so that every village has access to safe drinking water within the 10th Plan period. This is a stupendous task since only 62 percent of the population

(81.4 percent in urban and 55.6 percent in rural area) had access to safe drinking water in 1991. NSS 52nd Round report indicates that 78 percent of the households had access to safe drinking water (tap 36.3%, tube-well/hand pump 41% and tanker 0.5%) in 1995–96. Another 17.6 percent households could get drinking water from *pucca* well. Studies in metropolitan cities show that higher rate of diseases and longer duration of illnesses is due to poor quality of drinking water supply in slum areas. It is surprising that Kerala where death rates in all ages are one of the lowest in the country has less than 20 percent of the households' access to safe drinking water. Most of the households in Kerala obtain their drinking water from wells, water drawn from which is not considered safe for drinking purposes according to Census norm. Andhra Pradesh, Bihar, Assam, Madhya Pradesh, Orissa, Uttar Pradesh and Rajasthan have far less access to safe drinking water compared to that at the national level. Himachal Pradesh, Maharashtra and Tamil Nadu have already taken measures to supply drinking water through pipe lines to a great majority of their households. As per the NSS report, 92 percent of rural households and 94 percent of the urban households in Punjab have access to safe drinking water, hand pumps and tube-wells (65%) playing the major role. Uttar Pradesh and Bihar too rely mostly on tube-well and hand pumps for drinking water. In most hilly states, tap water is the predominant source of safe drinking water. NFHS II also confirms that a lot has been achieved in the supply of safe drinking water to households. NFHS I found 62 percent coverage for safe drinking water in 1993–94. NFHS II found safe drinking water reaching 78 percent households in 1998–99 (93% and 72% respectively in urban and rural areas).

Figure 11.16

% of households with safe drinking water

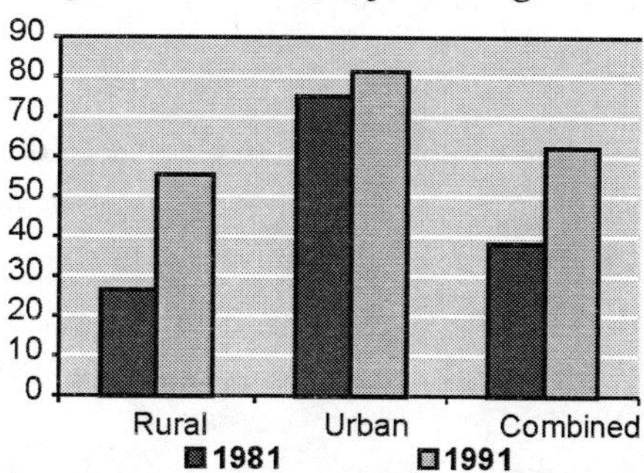

11.7.3.3 Access to Electricity[1]

Till 1991, only 42.37 percent of the households had electricity in their premises, 30.54 percent in rural areas and 75.78 percent in urban areas. Only a decade back the respective figures were 26.19, 14.69 and 62.51 respectively. As per NSSO survey (56th Round) electricity has reached to 91 percent of the urban and 51 percent of the rural households. This accounts for the huge difference in the percentage of villages electrified and the percentage of households actually receiving power supply in their living units.

There is large inter-state variation in the availability of electricity to the households. As per 1991 Census, Himachal Pradesh topped the list of states in percentage coverage (87.01%) for electricity connection to households followed by Punjab (82.31%) and Haryana (70.35%). Bihar (12.57%, 5.6% in rural area), Assam (18.74%), Uttar Pradesh (21.91%) and Orissa (23.54%) were at the bottom of the list in electricity connectivity to households. Nearly 28 percent of SC and 23 percent of Scheduled ST households at the national level had access to electricity against 48 percent for other households in 1991. In case of Punjab, 68 percent of rural and 87 percent of urban SC households had access to electricity compared to 84 and 97 percent respectively for other households.

1. A village is said to be electrified if electricity is supplied to at least 10 households no matter how big or small the village is or the total power consumption in the village.

NFHS II report gives an encouraging picture about the coverage of electrified households. At the national level 60 percent of households were provided with power supply, 91 percent in urban area and 48 percent in rural area. Bihar remained at the bottom of the table. Performance of Assam, Orissa, Uttar Pradesh and West Bengal in rural electrification were very unsatisfactory – the proportion of households that had access to power varied between 25 and 36 percent, far behind the national average. Gujarat, Karnataka, Maharashtra and Tamil Nadu had more than 80 percent households access to electricity.

Per capita electricity consumption continues to be very low in Northeastern states (80 to 172 kWh in 1996–97). Over 2,300 kWh per capita power consumption was recorded in two UTs – Dadra & Nagar Haveli and Daman & Diu. Among the larger states Punjab (792), Gujarat (694), Maharashtra (556) and Haryana (504) registered per capita annual electricity consumption (kWh) in excess of average 500 kWh per capita in 1996–97. There were as many as 5 larger states where per capita electricity consumption was less than 250 kWh in 1998–99: Assam (104), Bihar (138), West Bengal (194), Uttar Pradesh (197) and Kerala (241). As per the Planning Commission data, per capita consumption of electricity at the national level has increased from 191 kWh in 1986–87 to 334 kWh in 1996–97. UN Human Development Report 2005 indicates that per capita consumption of electricity in India has gone up to 569 kWh in 2002, far behind China (1,484 kWh) and the world average of 2,485 kWh.

11.8 Energy Sector in India

11.8.1 Growth of Energy Consumption

India ranks sixth in the world in total energy consumption. It needs to accelerate the development of the energy sector to meet the very fast growing demands (about 10% per annum). The country is rich in coal but has very small hydrocarbon reserves (0.4% of the world's reserve). The country is abundantly endowed with renewable energy in the form of solar, wind, hydro and bio-energy. More than 25 percent of primary energy needs in India are met through imports mainly in the form of crude oil and natural gas. The oil import bill due to rising oil prices in the world market is a serious concern for India's economy.

Coal and oil account for 54 and 34 percent respectively in energy production, with natural gas, hydro and nuclear contributing to the balance. Nearly 62 percent of power generation in India is from coal fired plants and 70 percent of the coal mined every year is used for thermal power generations.

The whole of South Asia accounts for only 0.5 percent of the world's crude oil and 1 percent of natural gas reserve. India's recoverable reserves of crude oil and natural gas have declined continuously after peaking at 806 million tons and 735 billion cubic meters, respectively, in 1991–92. The current recoverable balance reserves in India are estimated at 726 million tons of crude oil and 692 billion cubic meters of natural gas. Most of the crude oil production in South Asia is accounted for by India, which, in 1997–98, accounted for 93 percent (38 million tons) of the total oil production in the region. India is also the largest consumer and importer of crude oil and petroleum products. A few large reserves for oil and gas have recently been found out mostly in Southern part and in sea beds.

Table 11.30
Demand-supply gap in petroleum products and natural gas in India

	Petroleum products (million barrels per day)			*Natural Gas (million cubic meter per day)*		
	Demand	*Domestic production*	*% deficit*	*Demand*	*Domestic production*	*% deficit*
1997/98	1.68	0.69	61	52.1	49.3	5.37
2001/02	2.10	0.74	67	117.8	71.2	39.55
2006/07	2.89	0.80	74	167.1	57.5	65.59
2011/12	4.06	0.90	79	216.4	43.8	79.75

Source: Planning Commission 1998.

11.8.2 Energy Consumption

Per capita energy consumption in India is one of the lowest in the world as could be seen in Table 11.39 and Figure 11.19. India's per capita energy consumption in 1997 was 12.4 million Btu (British thermal unit), compared to 351.9 million Btu in the US and a world average of 64.8 million Btu. Per capita carbon emission in India was 250 kg of carbon per person, which was approximately one-quarter of the world average and less than 0.05% of that in the US. But, *energy intensity*, which is defined as energy consumption per unit of GDP, is one of the highest in the world. The industrial sector is the principal energy user, accounting for about 52 percent of commercial energy consumption.

Figure 11.17
Demand and domestic production of petroleum products

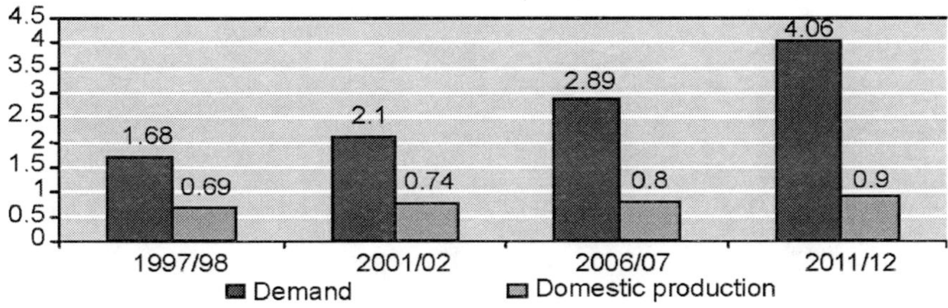

Figure 11.18
Demand and domestic production of natural gas

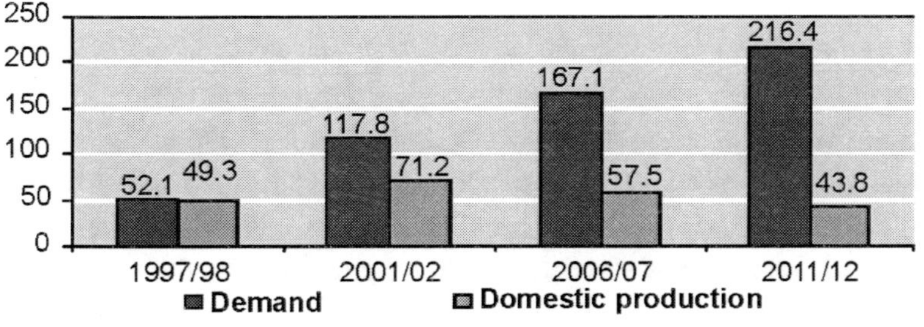

In the pre-reform period, the energy sector was totally regulated by government. Private sector participation in coal, oil, gas and electricity sectors is increasing in post-liberalization period. Energy prices in India have been under an administered regime with subsidies provided to meet certain socio-economic needs of the public. The government has taken some steps to deregulate the energy price. The prices of all grades of coal and to some extent the petroleum products have already been deregulated. In the electricity sector, most of the State Electricity Boards (SEBs) have started taking reform measures. Regulatory Commissions have been set up to determine tariffs based on economic rationale. But such reform in the power sector is not going to be easy in view of stiff opposition from political parties and trade unions.

Figure 11.19
Per capita energy consumption

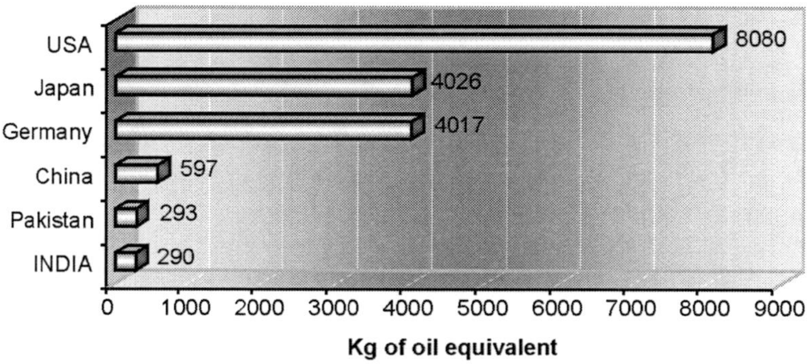

Country	Kg of oil equivalent
USA	8080
Japan	4026
Germany	4017
China	597
Pakistan	293
INDIA	290

Axis: 0 1000 2000 3000 4000 5000 6000 7000 8000 9000 — **Kg of oil equivalent**

Table 11.31
Energy consumption in India (in 10^{15} Btu)

Fuel type	*1973*		*1993*		*2010*	
	India	*% of world total*	*India*	*% of world total*	*India*	*% of world total*
Oil	20.0	0.75	62.4	2.00	164.0	3.56
Natural gas	1.4	0.14	14.6	0.82	63.0	2.35
Coal	39.9	2.39	117.0	5.46	271.0	7.40
Hydro electric	2.3	0.69	6.3	3.18	28.0	8.48
Nuclear and others	0.2	0.41	1.6	0.29	16.0	1.88
Total	64.9	1.10	201.9	2.59	542.0	4.45

Source: EIA 1995. 1996.

With over 17 percent of world population, the total energy consumption in India still is very low. From around 1.1 percent of world's total energy consumption (TEC) in 1973, India's share went up to 2.59 in the next 20 years, and by 2010 its share is expected to increase to 4.9 percent. India has a great potential for using its water resources. It is predicted that use of hydropower is likely to go up by over 12-fold in 2010 from the 1973 level. The largest increase is likely to be in the use of natural gas, mostly for generation of electricity. India is currently the fourth largest oil consumer in the Asia-Pacific region after Japan, South Korea and China. The country is reeling under the burden of a large oil import bill and spiraling oil prices – 70 percent of the petroleum used in India is imported at a cost of more than Rs 1,000,000 million a year.

The total demand of oil is expected to exceed 368 Mmt by 2025. It can go even further up if the GDP growth rate of 8–9 percent is attained on a sustainable basis. Number of motor vehicles per 1,000 population has made a big jump from 4.60 in 1971 to over 49 (two/three wheelers from 1.05 to 34.37) in 2000, and the per capita annual consumption of petroleum product has gone up from 13.3 kg in 1970–71 to 45.3 kg in 2001–02.

Figure 11.20
Energy production by fuel in India

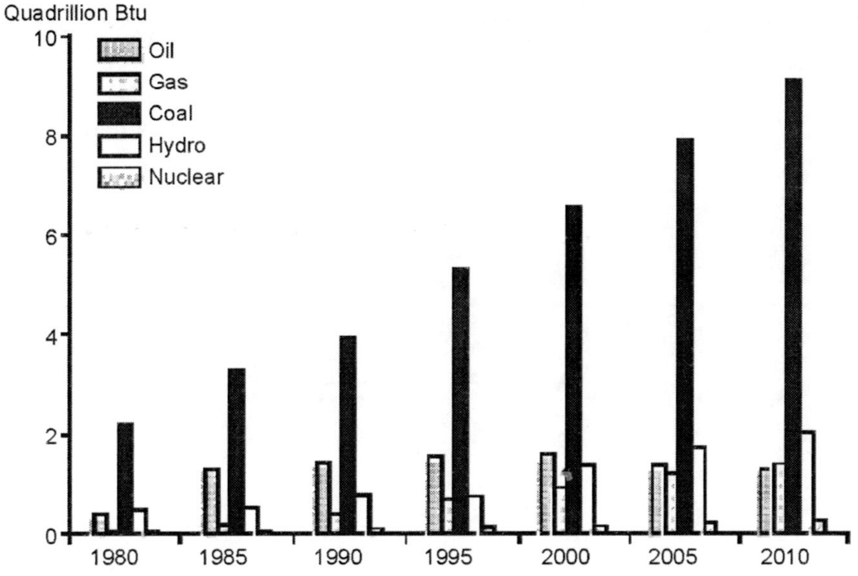

Table 11.32
Sectoral consumption (million ton oil equivalent) in India, 1997–98

	Coal	*Petroleum products*	*Natural gas*	*Electricity*	*Total*
Industry	60.93	11.74	2.91	8.49	84.08 (47.75%)
Agriculture	—	0.94	0.11	7.69	8.75 (4.96%)
Residential	—	12.80	0.27	4.14	17.21 (9.77%)
Transport	0.04	40.94	—	0.56	41.55 (23.60%)
Others	—	13.98	6.76	3.72	22.47 (12.61%)
Total	60.97	80.41	10.06	24.62	176.08 (100.00%)

Source: BPSR 1998.

Industry is the largest consumer of energy (47.75%) followed by transports (23.6%). The transport sector (road and railways) consume around 50 percent of petroleum products. Nearly 100 percent of coal is consumed by industries.

Table 11.33
Net imports of energy in primary commercial energy supply (%)

Year	Coal	Petroleum and natural gas	Electricity	Total
1953–54	(–)5.02	13.65	—	8.63
1960-61	(–)2.08	17.39	—	15.31
1970-71	(–)0.40	21.71	—	21.31
1980-81	0.25	25.45	—	25.70
1990-91	2.22	15.56	0.07a	17.85
1996-97	2.83	22.40	0.05a	25.28

a. Imported from Nepal and Bhutan.

11.8.3 Electricity Generation and Consumption

At the time of independence, India produced only about 1,370 MW of electricity. It has increased by 82 times, that is, installed generation capacity going up to 112,682 MW in 2004 (31,995 MW from hydro & wind, 77,974 MW from thermal and 2,720 MW from nuclear). A very small amount of electricity is imported from Nepal and Bhutan. The number of consumers, including households, is up from 1.5 million to 114 million, a 76 times increase. Electricity has reached to 91 percent of all inhabited villages by 2004. Transmission losses still remain a major concern in the power sector.

Table 11.34
Growth of the Indian power sector

Parameter	2004 status	Growth since independence (times)
Installed Capacity (MW)	112,682	82
Number of Consumers (million)	114	76
Agricultural Connections (million)	13	605
Transmission & Distribution Network ('000 Circuit Kilometer)	552	188
Electrified Villages ('000)	508	338
Per Capita Annual Consumption (kWh)	335	24

Source: Ministry of Power and Planning Commission.

Table 11.35
Installed electricity generation capacity, India (megawatt)

Year	Thermal	Hydro + Wind	Nuclear	Total
1991–1992	48,086	19,194	1,785	69,065
1995–1996	60,083	20,985	2,225	83,293
1999–2000	70,493	25,012	2,680	98,185
2001–2002	74,429	26,261	2,720	104,917
2003–2004	77,974	31,995	2,720	112,682
Compound growth (%) over 1991–2004	4.11	4.35	3.67	4.16

Source: Ministry of Power, Government of India.

Generation capacity of electricity in the period 1991–2004 increased by 4.16 percent annually (Table 11.35) and the GDP in the same years grew by over 6.4 percent. It is good to see that electricity from hydro and wind, which do not use fossil fuels and does not emit carbon, grew faster than both thermal and nuclear sources, which are known to pollute or may polute the atmosphere and the environment. The primary energy supply in the country is coal-dominant with the power sector accounting for about 40 percent of primary energy and 70 percent of coal consumption. Thermal energy still produces over 70 percent of electricity in the country. It is also the single largest consumer of capital, drawing over one-sixth of all the Indian investments over the past decades. Ownership of plants and electricity generation by fuel are shown in Table 11.36. Private players are likely to have a bigger role played in additional power generation in the coming years.

Table 11.36

Ownership of plants and generation of electricity by fuel (megawatt)

Ownership	*Hydel*	*Steam*	*Gas*	*Diesel*	*Wind*	*Nuclear*	*Total*
State	22636.02	36302.00	2661.70	582.89	62.86		62245.47
	(86.19)	(58.43)	(23.84)	(51.36)	(4.17)		(59.42)
Central	3049.00	21417.51	4419.00			2720.00	31605.51
	(11.61)	(34.47)	(39.59)			(100.00)	(30.12)
Private	576.20	4411.38	4082.40	551.94	1444.60		11066.52
	(2.19)	(7.10)	(36.57)	(48.64)	(95.83)		(10.54)
Total	26261.22	62130.89	11163.10	1134.83	1507.46	2720.00	104,917.5
Installed capacity	25.03	59.22	10.64	1.08	1.44	2.59	100.00

Source: Planning Commission (Power & Energy Division), 2002.

It is evident that the share of domestic consumption in the total sales of electricity has been increasing over the years (Table 11.37) and has increased from a level of about 13 in 1989–90 to 21.30 percent in 2001–02. The consumption share of agriculture sector has increased from about 25.9 percent in 1980–90 (only 3.9% in 1950) to 30 percent in 1995–96 and then dropped to 29.14 percent in 2000–01. The fast increase in electricity consumption in domestic and agriculture sectors brought down the share of consumption of electricity by industries and other commercial establishments. Share of industry in electricity consumption dropped from 62.6 percent in 1950 to 30.5 percent in 2000–01.

Table 11.37

Power consumption by sector, 2000–01

Sector	*Consumption share*	
	Billion kWh	*Percentage*
Domestic	66.99	21.28
Commercial	16.27	5.17
Agriculture	91.74	29.14
Industry	96.02	30.50
Traction (Railways)	7.19	2.28
Outside the State	3.91	1.24
Others	32.71	10.39
Total	314.83	100.00

Source: Planning Commission, 2001–02.

The domestic share increased mostly because of increased emphasis on rural electrification in the new economic policy. Out of 587,258 total inhabited villages in the country (1991 Census), about 86 percent of villages are declared electrified by March, 2001. As per the present estimates, around 80,000 villages in the country are yet to be electrified even on the basis of the current definition of village. Nine states have declared 100 percent electrification of their villages. The villages yet to be electrified are mostly located in Assam, Arunachal Pradesh, Bihar, Jharkhand, Madhya Pradesh, Meghalaya, Orissa, Rajasthan, Uttar Pradesh, Uttaranchal and West Bengal. Electrification through normal grid expansion may become possible only for 62,000 out of these 80,000 villages yet to be electrified. This is proposed to be done during the 10th Plan period. The remaining 18,000 villages are located in remote areas, hilly terrains, islands, deserts and often are very thinly populated. Such villages may be electrified economically through decentralized and non-conventional energy sources like solar, wind, small hydro and biomass. Private sector is likely to play a major role in electrification of these villages using renewable sources.

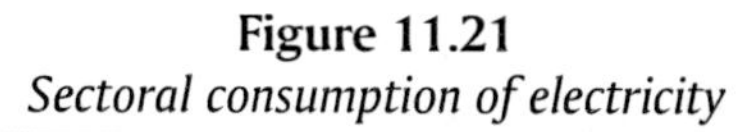

Figure 11.21
Sectoral consumption of electricity

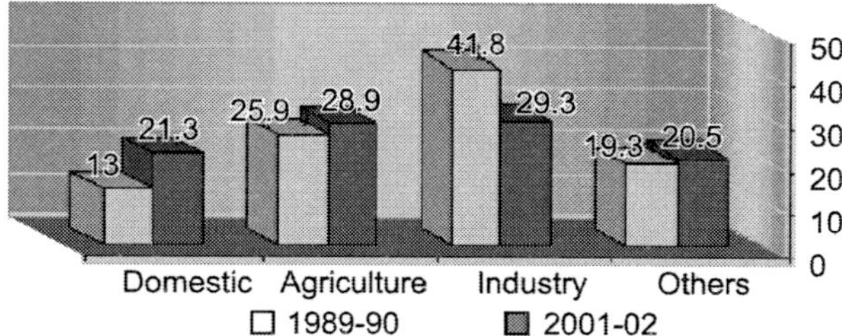

The Ninth Plan envisaged a capacity addition of 40,245.2 MW, comprising 24.4 percent of hydro electricity and 73.4 percent thermal and 2.18 percent nuclear power. The expected contribution from the state, central and private sector in capacity addition is 26.7, 29.6 and 43.7 percent respectively. The achievements of state, central and private sectors compared to their targets is 87.9 percent, 37.8 percent and 28.8 percent respectively. The major shortfall is in the central and private sector. Private sector projects have not come up mainly because of the poor financial condition of the SEBs who are the monopoly buyers of electricity from them.

Table 11.38
Addition to installed capacity (MW) in the Ninth Plan period

	9th Plan	*1997–98*	*1998–99*	*1999–00*	*2000–01*	*2001–02*	*9th Plan*	*% of plan target*
	Target	***Actual***	***Actual***	***Actual***	***Actual***	***Actual***	***Actual***	
I. Mode-wise								
Hydel	9819.7	233.0	542.5	1371.5	1285.0	1106.2	4538.2	46.21
Thermal	29545.5	2993.5	3699.5	2721.0	2173.9	2009.0	13596.9	46.02
Nuclear	880.0			440.0	440.0		880.0	100.0
Total	40245.2	3226.5	4242.0	4532.5	3898.9	3115.2	19015.1	47.24
II. Ownership								
State	10747.7	1676.0	1675.4	2329.1	2375.7	1393.9	9450.1	87.9
Central	11909.0	333.0	991.6	1615.4	659.0	905.0	4504.0	37.8
Private	17588.5	1217.5	1575.0	588.0	864.2	816.3	5061.0	28.8
Total	40245.2	3226.5	4242.0	4532.5	898.9	3115.2	19015.1	47.24

The National Thermal Power Corporation (NTPC), the world's sixth largest thermal power generating company, has gone from installing 200 MW units in 1982 to 17,735 MW units in 2002 and is expected to add another 16.000 MW by 2007. Over the years, the performance of NTPC power plants has become the benchmark for the Indian power sector.

11.8.4 Per Capita Energy Consumption

Per capita consumption of electricity has also recorded a significant rise. At the national level per capita consumption of electricity increased from 191 kWh in 1986–87 to about 355 kWh in 1999–2000 and to 569 kWh (HDR 2005) in 2002 (there is considerable difference in these estimates between HDR and Ministry of Power (MoP). Although close to hundred percent of villages would soon be electrified, it would not mean that every household would have access to electricity. Even with highly subsidized tariff, there would be many households that would fail to take the benefit of the rural electrification scheme. Per capita consumption of electricity in rural areas is far too small to make the rural electrification project in remote areas viable on cost-benefit analysis.

There are large inter-state and inter-regional variations in per capita electricity consumption. As against the all-India per capita consumption of 355 kWh (MoP) in 1999–2000, the per capita consumption in the Eastern and Northeastern region has been only 192 kWh and 103 kWh respectively. On the other hand, Western, Southern and Northern regions have per capita electricity consumption of 535 kWh, 400 kWh and 318 kWh respectively. The inter-state trends show large disparity between the states. States like Punjab and Delhi have per capita electricity consumption of 921 kWh and 653 kWh respectively, whereas it is about 69 kWh in states like Manipur and Arunachal Pradesh and about 141 kWh in Bihar.

Table 11.39

Per capita annual consumption of electricity and petroleum products in India

Year	*Electricity (figures in kWh) (domestic)*	*Petroleum products (in kg)*			
		Motor spirit	*High speed diesel oil*	*Kerosene*	*Others*
1950–51	NA	1.8	0.5	2.5	2.7
1955–56	NA	2.1	1.1	3.6	3.0
1960–61	NA	1.9	2.8	4.5	4.0
1965–66	NA	2.2	4.8	5.2	5.8
1970–71	7.0	2.9	7.7	6.6	13.3
1975–76	9.7	2.1	11.0	5.2	13.5
1980–81	13.5	2.3	15.5	6.3	16.4
1985–86	22.9	3.0	19.7	8.3	16.0
1990–91	38.2	4.2	25.0	10.0	26.0
1995–96	56.2	5.1	35.2	10.2	28.7
1996–97	58.6	5.2	36.0	9.6	29.5
1997–98	62.9	5.4	37.8	10.3	30.1
1998–99	66.7	5.7	38.0	10.9	37.8
1999–00	71.2	6.0	40.0	10.9	41.2
2000–01	75.2	6.4	36.9	10.4	43.8
2001–02 P	NA	6.8	35.6	9.8	45.3

Note:

(i) Total consumption excludes imports by private parties up to 1997–98. Thereafter, it includes private imports as well.

(ii) The population figures used for per capita consumption are taken from United Nations Population Division

Source:

1. Central Electricity Authority.
2. Ministry of Petroleum and Natural Gas.

Usually per capita consumption of energy estimate is based on combined consumption of energy by industries, railways and other commercial sectors plus agricultural and domestic consumptions and the transmission losses. Based on domestic consumption alone, per capita annual consumption of electricity is a meager 75 kWh. Table 11.39 gives estimates of per capita annual domestic consumption of electricity and other petroleum products. Per capita consumption has doubled between 1991 and 2001. Consumption of petroleum products also has risen fast.

11.8.5 Health of Power Sector

At this point let us take a look at the health of power sector in India. The demand of electricity is going up everyday, especially after the capital-intensive industrial growth since 1991. A modest estimate tells us that India must produce an additional 10,000 MW of electricity every year to meet the current and future demands. Generation capacity of electricity in the period 1991–2004 increased by 4.16 percent annually (Table 11.35) and the GDP in the same period grew annually by over 6.4 percent.

The basic requirement for the growth of the two key sectors – industry and service – which contribute both to employment generation and economic growth, is infrastructure. Infrastructural sectors – transport, power and telecommunication – have direct bearings on every modern production processes. The following graph shows how interrelated the growths of industry and infrastructure are.

The governments, both at the center and the state, are keenly looking for infrastructural investment from domestic and foreign players. Government's perspective plan for the power sector indicated an incremental capacity requirement of 1,420,000 MW during 1992–2007 to meet the increased demand. This implies that creation of the incremental growth would be in the region 10,000–12000 MW per year. To achieve this, the state needs to invite private players to participate in a big way both in power and other sectors.

Figure 11.22

Industry and infrastructure growth relationship (adapted from Reliance review of energy market, 2002)

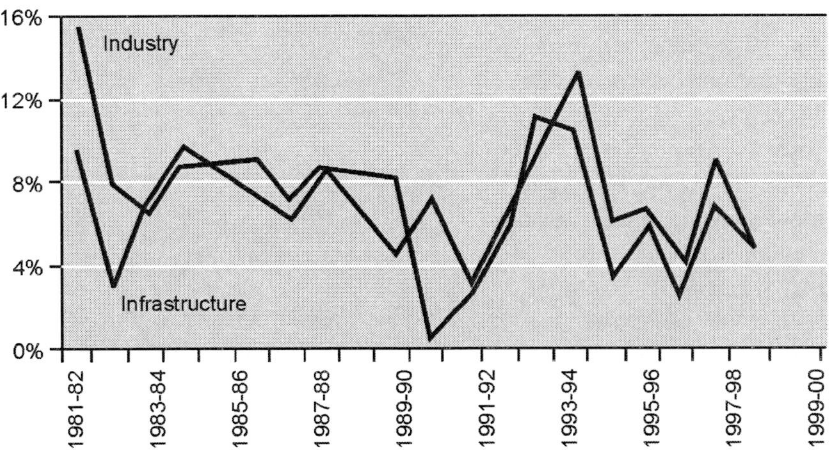

11.8.5.1 Plant Availability and Plant Load Factor (PLF)

The operational performance of utilities in terms of plant availability as well as plant utilization has been improving over the years. Table 11.40 indicates the improvement in the all-India plant availability of thermal units during 1991–92 to 2000–01. Table 11.41 shows improvement in Plant Load Factor (PLF) in thermal plants. While the plant availability improved from 72.8 to 80.5 percent between 1991–92 and 2000–01, the average PLF of the thermal plants increased from 55.3 to 69.9 percent in the same period. The gap between plant availability and PLF indicates that though the plants are available on 80 percent of the time, they are forced to shut down in some states, particularly in Eastern region, during the off-peak hours due to lower demand of power. Efforts need to be made to address this issue and utilize the plants optimally. There are wide variations in the PLF among the states. The low PLF in some instances could be attributed to poor quality of coal, age and size of units, equipment deficiency, etc.

Table 11.40
Plant availability of thermal plants

Year	*1991–92*	*1992–93*	*1993–94*	*1994–95*	*1995–96*	*1996–97*	*1997–98*	*1998–99*	*1999–00*	*2000–01*
Availability	72.8	74.7	78.0	76.6	77.8	79.0	79.4	78.7	80.3	80.5

Table 11.41
Physical performance of power generation (All India)

Year	*Plant availability (%)*	*PLF (%)*	*T&D losses (%)*
1996–97	79.00	64.40	24.53
1997–98	79.40	64.70	24.79
1998.99	78.70	64.60	26.45
1999–2000	80.30	67.30	30.80
2000–01	80.50	69.00	29.90
2001–02	NA	69.90	27.80

Source: Annual Report (2001–02): The working of SEBs and EDs

Table 11.42
Plant load factor of thermal power plants by ownership and regions

	1992–93	*1993–94*	*1994–95*	*1995–96*	*1996–97*	*1997–98*	*1998–99*	*1999–00*	*2000–01*	*2001–02*
I. Ownership										
State	54.1	56.6	55.0	58.1	60.3	60.9	60.7	63.7	65.6	67.0
Central	62.7	69.8	69.2	71.0	71.1	70.4	71.1	73.8	74.3	74.3
Private	58.8	57.0	65.8	72.3	71.2	71.2	68.0	68.9	73.1	74.7
II. Region										
Northern	62.0	63.9	59.1	62.1	64.8	66.7	67.2	70.9	73.1	75.1
Western	59.7	63.4	63.8	68.1	70.2	70.3	70.7	72.3	73.4	74.2
Southern	62.6	68.3	69.1	74.7	75.8	77.0	75.4	79.6	82.0	82.3
Eastern	39.8	44.8	43.7	42.7	42.2	43.0	44.1	46.1	47.9	48.7
Northeastern	24.3	19.9	26.8	28.6	27.1	21.3	18.8	18.2	18.5	16.8
All-India	57.1	61.0	60.06	3.0	64.4	64.7	64.6	67.3	69.0	69.9

Source: Annual Report (2001–02): The working of SEBs and EDs.

The plant load factor remains consistently higher both for central and private sectors compared to that in the state sector. PLF of thermal power stations in the Northern, Eastern and Northeastern

Figure 11.23

Plant load factor in percent (thermal plant)

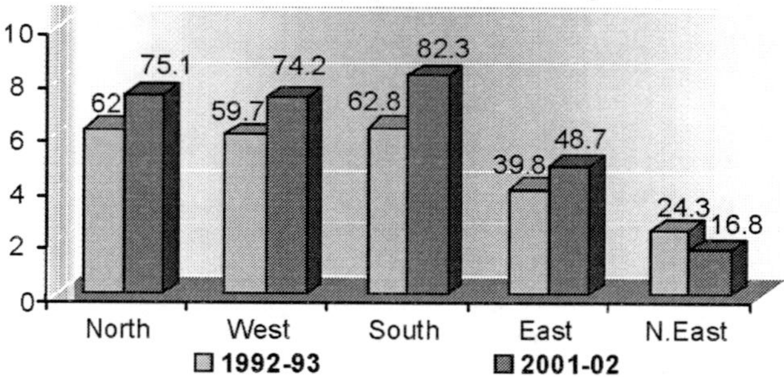

regions, particularly Delhi, Jharkhand, Bihar, West Bengal and Assam continues to be way behind the national average. Northern, Western and Southern regions usually have higher PLF compared to the all-India average.

11.8.5.2 Elasticity of Power

Elasticity of power both in generation and consumption with respect to GDP increased rapidly between first and third plan. It slowed down a little thereafter. While elasticity of electricity generation and consumption with respect to GDP between 1950–51 and 1999–2000 was 2.2 and 2.1 respectively, the same between 1990–91 and 1999–2000 was 1.09 and 0.89 respectively. This implies that a GDP growth by 1 percent resulted in increase in electricity generation and consumption by 1.09 and 0.89 percent respectively between 1990–91 and 1999–2000. Energy consumption in India per unit of GDP is one of the highest in the world. For example, it is 3.7 times that of Japan, 1.55 times that of USA and 1.5 times that of the world average.

11.8.5.3 Transmission and Distribution (T&D) Losses

Transmission and distribution losses (Table 11.41) remain a major concern in the developing countries. In the developed countries, the T&D loss is well below 10 percent. Even in China, T&D loss is 8–9 percent. The T&D losses at the all-India level has started increasing after the initiation of reforms and are reported to be more than 131 billion kWh annually. In percentage terms, the T&D losses have increased from 19.8 percent in 1992–93 to 31 percent in 1999–2000. The losses are expected to have declined to 27.8 percent in 2001–02.

The reforming states started reporting higher T&D losses after the restructuring of SEBs. For example, the T&D losses in Orissa before the restructuring of OSEB (1994–95) were 24 percent but it increased to a level of 50 percent after the unbundling of OSEB (1996–97). Similarly, other reforming states

Table 11.43

Elasticity of electricity generation and consumption with respect to GDP

	Generation	*Consumption*
First Plan	3.06	3.14
Second Plan	3.45	3.38
Third Plan	5.11	5.04
Fourth Plan	2.15	1.85
Fifth Plan	1.88	1.88
Sixth Plan	1.47	1.39
Seventh Plan	1.57	1.50
Eighth Plan	1.02	0.97

Source: Annual Report, 2001–02.

like Andhra Pradesh, Haryana, Karnataka, Uttar Pradesh, West Bengal and Rajasthan have also reported higher T&D losses after the reform process was initiated. It is stated that these states are now able to make a more realistic assessment of T&D losses in the power system, which earlier were partly camouflaged as agricultural consumption. Highest T&D losses are observed in Delhi and Jammu & Kashmir, 45 and 47 percent respectively followed by Uttar Pardesh at 39 percent, Karnataka at 36 percent, Haryana and Andhra Pradesh both at 33 percent and Assam, Madhya Pradesh and West Bengal at more than 30 percent. T&D losses in Himachal Pradesh, Kerala, Punjab and Tamil Nadu are lower than the all-India average.

For the major part of the last century power generation, transmission and distribution was totally under government control. State treasuries were empty and debt was already killing the loss-making state-run units. In the last two decades, however, the monopoly and control of power sector by the state has been seriously debated all over the world. The forerunner in the race was Chile followed by Argentina. The real momentum making this restructuring a global phenomenon was given by UK when it embarked upon its ambitious privatization reforms. The wave since then has swept countries like US, Japan, Norway, Netherlands, Canada, France and Australia. India, in spite of the socialistic clout still prevailing, needed to take lesson from the experiences of other countries.

11.8.5.4 Demand-supply Gap and the Subsidized Tariff

The ever-growing demand-supply gap forced the government to invite private players for setting up small power plants or 'Midgets'. It is also believed that the domestic private players might not have the necessary capital, especially for establishing mega-plants, as the foreign exchange component of funds required by such power plants could be large. The government liberalized the energy policy for easy flow of private investment and FDI in infrastructure development in the country including power generation. The Indian power industry has since independence faced the demand-supply gap besides some fundamental problems with the supply of the power produced – heavy transmission loss, frequent power cuts, erratic voltage and low or high supply frequency (quality of power).

Table 11.44

Demand-supply gap of electricity in India (in million units)

Year	*Peak demand*	*Peak met*	*Shortage*	*Shortage in %*
1996–97	63,853	52,376	11,477	18.0
1997–98	65,435	58,042	7,393	11.3
1998–99	67,905	58,445	9,460	13.9
1999–00	72,669	63,691	8,978	12.4
2000–01	78,037	67,880	10,157	13.0
2001–02	78,441	69,189	9,252	11.8
2002–03	81,492	71,520	9,972	12.2

Source: Annual Report 2002–03, Ministry of Power, Government of India.

The poor performance of SEBs with increasing financial strain resulting from low average tariffs and high cross-subsidies to agriculture and household sectors (most political parties are strongly opposed to tariff reforms in these two sectors) have stifled the growth of the power sector. Due to un-remunerative tariffs and irregular payment of subsidies by state governments, SEBs have not been able to invest in capacity additions and system up-gradation. In 2000–01, the total commercial losses of SEBs reached an alarming high of Rs 240 billion. Also SEBs have not been able to make full payments for the purchases they made; their creditworthiness has also become questionable. The picture would become clear from Table 11.45.

Figure 11.24

Demand-supply gap of electricity in India

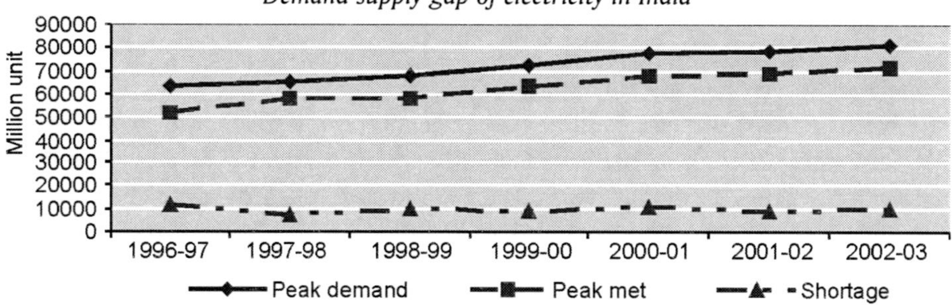

Table 11.45

Financial status of SEBs/Utilities

	1991–92	*1996–97*	*2000–01*	*2001–02*	*2002–03*
Gross Subsidy to specific sectors (Rs billion)					
(a) Agriculture	59.38	156.28	240.74	255.70	269.59
(b) Domestic (households)	13.10	42.34	99.68	108.94	116.51
(c) Inter-State Sales	2.01	2.85	3.86	2.47	2.26
Total Gross Subsidy	74.49	201.47	344.28	367.13	388.36
Subvention received from State Government	20.45	62.84	88.20	100.99	79.81
Net Subsidy	54.04	138.63	256.07	266.13	308.55
Surplus from sales to other sectors	21.73	78.49	34.35	36.15	74.99
Uncovered Subsidy	32.31	60.14	221.72	229.99	233.56
Commercial losses					
Excluding subventions	41.17	94.53	253.95	273.06	243.21
Including subventions	N.A.	N.A	165.75	172.07	163.40
Rate of Return (RoR) on Net Asset	–12.70%	–17.20%	–41.80%	–39.50%	–32.10%

Source: Ministry of Finance, 2002.

Figure 11.25

Subsidy by SEBs to agriculture and domestic subscribers

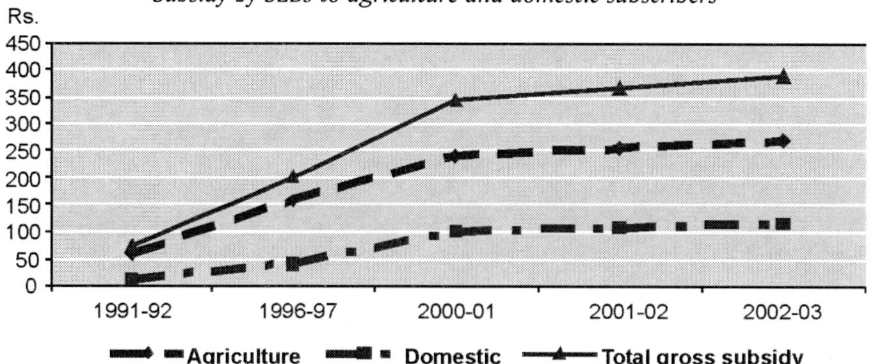

Agriculture alone was claiming subsidy over Rs 269 billion in 2002–03. Subsidy in agriculture has increased nearly by five folds between 1991–92 and 2002–03. Total uncovered subsidy by SEBs has increased by seven folds in the period. There are states that supply electricity to farmers totally free of cost or at a token 50 paise per unit (the recipients are mostly the big farmers). It is also in the knowledge of everyone that many of these farmers enjoying electricity subsidy makes huge profits by selling water to other farmers.

Figure 11.26
Cost of supply of electricity and average tariff, 1974–2002
(Reproduced from N. Swain et al.: Analysis of Power Sector in India)

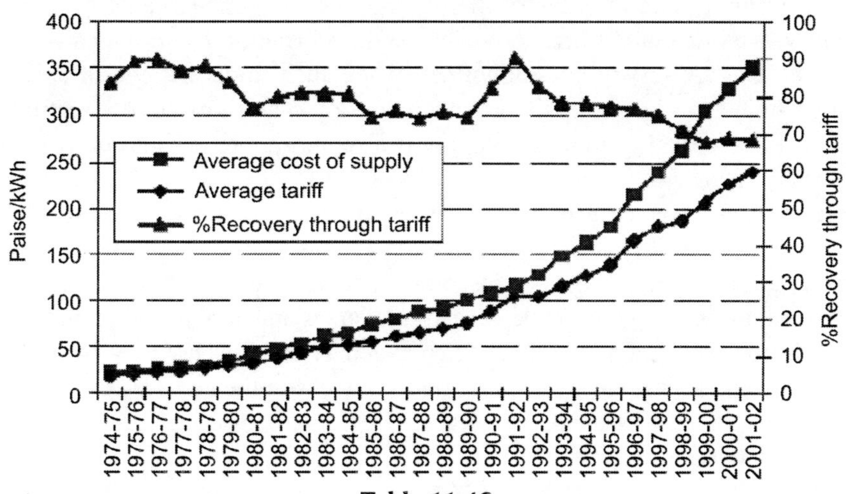

Table 11.46
Consumer category-wise average tariffs (Paise/kWh)

	1996–97	*1997–98*	*1998–99*	*1999–2000*	*2000–01*	*2001–02*
Domestic	105.7	136.2	139.1	160.7	183.1	195.6
Commercial	239.1	293.6	330.2	369.9	404.2	426.3
Agriculture	21.2	20.2	21.0	22.6	35.4	41.6
Industry	275.5	312.7	322.8	342.0	366.5	378.7
Traction	346.8	382.2	410.3	415.3	435.9	449.2
Outside State	151.4	138.1	163.8	190.1	187.9	194.4
Overall	165.3	180.3	186.8	207.0	226.3	239.9

Source: Annual Report (2001–02).

Table 11.47
Share of revenue from consumer sectors

Sector	*94–95*	*95–96*	*96–97*	*97–98*	*98–99*	*99–00*	*00–01*	*01–02*
Agriculture	4.77	4.37	3.95	3.54	3.62	3.19	4.55	4.99
Domestic	11.40	10.70	11.57	13.94	14.44	15.95	17.19	17.41
Industry	33.71	32.23	32.92	31.69	30.17	30.33	30.50	29.25

We have stated earlier that more than 86 percent of villages have already been electrified although only about 49 percent rural households have access to electricity in 1998 (NFHS II). Should the cross-subsidy now paid to domestic consumers, especially to the households that consume less than 50 units per month, are withdrawn, it is feared that a significantly high majority of these households would surrender their power line. Rural people often are not in a position to afford the cost of electricity; they meet their basic energy needs through the use of energy sources like firewood, cow dung, agricultural residues and subsidized kerosene. It must not be forgotten that these families are required to spend 60 percent or more of their income on their most fundamental necessity, food.

There is another important factor behind poor per capita domestic consumption of electricity. The voltage in the supply line in villages often is too low to operate even the simplest electrical gadgets. If there was a line fault or breakdown of the transformer, the entire area would be without power for several days. A survey has shown that when such faults happen in cities, the fault is mended usually within 2 to 4 hours. In villages it would take 48 hours or more to rectify even a minor fault. This uncertainty in quality in power supply is also an important factor why consumption of 'white goods' is not rising fast in rural areas.

The 1991 Census provides a cross-tabulation of access of households to electricity, safe drinking water and toilet facility within their living premises (Table 11.29). It is really unfortunate that nearly one-fourth of the households in the country had no access to any of these three vital provisions. The proportion was as high as 31 percent in rural areas and about 5 percent in urban areas. 28 percent of Scheduled Caste and 45 percent of Scheduled Tribe household's vis-à-vis 21 percent of other households had no access to any of these three services in their premises.

11.8.5.5 Policy Initiatives Since 1991

A number of policy initiatives have been undertaken since 1991 to encourage private investments in power sector. The Electricity Bill, 2001 eliminated the need for license for power generation and allows power trading. Many industries, as a result of this deregulation, are now in a position to set up power plants for their individual usage as also to trade power that are in excess of their plant requirement. Such plants mostly would be 'Midget' category. The much needed momentum in boosting power generation however came from Electricity Act, 2003. The Act gives substantial freedom to private players in the power sector – open access to transmission lines bypassing the SEBs and sell power directly to the distribution and trading licensees. In the long run, the end-users would benefit both in terms of choice of supplier and quality and reliability of the supply.

The new multi-player market-driven scenario since 1991 attracted private players to play an important role in power sector in India. The ever growing demand-supply gap can be kept under some control only if the private players enter the power market in a big way. State treasuries are perilously short of fund; the loss-making state-run power units are operating with cumulative debts running into billions. The shortage of fund has become a serious roadblock to faster growth of this key infrastructure sector for a sustainable GDP growth of even 6–8 percent. The influx of private capital in this capital-scarce venture, it is hoped by the planners, would solve, at least partly, this problem. Mega power projects are not in the priority list of the government, especially after the serious trouble with the Dabhol power project (Enron famed) in Maharashtra. The negatives of Mega Power Plants encouraged private players to look for Midgets or Small Power Plants, which are less capital intensive, less gestation period and less political pressure. Ideas of Midgets were further propelled with technological advancements in areas of small engine and turbine technology. Many industries have invested in on-site power generation, which as per CMIE estimates accounts for more than 10 percent of total capacity. This ratio is likely to increase as the Electricity Bill, 2001 eliminated the need for license for power generation and power trading.

21 SEBs and 14 Electricity Departments (EDs) are responsible for generation, transmission, and distribution, usually within their own states and territories. The central power utilities own and operate about 30 percent of the country's total generation capacity, while SEBs and EDs have 59 percent share of the total. The privately owned utilities, operating in certain urban centers and responsible for power distribution within their franchised areas, and some independent power producers have a share of 11 percent of the total power generation.

Some of the major reasons of hardship of the state controlled power units are

1. lack of injection of fresh capital,
2. low plant load factor (PLF),
3. un-remunerative tariffs (with every kWh sold, the utilities lose over 1.1 rupees on average),
4. enormous subsidy to agriculture (42 paise/kWh against cost of supply of Rs 3.50/kWh in 2002) and domestic consumers under intense political pressure (it almost took the shape of a political blackmail when coalition government of many different parties with different ideologies and political agenda became the pattern of the government at the Center since late 1980s); the commercial and industrial consumers cross-subsidize these sectors through very high tariffs,
5. the immense pressure of the environmental activists and the judiciary to keep under control the emissions,
6. enormous transmission and distribution (T&D) losses (well over 25%), and
7. the rising uncovered subsidies (rising from Rs 33.31 billion in 1991–92 to Rs 233.56 billion in 2002–03).

Agriculture, which consumes about one-third of the power in India, contributes less than 5 percent to the SEBs' revenue earnings. The burden of subsidized power has to be borne, at least partly, by industrial and commercial consumers. The benefits of subsidized power have not reached the poor, the marginal farmers and the rural households. It has gone mostly in favor of those who really are not entitled to receive it.

11.8.6 Alternative Sources of Energy

The Planning Commission believes that per capita income in 10 years can be doubled with GDP growth rate around 8.7 percent and the population not growing over 1.5 percent per annum. This would require huge increase in power generation besides upgrading the telecommunication and transport sectors. As it stands today, the additional generation of electricity would be primarily thermal, more specifically coal. Coal-fired thermal power stations not only emit huge quantity of GHG gases, disposal of fly-ash produced by thermal plants has also created a very serious problem. The governments at the center and the states have asked this fly-ash to be used in land filling, road construction and in construction of government buildings. There is, however, reservation from within various relevant establishments in strictly following this government guide line.

Though the world still has vast coal reserve, experts agree that natural gas needs to be used more aggressively for power generation for several reasons: though non-renewable, gas reserve is plenty, energy from it is cleaner than are obtained from burning of coal, and unlike crude oil the price of natural gas in the world market is likely to remain low and stable. Pressure is on the developing countries to produce as much cleaner energy as possible. China and India, who would be dominating the world scenario in electricity generation in the coming decades, have to find out alternative sources for power generation. India has already planned to bring natural gas from Iran and Myanmar through pipelines via Pakistan and Bangladesh respectively. India is also looking for procuring nuclear fuels and technologies from other countries to set up additional nuclear plants as also for a secured supply of nuclear fuels for its existing plants engaged in generation of electricity.

Planning Commission's Expert Committee on integrated energy policy forecasts that to sustain a GDP growth rate of 8–9 percent, the country needs by 2031 a power generation capacity of 778,095 MW and increased primary energy supply by three to four times to meet the electricity consumption which is likely to be five to seven times the current consumption level. Although India has 214 billion tons of hard coal reserve (about 7 percent of world's total reserve), only 84 billion tons are recoverable reserves of anthracite and bituminous coal. With 5 percent annual increase in production, the coal reserves are likely to be exhausted in about 40–50 years. We need therefore to look for alternative sources of energy fast.

India is trying to produce more electricity from gas. Recent surveys show that the country has large gas reserve. But to develop gas based generating stations on a sustainable basis, India needs to import gas from Iran and Myanmar. The gas pipelines are supposed to pass through difficult terrains and through countries that are not very friendly with India. Indian government is trying to enter into a long term agreement (25 years) with Iran for uninterrupted supply of gas throughout the year. There are many 'ifs' and 'buts' in all these deals.

11.8.6.1 Nuclear Energy

Going nuclear in a big way in energy production in India has been debated by the energy experts. The Department of Atomic Energy (DAE) predicted that by 2000 the Indian nuclear reactors would produce 43,500 MW of nuclear power. But as of 2005, DAE managed to produce only 3,310 MW. The nuclear reactors cost a lot to build and operate. After successful commissioning of TAPP 4, the authorities announced that power produced can be sold at Rs 2.65 per kWh. Certainly this cost analysis does not include costs dealing with disposal of nuclear wastes. Nuclear waste disposal is not only very costly, the wastes remain radioactive for tens of thousands of years. While we use nuclear electricity to run our AC machines, lifts and escalators, the future generation will have to face the consequences of our seeking comfort. There are many instances of accidents with nuclear reactors in various parts of the world. When such accidents happen, it can bring disaster to thousands, as was experienced in Chernobyl in Russia some 20 years back.

In spite of all the criticisms raised against nuclear power, there is a worldwide rethink about the greater urgency to use nuclear power as also power from other renewable sources in the context of GHG emissions from coal, natural gas and oil-fired thermal plants. Nuclear energy is green and clear and that is its greatest advantage; energy obtained from other renewable sources is also green. Nuclear power business has been growing fast in the last 30 years; the share of nuclear energy in the global energy generation has gone up by 13 percent, coal only by 1 percent, gas by 5 percent and hydro-electric's share has actually gone down. China is building one coal fired power plant almost every week. In spite of that it is planning to build at least 30 nuclear power plants (6 are already in the pipe line). USA has about 130 new coal-based power plants. Recently, USA has given license for 19 new nuclear power plants.

As of July 2007, 4,680 MW power is obtained from 17 nuclear plants (proposals are on to increase the life of the existing plants to 40 years from the present 20 to 30 years). Another 3,580 MW power would be generated from 5 new projects (500 MW would be generated by Prototype Fast Breeder Reactor, coming at Kalpakkam, by 2010). On March 6, 2005 the 540 MW power plant (Tarapore Power Project Unit 4) went 'critical' seven months ahead of schedule. TAPP–3 has also achieved criticality in 2007. TAPP–3&4 together are expected to generate 1,080 MW of electricity. In about another 10 years the nuclear generation would exceed 12,000 MW. Nuclear energy plants, many energy experts in India now admit, are definitely an important viable option for meeting the increased demand for power. The Expert Committee of the Planning Commission admits that theoretically nuclear energy offers the most potent means to long-term energy security. However, it has been argued by many, especially those opposing setting up new nuclear power plants (mostly as replacement to the existing plants reaching the age of retirement), that construction of gas-based power plants would be much more economical than construction of new nuclear plants by borrowing technology and buying equipments and fuels from other countries.

A few nuclear plants in India since 1970s have remained under international inspection (IAEA). This has hindered if not crippled the functioning of India's nuclear reactors. India has remained dependent for nuclear fuel and reactor technology on other countries. Since the first Pokhran test (1974) of indigenously built nuclear bomb, the nuclear suppliers group (NSG) imposed sanction on India. Such international pressure forced India to use its innovative skills to design and develop reactors that would not use uranium (U–235) or plutonium (Pu–239) as the fission material. India has only a modest reserve of uranium, 95,000 tons from which 61,000 tons may be obtained for power generation. The nuclear reactors require enriched uranium. Natural uranium contains 99.3 percent of U–238 isotope and only 0.7 percent of radioactive U–235 isotope. Nuclear reactors require enriched uranium or 'yellow cake' in which proportion of U–235 has been increased to at least 4–5 percent. Modern reactors require the enrichment to 20 percent or more for higher burn up. This enrichment process is really expensive (Nuclear bombs require more than 90 percent of U–235 or Pu–239). India has about 360,000 tons of monazite deposits (which are close to one-third of the world reserve) along the sea coasts (Orissa and Kerala) of which sixty-five percent may be mined to yield 225,000 tons of Thorium (a 'fertile' metal for use in reactor). India is planning to develop Fast Breeder Reactors (FBR) utilizing the massive reserve of monazite. It has been reported that the hundred percent indigenously produced FBR, at a cost well over 60 billion rupees would become 'critical' sometime in 2010. The advantage of FBR is that it will produce as much or more fuel in the process as the quantity of fuel used for generation of electricity. For example, if 10 MT of nuclear fuel is consumed by the reactor for generation of electricity, it will also produce more than 10 MT of nuclear fuel that can be used for a second reactor. Because of very unique and sophisticated technology, India has emphatically said in nuclear agreement with USA that FBR will not be open to safeguards of International Atomic Energy Agency (IAEA). An experimental FBR producing 40 MW of electricity was commissioned in 1985. KAMINI, the first thorium based FBR research reactor in the world is successfully operating at Kalpakkam (Tamil Nadu) for over a decade. Indian nuclear scientists working at Kalpakkam, in Tamil Nadu are confident that the technology they have developed would help India achieve its electricity requirement without investing much on conventional thermal plants within a decade or two. India would be in a position to stop import of fissile uranium from other countries. The nuclear scientists believe that India shall be in a position to market the technology and nuclear fuels to other countries. India is destined to become a super-power in electricity generation using FBR technology. It is a fact that one atom of U–235 or U–233 or Pu–239 can produce 10 million times of energy produced by the combustion of one atom of carbon from coal. Potential of obtaining energy is practically unlimited by using FBR nuclear technology.

The nuclear cooperation agreement between India and USA, signed on July 18, 2005 and the joint declaration by USA President George Bush and India's Prime Minister Dr Manmohan Singh on March 2, 2006 settled India's differences with Washington over the highly controversial separation plans for military and civilian use nuclear reactors. In spite of vehement opposition from the Left parties against the nuclear agreement and withdrawal of support to the Manmohan Singh government, the UPA government decided to go ahead with the operationalization of the nuclear deal. IAEA approved "India-specific safeguards" and the Nuclear Suppliers Group (NSG) lifted the ban against nuclear commerce with India. After IAEA and NSG waiver in 2008, the US Senate and the Congress have approved the agreement and the President of USA has put his signature on the 123 Indo-US nuclear agreement. India has signed nuclear agreement with France and Russia. The 40-year agreement, extendable by 10 years, commits the US to ensure uninterrupted fuel supplies to Indian reactors even if it terminates its cooperation and to help create strategic fuel reserve for Indian safeguarded nuclear reactors. It makes it incumbent upon the US to work with other countries in NSG to ensure that India can have nuclear cooperation with the international community. The civilian nuclear capacity in India after this agreement is likely grow by 100 percent, and electricity from the civilian reactors (not the FBR) is likely to produce 8 percent or even more of India's power requirement.

In the Indo-US nuclear cooperation agreement, India has agreed on an international inspection (IAEA) of the civilian nuclear reactors. India has succeeded to keep its nuclear reactors used for military purposes and the FBR out of bound for IAEA inspection. India is about to build the first commercial Fast Breeding Reactor which is expected to produce the same quantity of nuclear fuel or more as the amount it consumes for the generation of electricity. If the indigenously built FBR is successfully commissioned, the future energy position of India would become secured and the country's dependence on the conventional non-renewable energy source could be drastically cut. The Nuclear Power Corporation (NPC) wants 25–27 new nuclear power plants in the next 20 years. The estimated cost is about US$100 billion – a very good incentive for the nuclear industry in USA and elsewhere to cooperate with India in creation of nuclear power plants.

11.8.6.2 Other Renewable Sources of Energy

In today's hi tech development and increasing standard of living coupled with high population growth, electricity plays a very critical role. We have seen earlier that the mega thermal plants (coal-fired) will continue to have the largest share in generation of electricity. However to generate one unit of electricity, it needs three equivalent units of coal; two-thirds of this energy produced by burning coal is lost to atmosphere because of poor efficiency of the generation plants. After the government has invited private players to contribute to country's growing electricity requirement, the idea of Midgets has become a distinct reality. Midgets would use local resources and the units can be set up within a short time with a comparatively small investment using the most advanced technology. Gas-based power plants, wind energy, solar photovoltaic (PV), energy from biodegradable wastes, small scale hydro-power, etc. are coming up in various parts of the country. Today, wind energy plants costs about the same as a coal fired thermal power plant of the same capacity; it could even be cheaper at places with high wind speeds. The cost of biomass gasification and geothermal energy is going down too. Solar photovoltaic and wind energy now cost one tenth of what they did in early 1980s.

India now has a dedicated establishment – Ministry of Non-conventional Energy Sources (MNES) – probably first of its kind in the world. It was created in 1992. The non-conventional renewable energy covers three principal inputs, namely hydro, solar and wind. None of these has been exploited even moderately. India has huge hydel reserves. Every Indian states except Gujarat and Rajasthan have extensive water resources in the form of rivers. Virtually limitless hydro energy can be produced all along the Himalayan range, from Kashmir to Northeast as also in some central and Southern states. Hydro-based energy assessed around 2004 is approximately 30,000 MW. Anything up to three times this quantity can be produced if we really get down to it. Being a high 'monsoon' country, stored rain water can be used to produce electricity, support irrigation and supply drinking water.

We have over 7,500 km coastline. Besides trying to discover Narsapura-type oil rich basins, we must make as much use of wind as possible. India has the fifth largest installed wind capacity in the world at 2,400 MW. In 2004 alone, India added 615 MW of wind energy. The potential wind energy capacity could be anything between 20,000 MW and 45,000 MW. Every sea-facing state from West Bengal through Kerala to Gujarat has large expanses of beach. By March 2003, India had 484 MW of biomass power/cogeneration, 53 MW from biomass gassifiers and 2.5 MW of solar PVs. India enjoys anything up to 300 sunny days in a year. This is a great bonus for producing solar energy. This type of energy can be used effectively in cooking, water heating, lighting, running pumps for local irrigation and for other agricultural uses, power to hospitals, schools, street lights in villages and in remote areas. The "freed" regular energy as a result of this substitution can help augment the quantum of energy that industries and other establishments require. Installed capacity of all renewables by March 2004 was more than 4,600 MW. The Central government wants an additional 10,000 MW from renewable sources by 2012.

Table 11.48

Renewable energy potential in India

Source/Technology	***Potential/Availability***	***Potential exploited***
Biogas Plants	12×10^6	2.7×10^6
Biomass-based power	17,000 MW	69.5 MW
Efficient Woodstoves	120×10^6	20×10^6
Solar Energy	5 × 1015 Whr/yr	25 MW
Small hydro	10,000 MW	250 MW
Wind Energy	20,000 MW	1,000 MW
Ocean Thermal	50,000 MW	Nil
Sea Wave Power	20,000 MW	Nil
Tidal Power	9,000 MW	Nil

Source: Annual Report 1996–97, Ministry of Non-conventional Energy Sources

The Electricity Act 2003 completely de-licenses electricity distribution and captive generation. Persons who set up bio-gasification or wind plant are free to sell electricity. Some 20,000 remote villages, which cannot be connected through normal transmission lines, can be electrified through these plants. The Act asks every state Regulatory Commissions to fix a certain minimum target (percentage of total power) of electricity, which the power distribution licensees will have to be provided from renewable energy sources. Private investors in renewable energy have demanded uniform fixed tariff from all electricity boards. They also demanded a longer power purchase agreement, at least 10 years, to provide investment security to the investors in renewable power projects. Government of India has declared some promotional incentives (relief on import duty, sales tax and excise duty relief, soft loans, interest subsidy, tax holiday, etc. according to the nature of technology used). But the biggest impediment comes from the SEBs who are supposed to buy the surplus power from the private investors. The Boards collectively owed over Rs 400,000 million to various central public sectors and railways. Over one-sixth of the power distributed is pilfered. About 60 percent of the power is either free or subsidized. The decision to separate generation, transmission and distribution and allow the latter two to form separate bodies have been objected to by the Left and many others for fear of privatization of the power sector. They want the subsidies to continue indefinitely.

Table 11.49
Status of renewable energy technologies in India as on 30 April 2000

Technology	*Cumulative installations*
Family-size biogas plants	3 million
Improved cook stoves	32 million
Solar cookers	487 000
Solar hot water systems	500 000 million square meters
PV (Photovoltaic) water pumps (aggregate capacity)	3371
PV power units	1165 kip
PV community lights and street lights	39 000
PV home systems	117 000
PV lanterns	278 000
Water-pumping windmills	637
Small aerogenerators	55 kW
Wind farms	1167 MW
Biomass power	222 MW
Biomass gasifiers	34 MW
Wind-solar PV hybrid systems	76.5 MW
Small hydel	217 MW
Energy from wastes	15.2 MW

Source: MNES. 2000.

11.9 Transportation

The Pradhan Mantri Gram Sadak Yojana (PMGSY) had been launched in December 2000 to provide road connectivity to 160,000 habitations with population of 500 persons or more (250 in case of hilly, desert and tribal areas) by the end of the Tenth Plan period. The original estimate of Rs 600,000 million for the project has been revised to Rs 1,300,000 million. The program is scheduled to be financed by cess on diesel. Originally it was Re 1 per liter of diesel, which has since been revised to Rs 1.50 to provide the additional fund. The National Rural Roads Development Agency (NRRDA) provides the management and operations support for this massive rural road connectivity program.

There were about 3.3 million kilometers of roads by 2002, of which 1.4 million kilometers were surfaced and more than 1 million kilometers were covered with gravel, crushed stone, or earth. 150 national highways carry about 40 percent of road traffic on a total length of 65,569 kilometers. Around 85 percent of all passenger traffic and 70 percent of all freight traffic travel by road. By 2007, 13,146 kilometers are likely to be added to the highways with various road projects aiming at linking the country's major cities and spanning the entire country north-south, east-west. Modes of road transport are a mix of traditional and modern means. Urban transit is dominated by motor vehicles, with increasing use of automobiles, minibuses, buses, trucks, and particularly two- and three-wheelers. Bullock carts are still very familiar in villages. Camels, elephants and other animals still are extensively used in difficult terrains and even in local transport in some parts of the country. 72 percent of Indians still live in villages and 50 percent of the villages with population less than 1,000 are yet to be connected by metalled roads.

The road length per 100 square kilometers has increased at the national level from about 45 kilometers in 1981 to 75 kilometers in 1997. In the same period, road length per million populations has increased from 21.68 kilometers to 25.82 kilometers. Between 1991 and 2002, 600,000 kilometers of road have been added.

Table 11.50
Road length and motor vehicles in India

Year (as on 31st March)	*Road length (figures in km) per 1,000 persons*			*Number of registered motor vehicles per 1,000 persons*			
	Surfaced	*Unsurfaced*	*Total*	*Two/three wheelers*	*Car/Jeep*	*Other vehicles*	*Total*
1	*2*	*3*	*4*	*5*	*6*	*7*	*8*
1951	0.43	0.68	1.11	0.07	0.44	0.33	0.85
1956	0.53	0.68	1.21	0.10	0.51	0.46	1.08
1961	0.60	0.59	1.19	0.20	0.71	0.61	1.51
1966	0.70	0.87	1.57	0.46	0.93	0.85	2.24
1971	0.54	1.13	1.67	1.05	1.24	1.11	3.40
1976	0.90	1.14	2.04	1.73	1.27	1.41	4.41
1981	1.00	1.17	2.17	3.69	1.63	2.23	7.55
1986	1.08	1.18	2.27	8.10	2.28	3.28	13.66
1991	1.20	1.15	2.35	16.78	3.49	4.99	25.26
1996	1.40	1.16	2.57	25.22	4.56	6.86	36.64
1997	1.48	1.14	2.62	27.38	4.97	7.38	39.73
1998	1.44	1.09	2.53	29.98	5.38	7.94	43.30
1999	1.47	1.09	2.56	32.26	5.72	8.24	46.22
2000P	NA	NA	NA	34.37	6.12	8.56	49.05

Note: Midyear population figures as estimated by Registrar General of India for the respective years have been used to arrive at road length and vehicle for 1,000 persons since 1993–94.

NA: Not available.

Source: Ministry of Road Transport and Highways. Estimates have been worked out on the basis of figures published by Transport Research Wing, Ministry of Road Transport and Highways.

There are large differences between the states in coverage by roads. Among the major states, Kerala has the highest road length per hundred square kilometers (268 km in 1981 to 375 km in 1997). Tamil Nadu and Punjab are close second and third with about 35 percent of Kerala's road coverage. The rural-urban and rural-rural road connectivity in Kerala could be regarded as an important factor behind high human development in the state. In case of road coverage per million populations, one of the poorest states, Orissa was way ahead of others. In 1981, the coverage was 45 km (41 km in Kerala); it increased to 75 km in 1997. The improvement in road coverage was also impressive. The coverage by road has declined in Bihar and West Bengal.

Table 11.51
Index of growth for road length and motor vehicles (1991=100)

Year	*Surfaced road*	*Two/three wheelers*	*Car/ Jeep*	*Other vehicles*	*Total*
1991	100	100	100	100	100
1996	116.7	150.3	130.7	137.5	145.1
1997	123.3	163.2	142.4	147.9	157.3
1998	120.0	178.7	154.2	159.2	171.4
1999	122.5	192.3	163.9	165.1	183.0
2000		204.8	175.4	171.5	194.2

At the national level 50 percent of villages with 1,000 or less population were connected by roads. Nearly 100 percent villages in Kerala, Karnataka, Haryana and Punjab have achieved road connectivity. Madhya Pradesh and Rajasthan with 23 and 38 percent of their villages connected by roads are at the bottom of the list. The bigger villages (1,500 population or more) in almost all states are connected by roads except those in Bihar and West Bengal. The health of the roads and their maintenance are often very pitiable. Bihar and West Bengal are the worst performers in this respect.

With increase in road length in the country there is a simultaneous disproportionate increase in registered vehicles. Surfaced road has gone up by 400 percent between 1951 and 1999. Unsurfaced road per thousand persons has risen by 160 percent in the same period so that total road length has

Figure 11.27
Growth of road length and motor vehicles in India

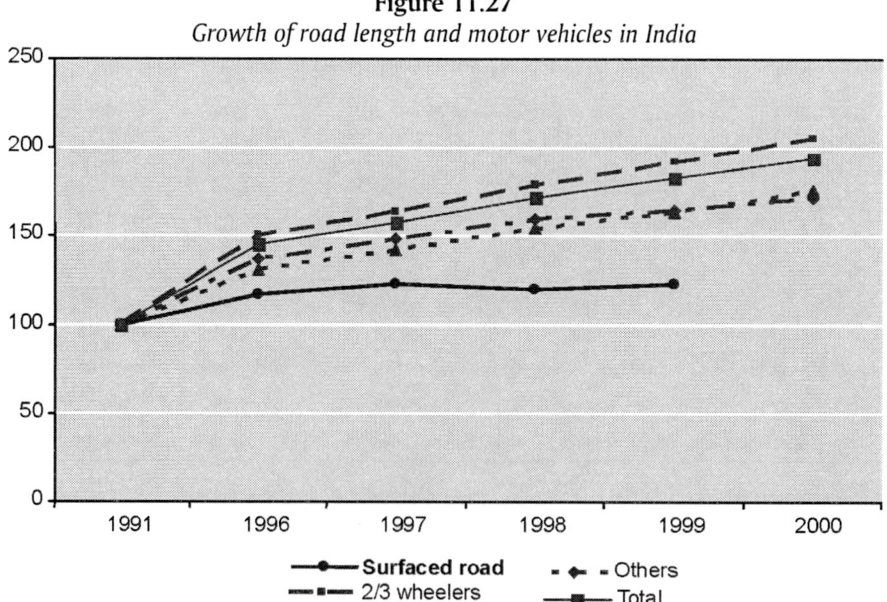

increased by 230 percent. In the same time frame motor vehicles of all types have gone up by 5,770 percent, two and three-wheelers by 49,100 percent, small cars by 1,300 percent and heavy vehicles including public buses and transport carriers by 2,497 percent. With 1991 taken as the base year, the growth index of length of surfaced road and number of different types of vehicles per 1,000 populations is presented Table 11.52.

The use of private vehicles is increasing by leaps and bounds in all parts of the world. Emission from automobiles is the principal source of air pollution, especially in cities and metros. Our judiciary had to intervene to restrict automobile emissions in congested cities. Some of the metropolitan cities have already mandated the use of compressed natural gas (CNG) in buses plying within the cities and has asked every vehicle to obtain compliance emission norm certificate periodically. The government is actively considering not issuing road-worthiness certificate to public transports that are on the road for 15 years or more. The share of public transport in meeting travel demand is diminishing fast. While buses accounted for about 11 percent of registered vehicles in 1951, the same now stands at 1 percent only. The share of public transport has gone down in most countries. Studies show that public transports need three times less energy and therefore emit three times less GHG than private fleet of cars. Energy use also can be brought down significantly with more public transport use.

Oil price in the international market has gone up very fast and reached $147 in July 2008. But that did not deter the expansion of automobile industry. Automobile industry, in fact, has been the fastest growing sector even in the developing countries especially after trade restrictions were lifted and customs and excise duties on such products were slashed under WTO agreement. Banks and other financial agencies even are offering 100 percent finance and other lucrative offers in pushing automobile sells (cars/jeeps/station wagons in Delhi showed a compounded annual growth rate of 9.3 percent in the decade ending 2003–04). While the developing countries have no option than to levy heavy taxes on petroleum products to make annual budgetary provisions for infrastructural development after meeting the enormous cost for import of crude oil, the developed countries like USA are reluctant to cut oil consumption or increase tax on fuel. Petroleum prices are very dear to the American citizens (as a matter of fact, in all developed countries) whose automobile-dependency life-style is accepted as non-negotiable. The auto giants like General Motors have a different plan in this global rise in fuel prices. GM has taken up a promotional scheme – the fuel price protection program. The GM was offering a gasoline subsidy ($1.99 a gallon for one year when the market price was over $3 a gallon) for cars that are gasoline guzzler – for luxurious vehicles that give a mileage of 5–6 km per liter of petrol. They also are offering discounts to soldiers who protect the oil lines to keep GM's gas guzzlers guzzling.

Over 90 percent of petrol in India is used by the private automobile sector. Because of huge price differentials, the cheap diesel is pushing automobile manufacturers in India to follow GM's car policy of making big guzzling diesel cars. Even the best of diesels sold in India is highly toxic and the motor vehicles departments in the country are quite lax in enforcing strict automobile emission norms.

It is indeed impossible to restrict the number of small cars on road since every car on road brings huge revenue in the form of various types of taxes. Consumption of the fuel and automobile emissions of toxic gases can be brought under sizeable control if the government can go-ahead with instituting some fuel economy norms (use of CNG, LPG, bio-diesel, electrically driven cars, etc.) for all types of vehicles. The use of cheaper fuel like diesel (which is costlier than even the super grade petrol in USA) for all private vehicles must be discouraged. But fuel savings and consequent check on GHG emissions can be attained by investing more on public transport and railways. Indian

Railways are taking measures to dedicate exclusive freight corridors between important cities and metros to facilitate movement of goods of all sorts at a cheaper rate and faster point to point delivery. Some important cities like London and Geneva have shown an increase in the share of public transports in the last decade.

11.10 Mass Communication

The number of radio stations and TV relay centers and consequently percentage of population covered by radio and TV have increased phenomenally since 1981. Whereas in 1981, about 19 percent of the population was covered by TV, the same increased to 87 percent in 1997. Similarly, the number and circulation of daily newspapers have increased significantly over the years. The estimated circulation of daily newspapers per thousand populations has increased from 27.5 in 1990 to 58.7 in the year 2000. But a more spectacular change has been observed in the field of telecommunication. The number of telephones per 100 populations, which was 0.60 in 1991, has increased to 5.11 in 2003, contributed largely by a sharp increase in the cellular mobile phones over the last few years. As of the middle of 2007, the total number of telephone connections through out the country is around 200 million of which cell phone alone accounts for more than 155 million. That is, there were 1 mobile phone for every 7 persons in India in 2007. Currently, in the use of cellular telephones, India is at the third spot after China and USA. Many international service providers (Vodaphone, AT&T for example) have expressed their intent to enter into the fast rising mobile market in India The internet connections have exceeded 9 million by the end of 2006.

Table 11.52

Radio and television in India

Year	*Number of*		*Percentage of population covered by*	
	Radio stations	*TV relay centers*	*TV*	*Radio*
1981	85	19	26	89
1986	93	185	67	91
1991	125	529	78	95
1992	143	535	81	96
1993	154	553	83	96
1994	173	564	84	96
1995	176	743	86	96
1996	185	792	86	97
1997	187	921	87	97

Source: Ministry of Information and Broadcasting.

Table 11.53

Telephones and post offices in India

Year	*Number of Telephones [Fixed + CMPs + Pvt. Basic + WLL] (million)*								*Availability of post offices per hundred thousand Population*
	Population (million)	*Fixed lines (DELs)*	*Cellular Mobile Tele-phones (CMPs)*	*Fixed lines (DELs) by private operators*	*Wireless In local Loop (WLL) (Fixed + Ltd. Mobile)*	*Total Tele-phones*	*Per 100 popula-tion*	*Per Sq. km*	
1	*2*	*3*	*4*	*5*	*6*	*7*	*8*	*9*	*10*
1951	361.10	0.10	NA	NA	NA	0.10	0.03	0.03	10.00
1961	439.20	0.33	NA	NA	NA	0.33	0.08	0.10	17.50
1971	548.30	0.98	NA	NA	NA	0.98	0.18	0.30	19.90

Cont'd...

Table 11.53 Cont'd...

1	*2*	*3*	*4*	*5*	*6*	*7*	*8*	*9*	*10*
1981	683.20	2.15	NA	NA	NA	2.15	0.31	0.65	20.30
1991	846.30	5.07	NA	NA	NA	5.07	0.60	1.54	17.60
1992	863.20	5.81	NA	NA	NA	5.81	0.67	1.77	17.80
1993	880.40	6.80	NA	NA	NA	6.80	0.77	2.07	18.00
1994	898.00	8.03	NA	NA	NA	8.03	0.89	2.44	17.20
1995	915.90	9.80	NA	NA	NA	9.80	1.07	2.98	16.90
1996	934.20	11.98	NA	NA	NA	11.98	1.28	3.64	16.60
1997	949.40	14.54	0.34	NA	NA	14.88	1.56	4.53	16.40
1998	964.70	17.80	0.88	NA	NA	18.68	1.94	5.68	18.20
1999	980.40	21.59	1.20	0.02	NA	22.81	2.33	6.94	15.90
2000	996.90	26.51	1.88	0.14	NA	28.53	2.86	8.68	15.90
2001	1027.02	32.44	3.58	0.27	NA	36.29	3.58	11.04	15.10
2002	1048.06	37.71	6.43	0.64	0.24	45.02	4.29	13.70	15.12
2003	1068.98	40.02	12.69	1.31	0.60	54.62	5.11	16.62	NA

Source:
—Department of Telecommunication
—Department of Posts
—Population projection for India & States–1996–2016 RGI
—For 1951,1961 & 1971 India: Towards population and Development goals UN population fund (UNDPA), 1997
—For 2001, population census of India, 2001 and for 2002, 2003 projection based on percentage Average Annual Exponential Growth Rates

Figure 11.28
Telephone per 100 population in India

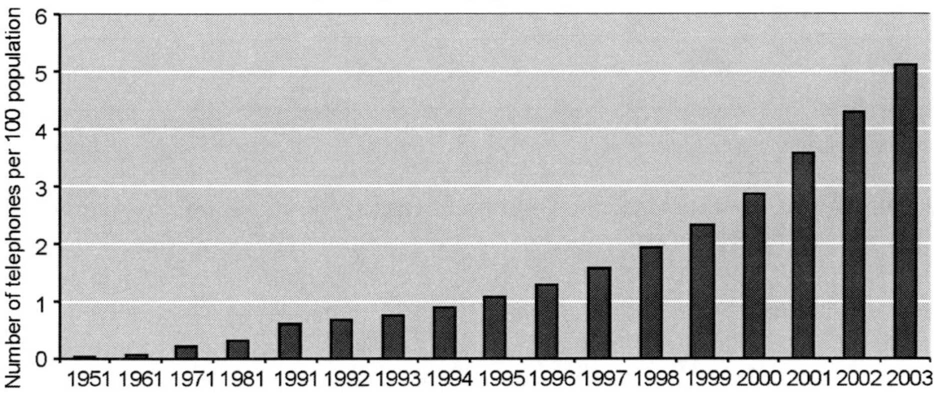

11.11 Physically and Mentally Disabled Persons

Disability refers to any restriction or lack of ability to perform an activity in the manner or within the range considered normal for a human being. NSSO survey on disabled estimated 1.8 percent of the total population in India with some disabilities in 1981 and the same rose in 1991 to 1.9 percent. About 81 percent of all disabled persons in the country and 84 percent of all those who were visually disabled in 1981 were from rural areas. The share of rural disabled to total disabled in the country came down to 78 percent while visual disability continued more or less at the same level. Visually disabled males constitute about 46 percent of all disabled persons. Of the total disabled persons 12.5 percent had more than one type of disability. Loco-motor and speech disabilities are much higher among males than in females.

There are considerable variations in the prevalence rate of disabilities among the states. 2.5–3 percent disability was observed in rural areas of Punjab, Andhra Pradesh, Himachal Pradesh and Maharashtra; Karnataka, Madhya Pradesh, Orissa and Tamil Nadu had such disabled persons between 2–2.5 percent in 1991. The national average of disabilities in urban areas was 1.4 percent. Orissa recorded the highest prevalence of disability in urban areas in 1991 followed by Andhra Pradesh, Tamil Nadu, Punjab and Kerala.

Only 2 percent of these disabled persons are educated and less than 1 percent of them are employed. According to a survey conducted by McKinsey and Company, it costs the nation as much as Rs 720,000 million every year for the care of these physically challenged citizens. Their families, friends and welfare organizations meet most of the expenses on fortunate physically disabled persons. The rest, a majority, roam about in places as beggars.

Problem of disabled persons is not peculiar to developing countries like India. But in terms of absolute numbers, India faces greater challenge than most other countries. In the developed countries 10 percent of physically disabled persons are given some sort of an employment after giving intensive training keeping an eye on the type of disabilities. Expenses for the rest are at least partially covered by social security provisions of the country. Even in Asia-Pacific countries 5–6 percent on an average of the physically challenged people is employed. Our physically disabled people struggle to get even the bare minimum for living. They suffer from lack of any medical attention, from social isolation and malnutrition.

Table 11.54

Number of disabled, 1981 & 1991 (per hundred thousand)

	Rural			*Urban*		
	Male	*Female*	*Person*	*Male*	*Female*	*Person*
1981	2,045	1,632	1,844	1,532	1,297	1,420
1991	2,277	1,694	1,995	1,774	1,361	1,579

Source: NSS report on disabled persons.

The national government passed the Disabilities (Equal Opportunities, Protection of Rights & Full Participation) Act in 1995. Although 3 percent reservation of physically challenged persons in government job is in place since 1977, the Act has so far not been implemented in letter and spirit in many states. Physically challenged girls and women in India, about 42 percent of all disabled persons, are most vulnerable even within the women population. They lack education and they have no voice. Not only does disabled person require greater resources to overcome their handicaps, they require additional resources to meet the requirements for education, training and skill formation. When the disabilities are right from the birth or from early childhood, the problem is more acute.

12
National Human Development

12.1 Points of Departure of NHDR from HDR

Human Development Report published by UNDP since 1990 is a hall mark enabling planners, administrators and social scientists all over the world to evolve development framework and strategies to concentrate on areas for achieving the greatest well-being of people. Once these areas have been identified, the key issue before a government is to develop the most effective and efficient use of the available resources and build up the delivery system for furthering the well-being of the common man.

UNDP annual Human Development Report is based on aggregate data at the national level. A person's life style, health, life expectancy, education and many other indicators of well-being is largely dependent upon the country where he is born. What is true at a global level is generally true at the national level as well – the social and economic diversity between states, urban-rural differences, religious and caste differences in opportunities and attainments and the gender of the person. A person born in Kerala can expect to live beyond 73 years; his birth is most likely to be attended by a professional person; he is likely to be fully vaccinated and would have more than 6 years of formal schooling. Had he born in Orissa, chances are that he would not survive beyond 57 years, chances are high that his birth will not be in any medical institution, chances of full vaccination is less than 50 percent and he would receive less than 4 years of schooling. Attainments of a person therefore depends quite largely on his place of birth and residence, whether it is in rural or in urban area, as also on the sex of the person besides the economic and social background of the family in which he is born.

National Human Development Report (NHDR) 2001 published by the Planning Commission, Government of India, presents the status of human development at the state level, both in terms of gender and rural-urban dimensions. A question has justifiably been raised in NHDR if the set of indicators developed by UNDP for cross-country comparisons across least to highly industrially developed countries is appropriate for comparisons at regional level for a country. NHDR has not changed the basic indicators and the modalities for computation of indices, but has modified or accommodated a few other variables to measure the basic indicators

Human Development Report published by UNDP is an annual feature. If we take a look at the HDRs for a few consecutive years, the change in the values of HDIs for countries across the globe would appear mostly due to changes in per capita GDP. This is especially true of countries in High HDI and most of the (High) Medium HDI countries that have in a large way concentrated on economic liberalization. For the least developed countries, especially in sub-Saharan Africa, life expectancy index has become a prime mover in the change in HDI because of high prevalence of HIV/AIDS in most of these countries. World aggregate gross domestic product GDP index has increased by 8.7 percent between 1997 and 2003. In the same period HDI, Life Expectancy Index and Education Attainment Index increased by 4.96, 1.45 and 5.47 percent respectively.

Table 12.1
Departures of NHDR indicators from UNDP indicators

Attainments	*UNDP indicators*	*NHDR indicators*
	I. Human Development Index HDI	
1. Longevity	Life expectancy at birth	1. Life expectancy at age 1 2. Infant mortality rate
2. Educational attainment	1. Adult literacy rate 2. Combined enrolment ratio	1. Literacy rate in 7+ age 2. Intensity of formal education
3. Economic attainment	Real per capita GDP in PPP$	1. Per capita real consumption expenditure adjusted for inequality 2. Worker-population ratio for Gender Equality Index GEI
	II. Human Poverty Index HPI	
1. Longevity deprivation	Probability at birth not surviving to age 40	Probability at birth not surviving to age 40
2. Educational deprivation	Adult illiteracy rate	1. Illiteracy rate for the population in age group 7+ 2. Proportion of children in age group 6–18 years not enrolled in schools
3. Economic deprivation	1. Population not using improved water sources 2. Underweight children under age five	1. Proportion of population below poverty line 2. Proportion of population not receiving medical attention at birth. This has been substituted in the alternate HPI for 1991 by proportion of children in the age 12–23 months not fully vaccinated 3. Proportion of population living in kutcha houses 4. Proportion of population without access to basic amenities – safe drinking water, sanitation and electricity
	III. Gender Equality Index GEI	
1. Equally distributed life expectancy index	1. Female life expectancy 2. Male life expectancy	1. Female life expectancy 2. Male life expectancy
2. Equally distributed education index	1. Female adult literacy rate 2. Male adult literacy rate 3. Gross enrolment ratio for females 4. Gross enrolment ratio for males	1. Female adult literacy rate 2. Male adult literacy rate 3. Gross enrolment ratio for females 4. Gross enrolment ratio for males
3. Equally distributed income index	1. Population share of male and female 2. Female income index 3. Male income index	1. Worker-population ratio for females 2. Worker-population ratio for males

A major objective of NHDR has been to developing a core set of indices that reflect the common concerns, social values and development priorities of all states. The core indices, it has been felt, must be decomposable at state and sub-state levels. Further, these indices must be amenable to inter-temporal and inter-spatial analyses, as well as their sensitivity to tracking developmental changes at more frequent interval of time.

Table 12.2

Change in HDI and other indices over the years

Region/Countries	HDR 1999				HDR 2001				HDR 2005			
	HDI	LEI	EI	GDPI	HDI	LEI	EI	GDPI	HDI	LEI	EI	GDPI
World	0.706	0.69	0.73	0.69	0.716	0.70	0.74	0.71	0.741	0.70	0.77	0.75
High HDI countries	0.904	0.87	0.95	0.90	0.914	0.87	0.96	0.91	0.895	0.88	0.96	0.85
Medium HDI countries	0.662	0.69	0.72	0.58	0.684	0.70	0.75	0.61	0.718	0.70	0.75	0.70
Low HDI countries	0.416	0.43	0.45	0.38	0.442	0.46	0.45	0.41	0.486	0.35	0.53	0.58
Norway	0.927	0.89	0.98	0.92	0.939	0.89	0.98	0.94	0.963	0.91	0.99	0.99
Italy	0.900	0.89	0.93	0.89	0.909	0.89	0.94	0.90	0.934	0.92	0.95	0.94
Brazil	0.739	0.70	0.83	0.70	0.750	0.71	0.83	0.71	0.792	0.76	0.89	0.73
Sri Lanka	0.721	0.80	0.82	0.54	0.735	0.78	0.84	0.58	0.772	0.79	0.85	0.68
China	0.57	0.75	0.78	0.57	0.718	0.75	0.80	0.60	0.755	0.78	0.84	0.65
INDIA	0.545	0.63	0.54	0.47	0.571	0.63	0.56	0.52	0.602	0.64	0.61	0.56
Pakistan	0.508	0.65	0.47	0.46	0.498	0.58	0.43	0.49	0.527	0.63	0.44	0.51
Nigeria	0.456	0.42	0.58	0.37	0.455	0.44	0.57	0.36	0.453	0.31	0.66	0.39
Uganda	0.404	0.24	0.56	0.41	0.435	0.30	0.59	0.41	0.508	0.37	0.71	0.45

Instead of using life expectancy at birth as the critical health indicator, NHDR uses a composite indicator consisting IMR and expectation of life at age one. Life expectancy at birth is a good and comprehensive indicator of health and well-being. NHDR, however, argues that life expectancy at birth is a slow moving indicator and is not that sensitive as are changes in IMR or under-five mortality or maternal mortality or vaccination. Changes in these health indicators are more sensitive to development efforts at the state and sub-state level. NHDR further argues that IMR in a developing country plays a critical role both in health attainments as also in determining the fertility level in the population. Longevity in NHDR therefore is measured by IMR as well as by the expectation of life at age one.

Adult literacy of HDI has been replaced in NHDR by total literacy rate in the population since inclusion of the age group 7 to 14 years would provide a measure of 'program effect' of universal school education for all children in that age group. Intensity of formal education also states what proportion of the literate population actually is in a position to utilize their formal education into developing 'literacy skills'.

Per capita GDP or per capita State GDP does not really capture economic well-being at household level for the fact that the state provides many services that are not directly reflected in household income. Moreover, a huge majority of the workforce in India, in all developing countries in fact, is in the agricultural sector and in the unorganized employment market. Statement about expenditure on principal items can be obtained more reliably than income from various sources and from different members of the same household. Economic attainments are better captured by per capita consumption expenditure. Economic deprivation of a household is better captured in the type of house they live in, access to safe drinking water, sanitation and other basic amenities as also the household's position in respect to poverty line in the population. The data from which HDI, GEI and HPI are calculated for urban and rural populations of different states in NHDR are presented in Appendix 12.1.

NHDR followed the general principle laid down for obtaining indices for each of the three indicators as also for obtaining a composite index of Human Development for different states and the rural-urban segments of the populations separately. In scaling each indicator, the major consideration was that attainments on each of them remain comparable and at the same time ensuring that the selection of end points (maximum and minimum values on the scale) remains stable for inter-temporal comparisons for a reasonable period of time. Planning Commission believes that the scaling norms adopted in NHDR 2001 would remain valid at least about 2020 even with a reasonable pace of development. Attainment of each indicator has been given the same weight, as are done in UNDP HDR. In case of IMR, the reciprocal of the indicator has been used.

Table 12.3

Scaling norm for NHDR 2001 : HDI

Indicator	*Minimum*	*Maximum*
Per capita per month Inflation Adjusted Consumption Expenditure (at 1983 prices)	Rs 65	Rs 325
Literacy Rate for 7+ years	0	100
Adjusted intensity of formal education	0	7
Life Expectancy at age one	50 years	80 years
Infant Mortality Rate	20 per 1,000	—

12.2 Computing HDI, GEI and HPI by NHDR

12.2.1 Composite Indicator of Health Attainments

$$X_1 = 0.65 \times \frac{X_1' - 50}{80 - 50} + 0.35 \times \frac{1/X_1'' - 1/20}{1/20 - 0},$$

X_1' being life expectancy at age one and X_1'' is infant mortality rate.

12.2.2 Composite Indicator on Educational Attainment

$$X_2 = 0.35 \times e_1 + 0.65 \times e_2$$

where $e_1 = \dfrac{X_2' - 0}{100 - 0}$ and $e_2 = \dfrac{X_2'' - 0}{7 - 0}$, X_2'being literacy rate for 7+ years and X_2'' is the adjusted intensity of formal education.

12.2.3 Inflation Adjusted Consumption Expenditure

$$X_3 = \frac{X_1 - 65}{325 - 65}$$

$$HDI_J = \frac{1}{3}\sum_i (X_i)$$

where HDI is for the *j*th state on the *i*th indicator, *i* goes from 1 to 3.

12.2.3 Gender Equality Index GEI

GEI is the same as GDI of HDR (UNDP) and uses the same indicators used in HDI, but captures inequalities between men and women. The index expresses level of females as percentage to that of males in various indicators. GEI differs from GDI of UNDP in computation of economic attainments of males and females. Instead of using per capita per month income (or expenditure), GEI captures the inequality that exists between males and females in their respective worker-population ratios. This has been done to avoid taking recourse to apportioning consumptions between males and females at the same household. Educational and health attainments have been captured using the same set of indicators used in computation of HDI.

Table 12.4

NHDR estimate of HDI and GEI (GDI) for the major states of India

State	HDI 1981			HDI 1991			HDI 2001	GEI (GDI)	
	Rural	Urban	Comb	Rural	Urban	Comb		1981	1991
1	2	3	4	5	6	7	8	9	10
Andhra Pradesh	0.262	0.425	0.298	0.344	0.473	0.377	0.418	0.744	0.801
Assam	0.261	0.380	0.272	0.326	0.555	0.348	0.386	0.462	0.575
Bihar	0.220	0.378	0.237	0.286	0.460	0.308	0.367	0.471	0.469
Gujarat	0.315	0.458	0.360	0.380	0.532	0.431	0.479	0.723	0.714
Haryana	0.332	0.465	0.360	0.409	0.562	0.443	0.509	0.536	0.714
Karnataka	0.295	0.489	0.346	0.367	0.523	0.412	0.478	0.707	0.753
Kerala	0.491	0.544	0.500	0.576	0.628	0.591	0.638	0.872	0.825
Madhya Pradesh	0.209	0.395	0.245	0.282	0.491	0.328	0.394	0.554	0.662
Maharashtra	0.306	0.489	0.363	0.403	0.548	0.452	0.523	0.740	0.793
Orissa	0.252	0.368	0.267	0.328	0.469	0.345	0.404	0.547	0.639
Punjab	0.386	0.494	0.411	0.447	0.566	0.475	0.537	0.688	0.710
Rajasthan	0.216	0.386	0.256	0.298	0.492	0.347	0.424	0.650	0.692
Tamil Nadu	0.289	0.445	0.343	0.421	0.560	0.466	0.531	0.710	0.813
Uttar Pradesh	0.227	0.398	0.255	0.284	0.444	0.314	0.388	0.447	0.520
West Bengal	0.264	0.427	0.305	0.370	0.511	0.404	0.472	0.556	0.631
INDIA NHDR	0.263	0.442	0.302	0.340	0.511	0.381	0.472	0.620	0.676
UNDP (2001)			0.438			0.513	0.577		

NHDR 2001 has published HDI for all the states and Union Territories, separately for urban and rural areas. HDIs for 1981 and 1991 have been calculated based on data covering the period 1981–1983 and the same for 1991 based on data covering the period 1991 to 1993–94. Using data for 1999–2001, HDI for 2001 for the major states has been estimated. UNDP estimates of HDI for the time points 1980, 1990 and 2000 for India are also presented in Table 12.4 (last row). The two sets of data are not comparable since the indicators used in NHDR are somewhat different from those used in computation of HDI by UNDP. That HDI is improving at the national level is documented by both sets of data.

There is marked difference in HDI values for rural and urban areas. Though urban-rural gap (0.442–0.263 = 0.179 for 1981, 0.511–0.340 = 0.170 for 1991) has marginally declined, it still remains strong. The urban-rural ratio of HDI has declined from 1.7 in 1981 to 1.5 in 1991. The rural-urban gap in early nineties was highest in Madhya Pradesh and least in Kerala. In fact, HDI in rural Kerala was even better than HDI estimated for urban area for all the other states.

There has been some change in relative positions in HDI for many larger states. Madhya Pradesh has improved its rank from 14 in 1981 to 12 in 2001; Assam went down from rank 10 in 1981 to rank 14 in 2001; Andhra Pradesh went down from rank 9 in 1981 to rank 10 in 2001; Karnataka and Maharashtra also recorded drops in their HDI rankings. Tamil Nadu has registered a maximum gain in raking, from 7 in 1981 to 3 both in 1991 and 2001. Rajasthan too improved its position, from 12 in 1981 to 9 in 2001. Kerala and Punjab have maintained their first two spots in all these years. Bihar remains the least developed state. Kerala is the only major state whose HDI exceeded 0.500 – 0.500 in 1981 and 0.591 in 1991. By 2001, four other states, namely Haryana, Maharashtra, Punjab and Tamil Nadu joined Kerala in this feat. Assam, Bihar, Madhya Pradesh and Uttar Pradesh still have HDI below 0.400. In general HDI was better for smaller states and UTs. All the UTs save Dadra & Nagar Haveli had HDI in excess of 0.500 in 1991. Chandigarh and Delhi had HDI more than 0.600 in 1991. The smaller states Goa, Manipur and Mizoram also had HDI above 0.500. The momentum gained in human development in the eighties by some states was lost in the nineties. Only three of the BIMARU states, namely Rajasthan, Madhya Pradesh and Uttar Pradesh maintained the momentum. A close correspondence between consumption expenditure level and HDI is observed both for economically advanced as well as the backward states. Such correspondence is less noticed for states in the middle-income category.

NHDR has estimated attainments of females on human development indicators vis-à-vis males. GEI (or GDI), which has been expressed as a ratio of attainments for females to that of males, ranges from zero to unity (complete equality). NHDR has tried to capture the inequality in economic attainments by taking worker-population ratio separately for males and females. GEI at the national level has increased from an estimated 0.620 in 1981 to 0.676 in 1991. GDI as per 1997 UNDP data was 0.525 for India, which improved to 0.586 in 2003. Gender inequality is least in Kerala (GEI 0.825 in 1991, a drop by 0.037 point from 1981 measure) and least in Bihar (0.469). Tamil Nadu and Andhra Pradesh are the two other major states where GEI is above 0.800. There are a few smaller states (Himachal Pradesh, Manipur and Meghalaya) and Dadra & Nagar Haveli, the only UT that registered GEI more than 0.800 in 1991. In general, women are better off in Southern states than in most other parts of the country. It is observed that the states doing well in improving female literacy have done well on GEI.

12.2.4 Human Poverty Index HPI

Human Poverty Index is a measure of intensity of deprivation. Like HDI and GEI, HPI is also a composite index involving three indicators, viz., health, education and economic. This has been captured through the proportion of population not expected to survive beyond age 40 (Health), proportion of illiterate population and children not enrolled in schools (Education), and proportion of population below the poverty line, proportion of the population without access to safe drinking water, sanitation and electricity, proportion of population deprived of medical attention at birth, full vaccination for children in age group 12–23 months and proportion of population living in *kutcha* houses (Economic). There are many publicly provided goods and services or benefits for which consumption share for a person cannot be measured even approximately. The proportion of population not able to attain a specified level of expenditure on all counts is identified as poor. The minimum consumption expenditure necessary for attaining an average energy (food) norm of 2,400 and 2,100 kcal per capita per day in rural and urban areas respectively, defines State Specific Poverty Line. HPI estimates reflect the deprivational perspective on development. HPI takes values from 0 to 100. It means the higher the value of HPI (closer to 100), the greater the deprivation. HPI is calculated by the following formula:

$$HPI_j = \left[\frac{1}{3} \times (P_1^3 + P_2^3 + P_3^3)\right]^{1/3}$$

where j refers to a particular state, P_i (i = 1, 2, 3) refers to the deprivation in the three identified dimensions, such that

P_1: Longevity deprivation captured by the indicator persons not expected to survive beyond age 40 years;

P_2: Composite indicator on educational deprivation; and

P_3: Composite indicator of economic deprivation.

Composite educational deprivation is calculated by using different weights for (1) illiteracy rate in the entire population age 7 and above (ed_1) multiplied by 0.35 and (2) proportion of children in age group 6–18 not enrolled in the schools (ed_2) multiplied by 0.65.

$$P_2 = (ed_1 \times 0.35) + (ed_2 \times 0.65)$$

P_3 is calculated by the following formula:

$$P_3 = \frac{1}{4} \times \sum_i (P_{3i})$$

where i goes from 1 to 4, such that

P_{31}: Proportion of population below the poverty line,

P_{32}: Proportion of population not receiving medical attention at birth (this has later been modified to include proportion of children, aged 12 to 23 months, not fully vaccinated);

P_{33}: Proportion of people living in *kutcha* houses; and

P_{34}: Proportion of population without access to basic amenities including access to safe dinking water, sanitation and electricity.

The same three indicators used in computing HDI and GEI are also used with equal weight for each for assessing HPI. Educational and Economic deprivations are measured using more than one

Table 12.5
Human poverty index, 1981 & 1991

*State/UT**	*1981*			*1991*		
	Rural	*Urban*	*Combined*	*Rural*	*Urban*	*Combined*
1	*2*	*3*	*4*	*5*	*6*	*7*
Andhra Pradesh	56.16	29.97	50.09	45.04	24.78	39.78
Arunachal Pradesh	62.03	30.04	59.86	53.71	24.56	49.62
Assam	60.19	33.37	56.00	52.57	21.79	48.95
Bihar	61.07	33.25	57.57	55.85	28.04	52.34
Goa	33.19	19.56	29.25	24.04	14.48	
Gujarat	47.46	24.71	37.31	33.59	20.29	29.46
Haryana	43.36	22.82	38.97	32.39	17.49	28.55
Himachal Pradesh	36.84	14.10	34.05	28.09	10.14	26.21
Jammu & Kashmir	52.37	28.42	46.94	39.34	17.81	34.19
Karnataka	50.11	27.40	43.96	37.54	20.69	32.70
Kerala	34.20	22.80	32.10	21.75	14.43	19.93
Madhya Pradesh	57.74	30.30	52.15	48.43	25.04	43.47
Maharashtra	47.29	20.53	38.63	36.53	16.23	29.25
Manipur	56.81	33.97	50.82	47.49	26.22	41.53
Meghalaya	60.64	23.43	54.02	56.45	18.05	49.19
Mizoram	54.39	29.62	47.97	45.96	17.39	32.20
Nagaland	53.80	35.70	49.37	46.83	21.70	42.07
Orissa	62.50	37.90	59.34	53.07	29.23	49.85
Punjab	37.33	21.73	33.00	27.95	18.26	25.06
Rajasthan	59.54	33.47	54.16	53.28	27.79	46.67
Sikkim	53.16	25.51	52.76	40.97	16.49	34.84
Tamil Nadu	49.23	25.28	42.05	33.98	18.71	29.28
Tripura	55.19	25.64	51.86	49.54	20.37	44.89
Uttar Pradesh	59.29	36.01	54.84	52.43	31.20	48.27
West Bengal	56.06	23.61	47.64	47.00	21.52	40.48
Andaman-Nicober Islands*	45.57	19.80	39.58	31.53	15.41	27.09
Chandigarh*	30.60	16.36	17.28	25.37	13.32	14.49
Dadra-Nagar Haveli*	54.65	25.34	52.53	52.25	21.80	49.59
Daman & Diu*	32.77	18.38	28.16	28.17	16.06	22.30
Delhi*	27.36	18.66	19.27	20.90	16.60	17.01
Lakshadweep*	30.38	23.44	26.82	19.04	13.88	15.88
Pondicherry*	44.82	27.24	35.79	30.87	20.01	24.16
INDIA	**53.28**	**27.21**	**47.33**	**44.81**	**22.00**	**39.36**

Source: National Human Development Report 2001, Planning Commission, Government of India 2002.

indicators with unequal weights reflecting priorities from development perspective and the policy focus in India's development planning.

Human Poverty Index has declined considerably from HPI of 49 in 1981 to 39 in 1991. The decline has been marginally more in rural areas resulting in bridging the rural-urban gap a little. Head count (HC) data on food adequacy norm and the HPI data for states and sub-state levels are closely comparable. There are considerable variations, both by rural-urban residences and by states. The rural-urban ratio of the poor by head count method is approximately half of that obtained by HPI analysis. HPI analysis of economic deprivation vis-à-vis poverty line is a more inclusive concept dealing with deprivation of basic minimum needs as accessibility to drinking water, sanitation, electricity, health facilities, quality of residence and purchasing power. The magnitude of rural-urban differences clearly implies that there is greater scarcity of these amenities in rural area compared to that in urban area. Opportunity for income/consumption expenditure is definitely an important factor, but not the only factor operating behind this rural-urban difference.

Although the magnitude of HPI has declined in all states/UTs in the nineties, inter-state differences are still substantial. The relative positions of different states/UTs over the period have not changed much. Significant decline in HPI was observed in Himachal Pradesh, Tamil Nadu, Maharashtra, Karnataka and Kerala.

Kerala, which did not feature in either of the extreme categories in the classification of the states/UTs for poverty level in their populations, does figure prominently both in HDI and GEI among the major states. Kerala still has a significant number of people below the poverty line (12.72% in 1999–2000). There are as many as 9 states/UTs that have higher inflation and inequality adjusted per capita consumption expenditure than that in Kerala (Rs 152.74 in 1999–2000), but most of these states/UTs are way behind Kerala in literacy, enrolment ratio and in all other social indicators including health and hygiene. The state has retained the top spot in HDI and GEI since 1981. During 1981–91, Kerala improved its HPI by more than 12 points when in the national level the change was by 8 points. Whereas rural-urban ratio for the people lying below the poverty line was 1.12 and 1.15 in 1983 and 1993–94 respectively, the rural-urban ratio for HPI had remained around 2 for the time points. This implies that huge shortage in basic amenities in rural areas still remain the major concern of the social planners.

Inter-state difference in HPI is very high. Goa (29.25) and Orissa (59.34) had the smallest and largest HPI in 1981 respectively among the states. In 1991, Kerala (19.93) and Bihar (52.34) displaced Goa and Orissa from their respective positions held in 1981. Most other states/UTs generally retained their HPI ranks for the time points. All the Southern states improved their HPI by a large margin, between 11 and 15 percentage points.

13
Family Planning (Welfare) Program in India

13.1 History of Family Planning Movement in India

Today, the population growth rate in India is around 1.5 percent a year. The 2001 Census recorded a decadal growth rate of 21.34 percent (average annual growth rate for the decade 1.93%). Growth rate relative to 1901 population in the first 50 years was 51.47 percent; in the next 50 years it went up to 330.8 percent. We have added 183,084,386 persons in 10 years between 1991 and 2001, which is 76.83 percent of the population enumerated in 1901 (238.4 million). We took thousands of years to reach the 1901 population total. In 1901, with the same geographical area as it is today, India's share to the world's surface area was 2.4 percent and its share of the world population was about 15 percent. After hundred years, its share of world population has risen to 16.7 percent. By 2050, population of India is likely to overtake the population of China, the most populous country in the world today. We are adding about 50,000 people everyday.

As we look at the "demographic transition" in developed West, we notice that the Western countries in pre-industrial era were economically backward; their economy was largely dependent upon traditional agriculture. Both birth and death rates were high, and the population was growing very slowly. With improvement in certain basic facilities – drinking water, sanitation, transport, education, etc., death rate started to fall. Birth rate however continued almost at the same level as when both death and birth rates were very strong. In consequence, population started to grow fast. This period of population growth in Europe, the "transition period", lasted for three centuries which brought about a seven-fold increase in their populations. European countries brought down their death rates without much assistance from preventive and curative medicines to which the world is used to today, especially the antibiotics and sprays for pest and insect control. The developing countries are expected to stay in the 'transition" phase for a comparatively short period, probably between 50 and 100 years and therefore most of them would experience "population explosion". This is due to the fact that despite poor health infrastructure in many of these countries, deaths in all ages has successfully been brought down by utilizing the fruits of medical research in the developed countries and some improvement in the nutrition factor.

Even in the late nineteenth century India, for which relatively reliable information about a few aspects of the populations are available, it was quite clear that when there was good monsoon, no famine, no epidemic, no outbreak of diseases, the population growth gathered some momentum. Usually such periods were brief; famines and epidemics soon prevailed bringing down the population growth rate. Malthusian Doctrine remained fully operational in the population growth history of India.

As early as 1831, Rammohon Roy, while arguing for a better and just treatment of the Indians before the Committee of the House of Commons in Britain, clearly expressed his thoughts about the problems associated with India's population. He told the House that child marriage and the tendency of the male folk not to venture outside their very restricted social and physical environment were the two key causes behind population growth in India. That the population did not grow fast, he argued, was because the natural checks on population growth in India were very strong at times. He cited the incidence of large scale break out of cholera in many parts of the country in 1817–19, which, he said, actually helped bringing in a balance between various segments of the population and also arrest the population growth. Prince Dwarakanath Tagore in his articles published in 'Sambad Koumudi' (founded by Rammohon) expressed his conviction that most issues relating to population was linked to the state of economy that prevailed in the country. He emphatically said that India needed domestic as also foreign capitals for economic prosperity of the nation. He also stressed on the need for more skilled labor force to push a faster growth of economy. Dwarakanath and many others did welcome European colonies in India for two reasons – foreign capital and new entrepreneurships. It was for these reasons he and many others came out with open support for *indigo cultivation* in India. Dwarakanath also wrote that the standard of living among Indians staying in indigo plantation areas was better off compared to those in most other areas. He supported population to pick up momentum to support the economic growth of the country.

The Bengali women's magazine "Bama Bodhini" published a number of articles on the role and status of women in Indian society. In one of its issues in 1866, reviews of two books were published. The author in one book tried to establish that the declining mental and health status of women was rooted in illiteracy among women. In the other book, the author tried to show that decline in birth and population growth rates was intrinsically related to the declining proportion of children in the total population. In the same magazine, some authors drew attention to the fact that Hindu religious order permitted marriage of girls at a considerable higher age and that there was enough support for widow remarriage in our ancient literature.

At the time of first ever complete Census in India in 1872 (though not simultaneous in all the provinces), the magazine "Sulav Samachar" asked people to cooperate sincerely with the census authority. The periodical also discussed some of the conventional and more scientific methods for birth control. It asked people to lay down their superstition and look at birth planning from objective considerations of the family and the nation. Every citizen, it urged, must try to realize why birth planning was necessary and the gains that would accrue from birth planning to individual families and the nation as a whole. The periodical also insisted on debates and discussions on family planning from social and medical points of view.

Bankim Chandra Chatterjee, the pioneer in modern Bengali literature and who gifted India with the National Anthem "Bande Mataram", wrote a few articles on population in the literary magazine "Banga Darshan" edited by him. Bankim Chandra was greatly influenced by Classical economics and Malthusian thesis on population. Like Malthus, Bankim Chandra believed that nature has the greatest say in population growth. All the sufferings of mankind are nature driven. Birth of a large number of children in the family invites hardship and misery to all. The only way out of this oppressing situation is economic prosperity. He pointed out that economic growth often would not match the population growth. To diffuse this discord between population and economic growth, he stressed on two paths: redistribution of the population through migration to less populated areas and a sizeable proportion of people remaining spinsters. But none of these two, Bankim Chandra observed, were applicable to Indian population since marriage was a universal phenomenon in Indian society and redistribution of the population through internal migration and emigration could not happen on a large scale since farming was the dominant occupation for the huge majority. The gap between the farm labors and others, he observed, had been widening and the living standard of the agricultural labor force was getting worse. This, he believed, had widened the gap between various sections of people both by economic and social indicators.

In one issue of the 1877 edition of the said periodical, it was pointed out that the size of population in India was much above the level that could be sustained by the usual agricultural production. Since a large quantity of food grains was exported, import of food grains could not be thought of as a remedial measure for food security. Even with land reform, the core problem would remain. Hunger and poverty would remain a constant factor for a great majority of people. Bankim Chandra asked for substantial cut in marriage rates, bringing large areas of fallow land under cultivation and use whatever internal resources are available for building new industries and expansion of trade and commerce. Though Bankim Chandra had repeatedly advocated for controlled population growth, he like Malthus, did not favor the use of contraceptives and other artificial means to control birth.

Iswar Chandra Vidyasagar, another great son of Bengal, who pioneered the movement of widow remarriage in India, showed through logical scrutiny that children resulting from child marriage are unlikely to be of high quality and that the society would suffer as a result. He used his mighty pen against polygamy and child marriage. Dadabhai Naoroji in 1876 drew attention of intelligentsia and the administration to the very damaging effect the growth of population had created on country's food security. Bhudeb Banerjee, a well-known educationist and social reformer from Bengal, after examining population related statistics for various countries wrote in his book "Samajik Prabandha" (Social Essays) in 1892 that population growth in India was relatively small (0.6% a year). He said this slow growth of population was a road block to country's economic growth. By comparing information from many other countries, he observed that the percentage of married women in India was among the highest in the world. He also demonstrated that proportion of widows among Hindus was not any different from that observed among Muslims and other religious groups. The Census Commissioner and many others had attributed the slow growth of population to the Indian marriage system. Bhudeb Banerjee did not agree with their views. He attributed the distortion in the age and sex structure of Indian population to high death rate and emphatically said that extreme poverty lay behind the high death rate.

The last decade of the nineteenth century remains very important for social, political and demographic reasons. On the one hand, the country was preparing for a ceaseless political fight against the British rules, spread of education to defeat superstitions and mass illiteracy became the motto of the enlightened people, on the other. The national leaders like Tilak, Gokhale, Joshi and others were busy devising ways and means to address various problems of Indian humanity. Their messages were very loud and clear: eradication of poverty and hunger and improvement of poor health conditions of teeming millions would be possible only if people of India realize the importance of birth control.

History tells us that philosophers, economists, historians, political scientists and social scientists from many other disciplines have raised, discussed and debated various population issues and their possible impacts on social, economic and general well-being of people of various countries. The political leaders and those in administration taking cues from these intellectual discourses augmented population programs and encouraged population researches. But in India, it mostly happened the other way round. It was the social reformers, activists and the political leadership that drew attention of academics to the wide-ranging and deep-rooted problems concerning the Indian population. True, there was less freedom for a scientist to work according to his plan when his country was under foreign rule. But that is a poor excuse since many other scientists like J. C. Bose, P C. Roy, C. V. Raman and others had earned international recognition and fame for their enlightened works even though they did not get any encouragement and help from the British rulers. The intelligentsia in India was late to react to the country's alarming population problems.

The first two decades of twentieth century saw the rising of people of India against the rule of British Raj. These two decades also registered heavy loss of lives due to frequent epidemics in various parts of the country – plague, cholera and influenza among others. The World War I in the second decade created some confusion among our leaders if it would be wise for Indian masses to toughen the freedom movement at that critical juncture.

In 1910, Sakharam Ganesh Deuskar came out with some analytical details of certain population trends from the last four census data of Indian population. People generally were made to believe that Hindus were losing their share in the population to other religious groups, especially to Muslims. Deuskar, after analyzing the growth pattern of population in various states as also the composition of their populations, came to the conclusion that population growth rate among different religious segments were almost similar except in East Bengal (now Bangladesh). Because of high birth rate, population growth rate in East Bengal was high relative to that in other areas and a slightly higher growth rate was noticed among the Muslims. After analyzing the migration data, Deuskar came to the conclusion that higher growth rate among Bengal's Muslims lay in inter-state migrations: a large number of Muslims from other states migrated to Bengal in search of jobs and a simultaneous exodus of large number of high caste Hindus from Bengal to other states. But the most significant publication on population in this period was P.K. Wattal's *The Population Problem in India* (1916). After analyzing the various Census data, Wattal was convinced that the high birth and death rates in India as also the poor state of living for the majority were rooted in our undefined social policy. He was convinced that high birth rate and heavy death tolls especially among young children and women in the country were mostly due to the effects of child marriage. He canvassed loud and clear that the custom of giving girls to marriage before they were physically and mentally matured to take on the responsibility of motherhood must be stopped by all means. The Sarda Act, passed in 1929, subsequently placed the minimum age at marriage of girls at 14.

The year 1921 is reckoned as the year of Great Demographic Divide in India. The population of India grew exceedingly slowly prior to 1921. Only 12 million increases in population were recorded in 30 years between 1891 and 1921. Since the beginning of the synchronous periodical census in 1881, the only decade when India registered a decline in the size of population was 1911–21. Famines and epidemics, especially the devastating influenza epidemic in 1918–19 were the causes behind the reduction of population in the decade. An estimated 6–7 million loss of lives in India occurred in the single year 1918–19. Between 1898 and 1918, about half a million deaths were recorded every year due to plague alone. Since 1921, India remained relatively free from the ravages of famines and epidemics. The consequent decline in the death rate, rather than any increase in the birth rate, saw India attain a faster growth of population.

India's population during 1961–71 grew by 109 million, which equals the growth of population in India in 30 years between 1921 and 1951. The population grew by 1.05 percent annually during 1921–31, by 1.34 percent during 1931–41 and by 1.26 percent between 1941 and 1951. The slowing down of growth during 1941–51 could be attributed to 1942–43 Bengal famine, World War II casualties and also to the dislocations caused by the partition of India in 1947. The period 1921–51 in

India's population planning history remains important for various reasons. Seeing the take off in growth rate in the last decade, the Census Commissioner in 1931 advised the government to initiate programs for birth control all over the country.

Indian economists had been talking quite loudly about how the growth of population has been increasingly impacting upon food supply and the labor market. Many social thinkers and social activists had been pressing the government to institute a population control program. Mahatma Gandhi too wrote in favor of birth control in 1925; but like Malthus, he too was opposed to artificial control of birth. He wrote:

> (T)here can be no two opinions about the necessity of birth control, but the only method handed down from ages past is *brahmacharya* or self control.

However, he said that if the male folks demanded, sterilization through vasectomy could be accepted. Gandhi was against any such surgical operation on females.

Probably the first formal birth control clinic in India was opened in Bombay (now Mumbai) by Prof. R.D. Karve in 1925. That was not taken kindly by the administration and the Professor had to resign from his post. Opinion of educated people favoring family planning was gaining momentum. The first government-initiated family planning clinic was opened in Bangalore in 1930. Two years later in 1932, the government of Madras (now Tamil Nadu) opened birth control clinics in the Madras Presidency. In the same year, the All India Women's Conference at Lucknow passed a resolution recommending that "men and women should be instructed in methods of birth control in recognized clinics". In 1935, the National Planning Committee, appointed by the Indian National Congress under the Chairmanship of Jawaharlal Nehru, strongly supported family planning. One of the recommendations of the Committee was:

> ... [I]n the interest of social economy, family happiness and national planning, family planning and a limitation of children are essential and the state should adopt a policy to encourage these.

In the year following, Dr A.P. Pillai conducted a family planning training course. In 1939, a few birth control clinics were set up in Uttar Pradesh and Madhya Pradesh. Subhash Chandra Bose, President of Indian National Congress in 1939, asked for a countrywide movement for birth control to keep the growth of population under check. A subcommittee under the Chairmanship of Radhakamal Mukherjee was formed to advice the National Planning Committee on matters relating to population. On the basis of the report submitted by this committee, the National Planning Committee urged that unless population pressure was curbed, the quality of population in India could not be improved. It said that the country needs to undertake a development plan to bring down the inequality in living standards among various segments of the population. The Committee also said that the state ought to develop a plan which would ensure people's participation in the family planning movement and inspire them to accept 'a small family norm'. The Committee recommended the following:

1. The age at marriage has to be increased gradually;
2. To obtain a genetically improved population, marriage of mentally retarded or deranged persons and those who have epileptic history must be prevented; if already married, they must be sterilized so that a check can be applied for transmissible diseases of serious nature;
3. Polygamy is strictly to be prohibited; and

4. Birth control clinics should be established all over the country so that people can benefit from expert advice on birth planning and contraceptive methods at a minimum cost.

The Committee also put emphasis on "self-control" in birth control.

P.N. Sapru in 1940 moved a resolution in the Council of States (the Upper House of the Parliament) for establishing birth control clinics all over India. The government appointed the Health Survey and Development Committee in 1943 under the Chairmanship of Joseph Bhore. The Bhor committee in its report in 1946 observed that since famines and epidemics were under reasonable control and provisions for improved public health had already been enlarged, the country soon would face the problems arising from population growth. The Committee recommended that birth control clinics needed to be opened in all government hospitals. The Committee preferred 'deliberate limitations' to 'self control' for family planning. The Committee recommended that doctors must advice on the use of contraceptives to those couples where conception could lead to health risk either to the mother or the child or both; it recommended further that contraceptives through public agencies are made available to people free of cost. Though there were differences of opinion if there should be a public policy on birth control, the Committee unanimously recommended that:

1. Various types of contraceptives are to be manufactured and their distribution outlets must be under direct control of the government.
2. The government must encourage research for contraceptive development and make provisions for this purpose.
3. There must be a provision for periodic review of the issues related to population and birth control.

In 1949, the Family Planning Association of India (FPAI) was formed in Mumbai under the presidency of Shrimati Dhanavanthi Rama Rao. Such associations are found in almost all developed countries. The FPAI played a noteworthy role in spreading the message of family planning through out the country. The first all India Conference on Family Planning was held in Bombay in 1951 under the auspices of FPAI, chaired by Prof. S. Chandrasekhar. In the very next year, an international conference on the same issue was held. In 1951, the Indian government in collaboration with United Nations instituted an in-depth population study in Mysore. The report of this hall-mark survey, popularly called Mysore Study, was published in 1960.

13.2 Launching of Official Family Planning Program

India is the first country in the world to officially promote family planning in 1952 with the expressed desire for a lower rate of population growth and stabilize the population at a level consistent with the requirements of the national economy. The ground work for the policy was worked out between 1931 and 1951. There was political consensus to undertake such a unique policy. Both Dr Rajendra Prasad, the first President of India and Jawaharlal Nehru, the first Prime Minister had no hesitation in their mind that something needed to be done to put a check on the growth of population if the social and economic objectives of this new Republic were to be realized. India needed huge investment in social sector, especially in health and education, as also in employment generation through rapid industrialization. A check on population growth rate would come handy for addressing these pressing needs.

The Planning Commission had no hesitation in admitting that a rapidly growing population can become a threat to economic development and therefore family planning must be made an integral part of the country's development program. Since family planning has not been in the state agenda for any country developed or developing, the Indian planners did not have any opportunity of taking lessons from others' experiences. The path India followed can be compared to surveys that are conducted on issues for which literatures are very scanty (experiencing survey). The program that India followed in the first two plan periods was really to gather experiences and assess the attitude of people, especially of rural folk, towards birth control.

Initially, family planning program was conceived as a movement to relieve the pressure of population on the supply of very basic necessities of life. In absence of improved technology and capital, production of consumer goods including food grains could not be increased at a pace consistent with the growth of population. The planners did not have a clear idea about what effect a long term population planning could have on the all-round development of the nation. This turned out to be an important cause why family planning in India at its initial phase did not receive the attention it really deserved. The participation of many internationally accepted family planning specialists in advisory capacity helped the government to modify family planning program from time to time. The review of the past performances in program implementation made it clear that family planning was needed to be integrated into the total development plan of the country.

The Planning Commission was aware that birth control, family planning, contraceptives, etc. are very personal issues, sensitive to a common man. For every innovative plan there are two equally important aspects – involvement of science and technology and the social and political environment to support the idea. The final decision about the course to be followed in the implementation of the plan of course is taken by politicians. In a democracy often public perception of an issue overwhelms the scientific and technological prescriptions associated with it.

Consistent with the democratic set up in the country, the policy formulators have emphasized on voluntary acceptance of birth control and family planning in India. A very large segment of Indian population is illiterate or poorly educated. The accountability of high population growth rate in the country squarely lies on these poor, uneducated and superstitious people. The imposition of birth control on them could have solved many problems of the country, but that would have violated the fundamental rights guaranteed by Indian Constitution. Keeping this in mind, the emphasis had been from the very beginning of the program on 'mass education and motivation'. The media, both print and audio-visual, has been extensively used for propagating the message of 'small family norm'. The fundamentals of the officially sponsored family planning agenda in India (except for a brief period during 'internal emergency' in 1975–77 when a great deal of coercive measure was taken for birth control) revolve around a few assertions on the part of the government:

1. The individual couples shall have the absolute say about the number of children they ought to have for their family;
2. Only those media agencies that have proven credibility in the eyes of common man are to be used for addressing the public on issues relating to family planning. For personal contact, only those persons would be reposed with the responsibility who commands respect of the common man and have proven credibility in the eyes of those whom they are to lead;
3. Public is to be instructed on the various methods of birth control in order to enable them to take decisions when they do decide to adopt some birth control measure;

4. Care should be taken so that people do not have to go to distance places to get expert advice and contraceptives;
5. Integrate family planning with public health programs, especially mother and child health care (MCH), which would improve its relevance and usefulness.

13.2.1 Clinical Approach

The family planning program in the first two Five Year Plans (1951–56 and 1956–61) had been an experience gathering exercise and the modus operandi of the program in this period is popularly referred to as Clinical Approach. By the end of the Second Plan, 4,165 family planning clinics were opened besides creating units in hospitals and health centers to cater expert advice and other services to couples seeking counsel on birth control. After a very limited progress in the First Plan period and the widely discussed remarks of the 1951 Census Commissioner about 'improvident maternities', the Central Family Planning Board was set up in 1956 and State Family Planning Committee in each state was appointed. Training schemes were set in motion. The Family Planning Committee of the Third Five Year Plan began to establish norms for family planning centers. Staff shortage has remained a major constraint, and little besides condoms and foam tablets could be offered to the clients. Sterilization was just beginning to show its relevance in Indian society although only 122,000 men and women were operated between 1951 and 1961. The Third Plan offered 100 percent financial assistance to states for training, staff and creating facilities for sterilization, which was to be offered free regardless of the economic status of the persons undergoing operation.

The Family Planning Committee felt that Community Development (CD) network was to be made responsible for motivational work and extensive education on family planning were to be given to the CD personnel so that they can operate as catalysts in infusing faith in family planning services offered by the state.

13.2.2 Extension Approach

This new plan was given a go signal after reviewing the performances and other feed backs from the first two Plan periods. It was realized that for the success of family planning program it is imperative that an uninterrupted campaign goes on to educate people of the benefits of a small family and help change their traditional beliefs, attitudes and mind-set that a large number of children are assets to a family. The government must use all its resources at hand to bring in a positive change in people's attitude towards birth control. That births can be and should be planned was a new concept for the majority of the population. The social scientists have repeatedly observed that there is always a resistant among people to accept any innovation, especially if they appear to go against the time-honored beliefs and customs. There is no ready market for every new commodity. Before the commodity is marketed, a well coordinated campaign needs to be organized to inform people about the salient features of the commodity and also explain how the acceptance of this product can improve and change peoples' life style. The social scientists have found five distinct layers in the process of adoption of an innovation (family planning is an innovation to many):

1. Unrelenting campaign;
2. All the information about the product (innovation);
3. Results of experimental application of this innovation;

4. A detailed and critical analysis of the negative and positive features of the innovation based on extensive surveys and experimentations;
5. Acceptance of the innovation only after developing confidence on the product or innovative ideas.

This clearly indicates that there would be a considerable time lag between awareness of the presence of a new commodity and its acceptance. The scientists also have observed that anything and everything that is communicated may not have a buyer even if there was a ceaseless campaign for the product. The source of information is as important as the person or the agency communicating it. When the message comes from someone very close to the individual or someone whose identity is clearly known and who is respected by the community for his knowledge and integrity, there is far less resistance to buy the views expressed by him than when the same comes from a stranger. It is a fact that an individual's perception on an issue can be molded with considerable ease by the pressure of his own community than by some one who is considered an outsider.

For effective implementation of this Extension program, persons selected by village councils were helped to understand the benefits that would accrue to the family and society once people accept 'small family norm'. They were also given extensive training in various aspects of family planning campaign and the methods that were commonly followed in birth planning. Being a son of the soil, the extension worker had easy access to families under his jurisdiction and the goal of reaching a large number of families in quickest time became possible. At the beginning of the extension program it was decided to concentrate on such communities where resistance was expected to be less. Success attained and experiences thus gained, it was believed, would make family planning campaign with other groups easier. The success of 'small family' campaign depended on how quickly and effectively the anti-birth-control mind-set of the poor and the illiterates could be transformed into a favorable one. The government asked the social scientists to get actively involved in this campaign.

Since 1950, innumerable KAP (knowledge, attitude and practice) surveys have been carried out in all parts of the country. But the family planning programmers did not use the observations from these studies much in formulating their plans. Quite a few excellent studies in 1950s and 1960s were conducted, which pointed to many shortcomings and lack of clear direction in the official family planning policy. Here we must refer to two very thought provoking studies. The first one is UN and Government of India sponsored *The Mysore Population Study* and the other the *Couple Fertility* by A. Dasgupta and others. Even the findings of these resourceful studies did not find much relevance in the formulation of our population policy. It is a fact that there was no *model* before the Indian planners to take lessons from. The ad-hoc-ism in family planning (and in many other issues) in India has for good reasons have been criticized by many.

It was only in the Third Plan that a target for birth control was set. It was urged that CBR was to be brought down to 25 per 1,000 populations as quickly as possible (How ridiculous the target was is borne by the fact that this target could not be reached even in 2001). To achieve this, the message of birth planning was to be conveyed to at least 90 percent of eligible couples. Three principal components of the mass campaign were

1. Acceptance of 'small family norm';
2. Let everyone know about the methods by which birth control could be achieved; and

3. Expert advice and service along with easy availability and access to all types of contraceptives are assured.

To make the Extension program work, emphasis was laid on the following:

1. Education of the masses;
2. Develop an efficient distribution system so that people do not have to walk long distances for advice and to collect the contraceptives;
3. Health centers are to be so equipped that they are able to provide all types of services;
4. A regular statistical evaluation is to be undertaken to asses the impact the family planning program has on birth rate;
5. Proper administrative coordination has to be established between various aspects of the family planning program; and
6. A good training program has to be arranged for those who would be connected with various aspects of the family planning program.

With the adoption of Extension Approach, some changes were made in the organizational set up in 1963. In 1966, a separate Directorate for Family Planning was created under the Ministry of Health and Family Planning.

1961 Census was a red herring to the planners since the population growth was faster than what was anticipated. In fact, Gopalaswamy, the Census Commissioner of 1951, asked the government to take some anticipatory measures when he made remarks about 'improvident maternity'. On the invitation of the Government of India, UN Evaluation Mission came to India in 1964 to make an assessment of the family planning program and advise the government on ways and means to make the program more effective. They stressed on a more elaborate and comprehensive strategy: integrate family planning into programs of general social development and health planning. It recommended widespread use of paramedical staff to fit Intra-Uterine Device, IUD – a recommendation whose wisdom was doubted by many. The Mission specifically stressed on a few other aspects:

- The Marriage Act is to be implemented strictly, and greater attention needs to be paid to education of women;
- Legalize abortion for certain social and health reasons;
- The facilities that are offered to women on account of pregnancy need revision so that women in reproductive age become less interested to become pregnant.

13.2.3 Cafeteria Approach

It was decided that every hospital in cities and districts was to have a family planning unit. More family planning clinics were to be established in urban areas. Primary Health Centers (PHC) were to have two doctors, one of who would be primarily responsible for family planning duties. Extending from PHCs, there would be sub-family planning centers for every 10,000 people. Auxiliary nurses, mid-wives (ANSs), extension educators and health assistants, lady health visitors (one for each 40,000 population) and statistical and other staff would also man the PHCs. Private voluntary agencies, such as Family Planning Association, would be encouraged to operate side by side with the official program and such agencies would be given some official assistance.

The new Department of Family Planning would coordinate the whole program. The administrative structure ran through the State Family Planning Departments to the district level. The perspective of this program was that a series of service points, aided by an extension system of male and female family planning workers, were to run in parallel with and sharing the functions and facilities of health services. Each service point was to deliver as many as possible of the contraceptive methods available so that people seeking advice would have the freedom to choose from among the birth control methods available. It is for this reason that the method was named Cafeteria Approach. A massive campaign for small family was organized through media. The inverted red triangle became the symbol of family planning. This symbol has been adopted in many other countries as well.

At the beginning of family planning movement, the major emphasis was on IUCD or IUD, popularly called 'Lippy's loop'. It was inexpensive, consisting of a small piece of inert plastic coil, and could be inserted even by a trained ANM. This was one of the most popular methods used all over the world prior to arrival of improved oral pills. Its contraception efficiency was very high though not 100 percent even when it remained securely in place. By 1966–67, only one year after the IUD campaign had started, 0.9 million women were fitted with IUD. The following year the number came down to 0.67 million and by 1970 it dropped to 0.5 million. It went up to 0.6 million in 1975–76. The ups and downs in IUD acceptors were mostly due to the reported side effects attended upon the use of loops. The near one million IUD acceptors at the very beginning of the program, some believe, happened because the motivated women came in large numbers to swell the acceptor level. In the later years, the less motivated clients were targeted and the size of acceptors fell. One major reason for drop of IUD acceptors in rural areas was that most often a woman had to travel miles to present her to the clinic to receive her IUD and subsequent advice. "Expulsion", i.e., 'spontaneous rejection' of the loop or 'removal', that is, deliberate taking out the device by the woman herself or by a doctor are reported common phenomenon in all countries. IUDs are quite effective when they are used for birth spacing.

Expulsion rate (called 'event rate') is least in the first year. The expulsion rates are smaller the greater the age of women. The 'loops' come in different sizes. Selecting the right size of IUD for insertion is important. This aspect of IUD was not given due attention when Indian women were fitted with the device. This caused problems for many. Larger size IUD has better contraceptive efficiency but is more uncomfortable to the acceptor. Their retention rate is better since their removal requires the help of doctors. It is also common that after insertion of the device, the acceptor may suffer from some pain, develop headache and excessive bleeding during menstruation. Bleeding probably constitute the most troublesome symptom which alarms the acceptor as well as the doctor. Excessive bleeding requires active treatment and sometimes the removal of the device.

The skill of the doctor fitting the IUD is very important. Indian doctors lacked the skill and training, at least in the initial stage. The doctors knew all the problems that were likely to follow after insertion. Since most acceptors were illiterate, the program coordinators felt that the number of acceptors could come down drastically if they were told in advance of the problems that were likely to happen after insertion of IUD. That was probably a wrong line pursued. Soon people came to know about these problems from other acceptors. This did have a negative effect on the prospective acceptors. The 'rumor effect' seems to have derailed India's family planning effort at various points of time. There have been innumerable cases of severe impairment of local programs by the spread of stories about the supposed or actual side-effects, the stories that influence the potential clients, even otherwise satisfied clients.

By 1965, it became clear that achieving fertility target of 25 per 1,000 populations by 1974 would not be possible. The think tank of the population program also felt that IUD could be a supplementary measure for birth control, but the real check was to be attained through sterilization. Sterilization had gained some momentum since 1956 (first official program became available in Madras in 1956). Whereas only 7,153 cases of sterilization (vasectomy and tubectomy combined) were recorded in 1956, it steadily rose to 269,565 in 1964. The program was expanded to offer sterilization in all hospitals and PHCs. It started picking up since 1965–66 (670,823 sterilizations) and reached the peak in 1967–68 (over 1.8 million) since the government introduced payment of a fee to the client in 1966. Vasectomy had gained popularity all through these years and in 1967–68 its share in total sterilization was as high as 90 percent. Mass vasectomy camps were organized in various parts of the country to reach the sterilization targets. It is worth referring to a mass vasectomy clinic organized by Dr D.N. Pai in the main Bombay railway station in 1970. The passenger traffic was of the order of 200,000 or more people daily. Soon vasectomies were carried out at a rate of 1,000 per month. Since a great majority of the passengers were regular travelers, the rate of operations soon came down. Bombay program went on to employ mobile clinics at markets and places with large gatherings. Inspired by Dr Pai's imaginative work in Bombay, the Collector of Ernakulam district in Kerala took over the Town Hall of Ernaculam and arranged 40 booths under trained doctors. An extensive campaign was carried out in the area and transports were arranged to bring clients from various parts of the town. A fairly large incentive, Rs 100 to each person undergoing sterilization including gifts in kind and lucky prizes were offered. Over 15,000 vasectomies were performed in one month. In 1971, another camp was organized in the same place, this time drawing people from wider regions, and carried out 63,000 vasectomy operations. In 1970–72, 14 percent of the couple in reproductive age in the district was protected by vasectomy, a proportion achieved in entire Kerala in six years 1965–71. The central government earlier showed little interest in vasectomy camps. But soon it became convinced of the efficacy of the camp approach, and encouraged the states to hold such camps. There was an invariable report of success when the first camp was organized in different states, but performances in repeat camps were disappointing. Stories also began to circulate about various malpractices connected with such camps.

More than two-thirds of plan allocation for family planning was spent in payment of fees to doctors, promoters/motivators and the clients. Normally, vasectomy is an extremely safe and effective procedure, and relatively free from side-effects though psychological trauma is often reported. Swelling and pain may accompany the operation for a brief period. But as it happened with most public programs (IUD, for example), the post-operative care was very inadequate, and many of those undergoing vasectomy, especially in camps, reported pain and illness. There was also opposition to vasectomy, especially in villages for a number of social reasons – vasectomized persons were ridiculed as 'eunuchs'; they became the object of great shame if their wives became pregnant; they were looked at suspiciously about their sexual morality, etc. Like the 'rumor' with IUD, these complaints too acted against intensification of the sterilization program. By 1970–71, total sterilization in the country came down to 1.3 million and the share of vasectomy to total sterilization dropped to 67 percent. In 1973–74, sterilization dropped to less than a million after the spurt in 1972–73 to 3.1 million, two-thirds of this in camps. The second UN Mission visited India in 1969. They examined India's family planning program and expressed their discomfort at the emphasis on sterilization. They recommended widespread use of IUD and training of paramedical staff to fit the device. The recommendations seem to have made not much impact on family planning program in India.

Proportion of vasectomy to total sterilization rose from 67 percent in 1970–71 to 84 percent in 1972–73. In 1973–74, sterilization figure was down to 0.95 million, vasectomy covering only 43 percent. By 1974, the Family Planning Department had abandoned major emphasis on the camp approach, partly because of the rumors associated with the organization of camps and partly because of financial stringency.

Indian family planning program from the very beginning had encountered a very nasty problem – hasty and enthusiastic adoption of a new strategy without going thorough review of the results of the previously adopted strategy. The despondency of mass sterilization path to curtail birth rate had something to do with the payment of fees to the 'motivator', especially when the 'motivator' himself was a person in authority. It is one thing to pay a modest incentive to the poor client, but it is altogether a different matter, unethical too, when a fee is paid to someone who brings in a client. 'Motivators' brought in men, some of who were too old, unmarried or even impotent or with sterile wives. They also coaxed many young men and others who may not have wanted the operation. They misled them about the nature of the operation and its consequences. They often took not only their own fee, but a good share of that due to the client. In fact, it often took the form of coercion. For instance, it has been reported that some farmers were told that they would be refused fertilizer supplies and credit unless they would give their consent to undergo sterilization. Such strong-arm measures became a very dominant feature in the 19 months period of Emergency.

The revised target of the Planning Commission in 1969 of CBR 32 by 1974 soon proved illusive. The Fifth Plan (1974–79) made population projections on the assumptions that the average CBR between 1976 and 1981 would be 30 and that CBR 25 could be achieved for 1981–85. The 1971 Census showed a decadal growth of 24.8 percent (geometric growth rate of 2.24) with population standing at 548 million, indicating an addition of 180 million in the last 20 years, 110 million since 1961. SRS data indicated CBR still at 37, CDR around 15 and IMR around 130. The Census estimates of these rates were still higher. There has been massive unemployment among educated as well as uneducated people. On the eve of emergency in 1975, an estimated 26 million people in India were unemployed out of a total labor force over 200 million. The momentum of the economy attained in the two World Wars accelerated considerably in the first two Plan periods. But the 1962 war with China, 1965 and 1971 wars with Pakistan and poor food grain productions in consecutive years and massive import of food grains in the mid-sixties totally jeopardized India's economic progress. Massive transfer from agriculture to non-agricultural occupations envisaged by the planners did not materialize. While the share of agriculture to the national income sharply declined from 57 percent in 1951 to 43 percent in 1973–74, share of agricultural population stood firmly at 70 percent indicating growing unemployment and disguised underemployment in the country. The land reform movement had been shunted and the 1971 Census clearly indicated a massive increase in the landless agricultural laborers.

The Bucharest Declaration (1974), "Development is the best contraceptive", appeared to many only a slogan in the context of population explosion in the country. Mrs Gandhi and her government felt intensely that all efforts for rapid economic development and improvement in the standard of living in the country would remain a casualty if stronger steps were not taken to bring down birth rates even if that meant going totally against the declared policy that birth control was a matter of personal choice and that the government was to act only as a facilitator in the choice-making.

During and after the Bangladesh Liberation War in 1971 a mass exodus from Bangladesh to India aggravated social and economic problems. Added to this, there were poor harvests in 1972, 1973 and 1974. There was oil crisis. There were numerous allegations how corruption had been rampant in public enterprises and the dubious methods of fund raising for the Congress Party. Jai Prakash Narayan's anti-corruption campaign was gathering momentum and most opposition parties got actively associated with it. Then came the final blow: Allahabad High Court in June 1975 annulled Mrs Gandhi's election to parliament in 1971. The judgment could not be reversed except through amendment of Constitution. The decline of her popularity among her own MPs and party workers, especially because an extra-constitutional power center that already had developed around her eldest son Sanjay Gandhi, could have forced her to take a drastic decision. She did not wait for the results of her appeal in the Supreme Court. On 26 June 1975, the infamous Declaration of Emergency was signed by the President of India. Mrs Gandhi's opponents including some of her own party men were put under detention and press censorship was instituted. With most prominent opposition members behind the bar, the government had little difficulty in clearing various measures to permit Mrs Gandhi to continue with programs legally as the Prime Minister.

13.2.4 The National Population Policy Statement 1976

The National Population Policy Statement was released on 16 April 1976. It was neither placed in the Parliament nor was it adopted. The opening paragraph of the Statement argued that

1. reducing the rate of population increase "will have to be treated as top national priority and commitment";
2. "to wait for education and economic development to bring about a drop in fertility is not a practical solution"; and
3. population control must play a crucial role in the movement toward economic independence and social transformation.

The National Population Policy Statement declared:

> Government have decided on a series of fundamental measures ..., which, it is hoped, will enable us to achieve the planned target of reducing the birth rate from an estimated 35 per thousand in the beginning of the Fifth Plan (1974) to 25 per thousand at the end of the Sixth (1984). Allowing for the steady decline in the death rate that will continue due to improvement in our medical and public health services and the living standards of our people, this is expected to bring down the growth rate of population in our country to 1.4 percent by 1984.

The rest of the Statement was a package of directives, disqualifications, and entitlements addressed to the state and the individual. The Policy Statement reminds one of the family planning policy followed in China to bring down the population growth rate to zero before the end of the millennium. Whereas issuing "birth card" and forced "abortion" for unauthorized conception were the principal mechanisms to bring down the birth rate in China, India followed the path of compulsory sterilization. The text of the Statement confirms the type of coercion that was to follow in the next nine months: "public opinion is now ready to accept much more stringent measures for family planning than before". How committed and rigid Mrs Gandhi was in enforcing compulsory sterilization would become very clear from this quote: "… some personal rights have to be kept in abeyance for the human right of the nations – the right to live, the right to progress." The government did not rule out enactment of a central law making sterilization compulsory. For the time being, the Policy Statement gave state legislators to go ahead to pass such laws. The Statement recommended compulsory sterilization only after a couple had had three children. Monetary compensation for sterilization acceptors was also increased. Some states like Maharashtra, Punjab and Haryana even were ready with draft bills for compulsory sterilization. These bills included even penalty clauses for those who violate the two-child norm (none of them physically or mentally crippled). The maximum number of excesses was committed in Haryana.

Probably the first sign of intimidation was seen in the Turkman Gate episode early in 1976. At the initiative of Sanjay Gandhi a demolition drive of hutments in the Jama Masjid area in old Delhi was carried out. Housing facilities for those evicted from their hutments were offered only to persons who would submit to sterilization. This 'slum clearance' drive and the greatest volume of sterilization excesses happened to have occurred in North Indian states where Sanjay Gandhi was very influential. Sanjay Gandhi became publicly identified with the sterilization drive in India. In addition to 20-point program, the Youth Congress, of which Sanjay Gandhi was the President, declared additional 5-point agenda, which included family planning program. The state governments were instructed even to use all employees under their command, directly or indirectly, for implementation of the family planning program. The state governments were given the option to grant additional privileges to those employees who would undergo sterilization. The center of course officially denied its backing, even deplored, for any coercive measure at the same time when such measures were in operation in full swing.

Compulsory sterilization was not really new in India in spite of its claim that the decision for birth control was left to individual couples. Sporadic cases of forced sterilization were known even in pre-1976 days. Many states had acquired clients for their sterilization camps by a variety of unsavory means. Although never accepted as the final solution, sterilization was accepted as inescapable as a major program for birth control in India. But the country was not prepared for the harshness with which the government sought to implement its family planning agenda taking the advantage of Emergency. Sterilization, which is the most effective method for birth control in a poorly literate country like India, became a symbol of denial of all that one was entitled to expect from its own elected government. Planning Commission in 1970 and the Operations Research Group, Baroda in 1976 carried out surveys among those who had accepted sterilization in mass sterilization camps. Both the studies came almost to the same stunning conclusion that a very large proportion of the acceptors of sterilization, especially vasectomy, admitted that their primary motivation for undergoing operation was financial compensation offered. That is, their extreme poverty level often led them to take such a vital decision.

The public anger that followed this coercion was clearly seen when Congress was voted out of power in 1977 parliamentary election. Family planning excesses during emergency became a major arsenal at the hand of united oppositions in the election campaign against Congress that followed the lifting of emergency and declaration of fresh poll in the country. The poor performance of Congress in 1977 election was also a clear alarm to prospects of family planning in India, at least in the short run. Foreign experts and international donor agencies were also bewildered about what had happened in India in the period of Emergency and soon thereafter. The international observers have been trying to make the Indian government realize that they had not been doing enough to take more aggressive and effective steps in family planning. The alarming scale of sterilization in nine months made them dismayed. Some international agencies involved in giving aids to India, became so nervous that they were in dilemma whether to continue their aid program and some, like International Planned Parenthood Federation, publicly dissociated themselves from the aid program to India.

In 1976–77, about 8.3 million sterilizations were done as against a target of 4.3 million. This was about 50 percent of sterilizations done all over the world in that year. Monthly salary of some government employees were withheld who in spite of having more than two children did not undergo sterilization. Government employees were asked to bring at least two clients every year for sterilization, failing which their yearly increments would be stopped. Each state during Emergency was given quotas for sterilization (comparable to distribution of birth card in China). Some states carried out sterilization much in excess of their quota. The number of sterilizations done in Delhi and Haryana were 475 and 425 percent respectively of their assigned quota. In Madhya Pradesh alone, one million sterilizations were carried out.

Desirability of a sharp reduction in birth rate to alleviate the adverse economic conditions is all too evident. A sharp reduction in child population would help transfer of some public fund from education and other welfare services to other sectors to enlarge and consolidate economic activity, savings and investments (*demographic dividend*). In the long run, a slower growth rate of labor force would help raise wages and create a demand for better quality workforce. It was a necessity for India at that stage paving the way for transition from labor-intensive, less efficient production to a more efficient capital-intensive economy. Many economists and demographers appreciated many features of the 1976 Policy Statement. A close examination of the Statement shows that some of the assertions were mere renewals of earlier initiatives and others could and should have been taken up earlier: *arrangement of state allocation of funds, the marriage age proposal, increased incentive to acceptors and disincentive for those who flout the norm, increased emphasis on female literacy and maternal and child health care, introducing 'population' in the educational curricula, etc.* Child Marriage Restraint Act, 1976 came into being fixing minimum age at marriage of girls at 18 years and 20 years for boys. Earlier in 1956 Hindu Code Bill raised the minimum age at marriage of girls to 15 years. The intelligentsia opposed the harshness and the selective manner in which they were implemented during Emergency. In reply to a question if sterilization drive has been a mistake, Mrs Gandhi said to BBC on 21 July 1977:

> The mistake was that it was left to officials largely, instead of citizens taking up and persuading people. The government's policy was not coercion at all. Somehow there were sort of both things – on the one side perhaps over-zealousness of people thinking that would each compete with the other in doing more, and some times people doing things deliberately in order to make the government and the program unpopular.

Although the Janata government under Morarji Desai was not opposed to family planning, it was against compulsory sterilization. Since the new political combine came into power on a negative campaign against the Congress government (corruption, nepotism, flouting all democratic norms, censorship of the press and media, making the administration a puppet at the hands of a few corrupt politicians, disrespect for the judiciary, coercion for compulsory sterilization, etc.), the Janata government imposed President's Rule in states under Congress rule and instituted Commissions to Enquire into many of the lapses of Mrs Gandhi's government. Shah Commission was appointed to enquire into the excesses committed by the previous government in family planning program. The family planning workers were apprehensive of the intensions of the government. The family planning program came almost to a dead halt. The number of sterilization slumped to a mere 90,000 in the very first year of Janata party rule from 8.3 million in the last year of 30 years of uninterrupted Congress regime.

Postmortem analysis of the Emergency seems to indicate that excesses committed in sterilization was a leading cause of popular disenchantment with Mrs Gandhi's government. The general apprehension was that the new government at the center would dismantle the family planning program (the Health Minsiter Raj Narayan, who was the victorious MP after Allahabad High Court annulled Mrs Gandhi's election to Parliament 1971, openly said that 'sterilization of human beings' was a barbaric act. He was removed from the cabinet by Morarji Desai probably because of his anti-family planning stanch). However, the government only replaced "family planning" by "family welfare" and issued a National Population Policy Statement, second in two years. The new Population Policy Statement of 29 June 1977 substantially reiterated the Statement of 1976 and indicated that sterilization would continue as the principal birth control method, but there would be no compulsion.

Morarji Desai government realized that the success of family welfare program rested upon voluntary participation of common man. The government launched a Community Health Program, under which one person was to be selected by the village council from each of around 600,000 villages for training as part-time village health worker to promote public health and family planning in villages. By the end of 1979, around 200,000 such workers had received three months training. Although the draft Sixth Plan (1978–83) was rather silent on the all round effect of rapid population growth on nation's welfare and economy, it did allocate larger funds for health and family welfare, education, agricultural extension, and organized labor. The Planning Commission emphasized on generating employment, improving the living conditions, primary and adult education, health services, environmental sanitation and supply of drinking water. The Planning Commission felt that improved status of women and children would play a major role in achieving fertility objectives in the long run.

The new government loudly expressed its official support for family planning, but its efforts at implementing it were weak. There were all indications that the family planning program had received a severe jolt in the first year of Janata rule. As Health Minister (after removal of Raj Narayan from Health Ministry, Morarji Desai kept the Health ministry under his personal control) and executive head of the government, Morarji Desai expressed his personal commitment to family welfare in many press releases. He asked every literate person, who understands the problem of unchecked population growth, to take the message to people around them that they must voluntarily come out with resolve for birth control. The Working Group on Population Policy (1978) submitted its interim report in March 1979. The recommendations of the Working Group were incorporated into the revised draft Sixth Plan. The recommendations included the following:

- Measures for bringing down death rate should receive as much attention as measures for decline in fertility. IMR, which was 120 per 1,000 at that time, must come down to 60 or even lower by 1996.
- Fertility and mortality goals should be expressed in terms of target dates for achieving replacement level fertility. The Working group recommended that the target date for achieving replacement level fertility should be 1996.

- The regional disparities in economic, agriculture, education, health and other services and provisions of physical infrastructure must be reduced as much as possible for they have considerable bearing on mortality and fertility. On the basis of the proportion of eligible couples effectively protected by contraceptives as of 1977, the Indian states be divided into three groups: Group A – fewer than 15 percent of all eligible couples effectively protected, Group B – the states with 15–25 percent couple protection rate, and Group C – those other states that had already registered more than 25 percent couple protection rate. Group C states were to attain IMR 60 and NRR 1 by 1991; For Group B and A, the respective dates should be 1996 and 2001. The population strategy should be to concentrate resources on family planning service delivery in the Group C states. For Group A as also for Group B states, the initial emphasis should be on "demand creation" with resources extensively used for making provision of education, social services, and creation of service delivery (particularly health) infrastructure. The emphasis was to be slowly shifted to family planning service delivery some years later.

It is unfortunate that India lost a very precious time because of Emergency fall-out. The baggy coalition of the Janata government (consisted of all rightist and leftist, secular and non-secular regional and national parties other than Congress) made it difficult to take firm decisions on policy issues. This state of indecision continued till the coalition government fell in 1979. Chaudhry Charan Singh formed an interim government but failed to muster majority support in Parliament. Without even facing the Parliament, he resigned and a mid-term poll was held in January 1980. Mrs Gandhi came back to power with a thumping two-thirds majority in Parliament. She dismissed nine state governments in mid-February where Janata party or its allies were in power (West Bengal under Left Front rule was spared). The quick change of events between 1976 and 1980 showed that Indian democracy was matured enough to vote out any government that failed to deliver on its promises. Sanjay Gandhi, who was believed to be the chief architect of the excesses committed during Emergency, had died in a plane crash. Mrs Gandhi and her party apologized for the excesses committed during Emergency.

Birth rate, which declined during Emergency from 35.2 in 1975 to 33.0 in 1977, went up to 33.9 in 1981. The return to an "all-out" results oriented family planning approach could not be expected from Mrs Gandhi, keeping in view the severe reaction of the 'illiterate masses' in the 1977 election. Initially, she was hesitant to take any firm stand on family planning program. Mrs Gandhi and her party apparently were not prepared to launch an aggressive birth control program to put at risk the popular support the Congress got back. She noticed that the number of sterilization acceptors started rising even when the bureaucracy under Janata regime was hesitant on implementation of a very positive program framed by the erstwhile government. However, she soon 'tightened up' policy implementation and delivery system with liberalization of the program – no compulsion, no intimidation. Her government could not risk recreating the climate of fear and revulsion that prevailed in the months of Emergency. The National Health Policy, 1983 emphasized the need for "securing the small family norm, through voluntary efforts and moving towards the goal of population stabilization". The Health Policy urged that replacement levels of TFR 2.1 should be achieved by 2000. While adopting the Health Policy, the Parliament emphasized the need for a separate National Population Policy.

Mrs Gandhi was assassinated in 1984. By the time her son Rajiv Gandhi took over the top executive post of the country, the level of sterilization acceptors crossed the 4 million mark (Table 13.1). Since then, the number of sterilization acceptors in a year generally was over 4 million but less than 5 million. Rajiv Gandhi followed the footsteps of his mother in family planning. He concentrated his attention on expansion of basic education and technology up-gradation of industries to ensure a faster growth of India's economy.

India passed the Medical Termination of Pregnancy Act (MTP) in 1971. The pre-natal techniques like amniocentesis and sonography are useful for the detection of genetic or chromosomal disorders or congenital malformations or sex linked disorders, etc. However, this technology is misused on a large scale for sex determination of the fetus. When the fetus is pronounced as female, it often prompts termination of the pregnancy. The person who contravenes the provisions of this Act is punishable with imprisonment up to 5 years and fine up to Rs 100,000.

MTP gave a useful option for carrying out the official family planning program forward. The inclusion of a provision in the MTP Act of 'failure of a contraceptive device' made abortion more or less available on demand. Abortion has remained an important method of birth control in all societies and at all times. It was not actively promoted in India till 1975. The number of abortions carried out (officially) was about 97,000 in 1974–75. The recorded incidences of abortion do not necessarily speak of the abortion rates in India. Small scale surveys carried out in different parts of the country seem to suggest that even in late 1970s, this could have been anything between 2 and 4 million. The official statistics presented in Table 13.8 point that MTP cases have increased by two-fold between 1980–81 and 2000–01 although the number of institutions approved for terminations increased nearly by three-fold. About 90 percent of abortions were performed before the pregnancies were 12 weeks old. The modern techniques are exceptionally safe provided abortion is carried out in certified clinics within the first 12 weeks of conception.

The National Development Council appointed a Committee on Population in 1991 under the chairmanship of Karunakaran. The Committee recommended the formulation of a National Population Policy to take a "a long term holistic view of development, population growth and environmental protection" and to "suggest policies and guidelines (for) formulation of programs" and "a monitoring mechanism with short, medium and long term perspectives and goals". Dr M.S. Swaminathan was entrusted with the task of framing a draft of the National Population Policy. The cabinet Group of Ministers prepared the final draft for the approval of the Cabinet.

13.3 National Population Policy 2000

India's annual increase in population at the time when NPP 2000 was tabled was 15.5 million which was large enough to neutralize efforts to conserve the resource endowment and environment. Before we present the brief sketch of NPP 2000, let us take a look at the milestones in the evolution of the population policy in India.

1929 **Sarda Act** fixing the minimum age at marriage of girls at 14 years

1939 National Planning Committee under the Chairmanship of Dr Radhakamal Mukherjee to advise on matters relating to population

1946 Bhore Committee Report

1952 **Launching of Family Planning Program**

1956 **Hindu Code Bill** raising the minimum age at marriage of girls to 15 years

1969 **Birth and Death Registration Act** making registration of all births and deaths compulsory.

1971 Medical Termination of Pregnancy Act.

1976 Statement of National Population Policy.

1976 **Child Marriage Restraint Act** fixing minimum age at marriage of girls at 18 years and 20 years for boys.

1977 Policy Statement on Family Welfare Program. Both statements (1976 and 1977) were laid on the table of the House of Parliament, but never discussed or adopted.

1983 **The National Health Policy** emphasized the need for "securing the small family norm, through voluntary efforts and moving towards the goal of population stabilization". While adopting the Policy, Parliament stressed the need for a separate National Population Policy.

1991 The National Development Council appointed a Committee on Population with Karunakaran as Chairman. The Karunakaran Report, endorsed by National Development Council in 1993, proposed the formulation of a National Population Policy.

1993 An Expert Group headed by Dr M.S. Swaminathan was asked to prepare a draft of a national population policy that would be discussed by the Parliament.

1994 **Pre-Natal Diagnostic Act (Regulation and Prevention of Misuse)** preventing pre-natal diagnosis of sex.

1994 Report on a National Population Policy by the Expert Group headed by Dr Swaminathan. This report was circulated among Members of Parliament, and comments requested from central and state agencies. It was anticipated that a national population policy approved by the National Development Council and the Parliament would help produce a broad political consensus.

1997 On the 50th anniversary of India's Independence, Prime Minister Gujral promised to announce a National Population Policy in the near future. During 11/97 Cabinet approved the draft National Population Policy with the direction that this be placed before Parliament. However, this document could not be placed in either Houses of Parliament as the respective Houses stood adjourned followed by dissolution of the Parliament.

1999 Another round of consultations was held in 1998, and another draft of National Population Policy was finalized and placed before the Cabinet in March, 1999. Cabinet appointed a Group of Ministers (headed by Dy. Chairman, Planning Commission) to examine the draft Policy. The Group of Ministers met several times and deliberated over the nuances of the Population Policy. In order to finalize a view about the inclusion/exclusion of incentives and disincentives, the GoM invited a cross-section of experts from among academia, public health professionals, demographers, social scientists, and women's representatives. The GoM finalized the draft population policy and placed the same before the Cabinet. This was discussed in the Cabinet on 19 November, 1999. Several suggestions were made during the discussions. On that basis, a fresh draft was submitted to the Cabinet.

2000 **NPP 2000** was adopted.

The National Population Policy was adopted by the National Democratic Alliance (NDA) government in February 2000. NPP 2000's immediate concern was to address the unmet needs of contraception, health care infrastructure, health personnel and to provide integrated service delivery for basic reproductive and child health care. The medium term objective was to bring down TFR to 2.1 (NRR 1) by 2010 and the long term objective was to achieve population stabilization by 2045. If things should go as proposed, CBR would come down to 21 and IMR to 30 (CBR 25.8 and IMR 68 in 2000) in 2010 and the population would be in the region of 1,107 million. NPP affirmed the commitment of the government towards voluntary and informed choice and consent of citizens while availing of reproductive health care services, and continuation of the target-free approach in administering family planning services. Following the recommendation of the NPP, National Commission on Population (NCP) was constituted on 11 May 2000 and Commission on Population at state/UT level in most states also came up.

The following interventions have been prioritized in the NPP 2000:

(i) Strengthen community health centers (CHC), primary health centers (PHC) and sub-centers;
(ii) Strengthen skills of health personnel and health providers;
(iii) Explore the possibility of accrediting the private practitioners for a year at a time and assign to each a satellite population, not exceeding 5,000 populations, for whom they provide reproductive and child health services.
(iv) Review the earlier system of the licensed medical practitioners who, after appropriate certificate from the Indian Medical Association, may participate in the provision of clinical services.
(v) Involve the non-medical fraternity in counseling and advocacy so as to demystify the national family welfare efforts.

The NPP 2000 admitted inter-sectoral differences in demographic transition among the states/UTs. The Policy asked for strengthening and energizing the family planning services in eight demographically weaker states, viz., Uttar Pradesh, Bihar, Madhya Pradesh, Rajasthan, Orissa, Jharkhand, Chhattishgarh and Uttaranchal. Population stabilization of the country largely would depend upon how the socio-demographic indicators in these states are attuned to the demands for the population stabilization.

NPP 2000 expressed concern about the declining sex ratios in many states. Although Pre-Natal Diagnostic Act was passed in 1994 and the Rules framed came into effect in January 1996, pre-natal determination of sex continues in many clinics in spite the fact that such sex determination was a punishable offence under the Act. Central Supervisory Board was constituted to look into the issue and advice the government on the steps to be taken for effective implementation of the Act. The Supervisory Board constituted the "Sub-committee on Implementation Strategy".

To attain a TFR 2.1 by 2010, the NPP 2000 concentrates on the following socio-demographic goals:

1. Address the unmet needs for basic reproductive and child health services, supplies and infrastructure.
2. Make school education up to age 14 free and compulsory, and reduce drop outs at primary and secondary school levels to below 20 percent for both boys and girls.
3. Reduce infant mortality rate to below 30 per 1,000 live births.
4. Reduce maternal mortality ratio to below 100 per 100,000 live births.
5. Achieve universal immunization of children against all vaccine preventable diseases.
6. Promote delayed marriage for girls, not earlier than age 18 and preferably after 20 years of age.
7. Achieve 80 percent institutional deliveries and 100 percent deliveries by trained persons.
8. Achieve universal access to information/counseling, and services for fertility regulation and contraception with a wide basket of choices.
9. Achieve 100 percent registration of births, deaths, marriages and pregnancies.

10. Contain the spread of Acquired Immunodeficiency Syndrome (AIDS), and promote greater integration between the management of reproductive tract infections (RTI) and sexually transmitted infections (STI) and the National AIDS Control Organization (NACO).
11. Prevent and control communicable diseases.
12. Integrate Indian Systems of Medicine (ISM) in the provision of reproductive and child health services, and in reaching out to households.
13. Promote vigorously the small family norm to achieve replacement level TFR.
14. Bring about convergence in implementation of related social sector programs so that family welfare becomes a people-centered program.

The NPP 2000 appears to give top priority to mother and child health care, with a view to bringing down IMR to 30 at the earliest. Repeated child births still are seen as an insurance against multiple infant and child deaths and accordingly, high infant mortality stymies all efforts at reducing TFR. To minimize maternal and infant mortality, institutional deliveries are a must. When that is not possible, the deliveries must be attended by trained persons. *The village council and health workers must insure 100 percent registration of pregnancies, marriages, births and deaths.* Even today about 50 percent of girls marry before they are 18 years (This can be averted only by compulsory registration of all marriages). This has to be stopped and their age at marriage needs to be increased to 20 years or more. Expecting mothers must receive vaccinations, other medicines and periodic check-up. Post-delivery nutritional status of mother must be looked into for the health of the mother and the child (one-time financial assistance to the mother for the first two children if they were born after the mother reached the age 19 plus an insurance program covering both mother and the child). Universal immunization of children against all vaccine preventable diseases is to be ensured.

The 73rd and 74th amendment of the Constitution provided an opportunity for decentralized planning and program implementation in the context of NPP 2000. Health, family welfare, and education now need to be made a responsibility of the *panchayati raj* institutions. To realize their potential, they need strengthening by further decentralization of administrative and financial powers, including powers of resource mobilization.

The 33 percent reservation of seats for women needs to be utilized to address the multi-sectoral agenda of population stabilization. Such committees, to be headed by an elected women panchayat member, will "think, plan and act locally, and support nationally". These committees will identify unmet needs for reproductive health services, be responsible for registration of births, deaths, marriages and pregnancies, and work for universalization of small family norm, bringing about a reduction in infant and maternal mortality, promoting compulsory child education, and such other related issues. Panchayats demonstrating exemplary performances will be nationally recognized and honored.

NPP 2000 is very serious about empowering women with health care and nutrition. A better health, prenatal and nutritional care insures not only lower maternal mortality, it adds to the nutritional and health care of the new born baby. The complex social and cultural determinants of women's health and nutrition have snowballing effects over a lifetime. Impaired health and low nutritional level is compounded by early child-bearing and consequent risk of serious pregnancy related complications. Women's risk of premature death and disability is highest during their reproductive years. Malnutrition, repeated pregnancies, delivery not attended by trained person, unsafe abortions, all combine to keep the MMR in India among the highest globally. Maternal mortality is not merely a loss of life; it speaks loudly of the social injustice to women. Low social and economic status of girls and women limits their access to education, good nutrition, as well as money to pay for health care and family planning services

An integrated package of delivery services at the village and household levels needs to be worked out for attaining the goal of population stabilization. The existing health infrastructure (limited personnel and equipments) in rural India is too inadequate to provide even the basic health and family planning services. This has to be addressed urgently. There is need to promote a more flexible approach, by extending basic reproductive and child health care through mobile clinics and counseling services. The government alone cannot resolve the unmet needs and make up for the inadequacies in health care infrastructure and services. To expand the coverage and extend the services, involvement of the voluntary and the non-government sector in partnership with the government is essential. A vast increase in the number of trained birth attendants, at least two per village, is necessary to universalize coverage and outreach of ante-natal, natal and post-natal health care. The corporate sector needs to play an active role through some specific commitments in areas of basic education, reproductive and child care, and involvement of women in labor force.

There continues to be unmet needs for contraceptives, supplies and equipment for integrated service delivery, mobility of health providers and patients, and comprehensive information both in rural and urban areas. It is important to strengthen, energize and make accountable the cutting edge of health infrastructure at all levels – village, sub-center and PHC.

Over 100 million people in India live in slums. The services like potable water, sanitation, and health care facilities are still pathetic in the slums. Their life becomes horrible during monsoon months. The municipal bodies must aggressively address to these and other issues relating to slums in the greater interest of the entire population under their charge.

Tribal communities, hill area populations and the sparsely populated areas often do not have access to affordable health care and educational services. The morbidity in such populations is often very high because of poor nutrition. Mostly poorly literate, they often have very high infant, child, and maternal mortality. These communities require special package of child and reproductive health care and education.

NPP 2000 also addresses its concern about the vulnerability of growing number of elderly people as a result of increasing life expectancy compounded by weakening of the family support system. Between 1996 and 2016, the elderly population (60 years and older) is likely to be doubled, from 62.3 million to 112.9 million. The Ministry of Social Justice and Empowerment has adopted in January 1999 a National Policy on Older Persons. It has become important to build in geriatric health concerns in the population policy. Since one of the major problems of the senior citizens is their health, it is urged that rural and urban health centers and hospitals be properly equipped for providing geriatric health care: screening for cancer, osteoporosis, and cardiovascular conditions. The NGOs need to be encouraged to design and implement formal and informal schemes that make the elderly economically self-reliant and build old-age homes for those who do not have helping hands to look after their necessities. The Apex Court also has said that children cannot disown their responsibilities to support their parents in their old age. Tax incentives have also been suggested to encourage grown-up children to look after their aged parents.

NPP 2000 recommended that the annual budget for Department of Family Welfare be doubled to enable government to address the shortfall in unmet needs for health care infrastructure, services and supplies.

The following promotional and motivational measures have also been proposed by NPP 2000:

(i) Panchayats and Zila Parishads will be rewarded and honored for exemplary performance in universalizing the small family norm, achieving reductions in infant mortality and birth rates, and promoting literacy with completion of primary schooling.

(ii) The *Balika Samridhi Yojana* run to promote survival and care of the girl child, will continue. A cash incentive of Rs 500 is awarded at the birth of the girl child of birth order 1 or 2.

(iii) Maternity Benefit Scheme will continue. A cash incentive of Rs 500 is awarded to mothers who have their first child after 19 years of age, for birth of the first or second child only. Disbursement of the cash award will in future be linked to compliance with ante-natal check up, institutional delivery by trained attendant, registration of birth and BCG immunization.

(iv) A Family Welfare-linked Health Insurance Plan will be established. Couples in BPL, who undergo sterilization with not more than two living children, would become eligible (along with children) for health insurance (for hospitalization) not exceeding Rs 5,000, and a personal accident insurance cover for the spouse undergoing sterilization.

(v) Couples below the poverty line, who marry after the legal age of marriage, register the marriage, have their first child after the mother reaches the age 21, accept the small family norm, and adopt a terminal method after the birth of the second child, will be rewarded.

(vi) A revolving fund will be set up for income-generating activities by village-level self-help groups, who provide community-level health care services.

(vii) Crèches and child care centers will be opened in rural areas and urban slums. This will facilitate and promote participation of women in paid employment.

(viii) A wider, affordable choice of contraceptives will be made accessible at diverse delivery points with counseling services to enable acceptors to exercise voluntary and informed consent.

(ix) Facilities for safe abortion will be strengthened and expanded.

(x) Products and services will be made affordable through innovative social marketing schemes.

(xi) Local entrepreneurs at village levels will be provided soft loans and encouraged to run ambulance services to supplement the existing arrangements for referral transportation.

(xii) Increased vocational training schemes for girls, leading to self-employment will be encouraged.

(xiii) Strict enforcement of Child Marriage Restraint Act, 1976.

(xiv) Strict enforcement of the Pre-Natal Diagnostic Techniques Act, 1994.

(xv) Soft loans to ensure mobility of the ANMs will be increased.

(xvi) The 42nd Constitutional Amendment has frozen the number of representatives in the Lok Sabha (on the basis of population) at 1971 Census levels. The freeze is currently valid until 2001, and has served as an incentive for state Governments to fearlessly pursue the agenda for population stabilization. This freeze needs to be extended until 2026.

13.4 Family Planning Achievements

In this section we present some statistical data relating issues connected to population and family planning. The accounts presented for birth prevention do not take into account if those who accepted one method of birth control or other would survive through the entire reproductive period remaining. The birth prevention account presented also does not make any adjustment for if there could be any further birth by those who had undergone sterilization after giving births to 4–5 children.

Preventable births cannot be the same for a woman who had been sterilized at the age of 25 and another sterilized at the age of 40. The innumerable cases of abortion not formally registered are likely to have tangible influence on birth prevention.

The Ministry of Health and Family Planning has prepared a scale for computing prevention of births and couple protection rates for various methods used for birth control:

> Every incidence of sterilization prevents 2.5 births in the next 23 years; 0.7 births are prevented in 10 years after insertion of an IUD; use of conventional contraceptives (CC) prevent 0.15 births for the next 3 years.

Obviously, the estimation of number of births prevented and couple protection rate based on this computation formula (or some other) can always be debated. However, if the same scale is used for all succeeding years, then an idea of relative performances for various years by various birth prevention methods can be obtained. Such computations however do not take into cognizance the fact that age specific fertility declines sharply after certain age. That is, chances of preventing birth by a woman undergoing operation at the age 35 or later is only marginal. Many studies confirm that vasectomy was performed even on very elderly persons, especially during Emergency. 'Motivators' were identified as the culprits for such unjust operations. Surveys conducted on acceptors of sterilization in mass sterilization camps in 1972 show that the average age of male and female acceptors of sterilization in camps was 39 and 31 years respectively. Most of them already had 4 or more children alive. 75 percent of those acceptors were either illiterate or had just primary education. Their average income was around Rs 100. Over the years the age of the sterilization acceptors have come down considerably.

13.4.1 Family Planning Acceptors and their Characteristics

Between 1965–66 and 2000–2001 a total of over 85 million sterilizations (over 8.3 million only in 1976–77) had been reported, of which over 62 million were tubectomies. Sterilization of males had been more popular in India till 1972–73. Thereafter, females gradually replaced males among sterilization acceptors, except for a short period between 1975 and 1977 when males in huge numbers were placed on the operation table. By 1999–2000, about 98 percent of sterilization acceptors were women. A total of 4.74 million sterilizations were done during 2000–01 as against 4.60 million in 1999–2000. Andhra Pradesh, Maharashtra, Rajasthan, Tamil Nadu, West Bengal, Arunachal Pradesh, Himachal Pradesh, Jammu & Kashmir, Manipur, Meghalaya, Mizoram, Nagaland, Dadra & Nagar Haveli, Daman and Diu and Lakshadweep reported better performances in 2000–01 than in 1999–2000. Sterilization numbers significantly dropped in Bihar, Madhya Pradesh, Orissa, Punjab and Delhi. Of the total number of 4,625,247 tubectomy operations reported for 2000–01, 38 percent were done by laparoscopic technique.

The mean age of wives of vasectomy acceptors in 1999–2000 was 29.1 years, down from 31.6 years in 1980–81, that of tubectomy acceptors 28.3 years down from 30.5 in 1980–81 and IUD acceptors 27.5 years down from 28.0 in 1981–81. IUD acceptors increased significantly in Maharashtra, Rajasthan and Mizoram. Proportion of IUD acceptors to total acceptors in the country declined in 2000–01 compared to that in precedent years in Bihar, Madhya Pradesh, Tamil Nadu, Uttar Pradesh, Andhra Pradesh, Karnataka, Punjab, Manipur and Delhi. The highest proportion of vasectomy acceptors by age of wife was in the age group of 25–29 years and that of tubectomy and of IUD acceptors were in the age group of 20–24 years. The age group of 20–29 years, which has the

Table 13.1
Sex-wise breakup of permanent sterilization performed

Year	Number of sterilizations				(4) as % of sterilization equivalent by all methods'000
	Vasectomy	Tubectomy	Total	(3) as % of (4)	
1	2	3	4	5	6
1965–66	576,609	94,214	670,823	14.0	68.9
1966–67	785,378	101,990	887,368	11.5	73.0
1967–68	1,648,152	191,659	1,839,811	10.4	88.1
1968–69	1,383,053	281,764	1,664,817	16.9	89.2
1969–70	1,055,860	366,258	1,422,118	25.8	85.7
1970–71	878,800	451,114	1,329,914	33.9	83.2
1971–72	1,620,076	567,260	2,187,336	25.9	88.2
1972–73	2,613,263	508,593	3,121,856	16.3	92.5
1973–74	403,107	539,295	942,402	57.2	78.5
1974–75	611,960	741,899	1,353,859	54.7	82.7
1975–76	1,439,337	1,230,417	2,668,754	46.1	87.0
1976–77	6,199,158	2,062,015	8,261,173	25.0	95.4
1977–78	187,609	761,160	948,769	80.2	76.4
1978–79	390,922	1,092,985	1,483,907	73.7	79.6
1979–80	472,687	1,305,237	1,777,924	73.4	82.1
1980–81	438,909	1,613,861	2,052,770	78.6	78.6
1985–86	639,477	4,262,132	4,901,609	79.5	87.0
1990–91	254,905	3,870,650	4,125,555	85.3	93.8
1991–92	174,201	3,915,838	4,090,039	85.4	95.7
1992–93	150,719	4,135,587	4,286,306	86.6	96.5
1993–94	150,235	4,347,215	4,497,450	96.7	96.7
1994–95	143,866	4,435,648	4,579,514	95.9	96.9
1995–96	123,748	4,298,571	4,422,319	97.2	97.2
1996–97	72,006	3,798,220	3,870,226	98.1	98.1
1997–98	71,352	4,167,162	4,238,514	98.3	98.3
1998–99	102,656	4,104,070	4,206,726	97.6	97.6
1999–00	86,742	4,508,724	4,595,466	98.1	98.1
2000–01	109,902	4,625,247	4,735,149	97.7	97.7
Since 1965–66	22,784,689	62,378,785	85,163,474	72.4	

Source: Family Welfare Program in India, Yearbook 1984–65 & 2001.

Figure 13.1
Sex-wise break-up of sterilization

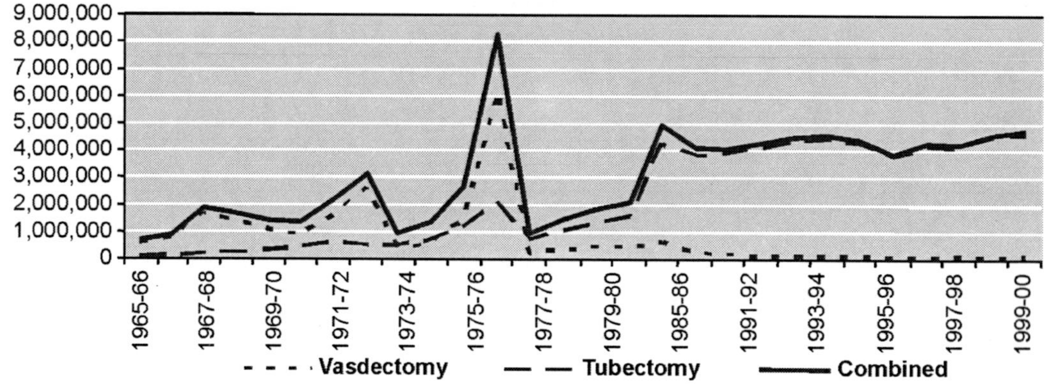

highest fertility, contributed 60.2 percent of vasectomy acceptors, 66.5 percent of tubectomy acceptors and 70.2 percent of IUD acceptors.

Table 13.2
Percentage distribution of sterilization and IUD acceptors by the age of women

Year	*<15*	*15–19*	*20–24*	*25–29*	*30–34*	*35–39*	*40–44*	*45+*	*<30*	*Mean age of wife*
1	*2*	*3*	*4*	*5*	*6*	*7*	*8*	*9*	*10*	*11*
					Vasectomy					
1980–81	—	0.3	10.4	29.3	33.1	20.1	6.5	0.3	40.0	31.6
1985–86		0.5	8.9	27.2	32.3	23.0	8.0	0.2	36.6	32.2
1990–91		0.4	8.6	26.6	33.2	24.0	6.9	0.2	35.6	32.2
1995–96		1.5	15.5	27.4	28.3	21.9	5.3	0.1	44.4	31.0
1996–97	0.2	1.2	19.9	33.8	29.4	11.8	3.6	0.2	55.1	29.6
1997–98	0.1	1.3	21.4	36.7	26.5	11.4	2.5		59.5	29.1
1998–99		0.9	24.2	39.0	24.1	8.9	2.8	0.1	64.0	28.7
1999–00		1.4	22.6	36.1	26.3	10.1	3.2	0.3	60.2	29.1
					Tubectomy					
1980–81		0.5	12.7	36.1	32.0	15.4	3.3		49.3	30.5
1985–86		0.9	14.5	35.1	30.8	15.3	3.3		50.5	30.3
1990–91		0.7	17.8	39.4	27.6	12.0	2.4		58.0	29.5
1995–96		4.3	25.1	38.1	22.5	8.4	1.7	0.1	67.4	28.0
1996–97		1.3	23.7	40.6	24.3	8.5	1.4	0.1	65.7	28.5
1997–98		1.7	23.2	41.6	22.7	9.7	1.1	0.1	66.4	28.0
1998–99		1.1	25.0	42.0	22.3	8.3	1.3		68.1	28.3
1999–00		1.3	25.4	39.8	23.5	8.7	1.2	0.1	66.5	28.3

Cont'd...

Table 13.2 Cont'd…

1	*2*	*3*	*4*	*5*	*6*	*7*	*8*	*9*	*10*	*11*
					IUD					
1980–81		4.4	28.3	34.0	21.8	9.3	2.2		66.7	28.0
1985–86	0.1	5.5	30.7	34.1	19.8	8.3	1.5	0.1	70.3	27.5
1990–91		5.6	30.9	33.6	19.1	8.5	2.2		70.2	27.5
1995–96	0.6	8.2	28.5	23.5	18.9	8.3	1.9		70.8	27.3
1996–97	0.1	6.4	26.7	31.0	25.7	7.7	2.3	0.2	64.1	28.0
1997–98	0.1	5.2	30.6	34.0	22.6	6.3	1.2	0.1	70.7	27.4
1998–99		5.2	32.1	34.1	20.3	6.9	1.4		71.4	27.3
1999–00	0.1	5.1	32.9	32.1	17.7	10.6	1.4	0.1	70.2	27.5

Source: Family Welfare Program in India, Yearbook 2001.

Table 13.3

Rural-Urban break-up of sterilization done in India

Year	***Number of sterilizations***				
	Rural	***Urban***	***Break-up not available***	***Total***	***% of rural to total@***
1	*2*	*3*	*4*	*5*	*6*
1980–81	1,363,105	633,839	25,826	2,022,770	68.3
1985–86	3,085,196	1,244,541	572,172	4,901,909	71.3
1990–91	2,504,683	1,178,730	442,142	4,125,555	68.0
1991–92	2,107,270	1,129,050	853,719	4,090,039	65.1
1992–93	2,209,074	1,081,951	995,281	4,286,306	67.1
1993–94	2,249,421	1,097,074	1,150,955	4,497,450	67.2
1994–95	2,396,313	1,123,266	1,059,935	4,579,514	68.1
1995–96	2,449,606	1,227,636	745,077	4,422,319	66.6
1996–97	2,495,663	1,182,393	192,170	3,870,226	67.9
1997–98	2,117,207	1,117,678	1,003,629	4,238,514	65.4
1998–99	2,125,322	1,109,140	972,264	4,206,726	65.7
1999–00	2,701,749	1,367,991	525,726	4,595,466	66.4
2000–01	1,936,702	741,855	2,056,592	4,735,149	72.3

@ Percentage of Column (2)+(3), the total figure for which rural/urban break-up is available.
Source: Family Welfare Program in India, Yearbook 2001

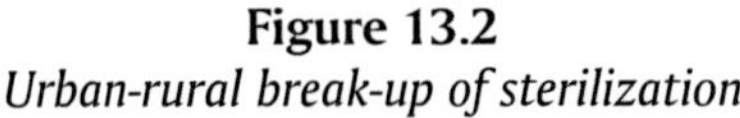

Figure 13.2
Urban-rural break-up of sterilization

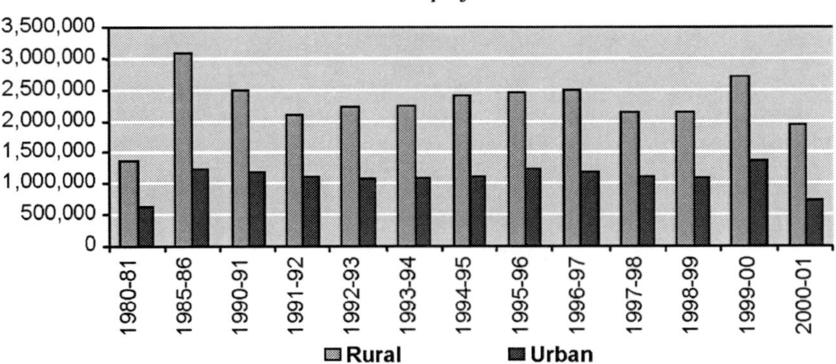

Table 13.4
Family planning acceptors by methods – All India ('000)

Year	*Sterilization*	*IUD insertions*	*Equivalent condom users*	*Equivalent oral pill users*	*Total acceptors*	*Equivalent Sterilizations*
1	*2*	*3*	*4*	*5*	*6*	*7*
1980–81	2,053 (31.6)	628 (9.7)	3,718 (57.3)	91 (1.4)	6,490 (100.0)	2,479
1985–86	4,902 (25.9)	3,274 (17.3)	9,387 (49.6)	1,358 (7.2)	18,921 $ (100.0)	6,665
1990–91	4,126 (15.1)	5,370 (19.6)	14,735 (53.9)	3,125 (11.4)	27,356 (100.0)	7,082
1991–92	4,090 (15.9)	4,386 (17.1)	13,875 (53.9)	3,366 (13.1)	25,717 (100.0)	6,697
1992–93	4,286 (15.9)	4,740 (17.5)	15,004 (55.5)	3,001 (11.1)	27,031 (100.0)	7,033
1993–94	4,497 (14.0)	6,017 (18.7)	17,283 (53.8)	4,302 (13.4)	32,099 $ (100.0)	7,941
1994–95	4,580 (13.5)	6,702 (19.8)	17,707 (52.3)	4,873 (14.4)	33,862 (100.0)	8,339
1995–96	4,422 (13.1)	6,858 (20.4)	17,297 (51.4)	5,091 (15.1)	33,668 (100.0)	8,235
1996–97	3,870 (12.1)	5,681 (17.7)	17,214 (53.8)	5,250 (16.4)	32,015 (100.0)	7,303
1997–98	4,239 (12.6)	6,173 (18.4)	16,796 (50.0)	6,395 (19.0)	33,603 $ (100.0)	7,940
1998–99	4,207 (12.1)	6,083 (17.5)	17,448 (50.3)	6,944 (20.0)	34,682 (100.0)	7,975
1999–2000	4,595 (12.5)	6,200 (16.9)	18,135 (49.4)	7,747 (21.1)	36,678 (100.0)	8,530
2000–01	4,735 (12.9)	6,046 (16.5)	18,202 (49.7)	7,640 (20.9)	36,623 (100.0)	8,610

$ Sum given under Cols. 2, 3, 4 & 5 may not tally with the figures under Col. 6 due to rounding off.

Note:

1. Equivalent Sterilisations have been calculated by revised formula by adding the number of Sterilisations, 1/3 the number of IUD Insertions, 1/18 the number of Equivalent Condom Users and 1/9 the number of Equivalent Oral Pill Users.
2. Figures in brackets indicate percentage to total acceptors for each year.

Source: Family Welfare Program in India, Yearbook 2001.

Table 13.5
Year-wise achievement of targets of family planning methods, All India ('000)

Year	*Sterilizations*		*IUD insertions*		*Eq. Condoms users*		*Eq. OP users*	
	Target	*Achieved*	*Target*	*Achieved*	*Target*	*Achieved*	*Target*	*Achieved*
1	*2*	*3*	*4*	*5*	*6*	*7*	*8*	*9*
1980–81	2,896	2,053	791	628	5,042	3,718	495	91
1985–86	5,560	4,902	3,244	3,274	9,515	9,387	960	1,358
1990–91	5,804	4,126	6,400	5,370	15,080	14,735	2,493	3,125
1991–92	5,434	4,090	5,956	4,386	16,151	13,875	2,650	3,366
1992–93	5,276	4,286	6,384	4,740	16,472	15,004	4,581	3,001
1993–94	5,183	4,497	7,330	6,017	19,345	17,283	5,004	4,302
1994–95	5,326	4,580	7,869	6,702	21,777	17,707	5,468	4,873
1995–96	5,032	4,422	7,423	6,858	$	17,297	5,793	5,091
1996–97	$$	3,870	$$	5,681	$$	17,214	$$	5,250
1997–98	$$	4,239	$$	6,173	$$	16,796	$$	6,395
1998–99	$$	4,207	$$	6,083	$$	17,448	$$	6,944
1999–2000	$$	4,595	$$	6,200	$$	18,135	$$	7,747
2000–01	$$	4,735	$$	6,046	$$	18,202	$$	7,640

$ No target fixed for condom users during 1995–96.
$$ No targets fixed since 1996–97.
Source: Family Planning Programs in India, 2001

The number of married couples (wife's age 15–44 years) gets divided between urban and rural areas (1991 Census) in the ratio 24.56:75.44. But the proportion of sterilization acceptors in rural area had remained confined between 65 and 68 percent in the 20 years since 1980–81 except in two years 1985–86 and 2000–01 when the proportion exceeded 71 percent (Table 13.3). The acceptance of sterilization by couples had been a little better in urban areas than in rural areas given the size of their respective populations. However, some notable improvement has been observed in the age distribution of the acceptors (Table 13.2). Whereas 40 percent of those accepting vasectomy had their wives in the age group 15–29 years in 1980–81, the same has gone up to 60 percent by the end of the millennium. The percentage of tubectomy acceptors in the age group 15–29 has gone up from 49.3 to 66.5 percent in the same period. Both are indications that birth planning has more and more been accepted by young married couples. For the IUD acceptors the changes are only marginal at the national level. IUD users have increased most in Assam, Gujarat, Maharashtra, Rajasthan, Meghalaya, and Mizoram; its use has declined in Bihar, Karnataka, Madhya Pradesh, Orissa, West Bengal, Manipur and Sikkim between 1997 and 2001. Condom users have declined in the years between 1997–2001 in many states – Bihar, Haryana, Karnataka, Kerala, Madhya Pradesh, Maharashtra, Punjab, Uttar Pradesh, West Bengal and some other smaller states; its use has increased in Andhra Pradesh, Assam, Gujarat, Rajasthan and a few other smaller states.

From the view point of birth prevention, it is more important to know the actual number of living children when a couple adopts any method of birth control. Those who opted for vasectomy in 1980–81 already had on an average 3.5 children. In 1999–2000, the average number of surviving children at the time undergoing operation came down to 2.5. With tubectomy, the drop was from 3.7 to 2.9 surviving children. For the IUD users the drop was from 2.6 to 2.1 numbers of surviving children on an average. The time series data for various indicators clearly indicate that family welfare program in India is in the right track, even though there is no coercion or serious disincentive for not adopting small family norm. The following table shows how the drop in number of surviving children has happened between 1980–81 and 1999–2000. Table 13.7 gives the educational status of wives of acceptors of various methods.

Table 13.6

Percentage of acceptors of vasectomy, tubectomy and IUD by number of surviving children in India

Children surviving	*Percentage of acceptors*											
	Vasectomy				*Tubectomy*				*IUD*			
	80–81	*90–91*	*95–96*	*99–00*	*80–81*	*90–91*	*95–96*	*99–00*	*80–81*	*90–91*	*95–66*	*99–2000*
1	*2*	*3*	*4*	*5*	*6*	*7*	*8*	*9*	*10*	*11*	*12*	*13*
One	1.0	1.0	3.3	7.1	0.6	1.2	1.8	2.5	19.2	28.5	32.5	32.8
Two	24.4	20.2	32.1	41.9	15.8	27.0	32.2	39.9	32.3	34.8	31.5	34.7
Three	34.8	36.3	40.5	30.5	35.0	40.4	37.9	35.6	24.8	21.6	22.9	20.0
Four	23.8	27.5	11.0	10.0	28.9	20.7	20.0	16.2	14.6	9.2	8.9	7.6
Average no. of children	3.5	3.5	3.1	2.5	3.7	3.2	3.1	2.9	2.6	2.2	2.2	2.1

Source: Family Welfare Program in India Year Book 2001.

Table 13.7

Percentage distribution of acceptors of vasectomy, tubectomy and IUD by educational status of wives, 1999–2000

Methods	*Illiterate*	*Literate below primary*	*Primary passed*	*Middle passed*	*Higher Secondary/ Matric*	*Graduate & above*
1	*2*	*3*	*4*	*5*	*6*	*7*
Vasectomy	37.4	14.7	16.2	14.0	11.3	6.4
Tubectomy	31.6	18.8	18.6	15.7	11.5	3.8
IUD	24.0	23.2	19.6	16.8	11.5	5.0

Source: Family Welfare Program in India Year Book 2001.

It is also to be noted that sterilization, which remains one of the most potent methods in India for birth prevention, has lost a large proportion of its share to IUD and CCs in recent years though the absolute number of sterilization is either increasing or maintaing a level (Table 13.5). Share of sterilization acceptors to all acceptors which stood at 31.6 percent in 1980–81, have been hovering between 12 and 13 percent between 1996–97 and 2000–01. Proportion of sterilization acceptors among all married couples (Table 13.15) was only 1.4 percent in 1970–71. It jumped to an all time high of 7.69 percent in 1976–77; it drooped to 1.8 percent in 1980–81. Between 1990–91 and 2000–01, the percentages of sterilization acceptors among all married couples were between 2.35 and 2.90.

IUD has started gaining enhanced acceptance from 1985–86 and its share to all acceptors has remained between 17 and 19 percent. Popularity of IUD indicates that the Indian couples increasingly are stressing on spacing of births between children. During the year 2000–01, 6,045,641 insertions were reported as against 6,199,845 in 1999–2000. Assam, Haryana, Maharashtra, Orissa, Rajasthan, West Bengal, Delhi, Himachal Pradesh, Mizoram, Tripura, Anadaman & Nicober Islands, Chandigarh, Dadra & Nagar Haveli, Daman and Diu, and Pondicherry reported better performances in 2000–01. Use of oral pills is also increasing. More than 50 percent of acceptors of family planning are using condoms. 18.6 million couples used condoms and 7.6 million oral pills in 2000–01. The year 2000–01 ended with 36.62 million total family planning acceptors at the national level as against 36.68 million in 1999–2000. Even though the government dropped 'target' from family planning program since 1995–96, it did not have any significant impact on the size of acceptors for different methods. The data on acceptors published refer only to those who took advantage of the services offered by public service points. Some additional couples must be added to this number of acceptors since many couples use the private clinics for getting their supplies and services or are resorting to their own techniques to prevent births. The number of such couples is likely to be small compared to those who took advantage of the state provisions. However, their number in urban areas, especially among middle and upper-middle income class must be appreciable.

The Government of India is keen to addressing the problem of unsafe abortion by improving the quality, accessibility and safety of abortion services countrywide. MTP is an important component of the on-going Reproductive Child Health program and it is one of the important methods of birth spacing and reducing maternal mortality. A significant proportion of maternal death is caused due to unsafe abortions. In order to increase availability and accessibility to abortion services, MTP equipments are procured centrally and provided to District Hospitals, CHCs and PHCs wherever required.

Table 13.8

Year-wise medical termination of pregnancies

Year	*No. of institutions approved for terminations*	*No. of MTP done*	*Year*	*No. of approved institutions for terminations*	*No. of MTP done*
1980–81	3,294	388,405	1994–95	8,511	627,748
1985–86	5,528	583,704	1995–96	8,722	570,914
1990–91	6,859	581,215	1996–97	8,891	538,075
1991–92	7,121	636,456	1997–98	9,119	512,823
1992–93	7,374	606,015	1998–99	9,528	666,882
1993–94	7,628	612,291	1999–00	9,565	708,512
			2000–01	9,806	723,142

Source: Family Welfare Program in India, Yearbook 2001.

Number of institutions approved for terminations and the number of MTP done in these centers have sharply gone up in the 20 years ending 2000–01 (Table 13.8). These figures refer only to the registered cases. But the number would be several times higher if information about abortions done in unapproved clinics and by quacks was taken into account. A close to 90 percent of abortions had taken place within the first 12 weeks of pregnancy (Table 13.9). Many women undergoing abortions either insert IUD or undergo tubectomy operation as well (Table 13.10).

Figure 13.3
Number of MTPs done

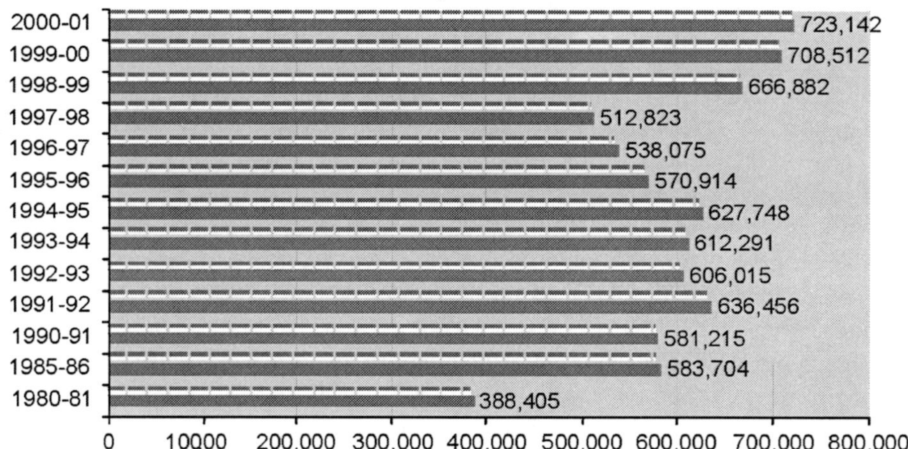

There is considerable variation in termination of pregnancies (official terminations) between the states. When the proportion of abortions in a state to total abortions in the country in a year in relation to their share of the total population of India is looked into, the most under performing states are Bihar, Andhra Pradesh, Karnataka, West Bengal, Madhya Pradesh and Gujarat; the high performing states are Maharashtra, Kerala, Tamil Nadu, Haryana, Rajasthan and Uttar Pradesh. Punjab is not included in either of the two categories of states though it is a common knowledge that predetermination of sex is as common in the state as in some others like Haryana and Uttar Pradesh.

Table 13.9
Distribution of MTP cases by duration of pregnancy

Year	*Duration of pregnancy*			*Total*
	Up to 12 weeks	*12–20 weeks*	*Not available*	
	Number	*Number*	*Number*	
1995–96	271,614 (88.0)	36,989 (12.0)	11,349 (3.5)	319,952
1996–97	339,691 (89.1)	41,350 (10.9)	84,664 (18.2)	465,705
1997–98	368,003 (89.3)	44,247 (10.7)	77,684 (15.9)	489,934
1998–99	508,065 (85.1)	88,692 (14.9)	34,037 (5.4)	630,794
1999–00	309,161 (89.5)	36,302 (10.5)	44,998 (11.5)	390,461
2000–01	410,406 (89.3)	49,147 (10.7)	64,245 (12.3)	523,798

Figures in parenthesis are percentages to total MTP cases for the year.
Source: Family Welfare Program in India, Yearbook 2001

Table 13.10
Medical termination of pregnancy with sterilization and IUD

	With sterilization		*With IUD*		*Without sterilizeation/IUD* $		*Total*
Year	*Number*	*%*	*Number*	*%*	*Number*	*%*	
1996–97	116,103	24.9	70,081	15.0	279,521	60.0	465,705
1997–98	132,729	27.6	81,776	17.0	266,718	55.4	481,223
1998–99	146,861	23.7	88,180	14.3	383,406	62.0	618,447
1999–00	111,471	30.0	54,670	14.7	205,548	55.3	371,689
2000–01	134,488	26.7	66,449	13.2	303,403	60.2	504,340

$ These figures may include cases for which break-up by acceptance of Sterilization/IUD is not available.
Source: Family Welfare Program in India, Yearbook, 2001.

Table 13.11
Age at the time of medical termination of pregnancy

Year	*Age at termination*							
	<15	*15–19*	*20–24*	*25–29*	*30–34*	*35–39*	*40–44*	*45+*
1	*2*	*3*	*4*	*5*	*6*	*7*	*8*	*9*
1997–98	0.1	3.3	23.5	36.8	24.5	9.5	2.0	0.2
1998–99	0.3	4.0	24.9	35.8	22.7	9.3	1.7	1.2
1999–00	0.3	4.7	26.6	36.7	21.5	8.4	1.5	0.2
2000–01	0.3	5.1	25.3	35.0	21.6	9.3	2.4	1.1

Source: Family Welfare Program in India Year Book 2001.

About 20.6 percent of approved clinics for MTP are located in Maharashtra; 18.6 percent of all recorded termination cases in India in 2000–01 were reported from this state. Although only 5.9 percent of authorized MTP centers are located in Uttar Pradesh, the state's share in pregnancy terminations is second highest (15.2%) in the country. Tamil Nadu has the second highest number of MTP institutions and recorded the third highest number of terminations (6.4%).

Neither the doctor nor the patient would feel comfortable for MTP when the patient is either very young or in their late thirties and beyond. The data also show that well over 80 percent of abortions were carried out for women in the age group 20–34 (Table 13.11) and most such abortions took place when the pregnancy was not beyond 12 weeks old (Table 13.9).

The mean number of living children in 1999–2000 in case of vasectomy acceptors was 2.5, 2.9 for tubectomy acceptors and 2.1 for IUD acceptors. The proportion of vasectomy acceptors with three or fewer number of living children was 85.4 percent whereas the corresponding figure for tubectomy acceptors was 78.4 percent. The proportion of IUD acceptors with one child was 32.8 percent of the total IUD acceptors recorded in 1999–2000 and that with two children was 34.7 percent. 30.7 percent of IUD acceptors had three or more children and all of them should have been advised for sterilization.

13.5 Impact of the Program

In a traditional society like India where marriage is considered sacrosanct, a reasonably important path to bring down birth rate is to curtail a woman's reproductive period. Although the government has passed the Child Marriage Restrain Act in 1976 and raised the minimum age at marriage of girls to 18 years, the government and the political parties showed little enthusiasm about its implementation. Birth and Death Registration Act, which made registration of these vital events compulsory, was passed as early as 1969. Yet, after 40 years of framing the Act, birth and death registrations in many states are extremely shoddy. Taking advantage of the 73rd and 74th amendments of the Constitution, the government expressed the need for decentralization of many basic welfare programs. Health, family welfare, and education were to be made the responsibility of the *panchayati raj* institutions. The NPP 2000 declared that 100 percent registration of marriages, pregnancies, births and deaths would become the additional responsibilities of village councils and health workers. But even today, a high proportion of girls marry before they are 18. After seven years of formulation of NPP 2000, the government is again talking about the necessity for compulsory registration of marriage (Supreme Court too has asked for compulsory registration of all marriages) since the ongoing reviews clearly indicate that the targets for TFR 2.1 by 2010 was unlikely to be met if the administrative machinery was not geared up to see that they perform what they have specifically been asked to do. The financial and health packages that are offered to women who give birth to their first baby after they reach the age 19 and register their pregnancy with the health center will necessarily have some impact on the age when they marry. But the more important issue is how to bring the girls to schools and enable them to extend their educational career as long as possible. When girls neither are attending schools nor providing any financial support to the family by undertaking some odd jobs (the government of India is determined to abolish child labor of any form), the poor parents have but little choice than to give their daughters in marriage as early as possible. If the government is really serious to abolish child labor and make flouting the Child Marriage Restraint Act a punishable offence, it needs to come up with compensation packages for millions of poor families that cannot survive without the services rendered even by their young kids.

Table 13.12

Eligible couples, 1970–71 to 2001–02 ('000)

Year	70–71	73–74	76–77	79–80	80–81	81–82	82–83	83–84	84–85	85–86	86–87	87–88	88–89
Couples	94489	100939	107389	113839	116033	118705	121377	124049	126721	129432	132572	135710	138850
Year	89–90	90–91	91–92	92–93	93–94	94–95	95–96	96–97	97–98	98–99	99–00	00–01	01–02
Couples	141990	145140	148430	151720	155020	158310	161593	164749	165869	168558	171198	176647	180056

The various components of the mass campaign on family planning, especially the catastrophic events that may follow to the mother and the child if girls were given to marriage before they were sufficiently physiologically and mentally equipped, have paid some dividend over the years. The proportion of married girls in the age group 15–19 years has progressively declined. Between 1961 and 1991, more than 53 percent cut in this regard has been achieved in urban area and 37 percent in rural area. The proportion of married couples with age of wives 20–24 years has also marginally declined both in rural and urban areas. Female nuptiality also indicates that the proportion of currently married women below the age 18 years has gone down by 4 percent (68% in urban and 3.2% in rural area) in the years between 1986 and 1991 compared to those married during 1981–86 (Table 13.16). It is an encouraging sign that the proportion of married girls in the age group 15–19 has been slashed to half in 1991 from the proportion it recorded in 1961 (69.6) and also a 10 percent reduction in the next age group (Table 13.17). Eligible couples have nearly doubled from 94,489,000 in 1970–71 to 180,056,000 in 2001–02 (Table 13.12).

Figure 13.4
Eligible couples ('000)

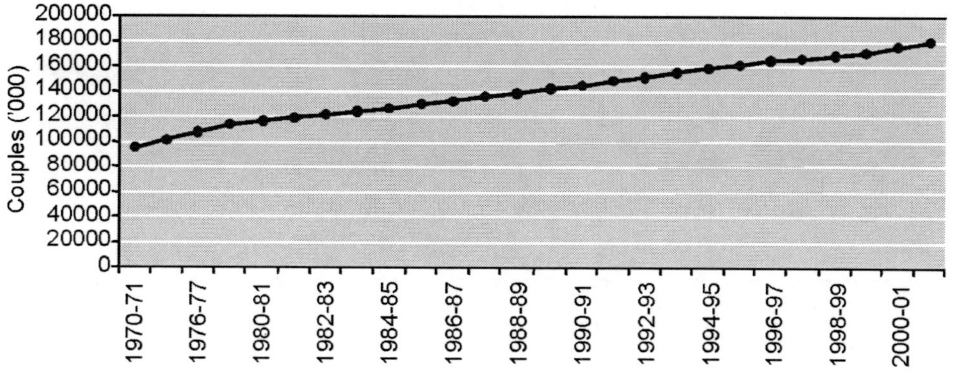

The number of married couples and the marriage rate per thousand populations in 1991 by age of wife (15–44 years) is presented below:

Table 13.13
Number of married couples by age of wife, 1991

	Total		*Rural*		*Urban*	
	Number	*Rate per 1,000 pop*	*Number*	*Rate per 1,000 pop*	*Number*	*Rate per 1,000 pop*
1	*2*	*3*	*4*	*5*	*6*	*7*
15–19	12983391	15	10794727	17	2188664	10
20–24	30236237	36	23033607	37	7202630	33
25–29	32599649	39	23816126	38	8783523	41
30–34	27103296	32	19808070	32	7295226	34
35–39	23454214	28	17001454	27	6452760	30
40–44	17871167	21	13358133	21	4513034	21
Total* (15–44)	144247954	172	107812117	173	36435837	169

* Excludes Jammu & Kashmir.
Source: Registrar General, India.

Table 13.14
Percentage distribution of married couples by age of wife, 1961–1991

Age of wife	***Percentage distribution of married couples***											
	Rural				***Urban***				***Total***			
	1961	*1971*	*1981**	*1991*	*1961*	*1971*	*1981**	*1991*	*1961*	*1971*	*1981**	*1991*
1	*2*	*3*	*4*	*5*	*6*	*7*	*8*	*9*	*10*	*11*	*12*	*13*
15–19	15.9	13.9	12.6	10.0	12.7	10.2	8.6	6.0	15.0	13.2	11.7	9.0
20–24	22.0	20.3	21.3	21.3	22.9	21.6	21.6	19.8	22.2	20.5	21.3	21.0
25–29	21.4	20.6	20.3	22.1	22.9	22.2	23.2	24.1	21.7	20.9	21.0	22.6
< 29	59.3	54.8	54.2	53.4	58.5	54.0	53.4	49.9	58.9	54.6	54.0	52.6
30–34	17.0	18.0	17.4	18.4	18.1	18.3	18.3	20.0	17.2	18.0	17.6	18.8
35–39	13.2	15.2	15.6	15.8	13.2	16.0	16.2	17.7	13.3	15.4	15.7	16.2
40–44	10.5	12.0	12.8	12.4	10.2	11.7	12.1	12.4	10.6	12.0	12.7	12.4

* Excludes Assam and based on 20 percent sample data
Source: Registrar General, India.

Table 13. 15
Percentages of eligible couples sterilized

Year	*Couples ('000)*	*Sterilization*	*% of couples sterilized*
1970–71	94,489	1,329,914	1.41
1973–74	100,939	942,402	0.93
1976–77	**107,389**	**8,261,173**	**7.69**
1979–80	113,839	1,777,924	1.56
1980–81	116,033	2,052,770	1.77
1990–91	145,140	4,125,555	2.84
1991–92	148,430	4,090,039	2.76
1992–93	151,720	4,286,306	2.83
1993–94	155,020	4,497,450	2.90
1994–95	158,310	4,579,514	2.89
1995–96	161,593	4,422,319	2.74
1996–97	164,749	3,870,226	2.35
1997–98	165,869	4,238,514	2.56
1998–99	168,558	4,206,726	2.50
1999–00	171,198	4,595,466	2.68
2000–01	176,647	4,735,149	2.68

Table 13.16
Selected indicators of female nuptiality

Description	Category	Total	Rural	Urban
Number of Currently Married Women (000s)	Total	192,602	145,401	47,201
	Who married during			
	1981–86	30,356	22,446	7,911
	1986–91	28,247	21,193	7,054
Mean Age at Marriage	Total	17.7	17.4	18.5
	Who married during			
	1981–86	18.0	17.7	19.0
	1986–91	18.3	17.9	19.6
Percent of Currently Married Women with Age at Marriage Below 18	Total	53.3	56.7	42.8
	Who married during			
	1981–86	49.3	54.0	36.1
	1986–91	45.4	50.8	29.3

Source: Census of India, 1991.

Table 13.17
Percentage of currently married females to all females for different age-groups over the years in India

Year	Age group						
	15–19	20–24	25–29	30–34	35–44	45–49	15–49
1961	69.57	91.76	94.17	91.43	82.56	69.73	84.42
1971	55.41	88.83	94.95	94.00	88.07	78.03	83.40
1981[a]	43.44	84.46	94.35	94.86	90.76	83.15	80.74
1991[b]	35.28	81.81	93.97	95.14	92.75	87.56	80.18

a. Excludes Assam.
b. Excludes Jammu & Kashmir.
Source: Office of the Registrar General, India.

Given the scale and diversity of India's population, it must be admitted that India has really done well to bring down TFR from 5.2 in 1971 to 3.2 (2.9 by NFHS II) in 29 years time. The steady decline has been observed both in urban and rural areas. NFHS II found 5 states (Goa, Kerala, Karnataka, Himachal Pradesh and Tamil Nadu) recording TFRs below replacement level or very close to it. Three other states, namely Punjab, Andhra Pradesh and West Bengal, must have attained replacement level TFR by now. The most disturbing picture noted in the survey was that TFRs in more populous states were still very high: Uttar Pradesh (TFR 3.99), Rajasthan (3.78), Bihar (3.49) and Madhya Pradesh (3.31). All the Northeastern smaller states also recorded high TFRs.

NFHS II (1998–99) clearly demonstrated a relation between education of women and their attained fertility: the survey observed TFR 1.99 among women who had completed school level education contrasted to TFR 2.26 who had middle school education, TFR 2.64 for those who were literate but did not fall in the 'middle school' category and TFR 3.47 for illiterates. The data when classified by religion, TFR for the different religious segments of the population stood as: Muslims (3.59), Hindus (2.78), Christians (2.44), Sikhs (2.26), Buddhists (2.13) and Jains (1.90). Both SCs and STs showed TFRs above 3. TFR for other backward castes (OBCs) were close to 3. TFR declined more than the all-India average decline in every state in the Northern region except Rajasthan, in both the states in the Central region, and in West Bengal, Arunachal Pradesh, Assam, and Karnataka. Bihar, Orissa, and all those in the Western and Southern regions except Karnataka where TFR declining by less than the all-India average. The TFR actually increased between the two surveys (NFHS I and NFHS II) in Rajasthan, Manipur, Meghalaya, Mizoram, and Nagaland.

Couples effectively protected have monotonically increased over the years both at the state and the national level. CPR in 1980–81 was 22.8 percent, the same has increased to 51.2 percent as on 31st March 2000 (Table 13.18). It is also noted that CPR in 1990s remained almost static at around 45 percent. A sudden jump observed in CPR from 44 percent in 1998–99 to 51.2 percent in 1999–2000 is due to doubling the percentage of couples protected by 'other methods' (which covers condoms, oral pills etc.). Very low CPR has been observed in Meghalaya (4.7%), Jammu & Kashmir (14.4%), Assam (15.2%), Manipur (17.8%) and Bihar (21.2%) in 1999–2000. Only four states [Punjab (65.6%), Karnataka (56.3%), Andhra Pradesh (52.8%) and Gujarat (52.8%)] showed CPR larger than the national average of 51.2 percent as on 31st March 2000. Surprisingly, Kerala, the pioneering state in the country in demographic determinants, did not come into the list of high CPR states although 13 out of 14 districts in the state achieved higher CPR than the national average.

One another thing comes out of the family planning acceptor data (Table 13.4) and effective couple protection data (Table 13.18) that family planning acceptors in 1980–81 were a meager 6,490,000, 31.6 percent of them were sterilization acceptors. CPR in that year was almost totally attained through sterilization. CPR in the 1990s varied between 43.5 and 51.2 and contribution of sterilization in achieving the CPR level still remained around two-third of all the couples effectively protected although sterilization acceptors share among all family planning acceptors came down to 12–13 percent. In the 1990s we observe that couples increasingly are moving towards IUD and other contraceptive methods. As the trends reveal, increase in effective protection in future is likely to come through increased acceptance of abortion, IUD and other contraceptives.

Table 13.18

Couples (women aged 15–44 years) effectively protected in India by using various methods of birth control

Year	*Estimated number of couples*	*Couples effectively protected by all methods*	*% of couples effectively protected*			
			Sterilization	*IUD*	*Other methods*	*Total by all methods*
1	*2*	*3*	*4*	*5*	*6*	*7*
1980–81	116033	26444	20.1	1.0	1.7	22.8
1985–86	129432	45163	26.5	3.7	4.7	34.9
1990–91	145140	64071	30.3	6.7	7.2	44.1
1991–92	148430	64655	30.3	6.3	6.9	43.6

Cont'd...

Table 13.18 Cont'd...

1	*2*	*3*	*4*	*5*	*6*	*7*
1992–93	151720	65946	30.3	6.3	6.9	43.5
1993–94	155020	70361	30.3	6.8	8.3	45.4
1994–95	158310	72552	30.2	7.2	8.5	45.8
1995–96	161593	75094	30.2	7.8	8.5	46.5
1996–97	164749	74746	29.6	7.4	8.3	45.4
1997–98	165869	75226	29.3	7.3	8.8	45.4
1998–99	168558	74221	29.1	7.4	7.5	44.0
1999–00	171198	87398	29.0	7.3	14.9	51.2

Note: The estimates of couple protected given in the above table are based on (a) age distribution of the acceptors and (b) estimates of joint survival ratios of husbands and wives in different age groups. Annual attrition rate for IUD acceptors is taken as 37.6 percent and average annual attrition rate for vasectomy and tubectomy acceptors are taken as follows:

Method/period	Ist Five years	2nd Five years	3rd Five years	4th Five years	5th Five years
Vasectomy	4.11%	7.14%	13.04%	18.74%	33.50%
Tubectomy	2.72%	6.20%	13.52%	28.65%	53.89%

Figure 13.5

Family planning performances in India, 1980–81 – 1999–2000

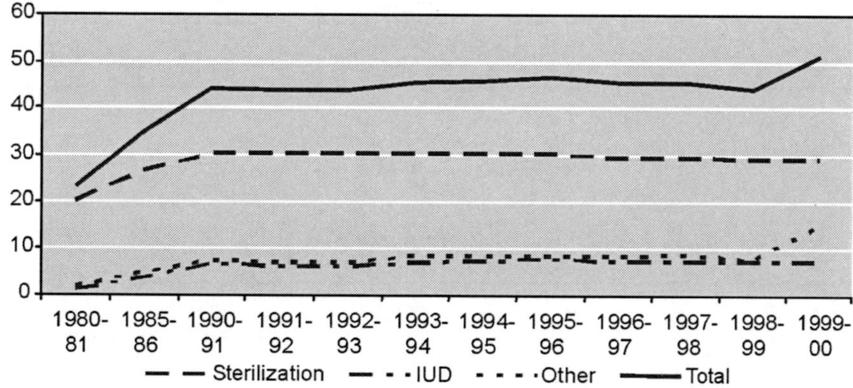

There is considerable variation in CPR among the districts. Of the 396 districts for which CPR data are available for the year ending 31st March 1998, 159 districts achieved more than 50 percent CPR, 135 districts attaining CPR in the range 40–50 percent. All the 17 districts in Punjab for which CPR data are available achieved more than 50 percent CPR. CPR more than 50 percent was achieved in 16 (19) districts in Gujarat, 13 (14) in Kerala, 23 (30) in Maharashtra, and 16 (20) districts in Karnataka. Only in 6 out of 63 districts in Uttar Pradesh, 2 (18) districts in West Bengal, 3 (17) in Assam, and 15 (45) in Madhya Pradesh recorded CPR more than 50 percent. The estimated number of births averted due to operation of the official family welfare program is 257.4231 million between 1980–81 and 1999–2000. The achievements of the Family Welfare Program at a glance since its inception are as under:

Table 13.19
Family welfare program achievement

Parameter	*1951*	*1981*	*1991*	*Current Levels*
Crude Birth Rate	40.8	33.9	29.5	25.8 (2000)
Crude Death Rate	25.1	12.5	9.8	8.5 (2000)
Total Fertility Rate	6.0	4.5	3.6	3.2 (2000) (2.9 by NHFS II)
Growth rate	1.25	2.22	2.14	1.93 (1991–2001) 1.73 (2000)
Maternal Mortality Rate (per 100,000 live births)	NA	NA	437 (NFHS I 1992–93)	407 (1998)
Infant Mortality Rate (per 1,000 live births)	146 (1951–61)	110	80	68 (2000)
Child Mortality Rate (0–4)Yrs. per 1,000 children	57.3 (1972)	41.2	26.5	20.4 (1999)
Couple Protection Rate (%)	10.4 (1971)	22.8	44.1	51.2 (2000)
Expectation of life at birth				
Male	37.1	54.1	60.6	63.9 (2001–06)
Female	36.1	54.7	61.7	66.9 (2001–06)

Source: Office of Registrar General of India
National Family Health Survey (NFHS) I & II.

Table 13.20
Fertility indicators – All India

	GFR			*GMFR*			*TFR*			*TMFR*			*GRR*		
	R	*U*	*C*	*R*	*U*	*C*	*R*	*U*	*C*	*R*	*U*	*C*	*R*	*U*	*C*
1	*2*	*3*	*4*	*5*	*6*	*7*	*8*	*9*	*10*	*11*	*12*	*13*	*14*	*15*	*16*
1990	133	96	124	170	136	162	4.1	2.8	3.8	5.4	4.6	5.2	2.0	1.3	1.8
1996	123	82	113	155	116	146	3.7	2.4	3.4	4.9	4.1	4.7	1.8	1.1	1.6
1007	120	87	110	154	115	145	3.6	2.4	3.3	4.9	4.1	4.7	1.7	1.1	1.6
1998	115	80	107	149	114	141	3.5	2.4	3.2	4.8	4.2	4.6	1.7	1.1	1.5
1999	113	78	103	148	112	139	3.5	2.3	3.2	4.9	4.2	4.7	1.7	1.1	1.5

R – Rural, U – Urban, C – Combined.
Source: Registrar General, India – Sample Registration System

Table 13.21

Age specific fertility rate in the major states, India 1997 & 2000

State	*Year*	*15–19*	*20–24*	*25–29*	*30–34*	*35–39*	*40–44*	*45–49*	*TFR*
1	*2*	*3*	*4*	*5*	*6*	*7*	*8*	*9*	*10*
Andhra Pradesh	1997	116.1	212.0	110.3	38.1	12.5	4.2	0.4	2.5
	2000	100.3	219.4	101.4	35.1	9.4	2.9	0.5	2.3
Assam	1997	55.0	182.5	178.8	131.7	67.3	23.4	5.2	3.2
	2000	60.6	174.4	183.0	103.3	67.7	24.2	3.8	3.1
Bihar	1997	54.8	241.9	231.3	178.1	98.6	51.8	15.4	4.4
	2000	66.2	247.3	259.5	160.5	107.2	49.9	18.3	4.5
Gujarat	1997	25.4	217.4	202.4	92.8	37.9	15.6	4.5	3.0
	2000	24.1	211.9	198.7	93.0	41.7	13.6	3.7	2.9
Haryana	1997	39.2	282.8	211.9	89.5	37.8	17.1	4.4	3.4
	2000	44.9	275.4	186.2	79.2	28.9	15.9	4.1	3.2
Himachal Pradesh	1997	22.9	223.0	152.0	60.0	15.4	3.8	0.0	2.4
	2000	23.0	202.6	167.6	43.1	17.3	5.1	0.0	2.3
Karnataka	1997	55.2	203.6	140.2	52.2	39.9	6.3	1.3	2.5
	2000	58.7	200.6	140.4	55.0	20.2	7.0	1.7	2.4
Kerala	1997	26.0	139.8	130.6	51.4	11.8	2.0	0.4	1.8
	2000	24.9	148.1	131.3	55.5	13.1	2.2	0.1	1.9
Madhya Pradesh	1997	87.6	274.5	213.6	126.4	63.2	28.3	5.1	4.0
	2000	74.6	289.1	271.4	122.7	61.8	26.4	9.4	4.0
Maharashtra	1997	54.2	245.1	155.4	60.8	20.9	6.7	2.2	2.7
	2000	50.0	231.2	133.5	56.3	17.7	5.5	1.6	2.5
Orissa	1997	43.3	202.9	190.8	97.4	49.2	18.0	3.8	3.0
	2000	38.9	182.9	179.9	92.7	44.5	16.0	4.9	2.8
Punjab	1997	16.4	199.6	204.3	82.5	31.0	9.5	0.5	2.7
	2000	16.5	203.4	181.6	62.3	20.1	3.3	1.3	2.4
Rajasthan	1997	60.5	277.6	233.6	137.2	79.7	35.0	13.0	4.2
	2000	65.2	283.7	233.3	131.9	68.9	31.4	10.8	4.1
Tamil Nadu	1997	30.7	179.4	124.2	44.8	11.0	2.9	1.0	2.0
	2000	32.9	177.7	134.4	51.4	15.1	2.1	0.3	2.1
Uttar Pradesh	1997	39.5	248.2	270.6	198.3	115.1	62.3	22.8	4.8
	2000	40.5	260.2	258.1	187.4	125.6	59.4	20.9	4.7
West Bengal	1997	67.0	201.0	130.7	66.6	28.1	14.1	2.7	2.6
	2000	58.2	178.2	128.4	63.6	24.8	11.6	4.9	2.4
INDIA	1997	54.0	220.3	182.8	104.2	54.3	25.0	9.0	3.2
	2000	51.1	218.7	184.5	100.8	53.1	21.7	7.7	3.2

Source: Registrar General of India: Sample Registration System.

But for the poor performance in the BIMARU and a few other states, India's family planning achievement would have been laudable. These four states still had TFR 4 or even larger at the beginning of this millennium compared to the national average close to TFR 3. As many as eight larger states must be very close to replacement level, some even lower in 2007.

The family planning campaign, especially the drive to encourage marriage of girls not before they are 18 and postpone the arrival of the first child till they are 20 or later had stronger impact on the urban women than the rural women, on the literate and educated women than the illiterates and those with very low level of formal education. The ASFR by residence and level of education of women clearly bring out the fertility differentials.

Table 13.22

Age specific fertility rate by education level of women, India 1999

Education level	*Rural/Urban*	*Age groups*						
		15–19	*20–24*	*25–29*	*30–34*	*35–39*	*40–44*	*45–49*
1	*2*	*3*	*4*	*5*	*6*	*7*	*8*	*9*
Illiterate	Rural	93.1	266.7	223.7	141.9	83.0	36.5	12.9
	Urban	60.8	220.1	179.3	103.5	55.2	18.6	6.3
Literate but without formal education	Rural	91.3	257.1	196.7	111.2	53.6	19.2	7.5
	Urban	58.1	236.2	209.2	118.1	42.7	24.7	4.0
Below Primary level	Rural	65.8	279.5	192.5	80.2	32.0	13.1	2.0
	Urban	57.6	266.5	196.2	80.7	34.9	7.9	1.4
Primary level	Rural	30.8	177.8	129.6	59.8	17.1	5.4	1.9
	Urban	24.5	186.7	141.8	47.0	12.8	2.8	0.5
Matric	Rural	22.9	134.8	133.2	66.3	18.2	6.4	1.9
	Urban	14.1	106.5	125.6	51.7	12.4	4.9	0.3
All levels	Rural	38.0	194.6	154.8	72.8	28.3	11.3	2.7
	Urban	22.5	143.2	136.6	58.2	19.4	5.3	1.0

Source: Registrar General, India.

13.5.1 Family Welfare Service Network

Family Welfare services are provided to the community through a network of sub-centers, PHCs and CHCs in rural areas and hospitals, dispensaries, etc. in urban areas. This network, being set up under the Minimum Needs Program (now reorganized as Basic Minimum Services (BMS) program), is also supported by an expanding number of Post Partum Centers at district and sub-district level. A Female Paramedical Worker (ANM) posted at every sub-center and supported by a Male Multi-purpose Worker (MPW) are the front line staff for providing family welfare services to the community. A Lady Health Visitor (LHV) posted at the PHC supervises the ANM's. As on 31–3–2001, 137,311 sub-centers, 22,842 PHCs and 3,042 CHCs were operating in the country. Ministries of Railways and Defense also provide Family Welfare services through their network of dispensaries, clinics and hospitals. NGOs all over the country are being involved in counseling, advocacy and for increasing awareness about the Reproductive and Child Health Program. The Department of Family Welfare is funding more than 1,000 NGOs to help in the RCH program. Under this program, NGOs generally have been involved in advocacy. The Department has decided to expand the activities of NGOs from mere advocacy to service delivery as well. A new program, RCH camps, has been launched in 2000–01 in remote rural areas not easily covered by PHCs. Though initially such camps were to be organized in selected districts, the Empowered Action Group (EAG) in the Ministry of Health and Family Welfare has decided to include this program in all the districts of demographically backward states. The government also has decided to train one *dai* from each village making deliveries safe.

Nearly two thousand referral units, identified under Child Survival and Safety of Mothers (CSSM), have become operational with skilled man-powers, especially anesthetists, gynecologists with adequate infrastructure and medicines. The obstetric and other complications do arise, especially in home deliveries in rural areas. The government has allocated funds for arranging referral transports for these cases.

However, a large proportion of the health centers, in spite of repeated assurance from state governments, do not have the minimum infrastructure, medicines, and more alarmingly doctors and nurses. About 30 percent of the doctors, asked to join these rural health centers, do not report for duty. Many of these health centers remain open only on days when some doctor from some other health center is deputed for selected few days. Media reports are plenty that paramedical staff, even the other supporting staff, attend to the ailing patients and prescribe medicines whatever there is in their stock. The central government is trying to bring out a bill in the parliament that would make mandatory for each doctor after he/she completes his/her internship to serve in rural health centers for one year ("barefoot doctors") before these doctors are granted permanent registration number. That probably would insure the presence of a doctor in rural health centers through out the year, but how much expert guidance and treatment the rural patients would receive from these doctors without any experience remains extremely doubtful. India, it seems, is taking lessons from China's experience on expanding health program to rural areas of the country.

Government of India launched CSSM in 1992–93 jointly funded by UNICEF and World Bank. India during 1997–98 launched the RCH Program for implementation during the 9th plan period by integrating CSSM program with other RCH services. In addition, a new component for management of Reproductive Tract Infection (RTI) and Sexually Transmitted Infection (STI) has also been incorporated.

MCH has remained at the center of these and other programs and projects instituted from time to time. The government realized that the key to birth control lies in bringing down IMR and child mortality and in reduction of MMR originating in pregnancy related causes. Vaccination program is a key intervention for protecting children from life threatening conditions. Universalization of immunization for infants and children (DPT, Polio, BCG and others) and vaccination against tetanus of mothers received top priority in India's family welfare program. A massive campaign for immunization through newspaper, radio and television is being carried out through out the year. The dates for nationwide polio vaccination are announced well in advance. The local political and community leaders often would take part in such campaigns especially in communities that have shown resistance to some of these vaccination programs. It is disconcerting to see a high dropout rate between first polio vaccine and the third in quite a few states/UTs (Arunachal Pradesh, Manipur, Meghalaya, Chandigarh, Delhi and Pondicherry). Immunization program has been strengthened in eight poor performing states (Assam, Bihar, Gujarat, Madhya Pradesh, Orissa, Rajasthan, Uttar Pradesh and West Bengal). Although the target for birth control has been abandoned and the decision to adopt family planning and choice of methods has been left to the personal decision of couples, immunization has not been left to individuals' decisions. The statistics prepared by the Health Department, Government of India, gives a genuine hope that universalization of mother and child care is progressing in the right direction. For a comprehensive picture on the execution of the immunization program, the reader is referred to Appendix 13.1.

The MCH program and the campaign for delayed marriage of girls and adoption of small family norm as also the various incentives offered to women who register their pregnancy, attend health centers for regular medical check-up and delay the birth of their child have definitely played some role in bringing down birth rates and in reduction of IMR and child mortality. Legalization of abortion has also brought down MMR since abortions in certified institutions cost less or no money, they are safe too. Yet maternal mortality in the country remains one of the highest in the world. What really is annoying is the fact that in spite large investment in MCH program, maternal mortality in rural India due to Bleeding of Pregnancy & Puerperium and Puerperal sepsis have been going up.

Table 13.23

Percentage of maternal mortality by causes related to child birth and pregnancy (rural India)

Specific causes	*1985*	*1990*	*1995*	*1997*	*1998*
1	*2*	*3*	*4*	*5*	*6*
Abortion	11.5	11.8	17.6	7.3	8.9
Toxaemia	6.7	15.2	9.9	6.6	8.3
Anaemia	23.1	19.4	17.0	17.3	19.0
Bleeding of Pregnancy & Puerperium	15.9	23.7	28.9	27.6	29.6
Malposition of child leading to death of mother	7.7	7.1	4.0	10.7	9.5
Puerperal sepsis	13.9	8.1	8.5	13.0	16.1
Not classifiable	21.2	14.7	14.1	17.5	8.6

Source: Model Registration Scheme – Survey of Causes of Death (Rural) 1985, 1990, 1994, 1995 – A report, RGI. Causes of Maternal Deaths and their percent distribution to total maternal deaths by SRS 1997,1998, RGI.

One other way of measuring the success of the family welfare program is the number of births averted through various methods adopted for birth control over the years. In the nineties, on an average an estimated 1.5 million births per year have been averted. Whereas in the 1980s the drop in birth rate per annum was 0.35 percentage points, it accelerated to 0.5 percentage point a year in 1990's. Death rate, on the other hand, declined by 1.2 percentage point in the 1990s. The trend curve (Fig 13.6) also clearly indicates that death rate has almost reached a stationary stage. Trend in birth rate decline clearly indicates that achievement of CBR 21 (or even lower) is possible by 2010 provided a faster decline in IMR and child mortality is achieved. Since the proportion of people in 60 years and older is likely to increase fast, the death rate trend may take a U-turn, resulting in faster decline in growth rate.

Table 13.24
Estimated number of births averted (in million)

Year	*Sterilization*	*IUD*	*Other methods*	*Total*	*Cumulative total*
1	*2*	*3*	*4*	*5*	*6*
1980–81	4.3003	0.2453	0.3677	4.9328	4 4.1571
1985–86	5.9745	0.8310	1.3154	8.1209	76.3333
1990–91	8.0387	1.9397	2.3263	12.3047	130.1443
1991–92	8.1896	2.0809	2.4233	12.6938	142.8381
1992–93	8.3113	2.0409	2.4020	12.7542	155.5923
1993–94	8.4669	2.1112	2.5780	13.1560	168.7483
1994–95	8.6398	2.3616	3.0475	14.0488	182.7971
1995–96	8.7979	2.6132	3.1837	14.5948	197.3919
1996–97	8.8853	2.7484	3.1815	14.8152	212.2070
1997–98	8.8597	2.6694	3.2342	14.7633	226.9703
1998–99	8.8944	2.6937	3.4822	15.0703	242.0873
1999–00	8.9268	2.7089	3.7002	15.3359	257.4231
Total	176.4481	35.9996	44.9755	257.4231	

Source: Family Welfare Program in India Year Book 2001.

Table 13.25
Decline in birth and death rates in India, 1981–2000

Year	*Birth rate*			*Death rate*		
	Rural	*Urban*	*Combined*	*Rural*	*Urban*	*Combined*
1	*2*	*3*	*4*	*5*	*6*	*7*
1981	35.6	27.0	33.9	13.7	7.8	12.5
1982	35.5	27.6	33.8	13.1	7.4	11.9
1983	35.3	28.3	33.7	13.1	7.9	11.9
1984	35.3	29.4	33.9	13.8	8.6	12.6
1985	34.3	28.1	32.9	13.0	7.8	11.8
1986	34.2	27.1	32.6	12.2	7.6	11.1
1987	33.7	27.4	32.2	12.0	7.4	10.9
1988	33.1	26.3	31.5	12.0	7.7	11.0
1989	32.2	25.2	30.6	11.1	7.2	10.3

Cont'd...

Table 13.25 Cont'd...

1	*2*	*3*	*4*	*5*	*6*	*7*
1990	31.7	24.7	30.2	10.5	6.8	9.7
1991	30.9	24.3	29.5	10.6	7.1	9.8
1992	30.9	23.1	29.2	10.9	7.0	10.1
1993	30.4	23.7	28.7	10.6	5.8	9.3
1994	30.5	23.1	28.7	10.1	6.7	9.3
1995	30.0	22.7	28.3	9.8	6.6	9.0
1996	29.3	21.6	27.5	9.7	6.5	9.0
1997	28.9	21.5	27.2	9.6	6.5	8.9
1998	28.0	21.1	26.5	9.7	6.6	9.0
1999	27.6	20.8	26.1	9.4	6.3	8.7
2000	27.5	20.7	25.8	9.3	6.3	8.5

Source: Registrar General,India, Sample Registration System, 1981–2000.

Figure 13.6
Birth and death rates in India, 1981–2000

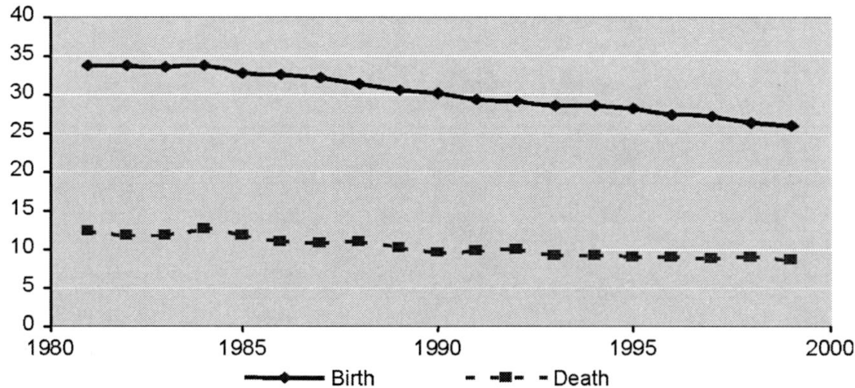

13.6 Fund Allocation

The RCH Program had an approved outlay of Rs 51,125.3 millions for 9th plan period. To mobilize funds, India obtained soft loans from World Bank, UNICEF, IDA and other donors and financial agencies. Allocation for family welfare program has increased considerably over the years. In fact, family welfare program has a very large share in the Plan and annual budget allocation for the Ministry of Health and Family Welfare. Probably this is the single department under the Ministry of Health and Family welfare where nearly 100 percent of the allotted sum is utilized every year. (For a greater detail of fund allocation and spending, see Appendix 13.2).

Table 13.26

Plan outlay on health & family welfare in different plan periods (Rs in crores)

Period	*Health*	*Family Welfare*	*Sub-total*	*Total Plan*	*% of health to Total*	*% of Family Welfare to*	
						Total	*Sub-total*
1	*2*	*3*	*4*	*5*	*6*	*7*	*8*
Third Plan (1961–66)	225.9	24.9	250.8	8576.5	2.6	0.3	9.93
Annual Plan (1966–69)	140.2	70.4	210.6	6625.4	2.1	1.1	33.43
Fourth Plan (1969–74)	335.5	278.0	613.5	15778.8	2.1	1.8	45.31
Fifth Plan (1974–79)	760.8	491.8	1252.6	39426.2	1.9	1.2	39.26
Annual Plan (1979–80)	223.1	118.5	341.6	12176.5	1.8	1.0	34.69
Sixth Plan (1980–85)	1821.0	1010.0	2831.0	97500.0	1.9	1.0	35.68
Seventh Plan (1985–90)	3392.9	3256.3	6649.2	180000.0	1.9	1.8	48.97
Annual Plans							
1990–91	960.9	784.9	1745.8	61518.1	1.6	1.3	44.96
1991–92	1042.3	856.6	1898.9	65855.8	1.6	1.3	45.11
Eighth Plan (1992–97)	7575.9	6500.0	14075.9	434100.0	1.7	1.5	46.18
Ninth Plan (1997–2002)	12072.98	14170.0*	26243.0	859200.0	1.4	1.64	54.00

*Figure excludes arrears
Source: Planning Commission.

Nearly 80 percent increase in fund allocation (current prices) to Family Welfare program has been made in the Tenth Plan (2002–07) over the allocation in the Ninth Plan. A huge sum has been allocated for rural family welfare sub-centers (38.5% of total allocation). Of the on-going schemes, RCH receives the maximum attention. Cost of free distribution of contraceptives and expenses relating to sterilization and IUD insertion together account for about 7.5 percent of the total allocation. About 2 percent of the Tenth Plan allocation is proposed to be used in National Maternal Benefit Scheme. India received assistances for the ongoing family welfare programs from international funding agencies.

Table 13.27

International assistance received for family welfare program in India (Rs million)

	1993–94	*1994–95*	*1995–96*	*1996–97*	*1997–98*	*1998–99*	*1999–2000*	*2000–2001*
1	*2*	*3*	*4*	*5*	*6*	*7*	*8*	*9*
Total*	3312.3	4564.3	4391.8	4815.5	3670.2	5586.4	7141.3	8148.5
World Bank	2407.1	3093.6	3122.5	2843.3	1473.7	1283.0	2816.0	4958.0

*Includes aids received from 12 international funding agencies including World Bank
Source: Family Welfare Program in India Yearbook 2001.

13.7 Population Research Centers (PRC)

The Ministry of Health and Family Welfare has established a network of 18 Population Research Centers scattered in 17 major states. 12 Universities and 6 institutes of national repute have been selected for PRC. These Centers are carrying on researches on various aspects of population stabilization, demographic, socio-demographic surveys and communication aspects of population and family welfare program. Government of India finances the research programs. Area specific studies are usually selected every year and cover a wide range of RCH program topics of current relevance. A very miniscule amount has been allocated for assistance to research institutes (only 0.6 percent in the Tenth Plan compared to over 0.8 percent in the Ninth Plan).

14

Census of India 2011

Provisional Populational Totals[1]

14.1 Growth of Population

On 31st March, 2011, the Census Commissioner C. Chandramouli presented in a press release the Provisional Population Totals for the Census 2011. The population total recorded is **1,210,193,422** [males 623,724,248 (51.54%) and females 586,469,174 (48.46%)], which almost is the same as the combined population of six countries, viz., USA, Brazil, Indonesia, Japan, Bangladesh and Pakistan. Actually, India in the last decade has produced as many people as the total population of Brazil. Population of Uttar Pradesh and Maharashtra together exceeds the population of the US. Two years back, the population projection was 1.19 billion for 2011. That missed the headcount result in 2011 by 18 million. The BIMARU states (Bihar, Madhya Pradesh, Rajasthan and Uttar Pradesh) together have a population of 444,604,691, i.e., 36.74 percent share of 2011 national population. In reality, these four states together have population numbers that exceed the entire India's population in the 1961 census count (439,234,771). The compiled distribution data for 35 states/UTs are presented in Appendix 14.1. This short write-up covers only the absolute population of various states/UTs in 2011, their decadal growth rates, population densities, sex ratio in different segments of the population and the attained literacy rates, separately for males and females.

The absolute decadal growth (2001–2011) is over 181 million, almost the same observed in 1991–2001 decade. We still are adding 18 million mouths every year (China is adding only 6.3 million a year). In effect, the change in absolute growth in population numbers in the last decade was –3,639,348 compared to 25,163,650 in 2001 (Table 14.2 Col. 5). In percentage term, the decadal growth has declined by over 4.3 percent – from 21.96 to 17.65 percent (growth of males 17.19% and females 18.12%). Even though the base data (2001) for 2011 census is far in excess of the base data for 2001 head count, the absolute decadal growth has come down from what it was in 2001 census. The 2001–2011 is the first decade – with exception of 1911–1921 – which actually has added lesser population compared to the previous decade.

The average annual exponential growth has declined from 1.93 percent (1991–2001) to 1.66 percent in the latest head count. That indicates that growth rate in the year 2011 could even be lower than 1.5 percent. India's share to world population has increased from 17 percent in 2001 to 17.5 percent in 2011. India is only about 2 percentage points behind China's share (19.4%) to world population. Earlier it was thought that India would overtake China in population at around 2045, the year when Indian population was expected to stabilize. US Bureau of Census after examining the latest demographic trends in China and India indicated that this may happen even as early as 2025 when China peaks her population at 1.395 billion. UN 2010 prejection indicates that India's population would peak at 1.718 billion in 2060, which at that point of time, would account for 18.45 percent of world population, projected at 9.31 billion. End of this century will see India's population

1. Most information are retrieved from the website.

dropping to 1.6 billion (16% of world population). Census 2011 only confirms that India would fail to reach many of the UN Millennium Goals; some of the NPP 2000 goals also would be missed.

Uttar Pradesh as usual has the largest population, 199.58 million and Sikkim the least, 0.608 million among the states. West Bengal, the fourth largest state with population 91,347,736, (13.93% increase over 2001 population) is behind Uttar Pradesh (199,581,477), Maharashtra (112,372,972) and Bihar (103,804,637), both in numbers and in decadal growth rate. North 24 Pargana in West Bengal is the second largest district with 10.08 million people, next only to Thane of Maharashtra which has a population of 10.1 million.

Regional share of the 2011 census population has been worked out. Male-female break-up of the regional population and the sex ratio, separately for each region, have also been computed (Table 14.1). The *Eastern region* has the largest number of states/UTs and together they have the largest share (26.114%) of population total of India, 2011. Eight states consisting of Assam, Bihar, Jharkhand, West Bengal, Orissa, Meghalaya, Manipur and Tripura collectively contribute over 98 percent to the region's population total. The two most densely populated states – Bihar and West Bengal – are located in this region. The population density of four states in the northeastern part of the region still has enough space for further growth. The *Eastern region*, which has as many as 13 states/UTs, (only four states and one UT registering decadal growth below 15%), is also growing fast and has added close to 50 million persons between 2001 and 2011. High growth of Bihar, Jharkhand, Meghalaya and other smaller states has contributed to the growth history of this region. The *Northern region* has remained the least populated area in the country. With exception of Himachal Pradesh and Punjab the other 6 states/UTs in the region have recorded decadal growth between 17.1 and 23.71 percent. The *Central region*, the second most populous region in the country, continues to grow very fast since all the 3 states (Uttar Pradesh, Madhya Pradesh and Chhattisgarh) in this region are growing by over 20 percent and have added 50 million in 2001–2011. The *Southern region* has 5 states/UTs showing decadal growth below 11 percent (3 below 8%); only 2 states have growth a little over 15 percent and Pondicherry, a UT, has the highest growth (27.72%) in the region. Its decadal addition is 29.3 million. The *Western region* has only 2 big states and 2 UTs. Gujarat and Maharashtra, recording growth rates 19.7 and 15.99 percent respectively, account for nearly 100 percent of the population in this region. Higher growth in these two industrially advanced states has invited migrants from all over the country. The region has added 25.6 million over and above 2001 population.

Table 14.1

Regional share, sex composition and sex ratio in 2011 population

	2011 population break-up by sex			*Percentage share of 2011 population*			*% share of females in region totals*	*Sex ratio in the region*
Region	*Persons*	*Males*	*Females*	*Persons*	*Males*	*Females*		
Northern	169,008,437	88,610,358	80,398,079	13.965	14.207	13.709	47.57	907.32
Eastern	316,033,895	162,757,597	153,276,298	26.114	26.095	26.135	48.50	941.75
Central	297,719,238	155,037,250	142,681,988	24.601	24.857	24.329	47.93	920.31
Western	173,342,364	90,186,957	83,155,407	14.324	14.459	14.179	47.97	922.03
Southern	254,089,488	127,132,086	126,957,402	20.996	20.383	21.648	49.97	998.63
INDIA	1,210,193,422	623,724,248	586,469,174		51.539	48.461		940.26

Male-female break-up of populations shows that females have the least share in the population in Northern region followed by Central region. There are almost equal number of males and females in populations in Southern states and the female-male ratio in the region is exceedingly close to 1000. Sex ratio in the population in these states as a combine is a mirror image of the percentage share of women in their total population.

14.2 Growth Rate

High growth is still observed in the BIMARU states (with 20–25% decadal growth they together share 36.74% of India's population) and in two northeastern states, viz., Arunachal and Meghalaya witnessing 25.92 and 27.82 percent decadal growth respectively and three union territories, Daman & Diu and Dadra-Nagar Haveli have growths much above 50 percent and Pondicherry grew by 27.72 percent. Jammu & Kashmir is still growing at an alarmingly fast rate, 23.71 percent, and Delhi by 20.96 percent. Of the 11 states/UTs recording less than 14 percent decadal growth (Table 14.3), five are either smaller states or UTs. Though population in Nagaland had been growing at a frighteningly fast pace between 1971 and 2001, the absolute population size in the state has declined in the

Table 14.2

Decadal population growth, 1951–2011

Census year	*Decadal growth*			*Change in absolute decadal growth*
	Absolute population	*Absolute*	*Percentage*	
1	*2*	*3*	*4*	*5*
1951	361,088,090	42,427,510	13.31	2,744,168
1961	439,234,771	78,146,681	21.64	35,719,171
1971	548,159,652	108,924,881	24.80	30,778,200
1981	683,329,097	135,169,445	24.66	26,244,564
1991	843,387,888	160,058,791	23.42	24,889,346
2001	1,028,610,328	185,222,440	21.96	25,163,650
2011	1,210,193,422	181,455,986	17.65	–3,639,348

Table 14.3

High and Low population growth rate states/UTs, 2001–2011

High		*Low*	
Dadra & Nagar Haveli	55.50	Nagaland	(-)0.47
Daman & Diu	53.54	Kerala	4.86
Meghalaya	27.82	Lakshadweep	6.23
Pondicherry	27.72	Andaman & Nicobar Islands	6.68
Arunachal Pradesh	25.92	Goa	8.17
Bihar	25.07	Andhra Pradesh	11.10
Jammu & Kashmir	23.71	Sikkim	12.36
Chhattisgarh	22.59	Himachal Pradesh	12.81
Jharkhand	22.34	Punjab	13.73
Rajasthan	21.44	West Bengal	13.93
Delhi	20.96	Orissa	13.97

Figure 14.1
Percentage decadal growth, 1951–2011

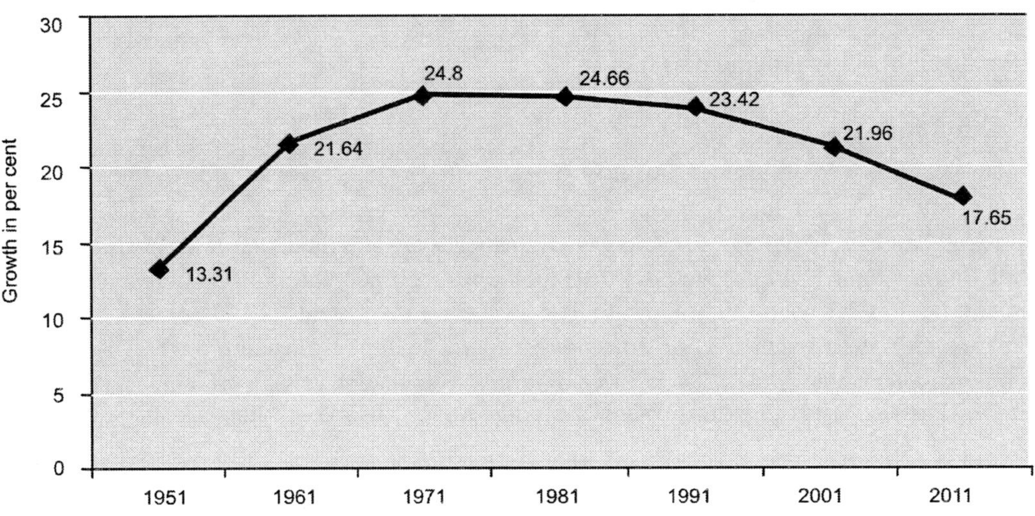

last decade (–0.47% growth). The reasons for such an abrupt drop in growth can be analyzed only when birth, death, migration and some other relevant data become available. Goa and Sikkim are very small states. Population share of 11 relatively low growth (below 14%) states/UTs in India's population in 2011 is only 24 percent (pooled population 290,399,435) as against about 44.59 percent (pooled population 539,681,146 (the BIMARU states together contributing 82.98% to this total) for the 11 relatively high growth (20% and over) states/UTs. In the remaining 13 states/UTs, growth rates varying between 14 and 20 percent, account for 31.41 percent of 2011 population. Whereas 21 states/UTs in 2001 recorded 20 percent or more decadal growth, the number has come down to 11 in 2011. In this highly skewed distribution, the fate of containing population growth in India appears to have been mortgaged to four big BIMARU states, all registering over 20 percent growth rate. The percentage decadal growth between 1951 and 2011 is displayed in Figure 14.1.

14.3 Population Density

Till 2001, West Bengal had the highest population density among all the states. In 2011, Bihar recorded population density of 1102 persons per km^2, overtaking West Bengal. West Bengal now stands second in population density with 1029 per km^2 against the national average of 382 per km^2. Kerala, which a few decades back topped in population density, now occupies the third spot with 859 people per km^2. Delhi accommodates the largest number (11,297) of people per km^2. The highest population density is in Delhi's north-east district (37,346 per km^2) and lowest si in Dibang Valley in Arunachal Pradesh (just 1 per km^2). Arunachal Pradesh has the lowest density, 17 per km^2. Andaman & Nicobar Islands is also very thinly populated with 46 per km^2. All the UTs, except Andaman & Nicobar Islands, are very densely populated. Northeastern states generally have space for further population expansion. Jammu & Kashmir (124 per km^2) and Himachal Pradesh (123 per km^2) have similar population density, but the former is still growing at a very fast rate (23.71%) and the latter has contained decadal population growth (12.81%) significantly. Even though Maharashtra (365 per km^2) and Gujarat (308 per km^2) because of their rapid industrial growth are receiving migrants from all over the country, still have population density much less than the national average.

14.4 Sex Ratio in the Total, Child and Age 7 and Above Population

Proportion of women in population has steadily declined between 1901 and 1981. Thereafter, in spite of fall in sex ratio among children, proportion of women in the population has been rising. This has happened because of higher survival rate of women in older ages and this higher survival rate over-compensated their shortfall in numbers in 0-6 age group. The 2001 census gave a clear indication that the gap between absolute numbers of males and females in the population was diminishing. The 2001 head count also showed that females registered a higher annual growth rate (0.0199977) than males (0.01958769) in the decade 1991–2001. The 2011 census count strengthened the perception that male-female gap in numbers has diminished further. Change in population share by females is shown in Figure 14.2

Apparently the most exciting information that this census brings out is the fact that the proportion of children below 6 years has declined from about 16 in 2001 to only 13.12 percent in 2011 (13.3% growth for boys and 12.93% for girls), i.e. over 5.5 million drop in absolute numbers (158.8 million in 2011 against 164.3 million in 2001, 2.88% drop). It clearly indicates that proportion of young age population (0-14) must have declined from around 34 percent in 2001 to around 30 percent in 2011. This declining trend of young age group in the population is clearly visible since 1981. That this decline is continuing is welcome since this will lift the median age in the population and India's "young" population has taken a decisive stride to attaining "adulthood" in the foreseeable future.

There are a few vital implications of this decline in child population: birth rate certainly has declined fast in the last decade [child-woman (in reproductive age group) ratio is a good indicator of

Figure 14.2

Proportion of females in population, 1901–2011

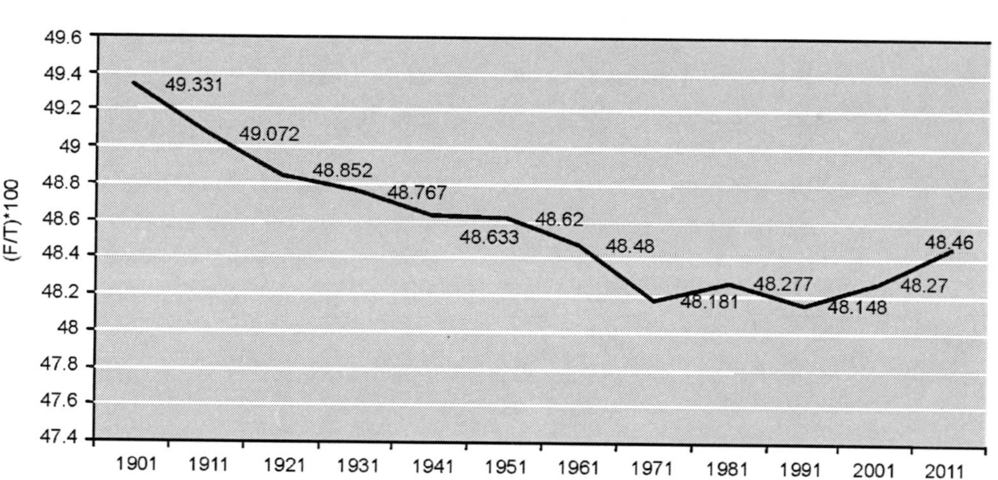

fertility level in a population]; this fast decline in child population will have a long term impact on the age-sex composition of the population; it would also push up the proportion of higher aged persons, especially the senior citizens, presenting challenging conditions to the social planners; in the long run there would be shortage of people in the workforce (15-59). Higher sex ratio is observed mostly in smaller states in northeast (Manipur, Mizoram and Meghalaya) besides some larger states like Kerala, Tamil Nadu and Andhra Pradesh, traditionally known for their healthier sex ratio in population.

Table 14.4

Sex ratio in total, child and age 7 and above population, 1991–2011

*States/UTs**	*Total population*			*Child population (0-6)*			*Age 7+ population*		
	1991	*2001*	*2011*	*1991*	*2001*	*2011*	*1991*	*2001*	*2011*
1	*2*	*3*	*4*	*5*	*6*	*7*	*8*	*9*	*10*
INDIA	**927**	**933**	**940**	**945**	**927↓**	**914↓**	**923**	**934**	**944**
Jammu & Kashmir	NA	892	883?	NA	941	859?	NA	884	887
Himachal Pradesh	976	968↓	974	951	896↓	906	980	980	983
Punjab	882	876↓	893	875	798↓	846	883	888	899
Chandigarh*	790	777↓	818	899	845↓	867	772	767↓	812
Uttaranchal	936	962	963	948	908↓	886↓	933	973	975
Haryana	865	861↓	877	879	819↓	830	862	869	885
Delhi*	827	821↓	866	915	868↓	866↓	810	813	866
Rajasthan	910	921	926	916	909↓	883↓	908	923	935
Uttar Pradesh	876	898	908	927	916↓	899↓	863	894	910
Bihar	907	919	916↓	953	942↓	933↓	895	914	912
Sikkim	878	875↓	889	965	963↓	944↓	860	861	883
Arunachal Pradesh	859	893	920	982	964↓	960↓	829	878	913
Nagaland	886	900	931	993	964↓	944↓	865	890	929
Manipur	958	974	987	974	957↓	934↓	955	977	995
Mizoram	921	935	975	969	964↓	971	911	930	976
Tripura	945	948	961	967	966↓	953↓	940	945	962
Meghalaya	955	972	986	986	973↓	970↓	947	971	989
Assam	923	935	954	975	965↓	957↓	910	929	953
West Bengal	917	934	947	967	960↓	950↓	907	929	946
Jharkhand	922	941	947	979	965↓	943↓	908	935	948
Orissa	971	972	978	967	953↓	934↓	972	976	985
Chhattisgarh	985	989	991	984	975↓	964↓	986	992	995
Madhya Pradesh	912	919	930	941	932↓	912↓	905	916	933
Gujarat	934	920↓	918↓	928	883↓	886	936	927↓	923↓
Daman & Diu*	969	710↓	618↓	958	926↓	909↓	971	682↓	589↓
Dadra & Nagar Haveli*	952	812↓	775↓	1,013	979↓	924↓	937	779↓	752↓

Cont'd...

Table 14.4 Cont'd...

1	*2*	*3*	*4*	*5*	*6*	*7*	*8*	*9*	*10*
Maharashtra	934	922↓	925	946	913↓	883↓	931	924↓	931
Andhra Pradesh	972	978	992	975	961↓	943↓	972	981	997
Karnataka	960	965	968	960	946↓	943↓	960	968	971
Goa	967	961↓	968	964	938↓	920↓	967	964↓	973
Lakshadweep*	943	948	946↓	941	959	908↓	943	946	951
Kerala	1,036	1058	1084	958	960	959↓	1049	1,072	1,099
Tamil Nadu	974	987	995	948	942↓	946	978	993	1,000
Pondicherry*	979	1001	1038	963	967	965↓	982	1,006	1,047
Andaman & Nicobar Is*	818	846	878	973	957↓	966	790	831	868
Declining sex ratio		**11**	**6**		**31**	**27**		**6**	**3**

↓ indicates that the sex ratio has declined from what was recorded in the previous census.

Table 14.4 presents the distributions of the states/UTs in sex ratios, separately for different population categories for different decades. It shows how the states/UTs improved/worsened their positions in various population categories. The 1991 data show that the sex ratio distribution for different population categories is essentially similar to that in 2011 except in 'below 850' class. The distribution of states/UTs is essentially alike both in 2001 and 2011 in 'all ages' and in 'age 7 and above population'. It appears that the sex ratio distribution in 'age 7 and above population' largely determines the spread of the same in 'all ages'. Both the population groups improved their positions almost in identical manner in 2011. It is in the children category that the number of states/UTs showing sex ratio below 951 worsened – from 17 in 2001 it slided further to 26 in 2011. That is the reason why child sex ratio fell from 927 to 914. No heed was paid to the warning sounded in 2001 census. The sex ratio in 0-4 age group plummeted by 58.5 points from the ratio recorded in 1991. Governments at the center and in states made no serious attempt to stop sex selective abortions in nursing homes and private clinics. The possibility of further drop in *sex ratio at birth* in 2001–2011 cannot be ruled out since the technology for sex determination of fetus, which largely remained confined to some states earlier, has now been expanded to most other states/UTs, even in rural areas due to wide spread use of

Table 14.5

Distribution of states/UTs by their sex ratio in different population categories, 1991–2011

	All ages			*0-6 years*			*Age 7 & above*		
	1991	***2001***	***2011***	***1991***	***2001***	***2011***	***1991***	***2001***	***2011***
Below 850	3	5	3	—	3	2	4	5	2
851-875	2	2	1	1	1	3	4	2	3
876-900	4	5	5	2	2	5	2	5	4
901-925	7	5	5	2	4	6	6	4	4
926-950	5	6	6	7	7	10	7	7	6
951-975	9	7	7	16	17	9	6	4	6
976-1000	3	3	6	5	1	—	4	6	8
1001-1025	1	1	1	1	—	—	1	1	1
1026-1050	—	1	1	—	—	—	—	—	1
1051+	—	—	—	—	—	—	—	1	—
	34	**35**	**35**	**34**	**35**	**35**	**34**	**35**	**35**
Declining sex ratio		**11**	**6**		**31**	**27**		**6**	**3**

Note: No census in Jammu & Kashmir could be conducted in 1991.

portable scanners. There are about 40,000 registered clinics in the country authorized to use scanners, and there are many more that are not on record.

Distribution of states/UTs in respect to their sex ratios for different population groups over the last three decades is presented in Table 14.5.

Sex ratio in age 7 and above population had been the key player in the rise or fall in sex ratio in the total population both in 2001 and 2011. The negative impact induced by child sex ratio had marginally been compensated by the improved sex ratio in age 7 and above population. From Table 14.5 we also see that out of the 35 states/UTs 31 recorded lower child sex ratio in 2001 vis-à-vis 1991. Of the 3 states/UTs (no census in Jammu & Kashmir in 1991) improving their child sex ratio vis-à-vis their 1991 levels, none having very large population, could not put much resistance to the strong pull exerted by the rest of the states/UTs. The push generated by 29 states/UTs that improved sex ratio by 1.19 percent in age 7 and above population in the same decade could neutralize the force of the pull and help register a 0.65 percent increase in sex ratio in the population in 2001. Presence of big states like Maharashtra and Gujarat among the 6 states where sex ratio in age 7 and above population had declined almost neutralized the push up effect. In the last decade the proportion of children in the population dropped by 2.88 percent. This resulted in increase in the population share for age 7 and above population by the same amount. Even with only 1.07 percent gain in sex ratio in this group, sex ratio in the population could increase by 7 points (0.75%) since the pull exerted by 3 states/UTs (only a marginal drop in Bihar) in 2011did not add much to the strength of pull exerted by 27 states/UTs which caused the child sex ratio in 2011 to drop by 1.42 percent. The movement of child sex ratio and that in the population is presented in Figure 14.3.

For comparative analysis, the high and low performing states/UTs (2011) in the three population segments (Tables 14.6-14.8) have been derived from Table 14.4. Six states/UTs – Kerala, Tamil Nadu, Mizoram, Meghalaya, Pondicherry and Chhattisgarh – consistently show higher sex ratio in all the three population segments – total, child and age 7 and above population in 2011. Similarly, names of six other states/UTs – Jammu & Kashmir, Chandigarh, Haryana, Punjab, Delhi and Uttar Pradesh – appear in the list of all the low sex ratio categories. Even though Delhi and Chandigarh improved their sex ratios in age 7 and above population by 53 and 45 points respectively, they still remain poor achievers in sex ratio, way behind the national average of 944. Bar

Figure 14.3

Sex ratio in population and child group

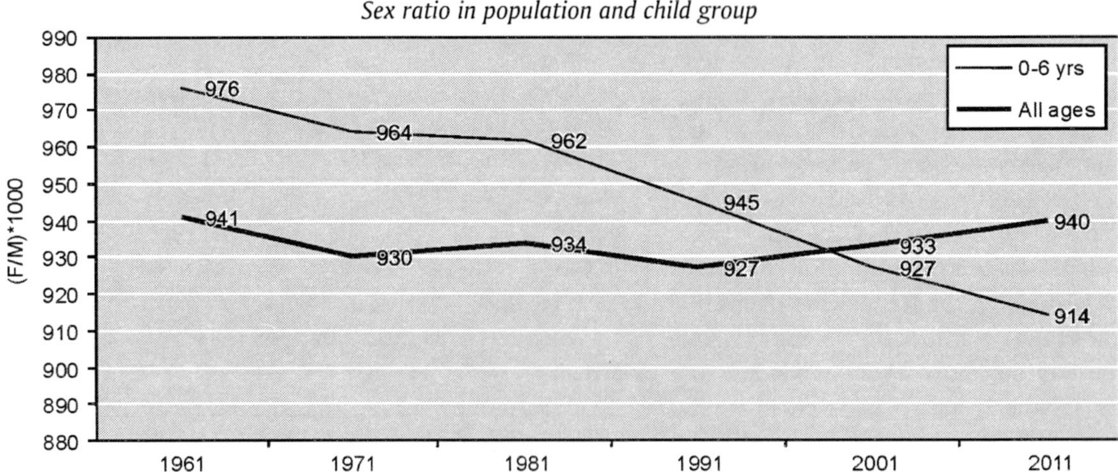

diagram for 21 states that recorded lower child sex ratio in 2011 compared to that in 2001 is presented in Figure 14.4.

Table 14.6
Sex ratio in all-age population

High		*Low*	
Kerala	1084	Daman & Diu	618
Pondicherry	1038	Dadra & Nagar Haveli	775
Tamil Nadu	995	Chandigarh	818
Andhra Pradesh	992	Delhi	866
Chhattisgarh	991	Haryana	877
Manipur	987	Andaman & Nicobar Islands	878
Meghalaya	986	Jammu & Kashmir	883
Mizoram	975	Sikkim	889
Himachal Pradesh	974	Punjab	893
Karnataka	968	Uttar Pradesh	908

Table 14.7
Sex ratio in child population

High		*Low*	
Mizoram	971	Haryana	830
Meghalaya	970	Punjab	846
Assam	967	Jammu & Kashmir	859
Andaman & Nicobar Islands	966	Delhi	866
Pondicherry	965	Chandigarh	867
Chhattisgarh	964	Rajasthan	883
Arunachal Pradesh	960	Uttarakhand	886
Kerala	959	Maharashtra	883
Tripura	953	Gujarat	886
West Bengal	950	Uttar Pradesh	899
Tamil Nadu	946	Lakshadweep	908

Table 14.8
Sex ratio in age 7+ population

High		*Low*	
Kerala	1099	Daman & Diu	585
Pondicherry	1047	Dadra & Nagar Haveli	752
Tamil Nadu	1000	Chandigarh	812
Andhra Pradesh	997	Sikkim	863
Chhattisgarh	995	Delhi	866
Manipur	995	Andaman & Nicobar Islands	868
Meghalaya	989	Haryana	885
Orissa	985	Jammu & Kashmir	887
Himachal Pradesh	983	Punjab	899
Mizoram	976	Uttar Pradesh	910
Uttarakhand	975	Bihar	912

Figure 14.4
Declining child sex ratio for 21 states, 2001 and 2011

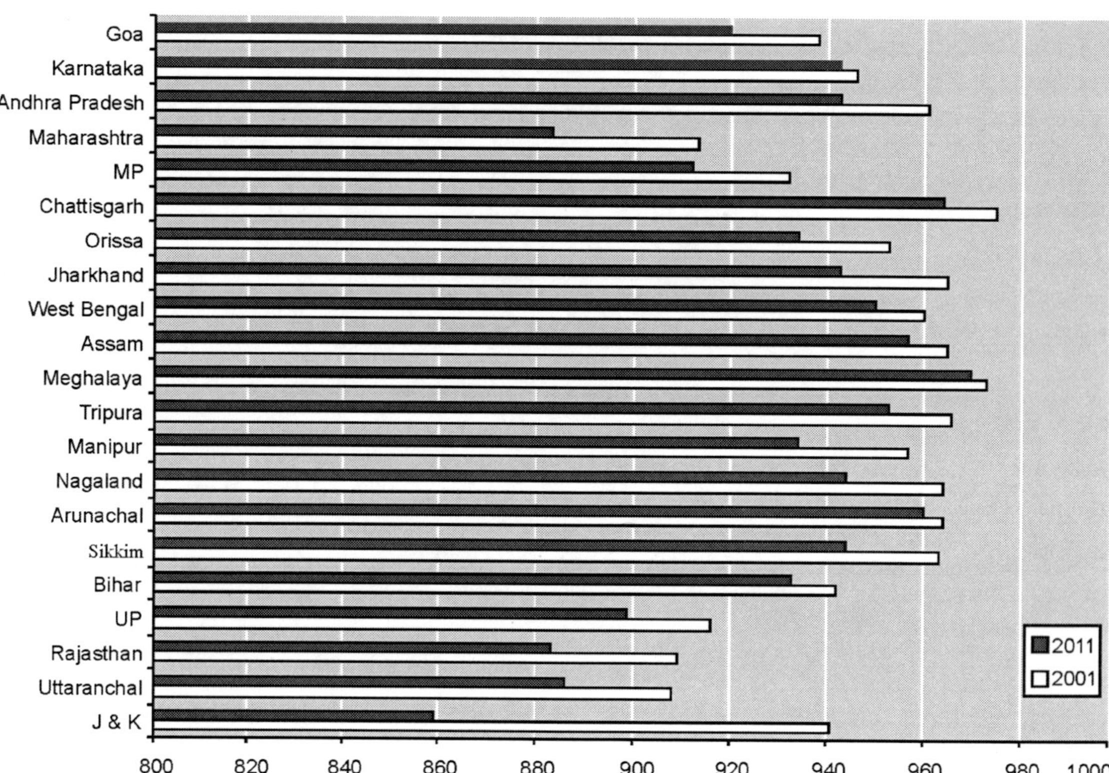

Sex ratio in any age is organically linked to that at birth and also to mortality differentials before the first birthday. Since 1941, female-male ratio in 0-4 age has progressively dropped below 1000. In 2001, the ratio recorded a massive drop by 58.5 points from 960.2 recorded in 1991 (vide Table 4.12 Chapter 4). That really was an astonishing event. If the entries in Table 4.12 are reasonably accurate, the sex ratio in some of the age groups as 10-14, 15-19, 20-24 and 25-29 in 2011 could be close to 900 or even less provided age-sex specific death rates did not change by a large margin in the decade. We have to wait for the full data to see how age sex distribution in the population has responded to changes in social and other demographic parameters in the last decade.

A correlation of the order 0.96 between sex ratio in the populations in 2001 and 2011 (Table 14.9) bear out that the relative positions of the states/UTs have changed only very marginally in the two consecutive census counts. The correlations in sex ratio (2001 and 2011) in child population and that for in age 7 and above population are 0.86 and 0.96 respectively. A slightly lower correspondence between 2001 and 2011 for the child group is due to erratic change in ratios for some states/UTs. The sex ratio observed in child population in 2011 would determine the nature of male-female composition of population in the years ahead, more importantly in the age segment 10-16 in the next census slated for 2021. There could again be an overall decline in sex ratio in the population if the sex ratio for children below 6 years drops further or continues at the same level as in 2001-2011. However, it is very likely that the birth rate in the population will continue to decline and that surely would bring down the share of the child population further. One can only sincerely wish that the child sex ratio would not drop further even if the dip in child population continues. The trends observed since 1991 make us optimistic that sex ratio in age 7 and above population for most of the states would improve further and the short falls in child sex ratio could largely be overcome.

Whereas decline in child population is welcome since it creates a condition for 'demographic dividend', a very alarming situation is in the offing – the sex ratio among children below 6 years has steadily been declining – 945 in 1981-1991, 927 in 1991-2001 and 914 in 2001-2011. The drop in child sex ratio (even the margin in drop) is not a new phenomenon. Only three states/UTs, viz., Punjab, Haryana and Chandigarh, recorded below 900 child sex ratio in 1991. The number increased to six in 2001 with the inclusion of Himachal Pradesh, Delhi and Gujarat in the list. In 2011, as many as ten states/UTs show the child sex ratio going down below 900 and nine states/UTs actually recorded decline by over 20 points. It is surprizing that Jammu & Kashmir lost additional 82 girls for every 1000 boys in 0-6 population in the last decade. Punjab is the only state where the number of 'missing girls' has declined by a large margin of 48; yet the state still has child sex ratio at a despicably below 850 level. Punjab (846) and Haryana (830) are the only two states, both in the same region, which recorded less than 850 girls per 1000 boys both in 2001 and 2011 counts. Apart from Himachal Pradesh, the whole of northwest (Jammu & Kashmir, Punjab, Haryana, Rajasthan, Gujarat, Maharashtra, Delhi and Chandigarh) recorded depressing sex ratio in the child population. All the BIMARU states showed sizeable decline in sex ratio in their child population. Two of them, Rajasthan and Uttar Pradesh, witnessed declines going even below 900 levels.

Table 14.9

Some correlation studies : growth rate, literacy and sex ratio

	Literacy rate by sex			*Sex ratio in population groups*						
	2011				*2001*			*2011*		
	Persons	*Males*	*Females*		*Total*	*Child*	*7+*	*Total*	*Child*	*7+*
Growth	-0.1822	-0.1310	-0.2554	Growth	-0.4901	0.0599	-0.5174	-0.611	-0.0638	-0.622
Persons		0.9569	0.9797	Total		0.3999	0.9956		0.4295	0.9985
Males			0.8825	Child			0.3148			0.382

Decadal growth (2001-2011) has been correlated both with literacy rates and sex ratio in the population. Almost a similar pattern of correlations between growth and sex ratio in different population groups is observed both for 2001 and 2011 data. Both 2001 and 2011 data also confirm that child sex ratio has no seminal impact on growth of population as yet. But, in the long run it will have significant effect on many demographic parameters including sex ratio in the population. With increase in missing girls, legitimate births may show signs of decline that will influence on the population growth rate and the sex ratio. Intensity of education, especially among women, and economic status of the family are likely to have larger impact both on birth as well as sex selective abortions.

Population scientists and social activists agree that the major reason for decline in child sex ratio is due to sex-selected abortion in huge numbers indicating that a large section of Indians still prefer sons to girls. Even Kerala, the most advanced state in the country on demographic parameters, did not improve sex ratio in the child population. Mostly the smaller states/UTs really showed enhanced sex ratio in child population. Maharashtra recorded a huge decline of 30 points from 913 to 883. In-migration (adult males) from other states could have the plummeting effect on the proportion of child group but not on the sex ratio in child population. The same is true of Gujarat, which is now a major destination for migrants from all over India for its booming industrial activity. It is obvious that the step the government has taken to prevent abortion of female foetuses (Pre-Natal Diagnostic Act 1994) has not produced desired results. Without a more proactive measure (exemplary punishment to the family and the doctor/technician involved in sex determination, de-licensing the clinics or the nursing homes involved in the racket and confiscating the equipments used for sex determination), this social menace cannot be eliminated.

It is surprising that Kolkata district in West Bengal has the lowest baby count – only 6.69 percent – among all the districts in India, close to 600. Kupwara in Jammu & Kashmir has the highest child population, i.e., 22.5 percent, in the country. The lowest child sex ratio in the population in 2011 since 1961 raises a few questions. Massive selective fetus wastage had earlier been observed mostly in a few northern states (Punjab, Haryana and Rajasthan in particular) and in some southern states. The scanning technology for sex determination of the fetus has now been expanded to most other states. Child population of Uttar Pradesh (29.7 million), Bihar (18.6 million), Maharashtra (12.8 million), Madhya Pradesh (10.5 million) and Rajasthan (10.5 million) together has a lion's share, i.e., 52 percent of children in India in 0-6 year age group. In the last two decades, on an average, they lost 33 girls for every 1000 boys (Bihar the least, 20, and Maharashtra the most, 53). All the BIMARU states continue to show very poor sex ratio in child population.

Though the sex ratio in child population has declined, the same in the total population has progressively improved, from 923 in 1991 to 933 in 2001 and then to 940 in 2011. This is the highest sex ratio recorded since 1971. Public health experts say the sex ratio across ages may have something to do with men dying earlier than women and the increasing widow population is due to their relatively higher life expectancy at higher age groups. Proportion of females in the all-age population has increased in 29 states/UTs. Exceptions are Bihar, Gujarat (though both have made considerable improvement in population growth rate in recent years) and Jammu & Kashmir (heavy loss of girls in child population). Sex ratio in age 7 and above population has been increasing monotonically in the last three decades – 923 (1981-1991), 934 (1991-2001) and 944 (2001-2011).

That sex-selective abortion is a critical reason for poor sex ratio (F/M) in child population is borne by improved sex ratio in the total as well as in age 7 years and above population. Whereas a 7-point increase in sex ratio is observed in the total population, the same improves to 10 points if the child group is left out of the computation of sex ratio in the population. Both sex ratios in the total population and in age 7 and above population were almost at the same level in 2001. Even with massive drops in child sex ratio between 1991 and 2011 (a total of 31 points), the sex ratio in the population continued to improve since the increase in sex ratio observed in 7 years and above population was based on increasing size of proportion of this vital population group. The states recording better sex ratio in the population find their names in the list of high achievers in 7 years and above age group. An almost similar observation is noticed for those who did badly both in total and other segments of population. Except Bihar, all the other BIMARU states did show appreciable improvement in the 7 years and above population.

69 percent of India's people live in 21 states/UTs where 'all age sex ratio' is below 950 (2011 census). The population share (25 states/UTs) rises to about 84 percent when the same criterion is shifted to the child group. In the child group, the usual expected level is 950 to 975 girls for every 1000 boys. This shows how the sex ratio in child population is going to shape the level of male-female balance in the population in coming years and decades. We cite here a very recent study on the fascinating history of changing sex ratio in child group in India in the last 30 years.

Funded by US, Canada and a few others, Prof. P. Jha and a few others studied the birth history of about 250,000 births in India (from three rounds of NFHS) between 1990 and 2005.[2] The study concentrated on the sex of the second and subsequent births. The researchers came to the conclusion that the sex selective abortion was high in families that already have one or two daughters and no sons. The analysis showed a steep decline in girls to boys' ratio (when the first child born in a family happened to be a girl, the decline was from 906 in 1990 to 836 in 2005, an average decline of 0.52 percent). But in cases where the first child was a boy, the girl-boy ratio was almost normal for the second child. The research found unquestionable affluence link to female feticide. The researchers observed that sex selective abortion was more frequent among educated (mothers with 10 or more years of schooling than in mothers with no education) and wealthy households. The notion that with increased education (especially among women) and income level, parents would rise above the tradition of 'son preference' was not corroborated in the study. The wealthier and better educated families have greater access to technology for sex determination of the fetus than the poorly educated and unwealthy families. The medical community often is too eager to oblige such parents, of course with an illegal hefty fee. The study also showed that sex selective abortion of girls was increasing by leaps and bounds since 1980 – from 0–0.2 million in 1980s to 1·2—4·1 million in the 1990s, and to 3·1—6·0 million in the 2000s. The study estimated that for every 1 percent decline in sex ratio at ages 0-6 years implied 1·2—3·6 million more selective abortions of girls.

The Lancet published study implies that people rich and poor, educated or illiterate, are eager to accept the small family norm, an argument the Indian government has been propagating since independence. The study did not notice any evidence of sex selective abortion of the first-born female feticides. This has prompted many researchers to speculate that sex selective abortion of first-born female fetuses may soon ensue if fertility in the population drops further. They also admit that the wealthy and knowledgeable families want to have a balanced family – a girl and a boy. They argue that the new technology has given them an instrument to determine the family composition. They even may undertake male feticide if the first child in the family is a boy. The upper echelon of society is moving towards 'one plus one' norm and therefore abortion would be more frequently used and with it would come the guidance from technology. A case in example is China where one-child norm has been thrust on the people. That brought down their sex ratio at birth to around 850. India is only second to China in the "missing girls" predicament.

The estimated crude birth rate in 2011 is 20.97 – a huge drop (18.73%) from 2001 level. A similar drop is observed in TFR – from 3.2 in 2001 to 2.62 in 2011. In the same period the death rate dropped by 25 percent from 2001's 8.5. The decline in birth rate would continue, though might be slowed down a bit, and the proportion of children below 6 years would also slide down further. That would threaten a further drop in child sex ratio. Death rate has reached a level wherefrom it may increase because of the increasing size of 60 years and above population. When such things happen, natural increase would also weaken.

'Missing women' will have a sustained impact on society. Researchers at the University College, London some five years back, indicated that skewed sex ratios could increase antisocial activity and violence in society. As men outnumber women, those males forced to live a bachelor's life, unable to find partners are likely to become marginalized, particularly in societies where marriage is nearly universal and accords social status and responsibility. Some researchers even went on to say that growing number of men with no partner by marriage, will lead to greater anti-social behavior and "ultimately present a threat to the security of society". The problem of 'missing women' is a serious issue both in India and China, the two largest countries in the world.

2. P. Jha, *et al*, *Trends in selective abortions of girls in India*, The Lancet, Early Online Publication, 24 May 2011)

14.5 Literacy Rate Among Males and Females

Literacy rate LR has increased by 9.2 and 11.8 percent respectively for males and females at the national level in the last decade. For males it is over 82.1 percent (444.2 million literate in absolute number) and that for females is over 65.6 percent (334.25 million). Thus, over 74 percent (778.4 million) Indians are literate today (who can read, write and understand written text) – a 10 percent increase over 2001 level. Males improved literacy by 31.8 and females by 48.5 percent over 2001 literacy levels for the respective absolute size of populations. In the total population it is 38.3 percent. The LR gap between male and female has also declined from 21.7 points in 2001 to 16.68 in 2011 in the population (Appendix 14.1), the least difference since 1951. Very small M-F gap is observed in Meghalaya (3.39), Mizoram (4.32) and Kerala (4.04). Highest gap is observed in Rajasthan (27.85). In the other three BIMARU states the gap ranges from 19.98 to 20.51 points. While 13 states/UTs show 15 points and above gap in literacy rate, 11 sates/UTs between 10 and 15 and in the other 11 states/UTs the gap is less than 10 points. Three most prosperous states, namely, Maharashtra, Gujarat and Karnataka, unexpectedly show quite large M-F gap – 14.30 to 16.50 points. But so long we do not have information on two other critical indices, viz., intensity of education and adult education, especially female adult education (age 15 years and above), nothing definitive can be said about the lasting progress in education in India.

Table 14.10

Absolute changes in literates and non-literates between 1991 & 2001 and 2001 & 2011

Literates/non-literates		*Persons*	*Males*	*Females*	*Gender gap M-F*
Literate					
	1991	358,402,626	228,983,134	129,419,492	99,563,642
	2001	562,010,743	336,969,695	225,041,048	111,928,647
	2011	777,400,000	444,200,000	334,250,000	109,950,000
Increase in 2001 over 1991		203,608,117	107,986,561	95,621,556	12,365,005
increase in 2011 over 2001		215,389,257	107,230,305	109,208,952	–1,978,647
Percent increase: 2001 over 1991		56.8	47.2	73.9	
Percent increase: 2011 over 2001		38.3	31.8	48.5	
Non-literate					
	1991	328,167,288	128,099,211	200,068,077	–71,968,866
	2001	296,208,952	106,654,066	189,554,886	–82,900,820
	2011	274,016,045	96,568,923	176,388,710	–79,819,787
Increase in 2001 over 1991		–31,958,336	–21,445,145	–10,513,191	–10,931,954
Increase in 2011 over 2001		–22,192,907	–10,085,143	–13,166,176	3,081,033
Percentage increase in 2001		–9.8	–16.8	–5.2	
Percentage increase in 2011		–7.5	–9.6	–6.9	

We have tried to estimate the absolute change in literates and non-literates between 1991 and 2001 and 2001 and 2011 (Table 14.10). Proportion of children below 6 years (13.12% for persons in the population) was deducted from the total population (literacy rate is calculated from persons in age 7 and above). Literacy rate for persons is calculated on this age 7 and above population: 1,210,193,422*(1-13.12/100) = 1,051,416,045. Size of the non-literate population is calculated by deducting the literates 777,400,000 from it: 1,051,416,045-777,400,000 = 274,016,045. The same procedure is also followed for the non-literates among males and females.

Compared to 2001, the improvement rate in LR for persons, males and females has weakened. As the final leg becomes shorter, chances of further improvement automatically gets restricted. The absolute size of non-literates progressively has become smaller and the pace of movement also got slower. The absolute size of non-literates in 2011 is closely equivalent to the combined populations of today's Uttar Pradesh and Tamil Nadu. Between 1991 and 2011, number of literates in the population increased by about 419 million and the number of non-literates has come down by over 54 million (31.5 million for males). The M-F gap has also come down progressively. In absolute numbers, females have exceeded males in adding literates to their population. Rate of decline of male non-literates is higher than that observed in females.

Table 14.11

Literacy rate (%) in male/female population

Male				*Female*			
High		***Low***		***High***		***Low***	
Lakshadweep	96.11	Bihar	73.39	Kerala	91.98	Rajasthan	52.66
Kerala	96.02	Andhra Pradesh	75.56	Mizoram	89.40	Bihar	53.33
Mizoram	93.72	Meghalaya	77.17	Lakshadweep	88.25	Jharkhand	56.21
Goa	92.81	Jammu & Kashmir	78.26	Tripura	83.15	Jammu & Kashmir	58.01
Tripura	92.18	Jharkhand	78.45	Andaman & Nicobar Is*	81.84	Uttar Pradesh	59.26
Pondicherry	92.12	Assam	78.81	Goa	81.84	Arunachal Pradesh	59.57
Daman & Diu	91.48	Uttar Pradesh	79.24	Chandigarh	81.38	Andhra Pradesh	59.74
Delhi	91.03	Rajasthan	80.51	Pondicherry	81.22	Madhya Pradesh	60.02
Himachal Pradesh	90.83	Madhya Pradesh	80.53	Delhi	80.93	Chhattisgarh	60.59
Chandigarh	90.54	Punjab	81.43	Daman & Diu	79.59	Orissa	64.36

Table 14.11 shows some of the states'/UTs' literacy achievement, separately for males and females. Accordingly, nine states/UTs appear both in male and female high achiever groups in literacy. Among the poorer performers, seven states are common in both the lists of males and females (for full data of LR for different states, see Appendix 14.1). The BIMARU states appear both in the lists of low performers. The male-female gap in high achievers ranges from 5 to 11.7 percentage points. But the gaps are much wider, varying from 16 to 28 percents for the low achievers in male and female populations. The BIMARU states show a consistently large gap, 20 to 28 percentage points, among male and female LRs. It is seen that the smaller states/UTs have done well in spread of education among the masses. It is the big states like Bihar, Andhra Pradesh, Uttar

Pradesh, Rajasthan and Madhya Pradesh that really have failed to capitalize the incentives given by the central government for universalization of education, especially among girls.

Spread of education generally applies an effective brake on birth rate, also on death rate. Spread of literacy does make a significant mark in arresting birth rate, but 'intensity of education', especially among women, would be a more efficient index for forecasting drop in birth rate in a time frame. Since data on intensity of education (also adult literacy) can be had only after detailed tabulation and analysis of the data by the census commissioner, one has to use the LR data to throw some light on the population growth. The correlation between literacy rate (persons) and population growth rate is weak negative, –0.182 (Table 14.9). More weak is the relation between male literacy and population growth (–0.13). Female literacy produces a slightly better correlation -0.26. The correlation between male-female literacy is 0.88. Many states have already reached a stage in male LR (some even in female LR) wherefrom further improvement would be exceedingly slow. Since females will have to go a long way to catch up with their male counterparts, it is they who would take the major responsibility for improving 'person literacy' in coming years.

14.6 Administrative Expenses for Conducting Census 2011

For covering 8,000 towns and cities and over 600,000 villages in 35 states/UTs, more than Rs 22,000 million were spent in conducting the census operations. Some 2.7 million enumerators and supervisors were employed. The cost incurred per person is estimated at Rs18. This gigantic operation involving huge investment in funds, people and other resources must appear as productive venture. Unfortunately, the office of the Census Commissioner takes very long time to come out with the final reports (in different phases), often after three or four years or more. Since 'caste' information has been included in the census schedule for the first time since 1931 census, a huge number of additional cross-tabulation needs to be undertaken which may delay considerably the publication of final results. China with a population over 1.35 billion and most other developed countries including USA bring out their census reports within a year or so of the census count.

Often delayed publication of this very useful exercise makes its utility as a base data for administrative planning, research and other use, both by public and the private sectors, doubtful. For excessive delay in publication of census reports, the data published in Human Development Report by UNDP, various rounds of NSSO, large surveys by NHS, Family Planning Year Book, DGHS, NCERT, Sample Registration Bulletins and many others have become important resources for many studies and analysis of changing demographic parameters that has real importance in many utility areas. Users of demographic data have often expressed their concern about the quality of the data produced by the gargantuan exercise. Better trained and qualified enumerators of ISI or other institutes of excellence could have been entrusted with the responsibility for conducting post enumeration checks (PEC), at least in some selected blocks. In the earlier days when data transfer and storage facility lacked the level of mechanization that we have today, committing some error in tabulation and computation was expected. Extreme care should be taken in cross-tabulation of today's extremely large data base for undertaking more complicated multifaceted analysis.

Appendices

Appendix 1.1

Three main languages in each state/UT, 1991

*State/UT**	*Languages*	*No. of speakers*	*%*	*State/UT*	*Languages*	*No. of speakers*	*%*
1	*2*	*3*	*4*	*1*	*2*	*3*	*4*
INDIA	**Hindi**	**337,272,114**	**40.2**	Andhra Pradesh	Telugu	56,375,755	84.8
	Bengali	**69,595,738**	**8.3**		Urdu	5,560,154	8.4
	Telugu	**66,017,615**	**7.9**		Hindi	1,841,290	2.8
Arunachal Pradesh	Nissi/Daffla	172,149	19.9	Assam	Assamese	12,958,088	57.8
	Nepali	81,176	9.4		Bengali	2,523,040	11.3
	Bengali	70,771	8.2		Bodo/Boro	1,184,569	5.3
Bihar	Hindi	69,845,979	80.9	Goa	Konkani	602,626	51.5
	Urdu	8,542,463	9.9		Marathi	390,270	33.4
	Santhali	2,546,655	2.9		Kannada	54,323	4.6
Gujarat	Gujarati	37,792,933	91.5	Haryana	Hindi	14,982,409	91.0
	Hindi	1,215,825	2.9		Punjabi	1,170,225	7.1
	Sindhi	704,088	1.7		Urdu	261,820	1.6
Himachal Pradesh	Hindi	4,595,615	88.9	Karnataka	Kannada	29,785,004	66.2
	Punjabi	324,479	6.3		Urdu	4,480,038	10.0
	Kinnauri	61,794	1.2		Telugu	3,325,062	7.4
Kerala	Malayalam	28,096,376	96.6	Madhya Pradesh	Hindi	56,619,090	85.6
	Tamil	616,010	2.1		Bhili/Bhilodi	2,215,399	3.3
	Kannada	75,571	0.3		Gondi	1,481,265	2.2
Maharashtra	Marathi	57,894,839	73.3	Manipur	Manipuri	1,110,134	60.4
	Hindi	6,168,941	7.8		Thado	103,667	5.6
	Urdu	5,734,468	7.3		Tangkhul	100,088	5.4
Meghalaya	Khasi	879,192	49.5	Mizoram	Lushai/Mizo	518,099	75.1
	Garo	547,690	30.9		Bengali	59,092	8.6
	Bengali	144,261	8.1		Lakher	22,938	3.3

Cont'd...

App. 1.1 Cont'd...

1	*2*	*3*	*4*	*1*	*2*	*3*	*4*
Nagaland	Ao	169,837	14.0	Orissa	Oriya	26,199,346	82.8
	Sema	152,123	12.6		Hindi	759,016	2.4
	Konyak	137,539	11.4		Telugu	502,102	1.6
Punjab	Punjabi	18,704,461	92.2	Rajasthan	Hindi	39,410,968	89.6
	Hindi	1,478,993	7.3		Bhili/Bhilodi	2,215,399	5.0
	Urdu	13,416	0.1		Urdu	953,497	2.2
Sikkim	Nepali	256,418	63.1	Tamil Nadu	Tamil	48,434,744	86.7
	Bhotia	32,593	8.0		Telugu	3,975,561	7.1
	Lepcha	29,854	7.3		Kannada	1,208,296	2.2
Tripura	Bengali	1,899,162	68.9	Uttar Pradesh	Hindi	125,348,492	90.1
	Tripuri	647,847	23.5		Urdu	12,492,927	9.0
	Hindi	45,803	1.7		Punjabi	661,215	0.5
West Bengal	Bengali	58,541,519	86.0	Andman & Nicobar Islands*	Bengali	64,706	23.1
	Hindi	4,479,170	6.6		Tamil	53,536	19.1
	Urdu	1,455,649	2.1		Hindi	49,469	17.6
Chandigarh*	Hindi	392,054	61.1	Dadra & Nagar Haveli*	Bhili/Bhilodi	76,207	55.0
	Punjabi	222,890	34.7		Gujarati	30,346	21.9
	Tamil	5,318	0.8		Konkani	17,062	12.3
Daman & Diu*	Gujarati	92,579	91.1	Delhi*	Hindi	7,690,631	81.6
	Hindi	3,645	3.6		Punjabi	748,145	7.9
	Marathi	1,256	1.2		Urdu	512,990	5.4
Lakshadweep*	Malayalam	43,678	84.5	Pondicherry*	Tamil	720,473	89.2
	Tamil	282	0.5		Malayalam	38,392	4.8
	Hindi	217	0.4		Telugu	34,799	4.3

Appendix 1.2

Population composition by religion, states and union territories

*State/UT**	*Hindus*	*Muslims*	*Christians*	*Sikhs*	*Buddhists*	*Jains*	*Others*	*Not stated*
1	*2*	*3*	*4*	*5*	*6*	*7*	*8*	*9*
INDIA	***82.00***	***12.12***	***2.34***	***1.94***	***0.76***	***0.40***	***0.39***	***0.05***
				States				
Andhra Pradesh	89.14	8.91	1.83	0.03	0.03	0.04	—	0.02
Arunachal Pradesh	37.04	1.38	10.29	0.14	12.88	0.01	36.22	2.04
Assam	67.13	28.43	3.32	0.07	0.29	0.09	0.62	0.05

Cont'd...

App. 1.2 Cont'd...

1	*2*	*3*	*4*	*5*	*6*	*7*	*8*	*9*
Bihar	82.42	14.81	0.98	0.09	—	0.03	1.67	—
Goa	64.68	5.25	29.86	0.09	0.02	0.04	0.04	0.02
Gujarat	89.48	8.73	0.44	0.08	0.03	1.19	0.03	0.02
Haryana	89.21	4.64	0.10	5.81	0.01	0.21	—	0.02
Himachal Pradesh	95.90	1.72	0.09	1.01	1.24	0.02	—	0.02
Karnataka	85.45	11.64	1.91	0.02	0.16	0.73	0.01	0.08
Kerala	57.28	23.33	19.32	0.01	—	0.01	0.01	0.04
Madhya Pradesh	92.80	4.96	0.65	0.24	0.33	0.74	0.09	0.19
Maharashtra	81.12	9.67	1.12	0.21	6.39	1.22	0.13	0.14
Manipur	57.67	7.27	34.11	0.07	0.04	0.07	0.77	—
Meghalaya	14.67	3.46	64.58	0.15	0.16	0.02	16.82	0.14
Mizoram	5.05	0.66	85.73	0.04	7.83	—	0.27	0.42
Nagaland	10.12	1.71	87.47	0.06	0.05	0.10	0.48	0.01
Orissa	94.67	1.83	2.10	0.05	0.03	0.02	1.26	0.04
Punjab	34.46	1.18	1.11	62.95	0.12	0.10	0.01	0.07
Rajasthan	89.08	8.01	0.11	1.48	0.01	1.28	—	0.03
Sikkim	68.37	0.95	3.30	0.09	27.15	0.01	0.09	0.04
Tamil Nadu	88.67	5.47	5.69	0.01	—	0.12	0.01	0.03
Tripura	86.50	7.13	1.68	0.03	4.65	0.01	—	—
Uttar Pradesh	81.74	17.33	0.14	0.48	0.16	0.13	0.01	0.01
West Bengal	74.72	23.61	0.56	0.08	0.30	0.05	0.67	0.01
Andaman & Nicobar Is.*	67.53	7.61	23.95	0.48	0.11	0.01	0.09	0.22
Chandigarh*	75.84	2.72	0.78	20.29	0.11	0.24	0.01	0.01
Dadra & Nagar Haveli*	95.48	2.41	1.51	0.01	0.15	0.38	0.06	—
Daman & Diu*	87.76	8.91	2.86	0.10	0.03	0.21	0.12	0.01
Delhi*	83.67	9.44	0.88	4.84	0.15	1.00	0.01	0.01
Lakshadweep*	4.52	94.31	1.16	—	—	—	—	0.01
Pondicherry*	86.16	6.54	7.23	—	0.01	0.06	—	—

Appendix 2.1

Decadal growth rate for states/UTs

*State/ UT**	*1961-1971*	*1971-1981*	*1981-1991*	*1991-2001*
1	*2*	*3*	*4*	*5*
Arunachal Pradesh	38.91	35.1	36.83	26.21
Assam	34.95	23.3	24.24	18.85
Bihar	20.91	24.1	23.38	28.43
Jharkhand	22.58	23.7	24.03	23.19
Manipur	37.53	32.4	29.29	30.02
Meghalaya	31.50	32.0	32.86	29.94
Mizoram	24.93	48.5	39.70	29.18
Nagaland	39.88	50.0	56.08	64.41
Orissa	25.05	20.1	20.06	15.94
Sikkim	29.38	50.7	28.47	32.98
Tripura	36.28	31.9	34.30	15.74
West Bengal	26.87	23.1	24.73	17.84
Gujarat	29.39	27.6	21.19	22.48
Haryana	32.22	28.7	27.41	28.06
Himachal Pradesh	23.04	23.7	20.79	17.53
Jammu & Kashmir	29.65	29.6	30.34	29.04
Punjab	21.70	23.8	20.81	19.76
Rajasthan	27.83	32.9	28.44	28.33
Uttaranchal	24.42	27.4	24.23	19.20
Uttar Pradesh	19.54	25.3	25.55	25.80
Maharashtra	27.45	24.5	25.73	22.57
Madhya Pradesh	29.28	27.1	27.24	24.34
Chhatisgarh	27.12	20.3	25.73	18.06
Andhra Pradesh	20.90	23.1	24.20	13.86
Goa	34.77	26.7	16.08	14.89
Karnataka	24.22	26.7	21.12	17.25
Kerala	26.29	19.2	14.32	9.42
Tamil Nadu	22.30	17.5	15.39	11.19
Andaman & Nicobar Islands*	81.17	63.9	48.70	26.94
Chandigarh*	114.59	75.5	42.16	40.33
Dadra & Nagar Haveli*	27.96	39.7	33.57	59.20
Daman & Diu*	70.85	26.0	28.62	55.59
Delhi*	52.93	53.0	51.45	46.31
Lakshadweep*	31.95	26.5	28.47	17.19
Pondicherry*	27.81	28.1	33.64	20.56
INDIA	**24.80**	**24.6**	**23.86**	**21.34**

Appendix 3.1

Live birth report (Form 2)

Registration Unit/ village/ Town/ Municipality – Taluk/ Tehsil
Thana
District

1. Date of birth
2. Sex: Male/Female
3. Name of Child
4. Place of birth*
5. Permanent Residential Address
6. Father's
   (i) Name
   (ii) Literacy
   (iii) Occupation
   (iv) Nationality
   (v) Religion
7. Mother's
   (i) Name
   (ii) Literacy
   (iii) Occupation
   (iv) Religion
8. Age of mother in completed years at confinement
9. Order of Birth
   (Number of live briths including the birth registered)
10. Type of attention at delivery**
11. Informant's
    (i) Name
    (ii) Address

Date Signature or left thumb mark of the informant

* If the delivery took place in hospital or any other institution, write "Hospital" or "Institution" giving its name, otherwise give full postal address of the place of birth,

** If the delivery was conducted in a hospital or maternity home, write the name of institution, otherwise mention whether it was conducted by a qualified or unqualified midwife and give her name.

Notes

1. In the case of illegitimate birth the word 'illegitimate' be entered in the remarks column, and no person's name should be entered as that of the father, unless there is joint request of the mother and the person acknowledging himself to be father of the child.
2. In the case of multiple birth make separate entry for each and a reference in the remarks column.
3. If the person is a non-worker, insert the word 'Nil' in the column for occupation

(The same form is used for recording a 'still-born' child. The questions in items 3 and 9 of the Form 2 are not asked)

Appendix 3.2

Death report (Form 4)

Registration Unit/ village/ Town/ Municipality – Taluk/ Tehsil
Thana
District

1. Date of Death
2. Full name of the deceased
3. Name of father/ husband
4. Place of death
5. Age
6. Sex: Male/Female
7. Marital status
8. Occupation
9. Religion
10. Nationality
11. Permanent residential address*
12. Cause of Death**
13. Whether Medically Certified: Yes/No
14. Kind of Medical attention received, if any
15. Informant's
    (i) Name
    (ii) Address

Date — Signature or left thumb mark of the informant

* The address of the parent, in case of a child, husband/ late husband in the case of married women/ widow and deceased if independent, are to be given in this column.

** Where the cause of death is medically certified, the cause marked (✔) in the medical certification Form No. 8 is to be entered here.

Note

1. If the deceased was over 1 year of age, give age in completed years. If the deceased was under 1 year of age, give age in completed months and if below 1 month, give age in completed number of days and if below one day, in hours.
2. If the person is non-worker, insert the word 'Nil' in the column for occupation.

Appendix 3.3

Census of India: Houselist schedule 2001

Location particulars (appropriate codes for each of the following particulars)

1. Name of the state/UT ...
2. Name of the district ...
3. Number and/or Name of the Ward ...
4. Name of the Town/Village ...
    1. Line number
    2. Building number
    3. Census house number

Predominant Material

4. Floor (1. Mud 2. Wood/Bamboos 3. Brick 4. Stone 5. Cement 6. Ceramic/floor tiles 7. Any other)
5. Wall (1. Grass/thatch/bamboos, etc. 2. Plastic/polythene 3. Mud/unburnt brick 4. Wood 5. G.I./metal/asbestos sheets 6. Burnt brick 7. Stone 8. Concrete 9. Any other)
6. Roof (1. Grass/thatch/bamboos/wood/mud, etc. 2. Plastic/polythene 3. Tiles 4. Slate 5. G.I./metal/asbestos sheets 6. Brick 7. Stone 8. Concrete 9. Any other)
7. Use of the census house (1. Residence 2. Residence-cum-other use 3. Shop/Office 4. School/College, etc. 5. Hotel/lodge/guest house, etc. 6. Hospital/Dispensary. etc. 7. Factory/workshop/work shed, etc. 8. Place of worship 9. Other non-residential use 10. Vacant)
8. Conditions of the census house if Code 1 or 2 in col.7 (1. Good 2. Livable 3. Dilapidated)
9. Household number

Total Number of Persons Normally Residing in the Household

10. Persons
11 Males
12. Females

Information Relating to the Head of the Household

13. Name of the head of the household
14. 1. Male 2. Female

If SC/ST or Others

15. 1. SC 2. ST 3. Others
16 Ownership status of the house 1. Owned 2. Rented 3. Any other
17. Number of dwelling rooms with this house
18. Number of married couples living in this household
19. Number of married couples having independent room for sleeping
20. Drinking water sources (1. Tap 2. Hand pump 3. Tube-well 4. Well 5. Tank/Pond/Lake 6. River/Canal 7. Spring 8. Any other
21. Drinking water sources (1. Within the premises 2. Near the premises 3. Away)
22. Source of lighting (1. Electricity 2. Kerosene 3. Solar 4. Other oil 5. Any other 6. No lighting)

23. Latrine within the house (0. No latrine 1. Service latrine 2. Pit latrine 3. Water closet)
24. Waste water connected to (1. Closed drainage 2. Open drainage 3. No drainage)
25. Bathroom within the house (1. Yes 2. No)
26. Kitchen within the house (1. Yes 2. No 3. Cooking in open space 4. No cooking)
27. Fuel for cooking (1. Firewood 2. Crop residue 3. Cowdung cake 4. Coal/Lignite/Charcoal 5. Kerosene 6. LPG 7. Electricity 8. Bio gas 9. Any other 0. No cooking)
28. Radio/transistor (1. Yes 2. No)
29. Television (1. Yes 2. No)
30. Telephone (1. Yes 2. No)
31. Bicycle (1. Yes 2. No)
32. Scooter/Motorcycle/Mopade (1. Yes 2. No)
33. Car/Jeep/Van (1. Yes 2. No)
34. Availing Banking services (1. Yes 2. No)

Appendix 3.4

Census of India: Household schedule 2001

Part I Location particulars

Name of the State/UT	...		
Name of the Tahsil/Taluk/PS	...	Name of District	...
Dev. Block/ Circle/ Mandal etc.	...		
Number and Name of Ward	...	Name of town/village	...

Part II Individual particulars Enumeration Block Number ...

(*These are recorded in a tabular sheet where the first column refers to each person in the household for whom information are collected individually on all the items 2 to 22. Item 23* (***fertility particulars***) *is intended to gather information on females who are already married. Only the code number that describes the individual are entered in relevant cells*)

1. Name of the person
2. Relationship to head (record the relationship in full)
3. Sex (1. Male 2. Female)
4. Age last birthday (in completed years)
5. Current marital status (1. Never married 2. Currently married 3. Widowed 4. Divorced or separated)
6. Age at marriage (in completed years)
7. Religion (1. Hindu 2. Muslim 3. Christian 4. Sikhs 5. Buddhist 6. Jain. For other religions, write name of the religion in full but do not give any Code number)
8. If Scheduled Caste, write the name of the Scheduled Caste from the list supplied (Scheduled Castes can be only among Hindus, Sikhs and Buddhists)
9. If Scheduled Tribe, write the name of the Scheduled Tribe from the list supplied (Scheduled Tribes can be from any religion)
10. Mother tongue
11. Other languages known (enter up to two languages in order of proficiency)
12. Literacy status: Male (1. Illiterate 2. Literate) : Female (1. Illiterate 2. Literate)

Cont'd...

App. 3.4 Cont'd...

13. Higher education level attained (for diploma and degree holder, also write the subject of specialization)
14. If attending educational institution (0. Not attending 1. School 2. College 3. Vocational institute 4. Other institute 5. Literary center)
15. If the person is physically/mentally disabled, give appropriate Code number (1. In Seeing 2. In Speech 3. In Hearing 4. In Movement 5. Mental)
16. Did the person work any time last year? (includes even part time help or unpaid work on farm, family enterprise or in any other economic activity) Yes: If worked for 6 months or more (Male Workers), write '1' and proceed to Q. 17 or If worked for less than 6 months (Marginal Workers) write '2' and proceed to Q. 17 or No: If not worked at all (Non-Workers) write '3' and proceed to Qs. 18 & 19
17. (i) Category of the economic activity of the Main or Marginal Worker (1. C: Cultivator 2. AL: Agricultural Laborer 3. HHI: Worker in Household Industry 4. OW: Other Worker)
    Economic activity of the Main or Marginal Worker. If Code '3' (HHI) or Code '4' (OW)
17. (ii) Occupation of the person (describe the actual work of the person)
17. (iii) Describe in detail the nature of industry, trade or service where the person worked or if self employment.
17. (iv) Class of worker: 1. Employer 2. Employee 3. Single worker 4. Family worker
18. If Code '2' (Marginal Worker) or Code '3' (Non-Worker), record code of non-economic activity from: 1. Student 2. Household duties 3. Dependent 4. Pensioner 5. Beggar 6. Others
19. If Marginal Worker or Non-Worker, is the person seeking/available for work? (1. Yes 2. No)
20. (i) Distance from residence to place of work in kilometers
20. (ii) Mode of travel to place of work (give Code number from: 0. No travel 1. on foot 2. Bicycle 3. Moped/Scooter/Motor cycle 4. Car/Jeep/Van 5. Tempo/Autorickshaw/Taxi 6. Bus 7. Tram 8. Water transport 9. Any other
21. Birth place: Is the person born in this village/town?
    Birth place:
    Q.21 (i) State/Country
    (If birth place within India, write the present name of the State or if birth place outside India, write the present name of the country)
    Q. 21 (ii) District
    (If birth place within India, write the present name of the district or if birth place outside India, put dash (-)
22. Place of last residence
    Has the person come to this village/town from elsewhere?
    If ' No', put dash (-) against Qs 22 (i) to 22 (v) or If 'Yes', give following particulars
    Q. 22(i) State/Country
    (If birth place within India, write the present name of the state or if birth place outside India, write the present name of the country)
    Q. 22 (ii) District
    (If birth place within India, write the present name of the district or if birth place outside India, put dash (-)

Cont'd...

Q. 22(iii) At the time of migration, was the place of residence: 1. Rural 2. Urban
Q. 22 (iv) Reason for migration of this person
Q. 22 (v) Duration of stay in this village or town since migration

23. Fertility particulars
Q. 23 (1) Number of children surviving at present *(also include daughters and sons presently not staying in this household)* Daughters: (like that in 23(ii)
Q. 23 (ii) Total number of children ever born alive *(including both living and dead daughters and sons)*: Daughters: Sons:
Q. 23(iii) Number of children born alive during last one year *(after 9th February, 2000)*: Daughters: Sons:

Part III For Households Engaged in Cultivation/Plantation

(i) Total net area of land under cultivation/plantation
Hectare Acres
(ii) Net area of irrigated land
Hectare Acres
(iii) Tenure status of land under cultivation/plantation
1. Owned 2. Rented 3. Owned and Rented

Appendix 5.1

Number of illiterates, decadal decrease in illiterates and percentage contribution in decrease : 1991, 2001

*States/Union Territories**	*1991*	*2001*	*Decadal decrease in number of illiterates*	*Percentage contribution in decrease*
1	*2*	*3*	*4*	*5*
INDIA[1,2]	***328,167,288***	***296,208,952***	***31,958,336***	***100.00***
Himachal Pradesh[3]	1,540,150	1,194,777	345,373	1.08
Punjab	7,043,608	6,379,994	663,614	2.08
Chandigarh*	121,185	144,413	–23,228	–0.07
Uttaranchal	2,454,593	1,984,993	469,600	1.47
Haryana	5,889,463	5,598,873	290,590	0.91
Delhi*	1,930,951	2,155,932	–224,981	–0.70
Rajasthan	21,597,410	17,935,918	3,661,492	11.46
Uttar Pradesh	62,313,875	57,810,542	4,503,333	14.09
Bihar	31,986,516	34,968,650	–2,982,134	–9.33
Sikkim	142,870	140,495	2,375	0.01
Arunachal Pradesh	398,323	403,266	–4,943	–0.02
Nagaland	384,323	561,941	–177,618	–0.56
Manipur	613,840	646,287	–32,447	–0.10
Mizoram	99,553	86,259	13,294	0.04
Tripura	894,103	727,997	166,106	0.52
Meghalaya	702,944	678,184	24,760	0.08
Assam	8,476,418	7,960,619	515,799	1.61

Cont'd...

App. 5.1 Cont'd...

1	*2*	*3*	*4*	*5*
West Bengal	23,906,271	21,266,590	2,639,681	8.26
Jharkhand	10,220,865	10,143,063	77,802	0.24
Orissa	13,396,318	11,472,584	1,923,734	6.02
Chhatisgarh	8,111,922	6,033,286	2,078,636	6.50
Madhya Pradesh	21,512,377	17,860,686	3,651,691	11.43
Gujarat[4]	12,661,634	12,469,293	192,341	0.60
Daman & Diu*	24,712	26,108	–1,396	0.00
Dadra & Nagar Haveli*	65,306	72,448	–7,142	–0.02
Maharashtra	22,985,512	18,998,379	3,987,133	12.48
Andhra Pradesh	31,056,061	25,689,502	5,366,559	16.79
Karnataka	16,486,397	15,132,802	1,353,595	4.24
Goa	252,881	212,484	40,397	0.13
Lakshadweep*	7,695	6,454	1,241	0.00
Kerala	2,575,157	2,559,343	15,814	0.05
Tamil Nadu	18,074,652	14,668,772	3,405,880	10.66
Pondicherry*	176,177	159,372	16,805	0.05
Andaman & Nicobar Islands*	63,226	58,646	4,580	0.01

Notes:

1. For making the data comparable the number of illiterates given in column 4 against India exclude the figures for Jammu & Kashmir for 1991 Census as this data. 1991 Census (since it) could not be held in this State due to disturbed conditions.
2. To make data comparable the number of illiterates shown in column 3 against India for the 1991 Census exclude the number of illiterates of entire Kachchh district, Morvi, Maliya-Miyana and Wankaner talukas of Rajkot district, Jodiya taluka of Jamnagar district of Gujarat state and entire Kinnaur district of Himachal Pradesh where population enumeration of Census of India, 2001, could not be conducted due to natural calamity.
3. To make the data comparable, the number of illiterates shown against Himachal Pradesh in column 3 for 1991 Census excludes the figures of illiterates of entire Kinnaur district where Census of India, 2001, could not be conducted due to natural calamity.
4. To make the data comparable, the number of illiterates shown against Gujarat in column 3 for 1991 Census excludes the figures of illiterates of entire Kachchh district, Morvi, Maliya-Miyana and Wankaner talukas of Rajkot district, Jodiya taluka of Jamnagar district of Gujarat state where population enumeration of Census of India, 2001, could not be conducted due to natural calamity.

Source: Provisional population totals (Web edition), Census of India 2001

Appendix 6.1

Number of towns and percentage of urban population, 1901–2001

Census year	*Number of towns by size class*							*Percentage of urban population by size class*					
	I	*II*	*III*	*IV*	*V*	*VI*	*Total*	*I*	*II*	*III*	*IV*	*V*	*VI*
1901	24 (1.33)	43 (2.37)	130 (7.18)	391 (21.59)	744 (41.08)	479 (26.44)	1811 (100)	26.0	11.2	15.6	20.8	20.1	6.1
1911	23 (1.21)	40 (2.28)	135 (7.7)	364 (20.75)	707 (40.31)	485 (27.65)	1754 (100)	27.4	10.5	16.4	19.7	19.3	6.5

Cont'd...

App. 6.1 Cont'd…

	I	*II*	*III*	*IV*	*V*	*VI*		*I*	*II*	*III*	*IV*	*V*	*VI*
1921	29 (1.53)	45 (2.38)	145 (7.66)	370 (19.54)	734 (38.75)	571 (30.15)	1894 (100)	29.7	10.3	15.9	18.2	18.6	7.0
1931	35 (2.05)	50 (2.92)	183 (10.7)	434 (25.37)	500 (29.22)	509 (29.75)	1711 (100)	31.2	11.6	16.8	18.0	17.1	5.2
1941	49 (2.24)	74 (3.38)	242 (11.05)	498 (22.74)	920 (42.01)	407 (18.58)	2190 (100)	38.2	11.4	16.3	15.7	15.0	3.1
1951	76 (2.72)	91 (3.26)	327 (11.71)	608 (21.78)	1121 (40.15)	569 (20.38)	2792 (100)	44.6	9.9	15.7	13.6	12.9	3.1
1961	102 (4.49)	129 (5.68)	437 (19.25)	719 (31.67)	711 (31.32)	172 (7.58)	2270 (100)	51.4	11.2	16.9	12.7	6.8	0.7
1971	148 (5.98)	173 (6.99)	558 (22.54)	827 (33.4)	623 (25.16)	147 (5.94)	2476 (100)	57.2	10.9	16.0	10.9	4.4	0.4
1981	218 (6.6)	270 (8.18)	743 (22.51)	1059 (32.08)	758 (22.96)	253 (7.66)	3301 (100)	60.3	11.6	11.3	9.5	3.5	0.5
1991	300 (8.12)	345 (9.33)	947 (25.62)	1167 (31.57)	740 (20.02)	197 (5.33)	3696 (100)	65.2	10.9	13.1	7.7	2.6	0.3
2001	393 (9.0)	401 (9.18)	1151 (26.35)	1344 (30.77)	888 (20.33)	191 (4.373)	4368 (100)	68.6	9.7	12.2	6.8	2.3	0.2

Appendix 7.1

Employment growth rate in organized sector, India 1961–2001

	Public/ Private	***Private + Public sector***			***Public sector***			***Private sector***		
		1961–81	***1981–91***	***1991–01***	***1961–81***	***1981–91***	***1991–01***	***1961–81***	***1981–91***	***1991–01***
	By Industry	***Exponential growth rate***								
0.	Agriculture	0.015	0.011	–0.004	0.048	0.022	–0.011	0.004	0.004	0.001
1.	Mining and Quarrying	0.021	0.011	–0.013	0.111	0.016	–0.012	–0.094	–0.033	–0.026
2.&3.	Manufacturing	0.026	0.003	0.005	0.063	0.020	–0.463	0.018	–0.004	0.016
4.	Elect, Gas & water supply	0.052	0.029	0.005	0.058	0.030	0.004	–0.009	0.012	0.016
5.	Construction	0.017	0.005	–0.008	0.028	0.003	–0.005	–0.054	–0.007	–0.016
6.	Wholesale & Retail Trade	0.015	0.014	0.011	0.033	0.030	0.008	0.018	0.007	0.013
7.	Transport, storage and communication	0.018	0.010	0.001	0.020	0.010	0.001	–0.033	–0.017.	0.035
8.	Finance, Insurance and Real Estate		0.041	0.013	0.119	0.044	0.006		0.023	0.039
9.	Community, Personal and Social services	0.036	0.022	0.008	0.032	0.021	0.006	0.064	0.019	0.015
	0–9 All sectors	0.030	0.015	0.005	0.038	0.020	0.001	0.010	0.002	0.014

Adapted from Organized Labor Market in India – Pre and Post Reform, by Suresh D. Tendulkar, 2003 (Web)

Appendix 7.2

Distribution of main workers by industrial categories, 1991

India	*Percent Main Workers*		
Industrial Categories	***Persons***	***Males***	***Females***
1	*2*	*3*	*4*
	Total		
1. Cultivation	38.7	39.9	34.6
2. Agricultural labor	26.1	20.8	44.2
3. Livestock, Forestry, Fishing, Hunting and Plantations, Orchards and allied activities	2.1	2.1	2.1
4. Mining and quarrying	0.6	0.7	0.3
5. Manufacturing, Processing, Servicing and Repairs in Household Industry	2.4	2.1	3.5
6. Manufacturing, Processing, Servicing and Repairs in Non-Household Industry	7.6	8.8	3.8
7. Construction	1.9	2.3	0.7
8. Trade and Commerce	7.4	9.0	2.2
9. Transport, Storage and Communications	2.8	3.5	0.3
10. Other Services	10.3	10.8	8.3
	Rural		
1. Cultivation	48.4	51.6	38.9
2. Agricultural labor	31.6	26.0	48.5
3. Livestock, Forestry, Fishing, Hunting and Plantations, Orchards and allied activities	2.2	2.3	2.1
4. Mining and quarrying	0.5	0.5	0.3
5. Manufacturing, Processing, Servicing and Repairs in Household Industry	2.2	1.9	2.9
6. Manufacturing, Processing, Servicing and Repairs in Non-Household Industry	3.6	4.0	2.3
7. Construction	1.0	1.3	0.3
8. Trade and Commerce	3.3	4.0	1.1
9. Transport, Storage and Communications	1.2	1.6	0.1
10. Other Services	6.0	6.8	3.5

Cont'd...

App. 7.2 Cont'd...

1	*2*	*3*	*4*
	Urban		
1. Cultivation	4.9	4.9	5.1
2. Agricultural labor	6.7	5.4	15.5
3. Livestock, Forestry, Fishing, Hunting and Plantations, Orchards and allied activities	1.7	1.8	1.5
4. Mining and quarrying	1.1	1.2	0.7
5. Manufacturing, Processing, Servicing and Repairs in Household Industry	3.1	2.5	7.5
6. Manufacturing, Processing, Servicing and Repairs in Non-Household Industry	21.9	23.1	14.1
7. Construction	5.1	5.3	3.3
8. Trade and Commerce	22.0	23.8	10.0
9. Transport, Storage and Communications	8.3	9.2	2.0
10. Other Services	25.1	22.8	40.4

Source :: Table C–1, Census of India 1991, Part IIB – Primary Census Abstract.
* Excludes figures for Jammu & Kashmir where the 1991 census could not be conducted due to disturbed conditions

Appendix 7.3
Employment in the organized sector by industry (in million)[1]

	1	*2*	*3*	*4*	*5*	*6*
			A. Public Sector[2]			
	By Industry	1961	1971	1981	1991	2001
0	Agriculture	0.18	0.28	0.46	0.56	0.50
1	Mining and Quarrying	0.13	0.18	0.82	1.00	0.88
2&3	Manufacturing	0.37	0.81	1.50	1.85	1.43
4	Elect, Gas and water supply	0.22	0.44	0.68	0.91	0.94
5	Construction	0.60	0.88	1.09	1.15	1.08
6	Wholesale and Retail Trade	0.09	0.04	0.12	0.15	0.16
7	Transport storage and communication	1.72	2.22	2.71	3.03	3.04
8	Finance, Insurance , Real Estate		0.29	0.75	1.19	1.28
9	Community, Social and Personal Services	3.73 (52.9)[3]	5.61 (52.3)	7.36 (47.54)	9.23 (48.43)	9.83 (51.36)
	Total	7.05 (58.31)[4]	10.73 (61.31)	15.48 (67.66)	19.06 (71.24)	19.14 (68.87)

Cont'd...

App. 7.3 Cont'd...

1		*2*	*3*	*4*	*5*	*6*
			B. Private Sector			
	By Industry	1961	1971	1981	1991	2001
0	Agriculture	0.67	0.80	0.86	0.89	0.93
1	Mining and Quarrying	0.55	0.41	0.13	0.10	0.08
2&3	Manufacturing	3.02 (59.9)5	3.97 (58.64)	4.55 (61.48)	4.48 (58.33)	5.01 (57.91)
4	Elect, Gas and water supply	0.04	0.05	0.04	0.04	0.05
5	Construction	0.24	0.14	0.07	0.07	0.06
6	Wholesale and Retail Trade	0.16	0.30	0.28	0.30	0.34
7	Transport storage and communication	0.08	0.10	0.06	0.05	0.08
8	Finance, Insurance , Real Estate			0.20	0.25	0.37
9	Community, Social and Personal Services	0.28	1.00	1.22	1.49	1.73
	Total	5.04	6.77	7.40	7.68	8.65
			Public + Private Sector (A + B)			
	By Industry	1961	1971	1981	1991	2001
0	Agriculture	0.85	1.08	1.32	1.45	1.43
1	Mining and Quarrying	0.68	0.59	0.95	1.10	0.95
2&3	Manufacturing	3.39	4.78	6.05	6.33	6.44
4	Elect, Gas and water supply	0.26	0.49	0.72	0.95	0.99
5	Construction	0.84	1.02	1.16	1.22	1.14
6	Wholesale and Retail Trade	0.25	0.34	0.39	0.45	0.50
7	Transport storage and communication	1.80	2.32	2.77	3.08	3.12
8	Finance, Insurance , Real Estate		0.29	0.94	1.45	1.65
9	Community, Social and Personal Services	4.01	6.61	8.58	10.71	11.56
	Total	12.09	17.50	22.88	26.74	27.79

1 Adapted from Organized Labor Market in India – Pre and Post Reform, by Suresh D. Tendulkar, 2003 (Web)
2 Public Sector employment includes those in Central and Non-central Public Sector Units (CPSU and NCPSU)
3 Percentage in respect to A total
4 Percentage in respect to A+B total
5 Percentage in respect to B total

Appendix 7.4

Distribution of main workers by industry and occupation and sex, India1991 ('000)

Industry	*Sex*	*Prof., technical and related workers*	*Admin. Executive & managerial workers*	*Clerical & related workers*	*Sales Workers*	*Service Workers*	*Farmers, Fishermen & retired workers*	*Prod. & related workers, transport equipment operators & laborers*	*Workers Not classified by occupation*	*Total*
1	*2*	*3*	*4*	*5*	*6*	*7*	*8*	*9*	*10*	*11*
Agriculture, forestry, fishing and hunting	Male	113	1.5	217	158	112	138445	224	90	139361
	Person	122	1.6	231	187	118	190324	241	116	191341
Mining and quarrying	Male	50	28	81	9	36	1	1312	20	1537
	Person	54	29	85	10	39	11	1509	24	1751
Manufacturing, processing, servicing & repairs in HHI	Male	11	23	12	53	54		4323	79	4555
	Person	13	26	13	72	86		6481	113	6804
Manufacturing, processing, servicing and repairs in other than HHI	Male	449	571	918	395	318	16	16581	167	19415
	Person	475	590	1002	422	337	18	18836	187	21867
Construction	Male	159	294	220	23	84	4	4298	40	5122
	Person	166	298	238	25	90	5	4677	44	5543
Trade and commerce	Male	503	974	1528	14592	1557	11	544	154	19863
	Person	533	1018	1715	15591	1681	12	578	168	21296
Transport, storage and communication	Male	110	167	1580	30	147	3	5688	84	7810
	Person	119	171	1685	32	163	3	5755	90	8018
Other services	Male	6231	738	4295	198	4393	73	5627	2440	23995
	Person	8676	787	4797	212	5809	79	6318	2634	29312
Total	Male	7627	2795	8852	15459	6701	138553	38597	3074	221658
	Person	10157	2923	9767	16550	8322	190442	44396	3375	285932

Source : Office of the Registrar General, India. (Excludes Jammu & Kashmir. Total may not tally due to rounding off).

Appendix 7.5

Female employment in organized sector in the larger states and India 2001

State	Total employment (in million)	% of women employment to total employment	State	Total employment (in lakhs)	% of women employment to total employment
INDIA	**27.79**	**17.8**	Madhya Pradesh	1.18	12.7
Andhra Pradesh	2.08	20.2	Maharashtra	3.69	15.2
Assam	1.12	31.3	Orissa	0.83	12.0
Bihar*	1.61	6.8	Punjab	0.85	15.3
Gujarat	1.70	12.4	Rajasthan	1.25	13.6
Haryana	0.65	13.8	Tamil Nadu	2.51	29.1
Himachal Pradesh	0.30	16.7	Uttar Pradesh	2.22	9.5
Karnataka	1.88	30.3	West Bengal	2.32	10.8
Kerala	1.24	39.5			

*The state of Bihar includes data of newly created state Jharkhand

Source : Directorate General of Employment and Training, Ministry of Labor

Appendix 7.6

Percentage distribution of workforce by industrial categories

Industrial categories	Rural						Urban					
	1972–73	1977–78	1983	1987–88	1990–91	1993–94	1972–73	1977–78	1983	1987–88	1990–91	1993–94
1	2	3	4	5	6	7	8	9	10	11	12	13
Primary Sector (Agriculture)												
1. Agriculture & allied	85.4	83.4	81.2	76.3	75.5	78.4	14.8	15.3	14.6	13.4	12.3	12.3
Secondary Sector (Industry)												
2. Mining & Quarrying	0.4	0.4	0.5	0.6	0.6	0.6	0.9	0.8	1.0	1.2	1.9	1.2
3. Manufacturing	5.3	6.2	6.7	7.2	7.7	7.0	26.5	28.0	26.7	26.0	25.8	23.6
4. Electricity, gas and water supply	0.1	0.1	0.1	0.2	0.4	0.2	0.7	0.8	0.9	1.0	1.4	1.0
5. Construction	1.4	1.3	1.7	3.3	2.2	2.4	4.3	3.8	4.7	5.4	5.0	6.3
Total of (2–5)	7.2	8.0	9.0	11.3	10.9	10.2	32.4	33.4	33.3	33.6	34.1	32.1
Tertiary Sector (Service)												
6. Trades, hotel and restaurant	2.5	3.3	3.5	4.0	3.9	4.3	18.1	18.8	18.4	19.0	17.3	19.4
7. Transport. storage and communication	0.7	0.8	1.1	1.3	1.5	1.4	7.5	7.9	8.1	7.8	7.6	8.0
8. Services	4.1	4.4	4.9	5.0	8.2	5.7	27.0	24.6	25.0	25.7	29.6	28.2

Cont'd...

App. 7.6 Cont'd...

1	*2*	*3*	*4*	*5*	*6*	*7*	*8*	*9*	*10*	*11*	*12*	*13*
9. Activities not classified	0.1	0.1	0.3	0.1			0.4		0.6	0.5		
Total of (6–9)	7.4	8.6	9.8	10.4	13.6	11.4	53.0	51.3	52.1	53.0	54.5	55.6
Total of (1–9)	100	100	100	100	100	100	100	100	100	100	100	100
Total employment (million)	198	221	243	252	268	290	38.5	49.2	59.6	69.5	73.6	81.8

Source: NSSO various Rounds

Appendix 7.7

Percentage share of GDP by service sector

Sectors	***1993 –94***	***1994 –95***	***1995 –96***	***1996 –97***	***1997 –98***	***1998 –99***	***1999 –00***	***2000 –01***	***2001 –02***
1	*2*	*3*	*4*	*5*	*6*	*7*	*8*	*9*	*10*
Trade, restaurant and hotel	12.72	13.12	13.99	13.97	14.35	14.49	14.65	14.69	15.06
(i) Trade	11.95	12.33	13.10	13.09	13.44	13.53	13.64	13.38	13.97
(ii) Hotel & restaurant	0.79	0.79	0.89	0.88	0.97	0.96	1.01	1.03	1.09
Transport, storage & communication	6.54	6.70	6.93	6.95	7.18	7.29	7.03	8.20	8.43
(i) Railways	1.23	1.17	1.18	1.15	1.12	1.07	1.10	1.10	1.10
(ii) Transport (others)	4.02	4.14	4.22	4.23	4.27	4.21	4.23	4.32	4.25
(iii) Storage	0.08	0.08	0.08	0.07	0.06	0.06	0.06	0.06	0.06
(iv) Communication	1.21	1.31	1.45	1.50	1.73	1.95	2.24	2.72	3.01
Finance, insurance, real estate and business services	11.53	11.35	11.43	11.34	12.08	12.18	12.70	12.59	12.46
(i) Banking & insurance	5.33	5.39	5.57	5.67	6.38	6.32	6.96	6.59	6.45
(ii) Others	6.20	5.95	5.86	5.67	5.70	5.67	5.74	6.00	6.01
Community social and professional services	11.98	11.54	11.59	11.43	12.18	12.62	13.36	13.51	13.51
(i) Defense and public administration	5.58	5.27	5.24	5.06	5.63	5.75	6.13	6.02	5.87
(ii) Other services	6.40	6.26	6.35	6.36	6.65	6.88	7.22	7.48	7.64
Total share of GDP	42.32	42.71	43.94	43.69	45.79	46.58	47.74	48.99	49.46

Source: Government of India: Economic Survey 2002–03.

Appendix 7.8

Total population, total workers, main workers, marginal workers and non-workers – India, states and union territories, 2001

State/UT*	Total / Rural / Urban	Persons / Males / Females	Total Population	Total Workers	Main Workers	Marginal Workers	Non-Workers
1	2	3	4	5	6	7	8
INDIA	Total	Persons	1025251059	402512190(39.26)	313173394(30.55)	89338796(8.71)	622738869(60.74)
		Males	530422415(51.74)	275463736(51.93)	240520672(45.35)	34943064(6.59)	254958679(48.07)
		Females	494828644(48.26)	127048454(25.68)	72652722(14.68)	54395732(10.99)	367780190(74.32)
	Rural	Persons	740255371(72.20)	310655339(41.97)	229672348(31.03)	80982991(10.94)	429600032(58.03)
		Males	380438194(51.39)	199199602(52.36)	169333233(44.51)	29866369(7.85)	181238592(47.64)
		Females	359817177(48.61)	111455737(30.98)	60339115(16.77)	51116622(14.21)	248361440(69.02)
	Urban	Persons	284995688(27.80)	91856851(32.23)	83501046(29.30)	8355805(2.93)	193138837(67.77)
		Males	149984221(52.63)	76264134(50.85)	71187439(47.46)	5076695(3.38)	73720087(49.15)
		Females	135011467(47.37)	15592717(11.55)	12313607(9.12)	3279110(2.43)	119418750(88.45)
Jammu & Kashmir	Total	Persons	10069917(0.98)	3688875(36.63)	2536509(25.19)	1152366(11.44)	6381042(63.37)
		Males	5300574(52.64)	2641348(49.83)	2189225(41.30)	452123(8.53)	2659226(50.17)
		Females	4769343(47.36)	1047527(21.96)	347284(7.28)	700243(14.68)	3721816(78.04)
	Rural	Persons	7564608(75.12)	2869319(37.93)	1798722(23.78)	1070597(14.15)	4695289(62.07)
		Males	3925846(51.90)	1929238(49.14)	1520448(38.73)	408790(10.41)	1996608(50.86)
		Females	3638762(48.10)	940081(25.84)	278274(7.65)	661807(18.19)	2698681(74.16)
	Urban	Persons	2505309(24.88)	819556(32.71)	737787(29.45)	81769(3.26)	1685753(67.29)
		Males	1374728(54.9)	712110(51.8)	668777(48.6)	43333(3.2)	662618(48.2)
		Females	1130581(45.13)	107446(9.50)	69010(6.10)	38436(3.40)	1023135(90.50)
Himachal Pradesh	Total	Persons	6070305(0.59)	2991448(49.28)	1964141(32.36)	1027307(16.92)	3078857(50.72)
		Males	3080781(50.75)	1685310(54.70)	1334033(43.30)	351277(11.40)	1395471(45.30)
		Females	2989524(49.248)	1306138(43.691)	630108(21.077)	676030(22.613)	1683386(56.309)
	Rural	Persons	5475424(90.20)	2771978(50.63)	1759474(32.13)	1012504(18.49)	2703446(49.37)
		Males	2749776(50.22)	1505312(54.74)	1163098(42.30)	342214(12.45)	1244464(45.26)

Cont'd…

App. 7.8 Cont'd…

1	*2*	*3*	*4*	*5*	6	7	8
		Females	2725648(49.78)	1266666(46.47)	596376(21.88)	670290(24.59)	1458982(53.53)
	Urban	Persons	594881(9.80)	219470(36.89)	204667(34.40)	14803(2.49)	375411(63.11)
		Males	331005(55.64)	179998(54.38)	170935(51.64)	9063(2.74)	151007(45.62)
		Females	263876(44.36)	39472(14.96)	33732(12.78)	5740(2.18)	224404(85.04)
Punjab	Total	Persons	24324749(2.37)	9141760(37.58)	7839111(32.23)	1302649(5.36)	15182989(62.42)
		Males	12983996(53.38)	7023757(54.10)	6487588(49.97)	536169(4.13)	5960239(45.90)
		Females	11340753(46.62)	2118003(18.68)	1351523(11.92)	766480(6.76)	9222750(81.32)
	Rural	Persons	16064238(66.041)	6382662(39.732)	5252672(32.698)	1129990(7.034)	9681576(60.268)
		Males	8508757(52.97)	4633197(54.45)	4199057(49.35)	434140(5.10)	3875560(45.55)
		Females	7555481(47.03)	1749465(23.15)	1053615(13.95)	695850(9.21)	5806016(76.85)
	Urban	Persons	8260511(33.96)	2759098(33.40)	2586439(31.31)	172659(2.09)	5501413(66.60)
		Males	4475239(54.176)	2390560(53.417)	2288531(51.138)	102029(2.280)	2084679(46.583)
		Females	3785272(45.82)	368538(9.74)	297908(7.87)	70630(1.87)	3416734(90.26)
Chandigarh*	Total	Persons	900914(33.96)	339021(33.40)	328906(31.31)	10115(2.09)	561893(66.60)
		Males	508224(54.176)	285136(53.417)	278377(51.138)	6759(2.280)	223088(46.583)
		Females	392690(45.82)	53885(9.74)	50529(7.87)	3356(1.87)	338805(90.26)
	Rural	Persons	92118(10.22)	39993(43.41)	38202(41.47)	1791(1.94)	52125(56.59)
		Males	56837(61.70)	36352(63.96)	35109(61.77)	1243(2.19)	20485(36.04)
		Females	35281(38.30)	3641(10.32)	3093(8.77)	548(1.55)	31640(89.68)
	Urban	Persons	808796(89.78)	299028(36.97)	290704(35.94)	8324(1.03)	509768(63.03)
		Males	451387(55.81)	248784(55.12)	243268(53.89)	5516(1.22)	202603(44.88)
		Females	357409(44.19)	50244(14.06)	47436(13.27)	2808(0.79)	307165(85.94)
Uttaranchal	Total	Persons	8483355(7E-05)	3133281(4E+01)	2323518(3E+01)	809763(1E+01)	5350074(6E+01)
		Males	4321041(50.94)	2005858(46.42)	1647759(38.13)	358099(8.29)	2315183(53.58)
		Females	4162314(49.06)	1127423(27.09)	675759(16.24)	451664(10.85)	3034891(72.91)
	Rural	Persons	6312415(74.41)	2501791(39.63)	1752827(27.77)	748964(11.86)	3810624(60.37)
		Males	3146031(49.84)	1446825(45.99)	1135357(36.09)	311468(9.90)	1699206(54.01)
		Females	3166384(50.16)	1054966(33.32)	617470(19.50)	437496(13.82)	2111418(66.68)

Cont'd…

App. 7.8 Cont'd…

1	2	3	4	5	6	7	8
	Urban	Persons	2170940(25.59)	631490(29.09)	570691(26.29)	60799(2.80)	1539450(70.91)
		Males	1175010(54.12)	559033(47.58)	512402(43.61)	46631(3.97)	615977(52.42)
		Females	995930(45.88)	72457(7.28)	58289(5.85)	14168(1.42)	923473(92.72)
Haryana	Total	Persons	21082989(2.06)	8382890(39.76)	6245402(29.62)	2137488(10.14)	12700099(60.24)
		Males	11327658(53.73)	5718804(50.49)	4941571(43.62)	777233(6.86)	5608854(49.51)
		Females	9755331(46.27)	2664086(27.31)	1303831(13.37)	1360255(13.94)	7091245(72.69)
	Rural	Persons	14968850(71.00)	6455946(43.13)	4521184(30.20)	1934762(12.93)	8512904(56.87)
		Males	8017622(53.56)	4079735(50.88)	3424251(42.71)	655484(8.18)	3937887(49.12)
		Females	6951228(46.44)	2376211(34.18)	1096933(15.78)	1279278(18.40)	4575017(65.82)
	Urban	Persons	6114139(29.00)	1926944(31.52)	1724218(28.20)	202726(3.32)	4187195(68.48)
		Males	3310036(54.14)	1639069(49.52)	1517320(45.84)	121749(3.68)	1670967(50.48)
		Females	2804103(45.86)	287875(10.27)	206898(7.38)	80977(2.89)	2516228(89.73)
Delhi	Total	Persons	13803085(1.35)	4526737(32.80)	4303812(31.18)	222925(1.62)	9276348(67.20)
		Males	7579849(54.91)	3957325(52.21)	3794300(50.06)	163025(2.15)	3622524(47.79)
		Females	6223236(45.09)	569412(9.15)	509512(8.19)	59900(0.96)	5653824(90.85)
	Rural	Persons	964943(6.99)	308766(32.00)	280858(29.11)	27908(2.89)	656177(68.00)
		Males	533255(55.26)	265067(49.71)	247291(46.37)	17776(3.33)	268188(50.29)
		Females	431688(44.74)	43699(10.12)	33567(7.78)	10132(2.35)	387989(89.88)
	Urban	Persons	12838142(93.01)	4217971(32.85)	4022954(31.34)	195017(1.52)	8620171(67.15)
		Males	7046594(54.89)	3692258(52.40)	3547009(50.34)	145249(2.06)	3354336(47.60)
		Females	5791548(45.11)	525713(9.08)	475945(8.22)	49768(0.86)	5265835(90.92)
Rajasthan	Total	Persons	56473122(5.51)	23781257(42.11)	17430143(30.86)	6351114(11.25)	32691865(57.89)
		Males	29381657(52.03)	14710049(50.07)	12871197(43.81)	1838852(6.26)	14671608(49.93)
		Females	27091465(47.97)	9071208(33.48)	4558946(16.83)	4512262(16.66)	18020257(66.52)
	Rural	Persons	43267678(76.62)	19877709(45.94)	13958254(32.26)	5919455(13.68)	23389969(54.06)
		Males	22394479(51.76)	11381353(50.82)	9786286(43.70)	1595067(7.12)	11013126(49.18)
		Females	20873199(48.24)	8496356(40.70)	4171968(19.99)	4324388(20.72)	12376843(59.30)

Cont'd…

App. 7.8 Cont'd…

1	2	3	4	5	6	7	8
	Urban	Persons	13205444(23.38)	3903548(29.56)	3471889(26.29)	431659(3.27)	9301896(70.44)
		Males	6987178(52.91)	3328696(47.64)	3084911(44.15)	243785(3.49)	3658482(52.36)
		Females	6218266(47.09)	574852(9.24)	386978(6.22)	187874(3.02)	5643414(90.76)
Uttar Pradesh	Total	Persons	166174612(16.21)	54180232(32.60)	39452928(23.74)	14727304(8.86)	111994380(67.40)
		Males	87560236(52.69)	41380607(47.26)	34655654(39.58)	6724953(7.68)	46179629(52.74)
		Females	78614376(47.31)	12799625(16.28)	4797274(6.10)	8002351(10.18)	65814751(83.72)
	Rural	Persons	131570779(79.18)	44865277(34.10)	31331667(23.81)	13533610(10.29)	86705502(65.90)
		Males	69117312(52.53)	33065880(47.84)	27181863(39.33)	5884017(8.51)	36051432(52.16)
		Females	62453467(47.47)	11799397(18.89)	4149804(6.64)	7649593(12.25)	50654070(81.11)
	Urban	Persons	34603833(20.82)	9314955(26.92)	8121261(23.47)	1193694(3.45)	25288878(73.08)
		Males	18442924(53.30)	8314727(45.08)	7473791(40.52)	840936(4.56)	10128197(54.92)
		Females	16160909(46.70)	1000228(6.19)	647470(4.01)	352758(2.18)	15160681(93.81)
Bihar	Total	Persons	82878796(8.08)	28080004(33.88)	21053153(25.40)	7026851(8.48)	54798792(66.12)
		Males	43153964(52.07)	20597085(47.73)	17571587(40.72)	3025498(7.01)	22556879(52.27)
		Females	39724832(47.93)	7482919(18.84)	3481566(8.76)	4001353(10.07)	32241913(81.16)
	Rural	Persons	74199596(89.53)	25856125(34.85)	19109705(25.75)	6746420(9.09)	48343471(65.15)
		Males	38510686(51.90)	18650188(48.43)	15811798(41.06)	2838390(7.37)	19860498(51.57)
		Females	35688910(48.10)	7205937(20.19)	3297907(9.24)	3908030(10.95)	28482973(79.81)
	Urban	Persons	8679200(10.47)	2223879(25.62)	1943448(22.39)	280431(3.23)	6455321(74.38)
		Males	4643278(53.50)	1946897(41.93)	1759789(37.90)	187108(4.03)	2696381(58.07)
		Females	4035922(46.50)	276982(6.86)	183659(4.55)	93323(2.31)	3758940(93.14)
Sikkim	Total	Persons	540493(0.05)	263320(48.72)	212478(39.31)	50842(9.41)	277173(51.28)
		Males	288217(53.32)	165957(57.58)	146666(50.89)	19291(6.69)	122260(42.42)
		Females	252276(46.68)	97363(38.59)	65812(26.09)	31551(12.51)	154913(61.41)
	Rural	Persons	480488(88.90)	239025(49.75)	190152(39.57)	48873(10.17)	241463(50.25)
		Males	255386(53.15)	147482(57.75)	129620(50.75)	17862(6.99)	107904(42.25)
		Females	225102(46.85)	91543(40.67)	60532(26.89)	31011(13.78)	133559(59.33)

Cont'd…

App. 7.8 Cont'd…

1	2	3	4	5	6	7	8
	Urban	Persons	60005(11.10)	24295(40.49)	22326(37.21)	1969(3.28)	35710(59.51)
		Males	32831(54.7)	18475(56.3)	17046(51.9)	1429(4.4)	14356(43.7)
		Females	27174(45.29)	5820(21.42)	5280(19.43)	540(1.99)	21354(78.58)
Arunachal Pradesh	Total	Persons	1096702(0.11)	482206(43.97)	413521(37.71)	68685(6.26)	614496(56.03)
		Males	579158(52.81)	293549(50.69)	266922(46.09)	26627(4.60)	285609(49.31)
		Females	517544(47.19)	188657(36.45)	146599(28.33)	42058(8.13)	328887(63.55)
	Rural	Persons	873633(79.66)	405998(46.47)	343181(39.28)	62817(7.19)	467635(53.53)
		Males	458482(52.48)	234433(51.13)	210871(45.99)	23562(5.14)	224049(48.87)
		Females	415151(47.52)	171565(41.33)	132310(31.87)	39255(9.46)	243586(58.67)
	Urban	Persons	223069(20.34)	76208(34.16)	70340(31.53)	5868(2.63)	146861(65.84)
		Males	120676(54.10)	59116(48.99)	56051(46.45)	3065(2.54)	61560(51.01)
		Females	102393(45.90)	17092(16.69)	14289(13.96)	2803(2.74)	85301(83.31)
Nagaland	Total	Persons	1988636(0.19)	849982(42.74)	708455(35.63)	141527(7.12)	1138654(57.26)
		Males	1041686(52.38)	487767(46.82)	424236(40.73)	63531(6.10)	553919(53.18)
		Females	946950(47.62)	362215(38.25)	284219(30.01)	77996(8.24)	584735(61.75)
	Rural	Persons	1635815(82.26)	737386(45.08)	606601(37.08)	130785(8.00)	898429(54.92)
		Males	846651(51.76)	398640(47.08)	341298(40.31)	57342(6.77)	448011(52.92)
		Females	789164(48.24)	338746(42.92)	265303(33.62)	73443(9.31)	450418(57.08)
	Urban	Persons	352821(17.74)	112596(31.91)	101854(28.87)	10742(3.04)	240225(68.09)
		Males	195035(55.28)	89127(45.70)	82938(42.52)	6189(3.17)	105908(54.30)
		Females	157786(44.72)	23469(14.87)	18916(11.99)	4553(2.89)	134317(85.13)
Manipur	Total	Persons	2388068(0.23)	1069578(44.79)	756520(31.68)	313058(13.11)	1318490(55.21)
		Males	1215664(50.91)	594642(48.91)	484240(39.83)	110402(9.08)	621022(51.09)
		Females	1172404(49.09)	474936(40.51)	272280(23.22)	202656(17.29)	697468(59.49)
	Rural	Persons	1812104(75.88)	846595(46.72)	592379(32.69)	254216(14.03)	965509(53.28)
		Males	928211(51.22)	464793(50.07)	373702(40.26)	91091(9.81)	463418(49.93)
		Females	883893(48.78)	381802(43.20)	218677(24.74)	163125(18.46)	502091(56.80)

Cont'd…

App. 7.8 Cont'd…

1	2	3	4	5	6	7	8
	Urban	Persons	575964(24.12)	222983(38.71)	164141(28.50)	58842(10.22)	352981(61.29)
		Males	287453(49.91)	129849(45.17)	110538(38.45)	19311(6.72)	157604(54.83)
		Females	288511(50.09)	93134(32.28)	53603(18.58)	39531(13.70)	195377(67.72)
Mizoram	Total	Persons	891058(0.09)	469597(52.70)	363858(40.83)	105739(11.87)	421461(47.30)
		Males	459783(51.60)	264162(57.45)	226637(49.29)	37525(8.16)	195621(42.55)
		Females	431275(48.40)	205435(47.63)	137221(31.82)	68214(15.82)	225840(52.37)
	Rural	Persons	450018(50.50)	257488(57.22)	202257(44.94)	55231(12.27)	192530(42.78)
		Males	233718(51.94)	139111(59.52)	120915(51.74)	18196(7.79)	94607(40.48)
		Females	216300(48.06)	118377(54.73)	81342(37.61)	37035(17.12)	97923(45.27)
	Urban	Persons	441040(49.50)	212109(48.09)	161601(36.64)	50508(11.45)	228931(51.91)
		Males	226065(51.26)	125051(55.32)	105722(46.77)	19329(8.55)	101014(44.68)
		Females	214975(48.74)	87058(40.50)	55879(25.99)	31179(14.50)	127917(59.50)
Tripura	Total	Persons	3191168(0.31)	1158190(36.29)	906487(28.41)	251703(7.89)	2032978(63.71)
		Males	1636138(51.27)	831318(50.81)	740153(45.24)	91165(5.57)	804820(49.19)
		Females	1555030(48.73)	326872(21.02)	166334(10.70)	160538(10.32)	1228158(78.98)
	Rural	Persons	2648074(82.98)	982635(37.11)	743447(28.08)	239188(9.03)	1665439(62.89)
		Males	1359288(51.33)	687956(50.61)	604711(44.49)	83245(6.12)	671332(49.39)
		Females	1288786(48.67)	294679(22.86)	138736(10.76)	155943(12.10)	994107(77.14)
	Urban	Persons	543094(17.02)	175555(32.32)	163040(30.02)	12515(2.30)	367539(67.68)
		Males	276850(50.98)	143362(51.78)	135442(48.92)	7920(2.86)	133488(48.22)
		Females	266244(49.02)	32193(12.09)	27598(10.37)	4595(1.73)	234051(87.91)
Meghalaya	Total	Persons	2306069(0.22)	956425(41.47)	742762(32.21)	213663(9.27)	1349644(58.53)
		Males	1167840(50.64)	557807(47.76)	471830(40.40)	85977(7.36)	610033(52.24)
		Females	1138229(49.36)	398618(35.02)	270932(23.80)	127686(11.22)	739611(64.98)
	Rural	Persons	1853457(80.37)	826334(44.58)	629401(33.96)	196933(10.63)	1027123(55.42)
		Males	939803(50.71)	470712(50.086)	392511(41.765)	78201(8.320)	469091(49.913)
		Females	913654(19.63)	355622(38.923)	236890(25.927)	118732(12.995)	558032(61.076)

Cont'd…

App. 7.8 Cont'd…

1	2	3	4	5	6	7	8
	Urban	Persons	452612(19.63)	130091(28.742)	113361(25.045)	16730(3.696)	322521(71.257)
		Males	228037(50.38)	87095(38.193)	79319(34.783)	7776(3.409)	140942(61.806)
		Females	224575(49.62)	42996(19.145)	34042(15.158)	8954(3.987)	181579(80.854)
Assam	Total	Persons	26638407(2.60)	9557064(35.88)	7083046(26.59)	2474018(9.287)	17081343(64.12)
		Males	13787799(51.76)	6884451(49.93)	5839050(42.35)	1045401(7.582)	6903348(5.07)
		Females	12850608(48.241)	2672613(20.80)	1243996(9.68)	1428617(11.12)	10177995(79.20)
	Rural	Persons	23248994(87.28)	8473127(36.45)	6078938(26.15)	2394189(10.30)	14775867(63.55)
		Males	11983157(51.54)	5963601(49.77)	4968101(41.46)	995500(8.31)	6019556(50.23)
		Females	11265837(48.46)	2509526(22.28)	1110837(9.86)	1398689(12.42)	8756311(77.72)
	Urban	Persons	3389413(12.72)	1083937(31.98)	1004108(29.62)	79829(2.36)	2305476(68.02)
		Males	1804642(53.24)	920850(51.03)	870949(48.26)	49901(2.77)	883792(48.97)
		Females	1584771(46.76)	163087(10.29)	133159(8.40)	29928(1.89)	1421684(89.71)
WestBengal	Total	Persons	80221171(7.82)	29503278(36.78)	23063800(28.75)	6439478(8.03)	50717893(63.22)
		Males	41487694(51.72)	22500480(54.23)	19632549(47.32)	2867931(6.91)	18987214(45.77)
		Females	38733477(48.28)	7002798(18.08)	3431251(8.86)	3571547(9.22)	31730679(81.92)
	Rural	Persons	57734690(71.97)	21897521(37.93)	16115110(27.91)	5782411(10.02)	35837169(62.07)
		Males	29606028(51.28)	16075548(54.30)	13619407(46.00)	2456141(8.30)	13530480(45.70)
		Females	28128662(48.72)	5821973(20.70)	2495703(8.87)	3326270(11.83)	22306689(79.30)
	Urban	Persons	22486481(2.19)	7605757(33.82)	6948690(30.90)	657067(2.92)	14880724(66.18)
		Males	11881666(52.84)	6424932(54.07)	6013142(50.61)	411790(3.47)	5456734(45.93)
		Females	10604815(47.16)	1180825(11.13)	935548(8.82)	245277(2.31)	9423990(88.87)
Uttar Pradesh	Total	Persons	26909428(2.62)	10127733(37.64)	6462736(24.02)	3664997(13.62)	16781695(62.36)
		Males	13861277(51.51)	6682839(48.21)	5158527(37.22)	1524312(11.00)	7178438(51.79)
		Females	13048151(48.49)	3444894(26.40)	1304209(10.00)	2140685(16.41)	9603257(73.60)
	Rural	Persons	20922731(77.75)	8590029(41.06)	5119383(24.47)	3470646(16.59)	12332702(58.94)
		Males	10660430(50.95)	5320278(49.91)	3939134(36.95)	1381144(12.96)	5340152(50.09)
		Females	10262301(49.05)	3269751(31.86)	1180249(11.50)	2089502(20.36)	6992550(68.14)

Cont'd…

App. 7.8 Cont'd…

1	2	3	4	5	6	7	8
	Urban	Persons	5986697(22.25)	1537704(25.69)	1343353(22.44)	194351(3.25)	4448993(74.31)
		Males	3200847(53.5)	1362561(42.6)	1219393(38.1)	143168(4.5)	1838286(57.4)
		Females	2785850(46.53)	175143(6.29)	123960(4.45)	51183(1.84)	2610707(93.71)
Orissa	Total	Persons	36706920(3.58)	14272764(38.88)	9572940(26.08)	4699824(12.80)	22434156(61.12)
		Males	18612340(50.71)	9818471(52.75)	8017115(43.07)	1801356(9.68)	8793869(47.25)
		Females	18094580(49.29)	4454293(24.62)	1555825(8.60)	2898468(16.02)	13640287(75.38)
	Rural	Persons	31210602(85.03)	12587554(40.33)	8058257(25.82)	4529297(14.51)	18623048(59.67)
		Males	15711853(50.34)	8386624(53.38)	6684924(42.55)	1701700(10.83)	7325229(46.62)
		Females	15498749(49.66)	4200930(27.10)	1373333(8.86)	2827597(18.24)	11297819(72.90)
	Urban	Persons	5496318(14.97)	1685210(30.66)	1514683(27.56)	170527(3.10)	3811108(69.34)
		Males	2900487(52.77)	1431847(49.37)	1332191(45.93)	99656(3.44)	1468640(50.63)
		Females	2595831(47.23)	253363(9.76)	182492(7.03)	70871(2.73)	2342468(90.24)
Chhatisgarh	Total	Persons	20810983(2.03)	9685260(46.54)	7059731(33.92)	2625529(12.62)	11125723(53.46)
		Males	10462337(50.27)	5542010(52.97)	4753649(45.44)	788361(7.54)	4920327(47.03)
		Females	10348646(49.73)	4143250(40.04)	2306082(22.28)	1837168(17.75)	6205396(59.96)
	Rural	Persons	16626637(79.89)	8384439(50.43)	5888778(35.42)	2495661(15.01)	8242198(49.57)
		Males	8294598(49.89)	4502529(54.28)	3783290(45.61)	719239(8.67)	3792069(45.72)
		Females	8332039(50.11)	3881910(46.59)	2105488(25.27)	1776422(21.32)	4450129(53.41)
	Urban	Persons	4184346(20.11)	1300821(31.09)	1170953(27.98)	129868(3.10)	2883525(68.91)
		Males	2167739(51.81)	1039481(47.95)	970359(44.76)	69122(3.19)	1128258(52.05)
		Females	2016607(48.19)	261340(12.96)	200594(9.95)	60746(3.01)	1755267(87.04)
Madhya Pradesh	Total	Persons	60252739(5.88)	25756485(42.75)	19077568(31.66)	6678917(11.08)	34496254(57.25)
		Males	31386566(52.09)	16202287(51.62)	14081689(44.87)	2120598(6.76)	15184279(48.38)
		Females	28866173(47.91)	9554198(33.10)	4995879(17.31)	4558319(15.79)	19311975(66.90)
	Rural	Persons	44288037(73.50)	20865600(47.11)	14748209(33.30)	6117391(13.81)	23422437(52.89)
		Males	22976980(51.88)	12195626(53.08)	10391973(45.23)	1803653(7.85)	10781354(46.92)
		Females	21311057(48.12)	8669974(40.68)	4356236(20.44)	4313738(20.24)	12641083(59.32)

Cont'd…

App. 7.8 Cont'd…

1	2	3	4	5	6	7	8
	Urban	Persons	15964702(26.50)	4890885(30.64)	4329359(27.12)	561526(3.52)	11073817(69.36)
		Males	8409586(52.68)	4006661(47.64)	3689716(43.88)	316945(3.77)	4402925(52.36)
		Females	7555116(47.32)	884224(11.70)	639643(8.47)	244581(3.24)	6670892(88.30)
Gujarat	Total	Persons	48387270(4.72)	20368797(42.10)	16288598(33.66)	4080199(8.43)	28018473(57.90)
		Males	25208865(52.10)	13870929(55.02)	12920179(51.25)	950750(3.77)	11337936(44.98)
		Females	23178405(47.90)	6497868(28.03)	3368419(14.53)	3129449(13.50)	16680537(71.97)
	Rural	Persons	30160219(62.33)	14341413(47.55)	10590157(35.11)	3751256(12.44)	15818806(52.45)
		Males	15506359(51.41)	8620383(55.59)	7816150(50.41)	804233(5.19)	6885976(44.41)
		Females	14653860(48.59)	5721030(39.04)	2774007(18.93)	2947023(20.11)	8932830(60.96)
	Urban	Persons	18227051(37.67)	6027384(33.07)	5698441(31.26)	328943(1.80)	12199667(66.93)
		Males	9702506(53.23)	5250546(54.12)	5104029(52.61)	146517(1.51)	4451960(45.88)
		Females	8524545(46.77)	776838(9.11)	594412(6.97)	182426(2.14)	7747707(90.89)
Daman & Diu*	Total	Persons	158059(0.02)	72654(45.97)	67603(42.77)	5051(3.20)	85405(54.03)
		Males	92478(58.51)	60627(65.56)	59034(63.84)	1593(1.72)	31851(34.44)
		Females	65581(41.49)	12027(18.34)	8569(13.07)	3458(5.27)	53554(81.66)
	Rural	Persons	100740(63.74)	52413(52.03)	48521(48.16)	3892(3.86)	48327(47.97)
		Males	63576(63.11)	45069(70.89)	43857(68.98)	1212(1.91)	18507(29.11)
		Females	37164(36.89)	7344(19.76)	4664(12.55)	2680(7.21)	29820(80.24)
	Urban	Persons	57319(36.26)	20241(35.31)	19082(33.29)	1159(2.02)	37078(64.69)
		Males	28902(50.423)	15558(53.83)	15177(52.51)	381(1.32)	13344(46.17)
		Females	28417(49.58)	4683(16.48)	3905(13.74)	778(2.74)	23734(83.52)
Dadra & Nagar Haveli*	Total	Persons	220451(0.02)	114121(51.77)	96333(43.70)	17788(8.07)	106330(48.23)
		Males	121731(55.22)	75939(62.38)	71355(58.62)	4584(3.77)	45792(37.62)
		Females	98720(44.78)	38182(38.68)	24978(25.30)	13204(13.38)	60538(61.32)
	Rural	Persons	169995(77.11)	91545(53.85)	75136(44.20)	16409(9.65)	78450(46.15)
		Males	91887(54.05)	56320(61.29)	52161(56.77)	4159(4.53)	35567(38.71)
		Females	78108(45.95)	35225(45.10)	22975(29.41)	12250(15.68)	42883(54.90)

Cont'd…

App. 7.8 Cont'd…

1	2	3	4	5	6	7	8
	Urban	Persons	50456(22.89)	22576(44.74)	21197(42.01)	1379(2.73)	27880(55.26)
		Males	29844(59.15)	19619(65.74)	19194(64.31)	425(1.42)	10225(34.26)
		Females	20612(40.85)	2957(14.35)	2003(9.72)	954(4.63)	17655(85.65)
Maharashtra	Total	Persons	96752247(9.44)	42053330(43.46)	35670836(36.87)	6382494(6.60)	54698917(56.54)
		Males	50334270(52.02)	26924764(53.49)	24485209(48.65)	2439555(4.85)	23409506(46.51)
		Females	46417977(47.98)	15128566(32.59)	11185627(24.10)	3942939(8.49)	31289411(67.41)
	Rural	Persons	55732513(57.60)	28106602(50.43)	22752088(40.82)	5354514(9.61)	27625911(49.57)
		Males	28443238(51.04)	15410854(54.18)	13589736(47.78)	1821118(6.40)	13032384(45.82)
		Females	27289275	12695748	9162352	3533396	14593527
	Urban	Persons	41019734(42.40)	13946728(34.00)	12918748(31.49)	1027980(2.51)	27073006(66.00)
		Males	21891032(53.37)	11513910(52.60)	10895473(49.77)	618437(2.83)	10377122(47.40)
		Females	19128702(46.63)	2432818(12.72)	2023275(10.58)	409543(2.14)	16695884(87.28)
Andhra Pradesh	Total	Persons	76111243(7.42)	34865117(45.81)	29001326(38.10)	5863791(7.70)	41246126(54.19)
		Males	38490506(50.57)	21725810(56.44)	19517524(50.71)	2208286(5.74)	16764696(43.56)
		Females	37620737(150.57)	13139307(34.93)	9483802(25.21)	3655505(9.72)	24481430(65.07)
	Rural	Persons	55296875(72.65)	28159160(50.92)	22943260(41.49)	5215900(9.43)	27137715(49.08)
		Males	27890340(50.44)	16309047(58.48)	14484219(51.93)	1824828(6.54)	11581293(41.52)
		Females	27406535(49.56)	11850113(43.24)	8459041(30.87)	3391072(12.37)	15556422(56.76)
	Urban	Persons	20814368(27.35)	6705957(32.22)	6058066(29.11)	647891(3.11)	14108411(67.78)
		Males	10600166(72.65)	5416763(51.10)	5033305(47.48)	383458(3.62)	5183403(48.90)
		Females	10214202(27.35)	1289194(12.62)	1024761(10.03)	264433(2.59)	8925008(87.38)
Karnataka	Total	Persons	52733958(5.144)	23521533(44.604)	19357600(36.708)	4163933(7.896)	29212425(55.396)
		Males	26856343(50.93)	15272725(56.87)	13944187(51.92)	1328538(4.95)	11583618(43.13)
		Females	25877615(49.07)	8248808(31.88)	5413413(20.92)	2835395(10.96)	17628807(68.12)
	Rural	Persons	34814100(66.02)	17129318(49.20)	13458918(38.66)	3670400(10.54)	17684782(50.80)
		Males	17618593(50.61)	10274566(58.32)	9218896(52.32)	1055670(5.99)	7344027(41.68)
		Females	17195507(49.39)	6854752(39.86)	4240022(24.66)	2614730(15.21)	10340755(60.14)
	Urban	Persons	17919858(33.98)	6392215(35.67)	5898682(32.92)	493533(2.75)	11527643(64.33)

Cont'd…

App. 7.8 Cont'd…

1	2	3	4	5	6	7	8
		Males	9237750(51.55)	4998159(54.11)	4725291(51.15)	272868(2.95)	4239591(45.89)
		Females	8682108(48.45)	1394056(16.06)	1173391(13.52)	220665(2.54)	7288052(83.94)
Goa	Total	Persons	1343998(0.13)	522565(38.88)	425702(31.67)	96863(7.21)	821433(61.12)
		Males	685617(51.01)	376113(54.86)	328349(47.89)	47764(6.97)	309504(45.14)
		Females	658381(48.99)	146452(22.24)	97353(14.79)	49099(7.46)	511929(77.76)
	Rural	Persons	675129(50.23)	274744(40.70)	205248(30.40)	69496(10.29)	400385(59.30)
		Males	339626(50.31)	186286(54.85)	154753(45.57)	31533(9.28)	153340(45.15)
		Females	335503(49.69)	88458(26.37)	50495(15.05)	37963(11.32)	247045(73.63)
	Urban	Persons	668869(49.77)	247821(37.05)	220454(32.96)	27367(4.09)	421048(62.95)
		Males	345991(51.73)	189827(54.86)	173596(50.17)	16231(4.69)	156164(45.14)
		Females	322878(48.27)	57994(17.96)	46858(14.51)	11136(3.45)	264884(82.04)
Lakshadweep*	Total	Persons	60595(0.01)	15349(25.33)	11739(19.37)	3610(5.96)	45246(74.67)
		Males	31118(51.35)	13229(42.51)	10332(33.20)	2897(9.31)	17889(57.49)
		Females	29477(48.65)	2120(7.19)	1407(4.77)	713(2.42)	27357(92.81)
	Rural	Persons	33647(55.53)	7998(23.77)	5910(17.56)	2088(6.21)	25649(76.23)
		Males	17196(51.11)	6999(40.70)	5240(30.47)	1759(10.23)	10197(59.30)
		Females	16451(48.89)	999(6.07)	670(4.07)	329(2.00)	15452(93.93)
	Urban	Persons	26948(44.47)	7351(27.28)	5829(21.63)	1522(5.65)	19597(72.72)
		Males	13922(51.66)	6230(44.75)	5092(36.58)	1138(8.17)	7692(55.25)
		Females	13026(48.34)	1121(8.61)	737(5.66)	384(2.95)	11905(91.39)
Kerala	Total	Persons	31838619(3.11)	10291258(32.32)	8236741(25.87)	2054517(6.45)	21547361(67.68)
		Males	15468664(48.58)	7790522(50.36)	6479350(41.89)	1311172(8.48)	7678142(49.64)
		Females	16369955(51.42)	2500736(15.28)	1757391(10.74)	743345(4.54)	13869219(84.72)
	Rural	Persons	23571484(74.03)	7675096(32.56)	5996288(25.44)	1678808(7.12)	15896388(67.44)
		Males	11450785(48.58)	5750087(50.22)	4689974(40.96)	1060113(9.26)	5700698(49.78)
		Females	12120699(51.42)	1925009(15.88)	1306314(10.78)	618695(5.10)	10195690(84.12)
	Urban	Persons	8267135(25.97)	2616162(31.65)	2240453(27.10)	375709(4.54)	5650973(68.35)
		Males	4017879(48.60)	2040435(50.78)	1789376(44.54)	251059(6.25)	1977444(49.22)

Cont'd…

App. 7.8 Cont'd...

1	2	3	4	5	6	7	8
		Females	4249256(51.40)	575727(13.55)	451077(10.62)	124650(2.93)	3673529(86.45)
Tamil Nadu	Total	Persons	62110839(6.06)	27811647(44.78)	23684611(38.13)	4127036(6.64)	34299192(55.22)
		Males	31268654(50.34)	18153275(58.06)	16346879(52.28)	1806396(5.78)	13115379(41.94)
		Females	30842185(49.66)	9658372(31.32)	7337732(23.79)	2320640(7.52)	21183813(68.68)
	Rural	Persons	34869286(56.14)	17572083(50.39)	14290211(40.98)	3281872(9.41)	17297203(49.61)
		Males	17508985(50.21)	10396912(59.38)	9067457(51.79)	1329455(7.59)	7112073(40.62)
		Females	17360301(49.79)	7175171(41.33)	5222754(30.08)	1952417(11.25)	10185130(58.67)
	Urban	Persons	27241553(43.86)	10239564(37.59)	9394400(34.49)	845164(3.10)	17001989(62.41)
		Males	13759669(50.51)	7756363(56.37)	7279422(52.90)	476941(3.47)	6003306(43.63)
		Females	13481884(49.49)	2483201(18.42)	2114978(15.69)	368223(2.73)	10998683(81.58)
Pondicherry*	Total	Persons	973829(0.09)	342101(35.13)	316851(32.54)	25250(2.59)	631728(64.87)
		Males	486705(49.98)	259309(53.28)	245878(50.52)	13431(2.76)	227396(46.72)
		Females	487124(50.02)	82792(17.00)	70973(14.57)	11819(2.43)	404332(83.00)
	Rural	Persons	325596(33.43)	127635(39.20)	113318(34.80)	14317(4.40)	197961(60.80)
		Males	163586(50.24)	89102(54.47)	82273(50.29)	6829(4.17)	74484(45.53)
		Females	162010	38533	31045	7488	123477
	Urban	Persons	648233(66.57)	214466(33.08)	203533(31.40)	10933(1.69)	433767(66.92)
		Males	323119(49.85)	170207(52.68)	163605(50.63)	6602(2.04)	152912(47.32)
		Females	325114(50.15)	44259(13.61)	39928(12.28)	4331(1.33)	280855(86.39)
Andaman & Nicobar Islands*	Total	Persons	356265(0.03)	136331(38.27)	113929(31.98)	22402(6.29)	219934(61.73)
		Males	192985(54.17)	109475(56.73)	97842(50.70)	11633(6.03)	83510(43.27)
		Females	163280(45.83)	26856(16.45)	16087(9.85)	10769(6.60)	136424(83.55)
	Rural	Persons	239858(67.33)	94035(39.20)	73635(30.70)	20400(8.51)	145823(60.80)
		Males	128837(53.71)	73497(57.05)	63502(49.29)	9995(7.76)	55340(42.95)
		Females	111021(46.29)	20538(18.50)	10133(9.13)	10405(9.37)	90483(81.50)
	Urban	Persons	116407(32.67)	42296(36.33)	40294(34.61)	2002(1.72)	74111(63.67)
		Males	64148(55.11)	35978(56.09)	34340(53.53)	1638(2.55)	28170(43.91)
		Females	52259(44.89)	6318(12.09)	5954(11.39)	364(0.70)	45941(87.91)

Figures in parenthesis indicate percentage.
Source: Office of the Registrar General, India.

Appendix 8.1

Vital rates based on sample registration system by sector for states, union territories and India during 2001

State/UT*	Birth rate			Death rate			Natural growth rate		
	Rural	Urban	Total	Rural	Urban	Total	Rural	Urban	Total
1	2	3	4	5	6	7	8	9	10
Andhra Pradesh	21.3	19.6	20.8	8.9	5.6	8.1	12.4	14.0	12.8
Arunachal Pradesh	22.9	12.8	22.0	5.9	2.3	5.5	17.0	10.6	16.5
Assam	27.8	18.5	26.8	9.8	6.6	9.5	18.0	11.9	17.3
Bihar	32.3	23.4	31.2	8.5	6.3	8.2	23.7	17.1	23.0
Chhatisgarh	29.0	22.4	26.3	10.1	7.0	8.8	18.9	15.4	17.5
Goa	14.0	13.9	13.9	8.1	6.5	7.5	5.9	7.4	6.5
Gujarat	26.6	21.5	24.9	8.8	5.6	7.8	17.8	15.9	17.2
Harayana	27.8	22.8	26.7	7.6	7.4	7.6	20.2	15.4	19.1
Himachal Pradesh	21.3	16.8	21.0	7.1	5.3	7.0	14.2	11.5	14.0
Jammu & Kashmir	21.1	16.3	20.1	6.1	6.0	6.1	15.0	10.3	14.1
Jharkhand	28.3	19.5	26.3	9.7	6.0	8.8	18.6	13.4	17.4
Karnataka	23.6	19.0	22.2	8.2	6.4	7.6	15.4	12.6	14.6
Kerala	17.4	16.6	17.2	6.8	6.1	6.6	10.6	10.5	10.6
Madhya Pradesh	32.8	23.0	30.8	10.8	7.2	10.0	22.0	15.9	20.8
Maharashtra	21.0	20.1	20.6	8.5	5.9	7.5	12.5	14.2	13.1
Manipur	19.0	15.9	18.2	4.8	6.1	5.1	14.2	9.9	13.1
Meghalaya	30.7	15.0	28.3	9.9	3.9	9.0	20.7	11.1	19.3
Mizoram	17.7	13.2	15.7	5.2	3.4	4.4	12.4	9.8	11.3
Nagaland	NA	12.4	NA	NA	2.6	NA	NA	9.9	NA
Orissa	23.9	19.6	23.4	10.7	6.8	10.2	13.2	12.8	13.1
Punjab	22.1	18.7	21.2	7.2	6.4	7.0	14.8	12.2	14.2
Rajasthan	32.3	24.7	31.0	8.3	6.2	7.9	24.0	18.5	23.0
Sikkim	21.8	16.7	21.6	5.2	3.2	5.1	16.6	13.5	16.5
Tamil Nadu	19.6	17.8	19.0	8.4	6.0	7.6	11.2	11.8	11.4
Tripura	16.6	13.5	16.1	5.6	5.2	5.6	11.0	8.3	10.5
Uttar Pradesh	33.2	27.0	32.1	10.6	7.8	10.1	22.5	19.2	22.0
Uttaranchal	21.1	16.6	18.5	10.0	6.1	7.8	11.1	10.5	10.7
West Bengal	22.8	13.8	20.5	7.0	6.4	6.8	15.8	7.4	13.7
Andaman & Nicobar Is*	17.8	14.2	16.8	5.0	4.1	4.7	12.8	10.2	12.1
Chandigarh*	20.6	15.6	16.1	2.2	3.7	3.5	18.4	11.9	12.6
Dadra & Nagar Haveli*	30.1	20.0	29.3	6.8	2.9	6.5	23.3	17.1	22.8

Cont'd...

App. 8.1 Cont'd...

1	*2*	*3*	*4*	*5*	*6*	*7*	*8*	*9*	*10*
Daman & Diu*	22.6	22.0	22.3	7.6	5.9	6.7	15.0	16.2	15.6
Delhi*	23.2	18.1	18.7	5.4	5.0	5.0	17.8	13.1	13.6
Lakshadweep*	22.1	18.7	20.4	4.7	5.2	5.0	17.4	13.5	15.4
Pondicherry*	18.7	17.3	17.9	7.7	6.6	7.0	11.0	10.7	10.8
INDIA	27.1	20.2	25.4	9.0	6.3	8.4	18.0	13.9	17.0

NA : Not available due to non receipt of returns
Source : Office of the Registrar General, India.

Appendix 9.1

Percentage distribution of deaths in rural India by major causes of death over the years

S.No	*Code*	*Major causes of death*	*1992*	*1993*	*1994*	*1995*	*1996*	*1997*	*1998*
1.	R	Symptoms, Signs and Abnormal Clinical finding not elsewhere mentioned	26.4	26.2	24.3	18.6	20.6	19.0	18.4
2.	J	Diseases of the Respiratory System	14.4	14.4	15.1	16.6	17.8	16.4	17.2
3.	I	Diseases of the Circulatory System	7.9	7.6	8.2	9.5	10.9	12.1	12.5
4.	A	Infectious and Parasitic Diseases	12.7	12.5	12.0	11.9	10.2	10.0	9.6
5.	P	Conditions Originating in the Peri-natal period	8.9	10.0	9.0	9.2	7.9	8.7	7.9
6.	G	Inflammatory Diseases of Central Nervous System	4.5	4.2	5.0	4.8	5.6	6.0	6.0
7.	X	With Venomous Animal Contact	5.0	4.7	5.0	6.0	5.5	5.9	6.7
8.	C	Neoplasm	3.2	3.1	3.9	4.2	3.9	4.3	4.3
9.	B	Viral infection	4.9	4.2	4.4	4.7	3.6	3.1	2.4
10.	D	Diseases of the Blood and Blood Forming Organs	2.9	3.1	3. 0	3.0	3.4	3.2	3.3
11.	V	External Causes of Mortality	2.1	2.1	2.2	2.4	2.1	2.3	2.2
12.	K	Diseases of the digestive System	1.4	1.4	1.6	1.6	2.0	2.1	2.1
13.	T	Injuries, Poisoning & Other Consequences of External Causes	1.2	1.3	1.3	1.4	1.1	1.4	1.3
14.	E	Metabolic Diseases	0.6	0.6	0.8	0.9	1.0	1.1	1.1
15.	N	Diseases of Genitourinary System	0.5	0.5	0.6	0.7	0.8	1.0	1.2
16.	O	Pregnancy, Childbirth and Puerperium injuries	0.9	1.1	0.9	0. 8	0.7	0.7	0.6
17.	W	Other External Causes of Accidental death	0.4	0.5	0.5	0.5	0.6	0.6	0.7
18.	F	Mental and Behavioral Disorders	0.3	0.6	0.4	0.5	0.5	0.5	0.6
19.	Q	Congenital Malformations, Deformations and Abnormalities	0.4	0.5	0.3	0.3	0.4	0.4	0.4
		Other Medically Certified Deaths	1.4	1.4	1.5	2.4	1.3	1.2	1.7

Source : Office of Registrar General, India : Survey of Causes of Death (rural) India; (As per International classification of diseases –X revision).

Appendix 11.1

Availability of forest and agricultural land in India

Year	*Per capita availability of forest land (in hectare)*	*Per capita availability of agricultural land in rural areas (in hectare)*
1950–51	0.113	0.638
1960–61	0.124	0.503
1970–71	0.115	0.410
1980–81	0.099	0.356
1985–86	0.089	0.327
1990–91	0.081	0.315
1995–96P	0.074	0.284
1996–97P	0.073	0.279
1997–98P	0.072	0.276
1998–99P	0.071	0.271

P : Provisional

Source : Estimates in this table have been worked out on the basis of area figures on land utilization published by the Ministry of Agriculture and Mid-Year estimates of population based on the reports of Standing Committee on Population Projections and Technical Group on Population.

Appendix 11.2

Percentage distribution of area by land use in India

Year	*Forests*	*Not available for cultivation*	*Permanent pastures & other grazing land*	*Land under misc. tree crops not included in net area sown*	*Cultivation waste*	*Fallow land & current fallow*	*Net area sown*	*Area sown more than once as percentage of net area sown*
1	*2*	*3*	*4*	*5*	*6*	*7*	*8*	*9*
1950–51	14.2	16.7	2.0	7.0	8.1	9.9	41.8	11.1
1960–61	18.1	17.0	4.7	1.5	6.4	7.6	44.6	14.7
1970–71	21.0	14.7	4.4	1.4	5.8	6.5	4 6.3	18.2
1980–81	22.2	13.0	3.9	1.2	5.5	8.2	46.0	23.3
1985–86	22.0	13.4	3.9	1.2	5.2	8.2	46.2	26.7
1990–91	22.2	13.3	3.7	1.3	4.9	7.7	46.9	29.9
1995–96P	22.6	13.6	3.6	1.1	4.6	7.8	46.6	31.8
1996–97P	22.6	13.6	3.6	1.2	4.6	7.6	46.8	32.8
1997–98P	22.6	13.8	3.6	1.2	4.5	7.9	46.5	34.3
1998–99P	22.5	13.8	3.6	1.2	4.6	7.7	46.6	34.3

P : Provisional

Source : Percentage figures have been worked out on the basis of area figures published by the Ministry of Agriculture

Appendix 12.1

Health, education and economic indicators for computing HDI and other indices

1. Health attainment indicators

States	Life expectancy at age 1								IMR			
	1981–85				1991–95				1981		1991	
	Rural		Urban		Rural		Urban					
	M	F	M	F	M	F	M	F	R	U	R	U
1	2	3	4	5	6	7	8	9	10	11	12	13
Andhra Pradesh	60.6	62.5	64.3	69.0	63.4	64.8	65.6	68.7	95	72	58	42
Assam	56.6	55.6	63.8	64.9	60.1	59.7	67.7	69.7			94	48
Bihar	58.9	56.1	64.7	63.8	63.3	60.8	67.1	69.9	98	62	77	50
Gujarat	60.0	65.0	63.1	65.8	63.3	64.6	64.2	67.8	129	85	83	64
Haryana	65.4	63.5	69.4	69.2	66.0	57.0	68.4	73.2	132	94	56	37
Karnataka	61.7	63.7	67.5	71.0	63.7	66.8	68.0	70.0	87	62	84	45
Kerala	67.0	72.9	65.9	71.0	70.2	75.0	69.4	75.4	56	49	45	42
Madhya Pradesh	57.3	56.9	63.2	65.7	60.3	59.3	65.4	66.6	158	105	142	84
Maharashtra	62.9	64.0	64.6	69.0	65.2	67.4	69.3	72.4	131	67	85	47
Orissa	60.0	59.3	62.5	64.3	62.1	61.0	65.6	70.1	171	111	130	72
Punjab	65.5	57.0	70.7	70.7	68.9	71.2	69.2	73.3	135	104	81	56
Rajasthan	57.8	58.0	63.6	66.0	62.4	62.6	67.8	67.6	153	97	93	55
Tamil Nadu	59.2	59.7	64.1	66.4	63.4	65.0	67.3	70.8	116	78	62	40
Uttar Pradesh	58.3	58.0	63.1	52.7	61.9	60.5	64.3	66.4	139	81	104	76
West Bengal	59.4	59.9	66.3	68.5	63.7	65.1	69.0	71.4	103	59	66	41
INDIA	**59.8**	**59.4**	**64.9**	**67.3**	**63.0**	**63.8**	**67.2**	**69.9**				

Source: RGI (1999): Compendium of India's Fertility and Mortality Indicators 1971 to 1997, and Census of India.

App. 12.1 Cont'd 2 ...

Health attainments Contd. 2

States	Probability of not surviving to age 40[1]				Proportion of children fully vaccinated (12–23 months)[2]				No medical attention at birth[3]
	1981		1991		NFHS 1992–93				
	R	U	R	U	R	U	M	F	
1	14	15	16	17	18	19	20	21	22
Andhra Pradesh	20.2	12.3	16.2	10.1	39.7	58.3	46.6	43.5	11.80
Assam	25.8	16.0	22.5	14.4	17.4	40.0	18.4	20.4	38.4
Bihar	27.3	15.2	19.8	12.8	9.1	21.5	12.5	8.8	46.4
Gujarat	22.4	16.4	18.2	13.3	46.2	57.0	51.3	48.3	16.6
Haryana	20.7	13.4	16.3	12.4	52.1	58.0	56.6	49.9	16.6

Cont'd...

App. 12.1 Cont'd…

1	14	15	16	17	18	19	20	21	22
Karnataka	19.1	10.9	17.9	10.0	49.9	57.6	50.7	54.0	26.1
Kerala	8.9	7.7	5.3	4.4	54.0	55.7	55.8	52.9	3.5
Madhya Pradesh	30.1	16.8	27.1	16.4	25.6	43.0	32.6	25.4	36.0
Maharashtra	19.3	12.5	14.4	8.7	65.6	61.6	61.2	67.1	20.1
Orissa	26.0	17.5	23.2	13.8	34.7	43.8	37.8	34.1	43.6
Punjab	17.6	12.1	15.3	9.8	57.7	75.6	68.9	54.2	1.8
Rajasthan	27.5	17.3	21.0	14.0	16.1	45.9	23.5	18.5	47.6
Tamil Nadu	23.3	13.5	15.2	9.1	60.3	73.3	68.3	61.9	9.6
Uttar Pradesh	32.0	20.2	23.5	13.3	17.4	32.9	22.5	17.0	48.1
West Bengal	22.0	11.7	16.1	9.8	31.3	44.1	31.8	36.5	13.1
INDIA	**25.2**	**14.1**	**19.6**	**11.4**	**30.9**	**50.7**	**36.7**	**34.1**	**32.2**

1. RGI: SRS abridged Life Tables, 1981–85 and 1989–93 2. National Family Health Survey I

App. 12.1 Cont'd.3…

States	*2. Educational attainments*							
	Literacy rate (7+ age)							
	1981				*1991*			
	R		*U*		*R*		*U*	
	M	*F*	*M*	*F*	*M*	*F*	*M*	*F*
1	*23*	*24*	*25*	*26*	*27*	*28*	*29*	*30*
Andhra Pradesh	38.7	16.8	72.6	48.7	47.3	23.9	75.9	56.4
Assam					58.7	39.2	84.4	73.3
Bihar	42.4	12.4	73.2	47.5	48.3	18.0	77.7	55.9
Gujarat	57.8	28.8	80.7	60.2	66.8	38.7	84.6	67.7
Haryana	53.4	18.8	76.1	55.8	64.8	32.5	82.0	64.1
Karnataka	51.1	23.8	76.5	56.4	60.3	34.8	82.0	65.7
Kerala	86.7	74.2	92.0	82.0	92.9	85.1	95.6	89.1
Madhya Pradesh	40.8	17.3	76.4	50.8	51.0	19.7	81.3	58.9
Maharashtra	61.7	29.5	82.9	63.9	69.7	41.0	86.4	70.9
Orissa	53.5	22.0	76.4	51.0	50.0	30.8	81.2	61.2
Punjab	49.6	32.7	70.8	58.1	60.7	43.9	77.3	66.1
Rajasthan	37.0	6.8	72.3	41.5	47.6	11.6	78.5	50.2
Tamil Nadu	60.1	29.8	83.8	62.7	67.2	41.8	86.1	69.6
Uttar Pradesh	43.4	11.7	64.8	42.7	52.1	19.0	70.0	50.4
West Bengal	52.8	26.8	77.2	62.5	62.1	38.1	81.2	68.3
INDIA 92–93	49.6	21.7			57.9	30.6		

App. 12.1 Cont'd.3...

States	*Educational attainments Contd. 2*							
	Intensity of formal education							
	1978				*1993*			
	Rural		*Urban*		*Rural*		*Urban*	
	M	*F*	*M*	*F*	*M*	*F*	*M*	*F*
	21	*22*	*23*	*24*	*25*	*26*	*27*	*28*
Andhra Pradesh	3.40	2.81	5.10	4.48	4.019	3.57	5.66	5.29
Assam	3.70	3.40	5.32	5.01	4.24	4.13	5.57	5.40
Bihar	3.26	2.57	4.66	4.06	3.87	3.35	5.63	4.95
Gujarat	3.69	3.34	5.30	4.94	4.49	4.13	5.63	5.43
Haryana	4.26	3.48	5.50	5.08	4.89	4.36	6.50	5.96
Karnataka	3.60	2.99	5.18	4.67	4.31	3.88	5.34	5.09
Kerala	4.87	4.80	5.45	5.47	5.34	5.40	5.57	5.69
Madhya Pradesh	3.67	2.94	5.08	4.54	4.41	3.61	5.72	5.20
Maharashtra	2.99	2.81	5.09	5.03	4.76	4.27	5.32	5.11
Orissa	3.78	3.20	5.24	4.84	4.25	3.92	5.09	5.00
Punjab	4.06	3.57	5.17	5.07	4.72	4.42	5.92	6.08
Rajasthan	3.81	3.06	5.26	4.48	4.13	3.10	5.55	4.91
Tamil Nadu	3.92	3.39	5.06	4.63	4.95	4.66	6.00	6.08
Uttar Pradesh	4.32	3.18	6.10	5.19	4.46	3.76	6.00	5.54
West Bengal	3.40	3.03	4.43	4.27	4.07	3.66	5.25	4.97
INDIA 92–93	**3.83**	**3.27**	**5.16**	**4.69**	**4.41**	**3.99**	**5.63**	**5.36**

Appendix 12.1 contd. 4...

State	*3. Economic attainments*							
	Inflation and inequality adjusted per capita consumption expenditure				*Percentage of population below poverty line*			
	1983		*1993–94*		*1983*		*1993–94*	
	Rural	*Urban*	*Rural*	*Urban*	*Rural*	*Urban*	*Rural*	*Urban*
1	*29*	*30*	*31*	*32*	*33*	*34*	*35*	*36*
Andhra Pradesh	81.59	107.36	95.62	106.10	26.53	36.30	15.92	38.33
Assam	91.30	116.38	90.13	150.54	42.60	21.73	45.01	7.73
Bihar	69.78	97.51	78.12	114.28	64.37	47.33	58.21	34.50
Gujarat	88.68	135.84	95.54	134.54	29.80	39.14	22.18	27.89
Haryana	108.64	126.31	102.15	136.79	20.56	24.15	28.02	16.38

Cont'd...

App. 12.1 Cont'd...

1	*29*	*30*	*31*	*32*	*33*	*34*	*35*	*36*
Karnataka	82.30	111.92	87.94	114.99	36.33	42.82	29.88	40.14
Kerala	97.32	111.58	112.92	142.46	39.03	45.68	25.76	24.55
Madhya Pradesh	71.77	103.01	78.71	106.59	48.90	53.06	40.64	48.38
Maharashtra	79.38	124.38	86.28	132.56	45.23	40.26	37.93	35.15
Orissa	71.45	106.61	91.93	117.25	67.53	49.15	49.72	41.64
Punjab	122.74	125.48	120.80	147.23	13.20	23.79	11.85	11.35
Rajasthan	83.84	111.25	88.68	121.85	33.50	37.94	26.46	30.49
Tamil Nadu	75.74	107.03	99.39	116.69	53.99	46.96	32.48	39.77
Uttar Pradesh	74.07	93.87	77.79	112.04	46.45	49.82	42.28	35.39
West Bengal	74.65	114.42	99.99	134.87	63.05	32.32	40.80	22.41
INDIA	**78.90**	**11.01**	**87.90**	**124.27**	**45.65**	**40.79**	**37.27**	**32.36**

App. 12.1 Cont'd. 5...

States	***3. Economic attainments contd. 2***									
	Households with kutcha houses				***Households with toilet facilities***		***Households with safe drinking water***			
	1981		***1991***		***1991***		***1981***		***1991***	
	R	***U***	***R***	***U***	***R***	***U***	***R***	***U***	***R***	***U***
1	***37***	***38***	***39***	***40***	***41***	***42***	***43***	***44***	***45***	***46***
Andhra Pradesh	55.5	29.1	45.0	20.6	6.6	54.6	15.1	63.3	49.0	73.8
Assam			76.1	28.8	30.5	86.1			43.3	64.1
Bihar	40.0	9.65	37.5	9.2	5.0	56.5	33.8	65.4	55.6	73.4
Gujarat	10.9	4.7	5.0	2.4	11.2	65.7	36.2	86.8	60.0	87.2
Haryana	29.5	9.2	17.2	6.0	6.5	64.3	42.9	90.7	67.1	93.2
Karnataka	30.4	14.2	20.2	8.4	6.9	62.5	17.6	74.4	67.3	81.4
Kerala*	44.0	26.4	27.9	16.0	44.1	72.7	6.3	39.7	12.2	38.7
Madhya Pradesh	27.0	7.8	17.3	3.1	3.6	53.0	8.1	66.7	45.6	79.5
Maharashtra	27.0	7.8	17.3	3.1	6.6	64.5	18.3	85.6	54.0	90.5
Orissa	73.2	34.5	64.4	26.7	3.6	49.3	9.5	51.3	35.3	62.8
Punjab	33.3	7.7	15.6	3.6	15.8	73.2	81.8	91.1	92.1	94.2
Rajasthan	30.3	9.2	45.5	5.8	6.7	62.3	13.0	78.7	50.6	86.5
Tamil Nadu	55.3	23.2	45.8	16.4	7.2	57.5	31.0	69.4	64.3	74.2
Uttar Pradesh	40.9	11.1	33.7	7.4	6.4	66.5	25.3	73.2	56.6	85.8
West Bengal	59.4	9.4	50.1	8.2	12.3	78.8	65.8	79.8	80.2	86.2
INDIA	**40.6**	**13.5**	**33.8**	**9.6**	**9.5**	**63.9**	**26.5**	**75.1**	**55.5**	**81.4**

* Traditionally Keralites depend on Pucca Well for obtaining water for drinking and other purposes. Pucca Well is not regarded as a safe source for drinking water as per Census classification.

Source: Census of India 1991

App. 12.1 Cont'd. 6...

3. Economic attainments contd. 3

States	Households with electricity connection				Households with safe water, toilet & electricity		Proportion of persons in age group 15 years and above who are in the workforce							
							1983				1993–94			
	1981		1991		1991		Rural		Urban		Rural		Urban	
	R	U	R	U	R	U	M	F	M	F	M	F	M	F
1	48	49	50	51	52	53	54	55	56	57	58	59	60	61
Andhra Pradesh	12.5	52.2	37.5	73.3	3.3	39.3	92.0	67.8	82.8	27.6	90.3	72.5	81.5	28.8
Assam			12.4	63.2	4.5	42.7	83.9	20.6	78.4	27.6	84.7	26.0	76.8	16.2
Bihar	3.5	50.1	5.6	58.8	2.0	41.2	88.8	38.5	80.8	17.3	86.7	27.1	73.8	12.0
Gujarat	30.8	74.4	58.4	83.0	8.8	58.6	88.9	61.7	80.3	20.4	89.1	58.1	80.9	21.6
Haryana	41.0	82.2	63.2	89.1	5.0	60.4	83.6	36.7	85.5	17.0	80.2	44.2	83.0	24.1
Karnataka	21.4	62.0	43.8	76.3	3.7	48.6	89.5	57.8	82.6	31.0	89.4	61.5	80.6	24.7
Kerala*	23.2	54.6	42.0	67.7	3.4	25.5	82.9	49.6	82.3	37.1	82.6	35.8	81.3	32.9
Madhya Pradesh	6.9	56.4	34.5	72.5	2.1	44.7	91.0	67.4	80.5	22.9	89.8	63.1	78.9	22.8
Maharashtra	24.1	70.5	53.5	86.1	4.2	58.8	88.9	70.7	82.5	23.6	85.9	70.7	78.9	25.3
Orissa	13.0	51.7	17.5	62.1	1.0	33.0	90.0	42.4	82.3	17.5	86.8	46.1	77.6	22.9
Punjab	50.6	85.4	77.0	94.6	13.9	68.8	88.1	47.4	85.0	20.4	84.3	32.8	84.3	14.7
Rajasthan	8.7	63.7	32.4	76.7	3.7	55.4	89.3	67.2	80.5	29.6	87.2	67.3	78.2	24.0
Tamil Nadu	26.0	61.6	44.5	76.8	4.0	40.5	90.3	64.0	85.4	31.6	86.9	65.1	83.2	33.7
Uttar Pradesh	4.0	54.6	11.0	67.8	2.9	53.7	89.7	39.7	83.4	15.8	88.4	34.7	79.0	16.2
West Bengal	7.0	57.9	17.8	70.2	5.5	57.2	88.2	30.4	82.9	20.1	89.7	29.1	81.5	21.9
INDIA	**14.7**	**62.5**	**30.5**	**75.8**	**3.9**	**50.5**	**88.7**	**51.0**	**82.5**	**23.5**	**87.6**	**48.8**	**79.9**	**23.4**

Source: Planning Commission, National Human Development Report 2001 (NSSO data).

Appendix 13.1

Year-wise achievement of targets of MCH activities – All India

(target in million)

Year	*Tetanus immunization for mothers*			*DPT immunization for children*			*Polio*			*BCG*		
	Target	*Achive ment*	*% of (2) achie-ved*	*Target*	*Achie-vement*	*% of (5) achie-ved*	*Target*	*Achie-vement*	*% of (8) achie-ved*	*Target*	*Achie-vement*	*% of (11) achie-ved*
1	*2*	*3*	*4*	*5*	*6*	*7*	*8*	*9*	*10*	*11*	*12*	*13*
1980–81	6.84	5.28	77.3	13.55	7.15	52.8	3.83	1.61	42.2			
1985–86	12.86	10.36	80.6	14.04	15.18	108.1	14.04	13.19	93.9	14.04	6.62	47.3
1990–91	25.27	20.14	79.7	22.34	22.50	100.7	22.34	22.68	101.5	22.34	23.01	103.0
1991–92	26.13	20.27	77.6	23.33	21.21	90.9	23.33	21.30	91.3	23.33	21.67	92.9
1992–93	27.01	21.45	79.4	24.29	22.00	90.6	24.29	22.12	91.0	24.29	23.46	96.6
1993–94	27.56	22.75	82.6	24.79	23.09	93.2	24.79	23.21	93.6	24.79	24.09	97.2
1994–95	27.53	23.07	83.8	24.77	23.40	94.5	24.77	23.58	95.2	24.77	24.70	99.8
1995–96	27.53	22.12	80.4	24.86	22.56	90.7	24.86	22.78	91.6	24.86	24.13	97.1
1996–97	28.11	22.98	81.8	25.40	23.25	91.5	25.40	23.55	92.7	25.40	24.95	98.2
1997–98	28.29	23.37	82.6	25.55	23.74	92.9	25.55	23.98	93.9	25.55	25.42	99.5
1998–99	27.749	23.28	83.9	25.12	23.55	93.7	25.12	23.93	95.3	25.12	24.54	97.7
1999–00	29.242	23.78	81.3	24.72	23.56	95.3	24.72	23.71	95.9	24.72	25.12	101.6
2000–01	28.813	24.78	86.0	24.35	25.01	102.7	24.35	25.34	104.1	24.35	26.34	108.2

App. 13.1 Cont'd. 2…

Year	*Measles vaccination*			*DT immunization for children*			*TT (10 years)*			*TT (16 years)*		
	Target	*Achie-vement*	*% of (2) achie-ved*	*Target*	*Achie-vement*	*% of (5) achie-ved*	*Target*	*Achie-vement*	*% of (8) achie-ved*	*Target*	*Achie-vement*	*% of (11) achie-ved*
1	*14*	*15*	*16*	*17*	*18*	*19*	*20*	*21*	*22*	*23*	*24*	*25*
1980–81				11.37	10.23	90.1						
1985–86				11.19	12.53	112.0	5.54	4.53	82.0	3.30	3.00	90.9
1990–91	22.34	20.29	90.9	17.13	13.94	81.4	15.47	11.03	71.3	15.43	8.31	53.9
1991–92	23.33	19.83	85.0	17.66	13.75	77.8	15.97	10.90	68.2	16.03	8.46	52.8
1992–93	24.29	20.86	85.9	18.16	14.13	77.8	16.31	11.32	69.4	16.36	8.74	53.4
1993–94	24.79	21.95	88.5	18.54	13.42	72.4	16.65	11.71	70.3	16.69	9.22	55.3
1994–95	24.77	21.60	87.2	21.45	14.56	67.9	20.31	11.92	58.7	18.15	9.27	51.1
1995–96	24.86	20.54	82.6	21.79	10.49	48.1	20.72	9.69	46.8	18.66	7.56	40.5
1996–97	25.40	21.14	83.2	22.17	13.77	62.1	21.08	12.16	57.7	18.99	9.39	49.5
1997–98	25.55	21.92	85.8	22.55	10.52	46.6	21.44	9.82	45.8	19.31	7.85	40.6

App. 13.1 Cont'd. 3...

Year	*Prophylaxis against nutritional anemia among mothers*			*Prophylaxis against Blindness due to Vit A Deficiency*					
				1st Dose			*2nd Dose to 5th Dose*		
	Target	*No. of beneficia-ries*	*% of achieve-ment*	*Target*	*No. of beneficia-ries*	*% of achieve-ment*	*Target*	*No. of beneficia-ries*	*% of achieve-ment*
1	*26*	*27*	*28*	*29*	*30*	*31*	*32*	*33*	*34*
1980–81	11.91	11.09	101.0@	24.20	68.8@				
1985–86	14.00	18.05	128.9	24.96	29.40	177.8			
1990–91	20.58	18.51	90.0	29.98	39 £	65.0 K			
1991–92	29.65	16.35	55.1	39.03	42 £	53.3 K			
1992–93	27.01	16.48	61.0	24.29	31 £	64.1 K			
1993–94	27.56	22.00	79.9	24.79	38 £	77.5 K			
1994–95	27.53	21.32	77.5	24.77	43 £	86.2 K			
1995–96	27.53	22.16	80.5	24.86*$*	16*$*	65.3 $*	22.45	31.34	36.7 K
1996–97	28.11	23.74	84.5	25.40 $*	16*$*	74.3*$*	22.84	31.37#	44.5 KK
1997–98	28.29	13.77	48.7	25.55 $*	17*$*	67.7*$*	23.23	34.20 #	38.7KK

@ Worked out after excluding the targets of those states/UTs for which figures have not been received
K Percentage of achievement of targets were worked out by taking half of the total doses given to the first time initiated, continued and completed dosed beneficiaries.
£ In doses
$$ Withdrawn from EPI schedule
$ Relates to Ist dose (Below 1 year + Above 1 year)
KK Percentage achievement of targets were worked out by taking 2 × 1.9 times of target
Source: Family Planning Program in India 2001

Appendix 13.2

Year-wise budget estimate and actual expenditure by the department of family welfare (Rs million)

Year	*Budget estimate*	*Revised estimate*	*Expenditure (actual)*	*(3) as % of (2)*
	1	*2*	*3*	*4*
1974–75	5,413.53	5,426.28	5,763.61	106.2
1975–76	6,319.90	7,149.42	12,199.19	170.6
1976–77	6,998.95	14,910.69	14,752.97	98.9
1977–78	9,817.67	8,977.03	8,603.52	95.8
1978–79	11,093.39	10,514.76	10,235.35	97.3
1979–80	11,519.23	11,069.61	10,836.41	97.9
1980–81	13,949.75	13,193.00	11,542.36	87.5
1981–82	15,477.50	16,848.38	18,079.90	107.3
1982–83	24,470.50	29,756.13	29,363.44	98.7

Cont'd...

App. 13.2 Cont'd...

	1	*2*	*3*	*4*
1983–84	32,971.92	37,470.92	37,423.84	99.9
1984–85	43,766.90	43,991.10	42,507.68	96.6
1985–86	49,986.40	49,986.40	48,866.67	97.8
1986–87	53,000.00	52,996.00	52,603.37	99.3
1987–88	58,486.00	57,286.00	57,314.50	100.0
1988–89	59,990.00	63,490.00	63,194.11	99.5
1989–90	65,295.00	63,795.00	63,521.98	99.6
1990–91	67495.00	78,479.00	78,219.49	99.7
1991–92	74,895.00	85,652.00	84,752.76	99.0
1992–93	100,000.00	104,100.00	102,902.46	98.8
1993–94	127,000.00	127,357.00	139,529.39	109.6
1994–95	143,000.00	153,800.00	153,412.00	99.7
1995–96	158,100.00	150,600.00	151,001.85	100.3
1996–97	153,500.00	154,700.00	156,225.13	101.0
1997–98	182,935.00	182,935.00	182,215.21	99.6
1998–99	248,935.00	225,300.00	234,274.54	104.0
1999–00	292,000.00	312,000.00	309,975.39	99.4
2000–01	352,000.00	320,000.00	309,010.54	96.6
2001–02	421,000.00	370,000.00	361,393.87	97.7

Appendix 13.3

Allocation of funds in the ninth and tenth plan on selected few schemes (Rs million)

Name of Schemes	*Ninth Plan*	*Tenth Plan*
Rural family welfare centers	15,000 (9.9%)	Transferred to state
Sub-centers	22,000 (14.6%)	10,4490 (38.5%)
Reproductive Child Health (RCH)	51,500 (34.1%)	77,860 (28.7%)
Sterilization and IUD insertion	6,000 (4.0%)	9,000 (3.3%)
Free distribution of contraceptives	5,300 (3.5%)	11,350 (4.2%)
National maternity benefit scheme	754.7 (0.5%)	5,000 (1.8%)
Research institutes	1,294.5 (0.8%)	1,595 (0.6%)
Total	**151,200 (100%)**	**271,250 (100%)**

Source: Family Welfare Program in India Yearbook 2001.

Appendix 14.1

Distribution of population, density, decadal growth rate, sex ratio, and literacy rate in the population, 2011

State/UTs*	Total population			Density per km²	Decadal growth rate	Sex ratio in population		Sex ratio in child population		Sex ratio in age 7 and above		Literacy rate (%)			
	Persons	Males	Females			2001	2011	2001	2011	2001	2011	Persons	Males	Femal es	M-F
1	*2*	*3*	*4*	*5*	*6*	*7*	*8*	*9*	*10*	*11*	*12*	*13*	*14*	*15*	*16*
INDIA	**1,210,193,422**	**623,724,248**	**586,469,174**	**382**	**17.64**	**933**	**940**	**927**	**914**	**934**	**944**	**74.04**	**82.14**	**65.46**	**16.68**
Jammu & Kashmir	12,548,926	6,665,561	5,883,365	124	23.71	892	883	941	859	884	887	68.74	78.26	58.01	20.25
Himachal Pradesh	6,856,509	3,473,892	3,382,617	123	12.81	968	974	896	906	980	983	83.78	90.83	76.60	14.23
Punjab	27,704,236	14,634,819	13,069,417	550	13.73	876	893	798	846	888	899	76.68	81.48	71.34	10.14
Chandigarh*	1,054,686	580,282	474,404	9,252	17.10	777	818	845	867	767	812	86.43	90.54	81.38	9.16
Uttarakhand	10,116,752	5,154,178	4,962,574	189	19.17	962	963	908	886	973	975	79.63	88.33	70.70	17.63
Haryana	25,353,081	13,505,130	11,847,951	573	19.90	861	877	819	830	869	885	76.64	85.38	66.77	18.61
Delhi*	16,753,235	8,976,410	7,776,825	11,297	20.96	821	866	868	866	813	866	86.34	91.03	80.93	10.10
Rajasthan	68,621,012	35,620,086	33,000,926	201	21.44	921	926	909	883	923	935	67.06	80.51	52.66	27.85
Uttar Pradesh	199,581,477	104,596,415	94,985,062	828	20.09	898	908	916	899	894	910	69.72	79.24	59.26	19.98
Bihar	103,804,637	54,185,347	49,619,290	1,102	25.07	919	916	942	933	914	912	63.82	73.39	53.33	20.06
Sikkim	607,688	321,661	286,027	86	12.36	875	889	963	944	861	883	82.20	87.29	76.43	10.86
Arunachal Pradesh	1,382,611	720,232	662,379	17	25.92	893	920	964	960	878	913	66.95	73.69	59.57	14.12
Nagaland	1,980,602	1,025,707	954,895	119	-0.47	900	931	964	944	890	929	80.11	83.29	76.69	6.60
Manipur	2,721,756	1,369,764	1,351,992	122	18.65	974	987	957	934	977	995	79.85	86.49	73.17	13.32
Mizoram	1,091,014	552,339	538,675	52	22.78	935	975	964	971	930	976	91.58	93.72	89.40	4.32
Tripura	3,671,032	1,871,867	1,799,165	350	14.75	948	961	966	953	945	962	87.75	92.18	83.15	9.03
Meghalaya	2,964,007	1,492,668	1,471,339	132	27.82	972	986	973	970	971	989	75.48	77.17	73.78	3.39
Assam	31,169,272	15,954,927	15,214,345	397	16.93	935	954	965	957	929	953	73.18	78.81	67.27	11.54

Cont'd...

App. 14.1 Cont'd…

1	*2*	*3*	*4*	*5*	*6*	*7*	*8*		*9*	*10*		*11*	*12*		*13*
West Bengal	91,347,736	46,927,389	44,420,347	1,029	13.93	934	947	960	950	929	946	77.08	82.67	71.16	11.51
Jharkhand	32,966,238	16,931,688	16,034,550	414	22.34	941	947	965	943	935	948	67.63	78.45	56.21	22.24
Orissa	41,947,358	21,201,678	20,745,680	269	13.97	972	978	953	934	976	985	73.45	82.40	64.36	18.04
Chhattisgarh	25,540,196	12,827,915	12,712,281	189	22.59	989	991	975	964	992	995	71.04	81.45	60.59	20.86
Madhya Pradesh	72,597,565	37,612,920	34,984,645	236	20.30	919	930	932	912	916	933	70.63	80.53	60.02	20.51
Gujarat	60,383,628	31,482,282	28,901,346	308	19.17	920	918	883	886	927	923	79.31	87.23	70.73	16.50
Daman & Diu*	242,911	150,100	92,811	2,169	53.54	710	618	926	909	682	589	87.07	91.48	79.59	11.89
Dadra & Nagar Haveli*	342,853	193,178	149,675	698	55.50	812	775	979	924	779	752	77.65	86.46	65.93	20.53
Maharashtra	112,372,972	58,361,397	54,011,575	365	15.99	922	925	913	883	924	931	82.91	89.82	75.48	14.34
Andhra Pradesh	84,665,533	42,509,881	42,155,652	308	11.10	978	992	961	943	981	997	67.66	75.56	59.74	15.82
Karnataka	61,130,704	31,057,742	30,072,962	319	15.67	965	968	946	943	968	971	75.60	82.85	68.13	14.72
Goa	1,457,723	740,711	717,012	394	8.17	961	968	938	920	964	973	87.40	92.81	81.84	10.97
Lakshadweep*	64,429	33,106	31,323	2,013	6.23	948	946	959	908	946	951	92.28	96.11	88.25	7.86
Kerala	33,387,677	16,021,290	17,366,387	859	4.86	1058	1084	960	959	1,072	1,099	93.91	96.02	91.98	4.04
Tamil Nadu	72,138,958	36,158,871	35,980,087	555	15.60	987	995	942	946	993	1,000	80.33	86.81	73.86	12.95
Pondicherry*	1,244,464	610,485	633,979	2,598	27.72	1001	1038	967	965	1,006	1,047	86.55	92.12	81.22	10.90
Andaman & N. Is*	379,944	202,330	177,614	46	6.68	846	878	957	966	831	868	86.27	90.11	81.84	8.27

Source: Census India, 2011 (Web) (compilation).

Selected Readings

Acharyya, Rajat and Saibal Kar (2004): *Trade Liberalization, Migration and Poverty.* www.gdnet.org/pdf2/gdn_library/global research_projects/macro_low_income/Acharyya.pdf _

Agarwala, S.N. (1962): *Age at Marriage in India*. Allahabad: Kitab Mahal

—— (1962): *Attitude Towards Family Planning in India*, Bombay: Asia Pub. House

—— (1964): "Sterilization as a population control device, its consequences", *The Econ. Weekly*, XVI

—— (1964): "Social and cultural factors affecting fertility in India", in, proceedings of the *7th International Parenthood Foundation*, NY

—— (1968): "Socio-economic and demographic characteristics of rural migrants and the non-migrants", *J.Inst. Econ. Res.* III (2)

—— (1977): *India's Population Problems*. ND: Tata-McGraw Hill

—— (1977): *Population*, ND: National Book Trust

Altekar, A.S. (1938): *The Position of Women in Hindu Civilization*. Benaras: India Book Shop

Ambannavar, J.P. (1969): "Comparability and adjustment of the Indian working force data, Census 1911–61", *Artha Vijnana*, 11(4)

—— (1975): *Population – Second India Studies.* ND: McMillan

Bardhan, Pranab (1974): "Some aspects of inequality", in, A. Bose *et al.* (eds): *Population in India's Development 1947–2000.* ND: Vikas

Beteille, Andre (1965): "Our Villages and Cities: A contrast between tradition and modernity", *Yojna*, Jan.26

Bhagat, R.B. and P. Praharaj (2005): "Hindu Muslim fertility differential", *Economic & Political Weekly*. Jan 29

Bhagawati, J.N. and M. Partington (eds): *Taxing the Brain Drain*, Amsterdam: North-Holland

Bhargava, P.K. (2002): "Changes in gender disparity in literacy rate during 1991–2001", Seminar on Progress of Literacy in India, NIEPA, New Delhi

Bhattacharyya, D. (1967): *Population of India, 1951–61 (mimeo)*, Cal: ISI

—— (1985): "Historical demography in India – scope, sources and materials and some crucial problems in outline", in Proceeding of the *Symposium on Historical Demography*, Bangalore

Bose, A. (1967): "Differential fertility by religion in India", in, A.K. Kamat (ed), *Population Problems in India*, ND: Kapur Printers

—— (1970): *Urbanization in India: An Inventory of Source Materials.* ND: Academic Books

—— (1978): *India's Urbanization, 1901–2001*. ND: Tata-McGraw Hill

—— P.B. Desai and S.P. Jain (eds) (1970): *Studies in Demography*. Lond: Allen & Unwin

—— P.B. Desai, A. Mitra and N. Sharma (eds) (1974): *Population in India's Development, 1947–2000.* ND: Vikas

Bose, N.K. (1965): "Calcutta – a premature metropolis", *Scientific American,* 213(3)

Caldwell, J.C., P.H. Reddy and Pat Caldwell (1984): "The determinants of fertility decline in rural south India", in, T. Dyson and N. Crook (ed): *India's Demography*. ND: South Asian Pub.

Caseen, R. (1978): *India – Population, Economy and Society*. Lond: McMillan

Central Statistical Organization (2002): *Selected Socio-Economic Statistics in India*. Web page.

Chandrasekhar, S. (1972): *Infant Mortality, Population Growth and Family Planning*. Lond: Allen & Unwin

Chattopadhyay, A., R.B. Bhagat and T.K. Roy (2004): "Hindu-Muslim Fertility Differentials: A Comparative Study of Selected Sates of India", in, T.K. Roy *et al.* (eds), *Population, Health and Development in India: Changing Perspectives*, Jaipur: Rawat Publications

Coal, A.J. and M. Hoover (1958): *Population Growth and Economic Development in Low Income Countries – A Case Study in India's Prospects.* Princeton: Princeton Univ. Press

Dasgupta, A., R.K. Som, M. Majumdar and S.N. Mitra (1955): *Couple Fertility* (NSS report 7), ND: Deptt. of Economic Affairs, Min. of Finance

Datt, Gaurav (1999): "Has poverty declined since economic reforms? Statistical data analysis", *Economic & Political Weekly,* December.

Davis, K. (1951): *Population of India and Pakistan*. Princeton: Princeton Univ. Press

Demographic Research Unit, Calcutta (1970): *Calcutta Fertility Survey.* Cal: IDRU

Desai, P.B. (1975): *A Survey of Research in Demography.* Bombay: Popular Prakashani

—— (1975): *Economic Development and Population Control in Aspects of Population Policy in India*. ND: CSD

Dhar, P.N. (2003): *The Evolution of Economic Policy in India; Selected Essays*, ND: Oxford Univ. Press.

Dharmalingam, A. and S.P. Morgan (2004): "Pervasive Muslim-Hindu Fertility Differences in India", *Demography*, 41(3)

Dreze, J. and Amartya Sen (1995): *India: Economic Development and Social Opportunity.* ND: Oxford Univ. Press

Driver, E.D. (1963): *Differential Fertility in Central India*. Princeton: Princeton Univ. Press

Dutta, M. and V.P. Vasin (1979): *Communicable Diseases, Pattern of Morbidity and Mortality in India.* ND: Central Bureau of Health Intelligence, DGHS

Dyson, T. (1983): "India's demographic transition – An appraisal of the provisional 1981 Census result", in, K. Srinivasan and S. Mukherje (eds):*Dynamics of Population and Family Welfare*. Bombay: Himalaya Pub. House

—— and M. Moore (1983): "On Kinship Structure, Female Autonomy and Demographic Behavior in India", *Pop and Dev Report*, 9(1)

—— and N. Crook (eds) (1984): *India's Demography: Essays on the Contemporary Population.* ND: South Asia Pub.

Ghosh, A. and R.R. Das (1985): "Demographic trends in India during 1757–1947", in, *Proceedings on the Symposium in Historical Demography*, Bangalore

Ghosh, D. (1946): *Pressure of Population and Economic Efficiency in India*. ND: Indian Council of World Affairs

Gosal, G.S. (1961): "Regionalism of sex composition of Indian population", *Rur. Soc.*, 26(4)

Goyal, R.P. (1975): "Shifts in age at marriage in India between 1961 and 1971", *Demography*, 4(2)

Halli, S.S. (1987): *How Minority Status Affects Fertility*. Westport: Greenwood Press

International Institute for Population Sciences (1995): *National Family Health Survey, India (NFHS I), 1992–93*, Mumbai

—— (2000): *National Family Health Survey (NFHS–2), 1998–99,* Mumbai

Jain, A.K. and P. Visaria (1988): *Infant Mortality in India – Differentials and Determinants.*ND: Sage Pub.

Jain, S.P. (1975): *Demography – A Status Study on Population Research in India.* ND: Tata-McGraw Hill

Kamat, A.R. (1973): *The Educational Situation and other Essays on Education.* ND: People's Pub. House

Kannan, K. and K.S. Hari (2002): Kerala's Gulf Connection – Emigration, Remittances and their Macroeconomic Impact 1972–2000, *CDS Working Paper 328*, Thiruvananthapuram, India.

Karve, D. (1936): *Poverty and Population in India*. Lond: Oxford Univ. Press

Kocher, J. (1973): *Rural Development, Income Distribution and Fertility Decline*. NY: Population Council

Lal, R.B. and V.B. Swami (1977): "Vital statistics: Sample Registration Scheme", in, A. Bose *et al.* (eds): *Population Statistics in India*. ND: Vikas

Mahalanobis, P.C. and D.P. Bhattacharyya (1961): "Growth of population of India and Pakistan", *Sankhya*, December.

Majumdar P.K. (2010): *Fundamentals of Demography,* Jaipur : Rawat Publications.

Majumdar, P.K. and B. Chaudhuri (1983): *Faltering First Step*. ND: Cosmo Pub

Malakar, C.R. (1972): "Female age at marriage and the birth rate in India", *Soc. Biology,* 19 (Sept)

Mandelbum, D.G. (1973): "Social components of Indian fertility", *Economic & Political Weekly*, VIII (4–6)

—— (1974): *Human Fertility in India*. Berkley: Univ. Calif. Press

Ministry of Health and Family Welfare (2004): India Country Report: *Population and Development*

Ministry of Human Resource Development (2001): Selected Educational Statistics, 1999–2000

Mitra, Ashok (1967): "Relationship between patterns of shift from agriculture to non-agriculture, 1951–61 and levels of development" and "Functional classification of India's towns and their broad features", in, A. Bose (ed): *Patterns of Population Change in India*. ND Allied Pub.

—— (1977): "Census of India – past and future", in, A. Bose, D.B. Gupta and G. Roychaudhuri (eds): *Population Statistics in India*. ND: Vikas

—— (1978): *India's Population Problems: Aspects of Quality and Quantity*. Bombay: Abhinav Prakashan

Mukherjee, S.B. (1976): *The Age Distribution of Indian Population: A Reconstruction for the States and Territories, 1881–1961*. Honolulu: East-West Population Institute

Myrdal, Gunnar (1970): *The Challenge of World Poverty*. Lond: Allen Lane

Nag, Moni (1962): *Factors Affecting Human Fertility in the Non-Industrial Society*. Pub. Division, Government of India

Naoroji, Dadabhai (1962): "Poverty in India" in, *Poverty and UnBritish Rule in India*. Pub. Division, Government of India

Natarajan, K.S. (1983): "Population projection up to 2001", in, *Studies in Family Planning*. NY: The Population Council, Vol. 35

NCAER (National Council of Applied Economic Research) (1999): *India Human Development Report*, ND: Oxford Univ. Press

National Literacy Mission (2000): Literacy Campaigns in India – National Overview (status as in March 1999), Directorate of Adult Education, MHRD

National Council of Educational Research and Training (1982): *Fourth All India Education Survey*, ND

—— (1999): *Sixth All India Education Survey*, ND

National Nutrition Monitoring Bureau (1999): *Report of Second Repeat Survey – Rural.* Hyderabad: National Institute of Nutrition, Indian Council of Medical Research

NSSO (1998): Attending an Educational Institution in India: Its level, nature and cost, NSS 52nd Round (1995–96)

—— (2001): *Employment and Unemployment Situation among Religious Groups in India 1999–2000*, Ministry of Statistics and Program Implementation, Government of India

Operation Research Group, Baroda (1971): *An All India Survey of Family Planning Practices*. Baroda

—— (1972): *Family Planning in India*. Baroda

ORGCC(1980): *Survey on Infant and Child Mortality, 1979 – A Preliminary Report.*

—— *Vital Statistics of India* – various issues

—— *Sample Registration Bulletin* – various issues

—— (2001): Census of India 2001: Provisional Population Totals, Paper 1 of 2001, Series 1

—— (2011): Census of India 2011 : Provisional Population Totals (Web).

Padmanava, P. (1982): "Mortality in India: A Note on Trends and Implications", *Economic & Political Weekly*, 32

Planning Commission (2002): *National Human Development Report 2001*, Government of India

Premi, M.K. (1972): *Educational Planning in India.* ND: Sterling Pub.

—— (1972): "Out-migrating towns in India: An analysis of their demographic characteristics", in, Census Centenary Seminar

—— (1980): *Urban Organization: A Study of its Nature, Causes and Consequences.* ND: Starling Pub.

—— (1982): *The Demographic Situation in India.* Honolulu: East-West Center

—— (2001): "The Missing girl child", *Economic & Political Weekly*, XXXVI (21)

Sachdev, A.S. (2002): "Urbanization in India: Past trends and future projections", *The Asian Journal,* 9(1)

Sachs, J.D., A. Varshney and N. Bajpai (eds) (1999): *India in the Era of Economic Reforms.* NY: Oxford University Press

Sharma, S.C. and C.L. Sapra (1971): *Wastage and Stagnation in Primary and Middle Schools.* ND: NCERT

Srivastava, S.C. (1972): *Indian Census in Perspective*, Census Centenary Monograph No. 1, Office of the Registrar General, India

Status of Physically Challenged Employees in Public Services. www.mobilityandhiv.org/docs/challenge.doc

Tendulkar, S.D. (2003): Organised Labour Market in India: Pre and Post Reform (web document for comment, suresh@econdse.org)

UNDP (United Nations Development Program): *Human Development Report*, various years, NY: Oxford Univ. Press

United Nations (1968): *An Evaluation of Family Planning Program of the Government of India.*

United Nations and Government of India (1961): *The Mysore Population Study.* NY: Population Division, UN

Visaria, P.M. (1980): *Poverty and Living Standards in India.* Washington: World Bank

Weiner, M. (1996): "Child labor in India: Putting compulsory primary education on the political agenda", *Economic & Political Weekly*, XXX1 (45–46)

World Bank: *World Development Report,* various issues, Washington

Zachariah, K.C. (1964): *Historical Study of the Internal Migration in Indian Sub-Continent, 1901–1931.* Bombay: Asia Pub.

—— (1968): *Migration in Greater Bombay.* Bombay: Demographic Training and Research Center

—— (1984): *Determinants of Fertility Decline in India*, World Bank, Washington

Sources of Macro-Level Demographic and Socio-Economic Data and Analysis

Office of the Registrar General and Census Commissioner (ORGCC)

Census publications

Occasional monographs

Pocket Book of Population Statistics

Sample Registration Bulletins

Vital Statistics of India

Government of India

Agricultural Census
Agricultural Prices Commission
Annual Survey of Industries (ASI)
Central Bureau of Health Intelligence
Central Statistical Organization (CSO)
Department of Atomic Energy
Department of Telecommunications
Directorate General of Health Service (DGHS)
Directorate of Statistics and Economics
Draft Report of Five Year Plans
Employment Review by Directorate General of Employment and Training (DGET)
Family Planning Communication Action Research Committee
Family Welfare Program Year Book
Ministry of Information and Broadcasting
Ministry of Finance
Ministry of Non-Conventional Energy Sources (MNES)
Ministry of Petroleum and Natural Gas
Ministry of Power
Ministry of Road Transport and Highways
Monthly Statement on the Progress on Family Welfare Program in India
National Commissions on Labor
National Council of Educational Research and Training (NCERT)
National Human Development Report (NHDR)
National Institute of Family Planning
National Nutrition Monitoring Bureau
Planning Commission
Planning, Monitoring and Statistical Division of Ministry of Human Resources & Development
Reserve Bank of India on Currency and Finance – Bulletins
State Human Development Report
Statistical Abstracts
University Grants Commission

Autonomous Bodies

International Institute for Population Sciences
Institute of Population Studies, Mumbai
National Council of Applied Economic Research (NCAER)
Operation Research Group, Baroda

Index